A CASEBOOK ON IRISH FAMILY LAW

by

WILLIAM BINCHY

B.A., B.C.L., LL.M.

Barrister-at-Law, Research Counsellor,
The Law Reform Commission

with a

FOREWORD

by

The Honourable Mr. Justice BRIAN WALSH

M.A. (N.U.I.), LL.D. (h.c.) (Dublin)

Senior Ordinary Judge of the Supreme Court of Ireland
Judge of the European Court of Human Rights
President, The Law Reform Commission

PROFESSIONAL BOOKS

1984

Published in 1984 by
Professional Books Limited
Milton Trading Estate, Abingdon, Oxon.
Typeset and printed in Great Britain
by Photobooks (Bristol) Ltd

ISBN: Hardback: 0 86205 084 7
Paperback: 0 86205 089 8

FOREWORD

The author of any book on family law must initially decide upon what he regards as the scope of family law. He can approach it simply on the basis that it deals with the legal relations of members of the family. If, on the other hand, he takes the view that it includes every branch of the law which may impinge upon the family it would not be possible to avoid dealing with the laws concerning social welfare, rent control, juvenile delinquency, the protection of children and even income tax. Education would also be included because in Ireland, by Article 42, section 1, of the Constitution, the family is acknowledged as the primary and natural educator of the child. In his selection of cases William Binchy has made a reasonable compromise between these two choices.

By its very nature family law reaches more closely into the life of the average person than almost any other area of law. It is one which occupies the attention not only of lawyers but also of psychologists, social scientists and politicians. The cases chosen illustrate not merely the very great increase in litigation in the area of family law in the last ten years in Ireland but also the expanding nature of the field of family law. A similar expansion of this type of litigation is to be found throughout the whole of the western world.

Although Ireland is situated on the western edge of Europe it eventually feels the effects of all social and political upheavals in Europe. However, the waves so generated tend to have diminished in force by the time they reach the shores of this country. While it might be claimed that the problems of family life are broadly similar throughout the western world yet any such statement must be qualified by the realisation that family life is so closely bound up with the socio-cultural life of a people that the problems arising do not lend themselves easily to a uniform solution. The development of family law in Ireland must be seen against the background of the social, moral and economic conditions prevailing in Ireland. But, most importantly, the moral concepts which are given the force of law by the Constitution play and have played a very important part in the development of family law as many of the cases in this book illustrate. To mention but a few, constitutional interpretation established the equality of parents and distinguished between the natural guardianship and the legal custody of children. It has led the courts to strike down legislation inimical to family life, even in the field of income tax. It has established the concept of marital privacy.

Legislators and judges alike must resist the temptation to embrace unquestioningly solutions adopted in other countries, whose socio-cultural life is significantly different, simply because they have been so adopted elsewhere. One must also avoid the tendency, already manifested in several areas of our laws and institutions, to borrow measures and ideas from other countries at the point when they are already being discarded in those countries where they have been tried and found wanting. Inferiority complex and timorousness often stifle innovation and originality. A new proposal often attracts suspicion if it has not first emerged outside our shores. The provisions in the Married Women's Status Act, 1957, which permits one spouse to sue the other in tort, was initially unacceptable to one member of the then Government on the grounds that if it were a good thing 'it would already have been thought of by the Mother of Parliaments'! The Succession Act, 1965, (a monument to the late Roger Hayes) a most important and far reaching piece of family law, was carried by the combined efforts of an enlightened and strong-minded Minister for Justice and a like minded leader of the Opposition to overcome the hesitation and the fears within and without their respective political parties.

Fundamental to the development of all family law must be the recognition that the family has always been a basic institution of human society or, as is stated in the words of

Article 41, section 1, of the Constitution, it is 'the natural, primary and fundamental unit group of society'. It does not depend for its existence upon positive law. Families serve the needs of their members and the needs of society. In the economic field they are of great importance both as incentives to work and as mechanisms in the distribution of wealth. But in addition to being an important social factor in the economic life of society the family is, above all, a moral institution and this must be reflected in all laws which purport to deal with the family. However, the laws must also recognise that each individual member of the family, whether spouse or child, has his or her own guaranteed personal rights which are co-existent with, but separate from, the rights of the family as a unit group. This becomes increasingly important with the emerging position of women in society and the recognition of the rights of children. Another factor that cannot be ignored is that the people of Ireland, whatever church they belong to, are a religious people. Those who would seek to advance the cause of secularism or even irreligion under the guise of family law are closing their eyes to reality and only place the obstacles of distrust and suspicion in the way of an orderly and acceptable development of a system of family law which reflects the true values of Irish society. For example, if legislation removes the advantages of a lawful marriage, or even penalises it, it could become redundant and obsolete as an institution unless prompted by a religious motive or rescued by the intervention of the courts in setting aside the legislation for invalidity having regard to the provisions of the Constitution.

The Constitution acknowledges that the family is founded upon the institution of marriage. Therefore family law in Ireland must have as its primary objective the protection of marriage and the provision of procedures and measures for adjusting affairs between individuals within the family, the protection of those individuals, the provision of social support for families and the protection of the family itself from attack. While the social policy of the State is reflected in its laws, which are inspired by the directive principles set forth in Article 45 of the Constitution, it must be carefully devised to deal adequately with these matters. Yet it must also lend itself to such questions as the equality of spouses and the legal status of illegitimate children. It is possible to deal justly with these matters without removing the special protection generally extended to the family. The question of illegitimacy in particular arouses deep, but not unmixed, feelings because of the resultant economic disadvantage in intestate succession and the social stigma of illegitimacy. While the first of these can be dealt with by legislation, and to some extent by judicial decision, the social stigma resides in the minds of people and does not lend itself to removal by legislation or by judicial intervention. The legislator and judge alike must be careful to approach such matters in a way which will avoid the risk of hardening social attitudes. It is probable that the increased growth of social, economic and cultural links with other countries in western Europe, together with ease of travel and communication, will bring about changes in social attitudes but nevertheless the sociological consequences of these factors will fall far short of bringing about the adoption of a uniform model of family law. For example, one factor which is notably absent from the Irish scene is the presence of large numbers of migratory workers such as are found in most countries in western Europe. Consequently our family law does not find it necessary to deal with the effects of the cultural shocks which in other countries in the European Economic Community affect both the migrant and the host.

A casebook on family law brings before the reader decisions of the courts in areas of the law where the courts have virtually no role in creating the conditions which would assist in bringing about successful family life and thus obviating resort to the courts. Therefore the cases must be looked at as the efforts of the courts to deal with family matters after damage has been done. This casebook gives an excellent overview of what the courts in Ireland have done in this troublesome area of law. The reader will learn a great deal about family law from these decisions. Yet, having read them, he will have to ask himself, firstly, whether the courts have done well and, secondly, whether the courts have been shown to be the best place in which to administer family law. If the courts are the best place in which to administer family law then a further question arises as to whether the present type of court sufficies or whether there should be a different type of one. Virtually all of the cases in this book are decisions of the High Court and the Supreme Court. However, it is undeniable that the cost of litigation in family law cases in the High Court is very great and is outside the means of most persons.

The Courts Act 1980 permits a great deal of family law litigation to be hived off to the Circuit Court and to the District Court. In a country where the population is not very dense one is always faced with the question of whether the courts should go to the people or the people to the courts. Most people would say that as far as possible the courts should go to the people. To that extent the District Court and the Circuit Court are more suitable than the High Court which spends most of its time in Dublin and is in any event already overloaded with work. Yet certain aspects of family law are of such fundamental importance, such as those cases which can alter the legal status of a person, that they should be decided in the High Court or by a High Court judge.

This prompts one to question the wisdom or the desirability of permitting legal adoptions to take effect without judicial intervention or confirmation. To use Mr. Binchy's words 'adoption in Irish law involves the irrevocable transfer of parental obligations and rights to a third party'. To raise this point is not to question the sterling work of the Adoption Board during the thirty two years of its existence. But its powers are limited. It cannot decide questions concerning the validity of the marriage of couples who seek to adopt. Yet if adoption is approved for a couple whose marriage is not a valid subsisting marriage in the eyes of the law of the State the resulting invalidity of the adoption may not be discovered until it is too late to avoid the consequent heartbreak and the inevitable legal consequences. One can but hope that no such case will reveal itself. It is worth recalling that one feared infirmity in our adoption procedure prompted the enactment of the Sixth Amendment of the Constitution.

There is much to be said for the creation of a unified family court which would be manned by a body of judges drawn from the different judicial levels of our courts. The particular type of case could determine the level of the judge to be assigned. Such a court could sit in any part of the country as frequently as was necessary and, depending on the type of case, it might consist of a judge of the District or of the Circuit Court or of the High Court. Without rushing to the extreme of having courts largely, if not entirely, manned by social workers or those who claim particular expertise in the field of family relations there is a place for them in the role of assessors to assist the judge. However, the primary function of a judge is to decide cases. When he has received all the guidance available from the parties, any expert testimony which may be available, and the assistance of assessors, he still has to come to a decision on matters which have concern not only for lawyers but also for other disciplines. While most cases may turn on resolution of disputed facts there are some which will require the division of property or perhaps even compel the compulsory transfer of property and these are matters which raise serious questions concerning fundamental rights. From the point of view of the courts it is more difficult for them to follow their previous decisions in this difficult area of the law than in other areas of law because by its very nature family law tends, albeit belatedly, to follow the continuous changes in social behaviour. Yet the courts must work within a framework of law set by the law makers who, however much they are conscious that society and the family are in a constant state of development and that many changes occur rapidly, nonetheless must fix the law for the immediate future at least.

All the cases in this work have been decided by courts in which the adversary system has been used. Each party's lawyer considers it his duty to achieve victory for his client and that may be achieved at the expense of making the other side appear in an unfavourable light. Those who have practised in this area of law can testify that the proceedings can be very acrimonious. The fact that most such cases are heard in camera encourages some parties to abandon all reticence and things are said and secrets are revealed which in many cases make it absolutely impossible for the parties ever to be reconciled. What is essential is a good pre-trial procedure so that every possible effort may be made to minimise the expenditure of money and emotion on the part of the litigants. However, one ought also to consider seriously the abandonment of the adversary procedure in family law cases, or at least in those concerning the custody of children, legal separation and maintenance, in favour of the system prevailing in civil law countries where the judge plays a far more important role in the elucidation of the facts than do the parties' own lawyers. There the judge conducts the inquiry and he is fully briefed and versed in the matter before he even sits in court. Indeed it would be to the advantage of all our practitioners in family law to have a greater appreciation of the large part played by family law, and the scope of family law, in civil law countries.

The nature of a large number of the important judicial decisions reproduced in this volume leads one to speculate on whether many of them might have been avoided altogether by the existence of extra-judicial conciliation agencies which would attempt to get the parties to settle their differences before having resort to court proceedings. Experience shows that by the time parties have reached the stage of issuing court proceedings a great deal of irreparable damage has already been done. The court atmosphere, irrespective of who occupies the bench and whether the procedures are adversarial or inquisitorial, produces its own adverse effect. The case for the existence of extra-judicial agencies to facilitate conciliation or reconciliation in family matters is overwhelming. Full use should be made of voluntary agencies as well as State-established agencies, provided that such agencies can be regarded as serious and objective agencies. One way to encourage this would be, perhaps, to have rules of procedure in the courts which would effectively prevent any case being brought to court unless it could be shown that the matter had already been thoroughly examined and investigated by the approved non-judicial agencies. These could be established on a local basis. Whether the local unit be a parochial one or a county based one or, in densely populated areas, a district based one does not really matter. The important thing is to make every effort to render it unnecessary for people to have resort to the courts and thus to reduce the risk of irreparable harm to the family.

Mr. Binchy brings to his subject a vast amount of experience in that field. He played a leading part in the preparation of the two most far-reaching modern statutes concerning family law, namely the Family Law (Maintenance of Spouses and Children) Act 1976 and the Family Home Protection Act 1976. He conducted the research necessary for the several working papers and reports of the Law Reform Commission in the field of family law and he has also written and lectured extensively on the subject. His selection of cases in the present work will greatly enrich the knowledge of students and practitioners alike in the field of family law. Many of the judgments reproduced are unreported and, save for those who are assiduous readers of all judgments, may be unknown to many persons. It is difficult to have a widespread knowledge of family law litigation because as most of the cases are heard in private only the practitioners actually engaged in a case will be in court and thus in a position to remember that particular case. This casebook will go a very long way towards filling the gaps which currently exist in the general knowledge of family law and should prove invaluable to all interested in this branch of the law whether they be lawyers, politicians or other students of the contemporary social scene. This work is another very welcome addition to the ever-growing number of excellent books on Irish law and the Irish legal system.

BRIAN WALSH
The Supreme Court
September 1984

PREFACE

For many reasons, Irish family law is a fascinating subject to study. We are all interested in family relationships in their complex variations. Most of us have views as to the role of the law in this area of our lives. In the Irish context, there are, moreover, the extra dimensions of politics, history and religion which have played an important part in shaping our present family law system.

This casebook is designed to incorporate most of the important judicial decisions on Irish family law. In recent years there has been an explosion of cases, in the wake of legislation on family maintenance, protection of the family home, barring orders, guardianship and adoption of children. Other areas of the law, where statutes have played a less significant role, have also involved a growing caseload. In the past eighteen months several important decisions on nullity of marriage and family property have been handed down. Moreover, the Constitution has played an important role in family law, which is likely to increase in coming years.

A major difficulty for Irish legal practitioners and law students has been that so few of the decisions on family law have been reported. Very many important Supreme Court and High Court decisions have never been published before; indeed, in my research, I discovered a number of decisions which had never before been brought to the attention of the legal profession in general.

In editing the unreported decisions, I have gone to some lengths to preserve as far as possible the privacy of the families involved in the litigation. This has on occasion made the judgments somewhat less easy to read and the use of initials such as X and Y reduces the impact of the account of the facts of the case. Nevertheless, this price is one which should be paid.

A casebook on family law must attempt to resolve two basic problems of structure. First, some decisions are difficult to categorise. For example, are *Nicolaon's* case and *G.* v. *An Bord Uchtála* to be part of the chapter on adoption or of the chapter on the family outside marriage? Both chapters would appear to have equal claims. I included these decisions in the latter chapter; the cross-referencing should ensure that the reader is kept in touch. The same question arose in relation to the recent Supreme Court decision of *O'Brien* v. *S.*, on the succession entitlements of children born outside marriage. This decision is included in the chapter on the family outside marriage rather than that on succession.

The other basic problem of structure results from the fact that, in many instances, decisions involve several separate issues – relating to maintenance, guardianship and the family home, for example. Extracts from these decisions are included in their appropriate chapters, with cross-referencing to one detailed statement of the facts.

While the book was at proof stage, the law maintained its inexorable progress. At a technical level, a number of the decisions included in the book have now been reported. Costello, J.'s important judgment in *D.* v. *C.* is reported in [1984] I.L.R.M. 173; the Supreme Court decision on divorce recognition in *M.T.T.* v. *N.T.* [1982] I.L.R.M. 217 has been reported (*sub nom. T.* v. *T.*) in [1983] I.R. 29; and O'Hanlon, J.'s decision on admission of paternity in *A.S.* v. *R.B., W.S. and the Registrar General of Births and Deaths*, [1984] I.L.R.M. 66 has been reported (*sub nom. S.* v. *S.*) in [1983] I.R. 68.

Some legal developments of substance should also be noted. In *A.L.* v. *J.L.*, High Ct., 27 February 1984, Finlay, P. rejected the argument that, so far as matrimonial property relationships are concerned, the trust on which a husband holds property for the benefit of his wife is conditional on each spouse honouring the obligations of the contract of marriage. Finlay, P. said (at p. 5):

'There is not, in my opinion, in the general principles of equity room for a voidable or conditional trust depending upon the maintenance of the marriage nor can the Courts investigate the true reasons for the unfortunate break-up of the marriage in order to ascertain the reality of the beneficial ownership of two people who agree jointly to purchase a house and make each of them contributions towards the redemption of mortgages standing upon it.'

(It is useful in this context to refer to *B.* v. *B.*, High Ct., July 1978 (1977–500 Sp.), another decision of Finlay, P. where a somewhat similar issue arose.)

The *Murphy* decision of the Supreme Court on income tax in 1980 has recently come under consideration. In *Muckley* v. *Attorney-General*, High Ct., 16 July 1984 (reported in the *Irish Times*, 17 July 1984, p. 8, cols. 2–4), Barrington, J. held unconstitutional section 21 of the *Finance Act 1980* which, in effect, permitted the revenue authorities a significant increase in tax rates for back assessment subject to a reduction to whatever figure the liability would have been if the *Murphy* case had not been decided. Counsel for the Attorney-General argued that those couples who had not paid the invalid tax for the years before *Murphy* should not be in a better position than those who, having done so, were not entitled to a rebate. Barrington, J. rejected this argument on the basis that in the *Murphy* case it had been found to be impracticable to vindicate the rights of married couples who had paid the invalid tax because directing the State to refund taxes unconstitutionally collected would have caused administrative and financial chaos; 'but there is no impracticability in defending the citizen against exactions which the State has no authority to impose'.

In another important decision, *Dennehy* v. *Minister for Social Welfare and Attorney-General*, High Ct., 26 July 1984 (reported in the *Irish Times*, 27 July 1984, p. 8, cols. 7–8), Barron, J. rejected a challenge to the constitutionality of the provisions of the *Social Welfare (Consolidation) Act 1981* which deal with deserted wives' benefit. Barron, J.'s judgment has not been circulated at the time of writing. From the newspaper report it appears that Barron, J. relied on the fact that the social problem of deserted wives was more extensive than that of deserted husbands; he considered, moreover, that as a matter of policy it would not be unreasonable, unjust or arbitrary for the Oireachtas to protect financially needy deserted wives who were mothers with dependent children residing with them, or to recognise that mothers who had care of children would have lost out in the labour market and so were likely to need similar protection when similarly deserted.

The recent decision of the House of Lords in *R.* v. *D.*, [1984] 2 All E.R. 449 on the subject of child kidnapping should also be noted. As is mentioned in the text [*infra*, p. 462], the Court of Appeal in this case had rejected the approach taken by the Irish Supreme Court in *The People (Attorney-General)* v. *Edge*, [1943] I.R. 115. Reversing the Court of Appeal, the House of Lords favoured a somewhat different approach. In its view, the absence of the consent of the person having custody or care and control of a child incapable of giving his or her consent is not a necessary ingredient in the common law offence of kidnapping; instead, the giving of such consent might be 'very relevant to the [defence of lawful excuse] in that, depending on all the circumstances, it might well support [such] a defence . . . .': *id.*, at 457 (per Lord Brandon).

At proof stage I was able to incorporate in chapter 14 some brief references to the Report of the Review Committee on Adoption Services, entitled *Adoption* (Pl. 2467), published in July 1984. The Report, which proposes radical changes, including the replacement of the present Adoption Board by an Adoption Court, merits detailed analysis.

Finally, the reader should be referred to the recent publication, entitled *Parent* v. *Parent*, edited by Eric Plunkett, which includes a most interesting paper by the President of the High Court, Mr. Justice Finlay, entitled *Legal Considerations in Custody Disputes*. Several of the questions raised in the notes to the decisions contained in chapter 15 are addressed by Mr. Justice Finlay.

I owe a debt of gratitude to several people who helped me in the course of preparing the book. First, I must thank Mr. Justice Brian Walsh for his encouragement and support and for having been good enough to write the Foreword for the book. I must also thank my colleagues, Mr. Joseph Brosnan, Barrister-at-Law, Mr. Charles Lysaght, Barrister-at-Law, and Mr. Frank Ryan, Barrister-at-Law, for their help and advice. Mr. Gary Lynch gave me considerable assistance, for which I am most grateful. Ms. Margaret Byrne, Librarian of the Law Society, and Miss Neylon, Librarian of King's Inns, also gave me a great deal of help. Ms. Peggy McQuinn, of the Supreme Court Office, once again could not have gone to greater lengths to provide assistance in tracking down Supreme Court decisions: I am very much in her debt.

WILLIAM BINCHY
20th August 1984

ACKNOWLEDGMENTS

The publishers and the author gratefully acknowledge permission from the following to reproduce materials from the sources indicated:

The Incorporated Council of Law Reporting for Ireland: *The Irish Reports.*
The Jurist Publishing Company: *The Irish Jurist Reports.*
Round Hall Press, Irish Academic Press: *The Irish Law Times Reports, The Irish Law Reports Monthly.*
Several members of the Irish Judiciary: the Unreported Judgments handed down in their names.
The Irish Times Limited: *The Irish Times.*
The Stationery Office and the Department of Justice: excerpts from statutory material and unreported judgments.

CONTENTS

TABLE OF STATUTES

STATUTES IN OTHER JURISDICTIONS

1. *Australia*

2. *Canada*

3. *New Zealand*

4. *United Kingdom*

THE CONSTITUTION

TABLE OF CASES

BIBLIOGRAPHY

Bromley	Family Law (6th ed., 1981)
Browne	Ecclesiastical Law of Ireland (2nd ed., 1803)
Burn	Ecclesiastical Law (9th ed., by R. Phillimore, 1842)
Cretney	Principles of Family Law (3rd edn., 1981)
Geary	Law of Marriage and Family Relations (1892)
Jackson	The Formation and Annulment of Marriage (2nd ed., 1969)
Kisbey	Law and Practice of the Court of Matrimonial Causes and Matters (1871)
Shatter	Family Law in the Republic of Ireland (2nd ed., 1981)
Shelford	Law of Marriage and Divorce (1841)
Wylie	Irish Land Law (1975)

Chapter 1

THE CONSTITUTIONAL AND JUDICIAL FRAMEWORK

This casebook examines several aspects of Irish family law – marriage, divorce *a mensa et thoro*, maintenance obligations, the family home, and so on – but to understand these aspects fully it is necessary to have regard to the constitutional and judicial framework of family law. This framework is considered in this chapter.

THE CONSTITUTION

Family law has been greatly influenced by Constitutional developments over the past half century. Article 41 of the Constitution provides as follows:

> 1.1° The State recognises the Family as the natural primary and fundamental unit group of Society, and as a moral institution possessing inalienable and imprescriptible rights, antecedent and superior to all positive law.
>
> 1.2° The State, therefore, guarantees to protect the Family in its constitution and authority, as the necessary basis of social order and as indispensable to the welfare of the Nation and the State.
>
> 2.1° In particular, the State recognises that by her life within the home, woman gives to the State a support without which the common good cannot be achieved.
>
> 2.2° The State shall, therefore, endeavour to ensure that mothers shall not be obliged by economic necessity to engage in labour to the neglect of their duties in the home.
>
> 3.1° The State pledges itself to guard with special care the institution of Marriage, on which the Family is founded, and to protect it against attack.
>
> 3.2° No law shall be enacted providing for the grant of a dissolution of marriage.
>
> 3.3° No person whose marriage has been dissolved under the civil law of any other State but is a subsisting valid marriage under the law for the time being in force within the jurisdiction of the Government and Parliament established by this Constitution shall be capable of contracting a valid marriage within that jurisdiction during the lifetime of the other party to the marriage so dissolved.

Later in this casebook we will be examining in detail many of the specific implications of this Article in relation to family law. We will be considering, for example, the prohibition on divorce legislation (*infra*, pp. 259–60), the rules relating to recognition of foreign divorces (*infra*, pp. 226–59), the Constitutional position of families (and their members) where the parents are not married to each other (*infra*, pp. 119–65) and the right to marital privacy (*infra*, pp. 357–69).

Article 41 is not the only Constitutional provision that affects family law. Other Articles, notably Articles 40.1, 40.3 and 42, have had an important influence in the development of our law in respect of such matters as sex equality (*infra*, chs. 5 and 15), contraception (*infra*, pp. 357–69) and homosexual conduct (*infra*, pp. 374–88). As recently as 1983, the Constitution was amended so as to give explicit Constitutional protection to 'the right to life of the unborn' (*infra*, pp. 370–73).

The literature on Constitutional aspects of family law has been growing rapidly in recent years. In the chapters which follow, detailed bibliographical references are provided on the specific aspects of the Constitution which touch on family law. More general analyses include *Shatter*, ch. 1; J. Kelly, *The Irish Constitution*, (2nd ed., 1984); Staines, *The Concept of 'The Family' under the Irish Constitution*, 11 Ir. Jur. (n.s.) 223 (1976); the Law Reform Commission's *Report on Illegitimacy*, paras. 31ff (LRC 4–1982).

THE JUDICIAL FRAMEWORK

The law of marriage and matrimonial causes had originally been part of the canon law of the Catholic Church; Ecclesiastical Courts throughout Europe administered and applied the canon law with a right of appeal to Rome. After the Reformation, and Henry VIII's dispute with the Pope, the right of appeal to Rome was abolished; legislation recognised the jurisdictional autonomy of the Ecclesiastical Courts of the Church of England and the Church of Ireland, which continued to administer canon law, subject to statutes and the common law. Thenceforth the Ecclesiastical Courts in both countries slowly developed these canon law principles without any further reference to what was happening in the Catholic Church's jurisprudence.

After the disestablishment of the Church of Ireland on 1st January 1871 the jurisdiction of the Ecclesiastical Courts of the Church of Ireland was transferred to a newly established civil court, the Court of Matrimonial Causes and Matters. With a view to encouraging some degree of continuity, section 13 of the *Matrimonial Causes and Marriage Law (Ireland) Amendment Act 1870* provided that, in all matrimonial proceedings, the new Court was to:

> proceed and act and give relief on principles and rules which in the opinion of the said Court shall be as nearly as may be conformable to the principles and rules on which the Ecclesiastical Courts of Ireland have heretofore acted and given relief.

Over the years since the 1870 legislation came into force, the Courts have generally been affected by the principle of minimal change required of them by section 13 of that Act. Recently, however, the judiciary have become increasingly willing to develop the law, where they consider that the advances in modern psychology and psychiatry make this necessary. We will be examining this development later, especially in relation to decisions on nullity of marriage, including Kenny, J.'s judgment in *S.* v. *S., infra*, pp. 76–79; Barrington, J.'s judgment in *R.S.J.* v. *J.S.J., infra*, pp. 24–29; and Costello, J.'s judgment in *D.* v. *C., infra*, pp. 29–41.

The basic jurisdiction in matrimonial matters is now vested in the High Court, with a right of appeal to the Supreme Court: see *Shatter*, 17. Several statutes have also explicitly conferred jurisdiction on the High Court, and on the Circuit and District Courts in relation to various aspects of family law: see *Shatter*, 17–18.

E.R. v. D.R.

Unreported, High Ct., Gannon, J., 16 February 1984 (1982–520Sp.)

Gannon, J.:

The above-named plaintiff caused a Notice dated the 18th October 1983 pursuant to Order 60 of the Superior Courts Rules 1962 to be served on the Attorney General requiring the determination by the Court of issues as to the validity under the Constitution of the statutory provisions referred to in the Schedule to that Notice. The Schedule to the Notice is as follows:

'Schedule

1. Section 5 of the *Guardianship of Infants Act 1964* as amended by Section 15 of the *Courts Act 1981.*
2. Section 23 of the *Family Law (Maintenance of Spouses and Children) Act 1976* as amended by Section 12 of the *Courts Act 1981.*
3. Sections 1 and 2 of the *Family Law (Protection of Spouses and Children) Act 1981.*'

This hearing has been concerned only with such issues. The Notice was not served upon the defendant, but the Attorney General appeared by Counsel to argue for the constitutionality of the statutory provisions.

The plaintiff is the wife of the defendant and they have three infant children. By special summons the plaintiff claims against the defendant the following reliefs:

(1) Pursuant to section 11 of the *Guardianship of Infants Act 1964* sole custody of the infant children and contribution for their maintenance and education.

(2) Pursuant to sections 5 and 7 of the *Family Law (Maintenance of Spouses and Children) Act 1976* payments of maintenance for herself and the three children.

(3) Pursuant to section 2(1) of the *Family Law (Protection of Spouses and Children) Act 1981* the exclusion by Court order of the defendant from the Family Home.

(4) Pursuant to section 12 of the *Married Women's Status Act 1957* the exclusive, or alternatively a share of, ownership of the family home.

(5) Pursuant to section 5 of the *Family Home Protection Act 1976* protecting the family home from the defendant's conduct.

(6) Restraining orders by way of injunction as primary or ancillary relief restraining the defendant from the use of the home as a residence and from access to herself and the children.

The plaintiff failed to serve the special summons on the defendant personally in the ordinary manner, and on the 4th March 1983 obtained an order of this Court for substituted service and subsequently obtained an order of the Master of the High Court giving the 23rd March 1983 as the return date. Although service was effected in the manner prescribed by Court order the defendant did not appear on the return date. Upon the special summons coming before the Court in the absence of the defendant the Court could proceed with the hearing in his absence if satisfied on the balance of probability that he was aware of the nature of the claim and issues for determination by the Court, and of the time and place of the intended Court hearing, and had reasonable opportunity of preparing for and attending at the hearing. However, if his failure to appear or to take any step in the proceedings could be consistent with an intention to not admit, nor submit to, the jurisdiction in this Court on reasonably arguable grounds that the jurisdiction of the Court is questionable, it would be undesirable to proceed in his absence without first examining the Court's jurisdiction in the matters. In such circumstances the plaintiff served the notice under Order 60 of the Superior Courts Rules expressed in the indefinite way that an issue as to the validity of the statutory provisions 'may arise in this action'. The notice as served on the Attorney General states:

'Take notice that as party having carriage of the above-entitled proceedings, we hereby give you notice pursuant to Order 60 of the Superior Courts Rules 1962, that an issue as to the validity of the sections of the Acts specified in the Schedule hereto may arise in this action. A preliminary issue as to the jurisdiction of the High Court to hear claims pursuant to (1) section 11 of the *Guardianship of Infants Act 1964* (2) section 5 of the *Family Law (Maintenance of Spouses and Children) Act 1976* and (3) section 2 of the *Family Law (Protection of Spouses and Children) Act 1981* has arisen in these proceedings and the plaintiff will contend at the trial of the said preliminary issue that if the various sections of the Acts set out in the Schedule hereto purport to restrict or remove the jurisdiction of the High Court to hear such claims by originating summons, the sections are unconstitutional.

Under the adversary system of adjudication by the Court an issue arises only upon an adverse contention made by an opposing party. None such had been made. Rules 1 and 2 of Order 60 seem to require that before proceeding under the rule a question or dispute must have arisen involving an adverse contention. Order 60 is as follows:–

1. If any question as to the validity of any law, having regard to the provisions of the Constitution, shall arise in any action or matter the party having carriage of the proceedings shall forthwith serve notice upon the Attorney General, if not already a party.
2. Such notice shall state concisely the nature of the proceedings in which the question or dispute arises and the contention or respective contentions of the party or parties to the proceedings.
3. The Attorney General shall thereupon be entitled to appear in the action or matter and become a party thereto as regards the question as to the validity of the law.

There was no one before the Court to argue that 'the various sections of the Acts set out in the schedule hereto purport to restrict or remove the jurisdiction of the High Court to hear such claims by originating summons' or to argue that on those grounds the said sections are unconstitutional. Because the defendant was not served with this notice and was not represented nor called upon to argue against the validity of the statutory provisions mentioned both the plaintiff and the Attorney General had difficulty in presenting arguments on the issue.

To support her argument that the said various sections are unconstitutional the plaintiff argued that they purported to deprive the High Court of jurisdiction to hear the claims in the originating summons. She also submitted arguments to show that the said sections are not unconstitutional and do not deprive the High Court of such jurisdiction. The Attorney General, in this adversarial system of adjudication, was faced with uncertainty as to the adversarial content of the argument he had to meet. His argument of necessity was confined to establishing that the statutory provisions called in question were duly enacted within the constitutional authority of the Oireachtas and that, properly construed, they are entirely consistent with the Constitution.

The first of the various sections of the three statutes referred to in the schedule to the Notice under Order 60 is section 5 of the *Guardianship of Infants Act 1964* as amended by section 15 of the *Courts Act 1981.* By sub-section 1(a) of section 15 the 1981 Act amends the 1964 Act by substituting the following as section 5:–

> 5(1) Subject to sub-section (2) of this section, the jurisdiction conferred on a court by this Part may be exercised by the Circuit Court or the District Court.
> (2) The District Court and the Circuit Court, on appeal from the District Court, shall not have jurisdiction to make an order under this Act for the payment of a periodical sum at a rate greater than £30 per week towards the maintenance of an infant.
> (3) The jurisdiction conferred by this Part is in addition to any other jurisdiction to appoint or remove guardians or as to the wardship of infants or the care of infants' estates.

The part of the Act referred to in section 5 as 'this Part' includes section 11 of the *Guardianship of Infants Act 1964* which is a section which specifies certain classes of orders relative to the welfare including custody and maintenance of an infant which may be made by a Court. It is this section 5 as now enacted which the plaintiff challenges as being unconstitutional if it restricts or removes the jurisdiction of the High Court or alternatively as not having such effect and therefore not unconstitutional.

The second of the statutory enactments referred to in the schedule to the plaintiff's Notice under Order 60 of the Superior Courts Rules is the new section 23 of the *Family Law (Maintenance of Spouses and Children) Act 1976* introduced into that Act by way of amendment by substitution effected by section 12 of the *Courts Act 1981.* Section 23(1) of the section as now amended is as follows:

> 23(1) Subject to sub-section (2) of this section, the Circuit Court and the District Court shall have jurisdiction to hear and determine proceedings under sections 5, 6, 7 and 9 of this Act.

Sections 5, 6, 7 and 9 of the 1976 Act are provisions for the making of Orders for periodic payments for maintenance, variation orders, interim orders and orders for transmission of such maintenance payments, and come within the definition of 'antecedent order' in section 3 of that Act. Sub-section (2) of section 23 as introduced by substitution contains six sub-paragraphs which provide limitations on the jurisdiction conferred in sub-section (1) quoted. For the purpose of this judgment I will summarise their effect rather than quote them in full. Sub-paragraph (a) of sub-section 2 of the new section 23 puts a limit to the jurisdiction of the District Court to order periodic payments, the limit being £100 per week for the support of a spouse and £30 per week for the support of a child. Sub-paragraphs (b) and (c) are both subject to the provisions of sub-paragraph (d) of subsection 2. Sub-paragraph (b) excludes from the jurisdiction of both District Court and Circuit Court the making of any order or direction under sections 5, 6, 7 and 9 'in any matter in relation to which the High Court has made an order or direction under any of those sections'. Sub-paragraph (c) excludes from the jurisdiction of the District Court the making of any order or direction under sections 5, 6, 7, and 9 'in any matter in relation to which the Circuit Court (except on appeal from the District Court) has made an order or direction under any of those sections.' Sub-paragraph (d) of sub-section (2) of the new section 23 relaxes the exclusion by sub-paragraphs (b) and (c) from the jurisdiction conferred on the statutory Courts of the power of variation or revocation of orders or directions of the High Court. The effect of sub-paragraph (d) is that notwithstanding paragraphs (b) and (c) the District Court and Circuit Court may vary or revoke such High Court orders as were made under sections 5, 6, 7 and 9 before the amendment of section 23 effected by section 12 of the *Courts Act 1981* provided the circumstances, to which the High Court order or direction related, changed for reasons other than the amendment of the section 23 and, as far as the District Court is concerned, it would have to come within the range of the new District Court limit of jurisdiction. It is this section 23 of the *Family Law (Maintenance of Spouses and Children) Act 1976* as now enacted which the plaintiff challenges as being unconstitutional if it restricts or removes the jurisdiction of the High Court or alternatively as not having such effect and therefore not being unconstitutional. Sections 1 and 2 of the *Family Law (Protection of Spouses and Children) Act 1981* comprise the third of the statutory enactments of the Oireachtas referred to by the plaintiff in the schedule to the Notice under Order 60 of the Rules of the Superior Courts as being of questionable validity for want of constitutionality. Section 1 of this Family Law Act of 1981 consists of definitions of terms used throughout the Act, which is declared to be an Act to make further provision for the protection of a spouse and any children whose safety or welfare requires it because of the conduct of the other spouse. The definitions include definitions of 'child', 'applicant spouse', 'respondent spouse', 'barring order', 'protection order', 'proceedings under this Act', and 'the Court'. Sub-section (2) of section 1 of that Act provides that an order made by a court upon appeal from another court should be 'treated as if it had been made by that other court'. Section 2 contains six sub-sections and provides for the making of barring orders by the Court as defined in section 1 with an expiry limit of 12 months on orders of the District Court. This limit is expressed to be subject to section 11, being a section which makes provision for the obtaining of a Court order for discharge of a barring order. Of these two sections of the new Act of 1981 the plaintiff takes particular exception to the definition in section 1 of 'the Court' which is given in the definition section as 'means the Circuit Court or the District Court'. Of the nineteen sections of the *Family Law (Protection of Spouses and Children) Act 1981* the plaintiff challenges as being unconstitutional only sections 1 and 2 and to the extent only that they may have the effect of restricting or removing the jurisdiction of the High Court.

It was not contended for the plaintiff nor argued that the amending Statute, namely the *Courts Act 1981*, was itself, nor any part of it, unconstitutional or that by effecting these amendments that Statute was invalid and ineffective to the extent that it thereby purported to deprive the High Court of any part of its jurisdiction. The effect in the case of section 15(1)(a) of that Act by amending by way of substitution in its result is the same as if it had repealed and re-enacted with variations the pre-1981 provisions of the *Guardianship of Infants Act 1964* but omitting therefrom any reference to the High Court. Section 15(1) (a) of the *Courts Act 1981* does not alter the definition of 'the Court' in Part III of the 1964 Act. This is done by section 15(1)(b) of the *Courts Act 1981* in such manner as to omit reference to the High Court. The effect in the case of section 12 of the *Courts Act 1981*, by amending by way of substitution, in its result is the same as if it had repealed and re-enacted with variations the pre-1981 provisions of the *Family Law (Maintenance of*

Spouses and Children) Act 1976 but omitting therefrom provision for further orders of the High Court. Sub-section (1) of section 23 of the 1976 Act before amendment reads as follows:–

> (1) Subject to sub-section (2) of this section, the High Court, the Circuit Court (on appeal from the District Court) and the District Court shall, concurrently, have jurisdiction to hear and determine proceedings under sections 5, 6, 7 and 9 of this Act.

The omitted words on amendment by substitution are 'the High Court' and the word 'concurrently'. Because of the device in the *Family Law (Maintenance of Spouses and Children) Act 1976* of giving in the definition section a reference to another section of the Act, namely section 23, for the interpretation of 'Court' the repeal of section 23 and its re-enactment effected by section 12 of the Courts Act 1981 without specifying the High Court gives a new meaning to the definition of 'Court' in the 1976 Act which affects other sections of that Act not expressed to have been amended. Section 17 of the *Family Law (Protection of Spouses and Children) Act 1981* expressly repeals section 22 of the *Family Law (Maintenance of Spouses and Children) Act 1976*. The repealed section 22 contained a definition of 'the Court' incorporating the High Court but the 1981 Act in the definition therein of 'the Court' omits the High Court. By sub-sections (3) and (5) of section 17 the *Family Law (Protection of Spouses and Children) Act 1981* makes provision in relation to orders made in the High Court prior to the repeal of section 22 of the 1976 Act thus showing a clear purpose of excluding the High Court from the scope of the 1981 Act. But the *Family Law (Protection of Spouses and Children) Act 1981* (by section 17 of which section 22 of the *Family Law (Maintenance of Spouses and Children) Act 1976* is repealed) is not confined to repealing and re-enacting with variations the repealed section of the 1976 Act. It is a new enactment fulfilling a different although somewhat similar purpose but in a more extensive manner and creates criminal offences. It was no part of the argument for the plaintiff that section 15(1)(a) or (b) or section 12 of the *Courts Act 1981* or section 17 of the *Family Law (Protection of Spouses and Children) Act 1981* or any of them is unconstitutional. The declared purpose of the plaintiff's argument is to obtain a construction by this Court of section 5 of the *Guardianship of Infants Act 1964* as now enacted and of section 23 of the *Family Law (Maintenance of Spouses and Children) Act 1976* now enacted by the *Courts Act 1981* which will enable the plaintiff to proceed in the High Court with claims for relief under section 11 of the *Guardianship of Infants Act 1964* and sections 5 and 7 of the *Family Law (Maintenance of Spouses and Children) Act 1976*. The plaintiff also seeks a construction by this Court of sections 1 and 2 of the *Family Law (Protection of Spouses and Children) Act 1981* which will enable the plaintiff to proceed in the High Court in the first instance for an order under section 2(1) of that Act.

In approaching the matter of construction of the sections of the Statute it must be borne in mind that the sections the subject of challenge must be read and construed in the context of the entire statute in each case and in accordance with the ordinary meaning of the words as expressed. It must be assumed that the Oireachtas intended the enactments to be valid in accordance with the Constitution and that the draftsman exercised the degree of skill and care required and to be expected by the Oireachtas. In this way the statutes and their sections may be construed in a manner consistent with the presumption of validity under the Constitution. Any construction of which the sections may be capable which would be inconsistent with the Constitution must be rejected. If the statutes and sections are not capable of interpretation and sensible construction and effective implementation consistent with the Constitution only then may they be declared invalid to the extent that they are found inconsistent with the Constitution.

As to the plaintiff's application for an order under section 11 of the *Guardianship of Infants Act 1964* it is clear that under the provisions of that Act both before and since the amendment by the *Courts Act 1981* such applications could be made to the Circuit Court. Since the 1981 Act the District Court now has a limited jurisdiction under the section which it did not have under the 1964 Act. The *Guardianship of Infants Act 1964* is a consolidating Act and repeals and re-enacts with amendments statutes in relation to the custody and guardianship of infants which had been in force prior to the adoption of the Constitution. The duties and functions of the Court as expressed in the 1964 Act always have been exercised by the High Court, and section 3 of the 1964 Act does not create or confer any new or original jurisdiction on the High Court. Although expressed in mandatory terms the standard that that section imposes for the exercise of judicial discretion is one which was adopted by the High Court prior to 1937. An order upon an application pursuant to section 11 of the 1964 Act falls within Part II of the 1964 Act. Under sub-section (3) of section 5, which has remained unaltered it is declared:–

> (3) The jurisdiction conferred by this Part is in addition to any other jurisdiction to appoint or remove guardians or as to the wardship of infants or the care of infants' estates.

This section as amended and as read in the context of the *Guardianship of Infants Act 1964* as now amended taken as a whole does nothing to affect the jurisdiction of the High Court to make orders under Part II of that Act and in particular under section 11 thereof. I can find nothing in this section 5 of this 1964 statute as now amended in 1981 expressing a withdrawal or withholding from the High Court of jurisdiction to entertain applications or to make orders under Part II of that Act. In my opinion the argument of the plaintiff that section 5 as amended of the *Guardianship of Infants Act 1964* restricts or removes the jurisdiction of the High Court to hear claims under Part II of that Act is unsustainable, and there is no ground for declaring that section to be invalid having regard to the provisions of the Constitution.

The *Family Law (Maintenance of Spouses and Children) Act 1976* as amended is an Act which imposes upon a married person in specified circumstances the obligation of providing in pursuance of Court orders periodic payments for the maintenance of the other spouse and of any child. The Act also creates powers and functions for collecting payments and enforcing the orders of the Courts. It permits all such applications to the Court, including to the High Court (section 25), to be made in a summary manner and to be heard otherwise than in public. The jurisdiction to hear applications and make orders under sections 5, 6, 7 and 9 of that Act is, by the combined effect of the definition of the word 'Court' and the amended section 23, conferred on the Circuit Court and on the District Court. Although section 23 as amended in 1981 does no longer declare such jurisdiction to be exercisable concurrently with the High Court there are a number of provisions which relate to applications to be made to the High Court. It is clearly the intention of the Oireachtas that all such summary applications should be made in the first instance to the Court of limited local jurisdiction. But as expressed in section 23 in its amended form and the entire 1976 Act there is not any wording in the section or the Act which may be interpreted as restricting or removing the jurisdiction of the High Court in relation to such matters. The statute taken as a whole is an Act conferring on the Courts of first instance of limited local jurisdiction a jurisdiction in relation to such matters and as such there is no ground for declaring the new section 23 of the *Family Law (Maintenance of Spouses and Children) Act 1976* as amended in the 1981 Act to be invalid having regard to the provisions of the Constitution.

The *Family Law (Maintenance of Spouses and Children) Act 1976* as amended has no section 22 in it by virtue of the repeal of that section by section 17 of the *Family Law (Protection of Spouses and Children) Act 1981.* This latter Act is more extensive in its scope and in significant respects differs from the purpose and effect of the repealed section 22 of the 1976 Act. (see *O'B* v. *O'B* [*infra*, p. 306].) That Act is expressed by the definition in section 1 of 'the Court' and section 12 to confer the jurisdiction at first instance conferred by that statute on Courts of limited local jurisdiction, but it does not require nor permit applications to such Courts to be heard in a summary manner although authorising the proceedings to be heard otherwise than in public. Neither section 1 nor section 2 nor in the entire of the *Family Law (Protection of Spouses and Children) Act 1981* is there any wording which may be construed or interpreted as restricting or removing any jurisdiction of the High Court in relation to the matters the subject of the statute. The statute taken as a whole is an Act conferring on the Courts of first instance and limited local jurisdiction a jurisdiction which they did not, and otherwise than by statute could not, have or have had in relation to such matters. Such being the nature, purpose and extent of the statute there is no ground for declaring the new Act of 1981 nor in particular sections 1 and 2 of that statute, the *Family Law (Protection of Spouses and Children) Act 1981*, to be invalid having regard to the provisions of the Constitution.

The burden of the plaintiff's complaint as stated in the argument presented by Mrs. Robinson is that it is not within the competence of the Oireachtas under the Constitution to withhold or withdraw from the jurisdiction of the High Court any issue which is justiciable, nor to restrict the jurisdiction of the High Court nor to deprive it of jurisdiction by statute. She argues that the deletion by amendment of a reference in these statutes to the High Court for the exercise of a jurisdiction previously exercised by that Court under these statutes before their amendment appears to effect, in an indirect manner, a subtraction or diminution of a jurisdiction with which the High Court is invested by the Constitution. She submits that by expressly conferring on the Circuit Court and the District Court but not on the High Court jurisdiction to grant relief of the nature sought the jurisdiction of the High Court in that respect has been withdrawn or withheld or precluded. She contends that the right of the plaintiff to have recourse to the High Court in the first instance for the orders sought is precluded by confining to the Circuit Court and to the District Court the provisions for granting and implementing such orders. She further contends that in their amended form the statutory enactments, prescribing reliefs in the first instance only upon application to Courts of limited local jurisdiction, effectively prevent recourse being had to the High Court for any such reliefs. In reply on behalf of the Attorney General Mr. Blayney pointed out firstly that the only issues which the Attorney General has been called upon to argue are as to the validity in accordance with the Constitution of the three statutory provisions as amended set out in the schedule to the Order 60 notice. He points out further that the notice does not indicate that any issue arises as to the validity in accordance with the Constitution of any of the statutory provisions by which the amendments are effected. The notice he claims does not challenge the constitutionality of any sections of the amended or new statutes other than those specified in that schedule. He argues that the only ground advanced to support the challenge to the constitutionality of the specified sections is an alleged ouster of the jurisdiction of the High Court either by removal or withholding of some area of jurisdiction from that Court. Mr. Blayney submits that as a matter of construction each of the three sections referred to in the schedule is expressed in clear and unambiguous language which does not give rise to any difficulty or doubt of meaning. He submits that each does no more and no less than confer on the Circuit Court and the District Court a particular type and range of jurisdiction. None of the three sections challenged on the issues before the Court, he submits, makes any express reference to the High Court. In the absence of any such express reference none of them, he contends, should be construed or interpreted as dealing in any way with the jurisdiction of the High Court.

On the construction and interpretation of these statutory provisions I have adopted the guidelines for the construction and interpretation of statutes or Acts of the Oireachtas which are laid down by the Supreme Court in *East Donegal Co-Operative* v. *Attorney General* [1970] I.R. 317 in particular at pages 340 and 341 of the Report. On the matters of the form of notice of issues for determination by the Court, the subject matter of enquiry, and the construction and interpretation of the statutory provisions specified I accept the arguments on behalf of the Attorney General as being entirely correct. But the range of argument which has been advanced on the issues as stated in the Order 60 Notice has gone beyond the bounds of enquiry indicated by the notice. The arguments by the plaintiff have raised a number of important questions which have been explored to some extent relative to the range of the jurisdiction of the High Court under the Constitution and the authority relative thereto of the Oireachtas. Implicit in the arguments on behalf of the plaintiff is the assumption that the jurisdiction conferred by the statutes which are challenged is in the nature of an exclusive jurisdiction confined to the Court named, and the further assumption that the plaintiff is entitled to have recourse or access to the Court of her choice as a constitutional right. For the Attorney General, however, it is submitted that the existence of Courts of first instance in addition to the High Court with such jurisdiction by which the High Court is invested by the Constitution. The simultaneous existence as provided for in the Constitution of Courts of first instance with limited local jurisdiction and the High Court indicates that the exercise of jurisdiction may not be exclusive to any Court, save in regard to questions of constitutional matters reserved by the Constitution to the High Court. A provision of access to some Court of first instance even to the exclusion of others it is submitted is a consistent protection of the constitutional right of access of a litigant. The right of access to the Courts is no more than a right of recourse to whatever Court may be designated by regulation of the Oireachtas and there is no constitutional right of an individual of access to the High Court at his choice save only in respect of the invested jurisdiction on constitutional issues which is reserved solely to the High Court.

In deference to the diligence applied in the preparation and submission of these arguments it is necessary to examine the provisions of the Constitution relative to the jurisdiction of the High Court, and to the powers and functions of the Oireachtas in regard to the jurisdiction of the Courts.

It is unnecessary to quote in full the provisions of Article 34 of the Constitution. It should be sufficient to point out that the Constitution requires that justice shall be administered in public in Courts to be established by law and that the Courts shall comprise Courts of first instance and a Court of final appeal. Article 34 paragraph 3 sub-paragraph 1 provides as follows:–

> 1° The courts of first instance shall include a High Court invested with full original jurisdiction in and power to determine all matters and questions whether of law or fact, civil or criminal.
>
> 2° Save as otherwise provided by this Article the jurisdiction of the High Court shall extend to the question of the validity of any law having regard to the provisions of this Constitution, and no such question shall be raised (whether by pleading, argument or otherwise) in any court established under this or any other Article of this Constitution other than the High Court or the Supreme Court.

Sub-paragraph 4 of paragraph 3 of Article 34 is as follows:–

> 4– The courts of first instance shall also include courts of local and limited jurisdiction with a right of appeal as determined by law.

It can be seen from these provisions that in addition to the High Court other Courts of first instance must be established by the Oireachtas. Such Courts may be only of limited local jurisdiction and may not be conferred with unlimited jurisdiction. (See *Grimes and others* v. *Owners of 'Bangor Bay'* [1948] I.R. 350). The extent of the jurisdiction to be conferred on such other Courts of first instance must be determined by the Oireachtas and such jurisdiction may be extended or restricted. As a corollary it is evident that the jurisdiction of such Courts may be wholly removed. The Courts themselves may be increased or reduced in numbers and a jurisdiction exercisable may, as the Oireachtas may determine, differ as between them. The establishment of such Courts of variable limited jurisdiction necessarily involves the regulation of their Constitution and organisation and the distribution of jurisdiction and business among them as provided for in Article 36(iii) of the Constitution. The range of this function of the Oireachtas is such that if any particular aspect of jurisdiction in respect of justiciable determination could be conferred exclusively upon any such Court of first instance of limited jurisdiction it would be possible for the Oireachtas to withdraw that particular aspect of jurisdiction completely from the Courts. The absence of Courts or of judicial jurisdiction in some Court over matters or questions justiciable would leave a person without remedy. That this could be achieved by the Oireachtas seems to be entirely inconsistent with the objectives of the Constitution. Consequently, there must be a Court to which recourse may be had upon any event or any occasion and in any circumstances where there may exist a wrong for which in justice a remedy may be required. This requirement of justice could not be satisfied by investing by legislation a Court constituted and established by legislation with exclusive but determinable jurisdiction. The provision in the Constitution at Article 34.3.1° that the High Court be invested with full original jurisdiction in and power to determine all matters and questions whether of law or fact, civil or criminal ensures that no wrong need go without remedy. This appears to be the principle upon which the judgment of the Supreme Court in *R.D. Cox* v. *Owners of M.V. Fritz Rabe* (unreported, Supreme Court, 1st August 1974) is founded. From that decision it is evident that the jurisdiction with which the High Court was invested by the adoption in 1937 of Article 34.3.1° of the Constitution is not limited to whatever jurisdiction theretofore was exercisable by the former High Court and then existing at law or by statute. In pursuing the objectives of promoting the common good and attaining true social order the Oireachtas necessarily makes laws which confer rights, impose duties, create offences, prescribe sanctions in the form of penalties and punishments. In so far as such laws give rise to disputable questions of law or fact, civil or criminal, for judicial determination it can be said they create new jurisdiction. Changes in social requirements and patterns and standards of behaviour which occur in the normal growth of the State and passage of time may give rise without the intervention of legislation to new and further matters and disputable questions of fact or law not in existence in 1937 but requiring judicial determination. It would be inconsistent, in my view, with the meaning of Article 34.3.1°, as interpreted by the Supreme Court in *Cox* v. *Owners of M.V. Fritz Rabe* if there could exist no jurisdiction in any Court in such matters unless and until conferred by enactment of the Oireachtas. From the amplitude of jurisdiction with which the High Court is invested by Article 34 of the Constitution it follows that the Oireachtas does not by legislation add to nor increase the jurisdiction of the High Court. It follows also that the Oireachtas cannot validly in accordance with the Constitution create a new juridical jurisdiction and withhold it from the High Court nor reduce nor restrict nor terminate any jurisdiction of the High Court. If I am correct in understanding the effect of Article 34.3.1° the jurisdiction, authority and powers with which the High Court is invested by that Article of the Constitution include all such functions, authorities, duties and powers as are incident to any and every part of its jurisdiction without any necessary intervention of the legislature. It follows that all such matters come within the ambit of the phrase 'foregoing provisions of this Constitution relating to the courts' in the introductory part of Article 36, and 'the said courts' referred to in sub-paragraph (iii) of that Article 36 are those Courts only which are referred to in sub-paragraph (ii) of the Article as 'all other courts'. For these reasons I would reject the contentions advanced on behalf of the Attorney General as wrong in law that the

Oireachtas may, under Article 36 of the Constitution, confer upon and withdraw from the High Court or confer to the exclusion of the High Court upon other Courts jurisdiction in the matters of family law and custody of children and maintenance under consideration in these proceedings.

The nature of the functions of the Courts under the Constitution is such that the Courts cannot initiate proceedings before them. The High Court can, as I have indicated, prescribe and regulate procedures for persons having recourse or desiring access to it. The procedures for access or recourse to other Courts of first instance must be regulated by law. Because of the constitutional provisions requiring Courts of first instance other than the High Court but of limited local jurisdiction to be established by law the jurisdiction of such Courts may be exercisable concurrently with the jurisdiction of the High Court. But where, and so long as, such concurrent but limited jurisdiction exists the High Court would not in my view be compellable as a matter of constitutional right by any person to provide him with access to the High Court and to enable him to have recourse to the High Court at his choice in lieu of recourse to the other Court of first instance established by law and having the jurisdiction sought to be invoked. On the other hand it would not be competent, in my opinion, for a Court of first instance of limited local jurisdiction to decline to exercise its jurisdiction in any aspect in which such jurisdiction is concurrent with the High Court jurisdiction on the ground merely that recourse may be had to the High Court. To that extent it seems to me that in relation to Courts having jurisdiction conferred only by law there cannot be any reality in the distinction between having jurisdiction and exercising jurisdiction. Such a distinction is valid in regard to the High Court in relation to matters in which recourse may be had as prescribed by statute to other Courts of first instance. It would not be a valid distinction in regard to the High Court in relation to questions affecting the validity of laws having regard to the provisions of the Constitution, as that is the only Court of first instance having such jurisdiction with which it is expressly and exclusively invested by Article 34.3.2° of the Constitution. I accept and agree with the views of my learned colleague, McMahon, J., on this distinction between the Court having and exercising jurisdiction expressed by him in *Ward* v. *Kenehan Electrical Limited*, unreported, 21st December 1979. The basic principle in relation to the question of access to the Courts appears to be that in justice no wrong (using that word in the wide general sense) should be without a remedy. What is called the right of access to the Courts is essentially a right to have recourse to justice and to have judicial determination in matters or questions of a disputable nature whether civil or criminal.

For these reasons I am of opinion that if and when and in so far as other Courts of first instance established by law have jurisdiction in matters of family law and custody of children and maintenance, of the nature under consideration in these proceedings, it is competent for the High Court to decline to entertain applications for orders obtainable in such other Courts, or to remit to such other Courts for hearing applications brought in the High Court which are within the jurisdiction of such other Courts.

My conclusions on the issues brought before the Court by the plaintiff's notice pursuant to Order 60 of the Superior Courts Rules 1962 dated the 18th October 1983 are as follows:–

1. The sections of the Acts specified in the schedule to the plaintiff's notice are valid and in accordance with the Constitution.
2. The jurisdiction of the High Court to hear claims of the nature set out in the plaintiff's originating summons has not been restricted nor removed.
3. The High Court may accept or decline to accept for hearing in accordance with its own procedures claims for relief of the nature set out in the plaintiff's originating summons.

Notes

1. After this decision a practice direction was issued in the following terms:

   In any case where relief is sought in the High Court under the [*Guardianship of Infants Act 1964*, the *Family Law (Maintenance of Spouses and Children) Act 1976* or the *Family Law (Protection of Spouses and Children) Act 1981*], the Summons shall be returnable before the Master in the ordinary way and thereafter shall be put in the list before the Judge sitting for Family Law on a Friday Motion day.

   The parties must on that occasion attend and submit such evidence or arguments as they see fit as to whether the case is one appropriate for The High Court to exercise its jurisdiction under one or other of the[se] Acts, or whether it is a case which should be remitted to the Circuit Court or District Court. A decision will then be made on that issue and, depending upon the nature of that decision, the case will be listed for hearing. Such listing will not determine the appropriate scale of costs, if any, to be awarded, which will be subject to the provisions of Section 17(4) of the *Courts Act 1981*.
2. The decision is summarised by O'Connor, 2 Ir.L. Times (N.S.) 88 (1984).
3. In recent years there has been increasing public discussion on whether the present framework of judicial proceedings in family law disputes should be replaced or supplemented by non-judicial processes. There has been much talk of non-judicial procedures for conciliation, mediation and arbitration. The literature has already grown to intimidating proportions. See, e.g., Prus, *The Decision to Divorce: The Functions of the Lawyer in Defining the Marriage as 'Unworkable'*, 4 R.F.L. 186 (1972); Conway, *To Insure Domestic Tranquility: Reconciliation Services as an Alternative to the Divorce Attorney*, 9 J. Family L. 408 (1970); Irving & Irving, *Conciliation Counselling in Divorce Litigation*, 16 R.F.L. 247 (1975); Felner, Primavera, Faber & Bishop, *Attorneys as Caregivers During Divorce*, 52 Am. J. Orthopsychiat, 323 (1982); Bellinson, *Changing Dynamics in Attorney-Client Relationship Due to No-Fault Legislation*, 14 Fam. L. Newsletter No.1, 5 (1973); Irving, Benjamin, Bohn & Macdonald, *A Study of Conciliation Counselling in the Family Court of Toronto: Implications for Socio-Legal Practice*, ch. 3 of H. Irving ed., *Family Law: An Interdisciplinary Perspective*, (1981); Cornwall, *Advice on Marriage Breakdown*, 12 Family L. 70 (1982); Etheridge, *Family Law*, [1973] Georgia State Bar J. 55; Hancock, *The Power of the Attorney in Divorce*, 19 J. Family L. 235 (1981); Callner, *Boundaries of the Divorce Lawyer's Role*, 10 Family L. Q. 389 (1977); Westcott, *Family Problems – The Solicitor and His Client*, 7 Family L. 24 (1977); Wolff, *Family Conciliation; Draft Rules for the Settlement of Family Disputes*, 21 J. of Family L. 213 (1983); Abella, *Procedural Aspects of Arrangements for Children Upon Divorce in Canada*, 61 Can. Bar Rev. 443 (1983); Day, *Techniques of Settlement of a Matrimonial Dispute*, ch. 3 of *Canadian Bar Association Continuing Seminars No.2: Family Law* (1974); Wade, *Negotiating Family Settlements: Benefits and Barriers*, 4 Can. J. of Family L. 49 (1983); *Matrimonial Problems: Counselling – Another Option?* 75 Gazette Inc. L. Soc. of Ir. 163 (1981); Yates, *Development of Conciliation in Divorce Proceedings*, 132 New L. J. 102 (1982); Graham Hall, *The Case for Conciliation Bureaux*, 6 Family L. 231 (1976); Parkinson, *Bristol Courts Family Conciliation Service*, 12 Family L. 213 (1982); Parkinson & Westcott, *Bristol Courts Family Conciliation Service*, 77 Guardian Gazette 513 (1980); Davis, *Settlement Seeking in Divorce*, 132 New L. J. 355 (1982); Parmiter, *Bristol In-Court Conciliation Procedure*, Law Society Gazette, 25 February 1981; Manchester & Whetton, *Marital Conciliation in England and Wales*, 23 Int. & Comp. L. Q. 339 (1974); McLoughlin, *Court Connected Marriage Counselling and Divorce – The New York Experience*, 11 J. of Family L. 517 (1972); Maddi, *The Effect of Conciliation Court Proceedings on Petitions for Dissolution of Marriage*, 13 J. of Family L. 495 (1974); Bates, *Counselling and Reconciliation Provision – An Exercise in Futility*, 8 Family L. 248 (1978); Fennell, *Before We Accept Divorce*, Irish Times, 8 January 1982; James & Wilson, *Conciliation – The Way Ahead*, 14 Family L. 104 (1984); National Family Conciliation Council, *The Code of Practice for Conciliation Services*, 14 Family L. 107 (1984); Wilkins, *Conciliation: 'A Friendly Feeling'?* 14 Family L. 122 (1984); Kubie, *Provisions for the Care of Children of Divorced Parents: A New Legal Instrument*, 73 Yale L. J. 1197 (1964); Woodhouse, *Family Law in Society*, 1 Auckland U. L. Rev. No.2, 44, at 56ff (1969); Spencer & Zammitt, *Arbitration: A Proposal for Private Resolution of Disputes Between Divorced or Separated Parents*, [1976] Duke L. J. 911; R. Coulson, *Fighting Fair: Family Mediation Will Work for You*, (1983) (including excellent bibliography at pp. 183–190).

   There is good reason to believe that the development of non-judicial procedures would have some benefits. Unfortunately, up to now there has been little hard analysis of what these procedures would involve; instead there has been a, perhaps understandable, tendency to prefer the softer option of referring to these procedures in general, laudatory terms, on the assumption that no-one could be *against* such positive-sounding concepts as 'mediation', 'conciliation' and 'non-adversarial procedures'. But is it all that simple? Are there not more important issues at stake which reasonable people should confront and attempt to resolve? We should try to avoid using the word 'conciliation' as 'a kind of woolly blanket which covers, and partially conceals, a variety of procedures and methods': Parkinson, *Conciliation: Pros and Cons (II)*, 13 Family L. 183, at 185 (1983).
4. Let us raise a few questions which appear central to the discussion but which so far have tended to be obscured.
   (i) Is the call for private non-judicial resolution of family disputes a call for the *removal of the present legal scaffolding* that has been constructed around family relationships? The norms of pluralism and individualism, coupled with scepticism about the objectivity of moral principles, might appear consistent with such a development. What would be the advantages? Greater autonomy? Less state control? The disadvantages?

Primarily that the 'freedom' could be a liberty to neglect or abuse one's spouse and children, a liberty to sell the home over their heads and generally to behave in a manner detrimental to their interests. (Cf. Davis & Westcott, 47 Modern L. Rev. 215, at 220 (1984).)

(ii) Is the call really for the removal or significant reduction in the role of the *courts* in the determination of legal rights and responsibilities relating to family life? Cf. Finlay, *Towards Non-Adversary Procedures in Family Law*, 10 Sydney L. Rev. 61, at 75 (1983). Such an approach springs from doubts expressed by some commentators as to whether judges are the best people to make decisions on issues which are primarily social and psychological rather than legal. Do you share these doubts? It is interesting to consider how the law as to guardianship of children would operate in practice in the hands of social workers, psychiatrists or psychologists rather than judges. One suspects that possibly the approach towards adultery and towards 'appropriate' parental roles might be somewhat different. If so, would such a change *improve the administration of the law,* or simply *replace one set of values as to family life by another set of values?*

(iii) Most of the public discussion in recent times has centred, not on the abolition of family law or the replacement of judges, but on the more modest contention that non-judicial processes of conciliation, mediation and arbitration should *supplement* the judicial structure. The obvious advantage to private negotiation is that the parties themselves arrive at a conclusion as to their future through their own efforts rather than by having a decision imposed upon them against the wishes of at least one of them – and possibly both. It is beyond the scope of this book to do more than mention some aspects of the subject which need consideration, in the hope that they will stimulate further thought and discussion:

(a) Is it possible that, in some cases at least, non-judicial procedures could facilitate rather than prevent the exploitation of one spouse by the other? Where one spouse has considerably more economic resources than the other, for example, is it wise to remove their negotiation from the objective scrutiny of the Court, whose function is to prevent injustice? Cf. Roberts, *Mediation in Family Disputes*, 46 Modern L. Rev. 537, at 540 (1983); Yates, *The Interdepartmental Committee Report on Conciliation – A Step Backwards,* [1983] J. of Social Welfare L. 335, at 336–337; Mnookin & Kornhauser, *Bargaining in the Shadow of the Law: The Case of Divorce*, 88 Yale L. J. 950, at 954–956 (1979); Winks, *Conciliation: Pros and Cons (II)*, 13 Family L. 183, at 184 (1983). See also Crouch, *Mediation and Divorce: The Dark Side Is Still Unexplored*, 4 Family Advocate No. 3, p. 27, at p 33 (1982).

(b) Who are intended to benefit from non-judicial procedures? The *spouses* or the *family as a whole?* If the former, why should the needs of children be downgraded? If the latter, how can non-judicial procedures effectively protect the interests of the children? Cf. Winks, *Divorce Mediation: A Nonadversary Procedure for the No-Fault Divorce*, 19 J. of Family L. 615, at 650–651 (1981); *Report of the Inter-Departmental Committee on Conciliation*, para. 1.13 (Lord Chancellor's Department, Chairman, P.D. Robinson, 1983); M. Freeman, *The Rights and Wrongs of Children*, 230–231 (1983).

(c) To the extent that third parties are involved in the non-judicial processes – counsellors, conciliators or mediators, for example – is there not a danger that the values of these third parties may affect the outcome of the negotiation process? Cf. Katz, *Family Law and Psychoanalysis – Some Observations on Interdisciplinary Collaboration*, 1 Family L. Q. No.2, 69, at 75–76 (1967); Parkinson, *Conciliation: Pros and Cons (II)*, 13 Family L. 183, at 184–185 (1983).

(d) *Delay* in taking the appropriate steps to protect his or her legal rights may sometimes result in serious prejudice for a spouse. Cf. de Brabant, *Techniques of Settlement of a Matrimonial Dispute*, ch. 4 of C.B.A. Continuing Education Seminars No.2, *Family Law*, at 7 (1974). At what point, therefore, should spouses seek legal advice – before, during or after the non-judicial process has begun? If *before*, how can the competing strategies of legal and non-judicial responses work in harmony? One advocate of conciliation procedures has said that:

> 'An offer of conciliation should not, however, deprive either party of legal advice or of immediate access to the court. On the contrary, a conciliator should alert an unrepresented party to the need for legal advice, and recognize possible emergencies for which legal advice should be sought immediately. Although any attempt to combine conciliation with adversarial legal proceedings is likely to undermine the conciliation, a conciliation procedure should not infringe people's legal rights, or subject them to other arbitrary kinds of control.' Parkinson, *Conciliation: Pros and Cons (II)*, 13 Family L. 183, at 184 (1983).

Does this analysis face up adequately to the full dimensions of the problem, in your view?

(e) The difference between *reconciliation* and *conciliation* should be noted. Reconciliation is successful if the spouses resume or establish a harmonious relationship, living together; conciliation, on the other hand, does not necessarily involve such a conclusion: it is designed to reduce bitterness between the spouses and to encourage them to come to an agreement about issues affecting their future life and the lives of their children. It is, of course, quite possible for a conciliator or mediator to seek *both* reconciliation and conciliation, in the sense that he or she would first examine the possibilities of reconciliation and, if there was no real chance of reconciliation in the particular case, he or she would encourage conciliation procedures. It is only prudent, however, to appreciate the importance of the conciliator's 'philosophy of conciliation' in this context. Some conciliators may be strong enthusiastists for a genuine and sustained attempt to reconcile the spouses; others may take the view that it is improper to make strong efforts to reconcile the spouses and that attention should be concentrated on conciliation. The point to notice here is that what is at issue is not reducible simply to a question of scientific prediction as to eligibility for reconciliation: a more fundamental question of values is involved.

(f) Should reconciliation procedures be compulsory or voluntary? Much has been written on this question. See, e.g., Spies, *Divorce in Pennsylvania: Is the Criticism Misdirected?*, 60 Dickinson L. Rev. 229, at 249 (1956); Law Review Staff, *Reconciliation and the Uniform Marriage and Divorce Act*, 18 S. Dakota L. Rev. 611 (1973); Robinson, *Joint Custody: An Idea Whose Time Has Come*, 21 J. of Family L. 641 (1983); Bates, *Family Law in Australia: A Long Engagement*, 3 Family L. Rev. 15 (1980); Bates, *Counselling and Reconciliation Provisions – An Exercise in Futility*, 8 Fam. L. 248 (1978); Milner, *Settling Disputes: The Changing Face of English Law*, 20 McGill L. J. 521, at 531 (1974); Woodhouse, *Family Law in Society*, 1 Auckland U. L. Rev. No.2, 44 (1969); Baum, *A Trial Judge's Random Reflections on Divorce: The Social Problem and What Lawyers Can Do About It*, 6 J. Family L. 61, at 77 (1966); Finlay, *Australian Divorce Laws and Marriage Conciliation*, 3 Family L. Q. 344, at 355 (1969); the English Law Commission's Report, *Reform of the Grounds of Divorce: The Field of Choice*, para. 30 (Cmnd. 3123, 1966).

(g) Are conciliation procedures successful and cost-effective? These questions were examined in England by an Interdepartmental Committee, which reported in 1983: see the *Report of the Inter-Departmental Committee on Conciliation* (Lord Chancellor's Department: Chairman, P.D. Robinson, 1983). The Report was generally unenthusiastic on both counts, concluding that the empirical data did not support many of the claims as to the effectiveness of out-of-court conciliation made by those involved in the conciliation process. In its turn the Report has come in for sustained critical analysis: see Yates, *The Interdepartmental Committee Report on Conciliation – A Step Backwards,* [1983] J. of Social Welfare L. 335; Davis & Westcott, *Report of the Inter-Departmental Committee on Conciliation*, 47 Modern L. Rev. 215 (1984); Bristol Courts Family Conciliation Service Trustees, *Conciliation – the Inter-Departmental Report Examined,* 14 Family L. 48 (1984). A consultation paper published subsequently by the Matrimonial Causes Procedure Committee, chaired by Mrs Justice Booth, expressed the view that conciliation as a recognised part of the legal procedure of divorce should be encouraged, but also took the position that it was outside the terms of reference of the Committee to consider the question of the availability of out-of-court conciliation schemes. James and Wilson comment that:

> 'As a result of the general tenor of the views of these two committees, therefore, the future, from the point of view of probable developments in policy, seems likely to offer no support for voluntary out-of-court schemes.' *Conciliation – The Way Ahead*, 14 Family L. 104, at 105 (1984).

(h) Would the best approach be to create a family court operating on non-adversarial lines? How exactly would such a court be constituted and function? Would the new structure require a change in the provisions in the Constitution relating to the judicial power? For general discussion of family courts, see *Shatter*, 28–30; B. Hoggett & D. Pearl, *The Family, Law and Society: Cases and Materials*, 625–636 (1983); Horgan, *Family Court: The Need and the Obstacles*, 27 N.I.L.Q. 120 (1976); Lynch, *Legal Status of Women in Ireland – I*, 23 Administration 61 (1975); *Call for Family Courts*, Sunday Independent, 20 February 1977; Gordon, *The Family Court: When Properly Defined, It is Both Desirable and Attainable*, 14 J. Family L. 1 (1975); J. Payne, *A Conceptual Analysis of Family Courts* (Law Reform Commission of Canada, 1973); Alexander, *The Family Court – An Obstacle Race?*, 19 U. Pittsburgh L. Rev. 602 (1958); the Ontario Law Reform Commission's *Report on Family Law, Part V: Family Courts* (1974); the Institute of Law Research and Reform of Alberta's Working Paper, *Family Courts* (1972); Brown, *A Two-Tier Family Court*, 133 New L. J. 310 (1983); Graham Hall, *Outline of a Proposal for a Family Court*, 1 Family L. 6 (1971); Neville Turner, *University of Birmingham – Institute of Judicial Administration, Family Courts (Comments on a Paper Prepared by the Family Courts Working Party to the Law Commission)*, 4 Family L. 39 (1974); Allard, *Family Courts in Canada*, ch. 1 of D. Mendes da Costa ed., *Studies in Canadian Family Law* (1972); MacQuaid, *The Unified Family Court of Prince Edward Island*, ch. 7 of I. Baxter & M. Eberts Ed., *The Child and the Courts* (1978); H. Andrews ed., *Family Law in the Family Courts*, (1973); Payne, *The Administration of Family Law in Canada: Proposals for a Unified Family Court*, ch. 24 of F. Bates ed., *The Child and the Law* (1976); Macdonald, *The Future of the Family Court in Canada*, 10 Family L. 123 (1980); Lindsley, *The Family Court: A Rational, Reasonable, and Constructive Revolution in Domestic Relations Law*, 5 Calif. W. L. Rev. 7 (1968); Cripps, *A Family Court for England*, 14 Family L. 72 (1984); Wade, *The Family Court of Australia and Informality in Court Procedure*, 27 Int. & Comp. L. Q. 820 (1978). New Zealand reforms are analysed in *Family Courts – An Interview with Judge Trapski,* [1981] N.Z.L.J. 383; Schäfer, *Family Courts – Reconsideration Invited,* [1983] Acta Jurid. 191.

The last, provocative, word on this subject goes to Michael Freeman:

'I do not think the implications of the Family Court have been properly thought through. The concept is not as unproblematic as most of those who urge its adoption have assumed. Rather than seeing it as something new we ought to place it and demands for it into the historical context of the therapeutic state. Could it be that moves away from formal adjudication, of which the Family Court idea forms an essential part, are moves towards an intensification of control?' *The State, the Family and Law in the Eighties*, 11 Kingston 1. Rev. 129, at 172 (1981).

Chapter 2

NULLITY OF MARRIAGE

Introduction

The law of nullity of marriage is concerned with the circumstances in which a marriage, on account of some vitiating element, is regarded by the law as not being valid. A marriage may be invalid for several reasons. For example, a 'marriage' celebrated between persons of the same sex will not be legally effective. Similarly a marriage celebrated by persons under the age of sixteen without the requisite approval of the President of the High Court will not be valid. Other cases of invalidity relate to bigamy, failure to observe the necessary formal requirements, mental incapacity, duress, mistake and fraud, marriages between close relations and impotence.

The law of nullity has developed historically from principles of canon law. When Henry VIII broke with Rome, ecclesiastical courts of the Church of Ireland continued broadly to apply these principles. In 1870, when the Church of Ireland was disestablished, jurisdiction in matrimonial matters was transferred to the civil courts. Section 13 of the *Matrimonial Causes and Marriage Law (Ireland) Amendment Act 1870* required the civil court to proceed on principles 'which, in the opinion of the . . . Court, shall be as nearly as may be conformable to the principles and rules upon which the Ecclesiastical Courts of Ireland have heretofore acted and given relief.' The courts have had regard to this provision but especially in recent years they have shown an increasing tendency to develop these principles, in the light of recent advances in psychiatry and psychology.

An important distinction should be kept in mind when reading the cases on nullity of marriage. This is between *void* and *voidable* marriages. Although the distinction did not originally exist in the law it has been present for several centuries and the courts have shown no desire in recent years to reject it. See generally *Shatter*, 60–61; Newark, *The Operation of Nullity Decrees*, 8 Modern L. Rev. 203 (1945); Tolstoy, *Void and Voidable Marriages*, 27 Modern L. Rev. 385 (1964); Moore, *Defences Available in Annulment Actions*, 7 J. Family L. 239 at 241–249 (1967); Goda, *The Historical Evolution of the Concepts of Void and Voidable Marriages*, 7 J. Family L. 297 (1967).

There are several important differences between these categories. Perhaps most important is the fact that in the case of voidable marriages a decree of nullity is required; but with void marriages, no decree is necessary. Any court and any person may treat void marriages as void without being concerned to obtain a judicial *imprimatur* (although in practice certain categories of void marriages would raise such a doubt as to their validity that a decree might be essential to resolve the issue).

The next most important difference is that the validity of a void marriage may be challenged by any person with a sufficient interest, even after the death of the parties, whereas a voidable marriage may be challenged only by one of the parties during the lifetime of both; until it is annulled it is regarded as valid.

Other differences may be noted. Children of a void marriage are illegitimate. Children of voidable marriages will be regarded as legitimate unless and until the marriage is annulled, whereupon they are retrospectively rendered illegitimate. Formerly it was not generally appreciated that there could be children of a voidable marriage where one of the parties was impotent. It is now realised that this is wrong: the child may have been conceived before the marriage at a time when the impotent condition did not exist, or may have been conceived by *fecundatio ab extra* or by artificial insemination homologous

(A.I.H.) (see further the Law Reform Commission's *Report on Illegitimacy,* paras. 100–101 (LRC4–1982)).

Marriages that are void include those null on the grounds of nonage, prior subsisting marriage, prohibited degree of relationship and formal defect. Impotence renders a marriage voidable. As to whether lack of consent renders a marriage void or voidable, the position is somewhat less clear. The view generally has been that it renders a marriage void, but recent decisions relating to mental incapacity (*R.S.J.* v. *J.S.J., infra*, pp. 24–29 and *D.* v. *C., infra*, pp. 29–41) and (possibly) the secret intention not to consummate the marriage (*S.* v. *S., infra*, pp. 76–79) indicate that marriages vitiated by lack of consent on these grounds at least should be categorised as voidable rather than void.

A general point should be noted. The courts have recognised a Constitutional right to marry, located in Article 40.3 of the Constitution: cf. J. Kelly, *The Irish Constitution*, 486 (2nd ed., 1984). Professor Kelly says that '[t]he whole constellation of rights expressly or clearly implied by Articles 41 and 42 in the field of the family and the upbringing and education of children must, one would have thought, necessarily include the right to marry, since Article 41 specifically commits the State to guarding "with special care the institution of marriage [and protecting] it against attack"': *id.* Wherever the right to marry is to be located, however, the question worth considering in relation to nullity is as follows: to what extent may legislation or court decisions relating to nullity of marriage circumscribe the right to marry? Is there some central core of capacity and consent which, if present, must be recognised as entitling a spouse to marry? What weight, if any, may (or must) be given to such factors as the common good, the rights of children and the prospects of success or failure of the marriage? Very little thought appears to have been given so far by Irish lawyers to this Constitutional dimension of the law of nullity of marriage.

We will examine the grounds for nullity of marriage in turn, beginning with a consideration of the ground of lack of prescribed formalities.

1. *FORMALITIES*

The law relating to formalities of marriage is complex, extending over a wide range of statutory provisions as well as incorporating important principles established at common law. The present law is under the shadow of history, reflecting religious and political considerations extending far beyond those of marriage itself.

Very briefly, it may be said that the law envisages a system whereby marriages may be celebrated according to the rites of certain religious denominations of the Judeo-Christian tradition or, at the option of the parties, according to secular rules. Marriages according to Catholic rites are largely free from legislative control, although registration (which does not affect the validity of these marriages) has been governed by statute since 1863. In an important respect the civil law takes a different approach from that of the Catholic Church on the question of formal requirements: the absence of witnesses (apart from a clergyman in Holy Orders) will not render a marriage celebrated according to Catholic rites void so far as the law of this country is concerned, although such a marriage may be regarded as void by the Catholic Church.

USSHER v USSHER
[1912] 2 I.R. 445 (K.B. Div.)

Lord O'Brien, L.C.J.:

The question to be determined in this case is, whether the petitioner, William Arland

Ussher, and the respondent, Mary Ussher, otherwise Caulfield, were lawfully married. The material facts are as follows:–

At about 10 o'clock at night on the 24th April, 1910, the petitioner went through what purported to be a ceremony of marriage with the respondent. Both the petitioner and the respondent were Roman Catholics at the time of the alleged marriage; upon this hypothesis the petition was presented. The ceremony, which is impugned as invalid, was performed by the Rev. Joseph Fahy, parish priest of the parish where they resided. The petitioner lived at a place called Eastwell, in the county of Galway, and the respondent was a housemaid in his establishment. The petitioner was about thirty years of age and the respondent about twenty. The petitioner had been born a Protestant, and had up to the date of the ceremony professed the Protestant religion; but immediately before the alleged marriage took place he had been received into the Roman Catholic Church. The ceremony was performed in accordance with the ritual, so far as it is expressed in words, of the Roman Catholic Church, but in the presence of one witness only – a woman of the name of Agnes Kavanagh, who was a cook in the petitioner's house. It appears that both the reception into the Roman Catholic Church and the ceremony of marriage took place in an unused bedroom at Eastwell, into which the Rev. Joseph Fahy was secretly introduced at night by the petitioner.

It was argued before us that this marriage was invalid by reason of the fact that only one witness thereto was present, and that it was invalid ecclesiastically and legally, both in the eye of the Roman Catholic Church, and in the eye of the law of the realm, the Common Law. The prohibitive and penal statute, the 19th Geo. II, c. 13, was referred to as invalidating the marriage.

There was an added, I might say, a special, ground of impeachment of the marriage; it was alleged to be subject to the condition that if the ceremony which was gone through was not effective as a valid marriage in the eye of the Roman Catholic Church, it was to be regarded as altogether invalid. The Rev. Joseph Fahy, who was examined at the trial, stated that he told the petitioner (who was not produced to give evidence) that two witnesses to the marriage were necessary; but afterwards alleged that he thought that a faculty which he got from his bishop, the Most Rev. Dr. Gilmartin, dispensed with the necessity of two witnesses, and rendered the presence of but one witness sufficient. As to this the Rev. Joseph Fahy lapsed into very great confusion. It is not now denied that the faculty from the bishop was confined merely to the authorization of the celebration of the marriage in a private house. The marriage certainly took place before but one witness, Agnes Kavanagh, the cook. The persons present were only four in number – viz., the petitioner, the respondent, the cook Agnes Kavanagh, and the Rev. Joseph Fahy. The ceremony of marriage was, as I have stated, gone through in the words (all the words having been used) of the Roman Catholic ritual. Did the fact that there was but one witness present invalidate the marriage from the standpoint of the Roman Catholic Church? In my opinion it did. The Decree of the Council of Trent has been promulgated in Ireland; it is applicable to and controls Roman Catholic marriages, and makes the presence of two witnesses necessary. A ceremony not in accordance with its requirements as to the presence of a priest and two witnesses is null and void. Not only is the marriage declared null and void by the Decree of the Council of Trent, but the parties purporting to contract are declared incompetent to do so, *omnino inhabiles ad contrahendum*. That is to say, the marriage is rendered invalid not by reason of any incompetency of a personal character attaching to, naturally inherent in, the persons purporting to contract, but by reason of the non-compliance with the external requirements, that is to say, the presence of the two witnesses rendered necessary by that Decree. It must be borne in mind that the Decree of the Council of Trent, though coercive and conclusive from the standpoint of the Roman Catholic Church, is not recognised by the law of the land, the Common Law. We must bear this distinction in mind when dealing with the question whether the marriage with which we are here concerned was good at common law. It is unnecessary to consider how, from the point of view of the Roman Catholic Church, a subsequent 'validation' of the marriage would operate. The word 'validation' is used, but what it really, essentially is, and how it precisely acts, I decline to speculate. No such thing has taken place in this case, nor has any such thing been attempted; in fact, the petitioner refused to give the consent said to be necessary for such 'validation.'

But, as was asked with much emphasis by counsel during the argument, how could the marriage be validated if it was altogether void? Such a proposition, it was contended, finds no support from 'reason.' I am afraid there are many things lying at the root, at the foundation, of the Christian religion, mysteries of faith, for an elucidation of which we should appeal to 'reason' in vain. The incredulity of scepticism is caused by making 'reason' the sole and exclusive touchstone of faith. One thing, however, 'reason' imperatively impresses: that, such are the difficulties which beset every form of the Christian religion, we should, no matter how great our devotion to the faith of our fathers, practise forbearance and toleration towards all men within the Christian fold, whatever their distinctive tenets may be. It is sufficient for me to say that the Decree of the Council of Trent, which has been promulgated in Ireland and forms part of the Roman Catholic Faith, declares a marriage with but one witness to be null and void, and no 'validation' has been even attempted.

I now turn from the law of the Roman Catholic Church to the law of the land, the Common Law. What, then, was regarded as a Common-Law marriage? Marriages that were made without formalities (see 'The Catholic Encyclopaedia,' vol. ix, page 692, col. 1), but by the mere consent of the parties, were at one time regarded by many as Common-Law marriages. In order to have made such marriages effective there should have been a present intention to make the contract, and it should have been expressed accordingly; in other words, *per verba de praesenti*. This was accepted, as I have said, by many as the true view of the essential conditions of marriage at Common Law before the well-known case of *Regina* v. *Millis* 10 Cl. & F. 534; it rested on the maxim, *Consensus facit matrimonium*. Then came the case I have mentioned – that of *Regina* v. *Millis* 10 Cl. & F. 534 – which was very elaborately argued, but in which, nevertheless, the noble and learned Lords who heard it were equally divided in opinion as to whether the presence of a clergyman in holy orders was essential to the validity of a Common-Law marriage. Next we have the equally well-known case of *Beamish* v. *Beamish* 9 H. L. C. 274, in which the House of Lords showed that, by virtue of the rule *Semper praesumitur pro negante*, the decision in *Regina* v. *Millis* 10 Cl. & F. 534 made the presence of a clergyman in holy orders necessary to the validity of a Common-Law marriage. (See Lord Campbell's judgment, pages 338, 339, 9th H. L. C.) He dealt with the matter at some length, and concluded his observations as to this head of his argument by saying:– 'It is my duty to say that your Lordships are bound by this decision (*i.e.*, the decision in *Regina* v. *Millis* 10 Cl. & F. 534) as much as if it had been pronounced *nemine dissentiente*' (page 338). Later on he says that it was 'settled by that case that, to constitute a valid marriage by the *Common Law* of England there must be present a clergyman in orders conferred by a bishop.' Lord Chelmsford is also reported to have said in the same case – '*The Queen* v. *Millis* 10 Cl. & F. 534 must be taken to have settled that *at Common Law* marriage was invalid unless contracted in the presence of a priest in holy orders'; and, to refer to the antecedent judgment of Lord Cranworth, it will be seen that he laid down that 'according to the Common Law of England and Ireland a marriage celebrated without the presence of a clergyman in holy orders was not merely irregular, censurable, and punishable, but was absolutely void.'

Now, why do I refer to these passages from the judgments of these noble and learned Lords? For this reason, that they deal with *the law of the land, the Common Law*; and because the Rev. Joseph Fahy, as has not been denied, fulfils the necessary conditions as to being a priest in holy orders. The substance, the essential conditions, of a valid marriage at Common Law are what we have here. The contracting parties, intending then and there to get married, interchanged their mutual consent, the one to be husband, the other to be wife, in the presence of a priest in holy orders. By the word 'priest' I mean not a mere physical sacerdotal entity, but a clergyman present to elicit and receive the consent of the contracting parties; to see that they intended to get married, and mutually understood each other, and who might act as a witness of the marriage if necessary. Here not only were *verba de praesenti* used, but, as I have already stated, the whole of the Catholic ritual, so far as it is expressed in words, was gone through. There was here the essence, the substance, of a Common Law marriage, clothed, as it were, in ecclesiastical garments. I find that in treatises on marriage law the priest is styled 'the official witness,' the *testis qualificatus*. At Common Law the presence of any other witness was unnecessary to constitute a valid marriage. The other witnesses essential under the Decree of the Council of Trent, but not essential at Common Law, were styled the *formal* witnesses. I am, therefore, of opinion that there was a good and valid marriage, according to the law of the land, the Common Law, between the petitioner and the respondent. It is not necessary to refer to those exceptional circumstances, such as a marriage at sea, or a case in which it is impossible to secure the presence of a priest, mentioned by Lord Cranworth and by Lord Wensleydale in their respective judgments in *Beamish* v. *Beamish* 9 H. L. C. 274, and in the Decree *Ne Temere*, which dispense with the necessity for the presence of a priest; such circumstances did not exist in the present case. Before I leave this part of the case, I desire to refer to the Report made on the Marriage Law of the United Kingdom, dated 1868; perhaps the most authoritative report (whether in regard to the position and qualifications of the signatories to it or of the witnesses examined before them) that was ever presented to either House of Parliament. Amongst the signatories were five Lords Chancellors, four English and one Irish; and among the witnesses were several Roman Catholic bishops, both English and Irish. The division under the head of 'Roman Catholic Marriages' consists of six short clauses, so succinct that their very succinctness causes me some compunctious visitings lest my observations be too great a trespass on the public time. All these clauses are relevant, but I will refer only to Clauses 1 and 6, which are as follows:–

Clause 1. – 'Until the year 1863 marriages between two Roman Catholics (being the great majority of the whole number of marriages annually solemnized in Ireland) were *left to the operation of the Common Law*, without any statutory enactment; and, so far as relates to the legal constitution of marriage between such parties, this is still the case; the provisions of the Act passed in that year being directory, with a view to the registration only of such marriages.'

Clause 6, after referring to the Council of Trent, the publication of banns, and dispensation with them by episcopal licence, continues as follows:–

'Of these matters, however (being requisites of marriage by the internal economy only of the Roman Catholic Church), the law of the land takes no cognizance; *and a marriage contracted in the presence of any Roman Catholic priest in Ireland between two Roman Catholics, although contrary to the law and discipline of their own Church, would be legally valid.'*

My brother Kenny most appropriately referred to these among other clauses of the Report; but there is one other antecedent clause, at page 3 of the Report, to the concluding lines of which, as I think them apposite, and entirely right, I shall refer. They are as follows:–

'In both countries (England and Ireland) provision is made for a general registry of marriages with a view to their greater publicity and more authentic proof; but the *validity* or *proof* of marriage is not made dependent upon such registration or upon any other particular kind of evidence.'

Palles, C.B. and **Gibson, J.** delivered concurring judgments

Notes

1. For critical analysis of the *Millis* decision, see Walshe, *Two Famous Irish Marriage Cases*, 31 Ir. Ecc. Record (4th series) 449, 579 (1912), 32 Ir. Ecc. Record 10, 118 (1913). See also Schwelb, *Marriage and Human Rights*, 12 Amer. J. of Comp. L. 337, at 355 (1963):–
   Th[e *Millis*] decision is believed by most competent scholars to have been without any real historical foundation . . . (Citing several judicial and academic authorities.)
2. Marriages celebrated otherwise than in accordance with the rites of the Catholic Church are subject to detailed statutory regulation, see *Shatter*, 41–42, 44–53. It appears, however, that in only a small number of cases will failure to comply with a statutory provision render a marriage void. Cf. *id.*
3. Marriages void on account of formal defect may not be ratified by subsequent cohabitation; nor, it seems, will the courts presume that such cohabitation was based on a valid subsequent marriage. In *Martin* v. *Shepherd*, I.L.T.R. 142, at 144 (1878), where parties had lived together for twenty eight years after a marriage ceremony that was void on account of formal defect, Sullivan, M.R. said:
   It has been contended very forcibly for the defendants that I ought to presume, from the length of time that has elapsed since 1850, that some other form of marriage has taken place between the plaintiff and her husband, and that I ought to turn a marriage that is null and void into a legal marriage by presumption, so as to ratify the course of life which she has been pursuing. I cannot hold that there is such a presumption in this case; I cannot here apply that doctrine. If it could be shown that she and her husband had gone to a foreign land, that they had lived there as man and wife for twenty, or any number of years, that she had passed as his wife, and that their children had been baptized as those of husband and wife, I am not at all certain that such a state of facts would not raise the presumption of a second marriage as against the illegal one of 1850. But I have not a shred of evidence to warrant that presumption.
4. As a general rule the law of the place of celebration determines the formal validity of a marriage: P. North, *The Private International Law of Matrimonial Causes in the British Isles and the Republic of Ireland*, 370 (1977); *Du Moulin* v. *Druitt*, 13 I.C.L.R. 212 (1860). Thus, a marriage celebrated in France by a religious rather than a civil ceremony is not valid, even if the parties celebrating it were Irish nationals, domiciled and living in Ireland at the time, both of them believing that the marriage was valid – as, of course, it would have been if celebrated in Ireland. It transpired that a number of Irish people had gone through religious ceremonies at Lourdes, without any prior civil ceremony. Accordingly section 2 of the *Marriages Act 1972* was enacted. It provided as follows:–
   (1) This section applies to a marriage:–
      (*a*) which was solemnised before the passing of this Act solely by a religious ceremony in the department of Hautes Pyrénées, France, and
      (*b*) was between persons both or either of whom were or was citizens or a citizen of Ireland on the day of the marriage.
   (2) A marriage to which this section applies shall be and shall be deemed always to have been valid as to form if it would have been so valid had it been solemnised in the State.
   (3) An tArd-Chláraitheoir may, on production of such evidence as appears to him to be satisfactory, cause a marriage to which this section applies to be registered in a register to be maintained in Oifig an Ard-Chláraitheora.
   (4) The register in which a marriage is entered under subsection (3) of this section shall be deemed to be a register maintained under the *Registration of Marriages (Ireland) Act, 1863*, and that Act shall apply and have effect accordingly.

   What would be the position if, before the Act, a party to a 'Lourdes marriage' had entered a subsequent marriage, on the basis that the first marriage was void? Cf. the discussion of this issue during the Seanad Debates by Senators Mary Robinson and Alexis FitzGerald and the Minister for Health, Mr. Erskine Childers: 73 Seanad Debates cols 986–988 (23 November 1972); *id.*, cols 1294–1295 (13 December 1972). See also *Shatter*, 53–54. Does the decision of *F.M.L. & A.L.* v. *An tArd Chláraitheoir na mPosadh*, *infra*, p. 79, throw any light on the problem?
5. The *Marriages Bill 1963* had favoured a different approach. Section 2(1) provided that:
   Where the following conditions are fulfilled in the case of a marriage solemnised before the commencement of this section, that is to say:
   (*a*) it was solemnised solely by a religious ceremony which took place in the Department of Hautes Pyrénées, France, and would for all purposes be recognised if the ceremony had taken place within the State,
   (*b*) one at least of the parties was for a period ending on the day of the marriage domiciled in the State, and

(*c*) the parties have, during a period subsequent to the marriage, been living together while domiciled in the State,

then, subject to subsection (6) of this section and with effect as from the day of its solemnisation, the marriage shall for all purposes be recognised as if the religious ceremony had taken place in the State.

Section 2(6) provided that:

Nothing in the foregoing subsections of this section shall operate to affect the validity of law of any marriage:–

(*a*) which, before the commencement of this section, was solemnised after the solemnisation of a marriage fulfilling the conditions specified in subsection (1) of this section while both of the parties to that marriage were alive, and

(*b*) which was between one of those parties and a third person,

and, in any such case, subsection (1) of this section shall not have effect.

Was this approach better or worse than what ultimately was preferred in section 2 of the *Marriages Act 1972?*

6. The complexities and difficulties involved in attempting to harmonise private international law rules relating to marriage were apparent in the drafting of the *Hague Convention on the Celebration and Recognition of the Validity of Marriage* in 1976: see Glenn, *Comment*, 55 Can. Bar Rev. 586 (1977); Reese, *The Thirteenth Session of the Hague Conference*, 25 Amer. J. of Comp. L. 393, at 393–394 (1977); North, *Development of Rules of Private International Law in the Field of Family Law*, 116 Receuil des Cours 9, at 92–98 (1980).

2. *NONAGE*

A marriage celebrated when either party is under the age of sixteen years is not 'valid in law' (*Marriages Act 1972*, section 1(1)), unless the President of the High Court (or a judge of that court nominated by the President) has first granted an exemption when the grant is 'justified by serious reasons and is in the interests of the parties to the intended marriage (*id.*, section 1(3)). It seems clear that a marriage contracted without this exemption is void rather than voidable.

Section 7 of the Act contains detailed provision requiring parental consent (or, in default, the consent of the President of the High Court or nominated judge) for a marriage celebrated by a minor who is aged sixteen years or older. It appears that failure to comply with these provisions does not render the marriage invalid: *Shatter*, 56. For an account of the practical operation of the President of the High Court's functions under sections 1 and 7, and relevant statistics, see the Law Reform Commission's Working Paper No.2–1977, *The Law Relating to the Age of Majority, the Age for Marriage and Some Connected Subjects.* More recent statistics are contained in the Law Reform Commission's *Report on the Age of Majority, The Age for Marriage and Some Connected Subjects.*

It has for long been recognised that there is a significant correlation between young age at the time a marriage is celebrated and subsequent marriage breakdown, see Monahan, *Does Age at Marriage Matter in Divorce?* 32 Social Forces 81 (1953); Glick & Norton, *Frequency, Duration and Probability of Marriage and Divorce*, 33 J. of M. & Family 307 (1971); H. Carter & P. Glick, *Marriage and Divorce: A Social and Economic Study*, 235–237 (1970); Podell, *The Case for Revision of the Uniform Marriage and Divorce Act*, 18 S. Dakota L. Rev. 601, at 604–605 (1973). A study carried out by Dr Helen Burke, of the Law Reform Commission and University College Dublin, found that those seeking a church annulment in the Dublin Regional Marriage Tribunal were younger than the Leinster average at the time of their marriage. Whether from this finding any *definite* conclusions may be drawn as to the risk factor of very young marriages, is however, not clear.

It would be tempting, but futile, to conclude from these studies that youthfulness was the cause of marriage breakdown and that the cure would be to prohibit young marriages. Unfortunately, life is not that simple. As to the complexities of the socio-economic factors impinging on young marriages, see R. Winch, *The Modern Family*, 600–601 (3rd ed., 1971). The psychological complexities are considered by Lee, *Age at Marriage and Marital Satisfaction: A Multivariate Analysis with Implications for Marital Stability*, 39 J. of M. & Family 493 (1977); Glenn & Weaver, *A Multivariate, Multisurvey Study of Marital Happiness*, 40 J. of M. & Family 269 (1978); Bahr, Chappell & Leigh, *Age at Marriage,*

Role Enactment, Role Consensus, and Marital Satisfaction, 45 J. of M. & Family 795 (1983). See also Adams, *Marriage of Minors: Unsuccessful Attempt to Help Them,* 3 Family L. Q. 13 (1969) (analysing an approach involving the prior consultation between the prospective spouses and a family agency).

The social implications of raising the minimum age for marriage are analysed by Wardle, *Rethinking Marital Age Restrictions*, 22 J. of Family L. 1 (1983), and by Fuller, *Washington's Statutory Restrictions on Marriage: Ripe for Legislative Review*, 12 Gonzaga L. Rev. 403, at 407–410 (1977). If the minimum age for marriage were raised to 18 or 21, would a Constitutional issue arise? As to the present law, it may be asked why the risk of marital instability can justify the prohibition and restrictions relating to young marriages when other risk factors (arising, for instance, in marriages between persons from different ethnic, educational or religious backgrounds) carry no similar limitations. Cf. W. O'Donnell & D. Jones, *The Law of Marriage and Marital Alternatives*, 36–37 (1982). So far as the parental consent requirement is concerned, it is interesting to investigate its rationale. If it is the promotion of the minor's welfare, why may a child undertake the lifelong commitment of a marriage which may have little chance of success, provided only that he or she has obtained the consent of his or her parents who in some, albeit rare, cases may have no particular concern for the child's welfare? If the policy is to protect parental authority independent of consideration of the child's welfare, is this a proper limitation on the minor's autonomy? Cf. *Anon., Note: The Uniform Marriage and Divorce Act – Marital Age Provisions*, 57 Minn. L. Rev. 179, at 192 (1972).

The Law Reform Commission, in its *Report on the Law Relating to the Age of Majority, the Age for Marriage and Some Connected Subjects* (LRC 5–1983) recommended that a marriage solemnised between persons either of whom is under the age of sixteen years should be void. This rule would apply to any marriage solemnised in the State, wherever the parties might have their habitual residence; it would, moreover, apply to any marriage solemnised *outside* the State where, at the time it was solemnised, the habitual residence of the parties, or either of them, was in the State. The idea behind this latter recommendation was to discourage 'forum shopping' by the sanction of invalidity.

The Commission also proposed that parental consent for the marriages of minors should be required. Where the parents *disagreed*, the minor would be entitled to seek the consent of the High Court, but where the parents were both *opposed* to the proposed marriage, there should be no recourse to the High Court. Having regard to the fact that, by reason of other recommendations, the age of majority (and consequently the right to marry without parental consent) would be reduced to 18, the Commission considered that:

> it would not be oppressive to require a minor in such circumstances to wait for what in many cases will be a period of months rather than years before being able to marry: para. 62.

3. *MARRIAGES FOR A LIMITED PURPOSE*

The Courts in this country have not been called upon to determine the validity of a marriage that has been entered into for some ulterior purpose, such as to gain immigration or tax privileges, or to legitimate a child. In England, the view has been taken that such marriages should be regarded as valid (*H.* v. *H.*, [1954] P. 258, at 267 (Karminski, J., 1953); *Silver (orse Kraft)* v. *Silver,* [1955] 1 W.L.R. 728 (P.D.A. Div., Collingwood, J.); *Vervaeke* v. *Smith (Messina and Attorney General Intervening),* [1982] 2 All E.R. 144 (H.L. (Eng.)), noted by St. J. Smart, 99 L.Q. Rev. 24 (1983)). In most other common law jurisdictions, the same view has been favoured but in the United States some Courts have preferred to hold that these marriages (at all events where they are designed to derive an immigration benefit) are void (cf., e.g., *U.S.* v. *Rubenstein*, 151 F. 2d 915 (1945)). Scottish law favours the same approach as in *U.S.* v. *Rubenstein*: cf. *Orlandi* v. *Castelli*, 1961 S.C. 113. In

Australia, courts have sometimes considered this type of problem under the heading of fraud: cf. *In the Marriage of Deniz,* [1977] F.L.C. 90–252, (noted by Bates, 128 New L. J. 403 (1978)); *In the Marriage of Suria,* [1977] F.L.C. 90–305; see further H. Finlay, *Family Law in Australia*, 175–176 (3rd ed., 1983).

A *dictum* of Barrington, J., in the recent decision of *R.S.J.* v. *J.S.J.* [1982] I.L.R.M. 263, at 264 (High Court, Barrington, J.), would suggest support for the view that marriages for ulterior, or limited, purposes should be regarded as valid. He stated:

> People have entered into a contract of marriage for all sorts of reasons, and their motives have not always been of the highest. The motive for the marriage may have been policy, convenience, or self-interest. In these circumstances it appears to me that one could not say that a marriage is void merely because one party did not love or had not the capacity to love the other.

See also *J.R. (otherwise McG.)* v. *P. McG., infra*, p. 68–70, and *E.P.* v. *M.C., (otherwise P.), infra*, p. 42–43. For consideration of the policy issues, see Bromley, *The Validity of 'Sham Marriages' and Marriages Procured by Fraud*, 15 McGill L. J. 319 (1969); Bates, *Limited and Extraneous Purpose Marriages – A Problem of Definition and Policy in the Law of Nullity*, 4 Anglo-Amer. L. Rev. 69 (1975).

4. *MENTAL INCAPACITY*

It is clear that, for a marriage to be valid, each spouse must have the mental capacity to marry. In determining the nature of that capacity the law has a difficult task. If the standard is set high at a high level then many people will not be capable of contracting a valid marriage. This raises Constitutional issues, as well as broader questions of human rights. Cf. Mecredy-Williams, *Marriage Law and the Mentally Retarded*, 2 Can. J. of Family L. 63 (1979); Jacobs, *Note: The Right of the Mentally Disabled to Marry: A Statutory Evaluation*, 15 J. of Family L. 463 (1977); Lazerow, *Mental Incompetency as Grounds for Annulment*, 7 J. of Family L. 442 (1967); Shaman, *Persons Who Are Mentally Retarded: Their Right to Marry and Have Children*, 12 Family L.Q. 61 (1978). A more practical consequence is a possible increase in the number of illegitimate children (assuming, of course, that the concept of illegitimacy has not been abolished). A further difficulty is that spouses might be tempted to seek to have their marriages annulled on the ground of mental incapacity when in truth they were capable of contracting a valid marriage but subsequently wished to be relieved of the commitments they undertook.

On the other hand, if the law set the standard of mental capacity for marriage at a very low level, this would mean that persons would be held to be validly married even in cases where they had not full capacity to understand the nature of marriage and the commitments that marriage involves.

There is no easy or obvious answer to this dilemma, which has come under increasing discussion in recent years. Historically the courts have annulled marriages where a spouse was unable to understand the nature of marriage and its obligations (*In the Estate of Park deceased; Park* v. *Park,* [1954] P. 89) (or, more rarely, where a spouse was suffering from very serious mental illness or was intoxicated (*Legeyt* v. *O'Brien*, Milw. 325 (1834); *Sullivan* v. *Sullivan*, 2 Hag. Con. 238, 161 E.R. 728 (1818); cf. *Roblin* v. *Roblin*, 28 Gr. 439 (1881)) or was under the influence of drugs or was hypnotised (*Jackson*, 281)). Recently a broader view has been taken.

R.S.J. v. J.S.J.

[1982] I.L.R.M. 263 (High Court, Barrington, J.)

The petitioner married the respondent on 21 June 1978, but the marriage was a failure and after 8 months the respondent left the matrimonial home. The petitioner was a farmer of comfortable circumstances. There was a history of psychiatric illness in the family. The respondent was a nurse who had left a very successful career on her marriage. The wife left the matrimonial home principally because she had become convinced that the husband did not want her there. On the husband's petition for a decree of nullity, two issues were raised for decision by the court; (i) whether the petitioner was induced to be a party to the ceremony of marriage through extreme pressure, fear, duress and undue influence imposed by the respondent, (ii) whether by reason of his mental capacity and state of mind at the time of the said marriage the petitioner was able to understand the nature, purpose and consequences of the marriage contract. By consent, a third issue was later added; in the form of the question: was the petitioner suffering from such disease of the mind on 21 June 1978 that he was unable to maintain and sustain a normal relationship with the respondent or any children there might be of the proposed marriage, and was he thereby incapable of contracting a valid marriage with the respondent? It was contended, *inter alia*, by the respondent that even if proven this last issue was not a good ground for declaring a marriage void.

Barrington, J. rejected the first two grounds of the petition, on the evidence. He continued:

THE THIRD QUESTION – THE LAW

The third question raises an issue for which, so far as I am aware, there is no precedent in the law of this country. The petitioner's counsel submit that even assuming the petitioner freely entered into the marriage and knew all the implications of the marriage contract he was still incapable of contracting a valid marriage because he was so ill that he was unable to maintain and sustain a normal relationship with his wife or with any children there might be of the proposed marriage. On the other hand Mr. Barron submits that even if the petitioner were to succeed in proving these grounds they would not entitle him to a decree of nullity in Irish law.

The substantial ground put forward on behalf of the petitioner is that he suffered at all material times from schizophrenia or some similar illness which disabled him from forming and sustaining a normal relationship with the respondent or with any other woman. I do not regard the reference to 'any children there might be of the marriage' as being a separate ground as, on the case as presented, the petitioner's alleged inability to form a normal relationship with any child there might be of the marriage was merely another symptom of the same illness which, it was alleged, would prevent him from forming a normal relationship with his wife.

In my opinion the illness of one of the parties, they both being in other respects capable of contracting a valid marriage, could not under any circumstances make a marriage void provided both parties knew of the illness and wished to get married. To hold otherwise would be an unwarranted interference with the right to marry. People have entered into a contract of marriage for all sorts of reasons, and their motives have not always been of the highest. The motive for the marriage may have been policy, convenience, or self-interest. In these circumstances it appears to me that one could not say that a marriage is void merely because one party did not love or had not the capacity to love the other. Mr Barr, however, on behalf of the petitioner submits that the matter goes deeper than this. He submits that marriage implies an intention on behalf of the parties to live in some form of society together and that if one of the parties – through illness it is suggested in this case – has not the capacity to maintain and sustain a relationship with the other a real marriage becomes impossible.

The law has always accepted impotence as a ground for avoiding a marriage. But in ways what is contended for here is a much more serious impediment to marriage. No doubt there have been happy marriages where one of the parties was impotent. But it is impossible to imagine any form of meaningful marriage where one of the parties lacks the capacity of entering into a caring, or even a considerate, relationship with the other. There is of course the distinction that in the case of impotence providing the grounds for a decree of nullity, the marriage will not have been consummated and there will be no children. In the present case the marriage was consummated and there could have been children. On the other hand there is no child and one should deal with this case as one finds it.

As Kenny J has pointed out in *S* v. *S* [*infra*. p. 77] the power of the High Court to declare a marriage null is derived from the Matrimonial Causes and Marriage (Ireland) Amendment Act, 1870 by which the jurisdiction exercised by the ecclesiastical courts of the Church of Ireland was transferred, on the disestablishment of that Church, to a court for matrimonial causes and matters, whose powers were subsequently transferred to the High Court. S. 13 of the Act provided that in all suits and proceedings the court of Matrimonial Causes and Matters was to proceed, act and give relief on principles and rules which, in the opinion of the court, were, as nearly as may be, conformable to the principles and rules on which the ecclesiastical courts of Ireland had up to then acted and given relief.

However, counsel for the petitioner rely upon a *dictum* of Kenny J [*infra*, p. 78] which is in the following terms:–

> S. 13 of the Act of 1870 did not have the effect of fossilising the law in its state in that year. That law is, to some extent at least, judge-made, and courts must recognise the great advances made in psychological medicine since 1870 make it necessary to frame new rules which reflect these.

I respectfully accept this dictum. If therefore it could be shown that, at the date of the marriage, the petitioner, through illness, lacked the capacity to form a caring or considerate relationship with his wife I would be prepared to entertain this as a ground on which a decree of nullity might be granted.

However, I think one can draw a further analogy with the case of impotence. Under the law of Ireland impotence makes a marriage voidable. But an impotent spouse can rely upon his own impotence to avoid the marriage only if the other party has previously repudiated the marriage. (*McM. v. McM.* [1936] I.R. 177 and *A v A (sued as B)* 19 LR (Ir.) 403).

THE THIRD QUESTION – THE FACTS

It has always been held that a heavy onus of proof rests on a person seeking to establish that a marriage – *prima facie* valid – is in fact void. How heavy Haugh J regarded the onus is illustrated by his judgment in *Griffith v Griffith* [1944] IR 35. In that case Haugh J stated (at p. 53) that he would not have acted on the mere telling of the petitioner's story 'even if I were inclined to believe it' but for the fact that there was very strong corroborative evidence. This appears to me to be putting the onus very high, and I prefer to regard it merely as a warning that a judge should be cautious before accepting the evidence put forward for a petition in a nullity suit.

In the present case I have considerable reservations about the petitioner's evidence. On the other hand I have the evidence of the petitioner's sisters from which it appears that the petitioner was, prior to the marriage, suffering from bouts of depression and that this depression had so undermined him that he was unable properly to cope with the management of his farm.

Against this I have the evidence of the respondent, which I also accept, that during their courtship, the petitioner presented to her as a man who was good company, had a good sense of humour and with whom she was happy to be. The petitioner did indeed complain about his health to her from time to time but such complaints as he made appeared, on investigation, not to be symptoms of any serious illness. I accept that the respondent, whom I accept as a practical, intelligent woman and a highly qualified nurse, was never at any time during their courtship, seriously concerned for the petitioner's health.

I have had the benefit of the evidence of three psychiatrists. Unfortunately, none of these psychiatrists saw the petitioner immediately before or immediately after his wedding. The most senior psychiatrist to see the petitioner was Dr Seamus Lennon. He saw him about four or five times between June and September 1977. At that time the petitioner was aged 45. He was complaining of panic attacks. He was particularly worried about the state of his heart. Dr Lennon drew the conclusion that the petitioner was rather eccentric (in the layman's sense of the term); that he was unduly concerned about himself; that he suffered from hypochondria; that he was introverted, and that he was a schizoid personality. A schizoid person I understand to be a person who, while not necessarily suffering from schizophrenia or any definite mental disorder, still shows some of the qualities of the person suffering from schizophrenia. Dr. Lennon treated the petitioner with anti-depressive drugs and with tranquillisers. The petitioner showed no permanent improvement from the treatment.

Dr. Lennon gave his opinion that while the petitioner might understand the nature of marriage he might find it difficult to understand and face up to relationships in marriage. Dr Lennon was not prepared to say, however, whether the petitioner would or would not make a success of marriage. He stated, 'I just don't know'.

Dr Lennon thought that the petitioner was in a better state of health at the date of the hearing than he had been when he (Dr Lennon) had seen him in 1977. In cross-examination Dr Lennon agreed that it would be a good thing for the petitioner to have a normal active relationship with any other person. It might be a good thing for him to have a girlfriend. He considered the petitioner needed emotional support. In the normal course he would be loath to advise any person to get married, but if he had been consulted, and if the prospective marriage partner appeared sympathetic, he might have advised the petitioner to go and marry. He considered the petitioner's capacity for emotional relationships was impaired, but he repeated that he was not saying that the petitioner was incapable of having a successful marriage. He (Dr Lennon) just did not know.

The second psychiatrist to give evidence was Dr. Morrisson. He first saw the petitioner on 28 November 1977. He saw him again on 5 December and on 19 December. The petitioner was complaining of depression, weakness, dizziness, palpitations, frightening dreams, of not feeling well, of having difficulty in meeting people, of being afraid to go into a public house, and an inability to manage his farm and do his work. During this period Dr. Morrisson saw very little change in the petitioner's condition. Dr Morrisson reached the conclusion that he was suffering from a schizo effective illness or some form of schizophrenia. Schizophrenia would affect nearly all the patient's thinking processes and would lead to disordered thinking. It would also result in a general blunting of his emotional reactions and lead to an inability to cope.

Dr. Morrisson next saw the petitioner on 1 May 1979. He then appeared depressed, uneasy and agitated. He appeared more depressed than in 1977 but Dr. Morrisson thought it would be reasonable to assume that the petitioner had continued in this or some similar condition throughout the intervening period.

Dr Morrisson considered that a man in the petitioner's condition would have great difficulty in marriage or in maintaining a relationship with anyone. He would find it hard to love anyone on a continuous basis. He would be incapable of loving someone in the accepted sense of the term. He would be capable of the marital act but would have difficulty in working, and in supporting a wife. Dr. Morrisson said that a very small percentage of men suffering from schizophrenia get married, and he was surprised that the petitioner did get married. Dr. Morrisson added that the petitioner would have difficulty in maintaining a relationship with anyone. He would not, in the generally accepted sense, be a father to a child. He would have difficulty in advising or controlling his child.

The third psychiatrist who had seen the petitioner was Dr Shanley under whose care the petitioner came when he was admitted to St Patrick's in November 1978. This was some four and a half months after the marriage. The petitioner was very depressed, his sleep pattern was bad, he was subject to bouts of crying and dizziness and suffering from palpitations. Dr. Shanley considered that the petitioner was suffering from endogenous depression and from a schizophrenic type illness. He said the petitioner would find it difficult to relate to people or to get close to them. The petitioner remained in St. Patrick's for fourteen days and then discharged himself before his treatment was completed.

In cross-examination Dr. Shanley repeated that the petitioner would not be able to have a meaningful relationship with another person. He may have felt he was close to his mother but he could be dependent without being close. He could have a similar relationship with other people whether a male or a female. Dr. Shanley considered that he had not the capacity for empathy.

The respondent, in evidence, gave an account of the period between the wedding and the petitioner's admission to St. Patrick's. She said the petitioner appeared alright on the day of the wedding. He was able to mix with people at the wedding and when he was with her he was fine. She admitted, however, that the marriage had its good and its bad times. However, the parties were sleeping together until just before the petitioner's admission to St. Patrick's. The petitioner suffered a bad cold in October 1978 and became cantankerous. He appeared very annoyed at having got married. The local doctor, Dr. Crowley, made the arrangements to have the petitioner admitted to St. Patrick's. She considered that the petitioner had brought pressure to bear on Dr. Crowley to have himself admitted. The respondent did not think that he, in fact, needed treatment in St. Patrick's.

CONCLUSION

Looking at the evidence as a whole, it appears to me that I must accept that the petitioner, both before and after his marriage, suffered from some form of personality defect or illness similar to schizophrenia. I must also accept that this made it difficult for him to have a successful marriage. I must also accept that the marriage in fact broke down. However, I found the petitioner's own evidence in many respects unsatisfactory, and I am not satisfied that he has proved that on the date of his wedding he was so incapacitated as to make the marriage void or voidable.

Even if the marriage in this case were a voidable marriage it appears to me that, *prima facie*, it would be a marriage voidable at the instance of the wife and not of the husband. In the circumstances of this case it appears to me that it would be necessary for the husband to show that the wife had repudiated the marriage. I asked the wife if she had ever considered applying for an annulment of the marriage herself. She totally rejected the idea. The statement to the contrary contained in Dr. Shanley's report to the court dated 7 January 1981 is a mistake. When the marriage ran into difficulties the couple sought ecclesiastical advice, but the wife thought they were seeking advice to save their marriage not to end it. She says, and I accept, that she was astounded when the husband raised the question of nullity. The wife accepts that the marriage has broken down, but that is a different matter. She appears to have left the matrimonial home for good and sufficient reason. When her husband invited her back she gave the invitation serious consideration before refusing it. In view of the history of the marriage and the husband's evidence as to his own state of mind when he extended the invitation, one cannot but feel that her refusal was justified.

In these circumstances I dismiss the petition.

Notes

1. How important is this decision, in your opinion? Does it 'open the floodgates'? For analysis of the decision, see Binchy, *Mental Incapacity and Nullity of Marriage*, 17 Ir. Med. Times No. 10, p. 32 (1983).
2. Could you define a 'caring or considerate relationship? Is this a matter to be determined by psychology? Psychiatry? Morality? Some other criterion? How does a 'caring or considerate relationship' contrast with a relationship where 'one party did not love or had not the capacity to love the other'?
3. Barrington, J. refers to 'illness' in spelling out his new ground for annulment. If a petitioner was not ill but nonetheless lacked the capacity to form a caring or considerate relationship with his or her spouse, would this be a reason for refusing a decree? Cf. *E.P.* v. *M.C. (otherwise P.), infra,* p. 42.
4. Should *physical* illness ever be a ground for annulment? Tuberculosis? Cf. *Davis* v. *Davis*, 90 N.J. Eq. 158, 106 Atl. 644 (1919), noted by *Anon.*, 2 Va. L. Rev. 465 (1915). Epilepsy? This was a ground in England until 1971 and is still a ground in some jurisdictions in the United States of America: see Mitchell, *The Legal Problems of Epilepsy*, 29 Temple L. Q. 364, at 366–368 (1956). Venereal disease? See England's *Matrimonial Causes Act 1973*, section 12(e); as to the United States of America, see H. Clark, *Domestic Relations*, 86 (1968); Foster, *Marriage: A 'Basic Civil Right of Man'*, 37 Fordham L. Rev. 51, at 64 (1968); W.A.S., *Annot.*, 5 A.L.R. 1016, at 1022ff (1920); Binchy, *Medico-Legal Aspects of Nullity of Marriage*, 17 Ir. Med. Times No. 13, p. 20 (1983).

D. v. C.

Unreported, High Ct., Costello, J., 19 May 1983 (26M–1982)

Costello, J.

INTRODUCTION

These are matrimonial proceedings in which the wife petitions for a decree of nullity, accepting that if she is to succeed the Court must extend the principles on which heretofore decrees have been granted and base its conclusion that the marriage was invalid on a ground which has not previously been successfully pleaded in our civil courts.

She and her husband were married on the 23rd of March 1974 and there are two children of the marriage, a girl aged nearly 7 and a boy aged 4½ years. She alleges that her husband's condition prior to marriage was symptomatic of manic depression and that since the marriage her husband has been diagnosed as a manic depressive, an alcoholic and a drug addict. She claims:

(a) that by reason of his mental capacity and state of mind at the time of the marriage her husband was unable to understand the nature, purpose and consequences of the marriage contract, and,
(b) that at the time of the marriage her husband was suffering from such disease of the mind that he was unable to maintain and sustain a normal relationship with her or any children there might be of the marriage.

It is claimed that either one or both of these grounds would justify the Court declaring that her marriage is and was null and void.

Whilst admitting in his answer that he has been treated in a psychiatric hospital after his marriage for 'bouts of mania, and bouts of depression,' whilst admitting that in or around 1978/1979 he began to take drugs that had not been prescribed for him, the Respondent claims that he was fully aware and appreciated the nature and purpose and consequence of his marriage at the time it was celebrated and denies that through mental instability he was incapable of contracting a valid marriage. At the hearing I allowed an amendment of the Answer. As a result there are now five main issues for determination which I can summarise as follows:

1. Whether the Respondent was at the time of his marriage suffering from a psychiatric illness;
2. If the answer to (1) is in the affirmative, whether as a result of this illness the Respondent:–
   (a) was unable fully to understand the nature, purpose and consequence of the marriage contract, and/or
   (b) was unable to maintain and sustain a normal marriage relationship with his wife and any children of his marriage.
3. If the Respondent suffered from the mental illness alleged and if the illness had one or other of the results referred to at (2) whether as a matter of law this rendered his marriage:–

(a) voidable, or
(b) absolutely void.

4. If the first two questions are decided in the Petitioner's favour and if the Respondent's illness is a ground for treating the marriage as *voidable*, (rather than *void*) whether the Petitioner has so approbated the marriage that she is now deprived of the right to a decree of nullity. (If the marriage is absolutely void because of the Respondent's psychiatric illness no question of approbation arises).
5. Prior to these nullity proceedings the Petitioner had instituted proceedings under the Guardianship of Infants Acts and the Family Law (Maintenance of Spouses and Children) Acts. In the light of the amended Answer a further issue arises from an Order of the High Court of 30th of June 1981 made in those proceedings; namely, whether the validity of the Petitioner's marriage is now res judicata so that she is now estopped from challenging its validity in these present proceedings.

Before examining the evidence and giving my conclusions on it there are some general observations which can usefully be made immediately.

The Respondent was first diagnosed as a manic depressive in England in the summer of 1978, i.e. a little over four years after his marriage. Later that year he commenced to attend a psychiatric hospital in Dublin where this diagnosis was confirmed. In addition he was diagnosed as suffering from alcoholism and a serious addiction to drugs. Since 1978 he has attended a psychiatric hospital both as an in-patient and as an out-patient for his drug addiction. It is important to bear in mind that the Respondent's addiction is only indirectly relevant to what the Petitioner has to establish, namely that her husband was a manic depressive *at the time of his marriage*. Attention therefore must be focused particularly on the evidence which assists in establishing the Respondent's psychiatric health prior to and at the time of his marriage. The post-marital history is of relevance in so far as it may help in throwing light on his pre-marital psychiatric health and also, to a more limited extent, on the issues of approbation and estoppel which have been raised.

There was no evidence arising from any psychiatric examination of the Respondent made before his marriage. The Respondent has called a psychiatrist who treated him since 1978 and the Petitioner has called a psychiatrist whose evidence to the effect that the Respondent was suffering from manic depression prior to and at the time of his marriage was based almost entirely on what he had been told by the Petitioner herself and, to a much less extent, on certain diaries and letters which the Respondent wrote. Whilst I will refer to these witnesses as the 'Respondent's psychiatrist,' and the 'Petitioner's psychiatrist' respectively, it should be made clear that both were scrupulously objective in the manner in which they gave their evidence and their assessment of the Respondent and by employing this nomenclature it must not be inferred that either was in any way partisan in his approach to this tragic case.

Here let me record a crucial conclusion of fact which I have reached. I found the Petitioner not only to be a truthful and intelligent witness endowed with a good and accurate memory but also a witness who gave her testimony in a calm, balanced and indeed detached manner. I had no difficulty in believing what she told me. My assessment of the Petitioner's reliability was the same as that of the psychiatrist called on her behalf. He stated that he was impressed by her as an intelligent, solid and steady personality, as a consistent, reliable and perceptive informant with a capacity for clear and detailed accounts of her husband's mental state and behaviour. The evidence which she gave in Court of her husband's moods and behaviour was in substance and very frequently in detail similar to the account which she gave to the psychiatrist whom she consulted about this case. In so far therefore as his professional opinion and diagnosis of the Respondent was based on the veracity and reliability of the Petitioner's evidence, I am satisfied that the Petitioner's psychiatrist was fully entitled to rely on it.

The area of difference between the Petitioner's psychiatrist and the Respondent's psychiatrist was a limited one. The Respondent's psychiatrist had treated him since 1978 (both as an in-patient and as an out-patient) but his main concern was to try to break him of his drug addiction and he accepted that he did not consider in any great detail either with the Respondent or with the Petitioner with whom his interviews were comparatively brief the underlying cause of the addiction. Nor did he reach any conclusions on his pre-marriage psychiatric state. He declined to make any comment about his mental health at the time of his marriage as he considered that it was not possible to make a retrospective diagnosis in this case. This was not the view of the Petitioner's psychiatrist. The Petitioner's Solicitor had asked that the Respondent be examined by the Petitioner's psychiatrist but this request was refused. In spite of this the Petitioner's psychiatrist was satisfied that he could make a clinically valid diagnosis about the Respondent's mental history and its effect on the relationship with his wife. His opinion was that the Respondent's moods and behaviour as detailed by his wife amounted to a classic diagnostic description of a manic depressive; that he had satisfied himself that the Petitioner had not been influenced in her account of events by any reading on the subject she may have undertaken or information about it otherwise obtained; and he was satisfied that he could make a clinically confident diagnosis. I accept his evidence on this point and in the particular circumstances of this case I am satisfied that I can act on the diagnosis which he made notwithstanding the Respondent's refusal to be examined by him.

The Petitioner's psychiatrist reached two important conclusions. Firstly, he diagnosed the Respondent as a person suffering from manic depression before and at the time of his marriage. Secondly, he was of the opinion that the Respondent's disorder was sufficiently serious as to incapacitate him from entering into and sustaining a viable marriage relationship. Whilst the Respondent's psychiatrist declined to make a retrospective diagnosis, he did not deny that a person suffering from a condition of manic depression might be incapable of entering into and sustaining a viable marriage relationship with the other partner to the marriage.

Finally, as to the other evidence in the case. The Respondent's relations and friends whom he called saw nothing untoward in his behaviour at the time of the wedding and did not recall any earlier psychiatric disorder from which he may have suffered. They were, it is hardly necessary for me to say, entirely honest witnesses. But their testimony does not displace the conclusions to be drawn from other more direct and more convincing evidence on these important aspects of the case.

THE FACTS

(a) *The relationship between the parties: a review*

I propose in this part of my judgment to summarise the conclusions I have reached on the evidence concerning the history of the relations between the Petitioner and the Respondent. I will then give my conclusions on the medical evidence and finally on the evidence relating to the Respondent's earlier medical history. Not unnaturally there have been differences in the testimony I have heard but the differences are by no means irreconcilable, and the areas of outright disagreement have been comparatively small. Where conflict exists I have had no difficulty in preferring the Petitioner's version of events to that of the Respondent.

The Petitioner first met the Respondent in the month of January 1972 in Germany. She was then eighteen years old. Her parents were Irish but she had been brought up and educated in England. When she left school she was uncertain whether to take up a nursing career or go to a University, and to give herself time to think over her future she took up a job as an attendant in a hospital in Germany. The Respondent was then a medical student in Dublin aged twenty-three and facing his finals in the summer of 1973. He had taken a short break from his studies to visit friends in Germany and was there introduced by a mutual acquaintance to the Petitioner. They obviously liked one another immediately and when his short visit was over it was arranged that the Petitioner would come over to Dublin to visit him. This she did a few weeks later staying in the Respondent's brother's house for a few days. She returned to London to her parents' house where the Respondent visited her and where out of the blue he proposed that they should get married. The Petitioner did not turn down or accept this proposal but in the following June the Respondent obtained a post in the same hospital in Germany in which the Petitioner was working and over the summer of 1972 they saw one another constantly and an understanding developed that they would get married as soon as the Respondent qualified as a doctor. In this, the first phase of their relationship, the Respondent appeared to the Petitioner to have a very bright and gay personality, and to be a person full of energy and given to a great deal of activity.

In the second phase of their relationship the Respondent's mood and behaviour toward the Petitioner changed. The Petitioner had decided to follow a University career and in September 1972 she obtained a position [at] Bangor University . . . The journey from Bangor to Dublin via Holyhead is not a difficult one and from September until the following June the Petitioner came regularly over to Dublin and stayed with the Respondent on weekends in a flat which he had rented on the North Circular Road. His attitude however to the Petitioner was now markedly different. He was working very hard for his final examination and on her visits he spent all day on Saturday immersed in his work and when he was not working he exhibited much less interest in the Petitioner and in her affairs than he had previously shown. On Saturday evenings it was his habit to go out drinking and on these occasions he drank a great deal too much and was regularly extremely drunk.

In June 1973 the Respondent sat his final medical examination and he took this failure extremely badly and was totally unable to cope with the disappointment. He became extremely upset and then extremely depressed. Through a friend a temporary position as a physician was obtained for him in a psychiatric hospital outside Dublin and he spent the summer there between June and September. The Petitioner's University term had finished and she joined him working as a cleaner in the hospital to which he was attached. She experienced for the first time the effects of the deep depressions to which he was subject. She tried to encourage him but could get no reaction from him and he would remain depressed and silent for long periods. Then for no apparent reason he would suddenly become quite elated and high spirited. The episodes of elation were of short duration and he would then sink back into a depression. Several years later the Respondent wrote to the Petitioner and confessed to her that in this period he had on one occasion taken drugs to relieve his depression, but it is clear that his behaviour and mood during this period were unconnected with the drug abuse to which unfortunately in later years he resorted.

In September 1973 the Respondent returned to Dublin and worked as an intern in a Dublin hospital preparing for his repeat examination in December. A further mood-swing then occurred. The Petitioner had decided to move from Bangor to Dublin to continue her studies in a University here. This was the best period of their relationship. The Respondent was now very calm and the Petitioner found him a pleasant relaxed companion. His depression had gone and his strange elated periods had disappeared. He passed his finals in December and it was agreed that they would get married in the following March, 1974.

About six weeks before their wedding the Petitioner found a small flat near the centre of Dublin and she and the Respondent went to live there together (previously the Petitioner had been staying in the house of the Respondent's parents). Around about this time a further change had come over the Respondent. He was working very hard as an intern in a hospital and the Petitioner saw very little of him but when they did meet there was very little communication between them. He went out drinking a lot with his friends and was drinking excessively and in an irresponsible fashion. Then a week before the wedding yet another shift of mood occurred. Quite suddenly the Respondent became extraordinarily active. He appeared to the Petitioner to be overbright and elated and although he was still working very hard in hospital he seemed to be full of energy and completely tireless. He insisted on going out when he was free from his professional duties but quite obviously he did not want to be with the Petitioner but sought out his companions and in their company insisted on being the centre of attraction. One day, quite unexpectedly, he produced an engagement ring for the Petitioner and on the same day he produced two air-drive tickets for a honeymoon in Paris. The Petitioner was extremely upset by these two actions on two different scores. Firstly, she fully realised how little money they had between them and both the Respondent and herself had agreed that they could not afford an engagement ring. (Previously they had exchanged simple gold bands in acknowledgement of their engagement). They had also agreed that they could not afford anything but a brief few days for a honeymoon, to be spent somewhere in Ireland. Secondly, the Petitioner was aggrieved that the Respondent had gone back on these decisions without discussing them with her and without giving any thought to the consequences. When the Petitioner expressed her disapproval the Respondent told her that the ring had cost £180 and that as she was going to be a Doctor's wife she would have to have it. When later he produced the tickets for Paris she again remonstrated with him saying that they could not afford them and that they had no money to spend on a holiday in Paris. The Respondent's response to this difficulty was to suggest that everything would be alright and that they would get the spending money as gifts on their wedding day.

At the wedding ceremony (which took place on the 21st of March 1974) and at the reception which followed the Petitioner felt that there was something wrong with the Respondent but she could not put her finger on the cause. She was very conscious that the wedding ceremony lacked solemnity and there was no closeness between her and the Respondent. He avoided having any communication with her but instead was chatting and giggling with his brother (the best man) throughout the ceremony and did not look at the Petitioner. At the reception his behaviour was the same. He moved from group to group entertaining everyone whilst the Petitioner sat quietly with relatives, largely ignored by the Respondent. He seemed to her to be over-happy and intent on giving the impression that everything was marvellous. The Petitioner however did have an opportunity to ask him about the money for their honeymoon and he told her that he had asked an old friend for a loan of £30.00 and that he had been given this sum as a present. The Petitioner with great reluctance was forced to tell her mother what the position was and obtained a sum of £80.00 from her. They had arranged to spend the first night of their honeymoon in an hotel near Dublin Airport. To the Petitioner's disappointment and concern when she and her husband left the wedding reception they were accompanied by the Respondent's brother and sister-in-law and when they got to the hotel they stayed to have an evening meal with the Respondent and the Petitioner. The Petitioner was more than ever convinced that something was wrong with the Respondent. His attitude towards her eventually caused her to break down. She became upset and started crying at the dinner table. The Respondent made no effort to comfort her and when they went to their bedroom she was still upset. The Respondent took no notice of her and give her no assurance of any kind. Sexual intercourse that night was a terrible experience for her. The Respondent refused her request to wait until she had composed herself and even though she was still crying he insisted on intercourse not once but several times. There was no affection shown by the Respondent to the Petitioner and no communication between them, his only comment being to compare favourably his sexual prowess with that of a mutual German acquaintance.

The Respondent's attitude to the Petitioner during their short honeymoon remained the same. He was anxious to seek out acquaintances in Paris and in their company he was in jocular form and good humour. But he did not want the Petitioner's company and when they were together there was little or no communication between them. His attitude to her was exemplified by his conduct when they both suffered from an attack of enteritis. The Respondent went to a hospital for treatment but did not tell the Doctor that his wife also needed medical care. Their money ran out and after six days they returned to Dublin. When the Petitioner telephoned her mother on her return she was unable to conceal the distress she was suffering and was crying so bitterly on the telephone that her mother thought that some fearful calamity had befallen her or her husband. The excuse which she gave to her mother for her tears was a lame one and her mother was left with the impression that her daughter was profoundly unhappy.

The beginning of their married life in Dublin together was far from auspicious. A week after their return the Respondent got extremely drunk at his brother's wedding and was very abusive towards his wife. Not long afterwards they went to a party in a friend's house and again the Respondent took much too much to drink and was again abusive to the Respondent. On his return to their flat his anger spilled over into violence and he assaulted her badly.

In view of the medical evidence to which I will later refer it has been necessary to refer with some particularity to the events of and surrounding the wedding. The months and years following do not require to be considered in such detail. For the remainder of 1974 the Respondent was working very hard in the same hospital to which he was attached prior to his wedding and the Petitioner did not see very much of him. At the beginning of 1975 he changed hospitals and this change seemed to bring about a further change in his mood. In the early part of 1975 he seemed to have much less energy and he again became very depressed and to the Petitioner's consternation he admitted to her that he had stolen some methedrin ampoules from the hospital pharmacy to relieve his depression. His mood changed again when he started working for membership of his professional body and coming up to June of 1976 he was then going through a period of intense hard work in which he gave all his concentration to his medical studies and paid very little attention to his wife and exhibited considerable irritation towards her. At this time, when his wife was six months pregnant, his irritation spilled over into anger and he assaulted her by kicking her on the leg.

On the day of the birth of their first child (a daughter) the Respondent's behaviour towards the Petitioner was in many ways similar to that of his behaviour at the time of his wedding. He paid what can only be described as a perfunctory visit to her in hospital and seemed incapable of showing her any affection leaving after only five minutes without even having seen his new child. He spent the rest of the day drinking with his friends. Following the birth of his first child the Respondent continued to work extremely hard giving the Petitioner the impression that he was tireless, but paying her very little attention. In the following year, however, his mood again changed. Their second child was born in November 1977 and a week before the birth the Respondent had again fallen into a deep depression and told his wife that he wanted to commit suicide adding (an item of information which has some significance for the issues I have to try) that he had wanted to commit suicide when he was a child and that as a student he had attempted to do so.

The Respondent's lack of attention towards, and communication with, the Petitioner and his periods of depression were not the only problems which faced the Petitioner in the year 1977. At the Respondent's suggestion she moved into residence in the hospital in which the Respondent was then attached and whilst there she discovered for the first time that he was administering drugs to himself on a regular basis. At first he denied that he was doing so but she found evidence of swabs, needles and syringes, and eventually he admitted that he was taking drugs. After his parents' death at the beginning of 1978 he excused his behaviour by saying that he was upset by their deaths, but the Petitioner was satisfied that this was an inadequate excuse and it became obvious to her that he was fast becoming an addict.

The Respondent resigned from the hospital to which he had been attached because he said he had had a disagreement with his superior and he moved to another hospital in Dublin. But his drug taking continued and his behaviour was getting out of hand. He travelled with his wife to England in the summer of 1978 and there for the first time he faced up to his problem. He freely confessed his addiction to his wife and was admitted to a psychiatric hospital in England for treatment. He discharged himself after six weeks and returned to Dublin. But he was still very ill on his return and went back to England for another period of six weeks. He told his wife that he had been diagnosed in England as a manic depressive, a drug addict, and an alcoholic. Back in Dublin he tried to continue to practise his profession in the hospital to which he was attached but he attended as an out-patient at the clinic of a well known Dublin psychiatric hospital.

Unfortunately out-patient treatment was not effective and he was admitted as an in-patient on the 2nd of May 1979. When first seen the assessment was not a conclusive one but later he was firmly diagnosed as suffering from a manic depressive illness of a circular type and from drug and alcohol abuse.

His first spell as an in-patient was a short one. After his discharge in the summer of 1979 the Respondent and the Petitioner went to Germany. This move came about in this way. Without any discussion with his wife the Respondent obtained a research position with a drug company and left his post in the Dublin hospital. At this time he was in a mood of considerable elation but the move to Germany only lasted six months and was a disastrous failure. The Respondent spent a great deal of his time in bed and due to his depression was unable to go out to work. He drank excessively and although he attended a psychiatrist his condition did not improve. Eventually he had to tell his superiors what was wrong with him and he was advised to go back to Dublin. During his stay in Germany he confessed to the Petitioner that he realised that he always had been sick, and that he had seen a psychiatrist in his student days who had diagnosed him as suffering from 'an oppressive, compulsive neurosis.' This diagnosis he said was obviously a wrong one and he told her that he had been in those days a manic depressive and should have been so diagnosed.

On his return from Germany the Respondent went straight back into hospital as an in-patient and was there from the 24th December 1979 to the 3rd January 1980. When he left however he was far from cured of his addiction. He had bought an expensive BMW motor car whilst in Germany with the aid of a bank loan and the first thing he did after leaving hospital was to obtain another bank loan and buy with it a new Renault 18 motor car. He obtained a position with a local authority outside Dublin but this was of short duration. He started taking drugs again and was re-admitted to hospital. He obtained another post this time in County Dublin but his addiction was getting worse and he was injecting himself so often that the Petitioner could see that his thighs were hardened, his vests were bloodied and he had no veins suitable for injection and used to inject himself under the skin. His situation deteriorated rapidly and finally came to a head when he took an overdose of drugs in an attempt to kill himself. On the 10th of April 1980 he was re-admitted to a psychiatric hospital and stayed there as an in-patient for nearly ten months.

In August 1980 the Petitioner had finally concluded that her marriage was at an end and she decided she would have to build a life for herself and her two children independent of the Respondent. She had obtained a degree in languages from her University and was able to find a part-time post which together with financial help from her parents enabled her to start a new life. But two very serious and terrifying assaults which the Respondent made on the Petitioner in the beginning of 1981 caused her to seek the help of a Solicitor and on the 11th of February 1981 an ex parte Order was made in the High Court barring the Respondent from the home where she was living with her children. Later a permanent barring Order and an Order granting custody of the children was granted to her.

I will consider the legal consequences of the 1981 proceeding later. But here I should record certain conclusions of fact relevant to the approbation issue which the Respondent has raised.

(a) The 1981 proceedings were instituted urgently for the purposes of the physical protection of the Respondent and her children and were maintained in the interests of the welfare of her children and herself.
(b) The Petitioner did not know that the Respondent had suffered from a psychiatric illness prior to her meeting him until told of this by the Respondent in 1977.
(c) The Petitioner did not appreciate that the Respondent's behaviour before and during his marriage was a manifestation of a psychiatric illness. She only became aware of this at the time she instituted these present proceedings in 1982.
(d) The Petitioner sought and obtained no legal advice as to her entitlement to a decree of nullity at the time of the 1981 proceedings. She was unaware that the Respondent's psychiatric illness might entitle her to a nullity decree until shortly prior to the institution of these proceedings.

One final matter of fact should here be mentioned. The attitude of the Respondent to his children is consistent with the conclusions I have reached about his mental state to which I will refer in a moment. In times of depression he would take to his bed and not talk to them. At other times he was aggressive and yet again over-indulgent towards them. I accept that it was very hard for the Petitioner to know what his attitude to them was likely to be at any given time.

(b) *The Medical Evidence*

I turn now to the medical evidence in the case.

As pointed out already the Respondent's psychiatrist declined to give any opinion on the Respondent's psychiatric condition prior to and at the time of his marriage in March 1974. His evidence is, however, of some relevance on this important aspect of the case. Firstly, although the Respondent was treated in hospital in 1978 primarily for his drug addiction he was also diagnosed as a sufferer from a manic depressive illness of a circular type, that is to say one in which the patient suffers from both mania and depression. Secondly, reporting on him in February 1981 his psychiatrist expressed the opinion that though the cyclical bouts of depression were 'certainly' present 'for the last three or four years at least' – i.e. at least as far back at 1977 or 1978.

On the Respondent's own evidence, therefore, it has been established beyond any doubt that certainly by the year 1978 and perhaps earlier the Respondent was suffering from a severe psychiatric illness in addition to alcoholism and drug addiction. The evidence of the Petitioner's psychiatrist is perfectly consistent with this evidence. I found his diagnosis a very convincing one. It was made by someone with very considerable professional experience and with outstanding qualifications. It gives a cogent and convincing explanation for the aberrant and at times bizarre behaviour of the Respondent towards the Petitioner and the swings of mood which she described. I have no hesitation in accepting it.

This diagnosis was to the effect that the Respondent suffered from a manic depressive illness which was present throughout the duration of his relationship with the Petitioner both before, at the time of, and after their marriage. It was possible to identify five clear stages in the cycle of this disorder until the pattern of the disease became clouded by the taking of drugs and alcohol abuse. The illness can be illustrated by drawing a horizontal axis showing mood changes and behaviour outside a midline range of normal variation. Above this range mood swings are classified as hypomanic and manic depending on the degree of their severity and functional incapacity. Within the midline range normal changes in moods occur in everyone which do not cause lasting functional impairment. Below the midline of normal mood variation degrees of depression occur ranging from mild through moderate to severe with various degrees of incapacity depending on the severity. Any given individual may have a pattern of his own with variable episodes of mania and hypomania followed by either depression, normality or even further episodes of mania without any intervening level phase.

The conclusions reached by the Petitioner's psychiatrist were as follows. When the Petitioner first met the Respondent in the first half of 1973 he was then in a manic state of his illness. This was followed during his final year's study (when, it will be recalled, the Petitioner was visiting him on weekends from Bangor University) by a period when he was in a hypomanic or early manic state. After the failure of his final examination the Respondent dropped into a stage of early depression which deepened during the summer of 1973 (when the Petitioner and the Respondent were working together in a psychiatric hospital outside Dublin). On their return to Dublin and in the Autumn and Winter of 1973 the Respondent achieved a period of sustained normal level mood state, followed by a brief return in the early part of 1974 to a hypomanic stage. But for the week before and during the period of his marriage (when it will be recalled he purchased an engagement ring and air tickets for Paris) the Respondent was again in a high manic phase. The Respondent's behaviour towards his wife on the night of their marriage was fully consistent with this diagnosis and indeed was a manifestation of his illness. In the first months after marriage the Respondent was again in the intensive high energy irritable state similar to the condition he was in prior to his final examination. After January 1975 his mood changed to depression and after six months he swung up into another high energy intensive irritable phase. On the day of his daughter's birth the Respondent swung into an even higher phase similar to that at the time of the marriage. Thereafter the mood changes occurred more frequently and evidence of drug taking became apparent.

In these five distinctive and separate mood stages the Respondent had a consistent mental state and behaviour each of which in a different way affected his ability to sustain a 'normal' relationship with his wife. The manic stage was characterised by intense hyperactivity, inexhaustible energy, inability to sleep or rest, continuous good humour, exaggerated stories, laughter at little cause, ambitious and expansive thinking together with extravagant spending bouts. Thinking was flippant with inability to sustain a single line of action or thought. Unrealistic decisions were made without awareness of the consequences and without planning in a coherent manner for their consequences. In such states a sufferer from mania relates more easily to strangers than to close relatives. The Petitioner was in transition from a stranger to a close relative in the early stages of their relationship. Once their relationship came closer to marriage and in the manic phases of his illness it is clear that the Respondent was unable to relate to her and his illness explains his conduct during and after the wedding ceremony.

In the next phase, the hypomanic or early manic phase, the Respondent exhibited a different set of personality characteristics. He then tended to be over-active, over-energetic and was obsessively concerned [with] his goals relating to his medical work to the exclusion of all other considerations. In this mood he was irritable, decisive and his relationship with the Petitioner changed. He showed no concern for her or interest in her activities.

When the Respondent was in a level and normal mood (which occurred very rarely indeed) he acted in a consistent and predictable way. In the next phase of moderate depression his mood and behaviour was again different. His talk content was depressive. He tended to be angry, critical and talked of suicide. In such moods he could not attend to his work and frequently missed work. Again during this period he could not relate to the Petitioner. All these characteristics were exacerbated in the periods of the deep depression from which from time to time the Respondent suffered.

Accepting as I do this diagnosis I am satisfied that the Respondent suffered from a psychiatric illness both before his marriage, at the time of his marriage and subsequent to his marriage. It was a cyclical manic-depressive disorder which resulted in disturbance in mood states which affected his personality and behaviour.

The sympathy which ought to develop between spouses did not occur because of these changes in mood and his erratic behaviour, and they explain why the Petitioner felt that at no time during her marriage did she have a sharing relationship with her husband. I am satisfied that the Respondent's illness at the time of his marriage was sufficiently severe as to impair significantly his capacity to form and sustain a normal viable marriage relationship with the Petitioner.

(c) *The Respondent's Early Medical History*

The conclusions which I have just stated are based on the evidence relating to the period since early 1972. But there is evidence that the Respondent suffered from mental illness before he met the Petitioner, evidence which supports these conclusions.

I have already referred to the admissions made by the Respondent to the Petitioner to the effect that he had suffered from some degree of mental illness in his childhood and youth. His admissions are corroborated by a witness who had befriended him in recent years and who with her husband took the Respondent into her home whilst he was a patient in the psychiatric hospital here in Dublin. This witness is a remedial teacher and obviously a highly reliable witness. The Respondent talked to her about his present illness and whilst doing so told her that he had suffered two serious bouts of depression once as a boy of fourteen for a period of six months, from which date he had formed the habit of pulling his hair out (a condition known as trichlomania), and once when he was a medical student whilst at college. The likelihood that he was telling this witness the truth is strengthened by other testimony. A student friend of his who gave evidence recalled that he had been particularly depressed at one time during their student days although he could not recall the exact date. Furthermore, the Respondent's diary for the early part of the scholastic year 1969/70 shows (a) that he had intended completing the whole year (although in fact he did not do so) and (b) that he recorded the fact that he was suffering from depression in the months of September and November 1969.

(d) *Conclusion*

I conclude therefore that the Petitioner has established that the Respondent was suffering at the time of the marriage from the incapacitating illness as alleged in the Petition. But I am not however satisfied that she has shown that the Respondent was unable fully to understand the nature, purpose and consequences of the marriage contract. It is true that he was in a manic state on the day of his marriage, but prior to this he had taken part in the arrangements for the wedding, and the decision to marry was a long-standing one. It has not, I think, been established that the Respondent did not fully appreciate what was involved in the marriage contract and so this ground of the Petitioner's claim fails. Her case for a decree must therefore stand or fall on the submission that the psychiatric illness which incapacitated the Respondent in the way I have described entitles her as a matter of law to a nullity decree.

THE LAW

(a) *The Validity of the Marriage*

The Petitioner accepts that a decree of nullity on the grounds now advanced has never previously been made in these Courts (or, for that matter, in the Courts in England) but she submits that our Courts have jurisdiction to develop the law of nullity and should do so in the manner she suggests. In relation to this submission she faces, however, an obstacle arising from the provisions of the statute under which jurisdiction in nullity matters was conferred on the Civil Courts in this country. The *Matrimonial Causes and Marriage Law (Ireland) Amendment Act 1870* transferred on the disestablishment of the Church of Ireland the jurisdiction exercised by the ecclesiastical Courts of that Church in matrimonial cases to a new Civil Court for Matrimonial Causes and Matters whose powers are now vested in the High Court. By Section 13 of that Act in all proceedings the new Court of Matrimonial Causes and Matters was required to act and give relief on principles and rules which in the opinion of the Court were as nearly as may be conformable to the principles and rules on which the ecclesiastical Courts had up to then acted upon and given relief. So, it is suggested on the Respondent's behalf that because the Ecclesiastical Courts of the Church of Ireland did not grant decrees of nullity on the grounds now advanced by the Petitioner this Court has no jurisdiction to do so.

The grounds on which the Courts in England will grant nullity decrees have been extended, but by Parliament and not by the Courts. This seems to be because of a restrictive interpretation of S. 22 of the 1857 Act which in terms similar to S. 13 of the Act of 1870 conferred on the Courts in England jurisdiction in nullity matters. A case in point is *Napier* v. *Napier* [1915] P. 184 in which a decree of nullity on the grounds of a wilful and persistent refusal to allow marital intercourse was refused on the ground that the Civil Courts had no power to alter the law as it was applied prior to 1857 in the Ecclesiastical Courts of the Church of England. A somewhat different approach, however, to the jurisdiction of the Irish Courts in nullity matters was expressed by Mr. Justice Kenny in *S.* v. *S.* (Unreported; 1st July 1976).

. . . Having concluded that the ground established by the Petitioner was not one on which the Ecclesiastical Courts would have granted a decree he nonetheless agreed that a decree be granted, holding that S. 13 of the 1870 Act did not fossilise the law, that the law had been to some extent at least, judge made and that the Court should recognise that great advances made in psychological medicine since 1870 made it necessary to frame new rules to reflect them. He held that a decree should be granted when one of the parties to it at the time of the marriage did not intend to have sexual intercourse with the other and when the parties to the marriage have not agreed before it that there will be no sexual relations between them or when the ages of one or both of them make it improbable that this will happen. The views of Mr. Justice Kenny were not part of the *ratio decidendi* of the majority decision of the Court. But I find his approach to the interpretation of Section 13 a persuasive one and I am strengthened in this opinion by the fact it found favour with Mr. Justice Barrington in a case of *R.S.J.* v. *J.S.J.* [1982] I.L.R.M. 263 (High Ct.).

That was a case in which the Petitioner sought a decree of nullity on the very ground on which the Petitioner relies in this case, namely, that he was suffering from a disease of the mind which incapacitated him from maintaining and sustaining a normal relationship with the Respondent or any children there might be of the proposed marriage. Mr. Justice Barrington (whilst on the facts refusing a decree) agreed with the interpretation placed on Section 13 of the 1870 Act by Mr. Justice Kenny and held that the Section did not have the effect of fossilising the law in its state in 1870 and that the Courts had jurisdiction to develop the law and declare marriages null and void on grounds other than those existing in 1870.

I respectfully agree with the views of Mr. Justice Kenny and Mr. Justice Barrington and I conclude that the statutory obligation created in 1870 to apply the long established principles and rules of the Ecclesiastical Court of the Church of Ireland does not prevent our Civil Courts from developing those principles in the light of the developments in modern medicine, provided of course such development is not inconsistent with those principles.

I conclude that the law should declare the Petitioner is entitled to have her marriage declared null and void on the facts established in this case, for the following reasons.

The Courts have never approached claims for nullity decrees merely by applying principles of contract law or statutory prohibitions and even when marriages have been entered into with complete freedom untainted with illegality, they may be declared null and void if one of the spouses is impotent at the time of the marriage and unable to consummate it. (See *McM* v. *McM* [1936] I.R. 217). But marriage is by our common law (strengthened and reinforced by our constitutional law) a life long union, and it seems to me to be perfectly reasonable that the law should recognise (a) the obvious fact that there is more to marriage than its physical consummation and (b) that the life long union which the law enjoins requires for its maintenance the creation of an emotional and psychological relationship between the spouses. The law should have regard to this relationship just as it does to the physical one. It should recognise that there have been important and significant advances in the field of psychiatric medicine since 1870 and that it is now possible to identify psychiatric illnesses, such as for example manic depressive illness, which in some cases may be so severe as to make it impossible for one of the partners to the marriage to enter into and sustain the relationship which should exist between married couples if a life long union is to be possible. Extending the law by reasoning by analogy is as old as the common law itself (in the thirteenth century it was pointed out that 'if any new and unwonted circumstance shall arise then, if anything analogous has happened before, let the case be adjudged in like manner, preceding a similibus ad similia' (Bracton *De Legibus* quoted in Cross *The English Doctrine of Precedent* p. 24) and so it seems to me (as it did to Mr. Justice Barrington in *R.S.J.* v. *J.S.J.*) that if the law declares to be null a marriage on the grounds that one spouse is through physical disability incapable of the physical relationship required by marriage it should do likewise where one spouse is through a psychiatric disability unable to enter into and sustain the normal inter-personal relationship which marriage also requires. Therefore in the light of the Respondent's psychiatric illness from which he suffered at the time of the marriage and which incapacitated him in the way I have described the Petitioner has made out a prima facie case for the relief claimed.

But before a decree can be made it is necessary to examine the defences which the Respondent has raised to it.

(b) *Is the marriage void or merely voidable?*

The Respondent submits that even if the Petitioner is correct on the legal principles to be applied by the Court and even if it is established that he suffered from the incapacitating psychiatric illness alleged nonetheless her claim must fail. The bar arises, it is claimed, because (a) if the alleged illness existed it merely rendered the marriage voidable and not void, and (b) the Petitioner has approbated the marriage and consequently has disentitled herself to a decree.

As the doctrine of approbation (which I will consider later in this Judgment) applies only to voidable marriages it is necessary to consider whether the ground now relied on to justify a decree is one which, as the Petitioner claims, renders the marriage void or whether, as the Respondent urges, it makes it merely voidable.

The distinction between an impediment which renders a marriage void and one which renders it merely voidable has an historical basis. At the beginning of the seventeenth century the civil courts were concerned with the ease with which marriages could be set aside and the children of such marriages thereby rendered illegitimate. By the use of the writ of prohibition the civil courts cut down the jurisdiction of the Ecclesiastical courts by forbidding them to annul marriages in certain cases after the death of either party. As a result impediments were divided into two kinds, civil and canonical. If the impediment was civil (for example the fact that one of the parties was married to a third person at the time of the ceremony) the marriage was void ab initio and its validity could be challenged by anyone at any time even after the death of one of the parties to it. If the impediment was canonical (for example the fact that one of the parties was impotent) the validity of the marriage could not be questioned after either party had died. Such a marriage must be regarded as valid unless it was annulled during the lifetime of both parties. (See Bromley's *Family Law* sixth edition pages 70–71). The reason underlying this distinction is illustrated and explained in one of the first cases which came before the civil courts in England after the transfer of jurisdiction had been effected (*A.* v. *B.*, L.R. 1 P. & D. 559). This was an administration suit in which the Plaintiff claimed a grant of administration as husband of the intestate and the Defendant made a rival claim, alleging that the Plaintiff's marriage to the deceased was null and void in law because of the impotence of the deceased. The Plaintiff successfully argued that the validity of his marriage could not be questioned after the death of his wife. The judgment (at pages 561–562) reads, in part, as follows:–

> The distinction between 'void' and 'voidable' is not a mere refinement but expresses a real difference in substance . . . It is obvious that this matter of impotence is one which ought to be raised only by the party who suffers an injury from it, and who elects to make it a ground for asking that the contract of marriage should be annulled . . . In all cases in which the incapacity to marriage is one in which society has an interest and which rests on grounds of public policy, it would be wrong and illogical that the validity or invalidity should depend upon the option of the parties, and in all such cases the marriage is absolutely 'void' and not 'voidable' only. But impotency has always hitherto been considered in the Ecclesiastical Courts (and since their abolition in the Divorce and Matrimonial Court), as a matter of personal complaint only . . . I must here take leave to point out that a contrary system would give rise to almost intolerable results. The question whether two people are married or not may arise on a great variety of occasions and be raised by third parties, as creditors or otherwise. Now, if the parties themselves in a case of impotency are content with the consortium vitae and prefer to maintain the bond of matrimony intact, would it not be almost intolerable that a third party should have the right to insist upon an enquiry into the nature of their co-habitation and the revelation of their physical defects?

By a parity of reasoning I can say that the illness alleged and established in this case is one which renders the marriage voidable and not void. There is no public interest in seeing that a marriage subject to this illness is void. Just as in the case of impotency when the law treats the marriage as valid until annulled during the lifetime of either of the spouses so it should, in my opinion, treat in a similar way a marriage where one of the spouses was suffering at the time of the ceremony of an incapacitating psychiatric illness of the type established in this case . . .

[**Costello J.** went on to consider whether the petitioner was barred by reason of approbation or estoppel *per res judicata*. (The passage from his judgment dealing with approbation is set out *infra*, p. 96). **Costello J.** held that neither applied and he granted a decree of nullity on the ground that the respondent at the time of the marriage:

> was suffering from a psychiatric illness and as a result was unable to enter into and sustain a normal marriage relationship with the petitioner.]

Notes and Questions

1. For analysis of *R.S.J.* v. *J.S.J.* and *D.* v. *C.*, see O'Connor, *Inability to Maintain and Sustain a Normal Marriage Relationship – A New Ground of Nullity*, 1 Ir. L. Times (n.s.) 60 (1983) and O'Connor, *Recent Developments in the Irish Law of Nullity*, [1983] Dublin U.L.J. 168 at 174–81.
2. Can *R.S.J.* v. *J.S.J.* and *D.* v. *C.* be reconciled? Is a 'caring or considerate relationship' the same as 'a normal marriage relationship' with one's spouse? If the concepts are not exactly the same, how do they differ? How do you understand the word 'normal'? As referring to statistical frequency ('normal' as opposed to 'rare')? Or as implying some form of value judgment ('normal' as opposed to 'deviant')? Is this distinction important?
3. Do you see any importance in the fact that in *R.S.J.* v. *J.S.J.* Barrington J. refers to 'illness', whereas, in *D.* v. *C.*, Costello J. refers to 'a psychiatric illness'?
4. In 1976, the Office of the Attorney General published a Discussion Paper entitled *The Law of Nullity in Ireland* (Prl. 5628). The Attorney General at the time was Mr. (later Mr. Justice) Declan Costello, S.C. Some of the central recommendations of the Discussion Paper were in relation to the ground of mental incapacity. The Discussion Paper referred to the position in England where a marriage is voidable on the ground that at the time of the marriage either party, though capable of giving a valid consent was suffering (whether continuously or intermittently) from mental disorder within the meaning of the *Mental Health Act 1959* of such a kind or to such an extent as to be unfitted for marriage: *Matrimonial Causes Act 1973*, section 12. 'Mental disorder' within the *Mental Health Act 1959* is defined by section 4(1) as meaning:

   > mental illness, arrested or incomplete development of mind, psychopathic disorder, or any other disability of mind.

   'Psychopathic disorder' is, in turn, defined by section 4(4) as meaning:

   > a persistent disorder or disability of mind (whether or not including subnormality of intelligence) which results in abnormally aggressive or seriously irresponsible conduct as the part of the patient, and requires or is susceptible to medical treatment.

The Discussion Paper recommended, first, that provisions on the lines of the English legislation should be introduced into our law; but the Discussion Paper went somewhat further:–

> The definition [of 'mental disorder' in the *Mental Health Act 1959*] deals with mental illness and psychopathic disorder. It is proper, however, that account should be taken of the insights which advances in psychiatry and psychology have given into aspects of human personality. It is clear that there exist defects of personality which though not capable of being characterised as 'mental disorder' (within the definition given above) may render the person suffering from them unfit for the responsibilities of a life-long union and the foundation of a family. . . . A modern statement of the law relating to marriage should take note of such facts. It must, of course, be recognised that it is not possible to define by statute the degree of personality defect which would justify an annulment decree being made. Accordingly, considerable discretion must be given to the Court to decide each case on its own evidence (including the evidence of psychiatrists and psychologists in appropriate cases). This fact, however, should not preclude the enactment of a provision which would allow an annulment of a marriage when the evidence establishes the unfitness of a spouse by reason of a defective personality. In this connection it is to be borne in mind that ecclesiastical Courts exercising nullity jurisdiction are required to consider and adjudicate upon evidence bearing on an allegation that the personality of a respondent spouse was subject to such a defect as to render him or her unfitted for marriage. It is recommended therefore that the term 'mental disorder' should be so defined as to include arrested or incomplete development of personality of such a kind as to render the person suffering from it unfitted for marriage and that where such a condition exists the marriage should be regarded as a void one. Para. 15(C).

This recommendation provoked much public discussion. Critics complained that it would bring the law of the State in line with developments of the Canon Law jurisprudence on marriage that had taken place in the Catholic Church over the previous decade or so. See Binchy, *Divorce in Ireland: Legal and Social Perspectives*, 2 J. of Divorce 99, at 104 (1978). To what extent does *D.* v. *C.* afford the basis for a decree of nullity in respect of 'arrested or incomplete development of personality'? In other words, when, if ever, may a spouse who is so affected nonetheless be considered capable of forming a 'normal marriage relationship'? It is worth reflecting also on the extent to which an arrested or incomplete personality may be attributable to 'a psychiatric illness', as *D.* v. *C.* appears to require.

5. Perhaps the courts and Oireachtas were wise not to prescribe too specifically the *type* of mental illness necessary to invalidate a marriage; to do so could create unnecessary problems for psychiatrists: cf. Walton & Presley, *Use of a Category System in the Diagnosis of Abnormal Personality*, 122 Br. J. of Psychiat. 259 (1973); Dumont, *The Nonspecificity of Mental Illness*, 54 Amer. J. of Orthopsychiat. 326 (1984).

E.P. v. M.C. (OTHERWISE P.)

Unreported, High Ct., Barron, J., 13 March 1984

The facts of the case are set out *infra*, pp. 71–72 where the ground of duress is analysed. Briefly, the petitioner alleged that he married the respondent, who was pregnant with his child, because she had told him that, if he did not do so, she would have an abortion. The parties lived together in the respondent's parents' home from the time of their marriage until four months after the birth of their child. They then moved into their own home. Within three days the respondent wanted to terminate the marriage. Her attitude then was that she had only married to avoid the shame of a pregnancy outside marriage and to provide a name for her child. She said that, having got what she wanted, the marriage was over. She left the petitioner less than six weeks later.

One of the grounds on which the petitioner sought a decree of nullity was that the respondent had 'never intended to enter into a proper and lasting marriage'.

Barron, J. disposed of this argument as follows:

In support of [this] ground, the petitioner relied upon the judgment of Barrington, J. in *R.S.J.* v. *J.S.J.* [*supra*, pp. 24–29] and the judgment of Costello, J. in *D.* v. *C.* [*supra*, pp. 29–41].

. . . Both of these cases proceeded on the basis that the respondent was suffering from a mental illness. There is no suggestion that the respondent in the present case is suffering from any illness whatsoever. Undoubtedly, the evidence shows that she was spoiled, that she preferred life as a single person, and that she was totally unprepared to accept the obligations of marriage. Nevertheless, there is no evidence whatsoever that she was ill. For these reasons, I would have refused the relief sought in any event.

Notes

1. Why should *illness* be so important? If a person by reason of his or her character, psychological profile – call it what you will – is unable to form a caring or a considerate relationship with his or her spouse, why would it matter whether this condition may or may not be categorised as an illness?
2. Would *S.*v. *S., infra*, p. 76, have any relevance to the present case, in your view? Should an undisclosed intention at the time of entering the marriage to desert the other party shortly afterwards be a ground for annulment?

M.F. McD. (OTHERWISE M. O'R.) v. W. O'R.

Unreported, High Ct., Hamilton, J., 24 January 1984 (1982–9M.)

Hamilton, J.:–

This is a Petition brought by the Petitioner, seeking a Decree that a marriage which purported to have taken place between the Petitioner and the Respondent . . . [i]n April 1972 is null and void.

As appears from the amended Petition sworn herein by the Petitioner on the 30th day of March 1983, the grounds of the Petitioner for her claim to a Decree of Nullity are that:

(a) At the date of the said marriage and prior to and subsequent thereto the Respondent was a homosexual and had had homosexual relationships, that he represented himself to the Petitioner as being a heterosexual person and that he was as a consequence guilty of gross misrepresentation and deceit, that he lacked the capacity to form or alternatively to maintain or sustain a lasting and marital relationship with the Petitioner by reason of his homosexual nature and temperament.

(b) By reason of the aforesaid matters the Respondent, prior to and at the time of the said marriage, had formed the intention not to develop or alternatively not to maintain a lasting and marital relationship with the Petitioner and had formed the intention not to be faithful to the Petitioner and since the marriage has continued to commit acts of homosexuality with the persons named in the Petition and with others whose names are unknown to the Petitioner.

The Petitioner claims that:–

(i) The Respondent did not give any true or valid consent to the said marriage.

(ii) Further or in the alternative the Respondent was incapable of giving true or valid consent to the said marriage.

(iii) In the further alternative, the Respondent was, by reason of his homosexual nature and temperament and incapacity to form and sustain a lasting marital relationship, incapable of performing or implementing a fundamental purpose or term of the contract of marriage.

(iv) The Petitioner did not give her full and free consent to the marriage and that she was not capable of giving her full and free consent to the said marriage in that she was not aware of the Respondent's lack of capacity or the deceit, misrepresentation, and the intention of the respondent not to fulfil fundamental features of the marriage.

In his answer, the Respondent, *inter alia* denies that he was at any time or is a homosexual or that he had or entered into homosexual relations with any of the persons named in the Petition or with any other person; he denies that he was lacking in the capacity or ability to form and maintain a lasting marital relationship and alleges that the Petitioner gave her full and free consent to the marriage and that his, the Respondent's, consent to the marriage was true and valid, that he had and exercised full capacity and capability in giving such true and valid consent and that he was fully capable and did perform and implement the terms and purpose of the contract of marriage.

Before proceeding to deal with these issues, I should say in the first instance, that I am satisfied that there is no collusion between the parties with regard to these proceedings and that I agree with the statement made by Mr. Justice Costello in the course of his Judgment in *D.* v. *C.* [*supra*, p. 29], where he stated that:–

> The Courts have never approached claims for nullity decrees merely by applying principles of contract law or statutory prohibitions and even when marriages have been entered into with complete freedom untainted with illegality they may be declared null and void if one of the spouses is impotent at the time of the marriage and unable to consummate it. (See *McM.* v. *McM.* [1936] I.R. 217). But marriage is by our common law (strengthened and reinforced by our constitutional law) a life long union, and it seems to me to be perfectly reasonable that the law should recognise (a) the obvious fact that there is more to marriage than its physical consummation and (b) that the life long union which the law enjoins requires for its maintenance the creation of an emotional and psychological relationship between the spouses. The law should have regard to this relationship just as it does to the physical one. It should recognise that there have been important and significant advances in the field of psychiatric medicine since 1870 and that it is now possible to identify psychiatric illnesses, such as for example manic depressive illness, which in some cases may be so severe as to make it impossible for one of the partners to the marriage to enter into and sustain the relationship which should exist between married couples if a life long union is to be possible. Extending the law by reasoning by analogy is as old as the common law itself (in the thirteenth century it was pointed out that 'if any new and unwonted circumstance shall arise then, if anything analogous has happened before, let the case be adjudged in like manner, preceding a similibus ad similia' (Bracton, *De Legibus* quoted in Cross, *The English Doctrine of Precedent*, p. 24) and so it seems to me (as it did to Mr. Justice Barrington in *R.S.J.* v. *J.S.J.*) that if the law declares to be null a marriage on the grounds that one spouse is through physical disability incapable of the physical relationship required by marriage it should do likewise where one spouse is through a psychiatric disability unable to enter into and sustain the normal inter-personal relationship which marriage also requires.

I also agree with the statement of Mr. Justice Kenny in *S.* v. *S.* [*supra*, p. 76] where he said:–

> Section 13 of the Act of 1870 did not have the effect of fossilising the law in its state in that year. That law is to some extent at least judge made and the Courts recognise the great advances made in psychological medicine since 1870 make it necessary to frame new rules which reflect these.

which statement was accepted by Mr. Justice Costello in *D.* v. *C.* and Mr. Justice Barrington in *R.S.J.* v. *J.S.J.* [*supra*, p. 24].

Consequently it appears to me that if the Petitioner establishes that the respondent was at the time of her marriage to him and by reason of his homosexuality incapable of entering into and sustaining the relationship which should exist between married couples if a life long union is to be possible, that she would be entitled to the relief which she seeks, a decree of nullity.

These are obviously questions of fact and the onus is on the Petitioner to establish them and, having regard to the nature of these proceedings and the allegations made against the Respondent, to establish them to a high degree of probability.

I do not propose to set forth the evidence adduced in this case with regard to these issues in any great detail.

To seek to establish that the Respondent was a homosexual prior to and at the time of his marriage to the Petitioner, the Petitioner relies mainly on the evidence of Mr. X and Doctor Y.

Having carefully considered their evidence and the manner in which they gave their evidence in Court and having regard to their friendship, particularly that of Mr. X, with the Petitioner, I consider them to be unreliable witnesses and where their evidence is in conflict with that of the Respondent, I accept that of the Respondent, whom I found to be an honest and truthful witness. He denies having sexual relations with either Mr. X or Doctor Y and I accept his evidence in this regard.

It is further suggested by the Petitioner that the Respondent had prior to and subsequent to her marriage a homosexual relationship with Mr. A.

It is quite clear from the evidence that the Respondent and Mr. A were very close associates and friends and the claim that their relationship was a homosexual one is based on the evidence of Doctor Y that on the occasion of a visit to Mr. A's home . . . in

June 1971 the Respondent slept with Mr. A and that on the following morning the Respondent informed Doctor Y that the relationship had come to an end and expressed sadness that it should have ended.

I accept Doctor Y's evidence in this regard but I cannot find on the evidence any basis for holding that it ever resumed other than on the basis of friendship.

There is no evidence that after his marriage to the Petitioner the Respondent engaged in any homosexual activities. I reject completely that he had a homosexual relationship with Doctor Z. The allegation made by the Petitioner in this regard was made without any reasonable basis on evidence and I accept the evidence of Doctor Z.

It seems to me . . . , having read the Petition and Answer and considered the evidence in this case, that there are two main issues which I have to decide in this case:–

1. Whether the Respondent was prior to and at the time of his marriage to the Petitioner a homosexual, and
2. If the answer to 1 is yes, whether the Respondent (a) was unable fully to understand the nature, purpose and consequence of the marriage contract, and/or (b) was unable to maintain and sustain a normal marriage relationship with his wife, and
3. If the answer is yes to both questions whether by reason thereof the Petitioner is entitled to a Decree of Nullity.

While I am satisfied as I said that the [Respondent] had a homosexual relationship with Mr. A[,] I am satisfied that that relationship had terminated prior to the occasion of the Respondent's marriage to the Petitioner. I am further satisfied that since the occasion of his marriage to the Petitioner there is no evidence that he engaged in or entered into homosexual relationships with any person. However it must be said that even if a person had a homosexual relationship prior to marriage that of itself is not a ground for a Decree of Nullity. It is submitted on behalf of the Petitioner and based on the evidence of Doctor S that a person with homosexual tendencies and who had engaged in homosexual practice would have extreme difficulty in forming, maintaining and sustaining a lasting marital relationship. It is only if this was established in respect of the Respondent that the Petitioner would be entitled on the basis of the decision of Mr. Justice Costello in *D.* v. *C.* to a Decree of Nullity. It is quite clear that the Respondent did have prior to his marriage a homosexual relationship with Mr. A. It is also equally clear from his evidence and indeed from the evidence of the Petitioner that the sexual relationship between the Petitioner and the Respondent was satisfactory and normal, that the marriage was consummated, that the relationship led to pregnancies which unfortunately resulted in miscarriages, that the sexual relationship between the Petitioner and the Respondent had continued on a satisfactory and normal basis from the date of the marriage until the date on which difficulties arose between the Petitioner and the Respondent.

With regard to these difficulties and the reasons therefor I accept the evidence of the Respondent whom, as I have said, I have found to be on the whole an honest and truthful witness. The difficulty with regard to Doctor S's evidence is that he was giving evidence on the basis of researches which had been carried out, that he never had an occasion and was not granted an occasion to examine or discuss the problems with the [Respondent] and consequently I cannot honestly hold on the basis of Doctor S's evidence that at the date of his marriage the Respondent was not capable of maintaining and sustaining a lasting marital relationship. I am satisfied that there was valid consent by both the Petitioner and the Respondent to this marriage and that the Petitioner is not on the law as it stands and on the evidence as it stands entitled to the Decree which she seeks and I refuse the application for a Decree of Nullity.

Note

For accounts of empirical evidence on the subject, see O'Gorman, *Difficulties Associated with Marriages Between Heterosexuals and Homosexuals*, 8 Br. J. of Sexual Med. 46 (May, 1981); Coburn, *Homosexuality and the Invalidation of Marriage*, 20 Jur. 441, at 447–8 (1960).

STATUTORY PROVISIONS

An Act of 1811 (51 Geo. III, c.37) renders void marriages contracted by 'a Lunatic by any Inquisition . . .' or by 'a Lunatic or Person under a Phrenzy, whose Person or Estate by virtue of any Act of Parliament . . . shall be committed to the Care and Custody of Particular Trustees', where the marriage takes place before the person has been declared of sound mind. A marriage contracted in breach of the Act, even during a lucid interval is void (*Turner* v. *Meyers (falsely calling herself Turner)*, 1 Hag. Con. 414, at 417, 161 E.R. 600, at 601 (*per* Sir William Scott, 1808); cf. *Browning* v. *Reane*, 2 Phill. Ecc. 69, at 90, 161 E.R. 1080, at 1087 (*per* Sir John Nicholl, 1812)) and there is no need to obtain a judicial decree to this effect (*Ex parte Turing*, 1 V. & B. 140, 35 E.R. 55 (1912), *Elliott and Sugden* v. *Durr*, 3 Phill. Ecc. 16, at 19, 161 E.R. 1064, at 1065 (*per* Sir John Nicholl, 1812)).

Questions

1. Is the 1811 Act consistent with the Constitution?
2. The Discussion Paper on Nullity published by the Office of the Attorney-General recommended the repeal of this Act. Do you?

5. *DURESS*

Duress is a ground generally considered to render a marriage void. What constitutes duress-

> must be a question of degree, and may begin from a gentle form of pressure, to physical violence, accompanied by threats of death. (*Griffith* v. *Griffith*, [1944] I.R. 35, at 42 (High Ct., Haugh, J., 1943)).

The reported decisions involve such matters as a threat to make the petitioner bankrupt if the marriage does not take place (*Scott* v. *Sebright*, 12 P.D. 21 (Butt, J., 1886)), a threat to injure or kill the petitioner (*Bartlett (falsely called Rice)* v. *Rice*, 72 L.T. 123 (Sir F.H. Jeune, P., 1894); *Hussein (orse Blitz)* v. *Hussein*, [1938] P. 159 (Henn Collins, J.)), fear of political persecution (*H.* v. *H.* [1954] P. 258 (Karminski, J., 1953)), or of conviction or imprisonment resulting from a false charge (*Griffith* v. *Griffith, supra; Buckland* v. *Buckland*, [1968] P. 296 (Scarman, J., 1965)), undue influence over the petitioner's personality (*B.* v. *D.*, unreported, High Court, Murnaghan, J., 20 June 1973) and a threat to commit suicide.

For general consideration of the ground of duress, see *Shatter*, 60–63; *Shelford*, 213–221; *Jackson*, 282–289; Brown, *Duress and Fraud as Grounds for the Annulment of Marriage*, 10 Ind. L.J. 473 (1935); Brown, *Shotgun Marriage*, 42 Tulane L. Rev 837 (1968); Coghill, *Nullity – Fraud and Duress*, 19 Austr. L.J. 9 (1945); Davies, *Duress and Nullity of Marriage*, 88 L.Q. Rev. 549 (1972); Hayes, *The Matrimonial Jurisdiction of the High Court*, 8 Ir. Jur. (n.s.) 55, at 63–66 (1973); Jackson, *Consent of the Parties to their Marriage*, 14 Modern L. Rev. 1, at 7–10 (1951); Kingsley, *Duress as a Ground for Annulment of Marriage*, 33 So. Calif. L. Rev. 1 (1959); Wadlington, *Shotgun Marriages by Operation of Law*, 1 Ga. L. Rev. 183 (1967); Waters, *Duress*, 116 Sol. J. 67 (1972); Ingman & Grant, *Duress in the Law of Nullity*, 14 Family L. 92 (1984); O'Connor, *Recent Developments in the Irish Law of Nullity*, [1983] Dublin U.L.J. 168, at 169–74.

S. v. O'S.

Unreported, High Court, Finlay, P., 10 November 1978 (1977–18M)

Finlay, P.:–

I am quite satisfied that I should not reserve judgment in this case, even though points of law arise, because it is a case affecting deeply the parties concerned. I am quite satisfied that this marriage must be declared null and void. I find the facts of the matter to be as follows – firstly, I am quite satisfied that there is absolutely no collusion between the

Petitioner and the Respondent. I have had the benefit of both their evidence and I have the benefit of certain medical evidence as well. The Petitioner's account of the material facts is strongly corroborated by the original letters written by the Respondent to her, which she has produced in Court. I see no reason to do otherwise than to accept as a completely truthful and conscientious witness, the Petitioner, and, as an equally truthful and conscientious witness, the Respondent. That is the first integral question in relation to any nullity proceedings. . . . [T]he second matter which is of great importance is that, not only is the Petitioner's account of the evidence corroborated by the Respondent himself, both of whom are witnesses of truth as far as I am concerned, but is also strongly corroborated by the psychiatric evidence given. I, therefore, find the facts proved to my total satisfaction to be very briefly these – The Petitioner and the Respondent were normal young people, attracted to each other, had a normal courtship and they became engaged in an unofficial way. This was at Christmas, 1973, or early January, 1974, and they were then thinking in terms, the Respondent believes as being a period of three years, the Petitioner believes they were thinking in terms of a date for marriage in July, 1975, with a pre-engagement about a year hence, Christmas, 1974, – July, 1975, being the anticipated time when the Respondent would have finished his medical studies and done his year's Internship and be a fully-fledged doctor, ready to earn. An event then occurred which was, to an ordinary outsider, of extreme[ly] minor importance. This was described as the dress dance which led to what can only be described as a lovers' quarrel, which led to a series of events which are proved to my total satisfaction. It had an extremely decisive emotional effect upon the Respondent, he re-acted by a development of a condition which is known to medical science and is known as Munchausen's Periodic Syndrome and that consisted of projecting with elaborate detail, bizarre conditions, the only cure for which was, in the first instance, the almost exclusive attention and physical presence of his fiancée as she then was and, secondly, as time went on, which required as the only consistent cure for it, an early marriage, earlier than the parties had intended and as soon as at all possible and earlier than he got his final. I have carefully studied the Petitioner giving her evidence about this matter. I am quite satisfied that she's an intelligent person and is now holding a responsible position, yet admitted that she was completely taken in by the wealth of the medical detail, medical jargon, given to her by the Respondent. The Respondent's explanation of why she couldn't check on all these matters, which she was anxious to do, had the sort of devious cleverness that is often manifested by people suffering from temporary psychiatric instability. She was persuaded, eventually, by April or May, 1974, around that time, that she had two choices open to her. One was to marry and marry immediately, within a six week period, some time in April, the other choice was to bear the responsibility either for the rapid decline and death of the Respondent or for his suicide. I believe he carried that stark alternative clearly to her mind and, from that time forward, notwithstanding some advice, some good advice from her father, that she was not capable of forming a free will to get married, she's described by Dr. Behan as having been, in his view, in the emotional bondage of the Respondent during that period. Essentially, it seems to me that the freedom of will necessary to enter into a valid contract of marriage is one particularly associated with emotion and that a person in the emotional bondage of another person couldn't consciously have the freedom of will. I am quite satisfied that, in effect, what was applied to the Petitioner was a form of duress and, in saying that, I think it only right for me to say as well that it is not a blameworthy question, it is something in a tragic situation that arose, not something for which anyone is to be blamed. In those circumstances, I am quite satisfied that there must be a declaration, as sought by the Petitioner, that the marriage entered into between the Petitioner and the Respondent, purporting to be entered into between the Petitioner and the Respondent, on the 26th June, 1974, is null and void.

REGISTRAR: Would you say on what grounds, the Judgment will have to be actually stated, 'by reason . . .'

JUDGE: The Petitioner was induced to go through a ceremony of marriage with the Respondent on the 26th June, 1974, by such threats and duress as made the marriage void for absence of real consent, those are the grounds, induced by duress.

Notes

1. Do you agree with the decision? Should the outcome have been any different if the respondent, in making the threat to commit suicide, suffered from no mental incapacity?
2. Courts in other countries have also been faced with cases based on similar threats: see *Hartford* v. *Morris*, 2 Hag. Con. 423, 161 E.R. 792 (1776); *Field's Marriage Annulling Bill*, 2 H.L.C. 48, 9 E.R. 1010 (1848); *Cooper (falsely called Crane)* v. *Crane*, [1891] P. 369 (Collins, J.); *Kecsemethy* v. *Magyer*, 2 Fed. L.R. 437 (N.S.W. Sup. Ct., Nield, J., 1961).
3. A medical bibliography on the Munchausen patient is set out by Wimberley, *The Making of a Munchausen*, 54 Br. J. of Med. Psychol. 121, at 128–9 (1981).

B. v. D.

Unreported, High Court, Murnaghan, J., 20 June 1973 (1971 26M)

Murnaghan J.:

In this case, the wife, who sues in her maiden name, claims that her marriage to the respondent which took place on 29th August 1970 should be annulled. Both parties are Catholics. There are no children of the marriage.

The Petitioner alleges that she was put in such terror and fear by the Respondent that, she agreed to the marriage, under such duress, that the marriage should be annulled by this Court.

The law relating to cases of annulment of marriage, which are rare in the Courts of this country, has been so fully and eruditely stated by Hanna J. in *McM.* v. *McM.* and *McK.* v. *McK.* [1936] I.R. 177, and by Haugh J. in *Griffith* v. *Griffith* [1944] I.R. 35, that it would be presumption on my part in this case to restate it in any detail. (The judgment of Haugh J. is referred to with approval by Karminski J. in *H.* v. *H.* [1954] P. 258).

When a Court in this country approaches the question as to whether or not a marriage is a nullity, it must proceed on the basis that the marriage is a solemn contract, which is presumed, as a matter of public policy, to be valid. The Court must therefore proceed with great caution before giving relief, by way of annulment and must always bear in mind that discontented spouses could mala fide attempt to circumvent the law. In this case there is no question that the spouses are, together, seeking to free themselves of the marriage bond. The petitioner undoubtedly wants to be rid of the respondent as her husband and has lately succeeded in persuading the appropriate local Church authority to declare the marriage null and void. The respondent on the other hand wishes to remain legally married to the petitioner, not in my opinion on any basis of affection, but because I believe, that, as a married man, his salary and emoluments, as a national school teacher, would be on a higher scale.

It is imperative, in this type of case that I should require the petitioner to establish what she alleges by strict and thoroughly satisfactory proof, and if possible by independent evidence.

It is clear on the authorities that if the apparent consent of the petitioner to the marriage was brought about by fraud or duress, the contract of marriage was not validly entered into, and was a nullity. In this case what is relied upon is the duress of the respondent. Duress must always be a question of degree. The degree of duress is a question of fact. The questions which I have to decide are first, whether there was duress, and second if there was duress whether it was of such a degree as to make the apparent consent of the petitioner to her marriage, not a real consent in law.

The petitioner who is now thirty years old first met the respondent who is now aged thirty seven years old in November 1965. They were both natives of the County Clare, both national school teachers, and both working in. . . . Beyond those basic facts they had nothing, as far as I have been able to judge, in common. I doubt that there was any real affection between them. The furthest the respondent went in this regard was to say that in the early stages he was not 'all that interested', but that around 1968 'I decided I was getting interested'. The petitioner on the other hand said that she 'was not in love with him' but at the same time, without my going into the details said that she 'did everything he asked, he always frightened me'.

The petitioner and the respondent in fact associated with each other over the period from the time they first met, until the marriage.

Generally the Petitioner's evidence was to the effect that the Respondent used the car, which she owned jointly with her sister B, as if it was his own; that he spent most of his leisure time gambling at the dogs and at horse racing; that he regularly borrowed, and in the latter stages demanded money from her which he did not repay, and which in total up to the time of the marriage amounted to over £1000; that from about February 1968 he was drinking heavily: and to use the Petitioner's own words, 'He always assumed I was his property'. The Respondent admits using the Petitioner's car, gambling and drinking, and that he borrowed money from the petitioner. He denies that he owes her over £1000 but he said he did not know how much he owed her. I accept the Petitioner's evidence in relation to the borrowing, and I am satisfied that more often than not the Respondent demanded the money. I am further satisfied to accept the Petitioner's evidence as to the amount owing by the Respondent.

The Petitioner's evidence was that the Respondent never displayed any affection or romance towards her.

It is very difficult in cases of this kind to be satisfied as to the relationship that existed between the parties, and this case is no exception. I am however satisfied, as I have already indicated, that whatever was the relationship between the Petitioner and the Respondent it did not proceed on the basis of a normal courtship, and I believe it lacked any real feelings of anything approaching affection.

I accept the evidence that the members of the Respondent's family did not think the Petitioner and the Respondent were suited to each other. This is an opinion I share. This is however not a reason in itself for annulling this marriage.

I have decided not to recount much of the evidence. It is necessary however that I should mention certain parts thereof.

On Thursday 27th August 1975 the plaintiff, being at home, and having told her mother (her father died in 1957) three sisters and a brother that she was supposed to be getting married the following Saturday in the Pro-Cathedral, then told them that she did not want to go through with the marriage, but that the Respondent was forcing her. I am satisfied that what the Petitioner told the members of her family then represented the state of her mind. Notwithstanding what she said to the members of her family the Petitioner met the Respondent, by prior arrangement, at the Old Ground Hotel in Ennis at midday on the following day Friday, and travelled with him to Dublin, when they met the Respondent's brother, a priest, his married sister and her husband, and his married brother and his wife. Arrangements had been made for the wedding at the Pro-Cathedral on Saturday at 11 a.m. Apart from that, the Petitioner had literally made no other arrangements for her marriage. I am satisfied that on the way to Dublin the Petitioner had phoned her sister in Kilkee from Port Laoise and told her that the Respondent was very aggressive and that she thought the best thing to do was to go on to Dublin and drop him at his lodgings and then return to Kilkee. I am satisfied that the Petitioner did not have the opportunity to carry out this intention. I am satisfied that the time of the wedding was changed by the Respondent's brother to 7 a.m. without reference to the Petitioner. I believe the reason for the change of time was to ensure that no member of the Petitioner's family would be present at the wedding.

Notwithstanding the facts I have just stated the Petitioner went through with the marriage ceremony.

Prima facie, having regard to her age and her social and educational standing, it is very difficult to take any other view but that the Petitioner consented to all that occurred. This I am bound to say was my initial reaction, but at the same time I had a feeling that I should take time before giving my decision. Having done so, I must say that I don't remember any decision I have found it more difficult to arrive at.

At this stage I commence by saying that I accept the Petitioner's sister [. . .] as a truthful and accurate witness. The picture of the Respondent which I get from her evidence, is that, towards the Petitioner, he was generally arrogant and domineering, and that he cut her off from her family, and friends [. . .]. [A] friend of the Respondent and called by him as a witness, said of the Respondent that 'when he had an opinion he had an opinion'; that 'he could bring you over to his way of thinking'; and that 'he always could bring words into his argument that would weight the case in his favour'. I was particularly interested by the evidence of this witness, who said that he knew both the Petitioner and the Respondent very well from around the year 1968, that 'maybe they were not suited, there were a lot of things between [the petitioner] and [the respondent] that were not normal': that 'I never accepted that love was the basis of their marriage' and that 'the basis of the marriage was some attraction [the respondent] has for [the petitioner] that was not an attraction for other girls'.

Having thought a great deal about this case I have come to the conclusion that [this witness] had an accurate insight into the relationship between the Petitioner and the Respondent but that the word 'attraction' was not the appropriate word to describe the basis for the marriage.

Having seen and heard the Respondent I generally find myself in agreement with the picture painted of his character by [two of the witnesses]. I consider that he is very forceful, mentally arrogant, and disinclined to take no for an answer.

Nobody gave evidence as to the character of the Petitioner. In the circumstances of the case I find it difficult to make what I consider would be a satisfactory judgment. She certainly had nothing resembling a strong personality. I can readily accept what [X, a witness] said when she said that 'he was all the time domineering her – she never answered at any time' as a description of the mental relationship between the Respondent and the Petitioner.

I have very little doubt but that gradually, from the first time they met, the Petitioner found herself in her relationship with the Respondent in a groove, which as time went on got deeper and deeper, and out of which she was constitutionally unable to extract herself, and in which perhaps she was prepared in the circumstances, if not content, to remain.

I return here to the evidence of [X, a witness]. I am satisfied that the Respondent had little or no 'attraction' for the Petitioner in the ordinary sense. I am however satisfied that he had developed a very considerable influence over her which was not based on any real affection, and that, as time went on, he exercised this influence on the Petitioner to get her to carry out his wishes, which she did. I am satisfied that the exercise of this influence, which was cumulative, resulted in the marriage on the 29th August 1970 and that in all the circumstances it amounted to duress. I have yet however to express my opinion as to whether the degree of duress was sufficient to enable me to grant the Petitioner the relief which she claims.

This latter question is the one which has given me the greatest difficulty. A subjective judgment based on hearing the evidence of the Petitioner and the Respondent giving evidence is almost impossible. Not without some misgivings, but having regard in particular to the immediate circumstances surrounding the wedding, I have in the ultimate result come to the conclusion after long consideration that the reasonable probabilities are that the degree of duress was such as to render the contract of marriage in this case one that the law should consider to be a nullity. I wish here to make it quite clear that in arriving at this decision I have not been influenced by the decision of the Clerical Court.

The Respondent very astutely took the point that, as there had been acts of intercourse subsequent to the date of the Petition, there had been condonation on the part of the Petitioner. I am satisfied that such intercourse that did take place, took place under the same duress as compelled the Petitioner to marry the Respondent. A further example in my opinion of the exercise of this duress is contained in the letter dated 11.3.1972 written by the Respondent to the Solicitor for the Petitioner, in which it is inter alia stated 'She now wishes to withdraw'.

For the foregoing reasons I therefore grant the prayer in the Petition and I decree that the marriage between the Petitioner and the Respondent which took place on the 29th August 1970 was null and void.

Notes

1. Is this a decision based on duress or undue influence? Does it matter? Cf. *McK. (otherwise F.McC.)* v. *F.McC.*, [1982] I.L.R.M. 277, at 281 (High Court, O'Hanlon, J.); *A.C.L.* v. *R.L.*, unreported, High Court, Barron, J., 8 October 1982 (28M 1981), at pp. 9–10.
2. Cf. *In the Marriage of S.*, [1980] F.L.C. 90–280, analysed by H. Finlay, *Family Law in Australia*, 176–177 (3rd ed., 1983).

GRIFFITH v. GRIFFITH

[1944] I.R. 35 (High Ct., Haugh, J., 1943)

Haugh J.:

This is a petition by Cyril Griffith to obtain a declaration from the Court that a ceremony purporting to be one of marriage, performed on the 18th November, 1925, did not constitute a lawful or valid marriage between the petitioner and the respondent, because of the want of a real consent on the part of the petitioner, who alleges that the respondent, Margaret Mary Griffith (otherwise Hayes) has been guilty of fraud and intimidation in procuring him to go through the ceremony.

As there has been no appearance by the respondent on the hearing before me, it is necessary that I should state the preliminary steps taken by the petitioner.

Proceedings were begun by petition instituted on the 14th August, 1942, and, by citation served on the respondent on the 15th August, 1942, she was informed of the nature of the proceedings, and directed to make answer thereto. She was further notified that, in default of her so doing, the Court would proceed to hear the said charge proved in due course of law, and would pronounce thereon, her absence notwithstanding. This initial step had only one result. In the month of October, 1942, the respondent moved the President of the High Court for the payment of alimony *pendente lite*, whereon affidavits were sworn by both parties, who were both represented by counsel. No order was made against the petitioner.

On the 31st October, 1942, the cause was set down for trial before a Judge without a jury, and the question to be tried was set out as follows:– 'Whether the petitioner was induced to go through the ceremony of this alleged marriage with the respondent by such threats and duress as to make the said marriage invalid for want of a real consent.'

The cause was listed and heard by me on the 25th February, 1943. Despite the service of the necessary documents on the respondent, she did not appear in person or through counsel on that day. The Registrar has informed me that she did visit the Central Office some time ago, where she was generally informed of the position, and of her rights to be heard. As an additional safeguard Mr. O hUadhaigh, solicitor for the petitioner, caused a letter to be delivered to the respondent at her address on the eve of the hearing, informing her of the time and the court in which the case would be heard.

I am therefore forced to the conclusion that the respondent has deliberately abstained from making answer to the charges made against her, with a full knowledge and appreciation of all that may be involved by her so behaving – a fact (if I exclude collusion between herself and the petitioner) which must weigh with me in determining the truth or otherwise of the story told by the petitioner.

The case is not brought on fraud alone, or intimidation alone, but on a combination of both. Despite the absence of the respondent the onus that lies on the petitioner to satisfy the Court that he is entitled to the relief he seeks is severe and heavy. I must be guided by principles well founded and long established. 'In all cases of this description it is the duty of the Court to be extremely cautious in pronouncing a marriage, solemnised between two parties, null and void, and to examine the whole of the evidence produced in proof of the nullity with great vigilance and jealously,' *per* Sir Herbert Jenner in *Wright* v. *Elwood* 1 Curt. 662, at p. 666. At the same time the law must be administered regardless of consequences, and though it sometimes happens that questions of nullity of marriage involve inquiries of the most unpleasant kind, the Court must go into them. 'The claim is for a remedy, and the Court cannot refuse to entertain it on any fastidious notions of its own,' *per* Sir Wm. Scott in *Briggs* v. *Morgan* 3 Phill. Ecc. 325. Where a marriage in fact is proved the presumption of law weighs heavily in favour of its validity, but this presumption can be rebutted by evidence. . . .

Duress must be a question of degree, and may begin from a gentle form of pressure, to physical violence, accompanied by threats of death; the same remarks apply to any form of fraud that may lead to a marriage; it, too must be a question of degree. The form of duress or intimidation alleged in this case is the threat of a criminal prosecution made by the respondent and her mother, whereby he was accused of unlawful carnal knowledge of the respondent then under seventeen years, with the result that she was then pregnant by him (the petitioner). This threat with the consequent scandal and publicity to him and to his family, along with the fear of conviction and imprisonment, resulted in the marriage, according to the petitioner. That is the case on duress.

Unfortunately, as I too well know from my experience at the Bar, and as Attorney-General, marriages frequently result from threats of this precise nature. Many such cases have passed through my hands in recent years. In some cases the marriage followed the threat of prosecution; in other cases the man charged did not agree to marry until after the preliminary hearing before a District Justice, and after he had been returned for trial. If that was the sole matter I had to consider and determine, this case would cause me no difficulty. Assuming that marriages have resulted from a fear so imposed, they are clearly valid and binding on both parties. The man is free to elect between the scandal and possible punishment, on the one hand, or the marriage to the girl he has wronged, on the other. But the fear imposed must be properly imposed, that is, the charge of paternity must be true.

However, in addition to the charge of duress, in this case there is the added and combined charge of wilful fraud, in that the charge of paternity was knowingly and falsely made by the respondent, upon which misrepresentation the petitioner acted and believed.

On this question there is ample authority in support of the statement . . . that fraudulent misrepresentation does not, apart from duress, affect the validity of a marriage to which the parties freely consented . . .

So much for the general principles, which I summarise as follows:- Duress or intimidation may produce a fear that may lead to marriage, but if such fear is justly imposed, the resulting marriage when contracted is valid and binding. Fraud or misrepresentation alone, and without duress, will not invalidate a marriage, unless it produces the appearance without the reality of consent.

As I have to consider the combination of both elements, it is well that I now state the story told by the petitioner, and then apply the law as I deem it to be.

He has sworn that during the year 1925, while aged nineteen years, he was an apprentice to the leather trade and working with his father at Messrs. Mullen Brothers, 132 Capel Street, Dublin, in receipt of a wage of £1 per week. That at that period he lived with his parents, brothers and sister at 54 Eccles Street, Dublin, and was then somewhat ignorant of, and vague about, what he described as 'the facts of life.' In July of that year he was camping with a friend on Howth Hill and then first met the respondent and another girl by chance on the 25th July, 1925, and that on the same evening, on his own admission, he attempted to defile this chance acquaintance, the present respondent. In paragraph seven of his petition he alleges 'he was familiar with the respondent, and attempted to have connexion with her, which attempt was broken off almost immediately.' In his evidence before me on that same topic, he swore that he met her for the first time on that evening in July; that they parted from the other two persons, and lay down together, and that familiarity took place; that he had not a full or real knowledge of the details of the sexual act, but that insertion of the penis did not, in fact, fully take place. The two then separated, and did not again meet until the 10th November following. On that day he was at his place of business in Capel Street, when the respondent and her mother (they lived in his neighbourhood) called and asked to see him. He went to them and her mother said, 'Is this him?' The respondent nodded. Her mother said to the petitioner:- 'Do you know this girl?' 'Yes, I remember I was with her some months ago, Mrs. Hayes.' 'I have had this girl examined by a doctor, and she is pregnant, and you are the cause of it.' I remember the date my daughter was in Howth; she took the liberty to go in my absence, and she has never gone there without me before.' In answer to that charge the petitioner swears that he denied the allegations, and said that as far as he knew he could not have the girl in that state, and Mrs. Hayes continued. – 'It could have been nobody but you, you needn't think you can hang about having your pleasure, and make a victim out of my daughter.' The petitioner continues by stating that the mother added that the girl was under age, and that she (Mrs. Hayes) would put him in his proper place, if he did not marry her daughter, and that she knew a lawyer named Fetherstonehaugh who would look after her daughter's interests. The petitioner then swore that following that conversation he believed he would be liable to a criminal prosecution, and would get gaol for it. He alleges that her mother also said the girl's father was drinking heavily as a result, and was like a raving lunatic. As a result he was terrified over the whole matter, that he and his father would lose their employment, and that he accordingly told the respondent's mother he would first like to speak with his father.

At this stage in my note of his evidence I have written:- 'I was so terrified, I told her I wanted to see my father. I was terrified over the whole thing, gaol, my, and my father's employment.' His father then came down and spoke to them for a short while. They were to call the next night, and they came about eight. My father was alone with them and later sent for me. He seemed very upset and annoyed over what he had heard. He said as I had admitted being in company with the girl I was bound by the Church to marry her. I denied I could have her in that state. He said no girl would tell such a story without grounds. He stressed what would take place and said he would go and see Father O'Doherty.

I later told Father O'Doherty that I did not believe I was the father of the child. Father O'Doherty explained things to me and said I was in duty bound to marry her, if she was, as he believed her to be, a respectable girl. I said I would go back and see my father. My father pressed me to go on with the marriage and repeated they could put me in gaol for it. I have a father, mother, sister and two brothers. They had me terrified. I was afraid of everything. Father arranged the marriage with Father O'Doherty. I saw her once only with my father before the marriage but had no conversation with her. The marriage was at 4 o'clock on a Wednesday. After the ceremony my father and I parted from her at the church gate and went home together. I next saw her shortly before Xmas, and had contributed nothing to her in the meantime. My father said that as we had married, and because of the child we should be living together. Arrangements were made that she was to come to live in a room in my father's house. She agreed to come. We slept together after she came but she took her meals with her mother. In the month of February the first and only act of intercourse as I now know it took place between us. After it had happened I said to her what took place now didn't take place when we were in Howth, and why have you blamed me for Howth? She immediately admitted it and said she had to find somebody to father her child – the other man knew too much about her. Petitioner continued:– 'I went out of the room to see my father immediately and told him of what she had said and he agreed we should go to Father O'Doherty on the following morning.'

They went to see Father O'Doherty on the next morning when an interview took place; he has given his account of that interview, but for precaution's sake I would prefer to deal with it as related by Father O'Doherty himself. After the interview they again parted on the steps of the vestry and the respondent went back to live with her mother. He, the petitioner, only saw her once since that event and that was some months later. At his father's instructions he sent her 10s. a week until the annulment of the marriage by Rome in the year 1935.

That is the substance of the story told by the petitioner and I have to consider it without the advantage of a proper cross-examination. It is a unique and remarkable story, and if it stood by itself, without reliable corroboration, told some eighteen years after the ceremony, I would be bound to reject it, because of its inherent improbability, and might with reason suspect that it was either the result of his own invention, or a collusive narrative prepared by both parties, for their mutual convenience. Accordingly, I now propose, before I deal with any legal principle, to discuss this story, and to state the various tests I have applied to ascertain if this story is collusive, invented, or true.

I begin by looking to see if there exists any evidence of an independent and dependable nature upon which I can safely rely. I have come to the conclusion that this story has been fully corroborated by Father O'Doherty, now Curate at St. Laurence O'Toole's Church, Dublin, and formerly Curate at Berkeley Street, and in particular, by an important document written and produced by that same witness.

My note of Father O'Doherty's evidence on the more important matters is as follows:– 'When I was at Berkeley Street church I knew Cyril Griffith and his father. I remember the interview before the marriage. I knew the allegations that had been made against him. At the interview his father seemed most anxious for the marriage. The boy seemed rather innocent – the father made up his mind for him. I said to the boy that he should be fair to the girl, if he had done anything wrong. I felt certain that the boy, through his father, realised he was guilty. The father was acting on the boy's mind. The marriage took place in the vestry on the 18th November, 1925. He, the son, was determined that he should not live with her. The father was anxious that the parties should live together.

'They came round to me the morning after they had come together. I don't know the date. In her presence Cyril Griffith said he had asked her, on the previous night, was he really the father of the child about to be born. She said no, another man was really the father of the child, but she was more fond of him, Cyril, and she would make a better match with Cyril, for which reason she told the story against him. She gave the same account to me. She seemed calm enough.' Father O'Doherty continued: 'I took up the first piece of paper and wrote on it what she had told me, read it to her, and got her to sign it. She seemed both penitent and intelligent.' That document is as follows:-

'I, Margaret Mary Griffith (maiden name Hayes), of 117 Upper Dorset St., Dublin, hereby state that Cyril Griffith, 54 Eccles St., Dublin, is not and could not be the father of the child I am bearing and that the statements which I made to the effect that no one else but he could be the father of this child – which statements forced him to marry me – were knowingly false. . . .

Father O'Doherty continued, 'As I foresaw the annulment I drew up the document in question. Nothing more then happened. I kept it until the annulment proceedings in the Diocesan Court were begun in Dublin.'

[**Haugh, J.**: noted that evidence had been given that the Roman Rota had annulled the marriage on the grounds of defective consent. He continued:]

. . . I must begin by the primary test of examining the petitioner's general attitude and demeanour in the witness box and his conduct for the eighteen years that elapsed between the marriage and these proceedings. I am not without some experience in dealing with matters of this sort, and I know it is common for a guilty man when first accused to deny such association and relationship with the girl who makes the complaint. That did not happen in this instance. On being accused the petitioner immediately sought his father and told him that intimacy and familiarity of a limited nature had taken place but that in his view it was not possible that he could be the father of her child. It is clear that the father did not fully accept this story, but took the view that this was only a part admission of the whole story and that the probability was that his son had been guilty of full sexual intercourse. The petitioner assumed the same attitude before Father O'Doherty, who also thought this was only a part confession. I have taken the view that the petitioner was a somewhat innocent young man, as stated by Father O'Doherty in his evidence, and was much influenced by his father's advice and wishes. As far as I judge by this test, he seemed a truthful and candid witness, and I believe the position was – having regard to his youth and general inexperience, but overborne by the advice and suggestions of his father and Father O'Doherty, and gravely influenced and frightened by the threat of prosecution with the consequent exposure and scandal to himself and his parents, along with the fear of possible imprisonment – that he married the respondent in the belief that he was possibly, but not probably, responsible for her pregnancy.

The next matter I have to consider is whether the interview that took place with Father O'Doherty, at which she made this important admission, is what it purports to be, or is something that has resulted from a collusive arrangement between the parties to this suit. If I must rule out 'collusion' the story told by him to me must be true in all its details, and must mean that he married the respondent in the erroneous and wilfully induced belief that he was the cause of her misfortune, and that his consent resulted from such wilful misrepresentation, and because of the fear it produced in his mind. In her absence, I must test 'collusion' by the general probabilities, having regard to all the facts and circumstances. I begin by asking myself what possible motive, other than its truth, could the respondent have had in making such admission which could only do her harm and could bring no possible benefit. She was then about to become a mother. She had a husband to father the child; and a home in which to live. If she had not made this admission, everything seems to suggest that this state of affairs would continue indefinitely. The making of this harmful admission meant that she would lose her husband and would be without her home on the same day and ever since. It might seem that she has done so, to enable herself to break the marriage bond. But eighteen years have since elapsed, and she has done nothing whatever in that direction. On the contrary, in support of the marriage tie, she attempted, as I have already stated, to obtain alimony *pendente lite* when these proceedings were begun. It appears she defended the suit before the Ecclesiastical Court in Dublin. Accordingly, as far as I can see, she had nothing to gain by inventing this story in collusion with the petitioner when interviewing Father O'Doherty, on the contrary, she literally had everything to lose.

The next question I have asked myself is:– was she induced to tell this story to Father O'Doherty by intimidation or duress exercised by the petitioner? I can find no reason whatever to suggest she was. Father O'Doherty has sworn that she was calm enough and seemed patient and intelligent. Even if that was only a guise or an appearance of her real self on that occasion, one might expect some form of recantation throughout the many years that have since elapsed. The evidence again points the other way. She agreed to leave her husband on that afternoon, and to return to her mother; the weekly sum of 10s. is given, not on her demand, but on the suggestion of the petitioner's father; this was stopped in 1935, and no demand was made by her for its continuance until the petitioner took these present proceedings in the year 1942, and lastly, but by no means least, she had every opportunity to come into this Court to show (if such be the case) that the statement in writing and signed by her was in any way improperly obtained. On this point two further letters written by her and produced by the petitioner are of the greatest importance, and go a long way in further corroboration of the story told by him.

The first of these was written to the petitioner, according to the postmark, on the 26th January, 1927, many months after the respondent had lost her twin children and returned to her mother. This letter has been produced and is as follows:–

'117 Up. Dorset Street,

'Dear Cyril,

'I ask you for God's sake to try and forgive all the wrong and harm I have done you. I know it is a lot to ask, but try to overlook it all.

'Margaret Griffith.'

The petitioner did not reply to this letter, or meet the writer as a result.

About two and a quarter years later, on the 3rd May, 1929, she again wrote.

'117 Up. Dorset Street,
3 May, 1929.

'My dear Cyril,

'I hope you will excuse this note, as you told me before not to write to you, but I want you to meet me on Monday night at the Mater Hospital, at 8 o'clock. Please meet me there, as there is something I would like to ask you.

'Ever yours,

'Margaret Griffith.'

Again he did not answer this letter, or comply with her request.

In view of the statements contained in the first letter I cannot possibly hold, let alone suspect, that the confession made to Father O'Doherty was other than free and voluntary. What can the words 'wrong' and 'harm' used in that letter refer to, other than the wrong and harm the petitioner has sworn to? There is no other harm suggested in this case. To my mind these two unsolicited letters clearly prove that the statement made by her, and reduced to writing by Father O'Doherty, was voluntary and true, which necessarily means that the events of the previous night as described by the petitioner are also true, collusion and intimidation by the petitioner being now ruled out. I must therefore conclude and hold that, prompted by conscience and possibly remorse, the respondent when taxed by the petitioner told the truth about the paternity of her child.

All this must mean that the consent to marry later given by the petitioner was in fact given, not because of the usual inspirations caused by love and affection, but because of a real and grave fear inspired by an unjust and fraudulent misrepresentation on a very grave and vital matter, going to the root of his consent; and that it was this fear, so unjustly imposed, that led to the marriage now impugned.

On my examination of the evidence, and on my view of the law, I feel bound to hold that a consent so obtained by this combination of fraud and fear, the first producing the second, is not a consent that binds the petitioner – and there being no real consent in law, there was accordingly no valid marriage. That is my conclusion on the evidence before me, independent of any other fact or circumstance.

Yet I cannot say I am untouched by the result of the proceedings finished at Rome, and I am glad that I can justly relieve the petitioner from the anomalous and unhappy position of being unmarried in the eyes of his Church and married according to the law of the land.

I have taken some trouble to ascertain, as well as I can, the law of the Church on such matters, and from an authoritative text book handed me, I find that the principles, in the main, seem to be similar. Under the heading Canon 1087 the text is as follows:–

'Marriage is invalid when contracted because of force or grave fear, caused by an external agent, unjustly, to free oneself from which one is compelled to choose marriage. No other fear can bring about the invalidity of a marriage. As all forms of fear are not sufficient, the following conditions must be fulfilled, before invalidity can be declared:–

'1. The fear must be grave.

'2. It must be imposed *ab extrinseco*.

'3. It must be unjustly caused, and it must be so compelling that marriage is really the only alternative in order to liberate oneself from it.'

On my view of the facts all these conditions clearly apply to this case. I conclude by saying, as Mr. Justice Hanna said, a nullity proceeding is a rare event in our Courts. It is still rarer to find an annulment granted. I have done so in this case, but its own special facts are unique, and stranger still, there is remarkable evidence of a reliable nature in support of the story told. It is difficult to foresee it repeated on a second occasion, with similar supporting evidence of so strong a character, and I must emphasise, in the public interest, that I would not have acted on the mere telling of such a story, even if I were inclined to believe it, were it not for the evidence of Father O'Doherty, the document he produced, and the two letters later written by the respondent.

I decree annulment in this case, and I direct the Registrar to communicate the result to the respondent forthwith, by special letter.

I will put a stay on the order for a period of fourteen days, so as to enable the respondent to take such steps as she may be advised. . . .

Notes

1. This decision has been widely discussed in other jurisdictions: see, e.g., *Szechter (orse Karjov)* v. *Szechter,* [1970] 3 All E.R. 905 (P.D.A.Div., Sir Jocelyn Simon, P.); *Buckland* v. *Buckland (orse Camilleri),* [1968] P. 296 (Scarman, J., 1965); *Kecsemethy* v. *Magyer*, 2 Fed. L. R. 437 (N.S.W. Sup. Ct., Nield, J., 1961); *Williams* v. *Williams,* [1966] V.R. 60 (Sup. Ct., Barber, J., 1965). See also H. Finlay, *Family Law in Australia*, 175 (3rd ed., 1983).
2. Do you accept the proposition that, where fear has been 'justly imposed', a marriage contracted as a result of that fear should be valid? See Manchester, *Marriage or Prison: The Case of the Reluctant Bridegroom*, 29 Modern L. Rev. 622 (1966), Neville Brown, *Shotgun Marriage*, 42 Tulane L. Rev. 837 (1968); Wadlington, *Shotgun Marriages by Operation of Law*, 1 Georgia L. Rev. 183 (1967); Kingsley, *Duress as a Ground for Annulment of Marriage*, 33 So. Calif. L. Rev. 1, at 4 (1959).
3. Is the decision authority for the proposition that fraud, *without any duress*, may invalidate the marriage? If not, is it inconsistent with this proposition? Why should not fraud invalidate a marriage, without any question of duress? Why should it be necessary to show that a party was frightened as well as fooled?
4. For a brief historical comparative survey of the 'just threat', see Schwelb, *Marriage and Human Rights*, 12 Amer. J. of Comp. L. 337, at 352–353 (1963).

K. v. K.

Unreported, High Court, O'Keeffe, P., 16 February 1971 (1969–34M)

O'Keeffe, P.:

This is a Petition . . . claiming a declaration that [the petitioner's] marriage to the respondent was and is null and void by reason of fraud and duress. The petitioner became acquainted with the respondent in the year 1956, and became friendly with her. He alleges that in the year 1960 he had sexual intercourse with her, but that it was interrupted before completion. He further alleges that he had no further intercourse with her until the year 1962. . . . He alleges that on the 28th January of that year he took the respondent to a picture and afterwards had intercourse with her in his motor car, but that again it was interrupted before completion. According to himself he never again had intercourse with her, and did not have any communication with her until August of that year, when she wrote to him alleging that she was pregnant by him, and when he did not answer this letter telephoned him making allegations to the like effect. By reason of her allegations, and the manner in which they were made, he, according to himself, agreed to meet her, and subsequently did so.

He swears that the telephone call to him was at a public telephone in the local shop, and that his conversation was open to anyone present to hear; that he agreed to meet her to discuss the matter with her, as she was making threats over the telephone, and he felt compelled to meet her as a result. He met her by appointment . . . and they went for a drive in his car, in which they later talked.

She alleged that he was the father of the child that she was expecting, and gave the likely date of birth as 1st November. He denied paternity, since, according to himself, he considered this impossible, but she told him that she had never had intercourse with any other man, and insisted that he was the father of the child. She threatened that if he did not marry her she would inform his parents . . . and also a sister of his who is a nun, and that she would bring legal proceedings against him which would result in adverse publicity. As a result, he says, he agreed to marry her, and did so in September, 1962. He swears that the marriage was never consummated.

The respondent did not give birth to any child on 1st November, 1962, and the petitioner alleges that about two weeks later he accused her of having deceived him, and that she did not deny this, but made a remark which could be taken as an admission of her guilt. On 23rd December, 1962, the respondent gave birth to twins, which were described by the owner of the nursing home in which they were born as premature – about [two] months or so – and which were still born.

. . . About a week after the respondent's return from the nursing home both went to live with the respondent's parents, on their farm. . . . Although they occupied the same house for some years, and indeed were both living there at the time of presentation of the petition, the petitioner swears that they occupied separate apartments, and that they never lived together as man and wife.

The respondent entered an appearance to the proceedings by a firm of solicitors, who afterwards withdrew from the proceedings by leave of the Court. They attended before the Master when the issues to be tried were fixed, but they did not appear at the hearing of the petition, and the respondent did not appear in person.

The principles to be applied in a case such as this have been very fully stated by Haugh, J. in *Griffith* v. *Griffith* [1944] I.R. 35, and I need not repeat them here. I consider that the petitioner has established that the marriage was induced by fraud and fear to the point that his consent to the marriage was no true consent. I believe his statement that the marriage was never consummated, and I take this as an important point in showing his mental attitude to the marriage at the time of the ceremony. His evidence is totally uncorroborated, but in spite of the sanctity of the marriage bond I do not feel justified in refusing the order he seeks on this ground. I think that the attitude of the respondent in entering an appearance in the proceedings, and instructing Solicitors up to a point, is indicative of there being no collusion between petitioner and respondent. Viewed in this light, her absence from the trial is almost an admission of the truth of the facts set out with considerable detail in the petition. Accordingly I feel disposed to grant to the petitioner the relief sought in his petition.

Following the precedent set by Haugh, J., in *Griffith* v. *Griffith*, I have decided to give to the respondent a last minute chance to protect the alleged marriage if she should be so advised. Accordingly I adjourn this case for fourteen days. I direct the Registrar to write to the respondent informing her that in default of special application by her within that period I intend to pronounce a decree of nullity for the reasons already indicated.

Notes

1. Do you agree with the holding in this decision?
2. What relevance (if any) to the outcome of the case should the threat to inform the petitioner's sister have had? Why?
3. Would spouses intending collusive proceedings welcome or be displeased with this decision?
4. See O'Reilly, *Fraud, Duress and Nullity*, 7 Ir. Jur. (n.s.) 352 (1974).

McK. (OTHERWISE M McC.) v. F. McC.
[1982] I.L.R.M. 277 (High Court, O'Hanlon J.)

O'Hanlon, J.:

The petitioner in this case asks the court to decree that her marriage to the respondent is null and void. Both parties were legally represented at the hearing, but neither in the answer filed in the proceedings nor in the conduct of the case did the respondent contest the claim, and it is apparent that a nullity decree is keenly desired by both parties. Indeed it would appear that the husband's lack of consent was relied upon in nullity proceedings before the ecclesiastical courts, which resulted in the making of a decree of nullity of marriage by Birmingham Metropolitan Tribunal on 5 November 1980. It is also important to note that the matter caused some difficulty to the ecclesiastical courts, since an affirmative decision in favour of the petition was given by The Dublin Regional Marriage Tribunal, followed by a negative decision given by the National Marriage Appeal Tribunal of Ireland, before the ultimate and binding decision was given by the third Tribunal to deal with the case.

The facts of the case are not in dispute and they reflect an unfortunate situation which must have arisen in relation to very many marriages in this country where the moral code has hitherto rested on a strong bedrock of religious belief.

Before summarising the relevant evidence, it is important to make the comment that I found the evidence of all the witnesses – the petitioner and her mother, the respondent, his mother and sister – completely credible and trustworthy. While the petitioner and the respondent are of one mind in seeking the relief referred to in the petition I am satisfied that there is no collusion between them to act from improper motives or to deceive the court in any way as to the true facts of the case in an effort to achieve release from a contract which is burdensome to both of them.

The petitioner was born in August, 1953, and the respondent in August, 1951. When they first met, while on holidays in the West of Ireland, the respondent was in rather poorly-paid employment as a storeman, and the petitioner was still a school-girl, about to embark on her last year at school. This was in 1970. They became friendly and in the following year, after the petitioner had completed her leaving certificate, they associated with each other on a fairly regular basis in 1971 and 1972. It was described as being a case of a group of friends going around together rather than a close personal relationship between two people, and both parties said they never contemplated marriage at that stage nor was the subject ever discussed between them. The petitioner secured a position in the bank, early in 1972, with a better income than that of the respondent, who had moved into different employment and taken a drop in salary in the hope of improving his prospects of progress to better things in the future.

Sexual intercourse took place between the parties in the summer of 1972; both testified that this was the one and only occasion on which it took place before their marriage, and both were stunned by the later discovery that the petitioner had become pregnant as a result of this single episode.

The petitioner was then just 19 years of age and the respondent just 21. The first to suspect that something was amiss was the petitioner's mother, and when pregnancy tests revealed that her suspicions were well-founded, a series of harrowing scenes took place in both households. The petitioner's mother, to whom the petitioner was very closely attached by bonds of affection and dependence, became terribly distressed; she told the petitioner that she would have to marry the respondent or leave home altogether. Her father, who was in poor health, having suffered two strokes, and with continuing high blood pressure, was even more agitated. The petitioner described the situation in her home at the time as 'tense and disastrous'; her mother was 'in bed, crying and broken up. – She said, "You are going to have to get out or get married" – I was in a state of shock'.

At the same time, stormy scenes were taking place in the respondent's home. His father refused to speak to him or have anything to do with him. His mother told him he could not stay on in the house. 'The trend was: "You are to get married" – no options open – no advice by anyone – I had nowhere to go.' 'I was told I would have to get married. I was led to believe there was no other option open to me. I cracked up under pressure – acted irresponsibly.' The situation in the respondent's home was so bad that he had to leave home and go to live with a friend who later acted as best man at the wedding.

In the meantime, the two sets of parents met in the petitioner's home, neither petitioner nor respondent being present or consulted in any way, and the decision was taken that the respondent would have to marry the petitioner as quickly as possible, before her pregnant condition became obvious to everyone. She was told by her mother to go and arrange it with a priest. She obeyed this directive, without communicating in any way with the respondent. The priest asked her why she was in such a hurry to get married, and when she explained that she was pregnant he made no further comment but arranged for the marriage to take place at an early date.

The respondent took no part in the arrangements for the wedding. He had to be put under great pressure to get the wedding ring, and arrived late for the ceremony. At that time he was earning only £15 per week, and he was not in a position to support a wife, nor had he done anything about providing a home for them after the marriage. After a honeymoon spent in a friend's house, and characterised by lack of affection and harmony between the husband and wife, they were taken in by his sister to live with her until they could provide a home of their own.

There followed a year spent in Scotland. The parties had marital relations on a number of occasions but their general relationship towards each other was deteriorating all the time. The petitioner suffered a miscarriage only two weeks after the marriage had taken place and there were no children born to them thereafter. They separated in or about the month of February 1975 and have not lived together since that time.

The respondent said in evidence: 'I was told our parents had agreed we were to be married. I felt trapped – no way out – if they had sent me to a gas chamber I would have agreed.'

The petitioner gave the impression of being a shy, reserved, and very sensitive type of girl, closely-attached to both her parents and very dependent on them, and it is easy to credit her story that her whole world fell in on her when she felt herself in a sense rejected by them.

The respondent appeared to be of tougher mould, but was clearly very immature in many respects at the time of the marriage. He felt himself condemned by his parents and by anyone to whom he turned for advice; any decision was effectively taken out of his hands by the joint meeting of the parents, who obviously considered they were in a position to impose their will on both the petitioner and the respondent, and this is what occurred in fact. An unwilling bride and a resentful husband were dragged to the altar and went through a ceremony of marriage which neither of them wanted, and without any genuine feeling of attraction or affection which might have led on to a happy union in the course of time.

It now becomes necessary to examine the state of the law applicable to this unfortunate series of events. If one has regard to the decided cases in Ireland, England and in other common law jurisdictions, a situation of conflict appears to emerge. The basis for the claim in the present case is duress. There is a good deal of authority in support of the proposition that duress in matrimonial causes is dealt with in the same way and is subject to the same rules as in the law of contract generally, and that to avoid a marriage contract or any other contract on grounds of duress there must be something in the nature of actual violence or threats of violence to the person, i.e., threats calculated to produce fear of loss of life or of bodily harm. (Co. Litt. 153 b).

In *Szechter* v. *Szechter* [1970] 3 All E.R. 905, at 915, Sir Jocelyn Simon, P. concluded his judgment by stating:

> It is, in my view, insufficient to invalidate an otherwise good marriage that a party has entered into it in order to escape from a disagreeable situation, such as penury or social degradation. In order for the impediment of duress to vitiate an otherwise valid marriage, it must, in my judgment, be proved that the will of one of the parties thereto has been overborne by genuine and reasonably held fear caused by threat of immediate danger, for which the party is not himself responsible, to life, limb or liberty, so that the constraint destroys the reality of consent to ordinary wedlock. I think that in the instant case that test is satisfied.

In *Szechter*, a collusive marriage had taken place to secure the release of a Jewish girl from prison in Poland in 1968. In *Parojcic v Parojcic,* [1959] 1 All E.R. 1 the petitioner who was a refugee from Yugoslavia, was threatened by her father that he would send her back to Yugoslavia if she did not marry the respondent; he also used physical violence towards her on the day prior to the marriage. In *Buckland v Buckland,* [1967] 2 All E.R. 300, the petitioner, a dock policeman in Malta, who was falsely accused of misconduct with the respondent, was advised by his lawyer that he faced certain conviction and imprisonment if he did not marry her. In *Scott v Seabright*, (1886) 12 P.D. 21, the petitioner was threatened with financial ruin and disgrace, but there was also evidence of threats to shoot her if she showed that she was not acting of her free will. In all of these cases there was ample proof of danger to the life or liberty or physical well-being of the petitioner, and there was little difficulty in granting a decree of nullity as sought.

A second limiting factor on the grounds for seeking nullity appears to emerge in the course of the judgment of Haugh, J. in the leading case of *Griffith v Griffith,* [1944] I.R. 35 – a judgment which, incidentally, has been cited with approval in later decisions in England and Australia. Having reviewed many of the earlier decisions in some detail, Haugh J concluded:–

> So much for the general principles, which I summarise as follows: Duress or intimidation may produce a fear that may lead to marriage, but if such fear is justly imposed, the resulting marriage when contracted is valid and binding. Fraud and misrepresentation alone, and without duress, will not invalidate a marriage, unless it produces the appearance without the reality of consent.

In that case, Haugh, J. was dealing with a situation which found a parallel in the later case of *K.* v. *K.* [*supra*, p. 58] and in the English case of *Buckland v Buckland (supra).* In each case there was a false allegation of sexual misconduct coupled with threats of legal proceedings, unfavourable publicity, and either imprisonment or other unpleasant consequences. It may be inferred from Haugh, J.'s summary of the principles applicable, however, that he took the view that if the allegations made against the petitioner were well-founded, it could be permissible to apply pressure of such kind against him to induce him to enter into marriage, and that he would not be allowed to allege lack of true consent at a later stage.

These rather stringent principles were applied by the Court of Appeal in England in dealing with the case of *Singh v Singh,* [1971] 2 All E.R. 828, where a 17 year old Sikh girl, living in England, was betrothed by her parents to a bridegroom whom she had never seen and was induced to go through a civil marriage ceremony with him in reliance on her parents' representation (which proved untrue) that he was handsome and well-educated. On discovering the true state of facts she refused to cohabit with him or to go through the religious ceremony which should have followed, but her petition for nullity was dismissed. Once again, the court concluded that:

> In order for the impediment of duress to vitiate an otherwise valid marriage, it must . . . be proved that the will of one of the parties thereto has been overborne by genuine and reasonably held fear caused by threat of immediate danger, for which the party is not himself responsible, to life, limb or liberty, so that the constraint destroys the reality of consent to ordinary wedlock.

There are, however, some Irish cases, where less stringent requirements were accepted as being sufficient to ground an application for nullity, and where the facts seemed more consonant with the related topic of undue influence than with legal duress in the strictest sense of the term.

[**O'Hanlon, J.** summarised and quoted extracts from the judgments in *B.* v. *D., supra*, p. 48 and *S.* v. *O'S. supra*, p. 46. He continued:]

. . . In considering whether, in the circumstances of the present case, I should adopt the more stringent approach to the law of duress as applied to nullity cases which is illustrated by the English and American cases, and by some of the comments of Haugh J in *Griffith v Griffith*, or the broader application of principles of duress evident in the decisions of Murnaghan J and Finlay P, I have regard to the fact that the High Court in exercising its jurisdiction under the *Matrimonial Causes and Marriage Law (Ireland) Amendment Act, 1870*, S. 13 is 'to proceed and act and give relief on principles and rules which in the opinion of the said court, shall be as nearly as may be conformable to the principles and rules which the ecclesiastical courts of Ireland have heretofore acted on and given relief.'

The fact that the ecclesiastical courts in the present case concluded – although obviously not without some difficulty – that the facts and circumstances were sufficient to warrant the grant of a decree of nullity, is some indication that duress as understood under canon law may embrace, not merely violence or threats of violence to the person, but also moral pressures of the type illustrated by the evidence given in the present case. This is referred to also in a comprehensive survey of nullity cases by A. H. Manchester, MA (Oxon), in the Modern Law Review, Vol 29 p. 623, (*Marriage or Prison: The Case of the Reluctant Bridegroom*), at 626 n. 18:

> Certainly canon law has a well defined doctrine or reverential fear – 'The expectation of future harm as a result of displeasure on the part of a parent, superior or other person under whose authority one is and to whom one owes reverence. In itself, reverential fear is slight, but it may be grave from its circumstances. It becomes grave when to this reverence are added importunate and insistent entreaties, long and strenuous persuasion, constant nagging, imperious words and similar circumstances.

The author contrasts this principle of canon law with the approach adopted by an American court in *Fluharty v Fluharty*, (1937) 193 Atl. 838, where it was stated:

The mere commands of a father, based on the relation of parent and child, do not show the necessary legal subjection of one person to another to constitute coercion . . . No matter what the facts were, or what he thought they were, the mere fact that the petitioner's father urged, or even commanded her to marry the respondent, does not amount to such coercion as to justify this court in annulling a contract of that nature.

My conclusion is that in the present case I should take the broader view of the concept of duress and that there is justification for declaring the marriage null and void. I am satisfied that the will, not merely of one partner but of both husband and wife, was overborne by the compulsion of their respective parents and that they were driven unwillingly into a union which neither of them desired, or gave real consent to, in the true sense of the word, and which was doomed to failure from the outset.

In the case of the petitioner I accept her evidence that she found herself in a desperate situation; about to be expelled from her home; unable to keep on her post in the bank by reason of her pregnancy, with nowhere to go and no means to provide for her own support or for that of the child she hoped would be born to her. Viewed in the cold light of retrospect it seems most unlikely that her parents, who obviously loved her very much, would have continued to harden their hearts against her, but she was not to know that at the time, and marriage appeared to be the only option open to her. I am influenced in coming to this conclusion by the fact that she was little more than a schoolgirl at the time and by the apparent sensitivity and even timidity of her temperament.

In the case of the respondent, I am satisfied that he was stunned and shocked by what had happened, and found himself under so much pressure from both sets of parents that he was unable to think coherently or make any rational decision as to what was best for his own future or that of the petitioner.

In both cases I believe the will was overborne by compulsion by persons to whom they had always been subject in the parent and child relationship and that the duress exercised was of a character that they were constitutionally unable to withstand.

On these grounds I make a decree of nullity, as sought by the petitioner, in relation to the marriage of the petitioner and the respondent, which was celebrated on 30 September, 1972, on the grounds of duress exercised against the petitioner by her parents at the time of the said marriage.

Notes

1. In what circumstances (if any) would a court, following this decision, reject the petitioner's case on the basis that the threat to which he or she had succumbed was a 'just' one?
2. It is not always the man alone who may be threatened with criminal or quasi-criminal proceedings in this type of case: see *Pascuzzi* v. *Pascuzzi,* [1955] O.W.N. 853 (High Ct. of Justice, Aylen, J.) (15 year-old girl threatened with juvenile delinquency proceedings).
3. The relationship between pre-marital pregnancy and marital disruption has been studied in detail over the years. See the English Law Commission's Report, *Family Law: Illegitimacy*, para. 4.6 (Law Com. 118, 1982). Christensen and Rubinstein reported in 1956 that:

> Premarital pregnancy seems to be a part of the divorce-producing syndrome . . . [It] seems to intensify the conflict which a couple may already be in . . . Not only do premarital pregnancy couples get divorced more frequently than others but they get divorced earlier after the wedding. Of the premarital pregnancy couples, those who waited until 'the last minute' to marry showed higher divorce rates than those who married soon after the condition was discovered.: *Premarital Pregnancy and Divorce: A Follow-Up Study by the Interview Method*, 18 Marriage & Family Living 114, at 122 (1956).

See also Christensen, *Premarital Pregnancy as Measured by the Spacing of the First Birth from Marriage*, 18 Am. Sociological Rev. 53 (1953); Christensen & Meissner, *Premarital Pregnancy as a Factor in Divorce*, 18 Am. Sociological Rev. 641 (1953); Monahan, *Premarital Pregnancy in the United States*, 7 Eugenics Q. 133 (1960); Teachman, *Methodological Issues in the Analysis of Family Formation and Dissolution*, 44 J. of M. & the Family 1037, at 1046–1048 (1982); J. Eekelaar, *Family Security and Family Breakdown*, 36–39 (1971); Baum, *A Trial Judge's Random Reflections on Divorce: The Social Problem and What Lawyers Can Do About It*, 6 J. Family L. 61, at 89–90 (1966). A study was carried out by Dr. Helen Burke of the Faculty of Social Science, University College Dublin, when she was a member of the Law Reform Commission, entitled *Age at Marriage and Marital*

Breakdown: An Analysis of Applications for Annulment to the Dublin Regional Marriage Tribunal 1975. The study is published as Appendix D of the Commission's Working Paper No.2 – 1977, *The Law Relating to the Age of Majority, the Age for Marriage and Some Connected Subjects.* In her study, Dr. Burke found that, at a minimum, 94 of the 419 applicants for religious annulments in that year were pregnant at the time of marriage; that 38.5% of the brides who married under the age of 20 were then pregnant; and that among the grooms who were under 20 at the time of the marriage, 55.2% of their brides were pregnant when they were married: cf. *id.*, at 130–131. Dr. Burke considered that these figures 'do look rather high' (*id.*, at 131) and expressed as one of the two 'main findings [to] emerge from this research' that 'there was a high incidence of pre-marital pregnancy among the applicants for an annulment in 1975 who were very young at the time of their marriage . . .' (*id.*, at 134). But since we do not know the incidence of premarital pregnancy among the population at large, it is, as Dr. Burke notes (at 130–131) 'impossible to ascertain if the incidence of pre-marital pregnancy was higher among those who applied for an annulment than in the population at large.' Thus, however high the figures may look they cannot, of course, lead to any definite conclusion one way or the other as to the correlation between pre-marital pregnancy and marital breakdown.

Another study, by Dr. Gabriel Nolan, should also be noted. Dr. Nolan, a consultant psychologist with the Eastern Health Board, examined fifty cases referred to his unit from the Dublin District Court. He found that in half the cases the wife had been pregnant at the time of marriage: *Psychiatrist Finds that Marriages of Necessity Lead to Discord*, Irish Times, 3 April 1976.

4. In contrast to civil law jurisdictions, common law countries have very few express limitations on entitlement to marry. The tradition has been to let the law of nullity resolve the problem afterwards. Would it be desirable to prohibit marriages where the woman is pregnant? Would such a law be Constitutional or would it offend against the right to marry? Should the State introduce a compulsory waiting period where the parties are young and the girl is pregnant?
5. In England, in *Singh* v. *Singh*, [1971] P. 226 (mentioned by O'Hanlon J.) and in *Singh* v. *Kaur*, 11 Family L. 152 (1981), the Court of Appeal preferred the stringent *Szechter* test to the more indulgent and subjective approach of *Scott* v. *Sebright*. For criticism of *Singh* v. *Singh*, see Poulter, *The Definition of Marriage in English Law*, 42 Modern L. Rev. 409, at 413–418 (1979). More recently in *Hirani* v. *Hirani*, 4 F.L.R. 232 (C.A., 1983), the Court of Appeal adopted the latter approach, Ormrod L.J. relying mainly on *Pao On* v. *Lau Yiu Long*, [1980] A.C. 614, the Privy Council decision on economic duress in the law of contract. For analysis of *Hirani*, see Ingman & Grant, *Duress in the Law of Nullity*, 14 Family L. 92 (1984).

A.C.L. v. R.L.

Unreported, High Court, Barron, J., 8 October 1982 (28M 1981)

Barron, J.:

The parties in this case met . . . in 1975. The petitioner, who was aged 28 at that time, was a senior secretary . . . She was also the owner of a [shop] . . . which was run by [a relation of hers]. The respondent was aged 32 and at that time he was [a] teach[er] . . . The parties was attracted to each other and within a very short time the respondent proposed marriage to the petitioner.

Early in 1976, the respondent by mutual but unexpressed agreement went to live with the petitioner in her home. . . . He again proposed marriage in February of that year. The petitioner does not appear to have regarded either proposal seriously. Nevertheless their relationship became closer and intimate. In May, the petitioner became aware that she was pregnant. The petitioner was somewhat apprehensive, but the respondent was pleased at the news.

The petitioner sought to conceal her condition from her family. This became possible because she had intended in any event to give up her job . . . and to go to London to obtain further experience of the fashion trade. At this time also the respondent was appointed [to an administrative position in another town]. There was a house going with this job and the couple moved into it in June.

The respondent saw no reason to conceal the pregnancy from his friends or family. As a result, the petitioner's sisters heard of the pregnancy, but her parents never did. By September the petitioner was noticeably pregnant and she moved to London. She had already been over to London to visit a doctor for a pre-natal check-up. The respondent also came to London. He obtained a flat for them both and they lived together in that flat until the baby was born, with the exception of some weeks during which the respondent had to return to [Ireland] for the purpose of his appointment with [his employers].

The baby was born on the 19th December 1976 in London. The parties returned to Ireland shortly after Christmas. They came to a property owned by the respondent. Save for a few days immediately after their arrival home when the parties went to stay with the petitioner's sister as a result of the condition of. . . this house [,it] was at all relevant times the parties' family home.

Once she had returned home, the petitioner realised that she had a duty to tell her parents as soon as possible that she was not married and that she had a child. She and her husband went to visit her parents and in the course of that visit her parents were told that although they were not then married they were going to get married. In addition the petitioner's mother was told by the petitioner that she already had a child. This visit was followed by a return visit to the parties by the petitioner's parents for the purpose of seeing the child and to bring it presents. Subsequently, a visit was made to the parties by the petitioner's brother and sister. During both these visits and on at least two other occasions when a brother or sister of the petitioner met her the petitioner was being asked when she was going to get married. The general reaction from both her parents and her brothers and sisters was that she had to get married. Arrangements were, in fact, made for the wedding to take place in [a church] in . . . Dublin and the parties were married there [in] March 1977.

Unfortunately, the parties did not achieve a settled home life following the wedding ceremony. For the following nine months they had a normal married relationship. However, the petitioner miscarried and from then on their relationship deteriorated and they separated.

What I have to ascertain are the circumstances leading up to the marriage and the nature of the consent given by the petitioner. I should say that I am satisfied that there is no collusion between the parties.

The parties are both strong characters. They are intelligent and hard-working. However, the petitioner is more concerned with conventional moral standards than the respondent, although perhaps the respondent's attitude is in part a front which he has built up. I accept them both as witnesses seeking to tell the truth as they see it.

Their relationship matured quickly and from the time that the pregnancy was diagnosed they assumed in practice the relationship of husband and wife. The respondent provided a home for the petitioner first in [one Irish town], later in London and ultimately in [another Irish town]. The respondent wanted to get married, the petitioner did not. They agreed that they would not marry during the pregnancy. However, when they were in London, it was necessary for them to decide on their future.

The petitioner even then was not prepared to be pushed. She agreed that they would get married, but was prepared to let things slide. This seems to have been because of reservations about the respondent, which she admits she never expressed to him. To me it seems that she realised even though only subconsciously, that he did not exist on the pedestal upon which she had placed him, but even to herself was not prepared to admit this.

It was in this state of mind that the petitioner returned to Ireland with her baby. She dreaded the meeting with her parents. She had never been away from them at Christmas and perhaps hoped that the news would already have been broken to them. However, it had not been.

On the parties' return to [the petitioner's property in Ireland] the petitioner was dissatisfied with its condition and they spent some nights with her sister. The first of these the respondent remained in [the petitioner's property]. However, this did not affect the petitioner's relationship with the respondent.

The parties went to visit the petitioner's parents. They did not bring their child with them. It was thought that the news should be broken more tactfully. In the event, through embarrassment on the petitioner's part, her parents thought that they were being told that the couple were going to get married. It was necessary for the petitioner to follow her mother into the kitchen to tell her that they already had a baby. The respondent who saw nothing to be ashamed of thought that the news had been fully broken to the petitioner's parents.

The result of the breaking of the news was that the petitioner was immediately pressed to name a wedding date. Her parents came to see the baby and brought him presents. However, they made it clear to the petitioner that they expected her to become a married woman as soon as possible. Her brothers and sisters took the same view and pressed her to do so for their parents' sake.

The petitioner had told her mother that she would speak to the respondent. She did so. He was quite agreeable to be married, appreciated that her parents would not wish the ceremony to be performed locally, and suggested that they get married in . . . Dublin. The petitioner agreed and arrangements were put in hand by the respondent.

At this stage the petitioner says that she did not want to get married, that she had reservations about doing so and that she only agreed because her parents made her. The respondent says she was perfectly willing to get married and that he thought she was above reacting to the pressures caused by their unconventional relationship. In support of her present contentions, the petitioner says that she made no preparations for her wedding and was unhappy during the period she was in Dublin for it.

It is true that she apparently made no hotel reservation. However, the circumstances of the wedding were abnormal and much of the evidence in relation to events in Dublin are attributable to this. Her own personal unhappiness sprung partially from the fact that she had to leave her baby. She was breast feeding it at the time and this caused a physical as well as an emotional pain. Another and perhaps the real source of her unhappiness on that day was caused by the attitude of the priest who heard her confession. Instead of sympathy and understanding, for which she thought she was entitled, he was disapproving and critical of her conduct.

In my view, the petitioner's evidence is coloured by the break-down of her relationship with the respondent. I prefer the evidence of the respondent where it conflicts upon detail and accept it. On only one point do I not accept the respondent's evidence. It is when he says that he thought the petitioner was above all that. I feel that he was fully aware that the petitioner was allowing herself to be persuaded to get married almost immediately when he knew that she had wanted her decision to be reached gradually. Also he was aware of who was persuading her and why.

In conclusion, I am satisfied that the parties came home intending to live together as a family and to get married sometime in the future. On her return home, the petitioner realised this scheme of things could not be adhered to. It was causing conflict with her family. She accordingly agreed to get married as soon as possible to please them. Without their persuasion, the parties would have got married but not as soon.

The petitioner says that she was forced to get married by her parents. She describes her position as being like someone who gets on a train and cannot get off. I do not accept that this was the position. I believe that she had a free choice and that she expressed it to please her parents. Certainly, although as I have said, the respondent was aware that she was being persuaded by her parents to get married, he was unaware that she felt under any such compulsion as she alleges. There is nothing in any of the evidence which I heard, including that of a psychiatrist, which conflicts with the view which I have indicated.

The claim in the present case is based upon duress. The law on the subject has been fully considered by O'Hanlon, J. in *McK. (otherwise M. McC)* v. *F. McC.*, [1982] I.L.R.M. 277

and there is no need for me to further review the authorities. This case and the authorities to which he refers establish that duress may be imposed from any source and not necessarily by the other party to the marriage; and that it need no longer be physical violence or the threat of such violence, but may amount to undue influence. To this extent, the petitioner's case must not be automatically rejected because the duress is not physical violence or does not arise from the conduct of the respondent.

However, the compelling factor must be pressure improperly brought to bear: *Scott* v. *Sebright* 12 P.D. 21 (1886); and also the fear must arise from some external circumstance for which the Petitioner is not herself responsible: See the judgment of Scarman, J. in *Buckland* v. *Buckland* [1967] 2 All E.R. 300, at 302. That was a case where the Petitioner was unjustly charged with unlawful carnal knowledge of a young girl and was left with the alternative of marriage or prison.

A passage from *Buckland* v. *Buckland* cites a passage in the judgment of Haugh, J. in *Griffith* v. *Griffith,* [1944] I.R. 35 with approval. In that case, the Petitioner had been deceived into thinking that his wife, who was then under the age of 17, was pregnant and that he was responsible. At page 43, Haugh, J. says:–

> Assuming that marriages have resulted from a fear so imposed, they are clearly valid and binding on both parties. The man is free to elect between the scandal and possible punishment, on the one hand, or the marriage to the girl he has wronged, on the other. But the fear imposed must be properly imposed, that is, the charge of paternity must be true.

Haugh, J. was referring in that passage to the fear of scandal, publicity and punishment consequent upon a prosecution for unlawful carnal knowledge. The passage from *Szechter* v. *Szechter* cited by O'Hanlon, J. is to the same effect.

In the present case, there is no evidence that the petitioner's parents, brothers or sisters acted in any way improperly. They were doing what they believed was for her best. Undue influence, at least, is fastening on to another's weakness and seeking to obtain a benefit from such behaviour. No such suggestion can be made here.

The position in which the petitioner found herself was brought about by her own conduct. She had the choice between marriage on the one hand and possible alienation of her parents on the other. In the words of Haugh, J. in *Griffith* v. *Griffith*:–

> If that was the sole matter I had to consider and determine, this case would cause me no difficulty.

It seems to me that, even if the evidence supported a compelling pressure which would otherwise have justified the granting of the relief sought, such relief should be denied because the respondent would not have been aware that the will of the petitioner had in fact been overborne. Finally, there is no evidence which, in my view, supports the contention that the petitioner's will was so overborne and that her consent to be married was not a true consent.

I would dismiss the petitioner's claim.

Notes

1. For analysis of *McK. (otherwise M.McC.)* v. *F. McC.* and *A.C.L.* v. *R.L.*, see Binchy, 17 Ir. Med. Times No.3, p. 24 (1983).
2. After this decision, attempt to state the present law on the question of 'just' threats.
3. When is consent to marry *free*? When does it *cease* to be free? Are these legal questions at all? Do they not raise a more fundamental philosophical issue? Are all our actions (including the decision to marry) causally explained by psychological, economic and social influences? When does an influence become duress? Is it a question of the *extent* or the *impropriety*, of the pressure?
4. Would it be better for our law of nullity of marriage to have *no* ground of duress? Cf. D. Lasok, *Polish Family Law*, 50–53 (1968).
5. Why should the fact that the respondent was unaware of the fact that the petitioner was acting under duress disentitle the petitioner to a decree?

J.R. (OTHERWISE McG.) v. P.McG.

Unreported, High Ct., Barron, J., 24 February 1984 (1982–6M)

Barron, J.:

The petitioner seeks a decree of nullity upon the grounds of duress. To understand the nature of the duress alleged, it is essential to refer to the petitioner's family background. Her mother had been a member of the Salvation Army. She was English by birth and had come to Dublin to live. While in the Salvation Army she had met the petitioner's father who was a Roman Catholic and had fallen in love with him and had married him. As a result of her marriage she was obliged to leave the Salvation Army; she then became a member of the Church of Ireland. However, by reason of her background she appears to have become extremely bigoted and was not prepared to tolerate the society of Roman Catholics. It is not necessary to go into this aspect of the evidence in any detail. However, it was of such a scale that although there were six children of the marriage only three, of whom the petitioner was one, were brought up here, the other three being brought up by relatives in [Northern Ireland]. In addition to her religious bigotry, the petitioner's mother's attitude to sex was that of total intolerance.

The combination of these two attitudes had a serious and adverse effect on the petitioner. By reason of the religious intolerance, she was taken from [a] Technical School and went to work at the age of 14. By reason of her intolerance in relation to matters of sex, boyfriends were not permitted in the home and consequently the petitioner had no real knowledge of the other sex.

The petitioner went to work at the age of 14. At first she had a job obtained for her by her father and subsequently obtained employment in a [firm]. . . . She had been employed with this firm for about five years and was aged 20 when she met the respondent who was a fellow employee of the same firm. She started going out with him but as he was a Roman Catholic this association had to be kept secret from her mother. They had intercourse on two occasions, both induced so far as the petitioner was concerned by alcohol, something to which she was not accustomed. As was perhaps bound to happen in such a situation, the petitioner found herself to be pregnant.

The evidence as to the subsequent sequence of events is not totally clear. It seems to me that the salient facts are as follows. She discovered that she was pregnant in or about the 15th December, 1963. She immediately told her father since she was afraid to tell her mother. He agreed to tell her mother whose reaction was predictable and she was told to pack her things and go. This threat was not complied with because the petitioner's brother was being married on Christmas Day in [X] and her mother went up in advance of that date to [X].

Meanwhile the petitioner told the respondent. His immediate reaction was non-committal, but certainly when he realised the petitioner's home situation he offered to marry her. They became engaged in the 24th December, 1963 and the petitioner brought him with her to her brother's wedding the following day. Her mother's reaction was to refuse to remain at the reception and she took her husband and two of her children with her.

On her return to [her home town] the petitioner went to see the local Parish Priest. He regarded her as too young and did not wish to marry her and the respondent. Nevertheless he agreed to do so and the wedding was fixed for and took place on the 9th February, 1964. The reception was held at a local hotel and the party left for a week's honeymoon in [Northern Ireland] in accommodation provided for them by the petitioner's brother.

During the period between her brother's wedding and her own the petitioner was permitted by her mother to remain in the house but not as a member of the family. Her situation was fully known to the respondent who was physically assaulted by her mother when he called at the house on one occasion. As an alternative to marriage, the petitioner says that she approached her father's relatives who also lived in [her home town] but as they had previously experienced the antagonism of her mother they were sympathetic but not prepared to be involved.

The parties' history since the 9th February, 1964 was perhaps to have been predicted. The respondent became drunk on the train journey to [Northern Ireland] and assaulted the petitioner. On their return to Dublin they stayed in a flat for a few months and then moved to London in a hope that matters would improve. There were two children born of the marriage: [A] born on the 18th August, 1964 and [B] born on the 4th February, 1966. The move to London was not a success nor was the marriage. The respondent deserted the petitioner on many occasions and out of a period of approximately sixteen years during which the parties were nominally living together the respondent was absent for approximately half this period. The petitioner obtained a good job in a West End London store as a Buyer. Basically it was her earnings which kept the family together. They returned, though on separate dates, from England in 1977 and separated finally in 1980.

The respondent has not given any evidence and has not defended the proceedings. Nevertheless I am satisfied that there is no collusion between the parties. The petitioner's evidence in relation to the matters occurring before her marriage and to her mother's attitude was fully corroborated by the evidence of her sister. I accept all the evidence which I have heard on this matter. I am satisfied that no attempt is being made by the petitioner to give any evidence other than that which she genuinely believes to be true.

This evidence shows an unhappy state of affairs. The petitioner when she found herself pregnant knew that she would be unable to remain at home to have her child. She sought help from her father's relatives who lived in [her home town] but was unable to obtain any assistance from them. She did not have the financial resources to fend for herself. Marriage seemed to her to be the only course open. She says now that she was never really in love with the respondent and that he was only a means to get her out of her home in the evenings and that left to herself she would never have married him. She says that if she had not married him she would have been in [a mental hospital]. It is difficult twenty years later to be reasonably sure of the position in which the petitioner found herself. She herself looks back from an extremely bad marriage and with a maturity which she had not even begun to acquire at that stage. I do not accept totally what she now says. There must have been a greater bond of affection between herself and the respondent than she is now prepared to admit. There is no other explanation for the fact she immediately became engaged and that he accompanied her to her brother's wedding. There were undoubtedly pressures on her which resulted in her agreeing to get married, but these were resolved in an amazingly short time if she herself was against the idea of marriage.

The case that is made on behalf of the petitioner is that she was compelled by two main factors to get married. These were the attitude of her mother and financial position. There is no doubt that her mother's attitude was outrageous and had the effect of closing off avenues of assistance such as her father's relatives which might otherwise have been open to her. It is submitted that the effect on her will was the same as that of parents who require their daughter to leave home because of the disgrace which they regard her as having brought upon the family. In each case, if a girl has no financial or other resources, it is submitted that this may be tantamount to compelling her to getting married. It is said that if there is only one course open to you your choice is not a free one. In my view the pressures imposed on the petitioner were not nearly as serious or as compelling as she now imagines them to have been. Marriage to the respondent may not have been an ideal marriage from her point of view even at that date. Nevertheless I am satisfied that she was not totally averse to the idea. If she had been, I feel that other assistance would have been available to her and I am reasonably sure that even as a last resort her own brother in

[Northern Ireland] would have provided for her during her pregnancy and afterwards.

The petitioner relies upon the decision of O'Hanlon, J. in *M.K.* v. *McC., supra*, p. 59. In that case O'Hanlon J. deals very fully with the law of duress as it affects the validity of a marriage. That was a case where the evidence showed that the decision that the parties should marry was made not by the parties themselves but by their respective families and that the two parties to the ceremony were in fact given no choice in the matter and accordingly there was no true consent on either of their parts.

Duress must be such that the apparent consent to marry is not a true consent. It can operate in one of two ways. It can operate so that the party under the duress fails to apply his or her mind to the question of giving consent. In such cases, the duress creates a form of bondage. The party concerned may not even be aware that such bondage exists. *McK.* v. *McC.* and *S.* v. *O'S.* [*supra*, p. 46] are examples of this form of duress. Duress can also operate to compel the party under the duress to make a decision to give his or her consent to escape the consequences which will otherwise follow. Such a party knows that his or her consent is not a true consent and is in effect consenting not to being married but to escaping from the threat. Such a marriage is a sham or a device to procure a particular result, i.e. freedom from the particular threat to which he or she is subjected.

It is this latter type of duress which is alleged in the present case. Of course the attitude of the petitioner's mother was a compelling factor towards her decision to get married. Equally her economic situation was a further compelling factor. But this does not mean that when she agreed to become engaged and then to become married that these two factors were the only factors bearing on her mind and that her consent was not a true consent. To test whether or not duress has affected the mind of a party to a marriage so that the marriage is a mere device to escape the pressures imposed it is necessary to look to how that party acted not only before the marriage ceremony itself but also afterwards.

Three English cases indicate the nature of duress of this type. In *Parojic* v. *Parojic* [1959] 1 All E.R. 1 the petitioner was a political refugee from Yugoslavia. Her father threatened that unless she married as he required her to do she would be sent back to Yugoslavia. In *Szechter* v. *Szechter* [1970] 3 All E.R. 905 the whole purpose of the marriage was to enable the petitioner to leave Poland where she would otherwise have had to remain in prison where she was likely to die through ill-health. In *H.* v. *H.* [1953] 2 All E.R. 1229 the petitioner married to obtain a passport to leave her native Hungary. In none of these cases did the parties reside together after the ceremony nor was any of these marriages consummated. The ceremonies were clearly a sham and a device to ensure the safety of the petitioner.

These cases show a stark contrast from the present. I do not suggest that a decree of nullity cannot be granted unless the circumstances are as obvious as in these three cases. But they do show that wherever the dividing line must be drawn, the present case does not lie on the side where the marriage can be annulled. The petitioner intended to marry the respondent and to hold herself out as being so married. In my view the marriage was not brought about through duress. The relief sought will be refused.

Notes

1. Is there a difference between a 'sham' marriage and one that is 'a device to procure a particular result. . . .'?
2. Is the decision based on some logical or philosophical criterion of duress?
3. On Barron J.'s analysis, may a marriage *ever* be annulled on the ground of duress where the alleged victim of duress intended at the time of entering the marriage to make a success of the marriage?

E.P. v. M.C. (OTHERWISE P.)

Unreported, High Ct., Barron, J., 13 March 1984 (1982–22M)

Barron, J.:

The facts in this case are as follows. The parties both lived in [X] and had known each other since they were children. They started going out together in the month of February 1979 when they were then aged 21 and 20 years respectively. They saw each other at first a couple of nights a week and then more frequently. In August 1979 the petitioner went on holiday with some friends. While he was away the respondent telephoned him and told him that she thought she was pregnant. There was no doubt in the minds of either of them that if she was then he was the father. He advised her to have a pregnancy test and this she did and was found to be pregnant. When he returned from his holidays they discussed what they should do about the matter. She was not anxious to have the child unless she was married. She said that she had two uncles in England and that one of them would be in a position to arrange an abortion for her. She was emphatic that if he did not wish to marry her, she would adopt this course. In the face of this attitude on her part the petitioner found himself with no option but to agree to marriage. Having agreed to get married the couple told the respondent's parents. They indicated to them that the pregnancy was part of the reason for getting married. The respondent's parents apparently disapproved of the marriage but did not take any steps to prevent it. The petitioner's father is dead and when he discussed the matter with his mother her attitude was that it was a matter for him.

The evidence establishes that the parties would not have married when they did but for the respondent's pregnancy. The petitioner says that over the four months he had been going out with the respondent he was getting to know her and that neither had at that stage any idea of marriage. His wish would have been to wait until the baby was born before coming to any decision as to their future. He says that the respondent expressed the fear that her parents would put her out of her home and regarded abortion as the only alternative to marriage. Certainly no other course was considered. Once the parties became engaged, the pre-marriage arrangements took the normal course and included a pre-marriage counselling course for five weeks which they both attended.

The parties were married on the 3rd November, 1979 and went to live with the respondent's parents. The petitioner says that he did not fit in particularly well with the family and that to a large extent his presence in the home was resented by the respondent's parents. He says that his wife acted as if she was still single by which he meant that she did not alter her general life style. The baby was born on the 23rd April, 1980. By this time they were making plans for their own home. Their house was bought less than half a mile from the home of the respondent's parents. The respondent did not however show the expected interest in furnishing it and getting ready for their move. She and her mother did involve themselves though in minor ways such as making curtains for the home. To some extent the respondent's attitude was brought about by her parents who interfered between the parties more than was sensible. Nevertheless they did move into their own home in August, 1980. This move resulted in bringing their marriage effectively to an end. After no more than three days the respondent wanted to terminate the marriage. Her attitude then was that she had only married to avoid the shame of a pregnancy outside marriage and to provide a name for her child. She said that having got what she wanted the marriage was over. She left after six weeks in their new home and there was an unpleasant incident when the petitioner was severely assaulted by the respondent's father and brother totally without any justification. . . . The petitioner alone gave evidence in this case. The respondent was not called to give any evidence. I believe the petitioner's evidence in the sense that I believe that he was trying to tell the truth as he now saw it. . . .

In my view this onus has not been discharged. On this ground alone, the petitioner is not entitled to the relief sought.

The petitioner sought a decree of nullity on the ground [inter alios] of duress. . . .

Duress must be of such a nature that there is the appearance without the reality of consent. Where consent is procured through fear for the life of another, the party consenting is fully aware that he is giving his consent to a ceremony of marriage but at the same time is in reality consenting to save that life. For this reason, the marriage is a sham. It is merely a device to remove the threat to the life of that other. If the petitioner had given his consent in this case solely for the purpose of saving the life of his unborn child, this would have constituted a ground for a decree of nullity. But the petitioner would have had to establish that the marriage was such a device to procure this end. If, as in this case, the parties had a normal engagement followed by a normal marriage and held themselves out as being a married couple, it cannot be said that the marriage ceremony was a sham. . . .

[Barron, J. also rejected the petition on the ground of collusion (see *infra*, p. 100); he rejected the petitioner's argument that the marriage was invalid on the ground that the respondent had never intended to enter a proper and lasting marriage (see *supra*, p. 42.]

Notes

1. Is it realistic to require that the petitioner should have given his consent to marry '*solely* for the purpose of saving the life of his unborn child"? (Emphasis added).
2. Since the petitioner's purpose was to save the life of the child, how can it be said that 'the parties had a normal engagement. . . .'? No other course, it would appear, would have saved the life of the child.
3. After this decision, can you state the *degree* of duress necessary to render a marriage invalid?
4. Can this decision be reconciled with *McK. (otherwise M.McC.) v. F. McC., supra*, p. 59.
5. Do Barron, J.'s three judgments on duress involve the application of conceptual criteria or a more intuitive 'line-drawing' which seeks to establish whether or not the case was 'bad' enough to justify a decree?

(6) *FRAUD AND MISTAKE*

The law relating to mistake or fraud as a ground for annulling a marriage has historically been regarded as being of somewhat narrow compass in common law jurisdictions; in civil law jurisdictions a broader approach has been favoured. See generally Hunt, *Error in the Contract of Marriage*, 79 S. Afr. L.J. 423 (1962), 80 S. Afr. L.J. 94, 231 (1963); Kingsley, *Fraud as a Ground of Annulment of Marriage*, 18 So. Calif. L. Rev. 213 (1945). A relatively recent development in Irish law may indicate the possibility of an increasingly liberal judicial approach to the subject.

The accepted view in this country and in England has been that mistake or fraud will render a marriage void in only three instances: (a) where either party is mistaken as to the nature of the ceremony; (b) where either party is mistaken as to the identity of the other party; and (c) where fraud and duress combine to bring about the appearance, but not the reality, of consent.

(i) *Mistake as to the Nature of the Ceremony*

USSHER v. USSHER
[1912] 2 I.R. 445 (K.B.Div.)

The facts of the case have been set out *supra*, pp. 18–19. On the question of mistake as to the nature of the contract, **Palles, C.B.** stated:–

. . . The second contention of the petitioner is that the parties contemplated a ceremony which should be valid according to the law of the Roman Catholic Church; and that, as the ceremony performed was not valid according to that law, there was no contract of marriage whatsoever.

In the argument of this question there has been much rather loose reasoning. In it, 'contract' has been used in two senses.

Prior to the ceremony, there was, I assume, a contract to marry at some future time, according to the Roman Catholic rite. But that contract is not the contract which is material here. This is not an action for breach of promise of marriage. The only contract we have to consider is that which is involved in the ceremony itself. By this contract the spouses took each other for husband and wife. This they did freely, knowingly, in terms unconditionally, and with the intention of thereby becoming husband and wife. This is the contract. Why is it alleged that this contract is not binding?

Not because it was not made: it is admitted it was made; but because it was made under mistake; as the spouses believed such contract to constitute a valid marriage according to the law of the Roman Catholic Church. They wished, it is said, to enter into a marriage which should be not merely a valid civil contract, but a Sacrament of the Roman Catholic Church as well; and it has been argued that their consent to the civil contract was therefore conditioned by its being a Sacramental contract also; which, admittedly, it was not.

Now I assume that it was the intention of one, at least, of the parties to receive a Sacrament of the Roman Catholic Church; and that, had she known that this intention was bound to fail – as it did fail – because of non-compliance with that Church's law, she would most probably not have entered into the civil contract.

But it does not follow that her consent, any more than that of Mr. Ussher, was conditional on the marriage being Sacramental. No such condition was expressed by anyone during the ceremony; there is no suggestion that such a condition was present to the mind of anyone at the ceremony; and an intention, which neither of the contracting parties had, but which under other circumstances, or with other knowledge, they might, or even probably would, have had, cannot be held to avoid the contract. Many marriage contracts would fail were such a principle to be admitted. Were every husband and wife, who had made a grave mistake in contracting marriage, and who with clearer knowledge would have refused to contract at all, to be free to repudiate the contract, how many current marriages could be declared legally binding? I make no doubt that there can be a mistake which will avoid the legal contract. But such a mistake must affect the very substance of the legal contract itself – for instance, the personal identity of one or other of the contracting parties. It must not be concerned with something merely accidental to the person – as, for instance, his or her wealth, position, or religion; or wholly separable from the contract – such, for instance, as in the present case, its effect.

Besides, it has not been suggested that Mr. and Mrs. Ussher had any different intention, when going through the ceremony, from that which other Roman Catholics have universally on like occasions; and a conditional marriage is practically unheard of among Roman Catholics.

Finally, we have it in evidence that Mr. and Mrs. Ussher at once entered on their married life, and continued in it, without any misgivings, and without enquiry into the fulfilment or nonfulfilment of any condition whatsoever – clear proof that they themselves had intended their marriage to be absolute, and not conditional. Indeed, I have no doubt that, until the question was raised by the able counsel engaged in this case, neither Mr. nor Mrs. Ussher, had ever heard, or had even conceived it possible, that there could be a conditional marriage.

Hence, too, I cannot admit the argument based on the principle of 'predominant intention,' which was advanced so subtly by counsel for the petitioner. He represented Mr. and Mrs. Ussher to us as saying: 'We wish to enter into a contract and to receive a Sacrament; but, if we are not to receive a Sacrament, we wish not to enter into the contract'; and he spoke of this latter wish as predominant – as prevailing against the former, or rather part of the former, intention. On this I need only remark that the theory of 'predominant intention,' in so far as it may be thought applicable to the present case, is only another form of the argument of conditional contractual consent; and it is, therefore, open to all the objections by which I have already shown that the marriage consent of Mr. and Mrs. Ussher was not intended by them to be conditional; nor, in such a contract, could unexpressed intention, even if it existed, be allowed to prevail against the intention which was expressed.

Even, therefore, were marriage no more than a contract, I should still not admit the argument of the petitioner. I might, indeed, allow that, in such a case, a Court of Equity *might* entertain an application *to rescind* the contract, on the ground of mistake, were it not that there could not be a *restitutio in integrum*. But such an application, even had the marriage not been consummated, would have for its basis the capacity of the parties to rescind by joint consent; and the Court would do no more than compel one of them to do what he or she had already the power of doing without the intervention of the Court.

But marriage is something more than a contract. It confers a *status*, through which unborn children obtain a title; and it is not revocable by the consent of even both parties. Hence the jurisdiction of our Courts of Justice to rescind contracts is not applicable to the contract of marriage. They can, of course, carefully examine into any circumstances which show that there was *no contract*, such as absence of *any* contractual intention, or such undue influence as shows that there was not a consenting mind, or substantive mistake as to the person. But, once there is a contract, freely and knowingly made, neither fraud nor mistake is sufficient to avoid it.

This law is absolutely settled. The cases in which questions as to it arise are more usually those of fraud than of innocent mistake; but if mistake, induced by the gross fraud of one of the parties, is insufficient to procure avoidance at the suit of the defrauded party, innocent mistake must, *a fortiori*, be also insufficient.

As to this, I shall mention, but two cases, *Swift* v. *Kelly* 3 Knapp, 257, at p. 293, and *Moss* v. *Moss* [1897] P. 263, at p. 267.

In the judgment of the Privy Council, in the first of these cases, it is stated to be certainly the law of England that, unless there be some positive statute law requiring certain things to be done in a specified manner, no marriage shall be held void merely upon proof that it has been contracted upon false representations, and that, but for such contrivances, consent never would have been obtained. 'Unless the party imposed upon has been deceived *as to the person*, and thus has given no consent at all, there is no degree of deception which can avail to set aside a contract of marriage knowingly made.'

In the second of these cases, *Moss* v. *Moss* [1897] P. 263 at p. 267, the late Sir Francis Jeune states the law in these terms:–

'While habitually speaking of marriage as a contract, English lawyers have never been misled by an imperfect analogy into regarding it as a *mere contract*, or into investing it with all the qualities and conditions of ordinary civil contracts. They have expressed their sense of its *distinctive character* in different language, but always to the same effect. Lord Stowell said that it was both a civil contract and a religious vow: *Turner* v. *Meyers* 1 Hagg. Cons. Cas. 414, referring, no doubt, mainly to the *incapacity of the contracting parties to dissolve it*. Dr. Lushington spoke of it as *more* than a civil contract: *Miles* v. *Chilton* 1 Rob. 684, 694. Lord Hannen said:- 'Very many and serious difficulties arise if marriage be regarded only in the light of a contract. It is, indeed, based upon the contract of the parties, but *it is a status* arising out of a contract': *Sottomayer* v. *De Barros* 5 P.D. 94, 101. The late President, Sir Charles Butt, said, in the case of *Andrews* v. *Ross* 14 P.D. 15, that 'the principles prevailing in regard to contract of marriage differ from those prevailing in all other contracts known to the law."'

For these reasons, I am of opinion that the second proposition of the appellant is not sustainable. . . .'

Gibson, J.:

. . . Error or mistake as to religious consequences cannot affect the completeness or effect of the contract. Assuming that civil and sacramental wedlock were contemplated as one and inseparable, and that the spouses regarded the religious element as fundamental, the marriage, completed according to the requirements of municipal law, cannot be treated as wrecked and destroyed. The primary intention to which the Court must give effect was the constitution of the status, and where law and conscience cannot be reconciled, the former must prevail. Public policy and the claims of issue are paramount. . . .

[In **Lord O'Brien, C.J.'s** judgment the issue of mistake is considered in the broader context of the question whether the contract was subject to a condition that the marriage was valid according to the Canon Law of the Catholic Church.]

Note

The question of mistake as to the nature of the ceremony has arisen in several decisions in many jurisdictions. See e.g., *Hall (otherwise Barrar)* v. *Hall*, 24 Times L.R. 756 (Gorell Barnes, P., 1908) (decree granted although Gorrell Barnes, P. had difficulty in believing 'that two people could be such awful fools'), *Lieberman (otherwise Szapira)* v. *Lieberman, The Times*, 24 January 1899, p. 14 (P.D.A. Div., Gorell Barnes, J.), *Neuman* v. *Neuman (otherwise Greenberg), The Times*, 15 October 1926, p. 5 (P.D.A. Div., Lord Merrivale, P.), *Ford (falsely called Stier)* v. *Stier.* [1896] P. 1 (Gorell Barnes, J., 1895) (Italian count '"not quick on the uptake" when spoken to in English' induced by English woman to go through marriage ceremony, believing it to be a betrothal), *Kelly (otherwise Hyams)* v. *Kelly*, 49 Times L.R. 99 (P.D.A. Div. Lord Merrivale, P., (1932), *Mehta (otherwise Kohn)* v. *Mehta,* [1945] 2 All E.R. 690 (P.D.A. Div., Barnard, J.). Cf. *Swift* v. *Kelly*, 3 Knapp 257, 12 E.R. 648 (P.C., 1835) (contention that woman did not understand the nature of the ceremony rejected on the evidence).

(ii) *Error as to the Person*

It is clear that mistake as to the *identity* of a person will vitiate consent, but in only very rare cases have petitions on this ground been successful. Contrast *Allardyce* v. *Mitchell*, 6 W.W. & a'B (I.E. & M.C.) 45 (1869) with *C.* v. *C.,* [1942] N.Z.L.R. 346. An error concerning the *character* of the other party has, however, been regarded as insufficient to invalidate a marriage. As Falconbridge, J. said in the Canadian decision of *Brennan* v. *Brennan*, 19 Ont. Rep. 327, at 337–338 (1889):-

> The maxim *caveat emptor* seems as brutally and necessarily applicable to the case of marrying and taking in marriage as it is to the purchase of a rood of land or of a horse.

Thus concealed pregnancy by another man at the time of the marriage will not be a ground for annulment: *Moss* v. *Moss (orse Archer),* [1897] P. 263 (Sir F.H. Jeune, P.); *Lang* v. *Lang*, 1921 S.C. 44 (2nd Div. 1920), overruling *Stein* v. *Stein*, 1914 S.C. 903 (1st Div.). In *Ewing* v. *Wheatley* (2 Hag. Con. 175, at 182–182, 161 E.R. 706, at 709 (1814)), Sir William Scott stated that,

> in general, ... that a man should represent himself of superior condition or expectations will not of itself invalidate a marriage, as the law expects that parties should use timely and effectual diligence in obtaining correct information on such points.
>
> It is perfectly established that no disparity of fortune, or mistake as to the qualities of the person, will impeach the vinculum of marriage. . . .

The same judge seven years previously, in *Wakefield* v. *Mackey (orse Thorpe, orse Jackson, falsely calling herself Wakefield)*, 1 Phill. Ecc. 134n, at 137n, 161 E.R. 937, at 939 (1807), had stated that:

> Error about the family or fortune of the individual, though produced by disingenuous representations does not at all affect the validity of a marriage. A man who means to act upon such representations should verify them by his own enquiries; the law presumes that he uses due caution in a matter in which his happiness for life is so materially involved, and it makes no provision for the relief of a blind credulity, however it may have been produced.

(Victims of frauds of this type have also been denied relief in the law of contract, so far as property transactions are concerned: cf. *Hogan* v. *Healy*, I.R. 11 C.L. 119 (Exch. Cham., 1877). Whether this decision would command full support today is, however, uncertain.) In the Australian decision of *In the Marriage of C. & D. (falsely called C.)*, (1979) F.L.C. 90–636, a mistake as to the sexual identity of one of the spouses was held to invalidate the marriage. For criticism, see Finlay, *Sexual Identity and the Law of Nullity*, 54 Austr. L.J. 115, at 118–119 (1980).

(iii) *Fraud Combined with Duress*

We have seen that in *Griffith* v. *Griffith*, [1944] I.R. 35 (High Court Haugh, J., 1943), *supra*, pp. 51–57, and *K.* v. *K.*, unreported, High Court, O'Keeffe, P., 16 February 1971 (34M/1060), *supra*, pp. 58–59 marriages were annulled on the basis of a combination of fraud and duress.

(iv) *A New Development*

S. v. S.

Unreported, Supreme Court, 1 July 1976 (1–1976)

Henchy, J.:

The short-lived marital union between the parties in this case was but a marriage in name only. It does not seem to have been supported by any emotional or other affinity on the part of the husband.

The marriage took place in July 1969. They had met two years earlier at a dance. The friendship that sprang up between them ripened quickly into intimacy. For a year and a half they went out together every night of the week. Then, for six months before the marriage, they saw each other every night of the week except Tuesday and Thursday – omitting those nights because they felt they were seeing too much of each other. They also used to go away on camping weekends, and on those weekends they had sexual intercourse with *coitus interruptus* on about twenty five occasions. There is nothing in the evidence to suggest any lack on his part before the marriage of emotional or sexual commitment to her.

The marriage proved a sad anti-climax for the wife. As a husband he turned out to be cold, unaffectionate, alienated. The marriage was never consummated. They had an eight-day honeymoon in Ostend, but, although they slept in the same bed, he showed a total sexual disinterest in her. It was the same story when they returned from the honeymoon to the matrimonial home where they slept in the same bed.

For six months they lived together in disharmony, and then he left her for good. His sexual disinterest in her was apparently no perverse affectation. The wife says she once tried to get him to effect sexual intercourse with her, but he proved unresponsive. Shortly after the marriage he told her that he had no affection for her, that in fact she revolted him, that he had no interest in founding a family, that the marriage was a mistake, and that the only reason he went through with it was because the arrangements were too far advanced and he was too much of a coward to break off the engagement.

What the wife discovered after the marriage was that some weeks before the marriage he had met the woman with whom he has since gone to live (and whom, for convenience, I shall refer to as the other woman). The wife learned from him that both before and after the marriage he had sexual intercourse with the other woman. According to the wife, he claimed to have spent the night before the marriage with the other woman and to have had sexual intercourse with her that night. It appears to be the fact that shortly after returning from the honeymoon, he started to go out at night with this woman. He admitted to the wife that he was in love with the other woman. Before he turned his back on this pseudo-marriage in January 1970, by leaving to go off to live with the other woman, he disclosed that the other woman had been expecting a child by him and had just then 'lost it in England'.

In the High Court, where this petition by the wife for annulment of the marriage was dismissed by Murnaghan J., the case for the wife was put on the basis that she had been induced by fraud to marry the husband. The trial judge rejected that submission. So would I. Undoubtedly, if the wife had known of the husband's relations with the other woman, or of his emotional and sexual attitude to herself, she would not have married him. But that is a far cry from saying that the marriage was born of fraud. We have had only the evidence of the wife. We have no reliable insight into the mental processes that prompted the husband to go through with this marriage to a wife whom he did not love and who, in fact, revolted him. We only have his statement later to the wife that he lacked the courage to call off the marriage at that late stage. There is no evidence that the husband made any overt misrepresentation before the marriage, and such silence or non-disclosure as is to be attributed to him could not, without indulging in pure speculation, be said to amount to a misrepresentation of the true state of things from his point of view. There is no doubt but that the wife entered into the marriage on the inducement of a concealed falsity, but that falsity (by which I mean falsity as to emotional and sexual capacity on the part of the husband) may or may not have been known to the husband at the time of the marriage. For all we know, he may have genuinely believed or hoped that he would be able to make the marriage a success. Because of that, fraud must be discounted.

[**Henchy J.** went on to consider the ground of impotence; he held that the respondent was impotent *quoad hanc*. *See infra* pp. 90–91].

Griffin J. concurred with **Henchy J.**, agreeing that the respondent was impotent *quoad hanc*. On the question of fraud, **Griffin, J.** observed:

. . . In this Court, counsel for the wife, although they did not abandon the allegation of fraud, did not press their argument on that ground, in my view wisely. . . .

Kenny, J.:

. . . The only reasonable inference from the evidence is that the husband did not intend to consummate the marriage at the time he got married. He is undoubtedly potent and, in my opinion, the evidence does not justify a finding that he had become impotent when with the wife (*impotentia quoad hanc*). The issue in the appeal is therefore whether a valid marriage exists when one of the parties to it at the time of the marriage does not intend to have sexual intercourse with the other and when the parties to the marriage have not agreed before it that there will be no sexual relations between them or when the ages of one or both of them make it improbable that this will happen.

The power of the High Court to declare a marriage null is derived from the *Matrimonial Causes and Marriage Law (Ireland) Amendment Act 1870*, by which the jurisdiction exercised by the Ecclesiastical Courts of the Church of Ireland was transferred on the disestablishment of that Church to a Court for Matrimonial Causes and Matters whose powers were subsequently transferred to the High Court. Section 13 of that Act provided that in all suits and proceedings the Court of Matrimonial Causes and Matters was to proceed, act and give relief on principles and rules which, in the opinion of the Court, were as nearly as may be conformable to the principles and rules on which the ecclesiastical Courts of Ireland had up to then acted and given relief.

The law administered in the ecclesiastical courts in Ireland was not the general canon law of Europe as it existed before the Reformation but an ecclesiastical law of which the general canon law was the basis but which had been modified and altered by legislation and judicial decisions and which was known by the distinguishing title of the King's Ecclesiastical Law (*The Queen* v. *Millis* 10 Cl. and F.534: *Ussher* v. *Ussher* [1912] 2 I.R. 445). In that law two principles were fundamental in suits for nullity. The first was that the petitioner had to establish his or her case with a high degree of probability or, as Lord Birkenhead expressed it in *C (otherwise H)* v. *C* [1921] P. 399, 'must remove all reasonable doubt'. The second was that the ground of nullity had to exist at the date of the marriage: events or acts subsequent to the marriage were never a ground for a declaration of nullity (*Napier* v. *Napier* [1915] P. 184).

Section 13 of the Act of 1870 did not have the effect of fossilising the law in its state in that year. That law is, to some extent at least, judge made and Courts must recognise that the great advances made in psychological medicine since 1870 make it necessary to frame new rules which reflect these. Despite this, I think that the two fundamental principles I have mentioned are still basic to the law of nullity.

It seems to me that the intention to have sexual intercourse is such a fundamental feature of the marriage contract that if *at the time of the marriage* either party has determined that there will not be any during the marriage and none takes place and if the parties have not agreed on this before the marriage or if the ages of the parties make it improbable that they could have intercourse (*Briggs* v. *Morgan* (1820) 3 Phill. Ecc. 325), a spouse who was not aware of the determination of the other is entitled to a declaration that the marriage was null. The intention not to have or permit intercourse has the result that the consent which is necessary to the existence of a valid marriage does not exist.

As I have said, the only inference possible is that at the time of the marriage the husband had formed a determination not to have sexual relations with the wife. I would therefore reverse the order of the High Court and give a declaration that the marriage between the husband and wife was absolutely void.

Notes

1. What 'great advances made in psychological medicine since 1870' could have any bearing on the issue of a fraudulent disclosure of a secret intention not to have sexual intercourse?
2. What do you understand by the term 'falsity as to emotional and sexual capacity'? What relevance (if any) does it have to impotence?
3. To what extent was the respondent's possible belief or hope that he 'would be able to make the marriage a success' relevant to the outcome of the case, in the view of Mr. Justice Henchy?
4. Is the decision authority for the granting of a decree of annulment where the respondent had a secret intention not to have children?
5. The decision is analysed by Duncan, *Sex and the Fundamentals of Marriage,* [1979–80] Dublin U.L.J. 29.
6. Cf. the Australian decision of *In the Marriage of Deniz*, 31 Fed. L.R. 114 (Fam. Ct. of Austr., 1977), noted by Bates, 128 New L.J. 403 (1978).
7. In the United States, fraud has been the basis of annulment in fairly wide circumstances. This was particularly so in New York prior to the liberalisation of its divorce law in 1966: see Twiss, *Comment: Annulment for Fraud in New York*, 24 Alb. L. Rev. 125 (1960); Franck, *The Annulment of Marriage in New York: 'Until Fraud Do Us Part'*, 1 U.B.R. Col. L. Rev. 471 (1961); *Anon., Comment: Annulment of Marriage in New York for Fraud Based Upon Religious Matters*, 30 Fordham L. Rev 776 (1962); J.M., *Note*, 26 Brooklyn L. Rev. 305 (1960); R.D.K., *Note*, 19 Brooklyn L. Rev. 140 (1952); *Anon., Note*, 24 Fordham L. Rev. 491 (1955); Denton, *Note: Marriage – Annulment on the Ground of Fraud*, 5 Baylor L. Rev. 313 (1953); Wilcox, *Note* 23 Notre Dame L. 364, at 396*ff.* (1947); *Anon., Note*, 22 N.Y.U.L.Q. Rev. 480 (1947); Lull, *Comment: Domestic Relations: Annulment of Marriage for Fraud: New York Doctrine*, 32 Cornell L.Q. 424 (1947); Crouch, *Annulment of Marriage for Fraud in New York*, 6 Cornell L.Q. 401 (1921); *Anon., Fraud and Annulment in New York*, 41 Colum. L. Rev. 503 (1941); Gershenson, *Fraud in the New York Law of Annulment*, 9 Brooklyn L. Rev. 51 (1939); Elrod, *Note: Domestic relations – Annulment for Failure to Reveal Family Morals*, 5 Ark. L. Rev. 442 (1951); O'Connor, *Recent Developments in the Irish Law of Nullity,* [1983] Dublin U.L.J. 168, at 182–5.

7. *PRIOR SUBSISTING MARRIAGE*

A marriage contracted during the subsistence of a previous valid marriage is void. This is so irrespective of any consideration of the good faith belief by either or both of the spouses that the later marriage is valid (*Miles* v. *Chilton (falsely calling herself Miles*), 1 Rob. Ecc. 684, 163 E.R. 1178 (1849). Cf. *P.* v. *P. (by amendment M'D.)* v. *P.*, [1916] 2 I.R. 400 (C.A., aff'g K.B. Div.)).

F.M.L. & A.L. v. AN tARD CHLÁRAITHEOIR NA mPOSADH

Unreported, High Ct., Lynch, J., 2 March, 1984 (1983–4463P.)

Lynch, J.:

The plaintiffs' claim in this case is for a declaration that the marriage celebrated between them on the 5th September, 1979 is a valid and lawful marriage and that the defendant do permit the registration thereof and register the same in the Register of Marriages.

THE FACTS

1. The first named plaintiff married a Miss O'C on the 26th August, 1972 and that marriage was duly registered in the Register of Marriages.
2. On the 4th August, 1978 a Papal dispensation was granted in respect of the said marriage of the 26th August, 1972 the effect of which was so far as the Roman Catholic Church is concerned to release the parties from the bonds of the said marriage and thus to entitle either party to remarry. The said Papal dispensation and its effect in the law of the Roman Catholic Church is however irrelevant to the issues which I have to decide. Indeed the letter dated the 22nd August, 1978 notifying the first named plaintiff of the dispensation contains the following paragraph:

   'This papal dispensation does not purport to affect the civil status of the marriage in question. Should you wish to contract a further marriage in the Church, you alone will be responsible for the civil effects of such marriage. We would suggest that you would be well advised to take competent advice on this aspect of the matter.'
3. On the 5th September, 1979 the first named plaintiff went through a ceremony of marriage with the second named plaintiff in the Roman Catholic Church in the Parish of Rolestown in the County of Dublin. The plaintiffs did not seek to have the said marriage registered in the Register of Marriages at that time.
4. On the 15th October, 1980 a decree of nullity was made by the High Court in respect of the said marriage of the 26th August, 1972 between the first named plaintiff and the said Miss O'C by reason of the impotence of the said Miss O'C. Following the said decree of nullity the plaintiffs sought to have registered their said marriage of the 5th September, 1979 in the Register of Marriages.
5. The defendant refused to register or permit the registration of the said marriage of the 5th September, 1979 on the grounds that at the date of its celebration the first named plaintiff was already duly and properly registered in the Register of Marriages as being married to the said Miss O'C.
6. On the 20th October, 1983 a daughter was born to the plaintiffs. The birth of the said daughter was duly registered in the Register of Births with the plaintiffs referred to as parents and by their married names but this registration did not amount to any admission by the defendant as to the validity of the plaintiffs' marriage of the 5th September, 1979 as no such question arose or was adverted to on the registration of the said birth. Pending the birth of their said daughter the plaintiffs commenced these proceedings by the issue of the Plenary Summons on the 28th June, 1983.

THE LAW

During the course of the trial of the action I was referred to the following authorities: *Ussher* v. *Ussher,* [1912] 2 I.R. 445; *P.* v. *P.,* [1916] 2 I.R. 400; *Newbold* v. *Attorney General,* [1931] P. 75; *Inverclyde* v. *Inverclyde,* [1931] P. 29; *McM.* v. *McM. and McK.* v. *McK.,* [1936] I.R. 177; *The Constitution*, Article 41, Section 3; *Clarke* v. *Clarke,* [1943] 2 All E.R. 540; *Mason* v. *Mason,* [1944] N.I. 134; *Dredge* v. *Dredge,* [1947] 1 All E.R. 29; *De Reneville* v. *De Reneville,* [1948] P. 100; *R.* v. *Algar,* [1954] 1 Q.B. 279; *Wiggins* v. *Wiggins,* [1958] 2 All E.R. 555.

It is clear from the foregoing authorities that the marriage between the first named plaintiff and Miss O'C was voidable rather than void by reason of the impotence of the said Miss O'C. The real question for decision by me is as to the effect of the decree of nullity of the 15th October, 1980 on such a voidable marriage. *P.* v. *P., Newbold* v. *Attorney General* and *Mason* v. *Mason* are clear authorities for the proposition that such a marriage on the pronouncement of the decree of nullity becomes absolutely void ab initio or in other words that the decree operates in accordance with its express terms. The decree of nullity in this case dated the 15th day of October, 1980 is as follows:–

> And the Judge having found that the marriage between the petitioner and the respondent has not been consummated and that such non-consummation was due to the impotence of the respondent by his final decree ordered that the marriage had and solemnized on the 26th day of August, 1972 between the petitioner and the respondent be pronounced and declared to have been and to be absolutely null and void to all intents and purposes in the law whatsoever by reason of the impotence of the respondent and that the petitioner be pronounced to have been and to be free from all bonds of marriage with the respondent.

I think that *P.* v. *P., Newbold* v. *Attorney General* and *Mason* v. *Mason* are preferable to the English authorities cited such as *Inverclyde* v. *Inverclyde, De Reneville* v. *De Reneville, R.* v. *Algar* and *Wiggins* v. *Wiggins* especially in the light of Article 41 Section 3 of the Constitution. Therefore I adopt as a correct statement of the law the following passage from the judgment of Andrews L.C.J. in *Mason* v. *Mason* [1944] N.I. 134, at p. 162:

> It is a form of decree which in substance has been handed down from the time of the ecclesiastical Courts and was carefully settled by the House of Lords in *Lewis* v. *Hayward* 35 L.J. (P.) 105. No doubt in the case of a voidable marriage its validity might never be questioned and in such cases would be deemed valid and never could be regarded as a void marriage: but when once its validity is successfully challenged and it is declared null and void by decree absolute, the invalidity is established retrospectively as from the date of the marriage itself, and the status of husband and wife, which continued to attach to the spouses until the decree, is finally and irrevocably altered and determined. In other words the force of the decree is that of a judgment in Rem such as to make the marriage, which was previously voidable only, void *ab initio* a mere form and nothing else.

It follows that from and after the decree of nullity on the 15th October, 1980 the first named plaintiff was not on the 5th September, 1979 married to the said Miss O'C and accordingly his marriage on that date to the second named plaintiff is now and must now be taken always to have been valid and therefore capable of registration in the Register of Marriages.

I must point out however that the chronology of the steps taken by the first named plaintiff in this case is, so far as the civil and criminal law of the land is concerned, very undesirable and may give rise to many problems and is indeed very risky from the point of view of a person in the position of the first named plaintiff.

A marriage which is voidable for impotence is not known to be voidable nor consequently void *ab initio* unless and until the High Court shall have pronounced it to be so. In the meantime the spouse remains apparently validly married and open to prosecution for bigamy under Section 57 of the *Offences Against the Person Act 1861.* In this connection I quote again from the judgment of Andrews L.C.J. in *Mason* v. *Mason,* [1944] N.I. 134, at 164–165:

I find what I regard as strong corroboration for the view which I have expressed in the terms of Section 57 of the *Offences Against the Person Act 1861* relating to the crime of bigamy. This section, so far as is material for our present purposes, provides that:–

> whosoever, being married, shall marry any other person during the life of the former husband or wife shall be guilty of felony: provided that nothing in this section contained shall extend to any person who, at the time of such second marriage, shall have been divorced from the bond of the first marriage, or to any person whose former marriage shall have been declared void by the sentence of any Court of competent jurisdiction.

The language of this proviso merits careful consideration for, in my opinion, it clearly recognises the essential difference in character between the decree of dissolution in divorce and the decree of nullity. In the former case the decree of divorce from the bond of the first marriage must, in order to constitute a defence to a bigamy charge, be in existence 'at the time of such second marriage' for it dissolves a valid and existing marriage as of that date: but in the case of a marriage declared void there is no stipulation as to the necessity for such declaration being in existence at the time of the second marriage: it is sufficient if at his trial the accused person is able to establish that his former marriage has at any time previously been declared void: for, when made, the decree declares that such former marriage is, and, retrospectively, that it always was void.

The converse is also clearly valid namely that if a trial for bigamy should pre-date the decree of nullity the accused spouse would be liable to conviction and penalty. I express no views as to what would then happen or follow in law if a decree of nullity were subsequently to be granted. I merely emphasise the difficulties and dangers of the course and order of events adopted by the first named plaintiff in this case by quoting from O'Brien L.C. in *P.* v. *P.*, [1916] 2 I.R., at 424:

> Once there has been a ceremony of marriage, prima facie the marriage is good. If a person who has gone through that ceremony chooses to come to the Court to have it declared that there never was a marriage, the Court will consider the conduct of the person seeking its aid, and may, on general equitable principles, refuse to permit such person to obtain a decree of nullity. That of course recognises that, so far as the public are concerned, it is presumed to be a good marriage until set aside, and that as between the parties one of them may not be able to have it set aside by reason of the conduct of such party adopting and taking advantages under it. But once the Court considers that the party seeking relief has not done anything which prevents him or her obtaining the relief sought, and the impotency of the other party is proved, it pronounces a decree declaring the marriage to be a form only and to be absolutely null and void at the time it purported to be effected, and from that time on.

Having in fact obtained the decree of nullity of the 15th October, 1980 the first named plaintiff has now fully regularised his position and I accordingly declare that the marriage of the plaintiffs of the 5th September, 1979 is a good and valid marriage and ought to be registered and I direct its registration accordingly in the appropriate Register of Marriages.

Notes

1. The general question of retrospective validation has given rise to much discussion: see Newark, *The Operation of Nullity Decrees*, 8 Modern L. Rev. 203 (1945); *Jackson*, 93; cf. Duncan, *Second Marriages After Church Annulments – A Problem of Legal Policy*, 72 Inc. L. Soc. of Ireland Gazette 203, at 204–205 (1978).
2. What do you think are the 'many problems' which Lynch, J. apprehends may result from a person adopting the sequence of steps that the first named plaintiff chose? Could one of them relate to illegitimacy? Does a child born of a second 'marriage' become legitimated by a subsequent decree of nullity in respect of the first, voidable, marriage? If so is the legitimation retrospective? And what is the status of a child conceived before, but born after, the second, initially void, marriage?
3. Cf. *The People (at the suit of the A.G.)* v. *Ballins*, [1964] Ir. Jur. Rep. 14 (Circuit Ct., O'Briain, P.). See also Lee, *Canon and Civil Marriage Laws in Ireland*, 67 Ir. Ecclesiastical Record 154 (1946), Duncan & O'Reilly, *Marriage and the Law – 3: Civil and Canonical Annulments*, Irish Times, 14 March 1974.
4. Should the Court entertain an argument that the essential validity of a marriage celebrated according to Catholic rites should be determined according to Canon law? Cf. *O'Callaghan* v. *O'Sullivan*, [1925] 1 I.R. 90 (Sup. Ct.).

8. *PROHIBITED DEGREES OF RELATIONSHIP*

In Ireland, as in every other country, there are legal controls on marriages between persons closely related by blood (consanguinity). There are also controls on marriages between persons closely related through marriage (affinity). See *Shatter*, 40. Marriages celebrated in breach of those prohibitions are void (*Marriage Act 1835*, section 2 (5 and 6 Will. 4, c. 54) (Lord Lyndhurst's Act)). Relationships of the half-blood have the same effect as those of the whole blood.

The prohibited degrees are wide-ranging in relation to both consanguinity and affinity. They are the result of a complicated legislative history, which raises some degree of uncertainty as to their precise scope (cf. 28 Hen. 8, c. 2 (1537), 33 Hen. 8, c. 6 (1542), 3 & 4 P. & M., c. 8 (1556), 2 Eliz. I, c. 1 (1560), *Statute Law Revision (Ireland) Act 1878*, (41 & 42 Vict., c. 57), *Deceased Wife's Sister's Act 1907* (7 Edw. 7, c. 47), *Deceased Brother's Widow's Act 1921* (11 & 12 Geo. 5, c. 24), *Statute Law Revision (Pre-Union Irish Statutes) Act 1962 (No.29))*.

In many other countries the prohibitions based on affinity, if they exist at all, are more narrowly drawn (cf., e.g. the law in France (*Civil Code*, articles 161–164), Italy (*Civil Code*, article 87), the Netherlands (*Civil Code*, section 1, article 41) Australia (*Family Law Act 1975*, section 51(3)–(6); cf. Finlay, *Farewell to Affinity and the Calculus of Kinship*, 5 U. of Tasmania L. Rev. 16 (1975)). For an excellent discussion of the policy issues, see Chester & Parry, *Reform of the Prohibitions on Marriage of Related Persons*, 13 Family L. 237 (1983); Freeman, *Affinity – Can the Bar Be Justified?* 6 Family L. 179 (1976) and the Report by a Group Appointed by the Archbishop of Canterbury, *No Just Cause: The Law of Affinity in England and Wales: Some Suggestions for Change* (1984). Whether a person should be prohibited from marrying an adoptive brother or sister, as the case may be, must also be considered. Would this be a sound policy? Would it be Constitutional? Cf. *Israel* v. *Allen*, 195 Colo. 263, 577 P. 2d 762 (1978). See also the Report of the Review Committee on Adoption Services, *Adoption*, para. 13.11 (Pl. 2467, 1984).

9. *IMPOTENCE*

Impotence renders a marriage voidable. It consists of a spouse's inability, from time of the celebration of the marriage, to have sexual intercourse with the other spouse. This inability may be the result of physical or psychological causes. Why should impotence be a ground for nullity of marriage? In *B-n* v. *B-n*, 1 Sp. Ecc. & Ad. 248, at 259–260, 164 E.R. 144, at 150–151 (P.C., 1854), Dr. Lushington said:

> Without entering into any minute discussion as to all the purposes for which marriage was intended, it is obvious that the capacity for sexual intercourse is, in all cases, save when age may seem to preclude it, to be deemed a most important essential; essential, because the procreation of children is one of the chief objects of marriage; essential, because the lawful indulgence of the passions is the best protection against illicit intercourse; and to these considerations may be added that well-known fact that, in most cases where the incapacity is on the side of the husband, the health of the wife cannot escape serious injury.

For a medical bibliography on impotence and related conditions, see Hawton, *Major Common Symptoms in Psychiatry: Sexual Problems*, 27 Br. J. of Hosp. Med. No. 2, 129, at 135 (1982). Legal Aspects of the subject are analysed by *Shatter*, 68–75; *Bromley*, 83–87; *Cretney*, 49–52; *Jackson*, ch. 7; *Burn*, vol. 2, 50lk–50le; *Shelford*, 201–213; *Browne*, 273–276; *Poynter*, ch. 8.

R.M. v. M.M.

76 I.L.T.R. 165 (Supreme Court, 1942, affirming High Court, O'Byrne, J., 1941)

Petition (by husband) that the Court be pleased to decree the ceremony of marriage celebrated between Petitioner and Respondent null and void.

A petition for nullity of Marriage was brought by R.M. (the husband), claiming, *inter alia*:–

(2) That by reason of the frigidity or impotence or hysteria or repugnance of M.M. [the wife] or by reason of some defect in the said M.M. rendering her incapable of consummating the said marriage, your petitioner was at the time of the said marriage, and has ever since been, and still is wholly unable to consummate the said marriage.
(3) That such frigidity or impotence or hysteria or repugnance or other defect in the said M.M. as in the last paragraph set forth is incurable by art or skill, as will so appear on examination and inspection.
(5) That there is not any collusion or connivance directly or indirectly between your petitioner and the said M.M. or any other person whatever in relation to this petition.

There had been no previous proceedings.
The Answer of M.M., supported by Affidavit dated 16th June, 1941, stated *inter alia*:–

(2) In answer to the matters alleged in paragraph 2 of the petition the Respondent admits that the said marriage has never been consummated and that at the time of the said marriage the Respondent was, and has ever since been, and still is unable, owing to invincible repugnance or revulsion to consummate the said marriage. The Respondent does not admit that she is frigid or impotent or that she has any defect as alleged in paragraphs 2 and 3 of the said petition.
(3) That there is no connivance or collusion directly or indirectly between the Respondent and the said R.M. the Petitioner, or any other person whatever in reference to the subject matter. . . .

Medical inspectors were appointed 'to examine the Respondent and to report to the Court whether the Respondent is capable of performing the act of generation and if incapable of so doing whether such impotency can or cannot be relieved or removal by art or skill'. Their Reports were included as part of the evidence in the case.

O'Byrne, J.:
This is a suit for a declaration of nullity of marriage on the ground of the alleged impotency of the Respondent.

The parties were married on the 27th August, 1940, at the parish church at Kilbride. At the date of the marriage, the Petitioner was 37 and the Respondent 19 years of age.

The Respondent's parents live near S.; but, when she was slightly over nine years of age, the Respondent went to reside at K., as a companion for Miss A., daughter of the Reverend Mr. A., who was an uncle of the Petitioner. The two girls were educated and brought up together and the Respondent lived at K. until she was over seventeen years of age, when she returned to her parents' residence. She subsequently took up a position as a lady's companion.

The Petitioner came to know the Respondent while she was living in his uncle's house, which the Petitioner visited from time to time, and I am informed that in recent years a correspondence took place between them. None of that correspondence was put in evidence nor was I given any particulars as to its nature or extent.

In August, 1940, the Petitioner was engaged as cashier in a Bank. On the 20th August, 1940, he came to Dublin for a holiday. He met the Respondent that day in Dublin, made a proposal of marriage to her and was accepted, and it was arranged that they should get married on the 27th August, 1940. The marriage took place in accordance with that arrangement. I was told that the reason for the shortness of the engagement was that Miss A. had arranged to get married on the 27th August, 1940, and it was desired that the two girls should get married at the same time.

After the marriage the Petitioner and the Respondent went to the Railway Hotel at G., where they spent three nights. On the 30th August they came to Dublin and spent the night in the Standard Hotel. On the 31st August they went to B. and spent the following five or six weeks in rooms while a flat was being prepared for them. In the month of October, 1940, they moved into the flat and, save for a few days in November which the Respondent spent at her parents' home the parties lived together in the flat until the 7th December, 1940, when the Respondent returned to her parents' home. Since that date the parties have not lived together.

It was established, beyond question, that the marriage was never consummated and that the Respondent is still *virgo intacta*. It was also established that Petitioner was able and anxious to consummate the marriage and that he made frequent attempts to do so between the date of the marriage and the 7th December, 1940, when the Respondent left the matrimonial home. [O'Byrne J. here referred to the Petition and Answer in the case.]

. . . On the night of the 27th August, 1940, the Petitioner made several attempts to have intercourse with the Respondent but the latter resisted and jumped out of bed on each attempt. On the following night the same thing occurred and the Respondent again resisted and told the Petitioner to 'stop that altogether.' On the night of the 29th August, the Respondent again struggled and resisted: she became very excited but said nothing. On the night of the 30th August, in the S. Hotel, the Petitioner again made persistent attempts to consummate the marriage, but the Respondent again resisted. She said, on this occasion, that she would not allow any man to have intercourse with her. During the period when the parties were residing at B. the same efforts were renewed and the same resistance was offered. The Respondent sometimes jumped out of bed and cried. After the parties had moved to the flat no change took place. The Respondent attended to her household duties and was otherwise happy and affectionate; but she repelled any attempt at intercourse. On one occasion, about this period, she told the Petitioner that she looked upon it as a filthy business and that people could love one another without resorting to intercourse.

Early in the month of November, 1940, both the Petitioner and the Respondent communicated with the Respondent's mother, who, throughout these unhappy events, appears to have adopted a very reasonable, affectionate and helpful attitude towards both parties. It was arranged that both parties should go for a weekend to the home of the Respondent's parents, in order to discuss the matter. For this purpose the Respondent went to her parents' home on the 15th November and the Petitioner followed the next day, and discussion took place at which the Petitioner, the Respondent and the latter's parents were present. The parents said that something would have to be done and they suggested that the Respondent should see a doctor. The Respondent was upset and said that she was going to live her own life in the way she pleased and that no doctor could put there what wasn't there. She further said that she didn't like it at all, that people could live together without intercourse and that it was a filthy habit. However, it was arranged that she should see a doctor and she did in fact see a doctor. The Petitioner returned to B. and the Respondent joined him there on the 19th November, 1940. She told him she had seen the doctor and that he suggested that, in order to resort to intercourse, she would have to take drugs. Nothing definite was done and things continued as before until the end of November, when the Respondent refused, any longer, to share a bed with the Petitioner. She thereupon made up a bed on a couch in the sitting-room and occupied it during the remainder of the period she spent with the Petitioner. When he protested, she said she could not occupy the same bed with him any longer. On the 3rd December she told Petitioner that she was going home and would not come back any more. On the 7th December, 1940, she left the Petitioner and went to her parents' home, where she has since resided. After her departure, correspondence took place between the parties. The Petitioner's letters are forthcoming and were put in evidence: the Respondent's letters have been destroyed and I have no evidence as to their contents.

On the 22nd February, 1941, the Petitioner met the Respondent and her mother and sister in Dublin by appointment. It was then arranged that the Respondent should see Dr. Davidson. She did so on the 6th March and, shortly afterwards, these proceedings were instituted.

The foregoing narrative has been taken mainly from the evidence of the Petitioner, which I accept as being substantially true and accurate.

In the course of these proceedings, an Order was made for the medical examination of both parties and both submitted to such examination. Dr. Rowlette and Mr. William Doolin, who examined the Petitioner, made a joint report in which they state that, in their opinion, he has not any impediment on his part to prevent the consummation of marriage. I am quite satisfied by this report and by the sworn testimony of Dr. Rowlette that there is, in fact, no such impediment.

Dr. Spain and Dr. Ashe, who examined Respondent, submitted separate reports. Having regard to these reports and to the sworn testimony of Dr. Davidson and Dr. Falkiner, I am satisfied that there is no physical impediment on her part to the consummation of the marriage. I am also satisfied and find as a fact that there was persistent refusal on the part of the Respondent to consummate the marriage and that the marriage was never, in fact, consummated.

It then becomes necessary for me to determine, upon the evidence before me, the nature and cause of that refusal – whether, in the words of Lord Shaw of Dunfermline in *G.* v. *G,* [1924] A.C. 349, at p. 367, it is due to a mere hostile determination of the mind arising from obstinacy or caprice or, on the other hand, whether it evidences a paralysis and distortion of the will preventing the victim from engaging in the act of consummation, thereby causing incapacity.

On this question I have considered with great care the evidence of Dr. Davidson and Dr. Falkiner and also the evidence of the Respondent. Dr. Davidson said he questioned the Respondent closely and that she told him she had no experience of sexual matters before marriage; but that she discovered after marriage that she had an intolerable aversion to such things and that she violently resented and rejected several attempts on the part of her husband to consummate the marriage. She told him she feels she could never allow sexual congress with her husband or any other man and that she is ready to go to any length to get out of the situation which requires her to do so. She further said that she was quite prepared to live with her husband as a sister; but could not, in any circumstances, submit to physical union with him. The doctor formed the opinion that she has a lasting and unconquerable aversion to the sexual act and that she has formed a resolute determination not to allow herself to be a partner in the act. In forming these opinions the doctor told me that he proceeded on the basis that what she told him was true and that, on this assumption he considered that her repugnance to the sexual act would render it impossible for her to consummate the marriage.

The evidence of Dr. Falkiner, who examined the Respondent on the 25th May, 1941, was substantially to the same effect as that of Dr. Davidson. He told me that the Respondent said that her resistance was due to revulsion and that she felt physically sick when attempts were made. He said there are genuine cases where there is such a revulsion to the sexual act and that it produces incapacity. He further said that such cases are extremely rare but that he considered that the Respondent was one of these cases. He also spoke on the assumption that what the lady told him was true; but he said he considered that she was speaking the truth by reason of the very simple and open way in which she answered all enquiries.

I recognise the weight which must be attached to the evidence of two doctors of such eminence in their profession; but, consistently therewith, I must also recognise that the weight which ought to be attributed to the evidence of the Respondent (which agreed substantially with what she told the doctors) is finally a matter for me.

I come now to consider the evidence of the Respondent. In doing so, I wish to say, at the outset, that she impressed me as a truthful witness – *i.e.,* as a witness who was telling me what she believed to be the truth. At the same time I must realize that the Respondent has been living in a state of severe nervous tension, that she was necessarily brooding over the whole question and that, accordingly, extreme care is necessary in order to ensure that her evidence on a matter, in which she is so intimately involved, is in accordance with objective truth.

The Respondent told me that she knew that physical intercourse was part of the duty of a wife and that at the time of the marriage she was happy in every way. She said that when intercourse was attempted on the first night of her married life, she was rather overcome by it, that she didn't like it and that the thought of it made her sick. She said that her husband continued the attempt and that she resisted and that no intercourse took place.

With reference to the second night, she says that *we* attempted to have intercourse; but *we* didn't succeed. She further says that she felt the same as the first night, but that she made an attempt, that she felt it was disgusting, that her husband continued to try and that she also tried, but disliked it more so. As regards this portion of her evidence, I desire to say that, in so far as it suggests that Respondent made an attempt to consummate the marriage, I do not accept it. In my opinion, whatever the reason, she did not, on this occasion or at any time during her married life, make any genuine attempt to consummate the marriage. She says that on the night of the 29th August, her husband made another attempt, but that she pushed him away and told him to leave her alone.

She gives very little evidence with reference to the period spent in rooms in B., but says that her husband continued his attempts to consummate the marriage and that she disliked it still more. She says that, when they moved into the flat, the attempts continued and that she couldn't bear it any longer. She says that, in October her husband suggested that she should see a doctor, but she told him she couldn't do it – that it was a filthy business. After her return from her parents' home in November she says she couldn't stand it any longer and that she slept on a couch after that. When she suggested going to her parents' home in the early part of December, she says her husband suggested that she should go away for a year, but that she refused and told him that if she went away she would not come back.

She told me that there was no question of her being fond of any other man and I completely accept her evidence as to this.

I must now consider the inference to be drawn from this evidence and the conclusion of fact at which I should arrive.

At the time of the marriage, the Respondent was a young girl with very little experience of life. Though she had known the Petitioner for a number of years I am not satisfied that the relationship between them was very intimate or such as would lead one to expect such a hurried engagement and marriage as subsequently took place. It is, to my mind, tragic that the marriage should have been arranged and entered on with such haste that the Respondent cannot have had any real opportunity of considering her position. She says that she and the Petitioner were fond of one another before the engagement and that she was in love with him; but, in the absence of any particulars or of any scrap of correspondence, I accept this statement with great caution. My view is that she was surprised and rushed into this marriage and that she never gave sufficient thought or consideration to the grave step she was about to take. She also says that she knew that physical intercourse was part of the duty of a wife; but I am far from satisfied that she had any very clear ideas on this subject or any clear conception of the serious obligations which she was undertaking in entering into the contract of marriage.

When the marriage had been solemnised and her husband attempted to consummate the marriage, I am satisfied that she was genuinely shocked and disgusted by the attempt. I am also satisfied that she had and continued during her matrimonial life with the Petitioner, to have a strong and real aversion to the sexual act. I am, however, asked to say that this aversion was of such an invincible character as to produce a paralysis and distortion of the will and thereby prevent her from engaging in the act of consummation. I am far from being satisfied as to this. The Respondent, when in the witness-box, though over-wrought and suffering from severe nervous and emotional tension, struck me as being to some extent, a rather self-willed and determined girl.

It would be sufficient for me, in order to dispose of this case, to say that, in my opinion, the onus of proof has not been discharged. I am, however, after full and careful consideration of all the evidence, prepared to go so far as to say that, so far from the will of the Respondent being paralysed or distorted in the manner suggested, I am of opinion that it was a free and active participant in the continued resistence shown by the Respondent to all attempts, on the part of her husband, to consummate the marriage. This view is, in my opinion, fortified by the emphatic statements made by the Respondent to Dr. Davidson and others that she would never allow her husband or any other man to have sexual intercourse with her and other statements to the like effect.

In my opinion the questions directed in this case by the Order of the 30th June, 1941, *i.e.* (1. Whether at the date of the ceremony of marriage between the Petitioner and Respondent the Respondent was and still is incapable of the act of generation? 2. Whether if so incapable at said date and said incapacity still exists the same can or cannot be removed by art or skill? 3. Whether the Respondent at the said date suffered and still suffers from such invincible repugnance or aversion to the Petitioner as to render it impossible for her to consummate the marriage?) should be answered as follows:– 1. No. 2. Does not arise. 3. No.

For these reasons I am of opinion that the Prayer contained in the Petition herein should be refused and the Petition dismissed.

The petitioner appealed to the Supreme Court. The grounds of the appeal were that the learned Judge misdirected himself in law and in fact and that his findings were against evidence and the weight of evidence.

Sullivan, C.J., delivering the reserved judgment of the Supreme Court affirming the decision of O'Byrne, J., said that if there was evidence that at any time during her married life the Respondent had consented to consummate the marriage then there might be much force in a contention that her subsequent refusal when the time came for her to do so was not wilful but should be attributed to invincible repugnance which paralysed her will. It would seem from the speech of Lord Dunedin in *G.* v. *G.* [1924] A.C. 349 that it was such evidence that satisfied him that the respondent in that case was incapable of consummating the marriage and that his decision in *A.B.* v. *C.B.* 8 F. 603 was based on a similar ground. In this case there was no such evidence. Although the subject of their marital relations was discussed by the parties on several occasions there was no indication by the Respondent that she would yield to her husband's wishes. Her reply to his remonstrances was that she could not do it; that she did not like it at all and that people could live together without having intercourse.

Notes

1. Do you agree with the holding of the decision? Is it in accord with today's values?
2. If a person very firmly and consistently refuses to have sexual intercourse in any circumstances does this afford evidence of a resolute exercise of free will or of an eclipse of the will? Who is to say? How? Is the central question one of resolution by a psychologist? A psychiatrist? A philosopher? On what philosophy of freedom of will is our law premised? Do you think that psychiatrists generally work on the same premise?
3. Contrast this decision with *N.F.* v. *M.T. (otherwise known as F.), infra*, p. 88 and *R. (otherwise W.)* v. *W., infra*, p. 92. See also *E.M.* v. *S.M.*, 77 I.L.T.R. 128 (High Ct., 1942), analysed by Hayes, *The Matrimonial Jurisdiction of the High Court*, 8 Ir. Jur. (n.s.) 55, at 69 (1973).
4. In *McM.* v. *McM. and McK.* v. *McK.*, [1936] I.R. 177, at 200 (High Ct., 1935), Hanna, J. said:

> A husband is not entitled to enforce his marital rights of indignity or brutal violence nor in such a manner as would, if there were no marriage, amount to rape. But there is sometimes necessary and permissible the 'gentle violence' referred to by Lord Dunedin in *G.* v. *G.*, [1924] A.C. 349, at 357.

What do you understand by the notion of 'gentle violence'? Does it appeal to you? Is it part of Irish law today? Has the Constitution any relevance? The right to bodily integrity? To health? Have the Family provisions any role? See also Morris & Turner, *Two Problems in the Law of Rape*, 2 U. Queensland L.J. 247, at 259–261 (1953).

5. O'Byrne, J. was 'far from satisfied' that the respondent had had 'any clear conception of the serious obligations which she was undertaking in entering into the contract of marriage'. Would it be plausible to argue that she failed the test set out in *The Estate of Park deceased; Park* v. *Park*, [1954] P. 89? If you are hesitant to ascribe words such as 'insanity' or 'mental incapacity, to the respondent, is that a good reason for holding the marriage valid?
6. What do you make of the Supreme Court's approach?
7. Would Kenny, J.'s approach in *S.* v. *S., supra*, p. 77 offer any solution?
8. In 1942, the same year as *R.M.* v. *M.M.* was decided, the Supreme Court of Canada came to the contrary conclusion, on the facts, in a similar type of case: see *Heil* v. *Heil,* [1942] S.C.R. 160. See also *Greenlees* v. *Greenlees,* [1959] O.R. 419 (High Ct. of Justice, Walsh, J.).

N.F. v. M.T. (Otherwise known as F.)

[1982] I.L.R.M. 545 (High Court, O'Hanlon, J.)

O'Hanlon, J.: The parties in this case married on 8 January 1976, at a time when both were still university students. . .

The young couple were not in a financial position to set up a home, and the petitioner says that he was reluctant to embark on marriage, notwithstanding a deep attachment of the parties for each other, but that he gave in to pressure by the respondent and by her parents, who were unhappy at the thought of a prolonged engagement which might extend over several years.

In these circumstances the parents of both parties agreed to help out – the petitioner's parents contributing £15 and later £16 per week to the household budget, and the respondent's parents contributing £10 per week and supplying foodstuffs and other forms of material help from time to time.

Prior to marriage the parties had been associating on intimate terms for over a year, and had indulged in sexual contact stopping short of intercourse. The petitioner stated that he wished to indulge in pre-marital intercourse but that the respondent was not willing to participate.

After the marriage took place, the parties lived together until 26 June 1979, when they separated, and did not cohabit together again after that date. The petitioner said that he attempted to have intercourse with the respondent on the night of the wedding, but that she became upset and frightened; that she was crying and saying she was 'not ready', and that the attempt was a failure. He said that she had deep-rooted fears of becoming pregnant, both before and after the marriage had taken place, and after marriage used the contraceptive pill at all times and in the early stages insisted that he should wear a contraceptive device whenever he approached her sexually.

The petitioner gave evidence to the effect that he made repeated attempts over the weeks following upon the marriage to consummate the marriage, but without success; that on such occasions the respondent became upset, and said her hymen was too strong.

It quickly became apparent that the parties were failing to achieve physical union as man and wife, and there was considerable conflict as to their respective willingness to seek medical assistance in an effort to resolve their problems. Each asserted that the other refused to co-operate in this respect, and in this state of conflict I find the petitioner's evidence more convincing than that of the respondent, having regard to the fact that he has submitted to the medical examination directed in the course of the present proceedings, while the respondent refused to submit to such examination and conceded that she also refused to submit to a medical examination in the course of proceedings brought by the petitioner seeking a Church annulment of the marriage.

It is quite clear from a description given by the respondent of one particular occasion when she says the petitioner attempted to have intercourse with her, using a degree of force in the process to overcome her resistance, that the whole procedure was excruciatingly painful for her. She suggested, (contrary to what appears from the answer filed on her behalf in the present proceedings) that the marriage may, in fact, have been consummated on that occasion, but her evidence was not such as to carry any conviction in this respect, and she was unable to state whether or not her hymen was still intact even at the present time notwithstanding the fact that she has been examined by a gynaecologist within the last year for purposes unconnected with the present proceedings.

Having regard to the sworn testimony of both parties, taken in conjunction with the answer of the respondent supported by affidavit verifying same, and having regard to the refusal of the respondent to submit to medical examination when required to do so for the purposes of the petitioner, I am satisfied that the marriage was never consummated.

The respondent, while admitting in the answer that such is the case, denies that the failure to consummate the marriage was attributable to incapacity on her part. . . .

The evidence established that the failure of the parties to consummate their marriage was not attributable to any physical incapacity on the part of the petitioner. On his own sworn testimony, he had had sexual intercourse with other persons prior to his marriage with the respondent, and subsequent to his separation from her. He submitted to medical examination, and the evidence of Dr. McLean confirmed that he was physically normal and capable of consummating the marriage.

The parties were obviously very attached to each other for a long time before they married, and this attachment and affection continued for a time after the marriage. The respondent participated in sexual intimacy stopping short of intercourse both prior to and subsequent to the marriage and there was nothing to suggest that such contact inspired feelings of revulsion in her, or that there was wilful refusal on her part to allow the petitioner to approach her with that degree of intimacy that would in the normal course of events lead on to marital relations in the fullest sense of the word. She did complain, however, that after the early failures to achieve intercourse, the petitioner's attitude towards her underwent a marked change; that he quickly became rough and hostile in his approach, and ceased to be in any way gentle or affectionate in his treatment of her. She also confirmed that she did not like children, and did not want to have children, but claimed that this was in accord with the petitioner's feelings also.

The relations between the parties went from bad to worse; there appear to have been traumatic episodes when the petitioner put the respondent out of the house, and if her evidence and that of her father is correct as to the language used by the petitioner, it indicates a great lack of sensitivity on his part for the plight in which the respondent found herself.

I am satisfied that the respondent is and has at all material times been incapable of consummating the marriage by reason of difficulties referable to her physical make-up and also by reason of psychological problems which affected her. Whether the physical problems can be resolved by medical intervention is impossible to forecast, owing to the lack of co-operation of the respondent in providing such evidence, but even if it should transpire that at some future date it would be physically possible for the respondent to have normal marital relations with some other partner, I find that there is and will remain a complete incapacity *qua* the petitioner. . . .

[The question of approbation is considered *infra*, p. 96]

S. v. S.

Unreported, Supreme Court, 1 July 1976 (1–1976)

[The facts of the case have been set out, *supra*, pp. 76–77. The Supreme Court unanimously granted a decree of nullity, but the three judges differed as to the grounds. **Kenny, J.** appeared to base his judgment on the ground of fraudulent non-disclosure (cf. pp. 77–78 *supra*). He rejected the ground of impotence; he considered that the respondent was 'unquestionably potent'. **Henchy, J.** and **Griffin, J.**, however, took a different view of the evidence.]

Henchy, J.:

. . . In this Court the wife's case has been argued primarily on the basis that the marriage should be annulled because of the husband's sexual impotence vis-à-vis her.

The husband has not taken any part in these proceedings, so we have only the wife's version of things. However, there is no suggestion of collusion, and the trial judge, who saw and heard the wife in the witness box, apart from expressing doubt as to the correctness of her version of one conversation she had with the husband, does not question her veracity.

I find the evidence coercive of the conclusion that while the husband's failure to consummate the marriage was not due to any general sexual incompetence – his previous sexual relations with the wife and his sexual relations with the other woman are proof of that – it was the result of an obliteration of his sexual capacity with her from the time of the marriage or, possibly from the time shortly before the marriage when he became intimate with the other woman. This incapacity would seem to have been a corollary of his attachment to the other woman. If it is not viewed as a genuine incapacity, and not an affected and willed abstention, this husband of twenty three would have to be credited with powers of sexual restraint with this wife of twenty-two who shared his bed nightly, which are completely belied by his sexual activity otherwise – with herself before he had met the other woman, and with the other woman before, during and after the period of six months when he lived with the wife.

The evidence given by the wife does not, to me, give a picture of a man who was perversely and wilfully living out a resolution not to have sexual relations with her. I find no suggestion that he was subjugating his libido to his will. On the contrary, her evidence conveys an impression of a total absence of libido on his part towards her during the period when they lived together. For example, when she tells of an effort she made to get him to have sexual intercourse with her, she does not say that he in any way repulsed her advances. She simply says that 'it was no good'. Her evidence shows that he made clear to her that he had no affection for her, that she 'made him sick'. His failure to consummate the marriage would seem to have been a part of that revulsion. We have no medical or other expert evidence to identify the psychological or other factors that produced his condition, but the condition itself seems to have been one of sexual impotence in relation to the wife during the period when they lived together ostensibly as husband and wife.

That being so, the matrimonial law governing the position is not in doubt. Where a husband, while not generally impotent, is unable to consummate the marriage because of impotence vis-à-vis the wife (or *impotentia quoad hanc*, as the ecclesiastical lawyers put it), that is a good ground in the civil courts for an annulment of the marriage at the suit of the wife. See *C. (otherwise H.)* v. *C* [1921] P. 399, where Lord Birkenhead L.C. reviews the authorities showing the civil law to be to that effect and points out that in the ecclesiastical courts, both before and after the Council of Trent, the doctrine of the church admitted and, indeed, enjoined nullity on such a ground. In fact, the wife here has obtained a declaration of nullity in an ecclesiastical court. In my judgment, the order on this petition should be to the same effect.

I would allow the appeal and issue a decree of nullity.

Griffin, J.:

. . . These two young people, prior to the marriage, and prior to the husband's meeting the woman with whom he is now living ('the other woman') had a deep affection for each other and had sexual intercourse on a number of occasions. The husband, so far as the evidence goes, had no difficulty whatever on any of these occasions. There is no question of his being impotent generally; this has clearly been established by his pre-marital sexual relations with the wife and also by his sexual relations with the other woman who became pregnant by him although she apparently subsequently had a miscarriage. The husband and the wife occupied the same bed on their honeymoon and subsequently occupied the same bed in the flat in which they lived in Dublin for almost six months after their return from the honeymoon. During all this time there was on the husband's part a total lack of inclination towards the wife, which, in the light of the pre-marital events, was completely to be unexpected. On the one occasion on which the wife made overtures to have the marriage consummated, it was, as the wife put it, 'no good'. It afterwards transpired that the explanation for the continued failure on his part to consummate the marriage was that he had met the other woman some weeks prior to the date of the marriage, had fallen in love with her, that he had slept with the other woman on the night before the marriage, and that he no longer had any affection for the wife and that she, as he put it, revolted him and 'made him sick'.

In my opinion, the only reasonable inference to be drawn from these facts is that there was a complete incapacity on the part of the husband in relation to the wife and that this was and would continue to be an unconquerable aversion on his part. . .

I would allow this appeal and grant a declaration that this marriage be annulled.

Notes

1. Do you agree with the majority holding that the respondent was impotent *quoad hanc*?
2. See Duncan, *Sex and the Fundamentals of Marriage*, [1979–80] Dublin U. L. J. 29.
3. Where a person of indeterminate sex marries, some difficult problems of legal categorisation arise (cf. Kahn, *The True Hermaphrodite – Of No Sex?*, 98 S. Afr. L.J. 111 (1981), Bartholomew, *Hermaphrodites and the Law*, 2 U. Malaya L. Rev. 83 (1960)) although it seems that in such rare cases the practice has been for a petition for nullity to be based on impotence: cf. *Corbett* v. *Corbett (orse Ashley)* [1971] P. 83, at 105 (Ormrod, J., 1970). But where two persons of the *same* sex go through a ceremony of marriage, courts in England have held that the marriage is void: *Corbett* v. *Corbett (orse Ashley), supra, Talbot (orse Poyntz)* v. *Talbot (orse Talbot)* 111 Sol. J. 213 (P.D.A. Div., Ormrod, J., 1967). In other countries, changing mores and living patterns have led some to contend that a 'marriage' between persons of the same sex should be regarded as valid. They point to the fact that the status of marriage confers a wide range of legal and social benefits on the spouses; they stress that heterosexual marriages are not automatically invalid by reason of the lack of capacity for sexual intercourse on the part of either spouse, and that procreative incapacity does not affect their validity, and they contend that to deny persons of the same sex the capacity to marry is unjust and (in countries where there are constitutional guarantees respecting fundamental rights) unconstitutional (see, e.g., W. O'Donnell & D. Jones, *The Law of Marriage and Marital Alternatives*, 46–50 (1982); *Anon., The Legality of Homosexual Marriages*, 82 Yale L.J. 573 (1973); Rivera, *Our Straight-Laced Judges: The Legal Position of Homosexual Persons in the United States*, 30 Hastings L.J. 799, at 874–878 (1979); Harper & Clifton, *Heterosexuality: A Prerequisite of Marriage in Texas?* 14 S. Texas L. Rev. 41 (1976); Veitch, *The Essence of Marriage – A Comment on the Homosexual Challenge*, 5 Anglo-Amer. L. Rev. 41 (1976); Karst, *The Freedom of Intimate Association*, 89 Yale L. J. 624, at 682–686 (1980)). These arguments have met with little success so far in courts in the United States and Canada. How do you think a case on these lines would fare in an Irish court? Cf. *Norris* v. *A.G.*, unreported, Supreme Court, 28th April 1983, *infra*, pp. 374–87.

   A somewhat different problem arises in respect of persons known as transsexuals. Such persons are of a psychological disposition that makes them believe that they are really members of the other sex trapped in the body of the wrong sex. They may seek an operation designed to make their bodies as similar as possible to the preferred sex. There is a view in some (but by no means all) medical circles that such an operation may be therapeutically required, having regard to the severe depression – sometimes suicidal – that may affect these persons. See Belli, *Transsexual Surgery – A New Tort?* 17 J. Family L. 487, at 490–491 (1979); Smith, *Comment: Transsexualism, Sex Reassignment Surgery and the Law*, 56 Cornell L. Rev. 963 (1971); Armstrong,

Transsexualism: A Medical Perspective, 6 J. of Med. Ethics 90 (1980); Roth, *Transsexualism and the Sex-Change Operation*, 49 Medico-Legal J. 5, at 15–16 (1981); Oles, *The Transsexual Client: A Discussion of Transsexualism and Issues in Psychotherapy*, 47 Amer. J. of Orthopsychiat. 66 (1977); Baker, *Transsexualism – Problems in Treatment*, 125 Amer. J. of Psychiat. 1412 (1969); Green, Newman & Stoller, *Treatment of Boyhood Transsexualism*, 26 Arch. Gen. Psychiat. 213 (1972); Socarides, *The Desire for Sexual Transformation: A Psychiatric Evaluation of Transsexualism*, 125 Amer. J. of Psychiat. 125 (1969). Operations have been carried out in some countries. The question may arise later as to whether such persons should still be regarded as being of their original sex.

This issue has given rise to much discussion in other countries. See, e.g., Holloway, *Transsexuals – Their Legal Sex*, 40 U. Colo. L. Rev. 281 (1968); David, *Comment: The Law and Transsexualism: A Faltering Response to a Conceptual Dilemma*, 7 Conn. L. Rev. 288 (1977); Brent, *Comment: Some Legal Problems of the Postoperative Transsexual*, 12 J. of Family L. 405 (1972); Kremer, *An Examination of the Rights and Status of Post-Operative Transsexuals with a View to Reform*, ch. 4 of Legal Research Institute of the University of Manitoba, Law Reform Programme, vol. 1 (1973); D. Myers, *The Human Body and the Law: A Medico-Legal Study*, ch. 3 (1970). It is noteworthy that in England during the passage of legislation introducing wide-ranging changes in the law of nullity in 1971, discussion of the subject of transsexual marriages took up a considerable portion of the parliamentary debates. There has been no judicial pronouncement on the question in this country, and the authorities in other jurisdictions are divided.

In England (*Corbett* v. *Corbett (orse Ashley)*, [1971] P. 83 (Ormrod, J. 1970)) and South Africa (*W.* v. *W.*, 1976 (2) S.A. 308 (Witwatersrand Local Div., Nestadt, J., 1975), *Simms* v. *Simms*, 1981 (4) S.A. 186), it has been held that chromosomal, gonadal and genital criteria should determine the sex of a person for the purposes of the law of marriage and that it is not proper to apply a psychological criterion where these three criterian are consistent. This approach has been criticised: see Kennedy, *Transsexualism and Single Sex Marriage*, 2 Anglo-Amer. L. Rev. 112 (1973); Smith, *op. cit.*, at 1006–1007, Pannick, *Homosexuals, Transsexuals and the Sex Discrimination Act*, (1983); Thomson, *Transsexualism: A Legal Perspective*, 6 J. of Med. Ethics 92, at 93–94 (1980); cf. Taitz, *The Legal Consequences of a Sex Change – A Judicial Dilemma*, 97 S. Afr. L. J. 65 (1980); Thomas, *Can the Lawyer Keep Up With the Doctor?*, 97 S. Afr. L.J. 77 (1980). In the United States of America, a different approach has been favoured. In *M.T.* v. *J.T..*, 140 N.J. Super. 77, 355 A. 2d 204 (App. Div., 1976), Handler, J. expressed the view that:

> for marital purposes if the anatomical or genital features of a genuine transsexual are made to conform with the person's gender, psyche or psychological sex, then identity by sex must be governed by a congruence of these standards.

See Poulter, *The Definition of Marriage in English Law*, 42 Modern L. Rev. 409, at 424–425 (1979); Browell, 6 Capital L. Rev. 403 (1977). Somewhat similar developments have taken place in the Federal Republic of Germany: see Giesen, *Transsexual Surgery and the Law*, 1 Int. J. of Med. & L. 469 (1980). Particular difficulties may arise where a person with the physical characteristics of both sexes has undergone a medical operation designed to enhance the characteristics of one sex. Cf. *In the Marriage of C. & D. (falsely called C.)*, (1979) F.L.C. 90–636, critically analysed by Finlay, *Sexual Identity and the Law of Nullity*, 54 Austr. L. J. 115 (1980), and by Bailey, 53 Austr. L.J. 659 (1979).

It is possible that the European Convention for the Protection of Human Rights and Freedoms will play an important role in this area. In *Van Oosterwijck* v. *Belgium*, Series A, No. 40, 3 E.H.R.R. 557 (1981), the European Court of Human Rights rejected a claim by a post-operative transsexual resulting from the failure of the State of Belgium to give official recognition to the post-operative sex assignment. The Court rejected the claim because the claimant had failed to exhaust domestic remedies. It is noteworthy that the European Commission had held in favour of the claimant, on the merits, under Articles 8 and 12 of the Convention. Another claim is at present under consideration by the Commission. See Pannick, *Homosexuals, Transsexuals and the Sex Discrimination Act*, [1983] Public L. 279, at 296–298; Morton, *The Transexual (sic) and the Law*, 134 New L.J. 621 (1984).

R. (OTHERWISE W.) v. W.

Unreported, High Court, Finlay, P., 1 February 1980 (1977–22M)

Finlay P.:

This is a petition brought by the wife seeking a decree that a marriage which purported to have taken place between the petitioner and the respondent [in] June, 1974 is null and void. The short grounds are that the marriage was never consummated and that such non-consummation was due to an incapacity on her part to consummate the marriage.

The respondent did not defend the petition in the sense that he did not contest it but he appeared on it and was represented by Counsel and gave evidence. In addition to the evidence of the petitioner and the respondent I also had the benefit of the evidence of Dr. Paul McQuaid who examined the petitioner prior to the hearing of the petition.

Firstly, I was satisfied that the evidence given to me by both the petitioner and the respondent was true. In relation to the matters relevant to this petition there was no significant conflict of evidence between them. I am satisfied that they are not acting in collusion and that they are both credible witnesses. In particular I was impressed by the care and accuracy with which I believe the Petitioner gave her evidence and with its truth.

I find the facts proved before me to be as follows.

The petitioner and the respondent are both members of the same profession and first met in the year 1972 when they were working in the same institution. A friendship grew between them which eventually became a strong relationship and culminated in an informal and to some extent private agreement to marry in the Spring of 1973. The petitioner, who is an only child, had I am satisfied a relatively unhappy childhood due to the fact that her father was an alcoholic and given to considerable violence. She was closely and devotedly attached to her mother and candidly admitted that up to very recently when she took a more compassionate view of his condition she actually hated her father. For both her and the respondent who in the year 1973 were approximately 25 years of age their friendship and relationship was the first significant relationship of their adult life with a member of the other sex.

Prior to the marriage which took place in June of 1974 the parties had purchased a house in their joint names and the Petitioner had moved into it having previously lived close to her employment and away from her family home in a flat. On three separate occasions prior to the marriage sexual intercourse took place between the petitioner and the respondent. I accept the evidence of the petitioner corroborated to a large extent by the evidence of the respondent that on each of these occasions the petitioner was completely passive and I further accept her evidence that she found to have sexual intercourse with the respondent on these occasions increasingly distasteful and increasingly difficult for her to accept. Neither the petitioner nor the respondent before these occasions had sexual intercourse with any other person.

According to her evidence the petitioner with hindsight sees her decision to marry the respondent as largely a way out of what she considered to be an intolerable home and family situation. By the Spring of 1973 she was aware that her mother had a terminal illness and according to her her father was compounding the situation by failing to grapple his drink problem and continuing conduct which had a very damaging effect on both her mother and herself. She was, however, and this is an important finding on the facts in my opinion, quite definitely extremely anxious that the marriage should be a success and she had a genuine intellectual companionship and compatibility with the respondent and has still very honestly expressed considerable regard and respect for him.

Immediately after the marriage there was a very short honeymoon indeed during which the petitioner repulsed any advances for sexual intercourse made by the respondent on the grounds that she was tired and under strain and this was readily accepted by the respondent. The problems and crisis of the petitioner's mother's illness had by the time of the marriage increased and there were for some short time after it further family problems before the parties settled down to reside as man and wife in the house which they had purchased.

From that time onwards up to June of 1977 when the parties finally separated the marriage was not, I am satisfied upon the evidence, consummated.

It would appear that with relatively considerable frequency at the commencement of the marriage but with diminishing frequency in the succeeding years the respondent sought to have sexual intercourse with his wife. She, I am satisfied, had an invincible repugnance to accepting his advances and on the evidence it appears to me improbable that the marriage could have been consummated otherwise than by the exercise of considerable force by the respondent.

I accept the petitioner's evidence that notwithstanding her experiences on the three occasions when she had sexual intercourse with the respondent before the marriage she was hopeful at the time of the marriage that it would become possible and tolerable thereafter and that that particular problem would be solved. She felt that possibly her repugnance to it prior to the marriage was in part at least contributed to by a sense of guilt from having sexual intercourse before marriage. I am also satisfied that the petitioner was aware throughout the marriage that her failure to have sexual intercourse with her husband was something which would put the marriage at considerable risk that she consulted her mother about it and received that advice from her mother. Furthermore she consulted a member of the staff of a Family Planning Clinic which she was attending in the hope that a change of a contraceptive pill which she was taking since the parties had decided not to have children would increase her sexual desire and sexual drive and make the having of intercourse possible. It is probable on the evidence before me that the Respondent himself was a person, at that time at least, with a limited sexual desire and limited sexual drive but there is no doubt but that he was anxious to consummate the marriage and that his failure to do so was a factor in the unfortunate break-up of the relationship between these parties. The parties, who are both Catholics, had been married according to the rites of the Catholic Church. Immediately after they separated in June of 1977, they entered into an agreement which provided for all the financial consequences of their separation and in particular for the sale of the house which they had jointly purchased and the distribution of the proceeds of that sale. The respondent then instituted proceedings in the Ecclesiastical Courts of the Catholic Church for an annulment of his marriage according to Canon Law. Those proceedings are still pending but it is of significance that they were instituted by the respondent without any prior agreement with the petitioner and, in fact, probably actually instituted without notice to her. In the late Autumn of 1977 the petitioner instituted these proceedings again without agreement with the respondent and without notice to him.

Subsequent to the separation of the parties in 1977 the petitioner remained living on her own in a flat and carrying out her professional duties for a period of approximately a year but in 1978 she formed a relationship with another man and she has had sexual intercourse with him, now lives with him and has a child born of that relationship. The respondent has not formed, as yet, any permanent relationship with anybody of the other sex.

Dr. Paul McQuaid did not see the petitioner until after the parties had separated and she did not seek either from him or from any other psychiatrist advice during the time when she was living with the respondent.

He expressed the opinion that by reason of her childhood and background the petitioner had, certainly at the time of her purported marriage to the respondent and at the time when she was living with him, a significantly immature personality amounting to a personality disorder reflecting principally her relationship with the opposite sex. He had first interviewed and examined the petitioner from a psychiatric point of view before she had formed the relationship with the person with whom she is now living but stated that he was not surprised when he heard of this as there was an accepted personality disorder which would be classified as a psychosexual disorder in which the experience is quite common that a person of the intellectual, personality and emotional make-up of the petitioner would accept and be able to co-operate in sexual intercourse on her own terms and without what she would perceive as the obligations of matrimony but would not be able at a particular stage of her development to do so within the confines of matrimony. On these facts it has been strongly urged upon me on behalf of the petitioner, by Mr.

Shatter, that the case comes squarely within the decision of the Supreme Court in *S.* v. *S.* [*supra*, p. 76] [Finlay P. summarised the judgments in that decision. He continued:]

I am satisfied that in this case there was no fixed intention on the part of the petitioner not to consummate the marriage and, therefore, the case does not come within the principle laid down in the decision of Mr. Justice Kenny. I am satisfied after careful consideration and bearing in mind the onus of proof which in a petition for nullity on the basis of non-consummation is imposed by law upon the petitioner that this marriage was not consummated by reason of an insurmountable repugnance on the part of the Petitioner to having sexual intercourse after marriage with the respondent due probably to a psychosexual disorder arising from her personality and from the background which had developed that personality. Having regard to that finding only one matter remains for decision and that is as to whether the petitioner, being the person who has failed to consummate the marriage, is entitled to a decree of nullity.

In *A.* v. *A. sued as B.*, 19 L.R. Ir. 403 (1887) it was held that an impotent man cannot maintain a nullity suit merely on the ground of his own impotency but if the woman altogether repudiates the relationship of wife and the obligations of the marriage contract the impotent man may show that there is no *verum matrimonium* and maintain such a suit. In that case the act of repudiation by the wife successfully relied upon was that the parties being Catholics she had immediately after the parties had separated instituted proceedings in her own Ecclesiastical Court which she persisted with and brought to a successful conclusion.

The requirement for repudiation by the respondent of the *verum matrimonium* was again applied by Mr. Justice Hanna in *McM.* v. *McM.* [1936] I.R. 177.

. . . It seems to me that that reasoning properly applied to the facts of this case leaves it beyond any doubt that the respondent has repudiated this marriage. The parties were both Catholics at the time of the purported marriage and the marriage took place according to the rites of the Catholic Church. I have no doubt on the evidence that the respondent's immediate concern after the separation between the parties had become final and complete was to try and free himself of this marriage according to the law of the Church of which he was a member. There can be no other explanation of his very rapid institution of proceedings seeking a decree of nullity in the Ecclesiastical Courts. It is irrelevant to the issue at present before me that those proceedings have not been yet terminated since they are being persisted in by the respondent. That must, in my view, be a clear and unequivocal repudiation by him of the marriage and, therefore, in my view entitles the petitioner to a decree of nullity based on her own impotency in the particular manner in which I have found on the facts it exists.

It was urged on me in the course of the legal argument that there are grounds for doubting the necessity for a repudiation as is laid down in *A.* v. *A. otherwise B.* and in *McM* v. *McM* and that more recent decisions, in particular that of *Harthan* v. *Harthan* [1949] P. 115 (C.A.) containing a close analysis of the older decisions would indicate that repudiation is not necessary though there may be circumstances which may bar from relief a person petitioning for nullity on the basis of his own impotency such as a knowledge of the defect at the date of the marriage.

Having regard to my finding that the respondent has unequivocally repudiated this marriage it is not necessary for me to decide the larger question arising from the conflict between the reasoning in this decision and the reasoning of the Irish decisions to which I have referred and I expressly reserve my view on that point.

I am accordingly satisfied that the petitioner is entitled to a decree of nullity.

Notes

1. For consideration of English developments, see Bevan, *Limitations on the Right of an Impotent Spouse to Petition for Nullity*, 76 L.Q. Rev. 267 (1960). As well as *Harthan* v. *Harthan*, relevant English decisions include *Pettit* v. *Pettit,* [1963] P. 177 (C.A.) and *Singh* v. *Singh,* [1971] P. 226 (C.A.). Canadian decisions following *Harthan* v. *Harthan* include *Paikin* v. *Paikin,* [1959] O.W.N. 51 (High Ct. of Justice, Walsh, J.) and *M.* v. *M.*, 13 W.W.R. 505 (Manit. Q.B., Williams, C.J.Q.B., 1954). See also *R.* v. *R.*, 28 R.F.L. 283 (N.S. Sup. Ct., Cowan, C.J.T.D., 1976).
2. *R. (otherwise W.)* v. *W.* is analysed by Duncan, *Sex and the Fundamentals of Marriage,* [1979–80] Dublin U. L. J. 29.

BARS TO A DECREE

In certain circumstances, the Court may dismiss a petition for a declaration of nullity of marriage, in spite of the existence of a vitiating element. Some categories of void marriage may be *ratified* after celebration; others may not. Those that are not, namely, marriages void on the ground of bigamy, formal defect or prohibited relationship, are incapable of ratification because of a dominant public interest consideration. The judicial view is that, however unjust it may be as between the parties, this consideration cannot override the public policy served by the ground. In the case of marriages void on the ground of lack of consent (whether from mental incapacity, duress, fraud or mistake), however, the defect is primarily of personal, rather than public, dimensions, so ratification is permitted. (It should be recalled that at least some marriages vitiated by lack of consent are now considered voidable rather than void: cf. *supra*, p. 16).

Where a marriage is *voidable*, the bar of *approbation* may apply. The operation of this bar was analysed in *D.* v. *C.*

D. v. C.

Unreported, High Ct., Costello J., 19 May 1983 (26m 1982)

[The facts of the decision have been set out, *supra*, pp. 29–38. The case concerned a marriage where, the petitioner alleged, the respondent suffered from a psychiatric illness at the time of the marriage which rendered him incapable of entering into or sustaining a normal marriage relationship with her. **Costello, J.** disposed of the question of approbation as follows:]

The bar which the Respondent urges disentitles the Petitioner to relief is based on the doctrine of approbation (or lack of sincerity as it was called in the earlier cases). The principle underlying this plea was stated in *G.* v. *M.* (10 App. Cases 171 at p. 168) as follows:

> There may be conduct on the part of the person seeking this remedy (i.e. a decree of nullity) which ought stop that person from having it; as, for instance, any act from which the inference ought to be drawn that during the antecedent time the party has with a knowledge of the facts and of the law approbated the marriage which he or she afterwards seeks to get rid of, or has taken advantages and derived benefits from the matrimonial relation which it would be unfair and inequitable to permit him or her having received them to treat as if no such relation had ever existed.

It will be noted that the defence now relied on can only succeed where it is shown that the Petitioner acted not only with knowledge of the facts which entitled her to a nullity decree but also with knowledge that those facts would, as a matter of law, have entitled her to the right she now seeks to enforce. It is perfectly clear that in the present case the Petitioner (a) did not know that her husband had suffered from a psychiatric illness at the time of their marriage until several years after the ceremony had taken place and (b) until she obtained legal advice shortly before the institution of these proceedings she was unaware that her husband's illness entitled her to a nullity decree. I am satisfied that she never approbated her marriage and she is not barred by her conduct from the relief she now claims.

N.F. v. M.T. (Otherwise known as F.)
[1982] I.L.R.M. 545 (High Ct., O'Hanlon, J.)

[The facts of the case have been set out *supra*, pp. 88–89. **O'Hanlon, J.** found that the respondent was impotent relative to the petitioner. He continued:]

This finding, however, does not conclude the case, as there remain for consideration the arguments based on approbation and delay.

The element of delay is not, in my opinion, of such an order as should debar the petitioner from claiming the relief he seeks in the present proceedings. It was felt at one time that a period of three years should be allowed to elapse before the positive conclusion should be drawn as to the parties' incapacity to consummate a marriage. This concept is no longer favoured, but it has been repeatedly stressed that a reasonable period of cohabitation should take place before a finding may properly be made that there is an inability to consummate the marriage. See the judgment of the Earl of Selborne, L.C. in *G.* v. *M.* (1875) 10 A.C. 171.

In the present case the parties lived together for 3½ years before finally separating. The petitioner then delayed a further two years before instituting proceedings for nullity, and then only after the respondent had brought maintenance proceedings against him under the appropriate legislation. However, he had spoken about the possibility of seeking annulment from the early months of the marriage but had been dissuaded from doing anything about it by the pleas of the respondent, and the intervention of her parents. When the parties separated, he swore – and I have no reason to disbelieve his evidence in this respect – that he took legal advice and was advised by a solicitor friend of his that he had no real prospect of success and that he should do nothing until a change in the law had taken place. When the respondent commenced her maintenance proceedings he went back to the same solicitor, who then conceded that he was not sufficiently expert in matrimonial law and advised him to seek assistance from a firm of solicitors with more experience in this field. It was as a result of taking this advice that the petitioner says he first learned, in the year 1981, that he might well have grounds for bringing proceedings for nullity.

In the case of *Pettit v Pettit,* [1962] 3 All E.R. 37, at 41, Donovan L.J. makes the following comment:

> In a case where a potent spouse discovers after marriage that his partner is incapable, he may or may not know that the law grants him a remedy. If he does not know, and he goes on living with the incapable partner, he will almost invariably do things which afterwards can be used as evidence that he approbated the marriage. Outwardly, he may be just an ordinary husband taking his wife about as his wife, and no doubt asserting in writing year after year that is is a married man living with his wife and therefore entitled to the appropriate tax relief. But as from the moment that he knows he has a remedy, the situation alters. If he decides to seek it, it seems to me it would be quite unfair to deny it to him simply because, when ignorant of the law, he behaves like any ordinary decent husband. If, after knowing of his remedy, he acts in such a way as to show that he does not wish to avail himself of it, but on the contrary acquiesces in the situation, then it may well and fairly be said that he has approbated the marriage. I think therefore that knowledge of the facts and the law should be regarded as prerequisites of approbation.

I accept the foregoing as a correct statement of principle and I feel it is apt in the context of the present case. It appears to me that both parties allowed the marriage to drift along, hoping against hope that all would come right in the end, and that the petitioner moved with reasonable expedition when life together became intolerable for both of them. It is in his favour that as soon as the separation had taken place, he put in motion the necessary proceedings to secure an ecclesiastical annulment, and it is not without significance that the respondent has hitherto been rather uncooperative in the investigations which have to take place for the purpose of those proceedings.

I have considered carefully what has been urged by counsel for the respondent concerning the material benefits that the petitioner derived from the marriage, by way of financial and other assistance from the respondent's parents, and by way of services rendered by the respondent herself, but I do not conclude that the petitioner was any better off financially than if he had remained unmarried, and in many respects I think life would have been much more comfortable for him if he had not tried to set up house as a married man while still making his way through college as a medical student. Consequently I do not regard the history of the parties' life together as creating an equity in favour of the respondent which would render it unfair, or unjust, or contrary to public policy, to give the petitioner the relief he seeks.

Evershed MR said in the case of *W. v. W.*, [1952] P. 152, at 161:

> The question in my view in this case as in all such cases, is 'Has the husband or wife (as the case may be) by conduct or overt acts consistent only with such affirmation, approbated the existence and validity of the particular marriage, whatever may be its particular attributes'?

The opinion of Lord Watson in *G. v M.* 10 A.C., at 197 contains the following passage.

> I think that when those cases are dissected they do show the existence of this rule in the law of England, that in a suit for nullity of marriage there may be facts and circumstances proved which so plainly imply, on the part of the complaining spouse, a recognition of the existence and validity of the marriage, as to render it most inequitable and contrary to public policy that he or she should be permitted to go on to challenge it with effect.

I have had regard to these principles in considering all the circumstances of the present case, and I have concluded that while the conduct of the petitioner towards the respondent may have been harsh and unfeeling at times while they were living together and while he was enduring the frustration of being deprived of normal marital relations, there is not in evidence such delay or other forms of approbation of the marriage as would operate as a bar to the present proceedings for nullity.

I am indebted to the legal representatives of both parties for the exhaustive review of the law relating to nullity which they provided for the assistance of the court, and I only refrain from commenting in greater detail on the cases cited in argument by reason of the desirability of delivering judgment as expeditiously as possible.

I therefore pronounce and declare that the marriage which was had and solemnised on 8 January 1976 between the petitioner and the respondent was and is null and void by reason of the incapacity of the respondent to consummate the marriage.

Notes

Should the birth of a child be regarded as approbation? Cf. *Jackson*, 348. Should adoption be so regarded? Cf. *W.* v. *W.*, [1952] P. 152 (C.A.); *Slater* v. *Slater*, [1953] P. 235 (C.A., 1952); *B.* v. *B.* [1954] N.Z. L.R. 358 (C.A., 1952); *L.* v. *L.* [1954] N.Z.L.R. 386 (Sup. Ct., McGreson, J., 1953).

The Court may also dismiss a petition for a declaration of nullity of marriage where there has been collusion.

M. v. M.

Unreported, Supreme Court, 8 October 1979 (1978–109)

Henchy J.:

In these proceedings the wife as petitioner applied in the High Court for a decree of nullity. The ground relied on was the non-consummation of the marriage because of the husband's impotence. The primary questions settled by the Master of the High Court for the decision of the Court on the petition were:

1. Whether the marriage between the parties was consummated or not.
2. If the marriage was not consummated, was such non-consummation due to the incapacity of the husband to consummate the marriage?

When the case came for hearing in the High Court on the 9 May 1978 the wife gave full and detailed evidence to the effect that from the date of the marriage in April 1971 until she and the husband finally ceased to live together 6½ years later, in September 1977, they never succeeded in having sexual intercourse, and that this was due to the husband's incapacity. She was corroborated by a general practitioner who gave evidence that the husband came to see him about his impotence early in 1976, and by a consultant physician to whom the husband was then referred and who, because he considered the complaint of impotence to be due to psychological factors, referred the husband to a consultant psychiatrist (who was not called as a witness, but whose medical reports were referred to). The general practitioner, who saw the wife in October 1975, gave evidence that he was of the opinion that she was still a virgin. The husband, who was in court and was represented by counsel, gave evidence in which he admitted that, notwithstanding the best efforts of the wife and himself to act on the advice and guidance given to them by the consultant psychiatrist, consummation of the marriage had never been effected, and that the failure was due to his non-physical or psychological incapacity.

There the matter stood when the evidence concluded and the judge reserved judgment. Each of the four witnesses (the wife, the husband, the general practitioner and the consultant physician) left court without any suggestion having been made that their evidence was not truthful or credible. It was not suggested to the husband or the wife that they had acted collusively in the matter before the court. Nor was it suggested to the general practitioner or the consultant physician that they (or the consultant psychiatrist) had been misled into a wrong conclusion as to the husband's impotence and, therefore, as to the non-consummation of the marriage. The judge's note of the evidence adds up to an unrebutted and unquestioned case for the grant of a decree of nullity.

A fortnight later, however, when reserved judgment was delivered, the judge rejected the wife's case and dismissed the petition. He said he was not satisfied that consummation had not taken place. Nor was he satisfied as to the bona fides of the parties. He said he had little doubt but that they had mutually agreed if possible to have their marriage annulled, and he considered the attitude of the husband was to assist the case made by the wife. In effect, therefore, he held that he was not satisfied that the husband and wife had not acted collusively and had not given perjured evidence.

In my judgment, having regard to the unanimity of the evidence given and the conduct of the case generally, it was not open to the judge to refuse a decree of nullity for the reasons given. It is not in accordance with the proper administration of justice to cast aside the corroborated and unquestioned evidence of witnesses, still less to impute collusion or perjury to them, when they were not given any opportunity of rebutting such an accusation. To do so in this case was in effect to condemn them unheard, which is contrary to natural justice.

Having due regard to the degree of proof required to be established by a petitioner in a case such as this, I consider that a decree of nullity was the only verdict that was open on the evidence given. If the case were to be sent back to the High Court for rehearing, there is no reason to think that such a rehearing would yield any other verdict.

It is for the foregoing reasons that I concurred in the decision (which has already been announced) that this appeal should be allowed and a decree of nullity ordered on the ground that the marriage was not consummated because of the husband's incapacity.

Kenny and **Parke, JJ.** concurred.

Notes

1. A critic of the decision might say that it would impose on a trial judge who suspected collusion the obligation of entering the proceedings as a quasi-advocate, seeking to cross-examine the witnesses. Do you agree? Would the outcome of the case have been different if the Judge had merely gone through the formality of asking each of the parties whether he or she was telling the truth, and both had said that they were?

2. Compare Henchy, J.'s approach to uncontradicted evidence in *Norris* v. *A. G., infra*, p. 374 – a point noted by J. Kelly, *The Irish Constitution*, 276 (2nd ed., 1984).

E.P. v. M.C. (otherwise P.)

Unreported, High Ct., Barron, J., 13 March 1984

[The facts of the case are set out *supra*, p. 71, where the ground of duress is analysed. Briefly, the petitioner alleged that he married the respondent, who was pregnant with his child, because she had told him that, if he did not do so, she would have an abortion. On the question of collusion, **Barron, J.** said:]

The present attitude of the respondent is that she wants maintenance for her child but none for herself. This attitude has been expressed in two letters from the respondent's solicitors to the petitioner's solicitors. The first letter is dated the 24th May, 1983 and the body of the letter is as follows:–

> We have now taken instructions from our client and can state that provided proper arrangements are entered into by your client for the maintenance of the child of the marriage, . . . our client will not contest your client's petition. This is also conditional on your client maintaining both our client and the child of the marriage up until the decree is obtained.

The second letter dated 15th August, 1983 was even more explicit. The relevant part of this letter was as follows:–

> . . .our client instructs us that she is prepared to co-operate with your client and agrees that it was not her intention at the time of the alleged marriage to your client to cohabit with him. Clearly a consultation would need to take place to allow your counsel to clearly understand the nature of our client's proposed evidence. No doubt you will write to us about that in due course.

The rest of the letter dealt with the question of access to the child. This passage was certainly inaccurate in one respect. The parties did consummate their marriage on more than just an isolated occasion and the evidence shows that it was clearly their intention to cohabit as man and wife.

The petitioner alone gave evidence in this case. The respondent was not called to give any evidence. I believe the petitioner's evidence in the sense that I believe that he was trying to tell the truth as he now saw it. I am satisfied that the consultation suggested in the letter of the 15th August, 1983 did not take place and that in fact no efforts were made to follow up the suggestion contained in that or the earlier letter either by the petitioner himself or by his legal advisers.

The first question to be determined in any matrimonial suit is whether or not there is any collusion between the parties. The fact that one of them does not appear does not establish collusion. Collusion means essentially an agreement between the parties so that the true case is not presented to the Court. Its nature is fully discussed in *Churchward* v. *Churchward* [1895] P. 7. In that case, there was a written agreement between the parties. It provided that the husband should institute proceedings for divorce grounded upon the adultery of his wife – a fact which could not have been contested – against both his wife and the co-respondent with whom she was then living; that he would seek no damages against the co-respondent; and that he might retain out of his wife's assets an agreed sum for his costs.

Sir Frank Jeune P. at pp. 16 and 17 posed four questions in relation to collusion as follows:

> There would seem, therefore, to be four questions that may be asked. The first, is it collusion to procure the initiation and prosecution of a suit, and arrange the mode and terms of its conduct, by agreement, though there be no express stipulation that there shall be no defence, and no specific ground for suspicion that a false case is put forward or material facts concealed? Secondly, does the addition of a term that there shall be no defence

> render such an agreement collusion? Thirdly is it collusion when, besides such an agreement, there is ground for suspicion that material facts may be concealed? or, fourthly, is there collusion only when it is shown that, in consequence of such an agreement, false matter has been introduced into the case or material facts suppressed?

Having considered a considerable number of authorities he held that collusion had been established. He in effect answered the first three questions which he had posed in the affirmative and the fourth of them in the negative. At p. 31 he said:–

> In the present case, being of opinion, as I have said, that the initiation of the suit was procured and its results as to costs and damages settled by agreement, I think it must be held that there was collusion. If it be necessary to constitute collusion that there should be a compact not to defend, that also was present in this instance – there was evidence that such a term had been omitted from the agreement as the result of counsel's opinion – further, if it be needful that suspicion of the concealment of some facts be entertained, I entertain suspicion (I do not wish to say more) as to the facts of the husband's conduct from the expressions used by the wife in her letters. But I do not think it has been shown, nor in my opinion needed, that any specific facts of a material character exist which might have been brought before the Court.

In the present case, there is no specific agreement nor has any specific fact been concealed. Nevertheless the two letters to which I have referred show clearly the mind of the respondent which was to ensure that the relief sought in these proceedings was obtained on terms agreeable to her. This attitude must and does lead me to have a suspicion that if the respondent had given evidence the case might well have appeared differently. The onus of proof is on the petitioner to establish that there are no reasonable grounds for thinking that the true case has not been presented to the Court. In my view this onus has not been discharged. On this ground alone, the petitioner is not entitled to the relief sought. . . .

Notes

Do you agree with the holding in this decision? Why do you think that the two letters from the respondent's solicitors were put in evidence? Would it have been wrong for both parties to have failed to produce them in evidence? What, in your view, would have been the outcome of the case had the letter not been produced?

ALIMONY AND RELATED MATTERS

A wife is entitled to alimony *pendente lite* in nullity proceedings, provided that the fact of marriage is admitted or proved (cf. *Bird (alias Bell)* v. *Bird*, 1 Lee 209, 161 E.R. 78 (1753); *Countess of Portsmouth* v. *Earl of Portsmouth*, 3 Add. 63, 162 E.R. 404 (1826); *Smyth* v. *Smyth*, 2 Add. 254, 162 E.R. 287 (1824); *Miles* v. *Chilton*, 1 Rob. Ecc. 684, 163 E.R. 1178 (1849)). Permanent alimony may not, however, be awarded (*Bird (alias Bell)* v. *Bird*, 1 Lee 621, 161 E.R. 227 (1754)). Children of void marriages and of voidable marriages which have been annulled are illegitimate (subject to the possible limitations mentioned, *supra*, p. 81, note 2); it would normally be possible for maintenance proceedings to be brought on their behalf by the woman against the man under the affiliation code. The man would usually have 'contributed to the maintenance of the child within three years after the birth of this child' (section 2(2) (b) of the *Illegitimate Children (Affiliation Orders) Act 1930*, as amended by section 28(1) of the *Family Law (Maintenance of Spouses and Children) Act 1976*) in which case an order for maintenance may be made 'at any time after the contribution' (*id.*), provided paternity can be established – a requirement that should not prove difficult in many such cases. It should be noted that the affiliation code was not designed to deal with cases of void or voidable marriages and that the extent to which relief is available under it is to a large extent accidental.

As to the rules relating to property entitlements where a marriage is void or voidable, see *P.* v. *P. (By Amendment M'D.)* v. *P.* [1916] 2 I.R. 400 (C.A. 1916, aff'g K.B.Div., 1915); *In re Eaves: Eaves* v. *Eaves* [1940] Ch. 109 (C.A., 1939); *Dodsworth* v. *Dale* [1936] 2 K.B. 503 (Lawrence J.); *In re Rodwell deceased: Midgeley* v. *Rumbold* [1970] Ch. 726 (Pennycuick J., 1969); *Adams* v. *Adams* [1941] 1 K.B. 536 (C.A.)

Chapter 3

THE FAMILY OUTSIDE MARRIAGE

LEGITIMACY AND ILLEGITIMACY

The law makes important distinctions between 'legitimate' and 'illegitimate' persons. Legitimate status attaches to children born within marriage, whether they were conceived before or after the marriage was celebrated. Moreover, children conceived within the marriage but born after it has ended are legitimate. Thus, posthumous children are legitimate. There is no judicial authority on the status of a child conceived before marriage but born after the marriage has ended on account of the father's death. The Law Reform Commission in its *Report on Illegitimacy*, para. 3 (LRC4–1982), considers that, under present law, in such circumstances a legitimate status 'should on principle be recognised'. Finally, legitimacy may result from legitimation (considered *infra*, pp. 109–10).

Much has been written on the subject of illegitimacy in recent years. Worthy of particular attention are H. Krause, *Illegitimacy: Law and Social Policy* (1971), S. Hartley, *Illegitimacy* (1975) and D. Gill, *Illegitimacy, Sexuality and the Status of Women* (1977). For an historical account, are Elisofon, *A Historical and Comparative Study of Bastardy*, 2 Anglo-Amer. L. Rev. 306 (1973). The morality of imposing social stigma through the concept of illegitimacy is considered by Teichman, *Illegitimacy*, 8 J. of Med. Ethics 42 (1982).

PRESUMPTION OF LEGITIMACY

A.S. v. R.B., W.S. AND THE REGISTRAR GENERAL OF BIRTHS AND DEATHS

[1984] I.L.R.M. 66 (High Ct., O'Hanlon, J., 1982)

O'Hanlon, J.:

The first-named plaintiff, AS commenced proceedings by plenary summons dated 30 July 1981, followed by a statement of claim in which she averred that she was the wife of the defendant, WS; that she had been associating with one, RB, since in or about the month of January, 1980, and living with him since the month of May 1980; that on 19 February 1981, she gave birth to a male child, and that the said RB was the father of the said child.

She sought an order of the High Court declaring that the said RB is the father of the said child and directing the registrar-general of births and deaths to register the birth of the said child under the name RPB. The proceedings were later amended to include a claim that the registrar-general should be directed to register the name of RB as father of the said infant.

The defendant, WS, elected not to deliver a defence in the proceedings and he did not oppose any of the applications made. The registrar-general of births and deaths delivered a defence requiring formal proof of the matters averred in the statement of claim and referring to the presumption of law that the child was the child of the marriage of the plaintiff and of the defendant, WS. Subject to the matters thus pleaded, the registrar submitted to whatever order the court saw fit on the application of the plaintiff.

In the course of the proceedings an order was made striking out the name of RB as a defendant in the proceedings, and joining him as a co-plaintiff with AS and the plenary summons and statement of claim were amended to include a claim under the provisions of the *Guardianship of Infants Act, 1964*, seeking the appointment of the plaintiffs as joint guardians of the infant, RP, referred to in the proceedings. There was no formal objection to this application made by either of the two remaining defendants in the action.

Having regard to the nature of the proceedings in their final form, the first issue which arose for determination concerned the question of the paternity of the child, RP, Linked closely to that was the legal issue as to the evidence which was admissible to prove paternity. The three parties primarily concerned – AS, RB, and WS husband of AS – were all agreed that the child should be regarded as the child of AS and RB, and sought to establish this fact by oral evidence to be given by AS to confirm that sexual intercourse had not taken place between herself and her lawful husband, WS, for some considerable time before she finally left him in or about the month of January 1980 or at any time thereafter, and that the only person with whom she had sexual intercourse after leaving her husband was RB with whom she had been living as man and wife from an early stage in 1980. Counsel for the registrar formally drew the attention of the court to the fact that such evidence could not be allowed if what has come to be known as 'the rule in *Russell v Russell*' were applied. The evidence was tendered and admitted *de bene esse* pending the making of a ruling on its admissibility, as was the evidence of WS, who confirmed in every material respect what had been stated by his wife.

It is right to add that medical evidence was also adduced, based on blood tests taken from all four parties – the husband, the wife, the child, and the person alleged to be the true father of the child – which established to my satisfaction that the husband, WS, could not be the father of the child, and that there was a high degree of probability that RB was the father of the child. On this basis, strict proof by other evidence of non-access by the husband to the wife at the relevant times did not appear to be vital for the claim to succeed, but in deference to the care and research devoted by counsel to the preparation of the legal argument in relation to this part of the case I feel that I should express my views in relation to the important topic which was raised for consideration by the court.

The submission made by counsel for the wife and by counsel for her co-plaintiff, RB, was that the rule of evidence and procedure which would exclude evidence of non-access given by the husband or the wife, tending to prove that the child was illegitimate, never formed part of the law in this country, or if it did at any time that it was part of it no longer by reason of incompatibility with the provisions of the Constitution and the requirements of public policy.

The so-called 'rule in *Russell v Russell*' [1924] A.C. 687, derived from the majority decision of the House of Lords, was, in reality, an extension of a much older rule which the Lords found to have been recognised in a judgment of Lord Mansfield CJ in the case of *Goodright and Stevens v Moss* (1777) 2 Cowp. 591. In that case Lord Mansfield, founding himself upon an earlier statement of the law emanating from the Delegates, (formerly the Supreme Ecclesiastical Court of Appeal), declared the common law to be as follows:–

> The law of England is clear, that the declarations of a father or mother cannot be admitted to bastardize the issue born after marriage.

– and in a second passage from the same report:–

> As to the time of the birth, the father and mother are the most proper witnesses to prove it. But it is a rule founded on decency, morality and policy that they shall not be admitted to say after marriage, that they had had no connection and therefore that the offspring is spurious; more especially the mother who is the offending party. That point was solemnly determined at the Delegates.

What the House of Lords decided in *Russell v Russell* was, that the rule of procedure which, as formulated by Lord Mansfield, they found to have been acted upon in many decided cases in the intervening period, applied not merely to legitimacy proceedings in the strict sense of the term, but also to proceedings instituted in consequence of adultery seeking a dissolution of marriage.

In the present proceedings, the issue is one of legitimacy or illegitimacy and if the rule of law as formulated by Lord Mansfield now forms part of our law it would be necessary to reject out-of-hand the evidence of the husband and wife that such access did not take place between them as by the law of nature would be necessary for the husband to be the father of the child.

Some doubt has been cast by later text-book writers on the correctness of Lord Mansfield's statement of the law, and the 'solemn determination of the Delegates' to which he referred has never been discovered, but the general rule to which he referred was reiterated on so many occasions subsequently that it would be futile to contend that it did not form part of the common law of England at the time when it came be considered again by the House of Lords in *Russell v Russell.*

In a later Scottish case, *Burman v Burman* 1930 S.C. 262, the Lord Ordinary, Lord Murray, held that the rule in *Russell v Russell* did not form part of the law of Scotland, and that the evidence of spouses was admissible to bastardize a child born during wedlock. In that case a husband instituted proceedings after obtaining a divorce, seeking a declaration that a child born during the marriage was not his child and for a decree ordaining the defenders, (the mother and child), to desist from asserting that the child was the pursuer's child.

Lord Murray, having allowed evidence of non-access to be admitted 'under reservation of its competency', held that the evidence was admissible in accordance with Scottish law, but that the pursuer had failed to establish his case. He based his decision on the legal issue on a lengthy review of previous cases which had come before the courts in Scotland where evidence of this nature had been admitted, and concluded:–

> I am of opinion that the 'rule in *Russell*' has not, and never did have, any place in the law and practice of Scotland . . .It is not open to doubt that so far as the experience of the present generation goes, the practice of our court has been consistently conducted in view that no such rule obtains in our law . . . It is certain that the point was not overlooked.

I have been invited, in the present case, to come to a similar conclusion in relation to Irish law, and to hold that the 'rule in *Russell*', or more accurately, the rule as stated by Lord Mansfield in *Goodright & Stevens v Moss* in 1777, never became part of our law and should not now be applied in our courts. I am unable to conclude, however, that the rule did not form part of the common law of Ireland, just as it formed part of the common law of England. There is, and always has been, a considerable diversity as between the law of Scotland and the law of England, as Scotland after the Act of Union, 1707, retained its own system of law and legal terminology. The diversity has been particularly marked in matters of procedure, and I have found no line of authority here, corresponding to that relied upon by Lord Murray in *Burman v Burman*, which would support a conclusion that our common law in this important topic diverged from that applicable in England.

The application of the rule as part of Irish law was considered by the Supreme Court in *Mulhern v Clery*, [1930] I.R. 649, where an issue arose for determination as to whether PH and MS were married or were their children illegitimate and therefore unable to claim on intestacy. It was held that the will and codicils of PH were admissible in evidence as the rule excluding evidence of a parent tending to bastardize his children applies only where the fact of a marriage has been established and does not extend to a case where the question is whether there has been a marriage or not.
Kennedy C.J. said (at p. 667):–

> . . . If the will we had to consider was not a will of P.H. accepting paternity though unlawful, but a will of Daniel Sweeney repudiating paternity and disowning Margaret Sweeney's daughter, Ellen Harding, as begotten of him notwithstanding proof of the lawful marriage of Daniel and Margaret, Mr Bartley could make a strong case of the non-admissibility of the will in evidence upon the doctrine of Lord Mansfield in *Goodright & Stevens v Moss* as expounded by the majority of the Lords in *Russell v Russell.* But, to quote and adopt the opinion of Fry J in *Murray v Milner*, such a rule has nothing to do with a case in which the question is, marriage or no marriage.

Fitgibbon J., at p. 679, also proceeds on the basis that the rule formed part of Irish law, but had no application to the facts of that particular case. The third member of the court, Murnaghan J. accepted that the will was admissible in evidence, without referring to the legal argument to the contrary.

The legal issues which arose for determination in that case were obviously considered in great depth since it occupied the time of the Supreme Court for ten days or more, and at no stage does it appear to have occurred to counsel or to the court to suggest that what has come to be known as 'the rule in *Russell v Russell*' had no application in Irish law. I think it must be accepted that it formed part of our law up to the time of the enactment of the Constitution of Ireland in 1937, whatever may have been the position from that time forward. It was also accepted and acted upon by the Courts in Northern Ireland in the cases of *Park v Park and McBride*, [1946] N.I. 151, and *Smyth v Smyth and Gray*, [1948] N.I. 181. . . .

There remains for consideration the question whether the rule still forms part of our system of law following upon the enactment of the Constitution of 1937. In this regard it is relevant to consider the legal basis for the rule and the criticisms which have been directed against it from time to time.

The statements made by different judges to justify the existence of the rule have almost invariably been marked by an element of ambiguity. Lord Mansfield, when propounding the rule in 1777, said 'it is a rule founded on decency, morality and policy'. Lord Halsbury, in the *Poulett Peerage Case*, [1903] A.C. 395, at p. 399 referred to the rule in the following terms:

> My Lords, I can only say for my own part as regards the rule which I think most wisely and properly protects the sanctity of married intercourse and forbids it to be enquired into in any court of law . . .

Both of these statements were considered by the Law Lords in *Russell v Russell.* The Earl of Birkenhead said (at p. 699):–

> The rule . . . says, upon the contrary, that such evidence shall not be given at all; and the reason given is that it would tend, if given, to bastardize the issue and to invade the very special sanctity inherent in the conjugal relation; and the reason is assigned which led, first the delegates and then the ordinary courts, to a conclusion so widely expressed. It is a reason founded upon 'decency, morality and policy' . . .
>
> Lord Mansfield was not concerned with the grossness or indecency of the subject which the reception of such evidence might involve. Nor indeed, ought any judge who understands his business to trouble his head as to the indecency of evidence, if its examination be required for the elucidation of truth. No court is contaminated by examining any facts or reviewing any language which the administration of justice requires. Judges must do their duty, sacrificing if necessary their delicacy in the process. What Lord Mansfield meant was that a deeply-seated domestic and social policy rendered it unbecoming and indecorous that evidence should be received from such a source; upon such an issue; and with such a possible result. . . .

Lord Sumner, in a dissenting judgment, was highly critical of the rule, but felt bound to accept that it formed part of the law which had to be applied in cases where legitimacy was directly in issue. He refused to accept, however, that it should be extended to divorce cases or to any other area where the courts were not bound by precedent to apply it. His trenchant criticisms of the working of the rule in practice deserve serious consideration when assessing whether the rule survived the enactment of the new Constitution in our own jurisdiction. The relevant passages from his speech are as follows:–

> To say that the law does not permit married intercourse to be inquired into in any court of law is in conflict with the clear rule that it can be and always is inquired into in nullity cases, in condonation cases whether there is a child or not, and in cases where cruelty by the communication of venereal disease is alleged. My Lords, neither can I find any guidance in applying the rule in Lord Mansfield's words, 'decency, morality and public policy'. The last tells us nothing. All our law, even statute law, is supposed to rest on public policy, but as public policy is an evolving, not to say an unstable thing, the public policy of one century may not be quite the same as that of the next but one. In a matter like the present the word morality tells us nothing, for what moralists

condemn, the law ignores. What the petitioner described was outside the law but it was a matter of fact. Upon these three subjects, morality, decency and public policy, I will only say this. If it had been feasible for the petitioner to have given evidence of 'non access' by the mouth of some third person, some chambermaid or spy, or it may be by the wife's written confession that the child was not his and that nothing had taken place between the spouses that could have made it his, he could have taken his proceedings and called this evidence and if he failed to obtain his decree it would not have been decency or morality or the bastardizing of the child that would have defeated him but the incredulity of the jury. If, on the other hand, the evidence which his case required was merely something 'tending to prove non-access' as for example, absence from home, then a well-to-do man able to afford the search for and the production of the evidence of third persons to prove it would get his decree, but a labourer who had roamed the country in search of work and could only prove his absence from home by his own evidence would find his mouth closed on a vital point and would remain tied to an unfaithful wife and bound to maintain another's child in the name of a rule founded on public policy . . . (p. 743).

If he secures his decree, he can, on the question of the custody of the child, close her mouth as to its paternity and keep from her the child whom he and she both know to be her paramour's. As for the child, he must console himself for a bleak and unkindly childhood by reflecting, when of age, how scrupulously the law has safeguarded his status of legitimacy. (p. 745).

My Lords, I am afraid that the sanctity of married intercourse passed into the limbo of 'lost causes and impossible loyalties' in 1857. You cannot give spouses the legal right to have their married life investigated in open court with a view to its formal and legal termination without being prepared when necessary to violate the sanctity of that life. The law recognises this. The Divorce Court sits that the secrets of married life may be divulged. Its decorum is preserved by those who preside and those who practice in it, and is preserved with extraordinary success (p. 746).

To my mind the only logical and legal solution is to recognise what is legally true, that a divorce petition and a legitimacy issue are distinct; to apply the rule which is essentially a legitimacy rule when, but only when, the courts have been wont to apply it before and to establish in a court which exercises a separate and statutory jurisdiction the principle that all relevant evidence is admissible unless it is excluded by Act of Parliament.

My Lords, my own view is that in the administration of justice nothing is of higher importance than that all relevant evidence should be admissible and should be heard by the tribunal that is charged with deciding according to the truth. To ordain that a court should decide upon the relevant facts and at the same time that it should not hear some of those relevant facts from the person who best knows them and can prove them at first hand seems to me to be a contradiction in terms. It is best that truth should out and that truth should prevail. With this, if the matter were one of first impression and we were free to lay down an ideal procedure, I think all must agree. As it is, the rule in *Goodright's* case exists and must be applied, but only when it is applicable. It is of ancient origin, the product of conditions no longer clearly known and of social necessities no longer existing in the form in which they arose. The reasons for it have been variously stated, and have never been very clear. I can be no party to the extension of such a rule to new cases where it must work anomalously and cannot produce the results for which it appears to have been devised.

It is a matter of some significance that the rule in *Russell v Russell* survived for only 26 years in England after its enunciation by the House of Lords, and was then swept away – not merely for divorce proceedings but for the purpose of all legal proceedings – by the *Matrimonial Causes Act, 1950*, s. 32 of which provides as follows:–

32 (1) Notwithstanding any rule of law, the evidence of a husband or wife shall be admissible in any proceedings to prove that marital intercourse did or did not take place between them during any period.

I am of opinion that the rule did not continue as part of our law after the enactment of the Constitution of Ireland in 1937. Art. 50 carried forward the laws in force in Saorstát Éireann 'subject to this Constitution and to the extent to which they are not inconsistent therewith'. I have already indicated that I consider that the rule in *Russell v Russell* formed part of those laws immediately prior to the enactment of the Constitution. In what manner was it inconsistent therewith?

Art. 34.1 provides that 'Justice shall be administered in courts established by law by judges appointed in the manner provided by this Constitution . . .' The High Court is given 'full original jurisdiction and power to determine all matters and questions whether of law or fact, civil or criminal.' Art. 38.1 provides that 'No person shall be tried on any criminal charge save in due course of law.'

Art. 40.3.1°. The State guarantees in its law to respect, and, as far as practicable, by its laws to defend and vindicate the personal rights of the citizen.
2. The State shall, in particular, by its laws protect as best it may from unjust attack and, in the case of injustice done, vindicate the life, person, good name and property rights of every citizen.

That the Constitution guarantees a right of access to the courts has been recognised and stressed in a number of cases, notably in *MacAuley v Minister for Posts and Telegraphs* [1966] I.R 345; *O'Brien v Keogh* [1972] I.R. 144, and *In re Art. 26 of the Constitution and The Emergency Powers Bill, 1976,* [1977] I.R. 159.

The combined effect of the abovementioned constitutional provisions appears to me to guarantee (*inter alia*) something equivalent to the concept of 'due process' under the American Constitution in relation to causes and controversies litigated before the courts. It is not so long ago since the law applicable both here and in England excluded from the witness box the parties to an action and their husbands and wives, apparently to protect them from 'the temptation to forswear themselves'. This remarkable rule of the common law, which applied even to the defendant in a criminal proceeding, survived into the 19th century, until a series of statutes passed in the second half of that century made the parties and their spouses competent witnesses in civil and criminal proceedings. Similarly, an accused person in a criminal proceeding could not be represented by counsel until quite a late stage of the development of the criminal law. It appears to me that if our Legislature were now to attempt to reintroduce these outmoded rules of the common law as features of the administration of justice within our jurisdiction, such legislation could not withstand constitutional challenge as it would be repugnant to modern thinking as to what constitutes fair procedures and the due administration of justice in the courts.

The rule in *Russell v Russell* appears to me to be a lone survivor into the twentieth century of these narrow and outmoded rules of procedure and to be no more capable of surviving the test of consistency with the Constitution than the other and more extreme examples already referred to. So long as the rule could be invoked it affected in a vital manner the interests of four different parties – the husband, the wife, the child, and the person who was alleged to be the true father of the child. The rule appears to have evolved from a concern to protect the child from the stigma, and loss of status and property rights, involved in a finding of illegitimacy. Lord Dunedin in *Russell v Russell* said:

> The whole point of Lord Mansfield's dictum rests on the concluding words: 'and to make the issue spurious', in other words it is when conjugal conduct is used, not as a thing in itself, but as leading to other inferences that the harm comes in . . .

As other judges have pointed out, however, it is impossible to calculate the harm that may be done to the child, as well as to the true parents of the child, if issues of legitimacy and paternity have to be determined by the courts without permitting the parties who can give the most cogent evidence in relation to these issues to give that evidence. Custody of the child may be denied to its true parents and may be given to someone with no ties either of blood or affection with the child. A husband may be prevented from giving evidence which will prove that he is not the father of the child, and he may be left with the legal obligation to support and maintain the offspring of an adulterous relationship between his wife and a third party.

Just as parties have a right of access to the courts when this is necessary to defend or vindicate life, person, good name or property rights, so they have a constitutional entitlement to fair procedures when they get to court. (In *Re Padraic Haughey*, [1971] I.R. 217; judgment of ÓDálaigh, C.J., at pp. 263–264). I find the concept that a spouse shall not be allowed to rebut the presumption of legitimacy which exists in favour of all issue born to the wife during the subsistence of the marriage, by proving non-access at the relevant time by his or her own direct evidence, to be inconsistent with this constitutional guarantee of fairness in procedures. In the words of Lord Sumner: 'In the administration of justice, nothing is of higher importance than that all relevant evidence should be admissible and should be heard by the tribunal that is charged with deciding according to the truth . . . It is best that truth should out and that truth should prevail.'

The same principle was expressed in similar language by Lord Murray in *Burman:* 'Any public policy resting on the sanctity inherent in the conjugal relation . . . must yield to the paramount public policy of ascertaining truth and doing justice'.

Because the rule in *Russell v Russell* ran counter to that paramount public policy and was calculated to defeat the due and proper administration of justice, I would hold that it ceased to have legal effect in the State after the enactment of the Constitution in 1937.

I now have to consider the legal consequences of the findings already made in the course of this judgment. On the evidence before me I am satisfied that the infant, RP who was born to the plaintiff, AS on 19 February, 1981, is the son of RB, the second-named plaintiff in the proceedings as reconstituted.

The obligations of the registrar of births and deaths are spelt out in the *Registration of Births and Deaths (Ireland) Act 1863*, as amended by the *Births and Deaths Registration Act (Ireland) 1880* S. 7 of the later Act provides as follows:–

> 7. In the case of an illegitimate child, no person shall, as father of such child, be required to give information under this Act concerning the birth of such child, and the registrar shall not enter in the register the name of any person as the father of such child unless at the joint request of the mother and of the person acknowledging himself to be the father of such child, and such person shall in such case sign the register together with the mother.

Application was made to the registrar-general in the present case to register the details concerning the birth, and to register the name of RB as the father of the child. This the registrar declined to do without the direction of the court, having regard to the presumption of legitimacy when the child was born during the subsistence of the marriage of AS and WS. I think he was right in the course he adopted. For the future, if all three parties – the husband, the wife, and the putative father – concur in the application to have the putative father registered as the father of the infant, it would, in my opinion, be in order for the registrar to act on such an application but in a case where there is, or may be a contest as to paternity he is not given any jurisdiction under the Act to decide when the presumption of legitimacy has been rebutted.

In the present case I propose to give a direction to the registrar-general, as sought by the plaintiffs, requiring him to register the birth in the usual manner, and to register the name of RB as the father of the child.

I will award the custody of the child to the plaintiffs jointly, until further order, but I do not propose to make any order as to guardianship, save to make an order declaring that the mother, AS, is guardian of the infant, as provided by s. 6(4) of the *Guardianship of Infants Act 1964*, in relation to illegitimate infants. S. 11 (4) of the Act entitles the natural father of an infant to apply to the court in relation to the custody of the infant and the right of access thereto of his father (including the natural father) or mother, but where the infant already has a guardian the Act does not appear to me to contemplate that the natural father may be appointed as a guardian jointly with the mother.

The findings made in the course of this judgment on the issue of paternity, and any orders consequent thereon, are not intended to be binding on the infant, RP, who is not a party to these proceedings, and are made without prejudice to any proceedings that may at any time hereafter be instituted by or on behalf of the said infant as to the issue of his legitimacy or otherwise howsoever.

Notes

1. The decision is analysed by Binchy, *Marriage, Paternity and Illegitimacy*, 17 Irish Medical Times No. 6, p. 26 (1983), and by O'Connor, '*The Rule in Russell* v. *Russell*', 1 Ir. L. Times (n.s.) 76 (1983).

2. Do you agree with the holding? Did O'Hanlon, J. give sufficient consideration to the risk of fraudulent repudiation of paternity?
3. The rule in *Russell* v. *Russell* has been abolished in most jurisdictions for several years: cf. the Law Reform Division, New Brunswick Department of Justice Working Paper, *Status of Children Born Outside Marriage: Their Rights and Obligations and the Rights and Obligations of Their Parents*, p. 10 (1974).
4. Why were no relevant cases from the United States cited, when the concept of 'due process' was invoked? Courts and commentators in the United States have addressed the problem: see, e.g. *Davis* v. *Davis*, 521 S.W. 2d 603 (Tex. Sup. Ct., 1975); H. Clark, *Domestic Relations: Cases and Problems*, 251 (2nd ed., 1974).
5. Before the judgment was handed down, the Law Reform Commission, in its *Report on Illegitimacy* (LRC 4–1982) had made recommendations very similar in their effect to what *A.S.* v. *R.B. & the Registrar General of Births & Deaths* decided. Do you consider that this decision is a reason for greater or less urgency in relation to the general reform of the law on illegitimacy?

LEGITIMATION

Legitimation by subsequent marriage has been part of our law since 1931. Section 1 of the *Legitimacy Act 1931* provides as follows:–

—(1) Subject to the provisions of this section where the parents of an illegitimate person marry or have married one another, whether before or after the commencement of this Act, the marriage shall, if the father of the illegitimate person was or is at the date of the marriage domiciled in Saorstát Éireann, render that person, if living, legitimate from the commencement of this Act, or from the date of the marriage, whichever is the later.

(2) Nothing in this Act shall operate to legitimate a person unless the father and mother of such person could have been lawfully married to one another at the time of birth of such person or at some time during the period of ten months preceding such birth. . . .

Subsection (2) of section 1 is designed to prevent the legitimation of children conceived in adultery, although it is drafted in a manner that results in anomalies: cf. *Shatter*, 168–169.

Legitimation by subsequent marriage enables the legitimated person (and his or her spouse, children or remoter issue) to take only those interests in property specified in the *Legitimacy Act 1931*. Sections 3 to 6 of the Act provide as follows.–

3.—(1) Subject to the provisions of this Act, a legitimated person and his spouse, children or more remote issue shall be entitled to take any interest:–

(*a*) in the estate of an intestate dying after the date of legitimation;

(*b*) under any disposition coming into operation after the date of legitimation;

(*c*) by descent under an estate in tail created after the date of legitimation;

in like manner as if the legitimated person had been born legitimate.

(2) Where the right to any property, real or personal, depends on the relative seniority of the children of any person, and those children include one or more legitimated persons, the legitimated person or persons shall rank as if he or they had been born on the day when he or they became legitimated by virtue of this Act, and if more than one such legitimated person became legitimated at the same time, they shall rank as between themselves in order of seniority.

(3) Where property real or personal or any interest therein is limited in such a way that, if this Act had not been passed, it would (subject or not to any preceding limitations or charges) have devolved (as nearly as the law permits) along with a dignity or title of honour, then nothing in this Act shall operate to sever the property or any interest therein from such dignity or title of honour, but the same shall go and devolve (without prejudice to the preceding limitations or charges aforesaid) in like manner as if this Act had not been passed. This sub-section applies, whether or not there is any express reference to the dignity or title of honour, and notwithstanding that in some events the property or some interest therein may become severed therefrom.

(4) This section applies only if and so far as a contrary intention is not expressed in the disposition, and shall have effect subject to the terms of the disposition and to the provisions therein contained.

4.—Where a legitimated person or a child or remoter issue of a legitimated person dies intestate in respect of all or any of his real or personal property, the same persons shall be entitled to take the same interests therein as they would have been entitled to take if the legitimated person had been born legitimate.

5.—Where an illegitimate person dies after the commencement of this Act and before the marriage of his parents leaving any spouse, children or remoter issue living at the date of such marriage, then, if that person would, if living at the time of the marriage of his parents, have become a legitimated person, the provisions of this Act with respect to the taking of interests in property by, or in succession to, the spouse, children and remoter issue of a legitimated person (including those relating to the rate of death duties) shall apply as if such person as aforesaid had been a legitimated person and the date of the marriage of his parents had been the date of legitimation.

6.—A legitimated person shall have the same rights and shall be under the same obligations in respect of the maintenance and support of himself or of any other person as if he had been born legitimate, and subject to the provisions of this Act, the provisions of any Act relating to claims for damages, compensation, allowance, benefit or otherwise by or in respect of a legitimate child shall apply in like manner in the case of a legitimated person.

The general effect of section 3 is to treat the date of the child's legitimation as equivalent to the date of his or her birth, so far as property entitlements are concerned. This can be important in relation to deeds or wills coming into operation before the date of legitimation, which make entitlement to property contingent on seniority of birth: cf. *Shatter*, 169, Law Reform Commission, *Report on Illegitimacy*, paras. 27–28 (LRC 4-1982). For a practical example of the effects of section 5, see *Bromley*, 579. The private international law aspects of legitimation are discussed by the Law Reform Commission in Working Paper No. 10–1981, *Domicile and Habitual Residence as Connecting Factors in the Conflict of Laws*, pp. 52–54.

THE CONSTITUTIONAL POSITION OF THE LEGITIMATED CHILD

IN RE J., AN INFANT
[1966] I.R. 295 (High Court)

TEEVAN, J.:

The salient facts are these: the prosecutors are husband and wife and they are the parents of the child whom the respondents retain in their custody and refuse to deliver to her parents. When the baby was born the parents had not yet married, and at the time that the custody of the respondents commenced, the baby was the illegitimate child of the mother. At that time the putative father had no legal right over the child. The mother was most anxious then that her delivery of a child should be kept as secret as possible. She had possibly another selfish motive for parting with her baby as soon after the birth as would be possible or practicable. She was considering the suit of another man, that is, other than the father of her child. Her motives then for parting with the child were selfish but, although this is so, she had some concern for her baby's welfare. This is evidenced by the fact that, through the agency of the community of nuns with whom she stayed for her confinement, the baby was placed in the care of excellent adopters, the respondents, with the intention of ultimate legal adoption under the Adoption Acts. With the intending adopters was found a home and environment superior in every way to what the mother was likely to be able to establish for the baby. The intended adoption failed because of non-observance of a fundamental statutory requirement. After the baby was placed in the care of adopters, the father renewed his suit with the mother and she ultimately accepted him in preference to the other suitor and father and mother were married on the 2nd August, 1965. The effect of this marriage has been to legitimate the child, who is now the legitimate child of the prosecutors. Having arranged for marriage with the father, the mother requested the return of their child, and the respondents, having developed great affection for her, refuse to hand her over.

It is well established that not only has the child an excellent home and excellent prospects, but that the respondents bestow on her the affection of parents to a child, and the child by now accepts them as parents. If they must part, it will be a sad parting and one that must deeply affect the child, with the undoubted prospect of some permanent effect. While the father is not in as good a position or as firmly set up as the 'adoptive' father, he is in lucrative employment and of means ample to establish and maintain a comfortable home for his family. He has taken the first step in that direction in that he has arranged joint residence in a house in London with a friend and his wife. It may not be an ideal, or even prudent, plan, but that is his own affair. He is entitled to order his family life as seems best or commendable to himself. It is sufficient to say that the father has the means to provide adequately for the needs and welfare of his child.

Originally the respondents' custody of the child was legal, for it was with the consent, indeed on the desire and request, of the mother that the infant, then an illegitimate child, was placed in such custody. The mother has withdrawn her consent to the child remaining in the custody of the respondents. The respondents, nevertheless, refuse to return the child to her parents. The respondents are devoid of right in the matter. They have no legal right to or over the child. They cannot therefore set up a right in themselves as a cause against an order of *habeas corpus*. To my mind that is the end of the case. The parents' right to custody is absolute unless and until forfeited in a way already well defined in many authoritative cases and in s. 14 of the *Guardianship of Infants Act, 1964*, or, stated shortly, unless and until they have been shown to be unfit or unwilling or unable to discharge their complementary duties to the child.

It is contended, however, that as the Court is bound to look to the welfare of the child as the first and paramount consideration in virtue of s. 3 of the Act of 1964, the child's welfare takes precedence of the legal right of the parents to custody, which should be disregarded if such welfare would be better served by leaving the child with the adopters. It is contended that the evidence establishes that the welfare of this infant would be better served by leaving the custody with the respondents and psychiatric evidence has been adduced which establishes a risk to the future health of the child by severance from the respondents, whom the child now regards as her parents. In effect the answer is that the child's welfare will be more secure and be at less risk in the future in the adopters' home than in her parents' home. In my opinion this is irrelevant and erroneous. To be valid it would have to be shown that s. 3 of the Act of 1964 effects a change in the law as it stood prior to that enactment, and that the section purports to diminish or curtail the rights of parents to the absolute control over their children. If it does, then, as Mr. Justice Henchy will say in the judgment he is about to read, a question of its constitutionality might arise. We are not, however, confronted with any such question in the present case and, as Mr. Justice Murnaghan . . . show[s], while in form this is a proceeding for *habeas corpus* it is in reality a process to obtain determination by the Court of the issue of the proper custody of the child.

Whatever difficulties may call for resolution in some other case in the future, in the present case we have parents ready, willing, able and anxious to set up a family home. Nothing has been or can be urged to suggest their unfitness for their responsibilities and duties as parents – nothing of such an order that the Court should treat their legal right to custody of their child as forfeit. In such circumstances the Court must presume that restoration to her parents is the best thing for the child's welfare. It has not been shown by the respondents that to restore her to her parents would imperil the child's welfare.

Henchy, J.:

. . . The present position as to the legal status of the child is that the purported adoption is a nullity and, because the father was at all times domiciled in this State and he and the mother could have been lawfully married to one another when the child was born, the subsequent marriage of the parents operated to make the child their legitimate daughter from the date of the marriage (s. 1 of the *Legitimacy Act, 1931*). Notwithstanding the fact that the adoption has turned out to be of no legal effect under the Adoption Acts, the adopters have refused to give up the child to its parents, and the parents are the prosecutors in the present proceedings for an order making absolute a conditional order of *habeas corpus* against the adopters for the return of the child.

The prosecutors' claim for the custody of the child is this: they say that they and the child form a family for the purposes of Articles 41 and 42 of the Constitution and that this fact, in the circumstances of this case, gives them an absolute right to the custody of the child. The respondents, on the other hand, say that Articles 41 and 42 make no change in the pre-Constitution law governing the right to the custody of infants, that the question is to be decided by reference to the infant's welfare, and that this approach has been given statutory reinforcement by s. 3 of the *Guardianship of Infants Act, 1964*. . . .

In construing Articles 41 and 42 for the purposes of the present case, the first question to be decided is whether the father, mother and child together constitute a family. I am of the opinion that they do. It is true that the child was born illegitimate and, therefore, outside a family, but by its parents' marriage it has clearly become a legitimate child of the marriage. I find it impossible to distinguish between the constitutional position of a child whose legitimacy stems from the fact that he was born the day after his parents were married, and that of a child whose legitimacy stems from the fact that his parents were married the day after he was born. In the former case the child is legitimate and a member of the family from birth by operation of the common law; in the latter case, by operation of the statute, from the date of his parents' marriage. The crucial fact in each case is that the child's legitimacy and consequent membership of the family are founded on the parents' marriage. The Constitution gives no definition of the family, but it does recognise, in Article 41, section 3, sub-s. 1°, that it is founded on the institution of marriage. I am satisfied that s. 1 of the *Legitimacy Act, 1931*, operated to endow the child in this case with membership of a family founded on the institution of marriage. It is an example of the way in which certain constitutional rights – for example, citizenship and rights founded on citizenship – may be conferred by the operation of an Act of Parliament. It is, of course, essential that such a statutory provision should not offend against the Constitution; but there is no suggestion in the present case that s. 1 of the *Legitimacy Act, 1931*, is unconstitutional.

The fact that the parents and the child constitute a family enables the prosecutors to invoke Article 42, section 1, of the Constitution, by which the State acknowledges that the primary and natural educator of the child is the family and guarantees to respect the inalienable right and duty of parents to provide, according to their means, for the religious and moral, intellectual, physical and social education of their children. In the present case it would be impossible, because of the age of the child (17 months), to give effect to the parents' right and duty of education if they are not given custody of the child. The only way in which the parents' right and duty of educating this child could be supplanted would be by bringing the case within section 5 of Article 42, which provides that, in exceptional cases, where the parents for physical or moral reasons fail in their duty towards their children, the State as guardian of the common good by appropriate means shall endeavour to supply the place of the parents, but always with due regard for the natural and imprescriptible rights of the child. Assuming that it would be competent for this Court, functioning as the State in its judicial aspect, to endeavour to supply the place of the parents in a case where section 5 of Article 42 would otherwise apply, I am not satisfied that this is such a case. Even if it be said that the mother for physical or moral reasons failed in her duty towards the child, I am not satisfied that the father did so. And I am quite satisfied that since at least the date of their marriage (2nd August, 1965, when the child was some 8 months old) both parents have been ready, willing and able to educate the child. Whatever may have been the position before then, I do not think it could be said that since then the parents for physical or moral reasons have failed in their duty towards the child. The Supreme Court has said that 'sub-Article 5 does not enable the Legislature to take away the right of a parent who is in a position to do so to control the education of his child, where there is nothing culpable on the part of either parent or child': *Re Doyle, an Infant* (1955; unreported). If it does not enable the Legislature to do so, then it does not enable the courts; and it has not been suggested that there has been anything culpable on the part of the parents since at least the date of their marriage. I am of the opinion that this is not one of the exceptional cases provided for by section 5 of Article 42 and that the prosecutors' rights and duties recognised by section 1 of Article 42 can be met only by awarding them the custody of the child.

If I am correct in my application of the Constitution to the facts of this case, the parents' right to the custody of the child is conclusively established without looking further than Articles 41 and 42. But counsel for the adopters say that s. 3 of the *Guardianship of Infants Act, 1964*, requires that in deciding the question of custody we must regard the welfare of the infant as the first and paramount consideration; and s. 2 of the Act defines 'welfare' as comprising 'the religious and moral, intellectual, physical and social welfare of the infant.' Having regard to the inalienable right and duty of parents to provide for the education of their children, and their right in appropriate cases to obtain custody of the children for that purpose, I consider that s. 3 must be interpreted in one or other of the following ways; first, by regarding it as unconstitutional, or, secondly, by reading it in conjunction with Articles 41 and 42 as stating, in effect, that the welfare of the infant in the present case coincides with the parents' right to custody. I need not choose between these two approaches, as neither could affect the conclusion I have already reached that the parents must have the custody. I wish , however, to make it clear that I expressly reserve an opinion (counsel not having raised the matter) as to whether it was competent for the Legislature to provide that in a case such as this, where the parents are jointly seeking custody of their child for the purpose of giving effect to their inalienable right and duty to provide for its education, the court should be bound to decide the question of custody by regarding the welfare of the infant as the first and paramount consideration.

I would disallow the cause shown and make absolute the conditional order.

Murnaghan, J.:

. . . Mr. Bell submitted that by virtue of the provisions of Articles 41 and 42 of the Constitution the parents are now absolutely entitled to the custody of the infant. Neither of these Articles deals with custody as such. Article 40, section 4, sub-section 2°, of the Constitution deals with cases where it is alleged that a person is unlawfully detained and provides for the release of a person unlawfully detained from such custody. I am aware that on occasions that Article has been invoked in cases of this kind, but in my opinion its provisions do not provide an appropriate method of procedure for obtaining a decision on the proper custody of an infant. Mr. Bell did not specifically state on what basis he made his application. I take it that in the circumstances this application is based on the provisions of s. 10, sub-s. 2 (*a*), of the *Guardianship of Infants Act, 1964* (hereinafter referred to as 'the Act'), which provides, in so far as material, as follows:- '(2) . . . a guardian under this Act (*a*), as guardian of the person, shall, as against every person not being, jointly with him, a guardian of the person, be entitled to the custody of the infant and shall be entitled to take proceedings for the restoration of his custody of the infant against any person who wrongfully . . . detains the infant . . .'

Regarded as proceedings under s. 10, sub-s. 2 (*a*). the provisions of s. 3 of the Act apply. Applying those provisions, and having regard to all the circumstances of this case, I would award the custody of the infant to the parents.

The natural rights of parents to the custody of their infant, recognised by the common law, are limited by the provisions of s. 14 of the Act. The provisions of that section, and likewise of s. 16 of the Act, do not apply to the facts of this case. This leaves for consideration only the question of the welfare of the infant having regard to the provisions of s. 3 of the Act.

As a general principle, the best place for an infant is with its parents. This is not to say that, since the coming into operation of the *Adoption Act, 1952*, there is any great difference between parents and adopting persons under that Act, because experience has, I think, shown that there is little if anything to choose between the loving care of parents for their natural children and that of adopting parents for their adopted children. I find it unnecessary here to go into a minute consideration of the respective benefits which, on the reasonable probabilities, would accrue to the infant from the custody of the parents or from the custody of the adopters. From the purely material point of view, I would think that the advantage lies with the adopters. From the point of view of nurture, affection and control, I would think that there is little or nothing to choose between the parents and the adopters. There is, however, another aspect. If left in the custody of the adopters, it seems to me that the position of the infant would be anomalous. In the existing circumstances the infant is not an adopted child, while by reason of the marriage of the parents it is now legitimated and, as a result, can never be adopted, except in the unlikely event of the death of both the parents before the infant reaches the age of twenty-one. Further, the parents have an inalienable right and duty to provide for the infant's religious, moral, intellectual, physical and social education which if they sought to exercise them while the infant was in the custody of the adopters, would create difficulties that would not, in my view, be consistent with the infant's welfare. For these reasons, and looking broadly at the question of the welfare of the infant, I have come to the conclusion that the infant should now be returned to the custody of the parents.

Notes

1. What are the chances of success, in your view, of a challenge to the constitutionality of the *Legitimacy Act 1931* insofar as it restricts the property rights of legitimated persons?
2. Assume that legislation is enacted abolishing the status of illegitimacy and repealing the *Legitimacy Act 1931*. Consider the case of a child after this legislation who is born outside marriage but whose parents later marry. What is the constitutional position of the child (a) during the period between his or her birth and the parents' marriage; (b) after the marriage?

AFFILIATION PROCEEDINGS

Financial support obligations in relation to children born outside marriage are governed by the *Illegitimate Children (Affiliation Orders) Act 1930* as amended by the *Courts Act 1971* and the *Family Law (Maintenance of Spouses and Children) Act 1976.* The legislative structure is cumbersome and complex: the philosophy and 'tone' of the 1930 Act contrast strongly with those of the 1976 Act. The legislation is in its present state because in 1976, when family maintenance obligations of spouses were being fundamentally reformed, there was strong pressure to reform the law relating to affiliation as well. The Minister for Justice accepted the argument that it was better to take the available opportunity to introduce important reforms in relation to affiliation, even if this involved complexities in drafting, rather than leave the law unreformed until a comprehensive reform was possible. The position is explained in the Law Reform Commission's *Report on Illegitimacy*, paras. 72ff. (LRC 4–1982). The subject as a whole is analysed in detail by Horgan, *The Financial Support of Illegitimate Children*, 11 Ir. Jur. (n.s.) 59 (1976).

PROOF OF PATERNITY

Section 3(2) of the *Illegitimate Children (Affiliation Orders) Act 1930* provides that the Court is not to be satisfied that a person is the putative father of an illegitimate child:–

> without hearing the evidence of the mother of such child and also evidence corroborative in some material particular or particulars of the evidence of the mother.

Section 1 of the Act provides that:–

> In this Act – the word 'mother' means any of the following persons who is with child or has been delivered of an illegitimate child, that is to say, any single woman or any widow, or any married woman living separate from her husband, and includes any married woman not living separate from her husband who before her marriage was delivered of an illegitimate child; and the expression 'putative father' means a person adjudged by an affiliation order made under this Act to be the putative father of an illegitimate child.

MORRISSEY v. BOYLE

[1942] I.R. 514 (Supreme Court, 1941)

Sullivan, C.J.:

This case comes before us on a Case Stated by the Judge from the Dublin Circuit Court on the hearing of an appeal from an order of the District Justice dismissing an application under the *Illegitimate Children (Affiliation Orders) Act, 1930*, made by Johanna Morrissey against Michael Boyle.

On the hearing of the appeal evidence was given by the appellant, by her father J.P. Morrissey, and by Guard John Maher. At the conclusion of their evidence counsel on behalf of the respondent asked the learned Judge to dismiss the appeal on the ground that there was no evidence corroborative in any material particular of the evidence of the appellant, as required by s. 3, sub-s. 2, of the said Act. That application was refused, but the learned Judge stated this Case, in which this Court is asked to determine whether he was right in refusing that application.

Sect. 3, sub-s. 2, of the Act provides:–

'No Justice of the District Court shall be satisfied that a person is the putative father of an illegitimate child without hearing the evidence of the mother of such child and also evidence corroborative in some material particular or particulars of the evidence of such mother.'

A similar provision in s. 4 of the *Bastardy Laws (Amendment) Act, 1872*, was considered by the Court of Appeal in England in *Thomas* v. *Jones* [1921] 1 K. B. 22, cited by Mr. Casey in the course of his argument. In his judgment in that case Scrutton L.J. said–'What is meant by "corroboration in some material particular" – that is, in a material fact? The vital fact to be proved in a bastardy case is that a child has been born to the applicant as the result of sexual connection with the man. From the nature of the case it is almost inevitable that there never will be any direct corroboration of sexual connection. The evidence in corroboration must always be circumstantial evidence of the main fact, that is to say, evidence from which it may be inferred that the main fact happened. For instance, the fact that the man has had connection with the woman and a child has resulted is sometimes inferred from evidence of previous affection, that they had been seen together showing affection to each other. Sometimes it is inferred from the fact of subsequent affection – that the man and woman are seen together showing signs of affection. Sometimes it is inferred from the fact that the man has done acts which may be treated as recognising responsibility for the child as his child, statements that he will provide for the child, payments for the child, all facts from which as a matter of inference and probability it is more probable that the intercourse did take place than not. I quite agree with what Bankes L.J. has said, that if the fact is such that the probabilities are equal one way or the other, an inference cannot legitimately be drawn from it one way or the other. It must show, even only slightly, more probability that intercourse took place than not, and if there is that balance of probability it is not for the Court to say that it is so slight that it would not have acted upon it.'

The appellant in her evidence stated that on two occasions in the summer of 1939 the respondent, who had been introduced to her as Mr. Manning, had taken her with another girl named O'Connell and Guard Maher for a motor drive in the County Dublin, that on each occasion the car stopped at a public house where all the party had some drink, and that they then went walking through the fields in pairs, the respondent with her and O'Connell with Guard Maher. She alleged that the respondent had intercourse with her on these occasions and on subsequent occasions also, and that as a result of this intercourse a child was born on the 7th March, 1940. She said that after the child was born she tried to get in touch with the respondent, and that she saw his car in Marlborough Street at the end of March or beginning of April, and her account of her interview with him is as follows:–

'The defendant came to the car. My father, who was with me, spoke to the defendant. The defendant came up to me and said "Hello, Miss Morrissey, it's a long time since I saw you." I said "I have been in trouble since, the baby is in a nursing home." He asked me in what home, and I told him. I told him I had trouble with my parents and that my father wanted to speak to him. The defendant said he would arrange to meet my father, but that it was too late that night. My father approached. The defendant said he would meet my father at Ball's Bridge the following night at 8 p.m. but the defendant was not there.'

The evidence of the appellant's father, J.P. Morrissey, was as follows:–

'My daughter gave me the number of the car (*i.e.*, the respondent's car). I saw the car in Marlborough Street. After a while two men came along. I approached the defendant, Boyle. I said "Are you Mr. Boyle?" He said "Yes." I said "A lady wants to see you." Nothing else happened then. He came across. I said "Now, Mr. Manning, this is my daughter and she will tell you her tale." I left them talking for 10 or 15 minutes. I came back and said "Now Joan, you're long enough, come along." She said "Mr. Boyle wants to make an appointment to see you." He said "Meet me at Herbert Park, Ball's Bridge, at 8 p.m. to-morrow night." He didn't turn up. The following night I wrote to the defendent the letter dated the 10th April, 1940.'

That letter was in evidence and it reads:–

'I was surprised that you did not keep the appointment you made for last evening. However, if you intend to meet me. I am willing that you should do so, and will meet you any place or time after 7 p.m. which will suit you. I do not intend to allow the matter to remain longer in abeyance and should you wish to come to an amicable agreement I will expect an early reply to this letter.'

The answer to this letter was a letter from the respondent's solicitors, Herman Good & Co., in which they say – 'We are to inform you that if you desire to discuss any matter with our client you will please first communicate with us. We must ask you not to address any further communications to our client or to get in touch with him in any other way.'

The appellant's evidence, that shortly after the birth of her child she met the respondent and had a conversation with him, as a result of which he made an appointment to meet her father on the following night at Herbert Park, and that he did not keep that appointment, is corroborated by the evidence of her father.

Mr. Casey says that the appellant in her evidence did not state that in her conversation with the respondent on that occasion she told him that he was the father of her child, and that her father did not say that he had heard her say so, and he contends that in these circumstances the fact that an appointment was made to meet on the following night is not material, and, accordingly, that corroboration of the appellant's evidence that such an appointment was made is not corrobation of her evidence in some material particular within the meaning of the sub-section.

In my opinion, the only reasonable interpretation of the appellant's evidence is that in the interview in question she charged the respondent with the paternity of her child. That such a charge was made is, I think, the reasonable inference from the fact that the respondent without asking for any explanation of the letter of the 10th April instructed his solicitors to reply to it in the terms of their letter of the 11th April. If such a charge was made, then the fact that the respondent did not repudiate it in the presence of the appellant's father, but made an appointment to meet him on the following night, obviously with the object of discussing the matter, is to my mind a most material circumstance from which the more probable inference is that the charge was well founded.

The appellant's evidence as to that material circumstance was corroborated by the evidence of her father. I am therefore of opinion that the learned Judge was correct in holding that there was evidence corroborative in some material particular of the evidence of the appellant, and in refusing the application for a direction made by the respondent's counsel.

Murnaghan, J. (Dissenting):

I have to state my opinion that there is not, in this case, the evidence required by the *Illegitimate Children (Affiliation Orders) Act, 1930*, to enable the District Justice to make a decree against the defendant as putative father.

The case is full of suspicion. Facts have been proved as to motor drives, and as to the defendant and his companion going on these drives under assumed names, but there is a question of law involved as to whether there is in this proceeding the evidence required by statute, corroborative of the mother's evidence.

I agree with and accept the statement of the law in the judgement of Scrutton L.J. in *Thomas* v. *Jones* [1921] 1 K. B. 22, and I do not wish to dissent from any of the legal propositions in that judgment. The corroborative evidence required by the statute may be of two kinds:–

1 Evidence of facts tending to corroborate the story of the mother as to what happened.

2 Evidence of the conduct of the defendant.

Both these kinds of evidence are present in this case, there is the evidence of the mother and also the evidence of Guard Maher, which was offered as corroborative evidence. In so far as what Guard Maher said is relied on as corroboration, it disproves the evidence of the plaintiff in vital respects; thus, he places the dates of these drives as July and not June as the plaintiff positively says, and, further, he says that the party remained together and never separated, though the plaintiff says that the party separated. In my opinion, so far as this evidence is relied on as evidence of intercourse or to prove intercourse, not only does it not furnish corroboration, but it rather goes to the contrary. I do not leave out of consideration that Guard Maher was an unwilling witness and attended on subpoena, and it is possible that all his evidence is untrue, but even if it be untrue, its untruth is no corroboration of the plaintiff's evidence.

The real point of the case turns on whether what was said at the interview that took place on the 8th April can amount to an admission by the defendant that he was the father of the child. If a person being confronted and charged with being the father makes no reply, that may amount to an admission. I ask myself whether, in fairness and justice to the defendant, he can be held on the evidence to have admitted that he was the father; on my view of the evidence it was attempted to 'corner' him into some kind of admission that he was the father, but there is no express admission by him that he was. It has, however, been urged on the Court that because he consented to a later appointment to discuss the matter, that that was an admission that he was the father.

I notice on the evidence that there is a complete absence of any direct statement by the girl or her father to the defendant that he was the father; further, there is no direct statement or admission by the defendant that he was, and the question is whether the circumstances of this case can be so interpreted as to amount to an admission by the defendant that he was the father. I think that if the defendant denied the paternity before he was charged with it, that that might be sought to be construed into an admission on his part. The defendant was entitled to wait until he was charged before he made a denial; he may have had knowledge in his heart and mind that he was the father, but the question is whether his action and conduct amounted to an acknowledgment of his paternity.

No purpose would be served by my going over the evidence; to my mind the whole occurrence may have raised in the defendant's mind a suspicion that he would be charged, but it is clear that on the evidence he was not charged, unless it can be said that talking to him amounted to a charge. On the evidence he appears to me to have taken up the attitude that he was willing to confer with the applicant and her father. Such an attitude does not amount to an admission. It is probable that he intended to deny any charge when it should be made.

With regard to the letters, the first charge against the defendant is contained in the letter asking him to come to an agreement. It is, on my interpretation of what happened at the interview on the 8th April that I take the dissenting view on the facts; in my opinion no inference can be drawn that the defendant admitted the charge.

In my opinion the answer to the question submitted to us should be 'No.'

Meredith, J.:

I agree entirely with the statement of facts and of the law given by the Chief Justice, and I have nothing to add to it, but I should like to say how I would approach the matter in practice.

In applying the principles to the facts, I would begin by taking the statement of the applicants, and then put aside those portions of her story that merely prove opportunities of access and any details that are not material particulars. Then I would put on the other side the different facts in the case that point to the defendant being the father, and I would call those facts A, B, and C, etc., and each of these facts has to be such that any one of them would suffice to turn the scale; if there were two of them it would weigh down the balance more heavily, and, if there were three or more of them, I should regard them as overwhelming. Then, if no further evidence were called and there were no statutory requirements of corroboration, I would decide the balance of probability in favour of the applicant. If there were further evidence, I would weigh the evidence on the material facts.

Then I would turn to the statute. By reason of the statute I cannot rely on balance of probability alone, but must get in addition corroboration in some material particular. I cannot look to opportunities of access as corroboration, but I must look to facts A, B, and C, etc., which are the facts that weigh with me as showing defendant's paternity. I must find corroboration in one of them, and if I find that in one of them, the statute is satisfied, and I may approach the case as I would any other, with her story as part of the evidence. Corroboration has not to go the length of being an unambiguous admission, for that would be conclusive: it is enough if there be something which tends to make you believe the story of the applicant to be the truth.

I agree with the Chief Justice that the answer to the question submitted to us should be 'Yes.'

Geoghegan and **O'Byrne JJ.** delivered concurring judgments.

Notes

1. Do you prefer the judgments of the majority or that of Murnaghan, J.?
2. See also *McCarthy* v. *Hourihane*, [1935] Ir. Jur. Rep. 37 (High Ct.); *Seaver* v. *O'Toole*, [1937] Ir. Jur. Rep. 8 (Circuit Ct., Judge Shannon, 1936); *Oliver* v. *Jeffrey*, 89 J.P.Jo. 335 (High Ct., 1925); *Cahill* v. *Reilly*, [1957] Ir. Jur. Rep. 77 (Circuit Ct., Judge Deale); *Kiely* v. *Mulvihill*, 82 I.L.T.R. 1 (Circuit Ct. Judge O'Briain, 1947); *O'Neill* v. *Kelly*, [1957] Ir. Jur. Rep. 81 (Circuit Ct., Judge Deale); *The State (Smyth)* v. *Fawsitt*, [1950] Ir. Jur.

Rep. 25 (High Ct., 1948); *Norwood* v. *Scott*, 73 I.L.T.R. 200 (N.I., Belfast Recorder's Court, 1939); *Egan* v. *Wallace*, [1957] N.I. 64 (C.A., 1956).

3. If the defendant fails to give evidence in affiliation proceedings, could this ever amount to corroboration? Cf. G. Wilkinson, *Affiliation Law and Practice*, 32 (1958).
4. On the question of scientific evidence of paternity, see Horgan, *The Financial Support of Illegitimate Children*, 11 Ir. Jur. (n.s.) 59, at 73–80 (1976); the Law Reform Commission's *Report on Illegitimacy*, 7–11 (LRC 4–1982); Bartholemew, *The Nature and Use of Blood Group Evidence*, 24 Modern L. Rev. 313 (1961); the English Law Commission's Report, *Blood Tests and the Proof of Paternity in Civil Proceedings*, Appendix B (Law Commission No. 16, 1968): Larson, *Blood Test Exclusion Procedures in Paternity Litigation: The Uniform Acts and Beyond*, 13 J. of Family L. 713 (1974); Terasak, *Resolution by HLA Testing for 1000 Paternity Cases Not Excluded by ABO Testing*, 16 J of Family L. 543 (1978): Forrest, *The Legal Implications of HLA Testing for Paternity*, 15 J. of Family L. (1977); Lee, *Current Status of Paternity Testing*. 9 Family L.Q. 615 (1975); *Joint AMA – ABA Guidelines: Present Status of Serologic Testing in Problems of Disputed Parentage*, 10 Family L.Q. 247 (1976).

TIME WITHIN WHICH AFFILIATION PROCEEDINGS MUST BE TAKEN

The 1930 Act included in section 2(2) a general limitation period of six months after the birth of the child, within which affiliation proceedings had to be commenced. There were certain exceptional cases where this period was extended. The position is now covered by section 28(1)(b) of the *Family Law (Maintenance of Spouses and Children) Act 1976*, which substitutes a new section 2(2) as follows:

An application for the issue of a summons or other process under this section may be made only –

(*a*) before the birth of the illegitimate child in respect of whom the application is made, or
(*b*) within three years after the birth of the child, or
(*c*) where the alleged father of the child contributed to the maintenance of the child within three years after the date of the birth of the child, at any time after the contribution, or
(*d*) where the alleged father of the child was not resident in the State at the date of the birth of the child, at any time not later than three years after the alleged father first takes up residence in the State after that date, or
(*e*) where the alleged father of the child was resident in the State at the date of the birth of the child but ceased to be so resident within three years after that date, at any time not later than three years after the alleged father first takes up residence in the State after that cesser.

Notes

1. Is it fair to say that the limitation period should be set aside merely on proof that an alleged father contributed to the maintenance of the child within three years after the birth of the child? Is such conduct sufficiently unequivocal?
2. Cf. *O'C* v. *B.*, unreported, High Ct., McWilliam, J., 14 February 1977 (1975 – 300 Sp.), analysed by Horgan, *Affiliation Proceedings in the High Court: An Application by a Married Woman*, 11 Ir. Jur. (n.s.) 340 (1976).
3. Are the present time limits for taking affiliation proceedings constitutional? Are *any* time limits constitutional? Cf. *Mills* v. *Habluetzel*, 456 U.S. 91 (1982); see also Caton Cathey, *Note: Redefining the Methods of Middle-Tier Scrutiny: A New Proposal for Equal Protection*, 61 Texas L. Rev. 1501, at 1513–1514, 1545–1549 (1983).

THE CONSTITUTION AND THE NON-MARITAL FAMILY

The constitutional position of the non-marital family is in a number of respects uncertain. The courts have analysed several relevant issues: whether the child born outside marriage has constitutional rights and, if so, the basis of those rights; whether the parents (or the mother alone) and the child constitute a 'family' for the purposes of Article 41 of the Constitution; and the constitutional position of the mother and father respectively. The subject has given rise to much academic analysis including the following: *Shatter*, ch. 1, Staines, *The Concept of 'The Family' Under the Irish Constitution*, 11 Ir. Jur. (n.s.) 223 (1976); the Law Reform Commission's *Report on Illegitimacy*, paras. 31ff (LRC 4– 1982).

THE STATE (NICOLAOU) v. AN BORD UCHTÁLA

[1966] I.R. 567 (Supreme Court 1966, aff'g High Court 1965)

Walsh J. (for the Court):–

The appellant in this case is a Cypriot who at all material times resided and carried on business as a café proprietor in London. He is a member of the Greek Orthodox Church. He is not a citizen of Ireland. Kathleen Donnelly is a citizen of Ireland whose parents and family at all material times resided in Co. Galway. In 1959 she was employed by the appellant as a waitress and they were living together as man and wife. She is a member of the Roman Catholic Church. In July, 1959, her brother, Denis Donnelly, came to London and took her back to her family in Galway. Her return to Ireland was followed by a correspondence of an amicable and sociable character between the appellant on the one hand and Miss Donnelly and her parents on the other. About this time Miss Donnelly found that she was pregnant. The appellant asked her to marry him and she and her parents were willing that the marriage should take place provided that he became a Roman Catholic. He was willing to do so, and it was apparently on this understanding that she returned to him in London. The marriage was, however, delayed pending receipt of the necessary documentary evidence that he was free to marry. On the 23rd February, 1960, a daughter was born to Miss Donnelly, at the North Middlesex Hospital, Edmonton. The birth of the child was registered on the 4th March and the certified extract from the register shows that it was registered on the information and signatures of the appellant and Miss Donnelly, that the child's name was given as Mary Carmel, that the name of the father was given as Leontis Nicolaou and that the name of the mother was given as Kathleen Sheila Donnelly. The address of both father and mother was given as 19, Durham Road, London. The child was baptised in the Catholic Church of St. Mellitus, London, on the 6th March. Mother and child returned to live with the appellant at 19 Durham Road, where they remained until the 16th June. During this period the mother was depressed and emotionally upset. The necessary documentary evidence that both were free had become available but it appears that she was unable to make up her mind what to do. The appelant says in his second affidavit that his attitude at this time was that he was anxious to marry her in a Catholic Church but that he was prepared to live with her outside marriage. He also said he was willing if she wished that she should depart and leave the child with him and that he was also reluctantly willing that she should depart and take the child with her, hoping that she would return when she felt better. Her mother was urging her either to marry or else leave the appellant and have the child adopted. Both these alternatives were frequently discussed between the appellant and Miss Donnelly. The appellant made it quite clear that he would not agree to have the child adopted. Miss Donnelly says in her affidavit that during this period she was worried about the child being illegitimate; that she was not satisfied to continue living with the appellant; that she was not prepared to marry him unless and until he became a Catholic; and that she was not prepared to depart and leave the child with him for fear that it would not be brought up as a Catholic. She wished to go to a Catholic home where she could work to keep herself and the child and with that end in view she had been in touch with the Crusade of Rescue, an English Adoption Society, which had put her in touch with the Catholic Protection and Rescue Society of 30, South Anne Street, Dublin. She eventually decided to take that step.

On the 16th June she left the appellant, taking the child with her. She told him she was going to a home, such as that already mentioned, in Dublin. He agreed to let the child go with her. He said in his first affidavit that he understood she intended to reside in an institution in Ireland and that he considered it essential that the child should be with its mother. He believed that the child could not be adopted without his consent and he told Miss Donnelly that if any proposals were made for adoption they should be referred to him. In his second affidavit he says that he agreed to let her take the child with her only on the understanding that any proposal for adoption should be referred immediately to him. She travelled to Dublin and on arrival went to 30 South Anne Street, where she met certain officers of the Catholic Protection and Rescue Society. She was then admitted with the child to St Patrick's, Navan Road, a home owned by the Society, where she remained some months, working for her own and the child's maintenance. She had requested Miss Cassidy, the secretary of the Society, to try and find a home for the child. She was eventually told that the Society had secured a parent to adopt the child, and following instructions, brought it on the 23rd September, 1960, to 30 South Anne Street, where she left it in the custody of officers of the Society.

Not having heard from Miss Donnelly, and being unaware of her and the child's whereabouts, the appellant wrote to Mrs. Donnelly on the 20th July, 1960, making inquiries. Mrs. Donnelly replied on the 26th July, saying that Kathleen had come from London to Dublin; that she, Mrs. Donnelly, would let him know how Kathleen and the child were getting on when she heard from her. Early in August the appellant got a letter from Miss Donnelly. In this she said that she thought she had made it clear to him when leaving him that all was over between them, so why not forget about her and the child and start a new life for himself; that she quite agreed that he was the child's father and was interested in her, but that she could not leave the child with him fearing it might not be reared a Roman Catholic, and if he had any plans with regard to the child's future she would be very grateful if he would let her know before she got the child adopted, as that would mean that it would not be his any more. This letter was addressed from Miss Donnelly's home in Galway. The appellant did not reply to her letter; but towards the end of September he travelled to Galway and saw her personally. He asked her where the child was, and she told him that she had left it in Dublin; that she had given it away. He returned to Dublin where he instructed Messrs. John P. Redmond & Co., Solicitors, to write to Miss Donnelly. They wrote on the 30th September, stating, *inter alia*, that they had been instructed that she had indicated that she had disposed of the child by placing it in an institution, or with persons prepared to adopt it; and that unless she replied within seven days that she was willing to return the child to the appellant they would institute proceedings in the High Court to compel her to do so. She replied on the 5th October, referring, *inter alia*, to her letter of the previous August to the appellant, to which she had received no reply. She said that the Crusade of Rescue Society in Dublin had got a good home for the child; and that adoption became legal within six months. On the 7th October Messrs. Redmond & Co. wrote to the secretary of An Bord Uchtála (hereinafter called 'the Board'), confirming a previous telephone conversation; and stating that they acted for the prosecutor, who was father of a child born to Miss Kathleen Donnelly in London on the 23rd February, 1960, and registered under the name of Mary Carmel Nicolaou. The letter went on to say that they had been instructed to institute proceedings in the High Court to prevent any adoption of the child; that in accordance with the provisions of s. 16 of the *Adoption Act, 1952*, they were putting the Board on notice that such proceedings were pending; and that in the event of the Board being requested to make arrangements for the registration of the child's adoption they must ask them to take no further steps in the matter pending the outcome of the Court proceedings. On the 17th October the Registrar of the Board replied acknowledging receipt of the letter and saying that the matter had been noted. Messrs. Redmond & Co. had written a similar letter to the secretary of the Catholic Protection and Rescue Society, and on the 12th October had received a merely formal acknowledgment. No proceedings were at this time instituted in the High Court on account, as stated by the appellant, of the state of Miss Donnelly's health.

Miss Donnelly continued to be much upset as a result of the circumstances in which she found herself, a condition which was apparently worsened by the receipt of Messrs.

Redmond's letter and the threat of legal proceedings. She suffered something in the nature of a nervous breakdown and at the end of 1960 and beginning of 1961 spent some ten or eleven weeks under treatment in Ballinasloe Mental Hospital. During early 1961 the appellant had some correspondence with her family; but correspondence with her personally was not resumed until October.

Some time in August or September, 1961, while she was staying with her parents, she received certain papers in connection with the adoption of the child. She called to the office of Mr. John C. O'Donnell, Solicitor, Galway, and explained her position. He took her to the office of the County Registrar, who is also a commissioner for oaths, where the necessary papers were signed and an affidavit of some kind sworn. On the 13th September, 1961 the Board made an order for the adoption of the child by a married couple.

On the 26th October Miss Donnelly wrote to the appellant, stating that she was not working and asking for a few pounds. She did not tell him that the child had been adopted. Correspondence continued during 1961, 1962 and 1963, in the course of which she asked for, and was given, money from time to time. In the spring of 1963, and again in the summer, she had spells of treatment in Ballinasloe Mental Hospital. Her letters about this time are written in affectionate terms and it appears from them that she was contemplating a return to London and marriage with the appellant. She did return to his employment in August, 1963; and arrangements were made for the marriage. She appears to have suffered another emotional upset, and refused to go on with it. It was at this time that the appellant first learned definitely from her that the child had been adopted. He was not aware where the child was, and made various unsuccessful attempts to find out. He had consultations with his legal advisers in Dublin, and on 17th January, 1964, an application was made to Mr. Justice Henchy for a conditional order of *habeas corpus* directed to the registrar of the Board and the secretary of the Catholic Rescue and Protection Society. This was described by the appellant's counsel as being in the nature of a 'fishing' application. When refusing it Mr. Justice Henchy suggested that an examination of the Register of Adopted Children might possibly yield results.

On the 12th February the appellant's solicitors obtained a certified extract from the Adopted Children's Register, showing that an order had been made on the 13th September, 1961, for the adoption of a female child, bearing the names, Mary Carmel, who had been born on the 23rd February, 1960. On the 14th April they wrote to the Board asking to be furnished with a copy of this order; and on the 21st April the registrar replied, stating that as a matter of principle their request could not be granted. Counsel on behalf of the appellant then applied to the High Court for a conditional order of *certiorari* seeking to quash the adoption order, and this application was refused by Mr. Justice Murnaghan on the 17th July. On appeal this Court granted a conditional order on the following grounds: – (1) that the Board in making the adoption order failed to comply with the requirements of s. 16, sub-s. 1, (*d*) and (*i*), of the *Adoption Act, 1952*; and (2) that the said Act is repugnant to the Constitution in so far as it purports to deprive the applicant of his rights as a natural father to have the custody of his natural child, Mary Carmel Donnelly, without notice to him, or at all. The order was directed to the registrar of the Board and, in accordance with Order 60 of the Rules of the Superior Courts, it directed that the Attorney General should have notice thereof. These parties having shown cause counsel on behalf of the appellant moved the High Court to have the conditional order made absolute notwithstanding the cause shown. The hearing of the application by three judges of the High Court occupied several days, spread over a period of some months; and eventually, on the 31st May last, the application was refused and the conditional order was discharged. From that decision the appellant now appeals. . . .

[**Walsh, J.** considered and rejected a number of arguments made by the appellant in relation to his rights under the Act. **Walsh, J.** continued:]

It is now necessary to consider the submissions advanced in support of the second ground on which the conditional order was granted to the appellant. The first of these was based upon Article 40.1 of the Constitution. . . .

In the opinion of the Court section 1 of Article 40 is not to be read as a guarantee or undertaking that all citizens shall be treated by the law as equal for all purposes, but rather as an acknowledgment of the human equality of all citizens and that such equality will be recognised in the laws of the State. The section itself in its provision, 'this shall not be held to mean that the State shall not in its enactments have due regard to differences of capacity, physical and moral, and of social function,' is a recognition that inequality may or must result from some special abilities or from some deficiency or from some special need and it is clear that the Article does not either envisage or guarantee equal measure in all things to all citizens. To do so regardless of the factors mentioned would be inequality.

The argument for the appellant was as follows: – At the time the Constitution of Saorstát Éireann came into force, and subsequently on the coming into operation of the present Constitution, the law of this country recognised as a personal legal right the right of the father of an illegitimate child to its custody, inferior only to that of the mother, while alive, and after her death superior to that of any other persons, such as the mother's relatives, and that this legal right was founded upon a judicial recognition of a pre-existing natural right: that the *Adoption Act, 1952*, in its provisions as to those whose consent is necessary before an adoption order can be made, and as to those who are entitled to be heard on an application for an adoption order, has no regard to this legal right of the natural father: that this amounts to unfair discrimination and is therefore repugnant to the Article in question: that while the Article by its terms refers only to citizens it recognises the personal right to equality before the law of citizens by virtue of the fact that they are human persons and that as non-citizens share with citizens a common humanity they therefore share their constitutional rights.

Legal rights, unless guaranteed by the Constitution, may be adversely affected or completely taken away by legislation. It was, nevertheless, submitted that such legislation, if it discriminates unfairly against a particular class of citizens, would be invalid having regard to the provisions of the Article in question.

In support of the first branch of this submission counsel for the appellant relied on *Reg.* v. *Nash* 10 Q.B.D. 454; *In re Crowe* 17 I. L. T. R. 72; *In re Kerr* 22 L. R. Ir. 642 and 24 L.R. Ir. 59. *In re Hyndman* 39 I. L. T. R. 191; and *In re Connor* [1919] I. R. 361, and submitted that these cases established that a natural father had the personal legal right for which they contended. The Court is not satisfied that these cases do establish that the natural father has any such legal right; and in so far as counsel's submission is based upon this proposition it is not, in the opinion of the Court, well founded.

Over and above this the appellant argues as follows:– that under the provisions of s. 14, sub-s. 1, of the Act, when there is question of a child's adoption no consent is required from its natural father; that under the provisions of s. 16, sub-s. 1, he is not as such natural father entitled to be heard on the application for an adoption order; that in contrast, consent to adoption is required from the mother, the guardian, and any person having charge of or control over the child and that the several persons mentioned in s. 16, sub-s. 1, are entitled to be heard on the application for adoption: that these provisions discriminate against natural fathers on the ground of sex because rights are given to the mother which are denied to the father and on the ground of paternity because rights are given to persons, who may be more distant relations of the child or even strangers in blood, which are denied to natural fathers.

Under the provisions of these sections of the Act certain persons are given rights and all other persons are excluded. Whether or not the natural father is excluded depends upon the circumstance whether or not he comes within the description of a person who is given a right, and he may or may not come within some such description. If he is in fact excluded it is because in common with other blood relations and strangers he happens not to come within any such description. There is no discrimination against the natural father as such. The question remains whether there is any unfair discrimination in giving the rights in question to the persons described and denying them to others.

In the opinion of the Court each of the persons described as having rights under s. 14, sub-s. 1, and s. 16, sub-s. 1, can be regarded as having, or capable of having, in relation to the adoption of a child a moral capacity or social function which differentiates him from persons who are not given such rights. When it is considered that an illegitimate child may be begotten by an act of rape, by a callous seduction or by an act of casual commerce by a man with a woman, as well as by the association of a man with a woman in making a common home without marriage in circumstances approximating to those of married life, and that, except in the latter instance, it is rare for a natural father to take any interest in his offspring, it is not difficult to appreciate the difference in moral capacity and social function between the natural father and the several persons described in the sub-sections in question. In presenting their argument under this head counsel for the appellant have undertaken the onus of showing that in denying to the natural father certain rights conferred upon others s. 14, sub-s. 1, and s. 16, sub-s. 1, of the Act are invalid having regard to Article 40 of the Constitution. In the opinion of the Court they have failed to discharge that onus.

In so far as this Article has been invoked to show that the Act purports to permit an unconstitutional discrimination between children in relation to adoption it is to be noted that the Act does not confer a right of adoption on any child, nor does it permit any child to be the moving party in respect of its own adoption. The restriction as to the class of children who may be the subject of adoption orders is a restriction imposed upon the Adoption Board and this restriction in no way impinges upon the provision of Article 40, section 1.

The fact that under the *Adoption Act, 1952*, an illegitimate child or an orphan may be the subject of an adoption cannot be construed as a discrimination against such child. Article 42, section 5, of the Constitution, while dealing with the case of failure in duty on the part of parents towards the children, speaks of 'the natural and imprescriptible rights of the child.' Those 'natural and imprescriptible rights' cannot be said to be acknowledged by the Constitution as residing only in legitimate children any more than it can be said that the guarantee in section 4 of the Article as to the provision of free primary education excludes illegitimate children. While it is not necessary to explore the full extent of 'the natural and imprescriptible rights of the child,' they include the right to 'religious and moral, intellectual, physical and social education.' An illegimate child has the same natural rights as a legitimate child though not necessarily the same legal rights. Legal rights as distinct from natural rights are determined by the law for the time being in force in the State. While the law cannot under the Constitution seek to deprive the illegitimate child of those natural rights guaranteed by the Constitution it can, as in the *Adoption Act, 1952*, secure for the illegitimate child legal rights similar to those possessed by legitimate children. It provides opportunities for illegitimate children and orphans to secure the advantages of family life. The Act does not infringe any natural right of an illegitimate child. On the contrary, its purpose and effect is to redress the inequalities imposed by circumstances on orphans and illegitimate children.

It was also submitted on behalf of the appellant that the provisions of the *Adoption Act, 1952*, violate the guarantees contained in Article 40, section 3, 1, of the Constitution. . . .

The Constitution does not set out in whole what are the rights of the citizen which are encompassed in this guarantee and, while some of them are indicated in sub-section 2 of section 3, it was pointed out in the judgment of this Court in *Ryan* v. *The Attorney General*

[1965] I. R. 294 that the personal rights guaranteed are not exhausted by those enumerated in sub-section 2. It is, however, abundantly clear that the rights referred to in section 3 of Article 40 are those which may be called the natural personal rights and the very words of sub-section 1, by the reference therein to 'laws,' exclude such rights as are dependent only upon law. Sub-section 3 cannot therefore in any sense be read as a constitutional guarantee of personal rights which were simply the creation of the law and in existence on the date of coming into operation of the Constitution. For the reasons already indicated earlier in this judgment, in so far as a father has rights in respect of his natural child which were the creation of law, judge-made or legislative, they were of their nature susceptible to legislative change and if the *Adoption Act, 1952*, has effected such change it does not infringe the guarantee contained in section 3 of Article 40. It has not been shown to the satisfaction of this Court that the father of an illegitimate child has any natural right, as distinct from legal rights, to either the custody or society of that child and the Court has not been satisfied that any such right has ever been recognised as part of the natural law. If an illegitimate child has a natural right to look to his father for support that would impose a duty on the father but it would not of itself confer any right upon the father. The appellant has therefore failed to establish that any personal right he may have guaranteed to him by Article 40, section 3, of the Constitution has been in any way violated by the Adoption Act of 1952.

The provisions of the *Adoption Act 1952*, do not purport to deal with the legal position of the father and mother of an illegitimate child and their respective claims where questions of custody are concerned apart from legal adoption and the Court does not find it necessary to consider the position in such a case.

The appellant next claimed relief under the provisions of Article 41 of the Constitution. It was submitted on his behalf that the *Adoption Act, 1952*, was invalid having regard to the provisions of this Article in that it violates the constitutional guarantees to protect the family in its constitution and authority and purports to render alienable what are referred to in the Constitution as 'the inalienable and imprescriptible rights' of the family, rights which in the words of Article 41, section 1, are 'antecedent and superior to all positive law.' It is quite clear from the provisions of Article 41, and in particular section 3 thereof, that the family referred to in this Article is the family which is founded on the institution of marriage and, in the context of the Article, marriage means valid marriage under the law for the time being in force in the State. While it is quite true that unmarried persons cohabiting together and the children of their union may often be referred to as a family and have many, if not all, of the outward appearances of a family, and may indeed for the purposes of a particular law be regarded as such, nevertheless so far as Article 41 is concerned the guarantees therein contained are confined to families based upon marriage. This, in the opinion of the Court, is of itself sufficient to render the appellant's submissions in respect of this Article of the Constitution unsustainable and the Article avails him nothing.

For the same reason the mother of an illegitimate child does not come within the ambit of Articles 41 and 42 of the Constitution. Her natural right to the custody and care of her child, and such other natural personal rights as she may have (and this Court does not in this case find it necessary to pronounce upon the extent of such rights), fall to be protected under Article 40, section 3, and are not affected by Article 41 or Article 42 of the Constitution. There is no provision in Article 40 which prohibits or restricts the surrender, abdication, or transfer of any of the rights guaranteed in that Article by the person entitled to them. The Court therefore rejects the submission that the *Adoption Act, 1952*, is invalid in as much as it permits the mother of an illegitimate child to consent to the legal adoption of her child, and lose, under the provision of s. 24 (*b*) of the Act, all parental rights and be freed from all parental duties in respect of the child.

Lastly, the appellant sought to invoke Article 42, section 1, of the Constitution. Article 42 is the Article which deals with education. [**Walsh, J.** quoted the section. He continued:] The appellant submits that the *Adoption Act, 1952*, has infringed his inalienable right as a parent to provide in these respects for his child the subject-matter of these proceedings. It is the opinion of this Court that the parent referred to in Article 42, section 1, is a parent of a family founded upon marriage and this of itself disqualifies the appellant as a parent within the meaning of that term in Article 42, section 1. The appellant's case therefore can find no support in this section. It follows that it is unnecessary to consider what might be the effect of the provisions of section 5 of Article 42 upon the circumstances of the appellant's case so far as the appellant is himself concerned.

It was also suggested that the *Adoption Act 1952*, by permitting the adoption of a child by the parents of an existing family and by enacting that the child shall be considered as one born to them in lawful wedlock, with the property rights and the other legal rights of such a child, in some way infringes the provisions of Article 41 of the Constitution by encroaching upon the guaranteed rights of that family and its members. The Court rejects that submission. The adoption of a child by the parents of a family in no way diminishes for the other members of that family the rights guaranteed by the Constitution. Rights of succession, rights to compensation for the death of a parent and such matters may properly be the subject of legislation and the extension of such legal rights by legislation to benefit an adopted child does not encroach upon any of the inalienable and imprescriptible rights guaranteed by the Constitution to the family or its members or upon the natural and imprescriptible rights of children referred to in section 5 of Article 42.

The High Court judgments rested in part upon the fact that the appellant is not a citizen of Ireland. This Court expressly reserves for another and more appropriate case consideration of the effect of non-citizenship upon the interpretation of the Articles in question and also the right of a non-citizen to challenge the validity of an Act of the Oireachtas having regard to the provisions of the Constitution. The opinion which the Court has pronounced upon these Articles is not dependent upon or affected by the fact that the appellant is not a citizen of Ireland or by the fact that the Attorney General through his counsel informed this Court that he did not wish to submit in this case that the rights, if any, of the appellant under the Articles in question were any the less by reason of the fact that he was not a citizen of Ireland.

For the reasons stated the Court is of opinion that the appellant's case should be dismissed.

Notes

1. Do you agree with the decision? For critical analyses, see J. Kelly, *Fundamental Rights in the Irish Law and Constitution*, 242–245 (2nd ed., 1967); J. Kelly, *The Irish Constitution*, 487–488 (2nd ed., 1984); *Shatter*, 360–361; Staines *The Concept of 'The Family' Under the Irish Constitution*, 11 Ir. Jur. (n.s.) 223 (1976). More generally, see Dickey, *The Notion of 'Family' in Law*, 14 U.W. Austr. L. Rev. 417 (1981).
2. Contrast the United States Supreme Court decision of *Stanley* v. *Illinois*, 405 U.S. 645 (1972), where an unmarried father successfully challenged the constitutionality of an Illinois statutory provision depriving him of the custody of his three children without an individualised hearing (which would have been afforded a married father) as to whether or not he was an unfit parent. Delivering the opinion of the Court Mr. Justice White said:

> It may be, as the State insists, that most unmarried fathers are unsuitable and neglectful parents. It may also be that Stanley is such a parent and that his children should be placed in other hands. But all unmarried fathers are not in this category; some are wholly suited to have custody of their children. This much the State readily concedes, and nothing in this record indicates that Stanley is or has been a neglectful father who has not cared for his children. Given the opportunity to make his case, Stanley may have been seen to be deserving of custody of his offspring. Had this been so, the State's statutory policy would have been furthered by leaving custody in him.
>
> . . . [I]t may be argued that unmarried fathers are so seldom fit that Illinois need not undergo the

administrative inconvenience of inquiry in any case, including Stanley's. The establishment of prompt efficacious procedures to achieve legitimate state ends is a proper state interest worthy of cognizance in constitutional adjudication. But the Constitution recognizes higher values than speed and efficiency. Indeed, one might fairly say of the Bill of Rights in general, and the Due Process Clause in particular, that they were designed to protect the fragile values of a vulnerable citizenry from the overbearing concern for efficiency and efficacy that may characterize praiseworthy government officials no less, and perhaps more, than mediocre ones.

Procedure by presumption is always cheaper and easier than individualized determination. But when, as here, the procedure forecloses the determinative issues of competence and care, when it explicitly disdains present realities in deference to past formalities, it needlessly risks running roughshod over the important interests of both parent and child. It therefore cannot stand. [Footnote references omitted.]

Chief Justice Burger (Blackmun, J. concurring) dissented. In language closely reminiscent of *Nicolaou*, the Chief Justice said:

. . . The Illinois Supreme Court correctly held that the State may constitutionally distinguish between unwed fathers and unwed mothers. Here, Illinois' different treatment of the two is part of that State's statutory scheme for protecting the welfare of illegitimate children. In almost all cases, the unwed mother is readily identifiable, generally from hospital records, and alternatively by physicians or others attending the child's birth. Unwed fathers, as a class, are not traditionally quite so easy to identify and locate. Many of them either deny all responsibility or exhibit no interest in the child or its welfare; and, of course, many unwed fathers are simply not aware of their parenthood.

Furthermore, I believe that a State is fully justified in concluding, on the basis of common human experience, that the biological role of the mother in carrying and nursing an infant creates stronger bonds between her and the child than the bonds resulting from the male's often casual encounter. This view is reinforced by the observable fact that most unwed mothers exhibit a concern for their offspring either permanently or at least until they are safely placed for adoption, while unwed fathers rarely burden either the mother or the child with their attentions or loyalties. Centuries of human experience buttress this view of the realities of human conditions and suggest that unwed mothers of illegitimate children are generally more dependable protectors of their children than are unwed fathers. While these, like most generalizations, are not without exceptions, they nevertheless provide a sufficient basis to sustain a statutory classification whose objective is not to penalize unwed parents but to further the welfare of illegitimate children in fulfillment of the State's obligations as *parens patriae.*

Stanley depicts himself as a somewhat unusual unwed father, namely, as one who has always acknowledged and never doubted his fatherhood of these children. He alleges that he loved, cared for, and supported these children from the time of their birth until the death of their mother. He contends that he consequently must be treated the same as a married father of legitimate children. Even assuming the truth of Stanley's allegations, I am unable to construe the Equal Protection Clause as requiring Illinois to tailor its statutory definition of 'parents' so meticulously as to include such unusual unwed fathers, while at the same time excluding those unwed, and generally unidentified, biological fathers who in no way share Stanley's professed desires. . . . [Footnote references omitted.]

In *Quilloin* v. *Walcott*, 434 U.S. 246 (1978), the Supreme Court rejected a constitutional challenge to Georgia's adoption laws, which denied an unmarried father the right to prevent adoption of his child, while requiring the consent of a married father for adoption. The appellant was an unmarried father who had never lived with his child. The child's mother, who had lived with the child, married when the child was nearly three years old. Eight years later she consented to the adoption of the child by her husband. The appellant attempted to block the adoption and to secure visitation rights, but he did not seek custody.

In rejecting the appellant's constitutional challenge, Mr. Justice Marshall said:–

. . . We have little doubt that the Due Process Clause would be offended '[i]f a State were to attempt to force the breakup of a natural family, over the objections of the parents and their children, without some showing of unfitness and for the sole reason that to do so was thought to be in the children's best interest.' *Smith* v. *Organization of Foster Families*, 431 U.S. 816, 862–863 (1977) (Stewart, J., concurring in judgment). But this is not a case in which the unwed father at any time had, or sought, actual or legal custody of his child. Nor is this a case in which the proposed adoption would place the child with a new set of parents with whom the child had never before lived. Rather, the result of the adoption in this case is to give full recognition to a family unit already in existence, a result desired by all concerned, except appellant. Whatever might be required in other situations, we cannot say that the State was required in this situation to find anything more than that the adoption, and denial of legitimation, were in the 'best interests of the child.'

Appellant contends that even if he is not entitled to prevail as a matter of due process, principles of equal protection require that his authority to veto an adoption be measured by the same standard that would have been applied to a married father. In particular, appellant asserts that his interests are indistinguishable from those of a married father who is separated or divorced from the mother and is no longer living with his child, and therefore the State acted impermissibly in treating his case differently. We think appellant's interests are readily distinguishable from those of a separated or divorced father, and accordingly believe that the State could permissibly give appellant less veto authority than it provides to a married father.

Although appellant was subject, for the years prior to these proceedings, to essentially the same child-support obligation as a married father would have been . . . he has never exercised actual or legal custody over his child, and thus has never shouldered any significant responsibility with respect to the daily supervision, education, protection, or care of the child. Appellant does not complain of his exemption from these responsibilities and, indeed, he does not even now seek custody of his child. In contrast, legal custody of children is, of course, a central aspect of the marital relationship, and even a father whose marriage has broken apart will have borne full responsibility for the rearing of his children during the period of the marriage. Under any standard of review, the State was not foreclosed from recognizing this difference in the extent of commitment to the welfare of the child. . . . [Footnote references omitted]

3. For consideration of the Canadian approach, exemplified in *Children's Aid Society of Metropolitan Toronto* v. *Lyttle*, 34 D.L.R. (3d) 127 (Sup. Ct. Can., 1973), see Bala & Redfearn, *Family Law and the 'Liberty Interest': Section 7 of the Canadian Charter of Rights*, 15 Ottawa L. Rev. 274, at 289–291 (1983).
4. The Report of the Review Committee on Adoption Services, *Adoption* (Pl. 2467, 1984) proposes (in para. 5.40) that a natural father of a child born outside marriage should be permitted to apply to the Court for an order granting him parental rights in relation to the child. Where the Court makes such an order, the consent of the father to the various adoption procedures should be required unless dispensed with in accordance with the law. Even in cases where parental rights had not been granted, "the putative father should be contacted at an early stage in the adoption process wherever possible, and the Adoption Court [proposed elsewhere in the Report] should satisfy itself in each instance that all reasonable steps were taken to obtain the views of the father or that otherwise there were valid reasons for not doing so." *Id.*

G. v. AN BORD UCHTÁLA

[1980] I.R. 32 (Supreme Court 1978, aff'g High Court, Finlay, P., 1978)

O'Higgins, C.J.:

On the 14th November, 1977, the plaintiff give birth to a baby girl. The plaintiff is unmarried and the child was illegitimate. The plaintiff was and still is a civil servant. She is the second of a family of four girls, and both her parents are alive. The plaintiff had been friendly with the father of the child for some time but, although he is unmarried, marriage between them was neither contemplated before the birth nor considered practicable since. The decision in this respect was that of the plaintiff. When the plaintiff became aware of her pregnancy she kept the fact to herself and informed neither the father nor her sisters nor her parents. The birth, which was a normal one, took place in hospital, and the child was and is normal and healthy. The plaintiff spent less than one week in hospital and after the birth of her child she informed only one married sister of the fact but did not inform her parents or either of her other two sisters.

Upon leaving hospital she placed the child in a nursery. Having done so the plaintiff considered what decision she should make as to the child's future. In hospital she had been urged by a member of the nursing staff to have the child adopted. On leaving hospital, through the agency of the hospital's social worker, she sought the advice of the director of an adoption society. The plaintiff at that time hoped to keep the whole affair from her parents because she feared the effect on them. Living as she did, sharing a flat with three other girls, she could not look after the child herself. For this reason adoption had to be and was considered. The plaintiff had four interviews with the director of the adoption society and finally decided to place her daughter for adoption. Having so decided, the plaintiff on the 6th January, 1978, had an interview with a medical social worker attached to the adoption society, and on that date the plaintiff signed a form of consent to the placing of her child for adoption. The legal implications and consequences of what she was doing were explained to her and she received in addition a printed memorandum dealing fully with these matters. Amongst the matters so explained to her and detailed also in the memorandum was the nature and effect of s. 3 of the *Adoption Act, 1974*, to which I will refer in more detail later in this judgment.

Towards the end of January, 1978, the plaintiff decided to inform her parents of the birth of her daughter. Their reaction was that she should have told them earlier and that, if she had done so, they would have helped her. They also said that if she now wished to keep the child they would help and support her. As a result the plaintiff wrote on the 11th February, 1978, to the adoption society expressing a wish to keep her child. She later had an interview with the director of the adoption society in which she made it clear that she had changed her mind about adoption and wished to have her child back.

Following the placing by the plaintiff of her child for adoption with the society on the 6th January, 1978 the society on the 22nd January had given the child into the care of the notice parties for the purpose of adoption. The notice parties were married in 1968 and the wife learned that she could not bear children; in 1975 they adopted a daughter through the same adoption society. In the autumn of 1975 they had applied again to the society to adopt another daughter. It was in these circumstances that the plaintiff's child was placed with them. Having been informed through the adoption society of the plaintiff's change of mind and of her determination to take back her child, the notice parties decided to hold on to the child instead of availing of their rights under s. 3 of the Act of 1974.

The Plaintiff's Proceedings

On the 11th May, 1978, the plaintiff commenced these proceedings in the High Court against An Bord Uchtála (the Adoption Board) claiming the return of her child. The President of the High Court, having regard to the reality of the issue which had arisen concerning the future of the child and to the absolute necessity that the identities of those concerned should not be disclosed, put into operation the procedures set out at the commencement of his judgment. These procedures, as one would expect from him, were devised with great care and concern both for the preservation of this essential secrecy and in the interests of justice. The result is that the adoption society has been added as a defendant, and that the persons now having custody have been added as notice parties and a notice of motion on their behalf (seeking an order under s. 3 of the Act of 1974) has become the true nature of these proceedings. Evidence was taken from both the plaintiff and the notice parties with due regard to each other's rights but without any disclosure of their identities one to the other. The learned President, having considered this evidence and having reserved judgment, decided against the notice parties' claim for an order under s. 3 of the Act of 1974 and directed that the child be returned to the custody of her mother. Against this decision this appeal has been brought by the notice parties.

[The Chief Justice referred to section 3 of the *Adoption Act 1974* which provides

> (1) In any case where a person has applied for an adoption order relating to a child and any person whose consent to the making of an adoption order relating to the child is necessary and who has agreed to the placing of the child for adoption either–
>
> (*a*) fails, neglects or refuses to give his consent, or
>
> (*b*) withdraws a consent already given,
>
> the applicant for the adoption order may apply to the High Court for an order under this section.
>
> (2) The High Court, if it is satisfied that it is in the best interests of the child so to do, may make an order under this section–
>
> (a) giving custody of the child to the applicant for such period as the Court may determine, and
>
> (*b*) authorising the Board to dispense with the consent of the other person referred to in subsection (1) of this section to the making of an adoption order in favour of the applicant during the period aforesaid.

(3) The consent of a ward of court shall not be dispensed with by virtue of a High Court order under this section except with the sanction of the Court.

He continued:]
In considering the application of s. 3 of the Act of 1974 to this case, the learned President came to the conclusion that the constitutional rights of the mother to the custody of her child continued and prevailed, and concluded that she was entitled as of right in the circumstances to the return of her child. In so concluding the learned President, while recognising the co-existence of clear constitutional rights on the part of the child, was of the opinion on the facts that these were neither interfered with nor endangered. Therefore, it seems appropriate that at this stage I should have regard to the constitutional rights of the persons primarily involved in this sad story, namely, the mother and her child.

The Mother's Rights

In the first place it should be noted that the mother is not the mother of a family, in the sense in which the term is used in the Constitution. Article 41 of the Constitution, which recognises the family as the natural, primary and fundamental unit group of society and as a moral institution possessing inalienable and imprescriptible rights antecedent and superior to all positive law, refers exclusively to the family founded and based on the institution of marriage. It is this family which, in Article 41, s. 1, sub-s. 2, the State guarantees to protect in its constitution and authority as the necessary basis of social order and as indispensable to the welfare of the nation and the State.

But the plaintiff is a mother and, as such, she has rights which derive from the fact of motherhood and from nature itself. These rights are among her personal rights as a human being and they are rights which, under Article 40, s. 3, sub-s. 1, the State is bound to respect, defend and vindicate. As a mother, she has the right to protect and care for, and to have the custody of, her infant child. The existence of this right was recognised in the judgment of this Court in *The State* v. *An Bord Uchtála* [1966] I.R. 567. This right is clearly based on the natural relationship which exists between a mother and child. In my view, it arises from the infant's total dependency and helplessness and from the mother's natural determination to protect and sustain her child. How far and to what extent it survives as the child grows up is not a matter of concern in the present case. Suffice to say that this plaintiff, as a mother, had a natural right to the custody of her child who was an infant, and that this natural right of hers is recognised and protected by Article 40, s. 3, sub-s. 1, of the Constitution. Section 6, sub-s. 4, and s. 10, sub-s. 2(*a*), of the *Guardianship of Infants Act, 1964*, constitute a compliance by the State with its obligation, in relation to the mother of an illegitimate child, to defend and vindicate in its laws this right to custody. These statutory provisions make the mother guardian of her illegitimate child and give the mother statutory rights to sue for custody.

However, these rights of the mother in relation to her child are neither inalienable nor imprescriptible, as are the rights of the family under Article 41. They can be alienated or transferred in whole or in part and either subject to conditions or absolutely, or they can be lost by the mother if her conduct towards the child amounts to an abandonment or an abdication of her rights and duties.

The Child's Rights

The child also has natural rights. Normally, these will be safe under the care and protection of its mother. Having been born, the child has the right to be fed and to live, to be reared and educated, to have the opportunity of working and of realising his or her full personality and dignity as a human being. These rights of the child (and others which I have not enumerated) must equally be protected and vindicated by the State. In exceptional cases the State, under the provisions of Article 42, s. 5, of the Constitution, is given the duty, as guardian of the common good, to provide for a child born into a family where the parents fail in their duty towards that child for physical or moral reasons. In the same way, in special circumstances the State may have an equal obligation in relation to a child born outside the family to protect that child, even against its mother, if her natural rights are used in such a way as to endanger the health or life of the child or to deprive him of his rights. In my view this obligation stems from the provisions of Article 40, s. 3, of the Constitution.

At Common Law

At common law an illegitimate child was termed 'filius nullius' and was regarded as being no more than the 'unfortunate offspring of the common failing of a man and a woman' – a burden on the locality and a person to be shunned. In this unchristian treatment of a human being, natural rights were forgotten and a lonely life was ordained merely because of the accident of birth. Not only is this not so now under the Constitution, but the State has the added obligation to defend and vindicate in its laws all natural rights of all citizens. In relation to illegitimate children and certain others, the State has endeavoured to discharge this obligation by the Adoption Acts. The purpose of these Acts is to give to these children the opportunity to become members of a family and to have the status and protection which such membership entails. I turn now to look at the provisions of these Acts in so far as they bear on this case.

The Adoption Acts

The *Adoption Act, 1952*, enabled a child who was not less than six months and not more than seven years of age, to be adopted if he was resident in the State and was either illegitimate or an orphan. The *Adoption Act, 1964*, provided for the adoption of a legitimated child on certain conditions, and the *Adoption Act, 1974*, removed the lower and upper age limits originally provided. The Act of 1952 provided for a register of recognised adoption societies, and they were given the sole right to make arrangements for adoption. The Act of 1952 enabled such societies to make the necessary preliminary arrangements with the mother or guardian. While the term 'placing for adoption' (as used in the Act of 1974) is not defined, it seems clear that the phrase contemplates the originating arrangement for adoption made by a mother or guardian with an adoption society. The mother or guardian so entering into such arrangement, or placing, for adoption must be fully informed of her rights, including the right to give or withhold consent at any time before the making of the adoption order.

Up to 1974 the final adoption order, irrespective of what was said or done at the original placing for adoption, could not be made without the final consent of the mother or guardian – except in exceptional circumstances where such consent could be dispensed with by the Board. This meant that, despite the placing for adoption and the giving of the child to the hopeful adopting parents and the passing of time, adoption would become impossible if the mother or guardian, at any time before the making of the adoption order, finally refused consent or withdrew a consent already given. The consent in question here is the consent to the making of the adoption order.

It was to deal with anxieties and difficulties caused by this situation that s. 3 of the Act of 1974 was passed. Two conditions must be satisfied for the section to operate on the application of a person entitled to apply. First, a person whose consent is necessary to the making of an adoption order must have 'agreed to the placing of the child for adoption.'

Secondly, that person must have either failed, neglected or refused to consent to the final order or have withdrawn a consent already given. The constitutionality of this section is to be assumed and, therefore, it must be interpreted in so far as is possible to accord with this assumption. Applying this principle, it seems to me that the section cannot be regarded as an attempt to diminish or restrict constitutional rights if another interpretation is open. Accordingly, in relation to a mother and her child, the words 'who has agreed to the placing of the child for adoption' must contemplate a mother who has so agreed and acted in such a manner as to abrogate her constitutionally-recognised rights to the custody of her child. This requires a free consent on the part of the mother given in the full knowledge of the consequences which follow upon her placing her child for adoption.

If the mother's agreement to the placing for adoption is not such as to extinguish or drastically modify her constitutional rights to custody, the section could not be operated against her. Once her agreement is such as to permit the operation of the section then, in my view, the decision to grant or refuse the order sought must be taken on the sole test as to what, in relation to the grant or refusal of the order sought, is in the 'best interests of the child.' This will involve a consideration of the circumstances of the mother, her reasons for refusing or withdrawing her consent, and the prospects of how the child's future will be served by refusing the order sought. While the making of the order merely permits the Board to proceed towards an adoption order (which it may or may not make), it does have the effect of finally deciding the mother's claim. Obviously to be considered also are the probabilities as to the child's future if the mother's consent is dispensed with. In suggesting matters to be considered, I am doing no more than that, for I conceive that many other matters which I have not adverted to may have to be considered in assessing 'the best interests of the child.'

This being my view as to the meaning and effects of s. 3 of the Act of 1974, I now turn to the evidence adduced before the learned President and to the facts as found by him.

Placing for Adoption

The plaintiff, being pregnant of her child, concealed the fact from everyone close to her. As she said in evidence, 'the pregnancy was not showing.' She went on to say that she was able to continue at her work and to wear ordinary clothes right up to the time she entered the hospital. Having gone to hospital and having given birth to her baby, the plaintiff confided in one of her sisters, who was married and who lived nearby. The question of adoption then arose and was urged on the plaintiff by a member of the nursing staff. On leaving hospital the plaintiff had four interviews with the director of the adoption society and, finally, she had an interview on the 6th January, 1978, with a social worker employed by the adoption society. Some seven weeks had then elapsed since the birth of her child. It is clear on the evidence that the full implications of adoption were explained to the plaintiff: and also explained were what her rights would be once she placed her child for adoption. These rights included a right to refuse or to withdraw consent to final adoption, subject to the possibility of an application being made to the High Court by a person seeking to adopt her child for an order authorising the Board to dispense with her consent.

I am satisfied that it was explained to her that such an order could be granted if it was then decided by the High Court that it was in the best interests of her child to do so. The evidence shows that not only was this fully explained to her orally, but that she was given a typed memorandum setting out the position in detail. It is clear that she was considering adoption because of her view, which subsequently turned out to be incorrect, as to the possible reaction of her parents. Nevertheless, can it be said on the evidence that she did not know what she was doing? In my view this cannot be said. It is, therefore, not surprising that the learned President of the High Court found as a fact that the various interviews with the director of the adoption society 'concluded with a clear decision by the plaintiff to place her child for adoption.' The plaintiff signed this consent later on the 6th January, 1978, having again been fully advised and having received beforehand the written memorandum already mentioned. Therefore, it seems to me on the evidence and the findings of fact made by the learned President of the High Court that one is driven to the conclusion that the plaintiff agreed to the placing of her child for adoption with knowledge of the consequences. One of these consequences [was] that, if she changed her mind before final adoption, her consent to such adoption could be dispensed with by the High Court if it were satisfied that it was in the best interests of the child to do so.

In my view, in agreeing so to place her child for adoption in the circumstances, the plaintiff dispensed with her constitutional rights to insist on the custody of her child and agreed to its custody being decided in accordance with the statutory provisions of which she was made fully aware.

Incorrect Test Applied

I am of the opinion, therefore, that this case was proper to be dealt with under the provisions of s. 3 of the *Adoption Act, 1974*, because the constitutional rights of the mother to the custody of her child had been dispensed with by her in the manner indicated. To the extent, therefore, that it came before the learned President to be dealt with in accordance with the provisions of that section, I am in agreement with what happened in the High Court.

However, I am concerned as to the tests applied by the President in coming to his decision. In my view, the section could not apply if the constitutional rights of the mother continued to exist, since legislation could not affect or prevail over these rights. Accordingly, the section could only be operative in circumstances in which the agreed 'placing of the child for adoption' constituted a consensual abandonment of constitutional rights and an acceptance by the mother of the provisions of the Adoption Acts in so far as her rights were concerned. As already indicated, I conceive this to be the effect of the learned President's finding on the evidence before him.

Nevertheless, in deciding in favour of the plaintiff's point of view, the President was clearly guided by the constitutional rights of the mother on the basis that these survived her clear and definite agreement to place for adoption. This being his view and there being, as he put it, no 'overwhelming demands' otherwise in relation to the welfare of the child, he felt bound to make the order required by these prevailing constitutional rights. While he dealt with the welfare of the infant, having regard to the circumstances of each of the parties, he does not appear ever to have considered the one question which arises under s. 3 of the Act of 1974, namely, what was 'in the best interests of the child.' He came down in favour of the mother because of her constitutional rights and the absence of any overwhelming reason to the contrary in relation to the child's welfare. He might have come to the same conclusion, having regard to the child's age, its relationship with the plaintiff and the probable home circumstances which the plaintiff could arrange, had he considered the issue solely as to what was in the child's best interests. But he did not do so. I would like to feel that this Court could do so, but I do not think it can. To do this, without seeing the witnesses, and by applying to the cold words of a typed transcript a test which was not applied in the Court below, would be to subvert this Court's function as a court of appeal. For this reason, with very much regret, I must conclude that this case should go back to the High Court to have the issue under s. 3 of the Act of 1974 determined in accordance with what is 'in the best interests of the child.'

I wish to add that I interpret s. 3 as giving to the child the statutory right to have her interests considered without regard to the clashing claims and competing rights of others. Further, I conceive it to be the clear duty of this Court to ensure that this right is both recognised and protected. For these reasons I would allow this appeal.

I wish also to add that I have had the opportunity of reading the judgment about to be delivered by Mr. Justice Walsh. In his judgment he expresses opinions, with regard to whether judicial powers are exercised by the Adoption Board and as to categories of persons who may be adopted, which do not directly arise in this case. As these matters have not been the subject of examination or argument in the present case I express no opinion with regard to them.

Walsh, J.:

. . . . While the facts of the case are relatively simple, the points of law raised are complex. The position of the unmarried mother and her child has always been an extremely difficult one in the common law of England and subsequently in Ireland when the English common law came to be the law of the land. It was not without justification that the late President of the High Court, Gavan Duffy P., in *In Re M.* [1946] I.R. 334 described the approach of the common law to illegitimacy as 'barbarous.' In his review of the law in that case, which I need not here repeat, he dealt with the position of the illegitimate child and its mother under the common law of England.

It is a matter of history that the civil and canon laws did not allow a child to remain illegitimate if the parents afterwards married, but a proposal by the Bishops in England to assimilate the law of England to the canon law in this respect was rejected by the English Parliament in 1235 in the first Act of Parliament ever passed in England, namely, the Statute of Merton. In this respect the law of England remained unchanged for almost 700 years until the *Legitimacy Act, 1926*. The common law in Ireland in this matter remained unchanged until the *Legitimacy Act, 1931*. In Scotland, however, and in most other Christian countries, including other countries of the common law, legitimation of the children has always followed the marriage of the parents.

As Gavan Duffy P. pointed out at p. 344 of the report of *In Re M.* [1946] I.R. 334 the harsh approach of the English common law to illegitimacy induced Victorian jurists in England to prop a mother's claim to the custody of an illegitimate child upon her primary statutory duty to maintain it. He went on to say:– '. . . the accident that the law for vagabonds imposes that maternal liability is a sorry substitute for the authentic claims of nature, which should not be thus depreciated under a Christian polity.' When Gavan Duffy P. spoke of the 'authentic claims of nature' he was speaking of the natural right or rights of a mother in respect of her child and the natural rights of the child in respect of its mother. These rights spring from the natural relationship of the mother and the child. So far as these particular natural rights are concerned, it is immaterial as between the mother and her child whether the mother is or is not married to the father of the child. During the hearing of this appeal counsel for the notice parties advanced the bold but, in my opinion, totally untenable view that the mother of an illegitimate child has no natural rights in regard to that child. This Court, in its decision in *The State (Nicolaou)* v. *An Bord Uchtála* [1966] I.R. 567 (at p. 644) clearly recognised the natural right of the mother of an illegitimate child to the custody and care of her child and held that this, and other natural personal rights which she has, fall to be protected under Article 40, s. 3, of the Constitution. The fact that such rights are not specifically enumerated in the Constitution does not support in any way the submission made in this Court on behalf of the notice parties. It is now well accepted that the view, first enunciated by my learned colleague, Mr. Justice Kenny, in the High Court in *Ryan* v. *The Attorney General* [1965] I.R. 294 and confirmed by this Court on appeal in the same case (that there are rights guaranteed by the

Constitution other than those which are enumerated in the Constitution itself) is the correct view.

At p. 344 of the report of *In Re M.* [1946] I.R. 344 Gavan Duffy P. said:– 'Under Irish law, while I do not think that the constitutional guarantee for the family (Art. 41 of the Constitution) avails the mother of an illegitimate child, I regard the innocent little girl as having the same "natural and imprescriptible rights" (under Art. 42) as a child born in wedlock to religious and moral, intellectual, physical and social education, and her care and upbringing during her coming, formative years must be the decisive consideration in our judgment.' That view was confirmed by this Court in its judgment in *Nicolaou's Case* [1966] I.R. 567 at p. 642 of the report. . . .

The mother and her illegitimate child are human beings and each has the fundamental rights of every human being and the fundamental rights which spring from their relationship to each other. These are natural rights. It has already been decided by this Court in *Nicolaou's Case* [1966] I.R. 567 that among the mother's natural rights is the right to the custody and care of her child. Rights also have their corresponding obligations or duties. The fact that a child is born out of lawful wedlock is a natural fact. Such a child is just as entitled to be supported and reared by its parent or parents, who are the ones responsible for its birth, as a child born in lawful wedlock. One of the duties of a parent or parents, be they married or not, is to provide as best the parent or parents can the welfare of the child and to ward off dangers to the health of the child. As was pointed out by this Court in *Ryan* v. *The Attorney General* [1965] I.R. 294 (at p. 350), there is nothing in the Constitution which recognises the right of a parent to refuse to allow the provision of measures designed to secure the health of the child when the method of avoiding injury is one which is not fraught with danger to the child and is within the procurement of the parent.

In my view, in this respect there is no difference between the obligations of the unmarried parent to the child and those of the married parent. These obligations of the parent or parents amount to natural rights of the child and they exist for the benefit of the child. The child's natural rights in these matters are primarily to be satisfied by the parent or parents.

In so far as children born out of wedlock are concerned, it has been pointed out in *Nicolaou's Case* [1966] I.R. 567 (at p. 644) that there is no provision in Article 40 of the Constitution which prohibits or restricts the surrender, abdication or transfer of any of the rights guaranteed in that Article by the person entitled to them. Thus, in an appropriate case, the mother may transfer her rights in favour of another or abandon them, but in a way in which the essential natural rights of the child in respect of its care, welfare, health and upbringing are not infringed. The Adoption Acts provide such a way. As in *Nicolaou's Case* [1966] I.R. 567, it is not necessary for me in this matter to explore, or endeavour to give an exhaustive enumeration of the guaranteed rights of either the mother or of the child. However, I think I should draw attention to the words of my learned colleague, Mr. Justice Henchy, in *McGee* v. *The Attorney General* [1974] I.R. 284 where he said at p. 325 of the report:–

> As has been held in a number of cases, the unspecified personal rights guaranteed by sub-s. 1 of s. 3 of Article 40 are not confined to those specified in sub-s. 2 of that section. It is for the Courts to decide in a particular case whether the right relied on comes within the constitutional guarantee. To do so, it must be shown that it is a right that inheres in the citizen in question by virtue of his human personality. The lack of precision in this test is reduced when sub-s. 1 of s. 3 of Article 40 is read (as it must be) in the light of the Constitution as a whole and, in particular, in the light of what the Constitution, expressly or by necessary implication, deems to be fundamental to the personal standing of the individual in question in the context of the social order envisaged by the Constitution. The infinite variety in the relationships between the citizen and his fellows and between the citizen and the State makes an exhaustive enumeration of the guaranteed rights difficult, if not impossible.

In my judgment in the same case, I referred (at p. 310) to Articles 41, 42 and 43 of the Constitution and expressed the view, which I still hold, that these Articles 'acknowledge that natural rights, or human rights, are not created by law but that the Constitution confirms their existence and gives them protection. The individual has natural and human rights over which the State has no authority . . .' Later, at p. 317 of the report, I stated:– 'The natural or human rights to which I have referred earlier in this judgment are part of what is generally called the natural law.'

Not only has the child born out of lawful wedlock the natural right to have its welfare and health guarded no less well than that of a child born in lawful wedlock, but *a fortiori* it has the right to life itself and the right to be guarded against all threats directed to its existence whether before or after birth. The child's natural rights spring primarily from the natural right of every individual to life, to be reared and educated, to liberty, to work, to rest and recreation, to the practice of religion, and to follow his or her conscience. The right to life necessarily implies the right to be born, the right to preserve and defend (and to have preserved and defended) that life, and the right to maintain that life at a proper human standard in matters of food, clothing and habitation. It lies not in the power of the parent who has the primary natural rights and duties in respect of the child to exercise them in such a way as intentionally or by neglect to endanger the health or life of the child or to terminate its existence. The child's natural right to life and all that flows from that right are independent of any right of the parent as such. I wish here to repeat what I said in *McGee's Case* [1974] I.R. 284 at p. 312 of the report:– '. . . any action on the part of either the husband and wife or of the State to limit family sizes by endangering or destroying human life must necessarily not only be an offence against the common good but also against the guaranteed personal rights of the human life in question.' In these respects the child born out of lawful wedlock is in precisely the same position as the child born in lawful wedlock.

The Constitution rejected the English common-law view of the position of the illegitimate child in so far as its fundamental rights are concerned. It guarantees to protect the child's natural rights in the same way as it guarantees to protect the natural rights of the mother of the child. . . .

The Act of 1952 provides for the adoption of children who are illegitimate and children who are full orphans. . . . They are children who might not otherwise have the advantage of a safe and secure home because of the circumstances prevailing in their particular cases.

It is interesting to note that these two classes of children are subject to one important difference. As has been held in *Nicolaou's Case* [1966] I.R. 567, the illegitimate child and its mother do not constitute a family within the meaning of Article 42 of the Constitution. On the other hand there is no doubt, in my view, that orphaned children who are members of a family continue to constitute a family for the purpose of the Constitution even though their parents have died. It can scarcely be contended that a unit consisting of four or five children who range in age between five and sixteen years, and whose parents may have been killed simultaneously in a car accident or may have died successively from illness, and who had been a family during the life of both parents or of the surviving parent, cease to be a family on the death of both parents. The family which is founded on marriage is recognised as the fundamental unit group of society; the fact that the married parents of the children have died does not alter the character of the unit.

In mentioning this aspect of the law, I am not to be taken as impugning in any way the validity of statutory provisions allowing for legal adoption. In my view, there is nothing whatever in the Constitution to prevent a member of a family passing out of that family. This happens naturally when a child sets out to establish a family of her or his own: or when, by reason of age or maturity or other circumstances, he ceases to be a member of a family in the sense of forming part of a unit which lives together as such and is a recognisable family within the meaning of the Constitution. I do not see any impediment in principle to a child passing out of one family and becoming a member of another family in particular circumstances. However, as this process may involve in those circumstances a consideration of the natural rights of the parents of the family which is being vacated and those of the child who is leaving the family, it must necessarily be based upon consent. Natural rights may be waived or surrendered by the persons who enjoy them, provided that such waiver is not prohibited either by natural law or by positive law. Likewise, circumstances may arise which necessarily lead to the inference that the rights have been waived or abandoned.

One of the most important questions of law to be examined in the present case is the provision in s. 3 of the *Adoption Act, 1974*, relating to the question of dispensing with the consent of the mother to the adoption of her child. This provision marked such a radical departure from the basic structure of the adoption system hitherto existing that it is necessary to examine that system in some detail.

The essential feature of the system established by the Act of 1952 was the fact that no adoption was possible without consent. In the first instance, the consent of the mother of the illegitimate child had to be obtained; where there was no mother or the mother could not be found, the consent of the legal guardian was required; where there was no legal guardian, the consent of the person having charge or control over the child had to be obtained. It followed that nobody could be compelled to adopt a child and that nobody would be given a child for adoption unless that person consented to the procedure. It would have been quite open for the Oireachtas to provide for legal adoption with the effects which it has without the intervention of any adoption board, simply by allowing it to be brought about by means of an intermediary or even by direct agreement between the person or persons who wished to have the child adopted and the person or persons who wished to adopt it. Thus adoption in our law is essentially a consent or voluntary arrangement. The Adoption Board is, in effect, a ratifying agency and a safeguard. The Board ensures that the particular adoption is made in accordance with the Acts of the Oireachtas and that the prospective adopters are suitable. It also preserves the anonymity of the parties to the procedure. Undoubtedly, there have been many cases where the arrangements for adoption have been made directly between the person seeking to have a child adopted and the person seeking to adopt the child, but they were routed through the Board for the simple reason that the statute provided that adoption would not amount to legal adoption unless the machinery of the Board was employed and an adoption order was made by the Board.

The Board has no function to settle disputes as to the custody of a child. Neither does it have a jurisdiction to adjudicate upon anything that could be said to be in controversy or dispute between parties, either in the cases where anonymity is maintained or in the cases where the parties are known to each other. The Board is simply concerned with what I am satisfied is the administrative function of seeing that the steps being taken are not contrary to the adoption legislation, are not inimical to the welfare of the child, and that everybody concerned has had a full opportunity of considering the matter carefully. It is quite clear that the Board was not invested with any power to settle or decide any question as to the existence of a right or obligation or duty. This appears to me clearly to have been the policy and the effect of the Act of 1952.

The Act of 1952 provides that certain persons, who are designated by reference to their occupation or relationship to the child, are entitled to be heard on an application for adoption as well as any other person whom the Board, in its discretion, decides to hear. It is obvious that there are instances where the Board, like many other administrative tribunals or designated persons exercising administrative functions, is bound to act judicially. As has already been pointed out by this Court in *McDonald v. Bord na gCon*

[1965] I.R. 217, the obligation to act judicially does not mean that the body or the person or persons so bound are thereby deemed to be exercising a judicial function or powers of a judicial nature: see also the decision of this Court in *East Donegal Co-Operative v, The Attorney General* [1970] I.R. 317.

The statutory consequences which flow from the making of an adoption order are that the mother or guardian loses all parental and guardianship rights and is freed from all parental and guardianship duties, and the child's legal status is substantially altered. By reason of the adoption, the child stands in relation to the adopters as a child born to them in lawful wedlock. Marriage also alters the status of the parties to it and, where it is one which results in the legitimation of a child, it alters the status of the child. Adoption, like marriage, has far-reaching effects in the law of succession. It is worth noting that all rights of succession, as distinct from the right to bequeath, derive from statute. The legal consequences of adoption are matters in respect of which the Board has no discretion or function. They are statutory consequences of the making of an adoption order and could equally well have been statutory consequences of an adoption permitted by law without the intervention of any adoption board.

As under the Act of 1952 no adoption order could normally be made in respect of a child exceeding seven years old, no general provision was made for giving consideration to the wishes of the child. However, in a special provision in s. 19 of that Act, which permitted the adoption of children over that age (but under the age of 21 years) who were in the care of persons seeking their adoption as from a date before the passing of the Act, the Board was obliged under the Act to give due consideration to the wishes of the child having regard to his age and understanding. That was a perfectly proper statutory provision because children also have constitutionally guaranteed natural rights. These rights must be safeguarded and a child's consent, in so far as its age and understanding warrant it, must be obtained before its status is altered by way of adoption. When a child has not reached that stage its interests must be represented. However, it may well be that in many cases the Board can adequately discharge that function. Naturally, where a child is of proper age and understanding, its natural rights or status may not be altered against its will. Where a child's welfare coercively requires a change in its custodial care, there is already ample power to deal with the matter under the *Guardianship of Infants Act, 1964*.

The Act of 1952 was amended by the Acts of 1964, 1974 and 1976. For the purposes of this case the Court is concerned principally with the Act of 1974. The first and, perhaps, most far-reaching change made by that Act is that contained in s. 11 which, in effect, removed the upper age limit of seven years and permitted the adoption of children where the Board was satisfied that in the particular circumstances of the case it was desirable to make an adoption order, provided that the adopted person was under 21 years old. It is to be noted in passing that no exception was made even for the case where such child might already have been married. The whole adoption procedure, except the exception with which I shall shortly deal, remained subject to the consents of all the concerned parties. In my view since 1974 these consents must also include the consent of the child where he or she is of the necessary age and understanding and, presumably, of the spouse of the child where the child is married – that is, of course, if the adoption of a married child is constitutionally possible. The fact that the Act of 1974, while increasing the age limit considerably, omitted to deal with the aspect of the child's consent does not alter the fundamental right of the child where his status is being altered. . . .

There is no definition in any of the Acts of the phrase 'the placing of the child for adoption.' However, I think one may reasonably assume that it means either the handing over of the child for the purpose of its being adopted or even, if the mother retains the child, the giving of a clear and unambiguous indication that it is her desire to surrender her natural rights in respect of the child and that it be adopted. I am satisfied that, having regard to the natural rights of the mother, the proper construction of the provision in s. 3 of the Act of 1974 is that the consent, if given, must be such as to amount to a fully-informed, free and willing surrender or an abandonment of these rights. However, I am also of opinion that such a surrender or abandonment may be established by her conduct when it is such as to warrant the clear and unambiguous inference that such was her fully-informed, free and willing intention. In my view, a consent motivated by fear, stress or anxiety, or a consent or conduct which is dictated by poverty or other deprivations does not constitute a valid consent.

It is significant that neither the question of the dispensing with consent (which, by its very nature, could in many cases raise a controversy as to rights) nor the question as to the custody of the child were placed within the powers of the Board but were assigned by the Oireachtas exclusively to the High Court, thus preserving the consenting and voluntary basis of the Board's role.

The function of the High Court in this particular area is to decide whether or not to authorise the Board to dispense with the consent of the mother, or guardian, or the person having charge of or control over the child. For the reasons I have already stated, the High Court must be satisfied that the consent already given (where it has been given) or the placing for adoption is such as to amount to a surrender or abandonment of the natural rights which exist in the mother. I refer to the mother in particular because a custodian or a guardian, or a person having charge of or control over the child, does not have these natural rights and the point arises only in a case in which the mother of the child is involved. As I have already indicated, the court should also take into account the wishes of the child in appropriate cases.

Hitherto I have referred only to adoption, which is quite distinct from guardianship or custody. The *Guardianship of Infants Act, 1964*, deals with questions of the custody of a child and it makes provision for the transfer of the custody of a child or the giving of a child  into the custody of a particular person or persons (whether the child be the child of married parents or not) where the welfare of the child so dictates. The Act also deals in a more restricted way with questions of guardianship. It is quite clear from that Act that guardianship and custody are two different concepts, and this has been made abundantly clear by the decision of this Court in *B.* v. *B.* [1975] I.R. 54. It is interesting to note in passing that s. 6, sub-s. 4, of the Act expressly states that the mother of an illegitimate child shall be the guardian of her child, thereby, in my view, reflecting a constitutionally protected natural  right, just as the parents of a child born in lawful wedlock are the guardians of the child because of the natural bond between them, as was also mentioned in *B. v. B.* [1975] I.R. 54; see also my own observations on the point in *McGee's Case* [1974] I.R. 284 at p. 311 of the report where I stated that in Articles 41 and 42 of the Constitution parents are the natural guardians of the children of the family. Guardianship may be surrendered or abandoned provided that doing so does not infringe any constitutional rights of the child and is not inimical to the welfare of the child. The test laid down in s. 3 of the *Guardianship of Infants Act, 1964*, is that the Court shall decide the matter having regard to the welfare of the child as the 'first and paramount consideration.' This phrase is found in s. 1 of the (English) *Guardianship of Infants Act, 1925.* A number of English judicial decisions have stated that the consideration of the welfare of the child is not to be regarded as the only consideration. The same phrase found its way into s. 2 of the Act of 1974 which provides.

> In any matter, application or proceedings before the Board or any court relating to the arrangements for or the making of an adoption order. the Board or the court, in deciding that question, shall regard the welfare of the child as the first and paramount consideration.

It was submitted to this Court that that is the test which should have been taken into account by the High Court in the present matter, notwithstanding that s. 3 of the Act of

1974, under which the High Court operates, uses quite a different test, namely, that of the course chosen being in 'the best interests of the child.' Prior to the setting up of the State in 1922 and prior to the enactment of the Constitution of Saorstát Éireann, it was clearly recognised by the Courts in this country when they came to deal with the question of the custody of a child, including an illegitimate child, that the paramount consideration was the welfare of the child in the widest sense of the term. I do not see that the position is made any stronger by the addition of the word 'first' to 'paramount' – if anything, it probably tends to weaken it because, as has been pointed out in one English decision, a reference to 'first' indicates that there may be second, third, fourth and successive considerations. The word 'paramount' by itself is not by any means an indication of exclusivity; no doubt if the Oireachtas had intended the welfare of the child to be the sole consideration it would have said so. The use of the word 'paramount' certainly indicates that the welfare of the child is to be the superior or the most important consideration, in so far as it can be, having regard to the law or the provisions of the Constitution applicable to any given case. However, when one turns to s. 3 of the Act of 1974 and comes to deal with another matter, one finds that a different phrase is used. Therefore it must be accepted that the test in s. 3 is not intended to be identical with the test in s. 2 of the Act of 1974; one must examine the test in s. 3 in the light of the procedure in which it is applicable. What is 'in the best interests of the child' relates obviously to a temporary situation. Custody orders are, of their nature, temporary only. The temporary nature of the situation is clearly indicated by the fact that what the High Court is called upon to do is to decide whether or not the Board should be given authority to dispense with the consent of the mother or the guardian or custodian, as the case may be.

[Having referred to the provisions of s. 3 of the *Adoption Act, 1974,* Walsh, J. continued]. It is not very clear from s. 3, sub-s. 2, of the Act of 1974 whether the High Court must couple paragraphs (*a*) and (*b*) or whether the High Court can refrain from making an order under paragraph (*a*) but make an order under paragraph (*b*). If the provision means that the granting of custody of the child to the applicant for such period as the court may determine is automatically to be coupled with authorising the Board to waive the consent of the mother, then there must be serious doubt as to its validity. If, however, it means that the High Court may do either, or both, then the grounds for the test to be applied for the purpose of authorising the Board to dispense with the consent may be utterly different from the grounds for the test to be applied in the giving or the refusal of custody, even though the custody is to be only for a temporary period. The fact that the authority to dispense with the consent may be given to the Board does not by any means end the case, because there still remains an application for adoption to be processed by the Board. If the Board does not make an adoption order then, if the custody of the child has been given to the applicant for adoption, the child will obviously have to be given back unless proceedings for custody only may be successfully maintained under the *Guardianship of Infants Act, 1964.*

In my view, the High Court must use the 'best interests' test in s. 3 of the Act of 1974 in considering whether or not to give custody for the temporary period and also in deciding whether or not it should authorise the Board to dispense with the consent. If the High Court is satisfied that it is in the best interests of the child that the Board should be permitted to examine and to process the application for adoption, the High Court is not thereby directing that there should be an adoption and is not in any way indicating to the Board how they should deal with the case.

I am quite satisfied that the President of the High Court did not err in adopting the test laid down in s. 3 of the Act of 1974 instead of the test laid down in s. 2, which latter test appears to be the one which binds the Board when it comes to consider whether or not it should approve of the arrangements to make an adoption order. The references to the 'court' in s. 2 are not very illuminating. Save for the purpose of reference in deciding questions of law, the court, apart from s. 3, has no function whatever in the matter of adoption as such. Section 2 specifically refers to 'the arrangements for or the making of an adoption order' and seems to imply that a court has some function in these matters.

In the course of the judgment of the learned President of the High Court, there are certain apparent ambiguities which might lead one to conclude that he had in mind the possibility that the consent of the mother might be dispensed with under s. 3 of the Act solely on the ground of her misbehaviour or, perhaps, on the ground of her general lack of fitness to have custody of the child. In view of the fact that he was obviously very conscious of the constitutional rights of the mother in this case, I do not think that this is the correct meaning to be attached to his judgment. I think that what he had in mind was that type of abandonment of her rights, or that type of misbehaviour or other activity on her part, from which it could be clearly inferred that she had in fact surrendered or abandoned her rights. However, I do not fully agree with the President of the High Court where he appears to suggest that, in a situation where there is a conflict between the constitutional rights of the child and those of the mother, the misbehaviour of the mother alone may justify a judicial intervention going so far as to dispense with the mother's consent to adoption in order to protect the child's constitutional rights. In my view, the situation envisaged could be dealt with appropriately by a custody order under the *Guardianship of Infants Act, 1964*, which is a completely different thing from an adoption order. The natural guardianship rights of the parent or parents may still be maintained although the custody may be given to a third person. For the reasons set out in the judgments in *B.* v. *B.* [1975] I.R. 54, the wishes of the parent or parents must in such a case be consulted on the upbringing of the child; it is only when there is a dispute which cannot be satisfactorily resolved that recourse to the court is necessary. Instances of the kind which worried the learned President of the High Court, namely, whether the constitutional rights of the child were to be upheld to the total or virtual exclusion of the constitutional rights of the mother, need not arise as the problem may be catered for in the manner I have indicated. The important question in cases such as the present one is whether there has been a surrender or an abandonment by the mother of her constitutional or natural rights in respect of the child, such as to give rise to the possibility of the child's being legally adopted.

There is nothing in the Constitution to indicate that in cases of conflict the rights of the parent are always to be given primacy. It is important to recall that in *In Re Frost* [1947] I.R. 3, Sullivan C.J., in delivering the judgment of all the members of the former Supreme Court of Justice said at p. 28 of the report:–

> I cannot, however, accept his second proposition which was that the rights of the parents . . . are absolute rights, the exercise of which cannot in any circumstances be controlled by the Court. That a child has natural and imprescriptible rights is recognised by the Constitution (Art. 42.5), and if Mr. Ryan's second proposition were accepted, it would follow that the Court would be powerless to protect those rights should they be ignored by the parents. I am satisfied that the Court has jurisdiction to control the exercise of parental rights, but in exercising that jurisdiction it must not act upon any principle which is repugnant to the Constitution.

Article 42, s. 5, of the Constitution speaks of the case where parents fail in their duty towards their children for physical or moral reasons: it provides that the State, *as guardian* of the common good, by appropriate means shall endeavour to supply the place of the parents, but *always with due regard for the natural and imprescriptible rights of the child.* Under that section the State may very well by legislation provide for the failure of the parents, and in appropriate cases it may very well extend the law beyond simple provisions for a change of custody. A parent may for physical or moral reasons decide to abandon his position as a parent or he or she may be deemed to have abandoned that position; a failure in parental duty may itself be evidence of such an abandonment. The fact that a parent fails in parental duty or abandons parental duty for no more than purely selfish reasons may well, by itself, be regarded in an appropriate case as a moral failure on the part of the parent, or as a failure which may be classified as arising from a moral reason.

In Article 42, s. 1, of the Constitution the State recognises that the family itself is the primary and natural educator of the child, but it goes on to say that the State guarantees to respect the inalienable right and duty of parents to provide in accordance with their means *for* the religious and moral, intellectual, physical and social education of their children. Therefore, such education is regarded both as a right and a duty of the parents; correlatively, it is the right of the children to look to their parents and family for the fulfilment of their duty to supply, arrange for, or provide that education. If there is a failure to perform the duty, then the circumstances may be such that a transfer of custody is warranted. Where there is a complete abandonment of the parental right and duty, the State may be justified in taking measures by statute or otherwise to protect the right of the child; these measures may include the enactment of adoption legislation. Where the *Guardianship of Infants Act, 1964*, defines 'welfare' it is, as has been remarked in other cases, following the wording of the Constitution itself. It is also to be borne in mind that some inalienable rights are absolutely inalienable while others are relatively inalienable.

So far interventions authorised by the Constitution have been examined in the context of a situation involving married parents and their children. In my view, they are no less permissible under the Constitution in situations involving an unmarried mother and her child.

The findings of fact made by the learned President of the High Court are such that there is no reason for holding that the defence of the constitutional rights of the plaintiff's child to an upbringing that will not be injurious or inimical to her own constitutional rights requires that the natural rights of the plaintiff (which are constitutionally protected) should be set aside. Neither the evidence nor the findings of the President would indicate the existence of any danger of the child's interests being in peril.

So far as the constitutional rights of the plaintiff are concerned, the findings of the President do not indicate that she has surrendered or abandoned her constitutional rights by a fully informed, free and willing surrender or abandonment of these rights, or at all, nor did the President so find. Before anybody may be said to have surrendered or abandoned his constitutional rights, it must be shown that he is aware of what the rights are and of what he is doing. Secondly, the action taken must be such as could reasonably lead to the clear and unambiguous inference that such was the intention of the person who is alleged to have either surrendered or abandoned the constitutional rights. The facts of the present case do not support any such conclusion. Less than eight weeks after the birth of her child, the plaintiff had already signed a form consenting to the placing of the child for adoption. Prior to that she had been subject to several representations urging her that it was in the best interests of the child and herself to have the child placed for adoption. When the representations were initially made to her, they were made to her within one week of the birth of her child and while she was still in hospital. It is not difficult to imagine the anxieties and troubled state of mind of this lonely young girl, who was but a short time past her twenty-first birthday and who, unknown to friend or family, had given birth to her child far from home.

There is no suggestion of any impropriety on the part of any of the persons who made representations or interviewed the plaintiff before and immediately after she had signed the form placing her child for adoption. However, it is regrettable that such a degree of haste should have arisen in a case such as this, especially having regard to the isolated position of the plaintiff and to her extreme youth. In so far as the evidence goes, she was not made aware of the possibilities which exist for aiding persons in her position or of the several excellent societies which exist for the purpose of enabling a woman who finds herself in the plaintiff's circumstances to retain her child and, at the same time, to carry on her life as normally as is possible in the circumstances. By the time the plaintiff did sign the form it may be that she was no longer confused but that is very far from saying that she was a completely free agent or that she was aware of the result if she withdrew her consent. All the circumstances indicate that she was not a free agent. The evidence discloses a reluctance and an anxiety on her part throughout the transaction; the matter which appears to have been operating mostly on her mind was her desire to maintain secrecy over the whole affair.

One can scarcely deny the great trauma and the medical, physical and psychological effects of the birth of a child on an unmarried mother, particularly if she is young. The fact that her mind may be such as to have a full appreciation of the fact and consequences of consent – even if such were possible in the present state of the law – does not mean that, having regard to the particular circumstances in which she finds herself, she should not have independent advice. This is specially so in the case of a young girl who is frightened at the possible reaction of her parents, who may be far away from her parents' home, and who is aware that her parents have no knowledge of the event – more particularly when it turns out (as in this case) that her appreciation of her parents' possible reaction is utterly wrong. Yet her fear and anxiety in regard to the reaction she expected from her parents was the dominant factor in her decision. The period before and after the birth of an illegitimate child can be very distressing for the mother of that child, much more so than for a married woman. The reasons for this are obvious. It must be taken into account that not infrequently the mother of such a child can have her judgment impaired at the time of, and even months after, the birth. This is recognised as being true also in the case of the mother of a legitimate child. Hence the introduction by statute into our criminal law of the offence of infanticide in place of that of murder where a mother takes the life of her baby within a year of the birth: see s. 1 of the *Infanticide Act, 1949.*

It is of the utmost significance that, the very moment the plaintiff discovered that her parents' attitude was far more understanding and helpful than she had feared it would be, she found herself for the first time in a completely free position where she could make a fully free choice. She made the choice without any hesitation. The choice was to keep and rear her baby.

I am satisfied that on the evidence the learned President of the High Court was correct in his decision not to authorise the Board to dispense with the consent of the plaintiff mother. On the view of the law that I have taken the question of 'the best interests of the child' only falls to be considered when the mother has surrendered or abandoned her rights. But even on the question of 'best interests,' if that point had been reached, I am satisfied that on the evidence the learned President of the High Court would be justified in holding that those interests would not have required him to authorise the Board to dispense with the plaintiff's consent. His findings of fact are to the effect that the constitutional rights of the child are not in any way exposed to danger and are much less likely to be damaged by being brought up in the manner contemplated and planned by the mother, and that the mother has not in any way surrendered or abandoned her own constitutional rights to both the guardianship and the custody of her child.

One has the utmost sympathy with the notice parties in the disappointment they must feel if they are not allowed to keep the child. However, their position is not comparable with that of the natural mother of the child. It is undoubtedly true that the notice parties have an excellent home and have brought up with loving care the child they have adopted. Even if they had received better legal advice than that which they received from somebody (who did not act for them in this litigation), I do not think that the position would be materially different. Be all that as it may, the fact remains that in matters of this kind and at the stage they have reached, the notice parties have no constitutional rights whatsoever in respect of the child they wish to adopt. The only legal rights they possess are the rights given to them to apply for adoption if the child is properly placed for adoption by the full and free agreement of the mother or, in a case where no consent is forthcoming after the child is properly placed for adoption, to apply to the High Court under the provisions of s. 3 of the Act of 1974. They have applied to the High Court but, in my opinion, their application must fail for the reasons I have already given.

I think I should not conclude my judgment in this highly important case without drawing attention to the danger of pressing, or urging, or advising the mother of an illegitimate child that the best thing for her to do (and do quickly) is to have her child adopted. Earlier in the course of this judgment I have referred to the possibilities that exist for aiding single mothers, and to the several excellent societies that have been established for the purpose of helping and advising persons in the position of the plaintiff to keep the baby and, at the same time, to carry on a reasonably normal life. Doctors, nurses, social workers, those working in hospitals, adoption societies and others concerned in these cases must always keep uppermost in their minds that the unmarried mother and her baby each have all the fundamental rights of other human beings and also those rights which spring from the relationship of the mother to her child and of the child to her mother, and that all these rights must be respected. Furthermore, it must never be overlooked that the Oireachtas instituted legal adoption in the interests of the child and not in the interests of those wishing to adopt a child legally, albeit for the most laudable reasons and thereby to make a child, or additional children, members of their family. If, as I hold, adoption is not possible without consent, express or implied (which, in the context, means a surrender or abandonment of constitutional rights), the question of competing or comparative material or other advantages should never arise as between the mother of the child and the applicants for adoption.

For the reasons I have given I am of opinion that this appeal should be dismissed.

Henchy, J.:

. . . . The single issue arising from those facts is whether, in pursuance of s. 3, sub-s. 2, of the *Adoption Act, 1974*, the Adoption Board should be authorised to dispense with the consent of the plaintiff mother in the making of an adoption order in favour of the couple (the notice parties) to whom the child was given for adoption. The case has been argued within the framework of the terms of reference imposed by that issue, so I shall confine this judgment accordingly. In so far as opinions or observations on wider and unargued topics emanate from this case, I do not wish my silence on those *obiter dicta* to be taken as concurrence. In particular, I refrain from expressing any opinion as to whether the making of an adoption order is the exercise of a judicial function, as the point does not arise in this case. . . .

Because of the central and fundamental position accorded by the Constitution to the family in the social and moral order, there is a necessary and inescapable difference of moral capacity and social function between parents or a parent within a family and the parents or a parent of an illegitimate child. While Article 40, s. 1, of the Constitution recognizes that 'all citizens shall, as human persons, be held equal before the law,' it adds the proviso that such a declaration 'shall not be held to mean that the State shall not in its enactments have due regard to differences of capacity, physical and moral, and of social function.' Thus one will find throughout the laws of the State many instances where parents within a family are treated differently from the parents of an illegitimate child. Likewise, with the same constitutional justification, instances may be adduced (*e.g.*, in the law of succession) where illegitimate children are treated differently from legitimate children.

While the moral capacity and social function of parents are, in constitutional terms, not alone distinguishable but necessarily distinguishable, depending on whether the children are legitimate or illegitimate, all children, whether legitimate or illegitimate, share the common characteristic that they enter life without any responsibility for their status and with an equal claim to what the Constitution expressly or impliedly postulates as the fundamental rights of children. Since Article 42 recognises the children of a marriage as having a natural and imprescriptible right (as the correlative of their parents' duty) to the provision for them of religious and moral, intellectual, physical and social education, a like personal right should be held to be impliedly accorded to illegitimate children by s. 3 of Article 40. That was the conclusion reached (correctly, in my view) by Gavan Duffy P. in *In re M.* [1946] I.R. 334 where the issue was whether the mother of an illegitimate child, who had given the little girl away for 'adoption' (there being then no Adoption Act), could later recover custody of the child. At p. 344 of the report Gavan Duffy P. summed up the legal position thus:–

> It is now universally recognised that the paramount consideration on such an application as this must be the welfare of the child, the word 'welfare' being taken in its widest sense. Under Irish law, while I do not think that the constitutional guarantee for the family (Art. 41 of the Constitution) avails the mother of an illegitimate child, I regard the innocent little girl as having the same 'natural and imprescriptible rights' (under Art. 42) as a child born in wedlock to religious and moral, intellectual, physical and social education, and her care and upbringing during her coming, formative years must be the decisive consideration in our judgment.

I share the view that, while the relevant constitutional rights of children are available equally to legitimate and illegitimate children, the constitutional guarantee for the family does not avail the mother (still less the father) of an illegitimate child. There is no parity of moral capacity or of social function which would justify reading s. 3 of Article 40 as importing for such a mother the natural and imprescriptible rights and duties of parents within a family.

In the normal state of things, the effectuation of the constitutional rights of an illegitimate child will require that the mother be given custody, particularly in the case of a very young child. In such a case the custody has a constitutional footing in so far as it satisfies a constitutional right of the child: while the mother's own right to custody has a legal, as distinct from a constitutional, foundation. In such circumstances the mother's legal right to custody must always yield to the constitutional rights of the child, so that the mother's claim to custody will not be given recognition if (because of factors such as physical incapacity, mental illness, personality defect, chronic alcoholism, drug addiction, moral depravity, or dereliction of parental duty) the mother's custody would be incompatible with the child's constitutional rights.

It is true that the mother's right to the custody and care of her child was said in *The State (Nicolaou)* v. *An Bord Uchtála* [1966] I.R. 567 (at p. 644 of the report) to be given constitutional protection by s. 3 of Article 40, but that observation was not part of the ratio decidendi of that case. The only matter in issue in that case was the nature and extent of the rights of a father of an illegitimate child. If the mother of an illegitimate child had a constitutionally-protected personal right to its custody, it is difficult to see how, in a case such as the present one she could be held to have lost that right when there is no evidence that she was ever made aware of the existence of the right. In my opinion, however, the mother's rights in regard to the child, although deriving from the ties of nature, are given a constitutional footing only to the extent that they are founded on the constitutionally-guaranteed rights of the child.

The *Guardianship of Infants Act, 1964*, clarified and enhanced the legal rights of a mother in regard to the custody, guardianship and upbringing of her illegitimate child. It repealed the *Guardianship of Infants Act, 1886*, the *Custody of Infants Act, 1873*, and the *Custody of Children Act, 1891.* Part II of the Act created a new judicial jurisdiction in regard to guardianship, but it was made clear that this jurisdiction is in addition to any other jurisdiction to appoint or to remove guardians: see s. 5, sub-s. 3, of the Act of 1964. The mother of an illegitimate infant (*i.e.*, a person under 21 years of age) is constituted guardian to the exclusion of the father (s. 6, sub-s. 4), and, as such guardian, is constituted guardian of the person and of the estate of the infant: see s. 10, sub-s. 1. However, the mother's rights as guardian are qualified (s. 3) by the general mandate that in any proceedings involving the custody, guardianship or upbringing of an infant, the court shall regard as the first and paramount consideration the religious and moral, intellectual, physical and social welfare of the infant. In other words, whatever statutory or common-law rights are vested in the mother of an illegitimate child, they must yield to the constitutional rights of the child in proceedings involving custody, guardianship or upbringing. . . .

If, contrary to my opinion, it could be held that the mother of an illegitimate child has a constitutional right to the custody of her child, a consent to placement for adoption could never amount, in itself, to an extinguishment of that right, for it amounts to no more than a consent by the mother to putting her rights (or some of them) in temporary abeyance. It is difficult to see how s. 3 of the Act of 1974 could be operated to defeat the mother's unforfeited or unabandoned constitutional rights, when the test is what is in the best interests of the child rather than the effectuation of the child's constitutional rights, which rights may be satisfied whether the adoption order is made or not. The objective to be attained by an order of the High Court under s. 3 is not simply the effectuation of the rights of either mother or child, but the attainment of a result which will be in the best interests of the child, by either granting or not granting to the mother a power to veto the adoption. . . .

Whether a distinction is to be drawn (and, if so, to what extent) between the 'welfare of the child' and the 'best interests of the child' is something I find unnecessary to consider for, in my opinion s. 2 and s. 3 of the Act of 1974 are directed to mutually exclusive situations. Section 2 is confined to one or other of two types of questions. The first is a question relating to the arrangements for an adoption. By reason of the stautory scope given by s. 4 of the Act of 1952 to 'the making of arrangements for the adoption of a child,' this type of question is limited to the sphere of the initiation of a placement; so it does not arise here. The second type of question envisaged by s. 2 of the Act of 1974 is one related to the making of an adoption order. While the question of whether or not the mother's consent to the making of an adoption order should be dispensed with might, broadly speaking, be said to be related to the making of an adoption order, it is so related only in a preliminary or indirect way. The juxtaposition of ss. 2 and 3 of the Act of 1974, with their differently worded specifications for the exercise of the court's discretion, must be held to indicate differing subject matters. In my view, s. 2 must be held to refer to questions relating to 'arrangements,' *i.e.*, the making of placements, or to the actual making of an adoption order. The question whether the mother's consent will be judicially dispensed with is a separate and distinct matter which arises only under s. 3 and is required by s. 3, sub-s. 2, to be decided in accordance with what is adjudged to be in the best interests of the child. That is the only test which the court may apply in a case such as this.

In the course of his judgment the President of the High Court said that he was holding that the plaintiff mother has a constitutional right to the custody and to the control of the upbringing of her child, that the child has a constitutional right to bodily integrity, and that she has an unenumerated right to an opportunity to be reared with due regard to her welfare, religious and moral, intellectual, physical and social. For the reasons I have given, I do not consider that the mother of an illegitimate child has a constitutional right to the custody or to the control and upbringing of the child. I consider that such a right vests in her as a legal right.

As to a constitutional right to bodily integrity, such a right arises for judicial recognition or enforcement only in circumstances which require that, in order to assure the dignity and freedom of the individual within the constitutional framework, he or she should be held immune from a particular actual or threatened bodily injury or intrusion. No such question arises in this case. There is no suggestion that, whether the proposed adoption goes through or not, the child will suffer any bodily injury or intrusion.

As to the constitutional right of the child, it arises under Article 40, s. 3, by analogy with Article 42, s. 1, and it amounts to a right to be accorded, with due regard to what the circumstances reasonably allow, an upbringing which will provide for the religious and moral, intellectual, physical and social education of the child. Whereas this right, as guaranteed by Article 42, s. 1, to legitimate children, is coupled with a correlative duty imposed on the parents – a duty which is related to their means – the analogous right of illegitimate children which is to be implied under Article 40, s. 3, cannot be necessarily exercisable in the context of a correlative duty imposed on the father or mother. Article 40, s. 3, allows certain personal rights, but not personal duties, to be impliedly recognized. So if it were held to justify the constitutional recognition of the mother's right as to education, it would do so without attaching the attendant constitutional duty imposed by Article 42, s. 1, on married parents. By that I mean that, whereas married parents are not allowed by the Constitution to cast off with impunity their duty to educate their children (the duty being an inalienable one), unmarried mothers are under no such constitutional inhibition. Indeed the Adoption Acts specifically recognize their right to surrender their children to adopters, while withholding from married parents the right to do so. To hold, therefore, that an unmarried mother has an implied constitutional right in respect of the education and, therefore, of the upbringing of her child would be to accord to her a preferred standing over that of married parents; and that would not be in concordance with the constitutional attitude to marriage and the family.

A judge hearing an application under s. 3 of the Act of 1974 is not necessarily concerned with the resolution of conflicting rights, legal or constitutional. He must, of course, ensure that the child's constitutional rights will not be violated if he makes the order sought by the applicants. In the present case it is clear from the transcript of the evidence and from the judge's findings that, whether the plaintiff's consent is dispensed with or not and whether her child remains with the notice parties or is returned to the plaintiff, there is nothing to suggest that the child will not receive, in the way of upbringing and education, her constitutional due. The question to be resolved is not whether on the merits an adoption order should be made in favour of the notice parties (for that is a decision which is reserved for the Board and which has to be decided on material not all of which is before the Court) but whether it would be in the best interests of the child to dispense with the mother's consent. And the onus is on the notice parties to show that it would be in the best interests of the child to do so.

It has for long been judicially accepted that in the case of a young child (the infant in this case is only one year old) a court will not, save for exceptional reasons, make an order which will have the effect of not recognising the right of the infant to be with its mother or the right of the mother to have the care of her infant. . . .

It would have to be shown that there has been or is something in the conduct of the mother, in her physical, mental or psychological capacity, or in the special needs of the child having regard to the religious, moral, economic or other relevant circumstances, before the court would be justified in passing over the prima facie valid claim of the mother.

I am satisfied that the notice parties have failed to satisfy the onus cast on them. There is nothing in the evidence to show any blameworthy conduct on the plaintiff mother's part in regard to the child. Her decision to place her child for adoption was made in her then known circumstances, and in the belief that it was all she could do and that it was in the best interests of the child. As soon as she discovered that her parents would help her and make it possible for her to bring up the child, she tried to get her child back. Having considered the child's welfare in its broad sense, the President of the High Court adjudged the mother to be a fit and proper person to have custody of the child; he did not think that the child would suffer any serious or permanent trauma as a result of being transferred from the notice parties to the plaintiff. Furthermore, looking at the child's 'welfare,' as that word is defined in s. 2 of the *Guardianship of Infants Act, 1964*, the President held that only a marginal difference could be drawn between the notice parties and the plaintiff. In short, all that can be said against the plaintiff's claim to be given the custody of her child is that she placed the child for adoption.

Prior to the passing of the Act of 1974, the mother's right to veto the adoption was absolute. Now that right is only a qualified one, in that s. 3 of the Act allows the High Court to dispense with her consent if it is satisfied that to do so would be in the best interests of the child. The two-stage nature of the adoption procedure, and particularly the requirement that the mother must be told at the time of placement that she may change her mind, means that there must be something more than a change of mind, something exceptional which is deleterious to the best interests of the infant, before an order should be made against the mother under s. 3 of the Act of 1974. There are no such exceptional circumstances in this case.

It is true that the President of the High Court, because of the view he took of the law, did not in terms make any finding as to where the best interests of the child lie. If I thought it would be open to him to make a finding adverse to the mother on that issue, I would favour remitting the case to him. But we have all the evidence before us in transcript together with the President's estimation of the witnesses, and it is possible to make an assessment of the full strength of the case for the notice parties. In my judgment, it is not such as could possibly support the making of an order against the mother under s. 3 of the Act of 1974. So I do not think that any necessary or useful purpose would be served by sending the case back to the President.

Accordingly, I would dismiss this appeal and uphold the order made in the High Court.

Kenny, J.:

. . . The President said that the plaintiff has a constitutional right to the custody of her daughter and to the control of her upbringing. When he said this he was, very properly, following a passage in the judgment of this Court in *Nicolaou's Case* [1966] I.R. 567 which appears at p. 644 of the report. That case related to the alleged rights of the father of an illegitimate child and so the passage is *obiter* and does not bind the members of this Court, at least when they are free of the considerable handicap of Article 34, s. 4, sub-s. 5, of the Constitution. As it has found favour with some members of this Court, I think it right to say that I do not agree with it and to give my reasons for doing so.

At common law, an illegitimate child was *filius nullius* and so, neither the father nor the mother of an illegitimate child was regarded as having the full parental rights which the law recognised in the case of legitimate offspring. The Courts protected the custody of whichever parent had had the child for some time: *R.* v. *Hopkins* 7 East 579 (1806) and the speech of Lord Herschell in *Barnardo* v. *McHugh* [1891] A.C. 388. The *Supreme Court of Judicature Act (Ireland), 1877*, provided in s. 28, sub-s. 10, that in questions relating to the custody and education of infants, the rules of equity should prevail and these were on the basis that the parents had not got an absolute right to custody but that the court should decide this issue having regard to the mental, moral and physical welfare of the child (*In re Elliot* 32 L.R.Ir. 504 (1893)); but in almost all cases this was achieved by giving the custody to the parents, or surviving parent, of a legitimate child: see *In re O'Hara*[1900] 2 I.R. 232 at p. 241 of the report.

The effect of the Act of 1877 was also seen in the approach to cases in which disputes arose in relation to the custody of illegitimate children. Because of the blood tie which exists between mother and child, the Courts held that the mother of an illegitimate child was entitled to its custody unless she had forfeited it by misconduct or unmindfulness of parental duty or inability to provide for its welfare – particularly as she was liable to maintain it. *R.* v. *Nash* 10 Q.B.D. 454 (1883): *Barnardo* v. *McHugh* [1891] A.C. 388. In some of the cases, the judges spoke of the 'natural' right of the mother of an illegitimate child to its custody, but in these cases the word 'natural' referred to the tie by blood which exists between mother and child; they were not thinking in terms of the philosophical doctrine of natural law and natural rights which the Victorian and Edwardian judges and lawyers regarded with contempt. The final step in the improvement of the legal position of the mother of an illegitimate child was the enactment of the provisions of s. 6, sub-s. 4, and s. 10 of the *Guardianship of Infants Act, 1964*.

While the Constitution deals with the rights of parents of legitimate children and 'the natural and imprescriptible rights' of the child, it says nothing about the custody of legitimate or illegitimate children. As Article 42 acknowledges that the family is the primary and natural educator of the child and guarantees to respect the inalienable right and duty of parents to provide, according to their means, for the religious and moral, intellectual, physical and social education of their children, it inferentially gives those who have married and are living together a constitutional right to the custody of their children. That Article does not do this for the mother of an illegitimate child for she cannot claim the benefits of Articles 41 and 42 and, in my opinion, is not given a constitutional right of custody by Article 40, s. 3, of the Constitution.

The passage at p. 644 of the report of *Nicolaou's Case* [1966] I.R. 567 which is relied on to establish that the mother of an illegitimate child has a constitutional right to its custody reads: 'For the same reason the mother of an illegitimate child does not come within the ambit of Articles 41 and 42 of the Constitution. Her natural right to the custody and care of her child, and such other natural personal rights as she may have (and this Court does not in this case find it necessary to pronounce upon the extent of such rights), fall to be protected under Article 40, section 3, and are not affected by Article 41 or Article 42 of the Constitution. There is no provision in Article 40 which prohibits or restricts the surrender, abdication, or transfer of any of the rights guaranteed in that Article by the person entitled to them.' It seems to me that in that passage there is an equation of 'natural rights' and 'constitutional rights.' I do not accept that there is such a connection, particularly as the word 'natural' is so ambiguous. When used in connection with the relationship of mother and child, it may mean the link between them formed by the facts that she has conceived the child, that it issues from her body and is fostered and nurtured by her; or it may mean that the theory of natural law, on which so much of that part of the Constitution dealing with fundamental rights is based, recognises such a right.

In my opinion the mother of an illegitimate child has a statutory right under the *Guardianship of Infants Act, 1964*, to the custody of her child but she has not a constitutional one. She has a natural right to it in the first sense which I have outlined above: I reserve the question whether she has such a right under the second sense of that word. Counsel for the notice parties properly conceded that the plaintiff has never abandoned or deserted her child, and is not unmindful of her parental duties. She was naturally distressed and overwrought after the birth of her child and she accepted the advice of a nurse that she should give the child for adoption. She had completely changed her mind by the 11th February, 1978, which was three months after the birth. The President said that, if the case were analogous to that arising where parents who have separated are seeking the custody of a child, he thought that the welfare of the child would be 'marginally' better served by leaving her with the notice parties, but that he was satisfied that the welfare of the child did not in any sense 'overwhelmingly' require that she should remain in the custody of the notice parties. I do not agree with the argument of counsel for the notice parties that this finding entitles his clients to succeed in their application to have the plaintiff's consent dispensed with. It seems to me that it is not in the best interests of the child to allow it to remain with the notice parties, though they would be wholly admirable in that role. The blood link between the plaintiff and her child means that an instinctive understanding will exist between them which will not be there if the child remains with the notice parties. A child's parent is the best person to bring it up as the affinity between them leads to a love which cannot exist between adoptive parents and the child. The child is now 12 months old and children of that age are infinitely adaptable.

In my opinion, if the matter be judged by legal rights only, the plaintiff has a statutory right to the custody of her child: if it be judged by psychological standards, everything favours her. I think the President was right when he refused to dispense with the plaintiff's consent and when he decided to give her custody of the child. He fixed £75 as a reasonable sum to be paid to the notice parties for their expenditure in connection with the child: see s. 15 of the Act of 1964. Counsel for the notice parties has now informed us that his clients did not ask for any sum for their expenditure, and that they do not now ask for anything for this. In my opinion, the President's order of the 19th September, 1978, should be affirmed in all respects.

Since writing this judgment, I have had an opportunity of reading that which has been read by my colleague, Mr. Justice Walsh. There was no adoption order made in this case and so the extremely difficult question whether the Board are exercising administrative or judicial powers when they make an adoption order was not mentioned during the argument. I reserve my opinion on that matter until it arises and is fully argued in a case before this Court.

Parke, J.:

. . . . I address myself at once to the fundamental question which arises in this appeal, namely, the ascertainment of the rights of the plaintiff in respect of her illegitimate child. I have no doubt whatever that such rights exist, but it is necessary to consider what is the nature and origin of such rights.

They do not arise under Article 41 of the Constitution because the family there recognised as the natural primary and fundamental unit group of society is that which is based upon the institution of matrimony. In my view, however, they are among the personal rights which the State guarantees in its laws to defend and vindicate under Article 40, s. 3, sub-s. 1, of the Constitution. The emotional and physical bonds between a woman and the child which she has borne give to her rights which spring from the law of nature and which have been recognised at common law long antecedent to the adoption of the Constitution. An example of the recognition and enforcement of such rights is to be found in *In re O'Hara* [1900] 2 I.R. 232. In one respect the State has given statutory recognition to these rights by providing in s. 6, sub-s. 4, of the *Guardianship of Infants Act, 1964*, that the mother of an illegitimate infant shall be the guardian of such infant. The right of such a mother to care for and protect and have custody of her child has been recognised by this Court in *The State (Nicolaou)* v. *An Bord Uchtála* [1966] I.R. 567.

However, the existence of such a right to custody does not decide the issue in this appeal because there is a clear difference between an application for custody of an infant under the *Guardianship of Infants Act, 1964*, and the relief which is sought by the notice parties under s. 3 of the *Adoption Act, 1974*; that distinction has been recognised by the learned President in the course of his judgment.

But before considering this, it is necessary to point out the important distinction which arises between rights which derive from Article 41 as against those recognised by Article 40. The former are declared to be 'inalienable and imprescriptible,' but the personal rights recognised by Article 40, like other personal rights, are capable of being waived or modified by the person entitled to them unless such waiver or modification infringes the constitutional rights of some other person.

Therefore, it is necessary to consider whether on the facts of this case the plaintiff waived or abandoned her rights by placing the child for adoption. The phrase 'placing for adoption' is not defined by any of the Adoption Acts but, in the context of the procedure involved in, and leading up to, an adoption order, its meaning seems quite plain. It is the act of handing over custody of the child so that it may be placed with persons who may subsequently seek and obtain an adoption order in respect of it.

On the evidence and on the facts found by the learned President there is no doubt that, during the interview which the plaintiff had with the social worker immediately before she signed a consent to the placing for adoption, the full implications and legal consequences of what she was doing were explained to her and that she understood them. In particular she was made aware that, although she could refuse her consent to an adoption order at any time before such order was made, if she did so the proposed adoptive parents could apply to the High Court under s. 3 of the Act of 1974 for an order dispensing with her consent if the court considered that it would be in the best interest of the child so to do. In these circumstances I am satisfied that she waived or abandoned her rights so as to leave the matter to be decided under s. 3 of the Act of 1974, unless by so doing she infringed or injured the constitutional rights of her child. The child has personal rights to life, to be fed, to be protected, reared and educated in a proper way; these rights are recognised by Article 40 of the Constitution. In my view, a child has no constitutional right to have these obligations discharged by his or her natural parent and, if there are other persons able and willing to satisfy such requirements, then a child's constitutional rights are sufficiently defended and vindicated. For these reasons, I consider the matter fails to be decided under s. 3 of the Act of 1974.

Because of the view which the learned President took of the mother's constitutional rights he precluded himself, in effect, from making a finding under that section; but he indicated that, had he been trying an issue relating to the custody of a child under the *Guardianship of Infants Act, 1964*, he would have awarded custody to the mother. There is, however, a clear distinction between such proceedings and applications under s. 3 of the Act of 1974. Custody orders are essentially transitory and may be (and frequently are) reviewed from time to time to meet changing circumstances. Orders under s. 3 of the Act of 1974, on the other hand, are perpetual in effect and it is difficult to imagine any decision which could affect as profoundly as such an adjudication the life and future of a child and, indeed, the lives of the mother and the proposed adoptive parents. It may be that this distinction provides an explanation for the rather puzzling difference between the words 'the best interests of the child' used in s. 3 of the Act of 1974 and the expression 'welfare of the infant' (as defined) used in the *Guardianship of Infants Act, 1964*, because in that context the court is only concerned with the welfare for the time being of the child. However, this is mere speculation.

Since there is no decision at first instance on the point, I respectfully agree with the Chief Justice that the matter must be remitted to the High Court to have this issue decided. Like the Chief Justice I do this with the greatest regret. Any course of action which could bring to an end as speedily as possible the heartache and anxiety which all the parties must be enduring would be greatly desired, but it seems to me that it would be beyond the powers of this Court, as an appellate tribunal, to reach a conclusion on the facts now before us on a matter which is essentially within the province of a court of first instance.

There is one other matter to which I wish to advert. In the course of his judgment, Mr. Justice Walsh has carried out a detailed analysis of the duties and obligations of the Adoption Board and of the manner in which it discharges its functions; he has also considered in some detail possible extensions in the scope and practice of adoption which had been brought about by the amending Acts and in particular by the Act of 1974. None of these matters were the subject of any submissions or arguments presented to this Court in the course of the appeal, nor do they appear to me to be germane to the matters which this Court is now called upon to decide. Therefore, I wish to say in the most explicit terms that I do not express any views upon such matters.

Notes

1. For analysis of the decision, see McGann, *G.* v. *An Bord Uchtála – The Best Interests of the Child and Constitutional Rights in Adoption*, 73 Inc. L. Soc. Gazette of Ireland 203 (1979).
2. In the light of this decision, attempt of state the constitutional position of the mother of a child categorised as 'illegitimate' by the law. Cf. the Law Reform Commission's *Report on Illegitimacy* pp. 21–25 (LRC 4–1983). What about the constitutional position of the child himself or herself? Cf. the *Report on Illegitimacy*, pp. 15–19. Which interpretation of Gavan Duffy, J's judgment in *In Re M.; an infant*, [1946] I.R. 334, at 344, do you favour?
3. How do you respond to Mr. Justice Walsh's view that 'a consent motivated by fear, stress or anxiety, or a consent . . . which is dictated by poverty or other deprivations does not constitute a valid consent'? Does this mean that children born to poor, anxious mothers may be ineligible for adoption for as long as these social and psychological constraints continue to apply? Cf. *McF.* v. *G. & G., The Sacred Heart Adoption Society & An Bord Uchtála, infra*, p. 423.
4. Do you agree with Kenny, J.'s statement that '[a] child's parent is the best person to bring it up as the affinity between them leads to a love which cannot exist between adoptive parents and the child'? Does the statement purport to be based on actual evidence? If so, what is this evidence? If not, why did Kenny, J. make the statement?
5. May constitutional rights be waived? Cf. J. Kelly, *The Irish Constitution*, 438–440 (2nd ed., 1984); Redmond, *Constitutional Law – Waiver of Rights*, [1979–80] Dublin U.L.J. 104.
6. On the subject of infanticide, mentioned in Walsh, J.'s judgment, see O'Donovan, *The Medicalisation of Infanticide*, [1984] Crim. L. Rev. 259.
7. On the question whether legislation providing for the adoption of legitimate children would be constitutional, see the Report of the Review Committee on Adoption Services, *Adoption*, paras. 3.7–3.8 (Pl. 2467, 1984).

THE STATE (K.M. & R.D.) v. MINISTER FOR FOREIGN AFFAIRS & OTHERS
[1979] I.R. 73 (High Court, Finlay P., 1978)

Finlay, P.:

This is an application to make absolute, notwithstanding cause shown, a conditional order of certiorari which was granted by the High Court on the 2nd February, 1978. The order directed the first and second respondents to send before the Court, for the purpose of being quashed, the record of the decision of the first respondent to refuse the request of the first prosecutor for a passport for her infant daughter. The Attorney General has been added as a notice party to the proceedings by reason of the fact that the ground on which the conditional order was granted involved (inter alia) an assertion that certain provisions of the *Adoption Act, 1952*, were repugnant to the Constitution.

The respondents have shown cause, but they have not contested any of the facts which are set out in the affidavit of the first prosecutor and which are the facts upon which the application is based. Those facts are that the first prosecutor is an Irish citizen who is aged 22 years and is unmarried. On the 22nd October, 1977, she gave birth to a baby girl. The first prosecutor states in her affidavit that the second prosecutor is the father of her child. It is not at present the intention of the first prosecutor to marry the second prosecutor. The second prosecutor is a Nigerian national who has been residing in Ireland since November, 1975, and is following a course of studies. It is stated to be his intention to return to Nigeria and to establish a home there in due course after the completion of his studies in Ireland. The birth of the child has been registered with the name of the second prosecutor as her admitted father. After her birth the child was transferred to a Children's Home in the county of Dublin pending a decision about her future. Discussions have taken place about that future between the two prosecutors, who are still on friendly terms, and it has been decided that it is in the best interests of the child that she should travel to Nigeria and there enter the home of the second prosecutor's parents who have been informed of her birth and have expressed a willingness to offer her a home with them until her father has established his own home in Nigeria. I was informed that these persons were in comfortable material circumstances. The reasons leading to the decision that this course of action was in the child's interest are partly the incapacity of the first prosecutor, who is working and living in a small flat in Dublin, to care for and look after the child properly, and partly the fact that the child is stated to have inherited the racial characteristics and a dark skin colour from her father and that she will grow up as a coloured, rather than a Caucasian, person.

In December, 1977, the first prosecutor applied to the Department of Foreign Affairs for a passport for her daughter and set out the appropriate information including, of course, the purpose of obtaining the passport and the purpose for which she wanted her daughter to travel to Nigeria. On the 16th January, 1978, she received a reply from the second respondent, as passport officer, stating that in the circumstances the Department was unable to accord passport facilities to the prosecutors' daughter. It is quite clear that the reason why the first respondent was not in a position to accord passport facilities to the prosecutors' daughter was not an exercise by him of any discretion but rather the fact that to do so would be the aiding and abetting by him of a breach of the provisions of the *Adoption Act, 1952*; that reason was not contested before me.

The granting or withholding of a passport does not appear to be of statutory origin but would appear to have derived originally from the Crown prerogative. However, it is provided in s. 1 (*xi*), of the *Ministers and Secretaries Act, 1924*, that the Department of External Affairs (now, of course, the Department of Foreign Affairs) shall comprise (inter alia) the administration and business generally of the granting of passports and of *visés* to passports, and all powers, duties and functions connected with the same. Apart from the provisions of the *Spanish Civil War (Non-Intervention) Act, 1937*, which are quite irrelevant to these proceedings, there does not appear to be any other statutory reference to a passport in our statute law.

The relevant provisions of the *Adoption Act, 1952*, are as follows. Section 40 of the Act of 1952 provides:–

> (1) No person shall remove out of the State a child under seven years of age who is an Irish citizen or cause or permit such removal.
>
> (2) Subsection (1) shall not apply to the removal of an illegitimate child under one year of age by or with the approval of the mother or, if the mother is dead, of a relative for the purpose of residing with the mother or a relative outside the State.
>
> (3) Subsection (1) shall not apply to the removal of a child (not being an illegitimate child under one year of age) by or with the approval of a parent, guardian or relative of the child.
>
> (4) A person who contravenes this section shall be guilty of an offence and shall be liable on summary conviction to imprisonment for a term not exceeding twelve months or to a fine not exceeding one hundred pounds or to both.

By virtue of the provisions of s. 3 of the Act of 1952 'relative' means 'grandparent, brother, sister, uncle or aunt, whether of the whole blood, of the half-blood or by affinity, relationship to an illegitimate child being traced through the mother only.' By the same section it is provided that 'parent' does not include the natural father of an illegitimate child.

The restrictions imposed on the removal of a child out of the State up to the age of seven years may be summarised thus.

1. In the case of an illegitimate child under the age of one year –
   (a) The child may not be removed except with the approval of the mother or, if the mother is dead, of a relative of the mother (as defined).
   (b) The child may not be removed even with such approval except for the purpose of residing with the mother or a relative of the mother (as defined).
2. In the case of an illegitimate child between one and seven years of age, the child may not be removed except with the approval of the mother, guardian or relative of the mother (as defined).
3. In the case of a legitimate child up to seven years of age, the child may not be removed except with the approval of either the mother or the father, a guardian or a relative of either the mother or the father (as defined).

The differences between the treatment in these sections of the position of an illegitimate and a legitimate child are, first, in all cases the consent or approval required in respect of an illegitimate child must be either that of the mother, or a guardian or of a relative of the mother; the consent or approval of the father, or any relative of the father, is irrelevant. Secondly, a further restriction, apart from approval, relating to the purpose of the movement of the child out of the State is imposed on an illegitimate child up to one year of age and is not imposed at all in relation to a legitimate child; that purpose is confined to residence with the mother or with a relative of the mother and is not applicable to residence with the father or any relative of the father.

An application having been properly and candidly made to the first respondent by the first prosecutor for the granting of a passport for her daughter, it was quite clear that to do so would be an act on the part of the first respondent which facilitated the commission of an offence created by s. 40 of the Act of 1952 and would be a decision which he could not make properly or lawfully.

On these facts, and having regard to the statutory provisions, two main attacks are made on behalf of the prosecutors against the constitutionality of the Act of 1952. The first is that it constitutes an invidious and unfair discrimination against an illegitimate child by reason of the differences which exist between the treatment of such a child and the treatment of a legitimate child. Secondly, it was asserted that upon being born the child has a constitutional right to travel outside the State, that this right is one of the unenumerated rights arising under the Constitution, that the sections quoted are a failure on the part of the legislature to protect and secure that right adequately and properly or are an unwarranted and unjustifiable invasion of the right. In argument some reliance was also placed on an assertion that the sections are an unwarranted and unconstitutional invasion of the rights of the natural father of an illegitimate child.

Briefly summarised, the argument on behalf of the respondents was that the entire provisions of the Act of 1952 contemplated a situation in which the mother of an illegitimate child, when compared with the mother of a legitimate child, for some significant period after the birth of her child was subjected to special and severe pressures of a social and economic nature in relation to the future and the disposal of the child; that it was proper that the legislature should protect not only the mother but the child from those pressures; that the manifest intention and purpose of s. 40 of the Act of 1952 (as read in conjunction with the definitions contained in s. 3 of the Act) was to afford such protection; and that the fact that in one particular case other protective provisions might have been more conducive to the welfare of the child was not a good ground for holding that the provisions of the Act of 1952 are repugnant to the Constitution.

With regard to the first submission made on behalf of the prosecutors, I am satisfied that for an illegitimate child and a legitimate child there is a difference of moral capacity and social function, at least in the context of the removal of the child out of the State. A legitimate child is part of a family unit; the rights and, in a sense, the duties of the family being specially provided for in the Constitution. In the generality of cases the legitimate child has the protection of a joint decision by its parents or, in the event of a difference of opinion between the parents as to the child's welfare, each parent has the right under the *Guardianship of Infants Act, 1964*, to apply to the court for orders protecting the welfare of the infant. In particular, each parent may apply for an order, which is frequently sought in the Courts, preventing the other parent from removing a child out of the State in defiance, or in contravention, of the welfare of the child. On the other hand, an illegitimate child has not the benefit of being a member of a family unit. In *The State (Nicolaou) v. An Bord Uchtála* [1966] I.R. 567 the Supreme Court decided that the constitutional rights of the family did not apply to the parents of illegitimate children. . . . Furthermore, the provisions of the Act of 1964 do not appear to permit of the father of an illegitimate child being a plaintiff before the court who is entitled to seek the directions of the court with regard to the welfare of the child. Such a general jurisdiction would appear to exist in the court exercising the powers under the Wards of Court jurisdiction, but the statutory protection of the child is certainly not identical to that of a legitimate child.

Further, in my view there is much weight in the submissions on this point made on behalf of the respondents to the effect that in the generality of cases the mother of an illegitimate child may be subject to strains, stresses and pressures arising from economic and social conditions which fully justify the legislature in making special provisions with regard to the welfare of that child, which provisions are not considered necessary for the welfare of a legitimate child.

I can find no distinction in principle between the special treatment afforded by s. 40 of the *Adoption Act, 1952* (coupled with the definitions contained in s. 3 of that Act) in the case of an illegitimate child as compared with the provisions contained in the same section in respect of a legitimate child on the one hand and, on the other hand, the special provisions contained in s. 49, sub-s. 2 (*a*) (ii), of the *Statute of Limitations, 1957*, in respect of a child in the custody of its parents at the time of the accrual of its right of action in tort as compared with the provisions of that statute affecting a child not in such custody. Therefore, following the reasoning and the principle of the decision of the Supreme Court in *O'Brien v. Keogh* [1972] I.R. 144, I am forced to the conclusion that the submission made on behalf of the prosecutors that the provisions of ss. 3 and 40 of the Act of 1952 constitute an invidious and unfair and, therefore, an unconstitutional discrimination against an illegitimate child [is] not well founded.

With regard to the second submission made on behalf of the prosecutors, this depends initially upon their establishing a right to travel out of the country as one of the unenumerated personal rights contained in the Constitution. The first statement of the existence of such unenumerated personal rights is to be found in the judgment of Mr. Justice Kenny in *Ryan* v. *The Attorney General* [1965] I.R. 294, which was subsequently confirmed by the Supreme Court. At p. 313 of the report the learned judge stated:– 'It follows, I think that the general guarantee in sub-s. 1° must extend to rights not specified in Article 40. Secondly, there are many personal rights of the citizen which follow from the Christian and democratic nature of the State which are not mentioned in Article 40 at all – the right to free movement within the State and the right to marry are examples of this. This also leads to the conclusion that the general guarantee extends to rights not specified in Article 40.'

I have considered carefully whether there should be any special reason why the learned judge, in taking examples of personal rights which are not enumerated in Article 40 but which arise from the Christian and democratic nature of the State, should have confined to a right to free movement within the State that which might be described ordinarily as a right to travel. Dealing with an absolute right which is subject only to public order and the common good, there would appear to be grounds for expressing it in this rather limited way. Without entering into and enforcing binding agreements with other sovereign States, the State can neither by its laws nor by the acts of its Executive guarantee its citizens freedom of movement outside the State as a personal right. It does not seem to me that the Constitution can or should be construed as imposing upon the State in any event or upon any terms an obligation to enter into or enforce such agreements.

However, where such agreements already exist in terms, and subject to conditions, acceptable to the State, it appears to me that the citizens of the State may have a right (arising from the Christian and democratic nature of the State – though not enumerated in the Constitution) to avail of such facilities without arbitrary or unjustified interference by the State. To put the matter more simply and more bluntly, it appears to me that, subject to the obvious conditions which may be required by public order and the common good of the State, a citizen has the right to a passport permitting him or her to avail of such facilities as international agreements existing at any given time afford to the holder of such a passport. To that right there are obvious and justified restrictions, the most common of which being the existence of some undischarged obligation to the State by the person seeking a passport or seeking to use his passport – such as the fact that he has entered into a recognisance to appear before a criminal court for the trial of an offence. Such a right to travel, which is inextricably intertwined with the right to obtain a passport, has been recognised by the constitutional law of the United States of America in such cases as *Kent* v. *Dulles* 357 U.S. 116 (1958). Furthermore, one of the hallmarks which is commonly accepted as dividing States which are categorised as authoritarian from those which are categorised as free and democratic is the inability of the citizens of, or residents in, the former to travel outside their country except at what is usually considered to be the whim of the executive power. Therefore, I have no doubt that a right to travel outside the State in the limited form in which I have already defined it (that is to say, a right to avail of such facilities as apply to the holder of an Irish passport at any given time) is a personal right of each citizen which, on the authority of the decisions to which I have referred, must be considered as being subject to the guarantees provided by Article 40 although not enumerated.

In the instant case, where I am dealing with a child who is under the age of one year and is, therefore, under the age of reason, such a personal right must be construed, in my view, in the same way as the Courts have consistently construed the right of liberty of such a child, that is to say, as being a right which can be exercised not by its own choice (which it is incapable of making) but by the choice of its parent, parents or legal guardian, subject always to the right of the Courts by appropriate proceedings to deny that choice in the dominant interest of the welfare of the child. So construed, the right of travel constitutionally arising for this particular child on the existing legal provisions for its welfare consist, in my view, of the right to travel with the approval or consent of its mother provided that such travelling, and the purpose of it, do not appear to conflict with the welfare of the child.

Having concluded that this child has a constitutional right to travel in the manner and for a purpose consistent with its welfare chosen by its mother, a question then arises as to whether the impugned provisions of the *Adoption Act, 1952*, constitute a discharge by the State of its obligations under s. 3, sub-s. 1, of Article 40 of the Constitution. . . .

If the facts stated in the affidavit of the first prosecutor (which has not been challenged) are accurate, and I have no reason to believe otherwise, then it seems to me to be clear that there is an important and vital advantage to the welfare of this child that it should be permitted to travel to Nigeria in order to become part of a family unit in that country as soon as possible. Having regard to the alternatives open to the child, in my view it is not in the child's interest in the first instance to continue in an institution or home. Secondly, if the child is to be assimilated into a family environment and background in Nigeria, the whole modern thinking on the importance of background and environment in the earliest possible formative years of a child indicate that the sooner that is commenced the more likely it is to be successful. Under the provisions of the Act of 1952 there is no machinery whereby that can be done lawfully, no matter how dominant that advantage may appear and no matter how clearly the welfare of the child may be served by an early removal from the State to Nigeria.

Apart from the facts of the instant case, it is easy to envisage probable, as opposed to fanciful, examples of similar cases affecting an illegitimate child. Within the first year of its life an illegitimate child might well require a very specialised form of treatment for a physical or mental ailment with which it was born and which would be carried out more appropriately and more efficiently outside this country. If such a necessity arose, the child's right to travel at the choice of its mother would become vital to its welfare. However, since the purpose of the child's journey outside the State would not necessarily be to reside with its mother, or with any relative of its mother, and since the practical necessity of the circumstances might well require the child to travel without any relative but with a medical or nursing companion for treatment, such a journey and the treatment associated with it would become legally impossible under the provisions of s. 40 of the Act of 1952.

Having regard to these considerations, I take the view that, by reason of the absence of any discretion vested in a court or otherwise for exceptional cases so as to permit the removal out of the State of an illegitimate child within the first year of its birth (otherwise than for the purpose of residing with its mother or a relative, as defined), the provisions of s. 40 of the Act of 1952 are unconstitutional because they fail to defend and vindicate the personal right of the child to travel in the manner in which I have defined it. To expand the definition of the right to travel which I am satisfied this child has, I am satisfied that such a child has a right to travel outside the State at the choice of its mother or legal guardian, subject to the power of the Courts to intervene in order to ensure the child's welfare. Having regard to the finding in the decision of the Supreme Court in *The State (Nicolaou)* v. *An Bord Uchtála* [1966] I.R. 567 that the father of an illegitimate child has not a right to its custody which is inferior only to that of the mother while she is alive and which is superior to that of any other person after her death, and having regard to the provisions of the *Guardianship of Infants Act, 1964*, which do not confer any such right of custody or guardianship on the father of an illegitimate child, I am not satisfied that the constitutional right to travel of an illegitimate child below the age of reason extends to a right to travel at the choice of its natural father.

It becomes necessary to consider, in the light of these findings, whether I must declare as invalid under the Constitution the entire of s. 40 of the Act of 1952 (as interpreted in accordance with the definitions contained in s. 3 of that Act) or whether it is necessary to delete only portions of that section so as to leave the remainder standing as valid. My understanding of the obligation imposed upon me by the presumption of constitutionality in favour of this Act, which was passed after the enactment of the Constitution, is that I should set aside only so much of the section as is necessary to render it constitutional. See [1973] I.R. at p. 147. I am satisfied that it is only necessary to declare as unconstitutional the entire of sub-s. 2 of s. 40 of the Act of 1952 and the words in sub-s. 3 of that section which are contained in brackets, that is to say:– 'not being an illegitimate child under the age of one year.' The section would then remain effective with the result that a child, either illegitimate or legitimate, who is under the age of seven years could not be removed out of the State except with the approval of a parent, guardian or relative of the child. 'Parent' and 'relative' in the case of the illegitimate child being construed as the mother or a defined relation of the mother; and 'guardian' for both the legitimate and illegitimate child being 'a person appointed, according to law, to be guardian of his person by deed or will or by order of a court of competent jurisdiction' – see s. 3 of the Act of 1952. In my view the section, so read, would be a sufficient vindication and protection by the State of the right of an illegitimate child to travel in the manner in which I have defined that as a constitutional right and, as such, would be a constitutional section. It follows from this decision that the conditional order of certiorari which has been obtained by the prosecutors must be made absolute and the cause shown set aside.

During the hearing a suggestion was made to me that it might be appropriate at this stage to make an order of *mandamus* directed to the Minister for Foreign Affairs to grant the passport. It does not seem to me to be appropriate to do so in these proceedings at this stage. However, it follows from my opinion that the child has a constitutional right to a passport, unless the respondents are in a position to bring Wardship proceedings before the court in the interest of this child as a result of which the court, exercising that jurisdiction, decides that it is contrary to the child's welfare for it to travel out of Ireland so as to remain with the family indicated in Nigeria.

Notes

1. For consideration of the decision, see J. Kelly, *The Irish Constitution*, 42–44 (2nd ed., 1984).
2. On the power of the Court in wardship proceedings to permit a child to be taken out of the jurisdiction, see *Re Medley, A Minor,* I.R. 6 Eq. 339 (Chy., 1871). See also *Kent County Council* v. *C.S., infra*, p. 472.
3. The decisions in the United States in relation to passports have generally been concerned with travel restrictions in the political and security contexts. As well as *Kent* v. *Dulles*, see *Aptheker* v *Secretary of State*, 378 U.S. 500 (1964); *Zemel* v. *Rusk*, 381 U.S. 1 (1965); *Haig* v. *Agee*, 453 U.S. 280 (1981). For academic analyses, see Parker, *The Right to Go Abroad: To Have and to Hold a Passport*, 40 Va. L. Rev. 853 (1954); Whelan, *Note: Passports and Freedom of Travel: The Conflict of a Right and a Privilege*, 41 Georgetown L. J. 63 (1952); James, *Note: The Right to Travel Abroad,* 42 Fordham L. Rev. 838 (1974): Kaplan, *Note: The CIA Responds to Its Black Sheep: Censorship and Passport Revocation –The Cases of Philip Agee*, 13 Conn. L. Rev. 317 (1981); Bowser, *Note: New Tension Between the Right to Travel Abroad and National Security Interests*, 13 N. Carolina Central L. J. 267 (1982).
4. Is section 11(4) of the *Guardianship of Infants Act 1964* consistent with the view that 'the provisions of the Act of 1964 do not appear to permit of the father of an illegitimate child being a plaintiff before the court who is entitled to seek the directions of the court with regard to the welfare of the child'?
5. Cf. *Abdelkefi* v. *Minister for Justice and the Attorney General*, unreported, High Ct., Barron, J., 27 January 1983 (1980–6410P), *infra*, p. 186.

IN THE GOODS OF WALKER DECEASED: O'BRIEN v. M.S. AND THE ATTORNEY GENERAL

Supreme Ct., 20 January 1984 (83–1982), affirming High Ct., D'Arcy, J. [1982] I.L.R.M. 327

Walsh, J. (delivering the judgment of the Court):

William Walker died a bachelor and intestate on 5th March 1975. He was survived by four sisters and one brother and one illegitimate daughter. The plaintiff is one of the sisters and the defendant is the illegitimate daughter. On 5th September 1975 the plaintiff applied to the Principal Probate Office for letters of administration to the estate of the deceased and on 7th October a caveat to the plaintiff's application was entered by the defendant. Proceedings were issued by way of plenary summons and a statement of claim by the plaintiff seeking an order setting aside the caveat and the warning and appearance which had been entered thereto and for an order granting liberty to the plaintiff to proceed with the application for a grant of administration to the estate of the deceased. The defendant in her defence claimed an order and declaration that she was 'the issue of the said deceased and she claims a share of the estate of the said deceased in such share and proportion' as to the Court might 'seem meet and just'. On the facts of the case if she were to be treated as issue for the purpose of that section she should as the only issue take the whole estate, there being no surviving spouse of the deceased. The pleadings in this case contain no express reference to the *Succession Act 1965* and no express reference to the

Constitution or any particular provision of the Constitution. Nevertheless the substantive claim in the case is that the plaintiff is entitled to succeed under section 67 of the *Succession Act, 1965* or, alternatively, and in the present case principally, by reason of being illegitimate and therefore being not entitled to succeed under section 67 of the *Succession Act*, a claim that sections 67 and 69 of the *Succession Act, 1965* are invalid having regard to the provisions of the Constitution. Because these issues concern the validity of the *Succession Act, 1965* notice was served on the Attorney General on 6th November 1981 pursuant to the provisions of Order 60 of the Rules of the Superior Courts. The proceedings therefore in the main became an issue between the defendant and the Attorney General on the validity of those provisions of the *Succession Act, 1965*.

The appeal before this Court is taken by the defendant against the decision of Mr. Justice D'Arcy who tried the case and held that the defendant was not entitled to succeed on intestacy not being issue within the meaning of section 67 of the *Succession Act 1965* and found also that sections 67 and 69 of that Act were not invalid having regard to the provisions of the Constitution for any of the reasons put forward by the defendant. In the view of this Court the conclusions reached by Mr. Justice D'Arcy on both issues are correct.

The constitutional questions in the case do not arise for consideration until one has first examined the issue arising under the *Succession Act*. If it were to be held that the defendant was entitled to succeed under section 67 of the *Succession Act, 1965* then none of the constitutional issues raised in this case would fail to be decided. It therefore becomes necessary to examine the provisions of the *Succession Act, 1965*.

The *Succession Act, 1965* (hereinafter referred to as 'the Act') abolished all the pre-existing rules of intestate succession both as to descent of realty to the heir at law and as to distribution of personalty to the surviving spouse, issue and next-of-kin and replaced them by new rules applicable to all property. Section 13 provides that where a person dies intestate (or dies testate but leaving no executors) his estate shall until administration is granted vest in the President of the High Court who for this purpose shall be a corporation sole. Therefore the estate the subject of the present suit which amounts to a modest £1,800 is vested in the President of the High Court.

Part VI of the Act in sections 66 to 75 introduced new rules for distribution on intestacy which are applicable to all property both real and personal. Section 67 subsection (3) provides that if an intestate dies leaving issue and no spouse 'his estate shall be distributed among the issue in accordance with subsection (4)'. The Act does not define the term 'issue'. As the Act was passed subsequent to the enactment of the Constitution it is presumed to be constitutional until the contrary is clearly established. . . . However, to apply that rule of construction one must first set about seeing whether there is more than one construction reasonably open on the words of the statute. It is true that the word 'issue' in general speech might well refer to children born within marriage or children born out of marriage. However, words have to be looked at in the context in which they appear and in this particular case they appear in a statutory context which relates to the succession to property. [After an examination of the question, **Walsh, J.** concluded that the word 'issue' in sections 67 and 69 referred solely to issue born within marriage. He continued:]

It therefore becomes necessary to consider whether such statutory discrimination between children born inside marriage and those born outside marriage in the law relating to intestate succession is invalid having regard to the provisions of the Constitution.

The defendant's attack upon the validity of the statutory provisions is based upon three provisions of the Constitution, namely Article 40 section 1, Article 40 section 3 and Article 43 section 1 subsection 2°.

It is logical to commence the examination of these arguments by dealing with Article 43 whose provisions have been invoked because they deal with matters wider than succession rights. Article 43 deals expressly with the natural right of man, by virtue of his 'rational being', to the private ownership of property and the State guarantees to pass no law to attempt to abolish the right of private ownership or the general right to transfer, bequeath and inherit property. Subsection 2° of Section 1 of that Article deals with the right to have private property and the right to transfer it. Transfer clearly may be effected either by transfer inter vivos or by testamentary disposition. If it is by testamentary disposition, obviously it is contemplated that the bequest will be effective or can be made effective by the prospective recipient receiving the property. The question raised in the present case, however, is whether the expression 'and inherit property' in subsection 2° confers a constitutional right to intestate succession. Obviously if there is no intestacy there can be no intestate succession. The defendant's counsel relied upon this particular expression by claiming in a case where there was an intestacy that there was a fundamental right guaranteed by the constitution vested in somebody to succeed on intestacy to the property. This, however, begs a very important question. Succession on intestacy has to be determined by some rules and the rules are and always have been determined by law. It cannot be maintained that as a basic natural right the eldest son was ever entitled to succeed to realty in preference to his brothers or sisters. Likewise it cannot be stated as a matter of natural right that the children of an intestate deceased were necessarily entitled to succeed at the expense of their mother, the intestate's wife, or alternatively, that she had any natural right to succeed on intestacy to the detriment of her children. Succession on intestacy does not depend on any act of the deceased property owner unless the omission to make a will can be deemed to be an act of positive intention. If the latter were to be regarded as an act on his part, then to die intestate in the present state of the law would be to indicate an intention not to benefit a person who could have been benefited by a testate succession; for example, a child of the deceased born outside marriage. In such an instance the constitutional rubric relied upon could not be put forward to justify defeating the intention so evidenced of the deceased property owner. Insofar as the deceased property owner makes a will he is quite free, subject to the provisions of the *Succession Act, 1965* relating to his wife and the possible claims of his children which might be exercised under section 117 of that Act, to bequeath property to any child of his outside marriage, or, indeed, to anybody else. If he decides not to bequeath property to his child born outside marriage and to dispose of all his estate by testamentary disposition subsection 2° of section 1 of Article 43 cannot be invoked to defeat his decision. It appears to the Court that the phrase 'and inherit property' must necessarily be related to the exercise of the power to transfer property by bequest and that what the State has guaranteed in that Article is to pass no law attempting to abolish the general right to inherit property so bequeathed. That does not mean that the State may not in appropriate cases prevent the succession to property. In this context the Court draws attention to the provisions of Part X of the Act of 1965 without offering any views whatsoever on its validity. For these reasons the Court is of opinion that the defendant has failed to show that the provisions of the Act of 1965 are invalid having regard to the provisions of Article 43 section 1 subsection 2° of the Constitution.

The defendant has also claimed that 'the right to inherit property' is one of the rights of property which is protected by Article 40 section 3 of the Constitution. In Article 40 section 3 subsection 2° the State undertakes by its laws to protect as best it may from unjust attack and in the case of injustice done to vindicate the property rights of every citizen. During the course of the argument the defendant, relying upon the claim of a right to inherit under Article 43 of the Constitution, claimed this to be a property right within the meaning of Article 40 section 3. The Court has already decided that no such right was vested in the defendant under Article 43 and therefore to that extent that ground of the claim based on Article 40 section 3 must fail. If the defendant has a vested right to property under the terms of the *Succession Act* then, of course, it would be a right falling to be defended and vindicated under Article 40 section 3. But so to decide, as the defendant claims, would be to beg the whole question in the case. Unless it can be shown that any such right exists that particular constitutional provision cannot be invoked. The Court has already decided that the *Succession Act* as it stands confers no succession rights upon the defendant and therefore there can be no question of the existence of any property right under the *Succession Act, 1965* being under attack. Indeed if it were to be held that the relevant sections dealing with intestate succession of the Act of 1965 were invalid having regard to the provisions of the Constitution it is difficult to know what property rights, if any, could be claimed by the defendant as the Act of 1965 repealed all pre-existing rules of intestate succession. In the light of this and in view of what the Court has already decided in relation to Article 43 the Court is satisfied that the intestacy of the defendant's father did not confer upon her any property right and thus there is no such right to be vindicated in this case. The Court is of opinion that as far as the claim is based on Article 40 section 3 it must also fail.

It is now necessary to examine the ground which was the one most relied upon in the present case, namely the claim that the relevant sections of the Act of 1965 are invalid having regard to the provisions of Article 40 section 1 of the Constitution.

It cannot be contested that a person born outside marriage is, as a human person, equal to one born within marriage. The Constitution provides that all citizens shall, as human persons, be held equal before the law. The meaning of this guarantee of equality before the law has been considered in many cases before this Court, In *The State (Nicolaou)* v. *An Bord Uchtála* [1966] I.R. 567 this Court stated that the guarantee was not one that all the citizens should be treated by the law as equal for all purposes but 'rather as an acknowledgment of the human equality of all citizens that such equality be recognised in the laws of the State'. The provisions have also been discussed by this Court in *The State (Hartley)* v. *The Governor of Mountjoy Prison* (21 December 1967, unreported), *Quinn's Supermarket* v. *The Attorney General* [1972] I.R. 1, *O'Brien* v. *The Manufacturing Engineering Co. Ltd.* [1973] I.R. 334, *O'Brien* v. *Keogh* [1972] I.R. 144, *De Burca and Anderson* v. *The Attorney General* [1976] I.R. 38, *East Donegal Co-operative Livestock Mart Ltd.* v. *The Attorney General* [1970] I.R. 317, *McGee* v. *The Attorney General* [1974] I.R. 284 at 315 (*per* Walsh J.), *Loftus* v. *The Attorney General* [1979]I.R. 221 and *Murphy* v. *The Attorney General* [1982] I.R. 241. It should be noted that the expression 'invidious discrimination' used by Ó Dálaigh C.J. in *O'Brien* v. *Keogh* is one borrowed from United States constitutional jurisprudence meaning unjust, unreasonable or arbitrary and constitutionally offensive. This meaning was noted in the judgment of this Court in *Murphy* v. *The Attorney General*, [1982] I.R., at p. 286.

In two of these cases, namely *East Donegal Co-operative Livestock Mart Ltd.* v. *The Attorney General* [1970] I.R. 317 and *De Burca and Anderson* v. *The Attorney General* [1976] I.R. 38, certain statutory provisions were found to be unconstitutional for infringing or being inconsistent with the guarantee of equality set out in the first part of section 1 of Article 40 already mentioned. It is correct to say that in the *De Burca* case O'Higgins C.J. and Walsh J. referred expressly to Article 40 section 1 as the basis of their judgments though arriving at different conclusions. Walsh J. held the statutory provision in question to be inconsistent with the provisions of section 1 of Article 40 while O'Higgins C.J. was of opinion that in the case of women serving on juries the statutory provision was saved by the proviso to section 1. In all of the cases mentioned above, the arguments of the parties included references to the second paragraph of Article 40 section 1 which hereafter will be referred to as 'the proviso'.

It is therefore necessary to examine the wording of the proviso. It is desirable to set out the exact text which is as follows:

> This shall not be held to mean that the State shall not in its enactments have due regard to differences of capacity, physical and moral, and of social function.

The Irish language text of the Constitution is as follows:

> Ach ni hiontuigthe as sin ná féachfaidh an Stát go cuibhe, ina chuid achtachán, don deifridheacht atá idir dhaoinibh ina mbuadhaibh corpordha agus ina mbuadhaibh morálta agus ina bhfeidhm chomhdhaonnaigh.

It would appear to be quite clear from the Irish language text that the proviso refers to the differences of capacity, physical and moral, and of social function of the citizens for whom or in respect of whom the State in its enactments has seen fit to have 'due regard' to their differences under these headings. In the present case no question arises of any difference of physical or moral capacity. Neither is there any question of a social function of the defendant arising from her illegitimacy. Indeed it could not be claimed that illegitimacy can in itself attribute any particular social function to the illegitimate person.

The essential difference between the defendant and the other persons claiming as next-of-kin under the estate of the deceased is the fact that the defendant is not the child of a family based upon marriage and the other next-of-kin are the issue of a family based on marriage.

It has already been well established in the case law of this Court that the family recognised by the Constitution, particularly in Article 41, is the family based upon marriage, that is to say a marriage which was a valid subsisting marriage under the law of the State. In that Article the State has undertaken and has guaranteed to protect the family in its constitution and authority 'as the necessary basis of social order and as indispensable to the welfare of the Nation and the State'. In the case of *Murphy* v. *The Attorney General,* [1982] I.R. 241, this Court held section 192 of the *Income Tax Act, 1967* to be invalid having regard to the provisions of Article 41 of the Constitution as it amounted to a breach of the guarantee to guard with special care the institution of marriage and protect it against attack. Section 192 of the *Income Tax Act, 1967* was one which aggregated the incomes of a married couple working and living together with the result that they would pay more income tax than two unmarried people living together and earning the same amount of income, thus in effect making it more profitable not to found a family based on marriage.

It has been argued in the present case that the State's special duty of protecting the institution of marriage can be a justification for ensuring that on intestate succession children born to either one of the married couple outside the marriage will not succeed on intestacy and that children born of the marriage will so succeed. Thus, it is claimed, the family patrimony will on intestacy be kept within the family and this is a reasonable and valid means open to the Oireachtas to adopt within the Constitution if it considers it necessary to do so. Thus the State ensures that the family based on marriage is maintained in a position superior to that of an unmarried union and thereby honours its guarantee under Article 41 section 1 subsection 2° of the Constitution. It is not claimed in the present case that there are any particular limitations placed upon the ability of the Oireachtas by legislation to allow intestate succession by children to their parents when they are born outside marriage nor is this Court called upon to express any opinion at this time on what limitations may exist in respect of any such legislative ability

The essential question is whether in recognising the undoubted social function of the family the validity of a law designed to protect the family depends upon compliance with the proviso to Article 40 section 1 in so far as it distinguishes, in questions of intestate succession, between those born inside marriage and those born outside marriage. Does a law aimed at maintaining the primacy of the family as the fundamental unit group of society require to come within the words of the proviso to be valid? This Court is of opinion that it does not. In its judgment in *O'Brien* v. *The Manufacturing Engineering Co. Ltd.*, [1973] I.R. 334, the Court in considering the applicability of Article 40 section 1 and the interpretation being placed upon it referred to *O'Brien* v. *Keogh* [1972] I.R. 144 and then used the phrase in relation to Article 40 section 1 that it 'only forbids invidious discrimination' in the sense in which that expression was used by Ó Dálaigh C.J. in *O'Brien* v. *Keogh* [1972] I.R. 144. . . .

The judgment of Walsh J. in *De Burca and Anderson* v. *The Attorney General* [1976] I.R. 38 stated that Article 40 section 1 does not 'require identical treatment of all persons without recognition of differences in relevant circumstances but it forbids invidious or arbitrary discrimination'. In *King* v. *The Attorney General* [1981] I.R. 233, section 4 of the *Vagrancy Act, 1824* was held to be inconsistent with several provisions of the Constitution and in particular with Article 40 section 1. In the course of his judgment Henchy J. stated that it failed to be consistent with Article 40 section 1 because of 'its arbitrariness and its unjustified discrimination'. Thus it may be seen from decisions of this Court referred to above that the object and the nature of the legislation concerned must be taken into account and the distinctions or discriminations which it creates must not be unjust or unreasonable or arbitrary and must, of course, be relevant to the legislation in question. Legislation which differentiates citizens or which discriminates between them does not need to be justified under the proviso if justification for it can be found in other provisions of the Constitution. Legislation which is unjust, unreasonable or arbitrary cannot be justified under any provision of the Constitution. Conversely, if legislation can be justified under one or more Articles of the Constitution, when read with all the others, it cannot be held to be unjust within the meaning of any Article: see the decision of this Court in *Dreher* v. *Irish Land Commission and the Attorney General* 1 July 1983, unreported) and also *Quinn's Supermarket* v. *Attorney General* [1972] I.R. 1, at p. 24.

The *Succession Act, 1965* must be seen as a most important part of what might generally be referred to as family law. . . . It can be scarcely be doubted that the *Succession Act* was designed to strengthen the protection of the family as required by the Constitution and for that purpose to place members of the family based upon marriage in a more favourable position than other persons in relation to succession to property whether by testamentary disposition or intestate succession. . . . Having regard to the constitutional guarantees relating to the family the Court cannot find that the differences created by the *Succession Act* are necessarily unreasonable, unjust or arbitrary. Undoubtedly a child born outside marriage may suffer severe disappointment if he does not succeed to some part of his parents' property on intestacy but he can equally suffer the same disappointment if the parent or parents die testate and leave that child no property – an event which could occur even if the *Succession Act* did enable intestate succession on the part of such child. However, the decision to change the existing rules of intestate succession and the extent to which they are to be changed is primarily a matter for the Oireachtas. Even if the present rules were to be found to be invalid having regard to the provisions of the Constitution it would avail the defendant nothing as the resultant absence of any rules would leave her without any claimable share.

It is unnecessary to speculate upon what would be the position under Article 40 section 1 of the Constitution if Article 41 did not exist. For that reason it is not necessary for the purposes of this judgment to consider on the basis of any such hypothesis the effect of the various United States cases cited during the hearing. No provision comparable to Article 41 exists in the United States Constitution and there is no part of the reasoning of the United States cases which is sufficiently persuasive to negative the compelling provisions of Article 41 which the Court is obliged to take into its consideration of the issue raised in the present case. . . .

The provisions of Article 41 of the Constitution of Ireland creates not merely a State interest but a State obligation to safeguard the family. . . .

Lastly, it is desirable to make reference to a decision of the European Court of Human Rights, namely *Marckx* v. *Belgium* (Series A. Judgments and Decisions, Vol. 31). This decision was relied upon by the defendant in the present case, although admittedly more in the nature of an indication of how the Court ought to decide if it was free to follow that case. The case can have no bearing on the question of whether any provision of the Act of 1965 is invalid having regard to the provisions of the Constitution. Insofar as that case may be in conflict with the provisions of the *Succession Act, 1965* this Court is obliged to follow the provisions of the Act of 1965: see Article 29 section 6 of the Constitution. That being said it should be pointed out that the case in question dealt exclusively with the relationship between an illegitimate child and her mother. Insofar as it dealt with the right of an illegitimate child to succeed on the intestacy of her mother that is already provided for in Irish law and the point does not arise in the present case. Insofar as it deals with the question of the obligation to establish the relationship between the mother and the child which was necessary under Belgian law that point does not arise in this jurisdiction as the maxim *mater semper certa est* did not apply in Belgian law but does apply in Irish law by reason of the provisions of sections 1, 7 and 28 of the *Births and Deaths Registration (Ireland) Act, 1880.* Furthermore, unlike the position discussed in the *Marckx* case there is no restriction in Irish law which prevents either the father or the mother of an illegitimate child bequeathing property to that child. Apart from noticing the distinctions between these two cases there is no object to be served by this Court entering into any examination of what conflict, if any, exists between the decision in the *Marckx* case and the provisions of the *Succession Act, 1965.* In view of the opinion already expressed in this judgment relating to the claims based on Article 43 and Article 40.3.2° of the Constitution it is of interest to note that in the *Marckx* case it was decided that Article 1 of the First Protocol of the European Convention on Human Rights and Fundamental Freedoms which enshrined the right of everyone to the peaceful enjoyment of his possessions applied only to a person's existing possessions and did not guarantee the right to acquire possessions on intestacy or otherwise.

For the reasons already given the Court is of opinion that the defendant has failed to establish that sections 67 and 69 of the *Succession Act, 1965* are invalid having regard to the provisions of the Constitution. The appeal will therefore be dismissed.

Notes

1. For analysis of the decision, see Paul O'Connor, *The Succession Rights of Illegitimate Children,* 2 I.r. L. Times (n.s.) 13 (1984). Earlier articles on the subject by Tom O'Connor should also be noted: see *Aspects of Our Present Law Relating to Illegitimate Children,* 72 Incorp. L. Soc. of Ireland Gazette 95 (1978); *Illegitimate Children and Succession: A Brief Constitutional Analysis*, 73 Incorp. L. Soc. of Ireland Gazette 53 (1979); *Illegitimacy and the European Convention on Human Rights,* 112 I.L.T. & Sol. J. 167, 173, 179, 185, 191, 203 (1978); and *The European Social Charter and Illegitimacy*, 72 Incorp. L. Soc. of Ireland Gazette 5 (1978).
2. Do you agree with the Court's rejection of the defendant's argument in respect of Article 43? Do you agree that the phrase 'and inherit property', properly understood, means 'and inherit property bequeathed by a will'?
3. After this decision, attempt to state what limitations, if any, there would be on the Government if it wished to implement in full the recommendations of the Law Reform Commission in its *Report on Illegitimacy*, that the status of illegitimacy be abolished and that the principle of equality should apply to all children, irrespective of the marital status of their parents?
4. If the Oireachtas were to pass a law giving a £500 'bonus' to every legitimate person in the country, but nothing to any illegitimate person, would this law be Constitutional?
5. For consideration of the United States decisions on illegitimacy, see Casey, *The Development of Constitutional Law under Chief Justice Ó Dálaigh*, [1978] Dublin U. L. J. 3, at 8–10; G. Douthwaite, *Unmarried Couples and the Law*, 117–129 (1979); Clark, *Constitutional Protection of the Illegitimate Child*? 12 U. Calif. Davis L. Ref. 383 (1979); Kellett, *The Burger Decade: More Than Toothless Scrutiny for Laws Affecting Illegitimates*, 57 J. Urban L. 791 (1981); Weber, *Comment: Illegitimacy and Equal Protection*, [1980] Arizona State L. J. 831; Hallissey,

Illegitimates and Equal Protection, 10 J. L. Reform 543 (1977); Vincent, *Comment: Equal Protection and the "Middle-Tier": The Impact on Women and Illegitimates,* 54 Notre Dame L. 303 (1978); Ford, *Casenote: Constitutional Law – A Less Than Most Exacting Scrutiny for Illegitimacy*, 42 Missouri L. Rev. 444 (1977); Isaacson, *Comment: Equal Protection for Illegitimate Children: A Consistent Rule Emerges*, [1980] Brigham Young U. L. Rev. 142; Note, *Illegitimacy and Equal Protection*, 49 N. Y. U. L. Rev. 479 (1974); Thompson, *Comment: Constitutional Law: Equal Protection for Illegitimates*, 17 Washburn L. J. 392 (1978); O'Brien, *Illegitimacy: Suggestion for Reform Following Mills* v. *Habluetzel*, 15 St. Mary's L.J. 79 (1983).

REFORM OF THE LAW RELATING TO ILLEGITIMACY

The Law Reform Commission have made radical proposals for reform of the law relating to illegitimacy. The basic premise during the Commission's deliberations was that, 'so far as the rights of children are concerned, it is unjust for the law to distinguish between children on the basis of the marital status of their parents': *Report on Illegitimacy*, para. 193 (LRC 4–1982). Briefly, the Commission propose the abolition of the concept of illegitimacy and the equalisation of legal rights of all children, irrespective of the marital status of their parents. For consideration of the Commission's proposals, see Duncan, 5 Dublin U.L.J. (n.s.) 29 (1983), Higgins, *In On the Act*, 14 Aim 7 (Spring/Summer 1984). See also 103 Seanad Debates, cols. 1365–1393 (16 May, 1984); 104 Seanad Debates, cols. 62–94 (23 May, 1984).

The English Law Commission, after a radical Working Paper (No. 74) on the subject in 1979, retreated in its Report (Law Com. No. 118) in 1982 to proposing retention of the status of illegitimacy, mitigated by certain improvements in the legal position of the illegitimate child. For analysis of the Working Paper, see Eekelaar, *Reforming the English Law Concerning Illegitimate Persons*, 14 Family L.Q. 41 (1980); Levin, *Reforming the Illegitimacy Laws*, 8 Family L. 35 (1978); Hoggett, *The Sins of the Fathers*, [1979] J. of Social Welfare L. 385; Hayes, *Note*, 43 Modern L. Rev. 299 (1980); Clarkson, *All Children Equal At Last?*, 9 Kingston L. Rev. 369 (1979). Commenting on the English Law Commission's subsequent Report, Alec Samuels states that the English Law Commission:

> took the cautious and not radical approach. They were looking for consensus politics, not confrontation politics and felt it better to educate the public than prematurely rush them. Evolution not revolution – pragmatism, not principle.
>
> But it is submitted that their conclusion is most disappointing, indeed their recommendation is a bad recommendation. Surely the Law Commission should have concentrated upon principle and refused to dodge the issue. Surely they should not have bowed to orchestrated or organized sectional pressure.
>
> They recommend the abolition of the legal disadvantages of illegitimacy which everyone will welcome. But they recommend the retention of the status so that the status of the child would continue to depend upon whether or not his biological parents were married at the material time. The child-father relationship would continue to depend upon the marriage or non-marriage of the biological father and mother. The child would continue to be differently or separately described and identified, and thus stigmatized. In the nineteenth century the child was a 'bastard', in the twentieth century he was 'illegitimate' and in the twenty-first century he would be 'non-marital'. Is there any advance, any change, anything more than semantics? *Illegitimacy: The Law Commission's Report*, 13 Family L. 87, at 88 (1983).

THE NON-MARITAL COUPLE

In recent years, there has been a significant increase internationally in unmarried cohabitation. The social causes of this development have been the source of much discussion. See, e.g. Part I of J. Eekelaar and S. Katz eds., *Marriage and Cohabitation in Contemporary Societies: Areas of Legal, Social and Ethical Change* (1980); Roussel, *Living Together Out of Wedlock: Socio-demographic Aspects*, ch.1 of *Legal Problems Concerning Unmarried Couples* (Proceedings of the Eleventh Colloquy on European Law, Council of Europe, 1982); Abadan-Unat, *The Non-Married Couple and Society: Socio-juridical Aspects of Cohabitation, id.*, ch.2.

In several countries, the law has responded to this increase in unmarried cohabitation, and further changes may be expected. In England, several books have been published in the past few years, discussing the present legal position there and recommending further changes. See, e.g. S. Parker, *Cohabitees* (1981); A. Bottomley, K. Gieve, G. Moon & A. Weir, *The Cohabitation Handbook: A Woman's Guide to the Law* (1981); M. Parry, *Cohabitation* (1981); P. Clayton, *The Cohabitation Guide* (1981).

In Ireland, there has so far been little recent judicial analysis of the subject directly although, of course, it is an important aspect of many decisions as to custody of children; (see *infra*, ch. 14). We may expect considerably more interest in the topic – in the courts and Oireachtas – in the future.

McGILL v. L.S.

[1979] I.R. 283 (High Ct., Gannon, J.)

Gannon, J.:

When the plaintiff and defendant first met in the year 1963 they were living in Munich where they were each employed in different American-operated Central European radio stations. The plaintiff was then living with his wife and his seven-year-old daughter. The defendant, who is an American citizen, was separated from her husband from whom she was divorced in 1964. The plaintiff left his wife and daughter in 1964 and made his home in the defendant's apartment in Munich until 1973, when his wife and daughter went to Australia. The plaintiff and the defendant spent holidays together in Ireland and on one of these, in 1967, the plaintiff purchased a house on 2 roods 25 perches of land in the townland of Leamcon in the barony of Carbery West. That property is comprised in folio 55796 of the register of freeholders for the county of Cork, and the plaintiff became the registered owner of the property on the 4th November, 1968. This property is the subject matter of an ejectment civil bill on title which was issued in the Circuit Court in Cork and was served on the defendant on the 2nd November, 1977.

In her defence to the claim the defendant disputes the plaintiff's right to recover possession of the property, and she does so on grounds which include the following:– '5. Further the defendant claims to be entitled to possession of the said premises as beneficial owner jointly with the plaintiff in the following circumstances namely – before and at the time that the said premises were acquired by the plaintiff in 1967 it was the common intention of the plaintiff and the defendant that the said premises should be acquired for the mutual benefit of both the plaintiff and the defendant and that the plaintiff and the defendant should be entitled jointly to the beneficial interest therein, and the defendant in the years between 1967 and 1973 provided for and made money available to the plaintiff out of her income and thereby enabled the plaintiff to spend money on and preserve keep maintain and improve the said premises out of his income, and further in the year 1973 the defendant gave up her then employment in order to and in the years since 1973 did use and occupy the said premises and preserve keep maintain and improve the same, and further in the said years since 1973 has spent money on the said premises. 6. Further or in the alternative the defendant pleads that the plaintiff is estopped from claiming that the defendant is not entitled to possession of the said premises by reason of the fact that the plaintiff, prior to the defendant's giving up her said employment, represented to the defendant that the defendant would not have to give up or leave the said premises and might continue to use and occupy the same as her home, in reliance on which the defendant so left her employment and Germany where she was then living and took up possession of the said premises.'

In her counterclaim the defendant asks for a declaration that the plaintiff holds the said premises in trust for the benefit of the plaintiff and the defendant jointly or, alternatively, in such manner as to the Court may seem fit. Following the hearing in the Circuit Court on the 18th October, 1978, the Circuit Court judge granted the plaintiff an order for possession but made no order on the counterclaim. The defendant appealed to the High

Court from that order and, with the leave of the Court, amended her defence by the addition of the following further paragraph:– '7. Further or in the alternative the defendant claims that, in consideration for the defendant's agreeing to give up her said employment to move to Ireland and to preserve keep maintain and improve the said premises, the plaintiff agreed to give the defendant leave or licence to have accommodation in the said premises to use or occupy the same as a home and to remain in possession of the same for so long as the defendant might wish or require. The said leave or licence is coupled with an interest and is irrevocable by the plaintiff and the plaintiff is not entitled to recover possession as alleged.'

The defendant also obtained leave to amend her counterclaim by the addition of the following further paragraphs:– '4. An injunction to restrain the plaintiff from determining or terminating the said licence referred to at paragraph 7. 5. £2,000 damages for breach of contract.'

. . . . The facts which are disclosed were that the plaintiff and the defendant commenced to live together as though husband and wife in her flat in Munich in 1964 and in Ireland on holidays until his employment took him to America towards the end of 1973. As the defendant's marriage had been lawfully dissolved she was free to marry, but the plaintiff could not or would not seek a dissolution of his marriage. Nevertheless it was their intention to live with each other for the rest of their lives. The defendant's flat was provided for her by her employers but she had to pay any expenses in connection with it and all her housekeeping costs and the cost of running her car. He used to take her out for meals frequently but all meals in the flat were provided by her. In 1965 they came to Ireland on holiday and talked about getting a holiday house in Ireland. In 1966 they came to Ireland on holiday and decided to look for a house in Ireland.

When on holiday together in Ireland in 1967, they came upon the house at Leamcon and he decided he would like to buy the house and she approved. It was then a deserted house in bad condition on a good site and he bought it for £1,775. She took no part in the negotiations in which he was engaged with the owner. He provided the entire purchase money. The legal requirements for effective transfer of ownership were not completed until November, 1968 – perhaps because it was necessary to get consent for sub-division, a new folio, and a land certificate. There was no provision made in that transaction to give her any legal estate or interest in the property nor was this aspect discussed. She believed then that it was a purchase by him of a permanent home for both of them although it had originated with the idea three years earlier of getting a place in Ireland for holidays. They spent their 1968 holidays together camping on the site and working at cleaning, restoring and repairing the premises and in getting water and electricity supplied. This was also the pattern of their joint holidays for the next few years and they moved furniture into the house from the defendant's flat in Munich. The total cost over the entire period for the work of renovation, repairs, decoration and so forth came to £9,750 of which the entire was paid by the plaintiff. For her part the defendant did a considerable amount of work mostly in the nature of cleaning, decoration and supervising tradesmen; she spent £1,000 of her own money on out-buildings which she said was by way of a present for him.

About the year 1968 the defendant had become friendly with a girl from England to whom she lent half the capital required by this friend in order to purchase a house, which is near Ballydehob in the county of Cork. The transfer of that property was effected in 1971 to the joint ownership of the defendant and her friend.

By 1973 American interest in radio broadcasting in Central Europe was diminishing and the defendant found that, if she were to remain with the company by whom she was employed in Munich, she would be required to transfer to America; this, she felt, would make impossible her continued association with the plaintiff and with the house at Leamcon. After discussions with the plaintiff, the defendant decided to give up her employment and the Munich flat, to live in Leamcon and to avail of a shipping allowance to move furniture from Munich to Leamcon. She received 30,000 D.M. which she invested in America with a view to providing herself with a subsistence income but her investment, through no fault of hers, became a total loss. She found herself reduced in income from £500 per month approximately to about £50 per month. Towards the end of 1973 the plaintiff had to go to America for a period of three months. It was about this time that the Watergate affair began to stir the news world and, as a journalist, he became involved in that area of news and his stay in America was extended. During 1974 the plaintiff became interested in another lady in America and disinterested in the defendant; correspondence between them ceased and their relationship came to an end.

On these facts Mr. Peart, on behalf of the defendant, submits that the property claimed by the plaintiff was purchased by him to be a permanent home for both of them in ultimate retirement and that he so represented to the defendant who, in consequence, changed her whole circumstances to her detriment in the belief that she had an interest to the extent of an undefined share in the property with a licence under an implied contract to allow her to have the use and occupation of it for as long as she wished. It is his submission that the Court should declare the plaintiff to be a trustee (upon a constructive or implied trust) for the defendant of a share or interest proportionate to her contribution, whether direct or indirect, towards the acquisition and improvement and maintenance of the property to the extent of the value it now has. He further claims that her licence to have possession has not been terminated lawfully and that it cannot be terminated without her consent or without making alternative provision, and that she should be compensated in damages for breach of the implied contract creating the licence for possession.

In support of his submission Mr. Peart relies upon the decision of the Court of Appeal in England in *Tanner* v. *Tanner* [1975] 1 W.L.R. 1246 and upon the judgments of Mr. Justice Kenny in *Heavey* v. *Heavey* 111 I.L.T.R.1 (1974) [*infra*, p. 261] and in *C.* v. *C.* [1976] I.R. 254 [*infra,* p. 265]. The two Irish cases were concerned with claims by wives against their husbands under s. 12 of the *Married Women's Status Act, 1957*, which is the modern substitute of s. 17 of the *Married Women's Property Act, 1882*, which was repealed by the Act of 1957 but is still invoked in England and Northern Ireland. Since the parties in this case are not married to each other, the defendant may find it necessary to call in aid the following extract from the judgment of Sir Robert Lowry (as he then was) in *McFarlane* v. *McFarlane* [1972] N.I. 59 at p. 78 of the report:–

> In my opinion the recent cases in the House of Lords clearly show that the rights acquired by a wife in property which at law belongs to her husband depend not on her deserts as a wife but on legal principles which are equally applicable between strangers: a direct contribution to the purchase price will, in the absence of a contrary intention, attract an equitable interest; an indirect contribution accompanied by an agreement will, and unaccompanied by an agreement will not, give the contributor an equitable interest. Two modifications apply between spouses, first that an arrangement is as good as an agreement, and second that the doctrine of advancement *may* operate against a husband contributor.

This concise but clear statement of legal principle demonstrates that, in the case of two persons who are not spouses, evidence of a consensus derived from words or conduct and intended to have legal consequences would support a trust expressed or implied or constructive. But whether the party having the legal estate and the party claiming an equitable interest be spouses or not, the Court will not impute a relationship of trustee and cestui que trust from the facts of a couple living together in (or seemingly in) the married state and sharing expenses without any more cogent evidence. I do not think that Mr. Justice Kenny intended to indicate anything short of this in the two judgments from which extracts were quoted in support of the defendant's counterclaim. . . .

[**Gannon, J.** quoted extensive passages from Kenny, J.'s judgments in *Heavey* v. *Heavey* and *C.* v. *C.* He continued:]

As the counter-claiming defendant is not a spouse but claims to be a cestui que trust by virtue of indirect contributions in circumstances of a close domestic relationship corresponding to that between spouses, I think it necessary to point out that indirect contributions which are unrelated to the acquisition of the property cannot found an equitable interest in it. I think it would be useful and appropriate to cite the following further extract from the speech of Lord Pearson in *Gissing* v. *Gissing* [1971] A.C. 886 at p. 909 of the report:–

> Difficult as they are to solve, however, these problems as to the amount of the share of a spouse in the beneficial interest in a matrimonial home where the legal estate is vested solely in the other spouse, only arise in cases where the court is satisfied by the words or conduct of the parties that it was their common intention that the beneficial interest was not to belong solely to the spouse in whom the legal estate was vested but was to be shared between them in some proportion or other. Where the wife has made no initial contribution to the cash deposit and legal charges and no direct contribution to the mortgage instalments nor any adjustment to her contribution to other expenses of the household which it can be inferred was referable to the acquisition of the house, there is in the absence of evidence of an express agreement between the parties no material to justify the court in inferring that it was the common intention of the parties that she should have any beneficial interest in a matrimonial home conveyed into the sole name of the husband, merely because she continued to contribute out of her own earnings or private income to other expenses of the household. For such conduct is no less consistent with a common intention to share the day-to-day expenses of the household, while each spouse retains a separate interest in capital assets acquired with their own moneys or obtained by inheritance or gift.

In this appeal the evidence of the defendant in support of her claim falls far short of what is required to enable the Court to hold, by the implication of a trust for her benefit, that she has acquired any beneficial interest in the property which is the subject of the claim. In spite of having the means and the opportunity, she took no part in the negotiations and contributed no amount of the purchase price for the acquisition of the property of which the plaintiff is sole owner. Such as were her indirect contributions all came after the acquisition of the property has been completed (without continuing instalment payments) and did not bear any significant relationship whatever to either the capital sum of £1,775 or to the sum of £9,750 spent by the plaintiff.

The decision in *Tanner* v. *Tanner* [1975] 1 W.L.R. 1346 has been cited in support of the contentions that the defendant has a licence to retain possession of the property, that the licence has not been revoked, and that it cannot be revoked as it is coupled with an interest. In that case the parties were not married but the defendant (who was in occupation and who opposed the claim for possession by the legal owner) was the mother of the owner's two children who never had had any other home but that claimed. The evidence in that case in support of the defendant's counterclaim, as to the indirect contributions of the mother to the acquisition of the premises by instalment payments by the father, was much stronger and clearer than on this appeal but the creation of a trust was rejected and a contract for a licence was implied.

While I have the greatest respect for the learned members of the Court of Appeal, I would not feel bound to adopt their decision in *Tanner* v. *Tanner* [1975] 1 W.L.R. 1346 which does not appear to be expressed as being founded on any clear principle. . . .

On the evidence before me on this appeal it is impossible to infer any particular point of time either for the commencement or the termination of the licence claimed. Both parties had been occupying the premises for many years in circumstances of mutual purpose or convenience which would not support a contractual relation of legal import. The concept of a wavering licence terminable not at the will of the grantor but upon the possibility of changeable circumstances affecting the licensee – such as was implied in *Tanner* v. *Tanner* [1975] 1 W.L.R. 1346 – is one which I find it difficult to reconcile with the law. On the facts of this case I am satisfied that the defendant was lawfully in occupation of the property which is the subject of the claim with the licence or permission of the plaintiff, but only as a licensee at will. For so long as the domestic and personal relations between the parties remained stable it was unlikely that the licence would be terminated, but the evidence does not support a licence by implied contract which could continue against the will of the plaintiff or even beyond the period of their mutual association. I am satisfied that the defendant's licence to occupy and have possession of the property was validly and effectively terminated by the institution of these proceedings at the latest. In my view, the defendant has no grounds for a claim to compensation for loss or damages arising out of such termination of the licence.

The defence and counterclaim raise matters which are very much outside the ordinary range of ejectment proceedings in the Circuit Court. These are matters of considerable importance in the area of domestic relations, disputes in relation to which are generally heard in camera and decisions thereon seldom reported. Consequently, it seems to me to be more helpful if, instead of reviewing the facts disclosed in evidence with meticulous detail as did the learned trial judge in *Richards* v. *Dove* [1974] 1 All E.R. 888 (where the facts corresponded closely to the facts of this case), I should give greater attention to the principles which are applicable to whatever facts the evidence might disclose. I have in mind also that, even if the facts of this case were as cogent (which they are not) as those in *Pascoe* v. *Turner* [1979] 1 W.L.R. 431, which was not cited to me, it would be more appropriate to be guided by the principles in *Pettitt* v. *Pettitt* [1970] A.C. 777; *Gissing* v. *Gissing* [1971] A.C. 886; and *McFarlane* v. *McFarlane* [1972] N.I. 59 than to follow the decision in *Pascoe* v. *Turner* [1979] 1 W.L.R. 431.

Lest it should seem (from the extracts which I have quoted from the several judgments) that the Courts can or should or will make a determination of law or in equity in favour of a party in the difficult area of domestic relations when sufficient evidence is difficult to obtain, I think I should conclude with the following extract from the speech of Lord Morris of Borth-y-Gest in *Pettitt* v. *Pettitt* [1970] A.C. 777 at p. 804 of the report:–

> The mere fact that parties have made arrangements or conducted their affairs without giving thought to questions as to where ownership of property lay does not mean that ownership was in suspense or did not lie anywhere. There will have been ownership somewhere and a court may have to decide where it lay. In reaching a decision the court does not find and, indeed, cannot find that there was some thought in the mind of a person which never was there at all. The court must find out exactly what was done or what said and must then reach conclusion as to what was the legal result. The court does not devise or invent a legal result. Nor is the court influenced by the circumstances that those concerned may never have had occasion to ponder or to decide as to the effect in law of whatever were their deliberate actions. Nor is it material that they might not have been able – even after reflection – to state what was the legal outcome of whatever they may have done or said. The court may have to tell them. But when an application is made under section 17 [*of the Married Women's Property Act, 1882*] there is no power in the court to make a contract for the parties which they have not themselves made. Nor is there power to decide what the court thinks that the parties would have agreed had they discussed the possible breakdown or ending of their relationship. Nor is there power to decide on some general principle of what seems fair and reasonable how property rights are to be re-allocated. In my view, these powers are not given by section 17.

These principles apply equally to the task before me. In the circumstances, it is my conclusion that the judgment of the Circuit Court judge was correct. I affirm the order of the Circuit Court and dismiss the appeal.

Notes

1. Are you surprised by the decision in any way?
2. Should the law treat a couple who are not married in the same way as married people? What legal distinctions, if any, does this decision draw between the two groups so far as their property is concerned?
3. What implication, if any, does this decision have in relation to the old common law rule that agreements based on future cohabitation outside marriage are illegal? Cf. Dwyer, *Immoral Contracts*, 93 L. Q. Rev. 386 (1977); Poulter, *Cohabitation Contracts and Public Policy*, 124 New L. J. 999, 1034 (1974); Gray, *A New Lease of Life*, 123 New L. J. 596 (1973) (proposing cohabitation contract in place of marriage). As to the present position in the United States, see Townsend Davis, *Comment: The Enforcement of Cohabitation Agreements: Theories of Recovery for the Meretricious Spouse*, 61 Nebraska L. Rev. 138 (1982); Freed & Foster, *Family Law in the Fifty States: An*

Overview, 17 Family L. Q. 365, at 438–447 (1984). For a jurisprudential analysis, see Hubbard & Larsen, *'Contract Cohabitation': A Jurisprudential Perspective on Common Law Judging*, 19 J. of Family L. 655 (1981). In Ontario, the *Family Law Reform Act, 1978* (St. Ont. 1978, c.2) introduced a new provision in section 52, which provides:

(1) A man and a woman who are cohabiting and not married to one another may enter into an agreement in which they agree on their respective rights and obligations during cohabitation, or upon ceasing to cohabit or death, including,
  (a) ownership in or division of property;
  (b) support obligations;
  (c) the right to direct the education and moral training of their children, but not the right to custody of or access to their children; and
  (d) any other matter in the settlement of their affairs.
(2) Where the parties to an agreement entered into under subsection 1 subsequently marry, the agreement shall be deemed a marriage contract.' [as to which see section 51 – ed.].

Would this be a good or a bad provision to introduce into our law, in your opinion?

4. For a thoughtful analysis of the decision in *McGill* v. *L.S.*, see Cooney, *Wives, Mistresses and the Law*, 14 Ir. Jur. (n.s.) 1, at 7ff (1979). More generally, see Hardingham, *The Non-Marital Partner as Contractual Licensee*, 12 Melbourne U.L. Rev. 356 (1980); Blake, *Towards a Definition of the Right to Occupy*, 8 Family L. 133 (1978); Harpum, *Adjusting Property Rights Between Unmarried Cohabitees*, 2 Oxford J. of Legal Studies 277 (1982); Girard, *Concubines and Cohabitees: A Comparative Look at 'Living Together', 28 McGill L.J. 977 (1983);* Bala, *Consequences of Separation for Unmarried Couples: Canadian Developments*, 6 Queen's L.J. 72 (1980); Hooper, *Cohabitees and the Family Home: Property Rights*, 6 Trent L.J. 57 (1982).
5. See also *P.* v. *C.*, unreported, High Ct., McWilliam, J., 22 February 1980 (1978–1484P.), which involved a dispute as to the beneficial interests in a home where a married man and an unmarried woman had lived. McWilliam, J. referred to the decisions of *C.* v. *C., infra*, p. 265 and *L.* v. *L., infra*, p. 268 (both relating to disputes between *spouses*) but not to *McGill* v. *S.* He said:

> From [*C.* v. *C.* and *L.* v. *L.*] it appears to me that the correct approach is to try to ascertain what sums have been paid by the parties towards the acquisition of the home and that, in doing this, I must take into account such contributions towards the household living expenses made by either party as enabled the other party to make such payments as were made by him or her. Having done this, I should treat the house as being held by the [man] on trust for the parties in the shares which they contributed either directly or indirectly towards its purchase.

6. It is useful to note Griffiths, L.J.'s statement in *Bernard* v. *Josephs*, [1982] Ch. 391, at 402 (C.A.), that:

> .... the nature of the relationship between the parties is a very important factor when considering what inferences should be drawn from the way they have conducted their affairs. There are many reasons why a man and a woman may decide to live together without marrying, and one of them is that each values his independence and does not wish to make the commitment of marriage; in such a case it will be misleading to make the same assumptions and to draw the same inferences from their behaviour as in the case of a married couple. The judge must look most carefully at the nature of the relationship, and only if satisfied that it was intended to involve the same degree of commitment as marriage will it be legitimate to regard them as no different from a married couple.

In *Burns* v. *Burns*, [1984] 1 All E.R. 244, at 256 (C.A., 1983), May, L.J. agreed with this passage from Griffith, L.J.'s judgment. See further O'Connor, *Indirect Contributions and the Acquisition of a Beneficial Interest in Property*, 2 Ir. L.T. (n.s.) 40, at 41 (1984). More generally, see Freeman & Lyon, *Towards a Justification of Rights of Cohabitees*, 130 New L.J. 228 (1980); Pearl, *The Legal Implications of a Relationship Outside Marriage*, 37 Camb. L.J. 252, at 263–265 (1978); Blake, *To Marry or Not to Marry?*, 10 Family L. 29 (1980), Deech, *The Case Against the Legal Recognition of Cohabitation*, 29 Int. & Comp. L.Q. 480 (1980); Oliver, *The Mistress in Law*, 31 Current L. Problems 81, at 83 ff (1978); Bissett-Johnson, *Mistress's Right to a Share in the 'Matrimonial Home'*, 125 New L.J. 614 (1975); G. Douthwaite, *Unmarried Couples and the Law*, ch.4 (1979) (reviewing developments in the United States).

7. On the question of the competing claims between the surviving spouse and the second partner on the death of a spouse, see *In the Matter of the Estate of E.J.D. Deceased*, unreported, High Ct., Carroll, J., 19 February 1981 (1979–596 Sp.)
8. If a person intentionally or negligently infects a person with whom he or she is cohabiting with a sexually transmitted disease, may he or she be sued in tort? Cf. *Hegarty* v. *Shine*, 4 L.R.Ir. 288 (C.A., 1878), discussed by B. McMahon & W. Binchy, *Irish Law of Torts*, 140–141 (1981). See also W. Prosser, *Handbook on the Law of Torts*, 105 (4th ed., 1971); J. Fleming, *The Law of Torts*, 74–76 (6th ed., 1983); Donnell, *Comment*, 20 Calif. W. L. Rev 61 (1983); *Duke* v. *Housen*, 589 P. 2d 334 (Wyo. Sup. Ct., 1979). Is the position different where one *spouse* infects the other? Cf *Crowell* v. *Crowell*, 180 N.C. 516, 105 S.E. 206 (Sup. Ct., 1920).
9. Until 1981, the action for 'breach of promise' enabled a party to an engagement to marry to sue for damages for

breach of contract where the other party wrongfully broke the engagement. The Law Reform Commission in its Working Paper No. 4 – 1978, *The Law Relating to Breach of Promise of Marriage* and its *First Report on Family Law*, pp. 21–24 (LRC 1–1981) recommended the abolition of the action and its replacement by more discretionary principles of property law and of unjust enrichment. The *Family Law Act, 1981* gives substance to these recommendations. Section 2 abolishes the action. Section 3 establishes a presumption (in the absence of evidence to the contrary) where property is given as a wedding present to an engaged couple or either of them, it was given to both as joint owners, subject to the condition that it should be returned at the request of the donor if the marriage for whatever reason does not take place. Section 4 provides that, where a party to an agreement to marry makes a gift of property to the other party, it is to be presumed, in the absence of evidence to the contrary that the gift–

(a) was given subject to the condition that it should be returned at the request of the donor or his personal representative if the marriage does not take place for any reason other than the death of the donor, or
(b) was given unconditionally, if the marriage does not take place on account of the death of the donor.

The English approach (*Law Reform (Miscellaneous Provisions) Act, 1970* section 3(2)) presumes that the engagement ring was given as an *absolute* gift, 'so as to preserve the right of the wronged woman to throw the ring into the river rather than return it to her former fiancé': Cretney, *Law Reform (Miscellaneous Provisions) Act, 1970*, 33 Modern L. Rev. 534, at 536 (1970), citing Mr. Leo Abse, M.P. (The fact that a 'wronged man' thus has no recompense, unless he can establish an implied or express condition to that effect, appears to have been ignored).

Section 5 of the *Family Law Act, 1981* provides as follows:–

(1) Where an agreement to marry is terminated, the rules of law relating to the rights of spouses in relation to property in which either or both of them has or have a beneficial interest shall apply in relation to any property in which either or both of the parties to the agreement had a beneficial interest while the agreement was in force as they apply in relation to property in which either or both spouses has or have a beneficial interest.
(2) Where an agreement to marry is terminated, section 12 of the *Married Women's Status Act, 1957* (which relates to the determination of questions between husband and wife as to property) shall apply, as if the parties to the agreement were married, to any dispute between them, or claim by one of them, in relation to property in which either or both had a beneficial interest while the agreement was in force.

Does this mean that the presumption of advancement now extends to transactions between engaged couples? If so, is this a sound policy?

Section 6 of the *Family Law Act, 1981* provides that, where an agreement to marry is terminated and it appears to the court, on application to it in a summary manner by a person other than a party to the agreement, that a party to the agreement has received a benefit 'of a substantial nature from the applicant in consequence of the agreement (not being a gift to which section 3 applies), the court may make such order (including an order for compensation) as appears to it just and equitable in the circumstances. Thus, for example, where the father of an engaged woman gave his prospective son-in-law the use of his car for a period of several months, he might consider making an application under section 6.

Section 7 provides that:–

> Where an agreement to marry is terminated and it appears to the court, on application made to it in a summary manner by a party to the agreement or another person, that, by reason of the agreement –
> (a) in the case of the party to the agreement, expenditure of a substantial nature has been incurred by him, or
> (b) in the case of the other person, expenditure of a substantial nature has been incurred by him on behalf of a party to the agreement,
>
> and that the party by whom or on whose behalf the expenditure was incurred has not benefited in respect of the expenditure, the court may make such order (including an order for the recovery of the expenditure) as appears to it just and equitable in the circumstances.

Thus, for example, where the father of one of the engaged parties paid for the air ticket of the other party to return from the United States to Ireland for the wedding, he could make a claim under this section if the wedding was called off. (The outcome of the claim would of course, depend on the courts' perception of what was 'just and equitable in the circumstances'). Where, however, the father of one of the parties to an engagement spent money on an expensive air ticket for *himself* (or some other person apart from either of the engaged parties) he would *not* normally be entitled to apply under section 7 (since this expenditure had not been incurred by him 'on behalf of a party to the agreement').

Jurisdictional aspects are dealt with in section 8 of the Act. The Circuit Court, concurrently with the High Court, has jurisdiction to hear proceedings under section 6 or 7; where a claim exceeds £15,000, however, this jurisdiction is subject to the like consents as are required for the purposes of section 22 of the *Courts (Supplemental Provisions) Act 1961*. The District Court has jurisdiction to hear proceedings under section 6 or 7 where the amount claimed does not exceed £2,500. A limitation period of three years from the date of the termination of the agreement applies to proceedings to enforce a right conferred by the Act: section 9.

Some intriguing questions may be raised about the present law. Perhaps the most important question relates to the possibility of getting around the statutory abolition on breach of promise actions by resorting to *other* remedies. Section 2(1) of the Act provides that:–

> An agreement between two persons to marry one another . . . shall not under the law of the State have effect as a contract and no action shall be brought in the State for breach of such an agreement, whatever the law application to the agreement.

Does this close the door to actions (in appropriate cases) for deceit, negligent misstatement, negligence or breach of trust? The question whether any specific exclusion of actions such as these was considered by the Law Reform Commission in its Working Paper No. 4 – 1978, *The Law Relating to Breach of Promise of Marriage*, p. 45; the Commission concluded that it would be better for the legislation not to include such a specific inclusion and this approach prevailed in the *Family Law Act, 1981.* On this question see generally Thomson, *The End of Actions for Breach of Promise?*, 87 L. Q. Rev. 158 (1971); L.C.B. G[ower], 87 L. Q. Rev. 314 (1971); the Law Reform Commission of British Columbia's *Report on Breach of Promise of Marriage*, pp. 18–19, 25–28 (LRC 64–1983); *Pavlicic* v. *Vogtsberger*, 390 Pa. 502, 136 A. 2d 127 (Sup. Ct., 1957).

The action for breach of promise has also been abolished in England (*Law Reform (Miscellanous Provisions) Act, 1970* section 1); Ontario (*The Marriage Act, 1977*, S.O. 1977, c.42, section 32 (now *The Marriage Act*, R.S.O. 1980, c.256, section 32); Australia (*Marriage Amendment Act, 1976*, section 23) and New Zealand (*Domestic Actions Act, 1975*, section 5). In the United States the action was abolished or greatly restricted in a burst of legislation in several states in the Nineteen Thirties. Courts have, however, been more circumspect: cf. *Stanard* v. *Bolin*, 88 Wash. 2d 614, 565 P. 2d 94 (1977). Abolition of the action has been proposed in Scotland (*Report on Outdated Rules in the Law of Husband and Wife* (Scot. Law Com. Report No. 76 1983)) Newfoundland (cf. R. Gushue & D. Day, *Family Law in Newfoundland*, p. 44 (1973)) and British Columbia (*Report on Breach of Promise of Marriage*, p. 27 (LRC 64–1983). This recent activism internationally may be traced in part of the impact of no-fault divorce: cf. *Stuwe* v. *Baron*, 121 D.L.R. (3d) 199, at 200 (B.C. Sup. Ct., Taylor, J., 1981).

Chapter 4

MARRIAGE AND THE LAW

In several important respects the law has for long treated married people differently from single people. Marriage has involved maintenance rights and obligations, property entitlements and succession rights, for example. These are considered in later chapters. The present chapter examines some other aspects of marriage.

TAXATION

MURPHY v. ATTORNEY GENERAL

[1982] I.R. 241 (Sup. Ct., 1980, aff'g. High Ct., Hamilton J., 1979)

Kenny, J. (delivering the judgment of the Court):

The plaintiffs, Mr. and Mrs. Murphy, are citizens of Ireland and a married couple with one child. They were married in July, 1975. They are employed as teachers in different schools. In this action the question is whether ss. 192 to 198 (inclusive) of the *Income Tax Act, 1967* ('the Act of 1967') which have the effect that, on marriage, the wife's income is aggregated with that of the husband for the purpose of assessment to income tax, are repugnant to the Constitution. . . .

Section 192 of the Act of 1967 provides that a woman's income chargeable to income tax shall, so far as it is income for a year of assessment during which she is a married woman living with her husband, be deemed for income tax to be his income and not hers. This is not, however, to affect the computation of her income in any way. Any income of hers which is deemed to be his is to be assessed on him and not on her. Sur-tax, which is referred to in s. 192, was formerly charged on the amount of income which exceeded a specific amount. It has been abolished by the *Finance Act, 1974*, a matter which, through inadvertence, was not referred to in the judgment of the trial judge. This Act provided that, subject to allowances given by the Act of 1967, (*a*) the taxable income which did not exceed £1,550 was to be charged at the rate of 26 per cent. (this was known as 'the reduced rate'); (*b*) so much of the taxable income which exceeded £1,550 but did not exceed £4,350 was to be charged at the standard rate (35 per cent.); (*c*) the taxable income in excess of £4,350 was to be charged, as to the first £2,000 at the rate of 50 per cent., as to the next £2,000 at the rate of 65 per cent.; and (*d*) the remainder of the income at the rate of 80 per cent. These higher rates have been altered by Finance Acts passed since then so that the highest rate is now 60%. The Act of 1974 also introduced a new relief for working wives which was to be deducted from gross income for the purpose of computation of liability to income tax. In 1974 it was fixed at £200 but it also has been altered by subsequent Finance Acts.

To make the scheme of taxation of husbands on their wives' income intelligible, it is now necessary to pass to s. 197 of the Act of 1967. It provides that if the husband or the wife make the appropriate application, income tax shall be charged and recovered on the income of the husband and that of the wife as if they were not married.

The Act of 1967 (ss. 138 to 145) gives allowances against the income of any individual to be assessed to tax. The reliefs which appear to be relevant to this case are:–

(*a*) a personal relief for a man who has his wife living with him;

(*b*) a relief for any man or woman in respect of each child of his or hers under 16;

(*c*) a relief for a married man in respect of life assurance premiums or contributions to provide for his widow or children;

(*d*) an exemption from tax of persons whose income does not exceed a certain amount;
(*e*) a relief for payments in respect of insurance or other provision to pay the costs of illness.

This list of reliefs is not exhaustive as there are many others: we have stated those which we think are relevant to this case.

If a claim for separate assessment is made by a husband or wife, the reliefs have to be apportioned between the husband and wife. However, s. 193 of the Act of 1967 provides that the total relief from tax given to the husband and wife who have applied for separate assessments is not to exceed that which would be given to them if they had not made such an application. The scheme of taxation for spouses who have made such an application was altered by s. 3 of the *Finance Act, 1978*, which, broadly speaking, provided that the income taxable when each of the spouses had the same income was to be one-half of the joint income, and where the separate incomes of husband and wife were different, provision was made for the amount which was to be assessed on each spouse. The result is that no tax advantage is obtained by the separate assessment of husband and wife: each becomes liable for an amount of tax and the two sums paid by them are the same as would have been payable if they had been taxed on a joint assessment. Separate assessment results in an apportionment between them of the amount of tax which would have been payable by the husband if they had not applied for separate assessments. Lastly, a married woman is to be treated for income tax liability as living with her husband unless they are separated under a court order or by a deed of separation or in such circumstances that the separation is likely to be permanent.

The consequence of the assessment on the husband in respect of his wife's income is to make the amount of tax which he pays greater than the aggregate of the amounts which would be payable by the two of them if they were either not married or married and separated. There are some cases of husband and wife having low incomes to which this generalisation does not apply. In the present case, however, the addition of the wife's income to the husband's gives him a bigger income for income tax purposes, which therefore makes him liable to a higher rate of tax. This is the ground of the plaintiff's complaint.

In the tax year 1976/77, the plaintiff Mr. Murphy had a gross salary of £3,711 and, after deductions, had a taxable income of £2,391. The plaintiff Mrs. Murphy, who had a gross salary of £3,483, had a taxable income of £2,223. When her taxable income was added to his, the total income tax payable by him was £1,579. If they had been separately assessed, their combined tax bill would have been £1,329. Thus, because they were married and living together, he had an extra liability to tax of £250. In the tax year 1977/78, when her taxable income was added to his, the total income tax payable by him was £2,070; if they had been separately assessed, his tax liability would have been £1,746. Thus, because they were married and living together, he had an extra liability to tax of £324. For the year 1979/80 their accountant has estimated (and the figures have not been challenged by counsel for the Attorney General) that the extra tax payable by Mr. Murphy, because he is married and living with his wife, will be £512. The aggregation of their incomes has the result that he has to pay income tax on some of his income at the rate of 45 per cent., on another part of it at the rate of 50 per cent., and on a third part at the rate of 60 per cent. If the plaintiffs were separately assessed, the highest rate at which each would be assessed would be 35 per cent.

Income tax was introduced as a temporary measure during the Napoleonic wars but was not renewed in 1815. It first became an annual feature of life in England under the Income Tax Act, 1842, which was subsequently extended to Ireland. The Act of 1842 contained a provision (s. 45) by which a husband became liable to be assessed to tax on his wife's income. Under the law before the *Married Women's Property Act, 1870*, was passed, payment to a married woman of her earnings did not give the employer a good discharge unless she has her husband's authority to receive them and a husband could, in his own name, recover his wife's wages (see Carson's *Real Property Statutes*, second edition (1910) at p. 338). The earnings and income of a married woman thus belonged to her husband. It was therefore thought just that he should be assessed to tax on them. Since the Married Women's Property Act, the earnings and income of a married woman belong primarily to her. The assessment of the husband on his wife's earnings is a survival from days when the law and social conditions were different. In 1979, when examples are to be found of married women holding high office in their own right, the assessment to income tax on the husband in respect of his wife's earnings is not easy to justify.

The plaintiffs contend that ss. 192 to 198 (inclusive) are repugnant to the Constitution of the ground that they violate Article 40, s. 1, and on the additional but separate ground that they are a breach by the State of the pledge by it in Article 41 to guard with special care the institution of marriage, on which the family is founded, and to protect it against attack.

Article 40, s. 1.

[Mr. Justice Kenny, having quoted Article 40, s. 1, of the Constitution, continued] This section is not a guarantee of equality before the law in all matters or in all circumstances. It is a qualified guarantee to all citizens *as human beings* that they will be held equal before the law. It therefore relates to those attributes which make us human: it is concerned with the essentials of human personality.

The second paragraph of Article 40, s. 1, is a recognition that inequality may be recognised and provided for, but only if it flows from or is related to a difference of capacity, physical or moral, or a difference of social function. The plaintiffs contend that aggregation of their assessable incomes subjects them, because they are married and living together, to a method and burden of taxation which bear unfavourably on them in comparison with two unmarried people living together. The method and burden, however, apply to all married couples living together.

There is, admittedly, an inequality for income-tax purposes between, on the one hand, married couples living together and, on the other hand, married couples who are separated or unmarried couples living together. That inequality, however, is justified by the particular social function under the Constitution of married couples living together. The mere fact that a heavier financial or other burden falls on some defined person or persons does not of itself constitute a repugnancy to s. 1 of Article 40. Having regard to the second paragraph of Article 40, s. 1, an inequality will not be set aside as being repugnant to the Constitution if any state of facts exists which may reasonably justify it.

The inequality alleged in this case is, first, as between married couples and, secondly as between, on the one hand, married couples living together and, on the other, unmarried couples living together. As to the former, since the impugned provisions apply only to married couples living together, and since all such couples are dealt with equally by a common set of rules, it is impossible to hold that the way in which married couples living together are dealt with amounts to unequal treatment contrary to s. 1 of Article 40. In so far as unequal treatment is alleged as between, on the one hand, married couples living together and, on the other, unmarried couples living together, the social function of married couples living together is such as to justify the legislature in treating them differently from single persons for income tax purposes. Numerous examples could be given from the income-tax code of types of income-tax payers who are treated differently, either favourably or unfavourably, because of their social function. This particular unfavourable tax treatment of married couples living together, set against the many favourable discriminations made by the law in favour of married couples, does not, in the opinion of the Court, constitute an unequal treatment forbidden by Article 40, s. 1, particularly having regard to the vital roles under the Constitution of married couples as parents, or potential parents, and as heads of a family.

The plaintiffs' counsel placed strong reliance on four cases decided in the United States of America, the Federal Republic of Germany, Italy and Cyprus. A close examination of these shows that they do not assist the plaintiffs' contentions on s. 1 of Article 40. . . .

Throughout the argument in the present case the phrase 'invidious discrimination' was used to indicate the type of inequality which is prohibited by s. 1 of Article 40. According to the 1979 edition of Collins English Dictionary 'invidious' means '1. incurring or tending to arouse resentment, unpopularity 2. (of comparisons or distinctions) unfairly or offensively, discriminatory.' While the second meaning can be used to describe the inequality prohibited by Article 40, s. 1, the primary meaning of the word is the first and its use in discussing Article 40, s. 1, is more likely to mislead than to help.

In his judgment the trial judge . . . referred to what he called 'the principle of individual taxation on an individual's income.' No section of our income tax code and no decision of any Irish Court was referred to which acknowledged the existence of such a principle. In our view there is no such principle in our taxation code.

Therefore, we are of opinion that the plaintiffs' case, in so far as it is based on s. 1 of Article 40, fails.

Article 41

[Mr. Justice Kenny, having quoted Article 41 of the Constitution, continued] It is to be noted that Article 41 has three sections. Section 1 recognises the family as the natural primary and fundamental unit group of society, and as a moral institution possessing inalienable and imprescriptible rights, antecedent and superior to all positive law. It is be-because of those fundamental features that the State gives the guarantee in s. 1, sub-section 2.

Section 2 stresses the importance of woman in the home and pledges that mothers shall not be obliged by economic necessity to engage in labour to the neglect of their duties in the home. Section 3, sub-s. 1, must be read not only in the context of the whole of s. 3 but in that of the whole Article. This means that the pledge given in s. 3, sub-s. 1, to guard with special care the institution of marriage is a guarantee that this institution in all its constitutional connotations, including the pledge given in Article 41, s. 2, sub-s. 2, as to the position of the mother in the home, will be given special protection so that it will continue to fulfil its function as the basis of the family and as a permanent, indissoluble union of man and woman.

The onus is on the plaintiffs to establish that the higher income-tax liability which may fall on the husband is a clear breach by the State of its pledge to guard with special care the institution of marriage and to protect it against attack.

Counsel for the Attorney General conceded that in some cases, but not in all, marriage could, as a result of s. 192 of the Act of 1967, have the consequence that the husband could become liable for more than the total sum of income tax which husband and wife would have to pay if they were assessed separately on what each of them earned. They argued, however, that to decide whether the State had failed in its pledge the whole of our law in relation to married couples should be looked at and that, when this was done, it would be found that in many respects numerous benefits are given to husband, wife and children. They submitted, accordingly, that when the Court took account of the many advantages and privileges given by the State to married couples and their children, they outweighed the disadvantage of the increased income-tax liability of the husband created by s. 192 of the Act of 1967.

The Court accepts the proposition that the State has conferred many revenue, social and other advantages and privileges on married couples and their children. Nevertheless, the nature and potentially progressive extent of the burden created by s. 192 of the Act of 1967 is such that, in the opinion of the Court, it is a breach of the pledge by the State to guard with special care the institution of marriage and to protect it against attack. Such a breach is, in the view of the Court, not compensated for or justified by such advantages and privileges.

The Court will, accordingly, declare that ss. 192 to 198 (inclusive) of the Act of 1967, in so far as these sections provide for the aggregation of the earned incomes of married couples, are repugnant to the Constitution.

Notes

1. Subsequently, counsel for the Attorney General requested the Supreme Court to indicate to the High Court on what basis the accounts and enquiries mentioned in the order of the Supreme Court dated the 25th January ought to be taken – whether the judgment ought to be held to operate prospectively only or retrospectively and, if retrospectively, relative to what precise period of time and to what taxpayers, if any, other than the plaintiff. The matter of the operation of the judgment of the Court was adjourned for argument until the 12th February, 1980, and was argued on the 12th–14th February, 1980.
   The Supreme Court held:–
   (1) (O'Higgins, C.J. dissenting) that the effect of the decision was that the sections were invalid *ab initio* and had never had the force of law;
   (2) (O'Higgins, C.J. and Kenny, J. dissenting) that the date from which the plaintiffs were entitled to be repaid the sums collected by way of tax invalidly imposed was the first day of the financial year immediately succeeding that in which they had challenged the validity of the imposition of the tax, namely, 6 April 1978);
   (3) (O'Higgins, C.J. and Kenny, J. dissenting) that, since before that date, the State had been entitled to act and to expend the revenue acquired from the tax on the *bona fide* assumption (no claim to the contrary having been made) that the tax had been validly imposed, the only taxpayers (other than the plaintiffs) entitled to seek restitution of tax in pursuance of the Court's decision where those (if any) who had already instituted proceedings challenging the validity of the sections impugned in the present proceedings.
   See further J. Kelly, *The Irish Constitution*, 275–276 (2nd ed., 1984).
2. Contrast Kenny, J.'s rejection of the relevance of *Hoeper* v. *Tax Commission of Wisconsin*, 284 U.S. 206 (1931) (on the basis that 'our Constitution does not provide for "due process" in the sense in which it was applied under the Fourteenth Amendment in that case') with O'Hanlon J.'s statement in *A.S.* v. *R.B. W.S. and the Registrar General of Births and Deaths*, [1984] I.L.R.M. 66, at 74–75, that 'the combined effect of the . . . constitutional provisions [contained in Articles 34.1, 38.1, 40.3.1 and 40.3.2] appears to me to guarantee (*inter alia*) something equivalent to the concept of "due process" under the American Constitution in relation to causes and controversies litigated before the courts.'
3. Is it proper to 'set' a particular unfavourable tax treatment of married couples living together, against the many favourable discriminations in favour of married couples? Why should this balancing process be attempted? If a particular unfavourable discrimination is made, why should it have to be endured simply because other favourable discriminations are made – bearing in mind (a) that these other favourable discriminations are justified and in some cases actually required, by the Constitution, and (b) that many of these other favourable discriminations may have been introduced without any reference to the unfavourable discrimination? Is there any inconsistency between the Court's handling of this issue under Article 40 and under Article 41, respectively?
4. On the Court's argument relating to Article 40.1, Professor John Kelly, *The Irish Constitution*, 456 (2nd ed., 1984) comments that it must be said that to use a difference in social function, where the quality of the difference is acknowledged to be one expressly supported by the State, as the basis for less rather than more favourable treatment, verges on the eccentric.
5. Could *Murphy* v. *The Attorney General* have been decided on grounds which stressed the sex discriminatory aspect of the aggregation provisions of the *Income Tax Act, 1967*? Cf. Forde, *Equality and the Constitution*, 17 Ir. Jur. (n.s.) 295, at 323 (1982).

NATIONALITY

SOMJEE v. THE MINISTER FOR JUSTICE AND THE ATTORNEY GENERAL
[1981] I.L.R.M. 324 (High Court, Keane, J., 1979)

The first-named plaintiff applied to the first-named defendant for a certificate of naturalisation relying upon ss. 15 and 16 of the *Irish Nationality and Citizenship Act, 1956*, he having married the second-named plaintiff, an Irish citizen, one year previous to the application. The Minister refused the application but reduced the residency requirement from 5 years to 2 years. S. 8 of the Act provides for a simpler, almost automatic, conferment of citizenship upon alien women who marry Irish citizens. The plaintiffs instituted proceedings claiming, *inter alia*, a declaration that ss. 8, 15 and 16 of the said Act are unconstitutional. The plaintiffs alleged that by virtue of the provisions of the said Act the second-named plaintiff was deprived of the right to confer automatic entitlement to Irish citizenship on her spouse and the right to marry the person of her choice was thereby abridged or trenched contrary to Article 40 of the Constitution. They also alleged that the differentiation between alien men and women contained in the said sections was a breach of equality before the law contained in Article 40 and also constituted a breach of Article 9.1.2°.

Keane, J.:
. . . It is also clear that the guarantee of equality before the law contained in Article 40 is not to be read as a guarantee that all citizens are to be treated by the law as equal for all purposes, but rather as an acknowledgement of the human equality of all citizens and a guarantee that such equality will be recognised in the laws of the State. The second paragraph of s. 1 is a recognition that inequality may or must result from some special abilities or some special need. (*See The State (Nicolaou) v An Bord Uchtála* [1966] I.R. 567, at 639).) It is also clear that Article 40 does not require a similarity of treatment for all persons. In the words of ÓDálaigh C.J. in *O'Brien v Keogh* ([1972] I.R. 144, at 156):

> As was said in the Judgment of this Court in *The State (Hartley) v Governor of Mountjoy Prison* (21st December, 1967) 'A diversity of arrangements does not effect discrimination between citizens in their legal rights. Their legal rights are the same in the same circumstances. This in fact is equality before the law and not inequality . . .' Article 40 does not require identical treatment of all persons without recognition of differences in relevant circumstances. It only forbids invidious discrimination.

I shall consider first the submissions advanced on behalf of the second-named plaintiff. The sections under attack provide for a diversity of arrangements as between male aliens and female aliens: the latter, upon marriage, are entitled automatically, at their option, to Irish citizenship, whereas the former are not. This does not mean that male aliens are precluded from acquiring Irish nationality upon marriage – or, to use the terminology employed on behalf of the second-named plaintiff, that Irish women are precluded from conferring the benefits of Irish citizenship upon their alien spouses – but the legislature has unquestionably made different arrangements so far as male aliens are concerned. It is not, however, sufficient for the plaintiffs to establish that such a diversity of arrangements exists; it must be shown to the satisfaction of the court that the diversity of arrangements constitutes a form of discrimination which is invidious and therefore prohibited by the Constitution.

It is to be observed at the outset that the Act does not provide for any discrimination between male and female applicants for citizenship as such. Persons of each sex are equally entitled to apply for and become Irish citizens by naturalisation. It is only in the case of aliens becoming married to Irish citizens (who are citizens otherwise than by naturalisation) that a distinction is drawn, and, in my view, the distinction is more properly regarded as conferring a form of privilege on female aliens rather than as being invidiously discriminatory against male aliens. I am entitled to presume that, in conferring this privilege, which does not necessarily involve any invidious discrimination, the Legislature was having regard to the social, economic and political condition which might prevail in the various jurisdictions from which alien aspirants for citizenship might come. It was open to the Legislature to take the view that, in some at least of these jurisdictions, the likelihood of females being engaged in any of the activities which might be relevant in considering an application for citizenship was sufficiently remote to justify the automatic granting of citizenship to female aliens upon their marriage to Irish citizens. It follows that, in my opinion the provisions of the sections in question do no more than provide a diversity of arrangements which is not prohibited by Article 40.1. The fact that, in the result male citizens may be able to confer the privilege of citizenship on their spouses where female citizens may not – and I am again employing the terminology used on behalf of the plaintiffs – does not affect this conclusion, since the distinction thus drawn is one which is not necessarily invidious.

It may well be, in any event, that it is an inappropriate use of language to treat a male citizen as being in a position to confer the privileges and burdens of citizenship on an alien spouse by his marriage to her. Under Article 9.1.2°. of the Constitution: 'The future acquisition and loss of Irish nationality and citizenship shall be determined in accordance with law'.

It is, accordingly, not the act of the citizen in marrying an alien which confers Irish nationality and citizenship upon the alien: it is the law enacted by the Oireachtas which confers those privileges and burdens upon aliens. It accordingly must remain doubtful whether the second-named plaintiff has any right in law to confer citizenship upon an alien of the nature contended for on her behalf: but even if such a right existed, it is clearly one which might reasonably be abridged in the interests of the common good provided that abridgment was on a basis which was not in itself unfairly discriminatory. If her right has been abridged, then, in my view, the abridgment has been effected for the common good and in a manner which cannot reasonably be regarded as unfairly discriminatory. For the same reasons, I am also of the opinion that, in so far as the second-named plaintiff's right to marry whomsoever she chooses has been abridged – and it may well be that it has not been abridged – such abridgment is also not constitutionally invalid.

I next consider the position of the first-named plaintiff. I have already said that the sections in question provide for a diversity of arrangements which, in my view, is not prohibited by the Constitution. As I have indicated, there is no question of the first-named plaintiff being excluded from Irish nationality and citizenship by reason of his sex alone. The fact that different arrangements are made, so far as the acquisition of citizenship is concerned in the case of female aliens, does not mean that male aliens are thereby excluded from Irish nationality and citizenship by reason of their sex. The sections in question, accordingly do not infringe the constitutional guarantee and undertaking of equality before the law; nor do they infringe the provisions of Article 9.1.2°., providing that no person may be excluded from Irish nationality and citizenship by reason of his or her sex. It has been pointed out by Walsh, J., delivering the Judgment of the Supreme Court in *East Donegal Co-operative Livestock Mart Ltd. and Others v The Attorney General* ([1970] I.R. 317, at 341) that the presumption of constitutionality carries with it the presumption that the Oireachtas intended that discretions which are provided for by an Act of the Oireachtas are to be exercised in accordance with the principles of constitutional justice. It follows that the Minister in exercising the various discretions conferred on him by ss. 15 and 16 of the Act must act in accordance with constitutional justice; and plainly would not be so acting if he purported to refuse an application solely on the ground of the sex of the applicant.

It follows that, on the assumption that the first-named plaintiff is entitled to rely on the constitutional guarantee contained in Article 40 of the Constitution, those rights have not been abridged by the sections under attack. It is, accordingly not necessary, in the context of this case, for me to express any opinion on the submission advanced on behalf of the defendants that, in any event, the first-named plaintiff was precluded from asserting such rights, a question which was expressly reserved for further consideration by the Supreme Court in *The State (Nicolaou) v An Bord Uchtála*, [1966] I.R. 567 at 645 (Walsh, J.).

There is, in my opinion, another and fatal obstacle to the claim of both plaintiffs. It was conceded on their behalf that, if s. 8 of the Act of 1956 was declared to be invalid having regard to the provisions of the Constitution, the section in its entirety would fall. Mr. O'Flaherty submitted that, in such circumstances, the court would be entitled to declare that the plaintiffs' rights had not been vindicated by the Oireachtas in the expectation that the Oireachtas would take whatever steps were necessary to ensure that their rights were in fact protected. No authority was cited in support of this proposition and I am satisfied that it is not well founded. The jurisdiction of this Court in a case where the validity of an Act of the Oireachtas is questioned because of its alleged invalidity having regard to the provisions of the Constitution is limited to declaring the Act in question to be invalid, if that indeed be the case. The court has no jurisdiction to substitute for the impugned enactment a form of enactment which it considers desirable or to indicate to the Oireachtas the appropriate form of enactment which should be substituted for the impugned enactment.

The result of the plaintiffs' argument, if well founded, would be to invalidate s. 8 in its entirety. It might also have the same effect so far as s. 16(d) and (e) are concerned. That would confer no benefit whatever on the plaintiffs: it would not redress any injustice to which either of them was subjected or in any sense known to the law vindicate their personal rights. While the possibility that there exists in our law a right of action akin to an *actio popularis* which would entitle any person, whether he was directly affected by an Act or not, to maintain proceedings and challenge the validity of that Act was left open by the Supreme Court in *East Donegal Co-operative v Attorney General* (see [1970] I.R. 317, at 338). I know of no basis on which such an action is sustainable where it cannot be shown that the right of any person will be thereby vindicated or protected. It is not the function of the court, in my view, to indulge in an academic exercise which will be utterly futile so far as the plaintiffs are concerned; and, apart from the other considerations to which I have referred, this seems to me to be a fatal obstacle to the granting of the relief which they have sought in the present proceedings. The plaintiffs' claim will accordingly be dismissed.

Notes and Questions

1. Do you agree with the analysis and holding of this decision? Cf. *Shatter*, 112, fn. 54.
2. If it could be shown that a particular foreign country practised absolutely no sex discrimination in any area of life – that women and men worked together in complete equality and home duties were spread evenly among them – would this subvert the rational justification for our law posited by Keane J., *so far as persons from that country were concerned*? In other words, why should conditions of sex inequality in foreign countries A, B and C provide a Constitutional justification for an Irish rule, premised on such inequality, so far as concerns persons from country D, where no such inequality prevails?
3. On Keane, J.'s statement that '[t]he court has no jurisdiction to substitute for the impugned enactment a form of enactment which it considers desirable . . . .', see Forde, *Equality and the Constitution*, 17 Ir. Jur. (n.s.) 295, at 336–337 (1982).

JACTITATION OF MARRIAGE

BODKIN v. CASE

Milw. 355 (Dr. Radcliff, 1835)

Dr. Radcliff.:

This is a jactitation charge by the promovent that the impugnant, on a certain day, falsely and maliciously alleged she was married to the promovent. To such a charge there are three defences available; first a denial of the boasting; second, a setting up of a fact of marriage; third, that he allowed her to assume the character of wife. The first asserts, that she did not boast; the second asserts, that she boasted truly; and the third, that the boasting was not malicious, though false. Here the second sort of defence has been relied on, and the jactitation attempted to be justified. She alleges an actual marriage, on or about the 14th of June, 1825, at 23, Great Ship-street (she does not say about what hour of the day), by the celebrated Joseph Wood, admitted to be in orders of the Established Church, in presence of two witnesses, one of whom is alleged to be dead; that after that there was cohabitation, and residence as man and wife for above three months, and that they were reputed so by their neighbours, acquaintances, and friends, and that at all times, and in all places, he acknowledged and introduced her to them as his wife; that Wood died in July, 1829, and the alleged witness, one Susan Wilson, died on the 30th of September, 1825. It is admitted, that the personal answer denies the marriage and cohabitation, &c.; indeed it not being read shows that.

This case is the most barren and destitute of circumstances that ever came before me. There is no circumstance of courtship, nor any fact that led to the marriage; no circumstance has been alleged, such as generally follows and accompanies the marriage of persons having no reason for concealment or mystery, even in respect of the lodgers of impugnant, two of whom have been produced. Her case at the bar is, that their condition in life was not so unequal as to make the marriage improbable; both were of age, and not living in their parents' houses, and if the marriage was therefore likely to take place, why was it so devoid of preparations and circumstances? No tea or wedding supper were prepared. The only witness produced to prove the fact is Maxwell, a tailor, who appears to be illiterate, and of no property. His story is, that about nine years before July, 1834, but on what day of the month he cannot say, he was present at the ceremony between those parties; he cannot say by whom it was celebrated, but he looked like a clergyman; and the witness cannot say, whether it was the Church of England ceremony or not; that the parson read from a book, but he cannot say whether he declared them husband and wife or not; and though he was present at the marriage and must have been intimate in impugnant's house, he cannot say whether they were since reputed and taken to be husband and wife; and no conversation at the time is alleged to have taken place. So much he states on his direct examination, which implies no doubt of the identity of both parties; but he is cross-examined, and in answer to the second interrogatory, will not take on him to swear he knew the promovent, or that he could not be mistaken in his person or appearance. To the third interrogatory he cannot say whether the ceremony was in Latin or English, but that the ceremony was in the evening; and he cannot identify the promovent, except on belief, and the person married might not have been him; that she (impugnant) brought him to be present, and he was but a short time in the room. But his answer to the sixth interrogatory sets his evidence aside. He says, 'He did call on a Mr. Hagarty in the month of June last, and tell him he (respondent) was afraid he would be summoned as a witness, to prove a marriage of the impugnant, and of respondent's uneasiness of mind to prove any such thing; and said respondent did mention at the time, that about nine years ago, respondent was sent for in a hurry, in the dark of the evening, to come to No. 23, Great Ship-street, in the city of Dublin, to the impugnant's house, and that having gone there, respondent was shown into a parlour where four persons were, and a candle lighting, and that one of the persons had a book in his hand, and another with his head down, and that respondent could not see by his face who was the person that was marrying to the impugnant on the occasion.' This is all very strange; no cause has been assigned for the sending for him at all, much less in such a hurry, when the priest and parties were standing up, and at so late an hour after dark in June; besides, there were several lodgers to be had in the house, to witness the ceremony. It is stranger still, that the man to be married should be let hide his face, when the only object for sending for Maxwell must have been that he might afterwards prove the marriage, and the man's identity; if that was not the object, there were enough without him. Why send for Wood to the house if secrecy was intended? especially if the only use of the ceremony was to silence her scruples; she was the actor in it, not the man.

So far as Maxwell goes, there is no evidence that the ceremony, if at all had, was between the parties here: I say, if at all had, which is very doubtful under the circumstances; it is for the first time set up after the death of the supposed clergyman and the supposed other witness. But it is said Maxwell is corroborated by M'Kenzie and Evans, who depose to their being reputed man and wife, to cohabitation, and to the promovent owning her as his wife. These witnesses have been examined only to general articles. M'Kenzie says, in general terms, that promovent lived and resided at No. 23, Great Ship-street, in June, July and August, 1825, but cannot say whether he did so constantly or not, though on the cross-examination she swears they cohabited there three months. Evans also swears, in general terms, to the cohabitation, reputation, and introducing and acknowledging her as wife, and their continual residence together for three months and more, except on his occasionally sleeping at the Hospital. That general swearing is not to be taken as corroboration; the corroboration should be by the proof of some fact leading to the supposition that the witness must have sworn truly: as, if the promovent, and Wood also, had been seen going into the house, that a supper was given as to new-married people, or such other facts, such as impugnant's appearing immediately after with a ring, or taking promovent's name then for the first time. That they cohabited as man and wife is rather a conclusion from circumstances, of which the Court is to judge whether it be correctly drawn. There is nothing to show by collateral circumstances that any marriage was had that evening in the house, much less that the marriage was of the promovent. Maxwell has not sworn, as matter to be corroborated, that he was the person; the corroboration must be of something he said, and not what he did not.

As to reputation, supposing it sufficient, there is no legal evidence of it from the family of either party, not even a conversation given from whence can be collected an acknowledgment of her as his wife. No house they were received at is mentioned, or any particular day that he was at Ship-street, or who were present, nor to whom any introduction took place, but by Mary-Anne M'Kenzie, who says he introduced or acknowledged her as his wife to witness and her father, who is also deceased, and they visited promovent and her at Ship-street; this has not been alleged, nor has any time been proved, and it has not been alleged so as to admit of contradiction. General swearing to cohabitation is not sufficient, though it might support the third line of defence, to shew he was accessary to the boasting, even if the marriage was not had; but those witnesses' credit is shaken as to the continued cohabitation at Ship-street by the evidence of Dr. Kirby, the porter, and others, making out nearly an *alibi* defence for the promovent. [Here the Court discussed some evidence given by the promovent to show that at the time assigned by the witnesses for his cohabitation with impugnant he was occupied from morning till night with professional duties at some distance.] It is proper to contradict a notion that a marriage, in such a case, could not be proved by circumstances, cohabitation, and acknowledgment; but here there are no circumstances sufficient, and only general swearing, uncorroborated by facts and circumstances, and such swearing is impeached by proof of the exception to the evidence.

[The Court, by its sentence, decreed that Eliza Case, pretended Bodkin, hath falsely and unjustly jactitated, given out, asserted, and declared that she was married or contracted in marriage with the said Thomas Bodkin; and that no marriage or matrimonial contract was entered into or solemnised between the parties at the time and place alleged, or at any other time and place, so far as appears; and enjoined the said Eliza Case to perpetual silence in this behalf, and declared that the said Thomas Bodkin was and is free from any marriage or matrimonial contract with the said Eliza Case, so far as appears.]

Notes

1. The main features of proceedings for jactitation of marriage are described by *Shatter*, 119–120; *Shelford*, 582–586 *Kisbey*, ch. 6; *Burn*, Vol. 2, 500a–500b, and the Law Reform Commission's *Report on Restitution of Conjugal Rights, Jactitation of Marriage and Related Matters*, ch. 3 (LRC 6–1983). Several decisions are also reported by A. Browne, *A Compendious View of the Ecclesiastical Law of Ireland*, Appendix 1 (2nd ed., 1803).
2. The Law Reform Commission, in ch. 4 of its Report, has recommended that the remedy of jactitation be abolished. In its place the Commission recommends a new remedy, consisting of an action for an injunction and, in appropriate cases, damages, against a person falsely claiming to be married to the plaintiff or falsely stating (with knowledge of the falsity of the statement or reckless indifference as to its truth) that another person is married to the plaintiff. The existing defences would continue to apply (with a minor modification as to the defence of acquiescence). Where an alleged party to a marriage is the defendant in the proceedings and he or she alleges that there is a valid marriage between the plaintiff and himself or herself, the Commission recommends that the proceedings should be suspended pending the disposition of this question in nullity proceedings.
   The Law Reform Commission also proposes (*id.*, pp. 24–25) the establishment of a new procedure for judicial declarations as to marital status, on the same general lines as contained in the *Legitimacy Declaration (Ireland) Act 1868.*
   The English Law Commission has taken a different view. It recommends that the remedy of jactitation of marriage should be abolished, arguing that:–
   > there is no valid reason why a false claim as to marriage should be treated differently from any other false claim. If a person makes a false claim, for instance, that he is someone's son or brother, or that the parties are engaged, such a claim does not of itself enable the person aggrieved to obtain an injunction, even though the allegation may be just as embarrassing as an allegation that the parties are married. *Family Law: Declarations in Family Matters*, para. 4.10 (Law Com. No. 132, 1984).
3. If jactitation proceedings were abolished and not replaced by any new procedure for judicial declarations as to status, could Article 40 of the Constitution be invoked by a plaintiff claiming wrongful appropriation of his or her name by a person making a false assertion as to marriage? Cf. Walsh, *The Judicial Power and the Protection of Privacy*, (1977) 1 Dublin U.L.J. 3, at 8.

RESTITUTION OF CONJUGAL RIGHTS

D. v. D.

Unreported, High Ct., Butler, J., 20 December 1966 (1965–5M, 1966–2M)

The facts of the case are set out *infra*, p. 290 in relation to Mrs. D's petition for divorce *a mensa et thoro.* Having rejected Mrs. D's petition, Butler J. went on to consider Mr. D's petition for restoration of conjugal rights.

Butler, J.:

I have had much difficulty in deciding the proper answer to the husband's petition for restoration of conjugal rights. While I have found that he was not guilty of such conduct as would entitle the wife to a divorce, he has not acted properly. He suffers from a condition which makes him difficult to live with and which has directly caused separation from his wife on at least three occasions. This condition can certainly be controlled and possibly cured by proper medical treatment but he refuses to face realities and to take proper advice or submit to treatment. Had I the jurisdiction to do so I would be inclined to hold that while the wife was not entitled to a divorce she had good grounds for withdrawing from cohabitation with her husband. Mr. Finlay [counsel for Mr. D] submits that I have no such jurisdiction.

The jurisdiction of this Court in matrimonial causes is a simple transfer effected by Section 7 of the *Matrimonial Causes (Ireland) Act, 1870.* There has been no enlargement of this jurisdiction by any subsequent legislation. The jurisdiction which undoubtedly exists in England to refuse to decree a divorce and also to refuse to decree restitution at the suit of the other party was first recognised by the Court of Appeal in *Russell* v. *Russell* [1894] P. 315 and upheld with strong dissent by the House of Lords on Appeal [1897] A.C. 395. It is based on the acceptance in England of desertion as a ground for relief by the *Matrimonial Causes Act, 1857* and the effect of Section 5 of the *Matrimonial Causes Act, 1884* which enacted that a respondent who fails to comply with a decree for restoration of conjugal rights shall be deemed guilty of desertion without reasonable cause. Thus understood, the jurisdiction established by the case does not exist in Ireland. In *Dunne* v. *Dunne* [1947] I.R. 227, Dixon J. pointed out that this Court is empowered to give relief only on principles and in accordance with rules conformable with those formerly acted upon by the former Ecclesiastical Courts of Ireland and that desertion was not a matrimonial offence within that code. It is also clear that the rule of the Ecclesiastical Courts was that unless a divorce *a mensa et thoro* could be granted the obligation of both husband and wife to live together was invariably recognised and enforced. Among the many authorities for that proposition I need only cite *Seaver* v. *Seaver* 2 Sw. & Tr. 665 (1845). In that case both parties had committed adultery and neither could, in consequence, obtain a divorce. The wife instituted a suit for restitution of conjugal rights in the Consistorial Court in Dublin and despite the most strenuous argument the relief was granted. The decision was upheld on appeal to the Court of Delegates. The decision of that Court was unanimous that a refusal of a decree of divorce was equivalent to a decree for restitution of conjugal rights. I am bound by these decisions that the matrimonial law, which I must apply, recognised no middle state in the relations of husband and wife between that of full cohabitation and divorce *a mensa et thoro.* Consequently, having held that Mrs. D is not entitled to a divorce I must make a decree for restitution of conjugal rights on Mr. D's petition.

Notes

1. Formerly, a wife who refused to accept her husband's choice of where to live risked the possibility of being held to be in desertion. This could affect her right to custody of their children: cf. *In re Mitchell*, [1937] I.R. 767 (Sup. Ct., 1937, aff'g High Ct., 1936) (Irish wife married Irishman who was then in permanent employment in Glasgow; having lived with him there for a short period, wife returned to Dublin and refused to go back to Glasgow; custody of their child awarded to the husband). The trend of the law in most jurisdictions has been to adopt a more egalitarian approach; see, e.g. *Dunn* v. *Dunn,* [1949] P. 98; *Simpson* v. *Simpson,* [1951] P. 320; H. Finlay, *Family Law in Australia*, 132 (3rd ed., 1983).

   Of course, the *Family Home Protection Act, 1976* has the effect, in result if not in express terms, of enabling a wife to 'sit firm' where her husband proposes to move the family elsewhere, and the Act allows her to have the reasonableness or unreasonableness of her veto to be put to external test – by the Court, under section 4.
2. When does the drunkenness of one spouse justify the other spouse's departure from the home? Cf. *Ruxton* v. *Ruxton*, 5 L.R. Ir. 455 (C.A., 1880).
3. If a wife is violent towards her children in the absence of her husband does this constitute cruelty which would justify him in leaving the home? Cf. *Manning* v. *Manning*, I.R. 6 Eq. 417 (Ct. for Mat. Causes, Warren, J., 1872), I.R. 7 Eq. 520 (Ct. for Warren J., 1873). Is the position different where the husband is present when the acts of violence take place? Are acts of violence by a husband on his children to be subject to the same rule as those by a wife?
4. Is there any justification in social policy for the retention of proceedings for restitution of conjugal rights today? Has it survived the coming into force of the Constitution? Cf. *infra*, p. 196.

5. The Law Reform Commission have recently recommended that proceedings for restitution of conjugal rights be abolished: *Report on Restitution of Conjugal Rights, Jactitation of Marriage and Related Matters*, p. 12 (LRC 6–1983). The Commission were impressed by the argument that it is contrary to the values of society today to require people to live with their spouses under sanction of committal to prison. Moreover, the remedy could be regarded as self-defeating in cases where the respondent chooses prison in preference to returning to the home: where the respondent is the source of family support, the effect of imprisonment might be to reduce the petitioner's chances of obtaining adequate maintenance. The Commission considered the argument that the remedy may induce some deserting spouses to come to their senses and return to their home, but took the view that reconciliation and conciliation would be more successfully encouraged where the procedures are voluntary rather than compulsory. The Commission considered that more support for these procedures should be made available by the State through financial subsidy of existing marriage guidance and conciliation agencies, as well as through the creation of new conciliation services, by way of pilot projects, if necessary.
6. In *Abdelkefi* v. *Minister for Justice and the Attorney General*, unreported, High Ct., Barron, J., 27 January 1983 (1980–6410P), an Irish woman, married to a Tunisian man whom the Aliens Registration Office refused permission to remain in Ireland, claimed that her constitutional right to the society of her husband had been denied. Barron J. disposed of this argument in the following passage:

   > The constitutional argument is unusual in form in that it does not seek to impugn the validity of any law having regard to the provisions of the Constitution. It claimed an absolute inalienable and imprescriptible right and by implication denies any authority as being empowered to deny this right. The argument put simply is, the authority in control of aliens is obliged, having regard to the guarantee of fair procedures, to hear the application of the [husband] to enter and to remain in the State when in the company of [his Irish wife]. On the hearing of any such application, it must be granted, because to refuse the permission would be to deny to [the wife] the constitutional right to the society of her husband.
   >
   > The [spouses] and their child have their home outside the jurisdiction and have no present intention of establishing a home within the State. The . . . wife wishes to travel to the State from time to time in order to visit her immediate family. When she does so, she wishes to do so in the company of her husband.
   >
   > Insofar as the [wife]'s claim is based upon the refusal by the Aliens Registration Office as being a denial of her personal rights under Article 40(3) of the Constitution, I do not regard the fulfilment of a desire to visit her immediate family in the company of her husband as being of such a fundamental nature as to be guaranteed by such constitutional provision. Insofar as the [wife']s claim is based on rights protected by Article 41(1) of the Constitution I can see nothing in the refusal by the Aliens Registration Office which could be said to weaken the family as an institution or to weaken its position in our society nor is there anything in such refusal which can be said to undermine the status of marriage. . . .

   Was Barron, J.'s rejection of the wife's case based on the *triviality* of the interference she alleged or on the *legitimacy* of the actions of the Aliens Registration Office? If the former, could there be a case – where the Irish spouse was obliged to remain in Ireland on account of sickness or old age, for example – where a Constitutional argument might arise on the perfectly legitimate exclusion of an alien? Cf. J. Kelly, *The Irish Constitution*, 613 (2nd ed., 1984). It is worth contrasting Finlay, P.'s analysis of the right to travel in *The State (K.M. & R.D.)* v. *Minister for Foreign Affairs & Others,* [1979] I.R. 73 (High Ct., 1978) *supra*, p. 152.

DOMICILE

The concept of domicile is important in private international law. Domicile is a link or 'connecting factor' between a person and the legal system of a particular country. It is of importance in relation to many aspects of family law, including marriage, matrimonial causes, succession, administration, matrimonial property, legitimacy, legitimation, adoption and guardianship. In simple terms it may be said that a person is domiciled in a country where he or she intends to reside permanently (or indefinitely). This simple definition belies the complexity of the concept: domicile is plagued with an elaborate scaffolding of rules and qualifications, which make the task of assessing a person's domicile in some cases very difficult and uncertain.

One aspect of this subject which gives rise to particular difficulties and uncertainties is the concept of a domicile of dependency. Historically the law has permitted adult males and adult single females to acquire a *domicile of choice*, but this privilege has been denied to married women, children and persons of unsound mind, who have a *domicile of dependency*. In the case of a married woman, the rule has been that her domicile depends on her husband's domicile. The domicile of a child is normally derived from the father's domicile: see Duncan, *The Domicile of Infants*, 4 Ir. Jur. (n.s.) 36 (1969); Binchy, *Reform of the Law Relating to the Domicile of Children: A Proposal Statute*, 11 Ottawa L. Rev. 279, at 280–282 (1979); Blaikie, *The Domicile of Dependent Children: A Necessary Unity?* [1984] Jurid. Rev. 1. Somewhat different and more elaborate rules apply to persons of unsound mind.

Whether the historic rules relating to the wife's domicile of dependency still continue with their full rigour today is not certain. The issue has been examined by the courts in the context of recognition of foreign divorces. The relevant decisions are included in Chapter 6, *infra*. For critical analysis of the existing law, see Duncan, *The Domicile of Women: A Submission to the Law Reform Commission*, (1977) 1 Dublin U.L.J. 38.

The Law Reform Commission, in its *Report on Domicile and Habitual Residence as Connecting Factors in the Conflict of Laws* (LRC 7–1983), recommended the abolition of domicile as a connecting factor in the conflict of laws and its replacement by habitual residence. The habitual residence of a person would be determined 'having regard to the centre of his personal, social and economic interests': Section 3(1) of the General Scheme of Legislation, *id*., p. 23.

The General Scheme is drafted with the purpose of ensuring that no equivalent of a wife's domicile of dependency should arise in relation to habitual residence. Section 3(3) provides that 'the habitual residence of any person shall not be determined by that of a spouse, a parent or any other person.' Section 4(1) provides that 'although the habitual residence of one spouse does not depend upon that of the other spouse, the habitual residence of one spouse may be taken into account in determining the habitual residence of the other spouse' and section 4(2) provides that, 'where the spouses are residing together, they shall each be presumed to have the same habitual residence, unless the contrary is shown.' Could it be argued that section 4(1) involves an unbreakable circularity of definition?

CRIMINAL LAW

THE STATE (D.P.P.) v. WALSH
[1981] I.R. 412 (Sup. Ct., Henchy, J.)

A wife was alleged to have been guilty of contempt of court. The defence of marital coercion was raised.

Henchy, J.:
. . . For a number of reasons, this submission is in my view lacking in persuasiveness. In the first place, it is to be noted that this offence of contempt was committed not in composing the statement but in causing it to be published in a newspaper. Whatever part the husband of the appellant Conneely may have taken in the composition of the statement, it is clear that he took no part in the dissemination of it. Her affidavit goes no further than to state that he was present when she was telephoning the statement to the newspaper. His physical presence is all that can be relied on as constituting the coercion which is said by her counsel to exculpate her.

There was undoubtedly a common-law defence of coercion available to a wife in regard to certain offences if the act in question was done by her in the presence of her husband. In an effort to compensate the wife for her inferior status, and in particular to make up for her inability to plead benefit of clergy, as her husband could, the law concocted the fiction of a prima facie presumption that the act done by her in the presence of her husband was done under his coercion. But, be it noted, it was only a prima facie presumption. The authorities are agreed in saying that the presumption could be rebutted by evidence that the wife was the instigator of the act, or was the more active party. The so-called coercion was recognized only when there was no evidence of initiative by the wife: see Smith and Hogan on Criminal Law (3rd ed. at p. 168). Here the presumption is plainly rebutted. On the appellant Conneely's own evidence on affidavit, as between her husband and herself, she was the prime mover in the commission of the *actus reus.* It was she, and she alone, who telephoned the statement to the newspaper. To do so was a duty committed to her (as honorary secretary of the Dublin Central Branch of the Association for Legal Justice) by the appellant Walsh as chairman of that branch. Her husband merely happened to be present when she did so. His mere physical presence in the room could no more provide a defence for her than it could form the basis of a conviction of him. It would be contrary to both reason and judicial authority to hold that in those circumstances the appellant Conneely could be acquitted of contempt simply because her husband was present when she telephoned the offending statement to the newspaper.

That is how I would dispose of this point if the presumption of coercion of a wife by the physical presence of her husband were applicable. But, in my judgment, that doctrine is no longer extant in this State. The idea that, where a wife performs a criminal act, there should be a prima facie presumption that the mere physical presence of her husband when she did it overbore her will, stultified her volitional powers, and drove her into criminal conduct which she would have avoided but for his presence, presupposes a disparity in status and capacity between husband and wife which runs counter to the normal relations between a married couple in modern times. The conditions of legal inferiority which attached at common law to the status of a married woman and which gave rise to this presumption have been swept away by legislation and by judicial decisions. Nowadays, to exculpate a wife for an *actus reus* because it was done when her husband was present is no more justifiable than if she were granted immunity from guilt because the act was done in the presence of her father, her brother or any other relative or friend. Any other conclusion would be repugnant to the degree of freedom and equality to which a wife is entitled in modern society and which has been extensively recognised in the statutes and judicial decisions of this State.

In particular, I would hold that the presumption relied on is inconsistent with the Constitution and was therefore, by virtue of Article 50, not given validity in the legal system after the Constitution came into force. A legal rule that presumes, even on a prima facie and rebuttable basis, that a wife has been coerced by the physical presence of her husband into committing an act prohibited by the criminal law, particularly when a similar presumption does not operate in favour of a husband for acts committed in the presence of his wife, is repugnant to the concept of equality before the law guaranteed by the first sentence of Article 40, s. 1, and could not, under the second sentence of that Article, be justified as a discrimination based on any difference of capacity or of social function as between husband and wife. Therefore, the presumption contended for must be rejected as being a form of unconstitutional discrimination.

Notwithstanding the fresh evidence adduced by the appellants, I see no reason to depart from the conclusion, reached unanimously by the full Court on the determination of this appeal, that no issue of fact as to the appellants' guilt remains to be decided. In my opinion, the curial part of the order of this Court should simply record that the appeal stands dismissed. The case will then go back to the High Court to be disposed of accordingly, that is to say, on the question of sentence only.

Griffin and **Kenny, J.J.**. concurred.

Notes

1. Can *any* case be made out for the old law relating to marital coercion? Cf. Pace, *Marital Coercion–Anachronism or Modernism?,* [1979] Crim. L. Rev. 82. On other aspects of this subject see Williams, *The Legal Unity of Husband*

and Wife, 10 Modern L. Rev. 16 (1947); Glover, *Conspiracy as Between Husband and Wife*, 9 Family L. 181 (1979).

2. The question whether rape within marriage should be treated by the criminal law in the same way as rape outside marriage has given rise to much discussion in recent years: see, e.g., Williams, *Marital Rape – Time for Reform*, 134 New L.J. 26 (1984); Freeman, *'But If You Can't Rape Your Wife, Who[m] Can You Rape?'*, 15 Family L. Q. 1 (1981); Freeman, *Rape by a Husband?*, 129 New L.J. 332 (1979); Maidment, *Rape Between Spouses – A Case for Reform*, 8 Family L. 87 (1978); *Anon., Note; The Marital Rape Exemption*, 52, N.Y.U.L. Rev. 306 (1977); B. Toner, *The Facts of Rape*, 111 (1977); Scutt, *Reforming the Law of Rape: The Michigan Example*, 50 Austr. L. J. 615, at 623–624 (1976); Sasko & Sesek, *Rape Reform Legislation: Is It the Solution?*, 24 Cleveland State L. Rev. 463 (1975); B. Babcock, A. Freedman, E. Norton & S. Ross, *Sex Discrimination and the Law: Causes and Remedies*, 820–821 (1975); Tutt, *Comment*, 11 Gonzaga L. Rev. 145, at 150–151 (1975); H. S.S. *Note*, 61 Va. L. Rev. 1500 (1975); Kaganas & Murray, *Rape in Marriage – Conjugal Right or Criminal Wrong?*, [1983] Acta Jurid. 125.
3. Section 9 of the *Married Women's Status Act, 1957* provides as follows:

   (1) Subject to subsection (3), every married woman shall have in her own name against all persons whomsoever, including her husband, the same remedies and redress by way of criminal proceedings for the protection and security of her property as if she were unmarried.
   (2) Subject to subsection (3), a husband shall have against his wife the same remedies and redress by way of criminal proceedings for the protection and security of his property as if she were not his wife.
   (3) No criminal proceedings concerning any property claimed by one spouse (in this subsection referred to as the claimant) shall, by virtue of subsection (1) or subsection (2), be taken by the claimant against the other spouse while they are living together, nor, while they are living apart, concerning any act done while living together by the other spouse, unless such property was wrongfully taken by the other spouse when leaving or deserting or about to leave or desert the claimant.
   (4) In any criminal proceedings to which this section relates brought against one spouse, the other spouse may, notwithstanding anything to the contrary in any enactment or rule of law, be called as a witness either for the prosecution or defence and without the consent of a person charged.
   (5) In any indictment or process grounding criminal proceedings in relation to the property of a married woman, it shall be sufficient to allege the property to be her property.

   How can subsection (3) be Constitutional? What rational goal does it seek to serve? The encouragement of family harmony? If so, is it likely to be effective? Contrast the approach in section 30(4) of the English *Theft Act, 1968*. For consideration of the historical background see Kenny's *Outlines of Criminal Law*, 290–291, para. 254 (19th ed., by J. Turner, 1966).

EVIDENCE

McGONAGLE v. McGONAGLE
[1951] I.R. 125 (Supreme Court, aff'g High Court, Davitt, J.)

O'Byrne, J.:

The Case Stated by the District Justice arose out of a prosecution under s. 12 of the *Children Act, 1908.* Catherine McGonagle, the respondent of this appeal and the mother of the child in question, was complainant and her husband, Richard McGonagle, the appellant in this appeal and the father of the child, was defendant. The respondent was a willing witness and her evidence was accepted by the District Justice, notwithstanding the objection of the appellant, who contended that she was not a competent witness. The Case Stated raises the question whether the District Justice was right in law in accepting the evidence of the respondent. That question has been answered in the affirmative by Mr. Justice Davitt and this appeal is taken from his decision.

With the exception of a very limited number of cases, to which it is unnecessary to refer in detail, the wife or husband of an accused person could not, at common law, give evidence either for the prosecution or the defence on the trial of such person. This position was radically altered in Great Britain by the *Criminal Evidence Act, 1898*; but that Act did not apply to Ireland. Further inroads on the common law doctrine were made from time to time by statutes dealing with special subject-matters.

The *Children Act, 1908*, applied to Ireland subject to certain modifications contained in s.

133. By clause 28 of that section it is provided that in any proceeding against any person for an offence under Part II of the Act (including s. 12) or for any of the offences mentioned in the First Schedule to the Act, such person shall be competent but not compellable to give evidence, and the wife or husband of such person may be required to attend to give evidence as an ordinary witness in the case and shall be competent, but not compellable, to give evidence. This was the position in this country at the time of the constitutional changes effected by the Treaty of 1921.

In 1924 the Oireachtas enacted a statute on substantially the same lines as the said Act of 1898; it is the *Criminal Justice (Evidence) Act, 1924.* By s. 1 it is provided that every person charged with an offence, and the wife or husband, as the case may be, of the person so charged shall be a competent witness for the defence at every stage of the proceedings, whether the person so charged is charged solely or jointly with any other person. The section contains various provisoes, including the following, viz., '(*c*) the wife or husband of the person charged shall not, save as in this Act mentioned, be called as a witness in pursuance of this Act except upon the application of the person so charged.' The clear intent and object of this section is to make the evidence of the accused person, and that of the wife or husband of the accused person, available for the accused person and only at his, or her, option.

Sect. 4 provides 1, that the wife or husband of a person charged with an offence under any enactment mentioned in the Schedule to the Act may be called as a witness either for the prosecution or defence and without the consent of the person charged, and 2, that nothing in the Act shall affect a case where the wife or husband of a person charged with an offence may, at common law, be called as a witness without the consent of that person. The Schedule contains:–

(*a*) The Vagrancy (Ireland) Act, 1847.	Sect. 2.
(*b*) The Offences Against the Person Act, 1861.	Sects. 48, 52, 53 and 54 so far as unrepealed and s. 55.
(*c*) The Married Women's Property Act, 1882.	Sects. 12 and 16.
(*d*) The Prevention of Cruelty to Children Act, 1904.	The whole Act.

It is contended on behalf of the appellant that the proceedings before the District Justice were governed by s. 1 of the Act of 1924 and that, under that section, his wife could not properly be called as a witness on behalf of the prosecution without his application, and could not be called against his consent. It is further contended that the Act of 1924 repeals the provision of the *Children Act, 1908*, to which I have referred.

The material provision of the Children Act is of a very special nature; it is confined to proceedings for an offence under Part II of that Act or for any of the offences mentioned in the First Schedule to the Act. The First Schedule sets out 1, certain sections of the *Offences Against the Person Act, 1861*; 2, the *Criminal Law Amendment Act, 1885*; 3, the *Dangerous Performances Acts, 1879* and *1897*; 4, any other offence involving bodily injury to a child or young person.

It is a general rule of construction that a prior statute is held to be repealed, by implication, by a subsequent statute which is inconsistent with and repugnant to the prior statute. This rule, however, does not apply where, as in the present case, the prior statute is special and the subsequent statute general. In such a case the Court applies the doctrine, '*generalia specialibus non derogant.*'

The reason for the application of this doctrine is clearly stated in the opinion of the Judicial Committee of the Privy Council in *Barker* v. *Edger* [1898] A. C. 748, at 754:– 'When the Legislature has given its attention to a separate subject, and made provision for it, the presumption is that a subsequent general enactment is not intended to interfere with the special provision unless it manifests that intention very clearly.'

The foregoing maxim is not in dispute; but, as I understand the case of the appellant, it is contended that, in this case, the Legislature, in the Act of 1924, has clearly manifested its intention to repeal the material provision of the Act of 1908. Reliance is placed on s. 4 of the Act of 1924, and it is argued that this section clearly indicates that Parliament had its attention directed to the special subject and considered that special provision was necessary only in the case of offences comprised in the Schedule to the Act. It will be noted that the Schedule refers to certain sections of the *Offences Against the Person Act, 1861, so far as unrepealed*; whereas, in the case of the *Prevention of Cruelty to Children Act, 1904*, it refers to *the whole Act*. The words which I have italicised would seem to indicate that, *per incuriam*, the Legislature overlooked the fact that a great deal of the Act of 1904 had been repealed and re-enacted in the Act of 1908.

In particular, s. 1 of the Act of 1904 was repealed and provisions to substantially the same effect re-enacted in s. 12 of the Act of 1908 under which the prosecution was brought. If, as contended by counsel for the appellant, the Legislature directed its attention to this special matter and considered that the wife or husband of the person charged with an offence under s. 1 of the Act of 1904 might be called as a witness either for the prosecution or defence and without the consent of the person charged, it is difficult to understand on what possible grounds it could determine that a different principle should be applied with reference to the trial of an offence under s. 12 of the Act of 1908. What I have to consider is whether the Oireachtas has clearly manifested its intention to repeal the provisions of clause 28 of s. 133 of the Act of 1908. Not only has it not done so, but, in my opinion, it has indicated a clear intention that the provisions to which I have referred should apply on the trial of a person for such offence as that which the District Justice had to investigate. It seems to me quite clear that these provisions are still operative notwithstanding the Act of 1924, and I do not consider it necessary to examine in detail the other enactments contained in the Schedule to the latter Act.

It was sought to place some reliance on the absence from clause 28 of the words, 'without the consent of the person charged,' and to suggest that the absence of these words implied that such consent was necessary before the evidence could be received. In my opinion, there is no substance in this contention.

For these reasons I am of opinion that the evidence of the respondent was properly received by the District Justice under clause 28 and that this appeal should be dismissed.

Black, J.:

. . . The appellant's counsel contended that s. 133, clause 28 of the *Children Act, 1908*, which makes a wife a competent, though not a compellable, witness in a prosecution against her husband for an offence under that Act, omits deliberately the words, 'without the consent of the person charged,' which words are contained in s. 4, sub-s. 1, of the English *Criminal Evidence Act, 1898.* The argument was that these words were inserted in s. 4, sub-s. 1, of the *Criminal Evidence Act, 1898*, in order to render it unnecessary to have the consent of the person charged before admitting the evidence of the husband or wife of that person under the said section, and that but for the said words, that consent would have been necessary. It was, therefore, contended that since those words are omitted from s. 133, clause 28, of the *Children Act, 1908*, the consent of the person charged in cases governed by s. 133, clause 28, of the *Children Act, 1908* (assuming that section to be still in force), is necessary before the evidence of the husband or wife of that person can be given against such person.

In my opinion, the effect of such an interpretation of s. 133, clause 28, would be to frustrate one of the obvious intentions of that section, namely, the intention that where a husband is on trial for an offence under s. 12 of the *Children Act, 1908* (which section is included in Part II of the Act), the wife shall be entitled (though not bound) to give evidence either for or against him. It seems plain that if in such a case the wife could not give evidence against the accused husband without his consent, she could not in practice give such evidence at all; for it is unlikely that the husband would ever consent to her doing so, and the result would be that the provision of the section making the wife a competent witness against her husband would, for practical purposes, be a nullity and a sham. I think it highly improbable that s. 133, clause 28, could have been intended to be interpreted so as to involve such a result, and I deem it more probable that the words, 'and without the consent of the person charged,' were inserted in s. 4, sub-s. 1, of the *Criminal Evidence Act, 1898, ex abundante cautela*. If they had been omitted from that section I do not think that the English Courts would have been justified in deeming them to have been inserted in it by implication. Therefore, it is my opinion that s. 133, clause 28, of the *Children Act, 1908*, ought not to be construed in the sense for which the appellant's counsel contended, and that its effect is to make the wife's evidence admissible against the husband on trial for an offence under Part II of that Act without the consent of the husband.

Next, and I think principally, it was contended that s. 133, clause 28, of the *Children Act, 1908*, was superseded and impliedly repealed by s. 4, sub-s. 1, and s. 5 of our *Criminal Justice (Evidence) Act, 1924.*

[**Black, J.** quoted section 4(1) and the Schedule to the Act. He continued:]

Now, s. 1, of the . . . *Prevention of Cruelty to Children Act, 1904* . . . creating the offence of cruelty to children under the age of sixteen has been repealed by the Third Schedule to the *Children Act, 1908*, though s. 12, sub-s. 1, of the *Children Act, 1908*, re-creates the same offence in word for word the same terms. But, the *Children Act, 1908*, is not mentioned in the Schedule to the *Criminal Justice (Evidence) Act, 1924.* Therefore, s. 4 of this last-mentioned Act, enabling a wife to give evidence against her husband when charged with any of the offences mentioned in the Schedule would not enable the wife to give such evidence on a charge against her husband under s. 12 of the *Children Act, 1908*, since that Act is not mentioned in the Schedule to the said Act of 1924. The wife could only give evidence in such a case against her husband by virtue of s. 133, clause 28, of the *Children Act, 1908*, and if that section is repealed, she could not give evidence against her husband at all on the hearing of a charge of cruelty to children under s. 12 of the *Children Act, 1908.* That such a repeal, which would have such a result, could have been intended by the Legislature of 1924 seems to me so extravagantly improbable as to make it unthinkable for me to imply it, and more especially when one remembers that such a change in the law would be highly retrograde, for the whole trend of legislation since as far back as the *Criminal Evidence Act, 1898*, has been to enlarge, rather than to narrow, the range of offences upon the trial for which a wife may give evidence against her accused husband.

There are also other offences on a charge of which a wife can give evidence against her husband provided for by s. 133, clause 28, of the *Children Act, 1908*, together with the First Schedule to that Act, which are omitted from the Schedule to our *Criminal Justice (Evidence) Act, 1924*, so that if the said s. 133, clause 28, is repealed, a wife could no longer give evidence against her husband charged with any of these offences. For instance, one of these offences omitted from the *Criminal Justice (Evidence) Act, 1924*, though included in the First Schedule to the *Children Act, 1908*, is the offence under s. 56 of the *Offences Against the Person Act, 1861*, of taking away a child by force or fraud with intent to deprive its parent of the possession of such child or harbouring such child knowing it to have been so taken away. Under the Act of 1908 a wife could give evidence against her husband when charged with such an offence. If the appellant's contention is right our Act of 1924 has impliedly taken that right of the wife away. In the same way our Act of 1924 would have taken away the wife's right to give evidence against her husband on trial for offences under the *Criminal Law Amendment Act, 1885*, for the Criminal Law Amendment Act is omitted from the Schedule to the Act of 1924, though it was included in the First Schedule to the *Children Act, 1908.*

Some colour was sought to be lent to the contention in question by pointing out that ss. 52 and 55 of the *Offences Against the Person Act, 1861*, are included in the Schedule to our *Criminal Justice (Evidence) Act, 1924*, although they were already included in the First Schedule to the *Children Act, 1908*, and it was argued that if s. 133, clause 28, and the First Schedule to the *Children Act, 1908*, were still in force, the repetition of the said ss. 52 and 55 of the Act of 1861 in the Schedule to our *Criminal Justice (Evidence) Act, 1924*, would be otiose. This is so, and, no doubt, there is a certain presumption against a statutory provision being otiose; but otiose provisions in statutes are not unheard of. They may be due to the draftsman's wish to lend them emphasis or they may be due to inadvertence; but, whatever the reason, such presumption as there may be against a provision being otiose is, in my view, far from strong enough to counteract the gross improbability that s. 4, sub-s. 1, and the Schedule to the *Criminal Justice (Evidence) Act, 1924*, could have been intended impliedly to repeal s. 133, clause 28, and the First Schedule of the *Children Act, 1908.*

Finally, we were pressed with s. 5 of the *Criminal Justice (Evidence) Act, 1924*, but in my view, when that section provides that the Act 'shall apply to all criminal proceedings,' subject to a specified exception, it does not mean that *only* that Act shall apply, or that s. 133, clause 28, of the *Children Act, 1908*, shall not continue to apply, to those criminal proceedings to which the First Schedule to the said Act of 1908 made it apply. In my opinion Mr. Justice Davitt was right in holding upon the Case Stated that the District Justice was correct in point of law in admitting the respondent as a witness against the appellant, and this appeal should be dismissed.

Maguire, C.J. concurred with **O'Byrne, J.**

Notes

1. If section 113(28) of the *Children Act, 1908* is not repealed by the *Criminal Justice (Evidence) Act, 1924*, does it follow that the same rule applies to other pre-1924 statutes making the accused competent or compellable to testify in criminal trials which were not listed in the Schedule to the 1924 Act? Cf. *Attorney-General* v. *Power*, [1932] I.R. 610 (not cited in *McGonagle* v. *McGonagle).*
2. Legislation subsequent to 1924 extending the competence of a spouse of the accused includes the *Married Women's Status Act, 1957*, section 9(4), the *Redundancy Payments Act, 1967*, section 45 and the *Social Welfare (Consolidation) Act, 1981*, sections 116(4) and 145(4).
3. Does section 1 of the *Criminal Justice (Evidence) Act, 1924* make the competent spouse compellable? See *Cross on Evidence*, p. 178 (5th ed., 1979), cf. Toswill, *The Accused's Spouse as Defence Witness,* [1979] Crim. L. Rev. 696, at 699. Does section 4 of the Act have this effect? Cf. *Leach* v. *R.*, [1912] A.C. 305.
4. What is the position regarding competence and compellability of spouses: (a) after a decree of divorce *a mensa et thoro* has been granted? Cf. *Moss* v. *Moss*, [1963] 2 Q.B. 799; (b) after a voidable marriage has been annulled? Cf. *R.* v. *Algar*, [1954] 1 Q.B. 279; (c) after a void marriage has been entered into? Cf. *Wells* v. *Fisher*, 1 Mood. & R. 99, 174 E.R. 34, *sub nom. Wells* v. *Fletcher,* 5 C. & P. 12, 172 E.R. 855(1831); *R.* v. *Algar, supra; Jackson,* 126.
5. In the United States, '[t]he enactment of legislation on this subject has been so general that it can be said that, except in one or two jurisdictions, the incompetency of husband or wife as a witness in a case when a spouse is a party no longer exists. The marital relations problems that continue to confront the courts are those of privilege rather than of competency'; D. Louisell, J. Kaplan & J. Waltz, *Cases and Materials on Evidence*, 899 (3rd ed., 1976). See further Lempert, *A Right to Every Woman's Evidence*, 66 Iowa L. Rev. 725 (1981).
6. Should any special rules regarding competence and compellability apply to members of the family other than spouses? Should persons who are cohabiting be subject to any special rules?
7. Section 1(d) of the *Criminal Justice (Evidence) Act, 1924* provides that:–

   > nothing in this Act shall make a husband compellable to disclose any communication made to him by his wife during the marriage, or a wife compellable to disclose any communication made to her by her husband during the marriage.

   It should be noted that only the spouse *to* whom the communication is made, and *not* the spouse *by* whom it is made, is entitled to the privilege.

Has our Constitution any effect on rules of evidence so far as it concerns spouses? Cf. *McGee* v. *A.G.*, [1974] I.R. 284 (Sup. Ct., 1973), *A.S.* v. *R.B., W.S. and The Registrar General of Births & Deaths,* [1984] I.L.R.M. 66 (High Ct., O'Hanlon, J., 1982). If a person maliciously refused to disclose an entirely unconfidential communication from his or her spouse and as a result a stranger was sent to prison, could this be justified under the Constitution? Could even the risk of such a contingency be defended?

8. Could it be argued that, by virtue of Article 41 the Constitution requires that communication between parents and their children should also be privileged? Or does the proviso to Article 40.1 justify the present distinction? For consideration of the merits of a parent-child privilege, see Stanton, *Child-Parent Privilege for Confidential Communications: An Examination and Proposals*, 16 Family L. Q. 1 (1982).
9. What policy goals are served by the marital communications privilege? Could they be better achieved by other strategies? See the Law Reform Commission of Western Australia's *Report on Competence and Compellability of Spouses to Give Evidence in Criminal Proceedings*, paras. 7.37–7.39 (Project No. 31, 1977); Fawal, *Comment: Questioning the Marital Privilege: A Medieval Philosophy in a Modern World*, 7 Cumb. L. Rev. 307, at 318–322 (1976); Boies, *Note: The Husband-Wife Testimonial Privilege in the Federal Courts*, 59 Boston U. L. Rev. 894 (1979).
10. Internationally, legislatures have adopted widely ranging solutions to the question of the marital communications privilege. In the United States of America, the privilege is recognised but subject to specified exceptions (cf. e.g., *Uniform Rules of Evidence*, rules 215, 217, California's *Evidence Code*, sections 970–972, 981–987; Good & Sharlot, *Article V: Privileges*, in *Texas Rules of Evidence Handbook*, 20 Houston L. Rev. 273, at 305–318 (1983); Bigelow, *Comment: The Marital Privileges in Washington Law: Spouse Testimony and Marital Communications*, 54 Wash. L. Rev. 65, at 94–95 (1978). The Law Reform Commission of Canada (*Report on Evidence*, p. 79 (1975)) has proposed that a person should have:–

> a privilege against disclosure of any confidential communication between himself and a person who is related to him by family or similar ties if, having regard to the nature of the relationship, the probable probative value of the evidence and the importance of the question in issue, the need for the person's testimony is outweighed by the public interest in privacy, the possible disruption of the relationship or the harshness of compelling disclosure of the communication.

E.R. v. J.R.
[1981] I.L.R.M. 125 (High Court, Carroll, J.)

Carroll, J.:

. . . On the first day of this action submissions were made on behalf of Fr. Brendan McDonnell that he is entitled to claim privilege in respect of communications made to him as marriage counsellor in relation to Mr. and Mrs. R.
Two cases were cited, *Cook v Carroll* [1945] I.R. 515 and *Pais v Pais* [1970] 3 W.L.R. 830.

The Irish case of *Cook v Carroll* is a judgment of Mr. Justice Gavan-Duffy in which he held that, where the relationship of parish priest and parishioner exists on a matter of confidentiality, the communications are privileged.

In deciding the issue he expressly mentioned Article 44.1.2 of the Constitution which recognised the special place of the Catholic Church – and which has now been repealed.

The principles on which his judgment are based are taken from the writings of John Henry Wigmore on Evidence and concern four fundamental conditions, the presence of which are essential to the establishment of privilege. These are:–

> (1) The communications must originate in a confidence that they will not be disclosed;
> (2) this element of confidentiality must be essential to the full and satisfactory maintenance of the relation;
> (3) the relation must be one which in the opinion of the community ought to be sedulously fostered; and
> (4) the injury which would enure to the relation by the disclosure of the communications must be greater than the benefit thereby gained for the correct disposal of litigation. These four conditions being present a privilege should be recognised and not otherwise.

The relationship of parish priest and parishioner is a relationship different to that of priest as marriage counsellor to spouses and this latter relationship must be examined to see if the four conditions apply.

The nature of the relationship is such that a priest acting as marriage counsellor will be consulted by a spouse or spouses in order to get advice in connection with difficulties in their marriage. I consider that confidentiality is an essential element in that relationship. I can imagine nothing less conducive to frank and open discussion between priest and the spouses, possibly leading to admissions of faults and failings on both sides, than the possibility that total confidentiality will not be observed.

Therefore the first two conditions are fulfilled.

The Constitution guarantees that the State will protect the family (Article 41). The provision of confidential marriage counselling which may help a married couple over a difficulty in their marriage is protection of the most practical kind for the family and should be fostered. The Article (now repealed) concerning the special position of the Catholic Church, while it may have influenced the decision of Gavan Duffy J. in *Cook* v. *Carroll*, [1945] I.R. 515, is neither relevant nor essential to deciding whether the relationship in question here should be fostered, even though it is a priest who is claiming privilege. The fact that the marriage counsellor is also a minister of religion adds weight to the proposition that a confidential relationship between such marriage counsellor and the married couple should be fostered. When I refer to a priest, I am including ministers of religion in general. Advice given by a minister of religion has an added dimension which is not present between lay people. The third condition is fulfilled to my satisfaction.

The last condition is one which presents the most difficulty. The court should be slow to admit new categories of privilege. The one here has not yet been recognised in this country, though it has been recognised in England. In the English case of *Pais v Pais* [1970] 3 W.L.R. 830 it was held that the privilege attached to communications made by spouses to a marriage counsellor was not the privilege of the counsellor but of the spouses and accordingly the evidence could only be given by the counsellor if both spouses had in unmistakable and unequivocal terms waived the privilege attaching to their communications.

The question to be answered is whether the injury to the relationship which would result from disclosure is greater than the benefit gained by not allowing a claim of privilege.

Mr. Danaher states that the interests of the children must come before the rights of the spouses, presumably on the basis that in any matter relating to children, privilege could not be claimed and, conversely, if there were no children, there would always be privilege. However, it seems to me that it would be impossible to separate, in marriage counselling, matters relating to children and matters unconnected with them. Where there are children, they are an integral part of marriage. To my mind either the privilege exists in respect of all communications or it does not exist at all.

It seems to me that a guarantee of confidentiality which will not be breached by giving evidence in court is an important element in building up confidence between the counsellor and the spouse or spouses. The family as such, i.e. both parents and children, benefit by successful counselling. Therefore, I am of the opinion that any benefit which could be gained in litigation by having the evidence available does not outweigh the possible injury to the relationship if disclosure can be compelled.

However, I do subscribe to the proposition that the privilege is that of the people consulting and not the priest. If both of them have taken part in the consultations, the privilege must be waived clearly and unequivocally by both. This has not happened in this case.

Since Fr McDonnell is both family friend and counsellor, the only matter to be determined is whether the occasion in respect of which the privilege is claimed was an occasion on which the relation existed and I will hear evidence to determine that issue. I reserve the question of whether privilege can arise where the counsellor is not a minister of religion. Since it does not arise in this case I am not deciding that issue here.

Notes

1. Do you consider that communications to a marriage counsellor who is not a minister of religion fulfill Wigmore's four conditions?
2. Cf. *S.M. & M.M.* v. *G.M.*, unreported, High Ct., Finlay, P., 7 March 1984 (1983–5624P.). To what extent, if at all, may the welfare principle in relation to children limit or override rules of evidence?
3. For consideration of the position in the United States see the excellent article by Yellin, *The History and Current Status of the Clergy-Penitent Privilege*, 23 Santa Clara L. Rev. 95, at 124ff (1983).

TORTIOUS INTERFERENCE WITH FAMILY RELATIONSHIPS

Tort law through a variety of actions has afforded members of a family some protection against intentional and negligent interference in the relationships with each other. The structure of these actions is antiquated, being based on legal fictions which have been regarded with increasing distaste in the community in recent years. The *Family Law Act, 1981* abolished three of these actions. The first was that of criminal conversation, which enabled a man to obtain damages from a person who had sexual intercourse with his wife. (The question where a woman had a similar right of action in respect of a woman who had sexual intercourse with her husband was never resolved by an Irish court.) The other actions abolished by the 1981 Act were for enticement and harbouring of a spouse. Whether the Constitution could be invoked in cases of intentional intrusion into the marriage relationship is not clear. The protection of the Family under Article 41 might suggest that it would: on the other hand, the rights of association and of privacy could be counterweights. For an attempt by a husband to invoke the machinery of *habeas corpus*, see *Burton* v. *Vandeleur*, L. Recorder 69 (1831). A modern analysis of the policy issues is presented by Huhn, *Comment*, [1982] S. Illinois U.L.J. 275. (See also Duncan, *Supporting the Institution of Marriage in Ireland*, 13 Ir. Jur. (n.s.) 215 at 226 (1978). As regards inter-spousal relationships, the action for tortious interference with *consortium* remains. See generally B. McMahon & W. Binchy, *Irish Law of Torts,* 412–415 (1981); B. McMahon & W. Binchy, *A Casebook on the Irish Law of Torts*, 421–430 (1983). Cf. *Collier* v. *Dublin, Wicklow & Wexford Ry. Co.,* I.R. 8 C.L. 21 (Com Pleas, 1873).

There is no Irish decision squarely recognising a wife's right to sue for tortious interference with consortium although a strong case (supported by the Law Reform Commission) may be made that a wife has such a right. On the aspect of the subject see Reeves Little, *Note: Consortium: A Survey of the Present Law*, 19 J. of Family L. 707 (1981). As to the scope of damages, a recent Canadian decision, *Jones* v. *Taylor*, 27 C.C.L.T. 84 (Sask. Q.B., Walker, J., 1983) has held that no compensation should be allowed to a husband for loss of commercial advantages by reason of the injury to his wife. The husband, who was blind, ran a modest family beekeeping operation with the considerable assistance of his wife. When his wife was injured the business suffered greatly. The decision may be compared with *Chapman* v. *McDonald*, [1969] I.R. 188 (High Ct., O'Keeffe, P.), where it was held that in an action for the loss of services of a child, damages for the loss of domestic services only could be claimed. Could it be argued that *Jones* v. *Taylor* would subvert the view of marriage as a partnership? If so, is this to be commended or condemned? Does the action for loss of *consortium* serve a useful purpose? Should it be abolished? Should any other action replace it? Cf. the Law Reform Commission's Working Paper No. 7–1979, *The Law Relating to Loss of Consortium and Loss of Services of a Child*, and its *First Report on Family Law*, pp. 9–11 (1981). See also *Shatter*, pp. 95–100. In England, Wales and Northern Ireland, the action was abolished by section 2 of the *Administration of Justice Act, 1982.* Similarly in Ontario in 1978: *Family Law Reform Act, 1978*, section 69(3) (St. Ont. 1978, c.2.). Should unmarried persons living together be entitled to sue for loss of *consortium*? In the United States in *Butcher* v. *Superior Court of Orange County*, 139 Cal. App. 3d 58, 188 Cal. Rptr 503 (1983), it was held that they should. See also *Bulloch* v. *United States*, 487 F. Supp. 1078 (D.N.J. 1980).

This approach has been rejected in several other decisions: cf. *Curry* v. *Caterpillar Tractor Co.*, 10 Family L. Rptr, 1241 (U.S.D.C.E. Pa., 1984) *Clifford* v. *White*, 526 F. Supp. 381 (D.D.C., 1983); *Weaver* v. *G.D. Searle & Co.*, 558 F. Supp. 720 (N.D. Ala, S.D., 1983): *Rieding* v. *Commercial Diving Center*, 143 Cal. App. 3d 72 (1983); *Hendrix* v. *General Motors Corporation*, 9 Family L. Reptr 2663 (Calif. Ct. App. 1st Dist. 1983); *Laws* v. *Griep*, 332 N.W. 2d 339 (Iowa Sup. Ct., 1983). The policy considerations are well analysed by Meade, *Consortium Rights of the Unmarried: Time for a Reappraisal*, 15 Family L.Q. 223, at 236–251 (1981); Wilson, *Note: Loss of Consortium Claims by Unmarried Cohabitants: The Roles of Private Self-Determination and Policy*, 57 Indiana L.J. 506 (1981); Treu, *Comment: Loss of Consortium and Engaged Couples: The Frustrating Fate of Faithful Fiancées*, 44 Ohio St. L.J. 719 (1983); Woods, *Comment: Loss of Consortium: Extending Recovery to Unmarried Couples in Texas*, 35 Baylor L. Rev. 543 (1983); Kaska, *Comment: Iowa Unmarried Cohabitants Denied Recovery for Loss of Consortium*, 69 Iowa L. Rev. 811 (1984).

Brief mention may be made of the legislation on fatal injuries. Part IV of the *Civil Liability Act, 1961* enables dependants of a deceased person whose death was brought about by a commission of a tort to sue the tortfeasor of compensation. A 'dependant' is any member of the family of the deceased who suffers injury or mental distress. 'Member of the family' is defined by section 47(1) as meaning that deceased's

> wife, husband, father, mother, grandfather, grandmother, stepfather, stepmother, son, daughter, grandson, granddaughter, stepson, stepdaughter, brother, sister, half-brother [or] half-sister.

Section 47(2) provides that in deducing any relationship in this context:

> (a) a person adopted under the *Adoption Act, 1952*, shall be considered the legitimate offspring of the adopter or adopters;
> (b) subject to paragraph (a) of this subsection, an illegitimate person shall be considered the legitimate offspring of his mother and reputed father;
> (c) a person *in loco parentis* to another shall be considered the parent of that other.

For consideration of the law on fatal injuries, see B. McMahon & W. Binchy, *Irish Law of Torts*, ch. 10 (1981); B. McMahon & W. Binchy, *A Casebook on the Irish Law of Torts*, 88–113 (1983).

Finally, although not strictly falling within the scope of the title of the present chapter, it is interesting to consider the position of the child who suffers injury as a result of a wrong done to his or her parents.

MULHOLLAND v. MURPHY & CO. LTD

77 I.L.T.R 212 (Circuit Ct., Judge O'Connor, 1943)

The plaintiff was aged about 14 months at the time of this action. His father was a member of the defendant Company and as a result of the negligence of defendant's servants the plaintiff's mother met with an injury. Plaintiff was at that time aged two months and was being nursed by his mother. As a result of her injuries the mother was unable to continue nursing the Plaintiff who was then fed on patent foods but did not appear to develop as a healthy child should. The mother had brought proceedings against the defendant Company in respect of the negligence and had recovered damages. The plaintiff now sought to recover damages for loss sustained by reason of the cessation of nursing and care of his mother, as a result of the negligence alleged in the mother's action.

Evidence was given by the plaintiff's mother and father that when his mother was unable to continue nursing he had to be put on patent foods and later milk and water. From that time onwards he did not thrive. He had been previously healthy. Medical evidence was tendered to show that the child was now underweight, puny and inactive. Four other children in the family were healthy and strong.

Counsel for the defendant Company submitted that, if there were any injuries to the plaintiff as a result of the negligence alleged, damages in respect of them had been included in the damages awarded to the mother. The cause of action was too remote. (Cited: *In re Polemis* [1921] 3 K. B. 560, on the question of remoteness.)

Judge O'Connor: This is a very unusual claim. If the plaintiff did suffer injury as claimed damages therefor should have been included in the mother's claim. I am of opinion that the cause of action is too remote.

Notes

1. The issues in this case appear to have been disposed of very inadequately. The decision can be attacked for its failure to distinguish between the concepts of duty, standard of care and remoteness of damage. On the substantive merits of the case, why should a defendant cease to be liable to plaintiff B for reasonably foreseeable injury to B simply because that injury was inflicted through the medium of another person (plaintiff A)? Cf. *Marx* v. *A.G.*, [1974] 1 N.Z.L.R. 164 (Sup. Ct., 1973), criticised by Binchy, *Note: Duty and Foresight in Negligence: The 'Control Devices' Out of Control*, 38 Modern L. Rev. 468 (1975). Presumably the court was reluctant to countenance an action by a child for loss resulting from injury to a parent akin to the spouse's action for loss of *consortium: cf.* J. Fleming, *The Law of Torts*, 136, 622 (6th ed., 1983). But were not the facts of the case sufficiently strong to allow for recovery of damages without conceding an unnecessarily broad principle?
2. The Law Reform Commission, in its *Report on Family Law* pp. 9–11 (LRC 1–1981) recommended the creation of a new statutory action for loss of *consortium* for the benefit not only of parents but also of children. In the United States some courts have conferred a right of action on children for interference in their relationship with a parent resulting from the negligent infliction of injury on the parent. In one such case, *Weitl* v. *Moes*, 311 N.W. 2d 259 (Iowa Sup. Ct., 1981), Justice Allbee quoted with approval the argument of one commentator (Dwork, 56 Boston U.L. Rev. 722, at 742 (1976)) that:

   > . . . . children are in even greater need of compensation for loss of the emotional benefits flowing from the family than are parents and spouses. Since the child in his formative years requires emotional nurture to develop properly, the loss of love, care and companionship is likely to have a more severe effect on him than on an adult; and society has a strong interest in seeing that the child's emotional development proceeds along healthy lines. Moreover, an adult is in a better position than a child to adjust to the loss of a family member's love, care and companionship through his own resources. He is capable of developing new relationships in the hope of replacing some of the emotional warmth of which he has been deprived. A child, however, is relatively powerless to initiate new relationships that might mitigate the effect of his deprivation. Legal redress may be the child's only means of mitigating the effect of his loss.

   See also *Ferriter* v. *Daniel O'Connell's Sons, Inc.*, 413 N.E. 2d 690 (Mass. Sup. Ind. Ct., 1980). Not all courts agree: see, e.g. *Norwest* v. *Presbyterian Intercommunity Hospital*, 652 P. 2d 318 (Ore. Sup. Ct., 1982), noted by Skerry, 17 Suffolk U.L. Rev. 776 (1983). For extended analyses of the issues, see Love, *Tortious Interference with the Parent-Child Relationship: Loss of an Injured Person's Society and Companionship*, 51 Indiana L.J. 590 (1976); Ronaldson, *Comment*, 17 John Marshall L. Rev. 113 (1984); Thornton, *Loss of Consortium: Inequality Before the Law*, 10 Sydney L. Rev. 259, at 272–3 (1984).

Chapter 5

FAMILY MAINTENANCE

Introduction

Before 1976, there were only limited legal means of enforcing family maintenance obligations. Under the *Married Women (Maintenance in case of Desertion) Act 1886*, a married woman who was deserted by her husband, could obtain a maintenance order against him for wilful refusal or neglect to maintain her. A comprehensive analysis of the 1886 Act is provided by Duncan, *Desertion and Cruelty in Irish Matrimonial Law*, 7 Ir. Jur. (n.s.) 213 (1972). The principal weaknesses of this legislation were that it applied only in cases of desertion and (until 1971) only the District Court had jurisdiction. The *Courts Act 1971* raised the jurisdiction of the District Court and extended jurisdiction to the High Court, where no maximum limit would apply.

The old poor law also provided some protection for unmaintained spouses. The *Public Assistance Act 1939* imposed on spouses a mutual obligation of maintenance and required a spouse to reimburse a local authority for money it paid for the maintenance of the other spouse. This obligation was reinforced by criminal sanctions. Legislation in 1975, now consolidated in the *Social Welfare (Consolidation) Act 1981*, has removed the criminal sanctions. See *Shatter*, 167.

Alimony, in the form of periodical payments, may be awarded in proceedings for divorce *a mensa et thoro*. The common law doctrines of agency of necessity and agency based on cohabitation, formerly of some significance, have played a greatly reduced role in securing maintenance of wives in recent years. See *Shatter*, 268–269.

Maintenance obligations in relation to legitimate children were of a restrictive nature until 1964. Section 11(2) (b) of the *Guardianship of Infants Act* of that year enables either parent to apply for a maintenance order in respect of a child, but an order may not be made unless the spouses have ceased to cohabit, and it ceases to have effect if they cohabit for a period of at least three months thereafter: section 11(3). For a creative application of section 11 in relation to the protection of children's occupation of the family home, see *E.D.* v. *F.D.*, *infra*, p. 345. For consideration of the relationship between orders for the maintenance of children under section 11 and orders for alimony in proceedings for divorce *a mensa et thoro*, see *M.* v. *M.*, unreported, High Ct., Kenny, J., 22 June 1970, p. 9 (1969–228 Sp.).

The Family Law (Maintenance of Spouses and Children) Act 1976

The Family Law (Maintenance of Spouses and Children) Act 1976 introduced wide-ranging changes in relation to family maintenance obligations. For detailed consideration of the Act, see Horgan, *The Irish Republic's New Maintenance Provisions*, 127 New L.J. 743 (1977); Binchy, *Family Law Reform in Ireland – Some Comparative Aspects*, 25 Int. & Comp. L.Q. 901 (1976). Many of the Act's provisions are based on the recommendations of the Committee on Court Practice and Procedure in its Nineteenth Interim Report, *Desertion and Maintenance* (Prl. 3666, 1974), analysed by Duncan, 9 Ir. Jur. (n.s.) 321 (1974). See also the *Report of the Commission on the Status of Women*, ch. 7 (Prl. 2760, 1972).

Section 5 contains the central provisions of the Act. It provides as follows:

(1) (*a*) Subject to subsection (4) of this section, where it appears to the Court, on application to it by a spouse, that the other spouse has failed to provide such maintenance for the applicant spouse and any dependent children of the family as is proper in the circumstances, the Court may make an order (in this Act referred

to as a maintenance order) that the other spouse make to the applicant spouse periodical payments, for the support of the applicant spouse and of each of the dependent children of the family, for such period during the lifetime of the applicant spouse, of such amount and at such times, as the Court may consider proper.

(*b*) Subject to subjection (4) of this section, where a spouse –
(i) is dead,
(ii) has deserted, or has been deserted by, the other spouse, or
(iii) is living separately and apart from the other spouse,
and there are dependent children of the family (not being children who are being fully maintained by either spouse), then, if it appears to the Court, on application to it by any person, that the surviving spouse or, as the case may be, either spouse has failed to provide such maintenance for any dependent children of the family as is proper in the circumstances, the Court may make an order (in this Act referred to as a maintenance order) that that spouse make to that person periodical payments, for the support of each of those dependent children, for such period during the lifetime of that person, of such amount and at such times, as the Court may consider proper.

(*c*) A maintenance order or a variation order shall specify each part of a payment under the order that is for the support of a dependent child and may specify the period during the lifetime of the person applying for the order for which so much of a payment under the order as is for the support of a dependent child shall be made.

(2) The Court shall not make a maintenance order for the support of a spouse where the spouse has deserted and continues to desert the other spouse.

(3) Where the applicant spouse has committed adultery, then –
(*a*) if the other spouse has condoned or connived at, or by wilful neglect or misconduct conduced to, the adultery, the adultery shall not be a ground on which the Court may refuse to make a maintenance order for the support of the applicant spouse,
(*b*) if the other spouse has not condoned or connived at, or by wilful neglect or misconduct conduced to, the adultery, the Court may, notwithstanding the adultery, make a maintenance order for the support of the applicant spouse in any case where, having regard to all the circumstances (including the conduct of the other spouse), the Court considers it proper to do so.

(4) The Court, in deciding whether to make a maintenance order and, if it decides to do so, in determining the amount of any payment, shall have regard to all the circumstances of the case and, in particular, to the following matters –
(*a*) the income, earning capacity (if any), property and other financial resources of the spouses and of any dependent children of the family, including income or benefits to which either spouse or any such children are entitled by or under statute, and
(*b*) the financial and other responsibilities of the spouses towards each other and towards any dependent children of the family and the needs of any such dependent children, including the need for care and attention.

Section 3(1) of the Act provides that the expression 'dependent child of the family', in relation to a spouse or spouses:

means any child –
(*a*) of both spouses, or adopted by both spouses under the *Adoption Acts, 1952* to *1974*, or in relation to whom both spouses are *in loco parentis*, or
(*b*) of either spouse, or adopted by either spouse under the *Adoption Acts, 1952* to *1974*, or in relation to whom either spouse is *in loco parentis*, where the other spouse, being aware that he is not the parent of the child, has treated the child as a member of the family,
who is under the age of sixteen years, or, if he has attained that age –
(i) is or will be or, if an order were made under this Act providing for periodical payments for his support, would be receiving full-time education or instruction at any university, college, school or other educational establishment and is under the age of twenty-one years, or
(ii) is suffering from mental or physical disability to such extent that it is not reasonably possible for him to maintain himself fully.

Section 3(1) also provides that 'desertion':

includes conduct on the part of one spouse that results in the other spouse, with just cause, leaving and living separately and apart from him, and cognate words shall be construed accordingly.

Other provisions of the Act, notably sections 8 and 27, raise issues related principally to separation agreements. These are considered in Chapter 10, *infra*.

E.D. v. F.D.

Unreported, High Ct., Costello, J., 23 October 1980 (1979–26Sp.)

Costello, J.:

The Plaintiff and the Defendant were married [in] 1966. They have three children [A, B and C] who are now aged 12½, 7½ and a little over 4½ years respectively. The Defendant left the family home in June 1978 for [England]. He never returned to reside in it and in effect deserted his wife and children. The Defendant was ordered to pay £130 per week maintenance on the 6th April 1979 after an interlocutory hearing at which he did not attend. In July of this year the proceedings were listed for hearing, but because of the pressure of the court's lists they were adjourned until this term. Because of the failure to comply with the terms of the maintenance order a motion was brought to commit the Defendant for contempt of court. I have heard both motion and substantive action together.

As to the sum claimed by the Plaintiff for future maintenance for herself and her children a schedule has been prepared which sets out the Plaintiff's estimated needs. This shows that she requires an average weekly payment of £207 to provide for herself and her children, apart from the mortgage. Plaintiff has however obtained part-time work which gives her £47 per week net and she is prepared to reduce her maintenance claim by this amount. In the past she was forced to take in a student as a lodger. I am satisfied that she is acting reasonably in not wishing to have the privacy of her home intruded upon by the presence of a stranger in the house, and that she should not be required to make further efforts to obtain an income from this source. Her claim, then, is for the sum of £160 per week, or £170 per week if she is liable to discharge the mortgage and insurance outgoings on the family home.

I am satisfied that her estimated requirements are reasonable and in no way inflated and that she would need the sum of £170 per week to maintain adequately herself and her children at a reasonable living standard.

The Defendant, however, says he is not in a position to pay this sum, and that he can only pay £120 – £125 per week. He is . . . now living in England, and mainly employed under contract with [employer X]. For the year ending the 5th April 1979 he received over £15,800 from [employer X]. For the year ending the 5th April 1980 he received nearly £22,000 from the same source. In addition he received from [employer Y] last year a sum of £1,268.35 and in addition was in receipt of other fees. He says however that his income for the year 1980/81 will only be in the region of £13,000 – £14,000. This is, he says, because he has given up [part of his work with employer X] because of cut-backs in the expenditure of [employer X] and because he has given up his contract with [employer Y]. I am, however, quite satisfied that the Defendant has seriously under-estimated his likely earnings in the current year. He has made an outstanding success of his profession and I cannot accept that there will be any serious reduction in his earnings in the current year. He said that he gave up [the] contract [with employer Y] because he thought his time could be more profitably employed. If this is so, then he should be able to compensate for the loss of earnings under this head. Already this year he was offered and accepted [another] position . . . and received a fee of over £1,000 for it. I will approach, therefore, the question of maintenance on the basis that his earnings this year will be in the region of £22,000 gross.

I must make such order as is 'proper in the circumstances'. In fixing maintenance I do not accept the view which was urged on the Defendant's behalf that because the overall family expenses rise when a husband deserts the family home the extra burden should be borne equally by the husband and the wife and children who are living with her, and that all must be prepared to accept a reduction in their living standards. When a husband deserts his wife and children the Court should be concerned to ensure that their financial position is protected, even if this means causing a drop in the husband's living standards. In this particular case, it is clear that the Defendant has not been aware of this fact, and part of the serious financial difficulties he now is in stem[s] from the fact that he has in the last two years attempted to live on a scale wholly inappropriate to his family responsibilities. These difficulties have been further aggravated by his failure to meet his past financial commitments and it is to be observed that a great deal of the sums which he expended in the past fifteen months on behalf of his family were in respect of earlier liabilities which he had failed to discharge.

I am satisfied that out of the income which I estimate the Defendant will receive he should be able to pay the sums the Plaintiff needs for herself and her children, namely £170 per week. In reaching this decision I am aware that the estimated income is a gross one. The Defendant in evidence told me that he had employed an accountant to assist in the tax liability to the U.K. government but that he thought it would be very slight. I am prepared to accept that his evidence was over optimistic in this regard and to make my award on the basis that his current income will be reduced by a tax liability which, although presently unascertained, will not be insignificant. The fact that no reliable estimate can be made of it now is the responsibility of the Defendant who no doubt could have made available estimates from his accountant. But I am also entitled to take into account that most of the Defendant's earnings in the current year are likely to be in sterling. Currently sterling is standing at 17% over the Irish pound, but I will assume for the purpose of this judgment that over the forthcoming year it will stand on average at 10% above the Irish pound as it has in the past year. This increases the Defendant's ability to pay the weekly sum of £170 by about 10%. Taking all the circumstances into account, including the serious financial situation which is facing the Defendant and to which I will not refer, I think that the sum I have mentioned is a reasonable and proper one. I will order that it be paid monthly in advance, on the first of each month by means of a bank transfer from the Defendant's to the Plaintiff's Bank. The monthly sum should be such as to produce £746 Irish pounds to the Plaintiff, apportioned as to £80 for A £60 for B £40 for C and £566 for the Plaintiff. The order will declare that the Defendant is not to be liable for any outgoings in respect of the family home. . . .

[**Costello, J.** went on to consider the position in relation to the family home. See *infra*, pp. 345–46]

Notes

1. Cf. *Shatter*, 271:

> On the evidence given in th[is] case the husband's earnings were considerable. It is clear, however, that if the husband's earnings had been at a lower level a reduction in the living standards of the wife should have been inevitable.

2. This decision is important in spelling out the value judgment that for a man to walk away from his family does not mean that he may also walk away from his responsibility to maintain his wife and children. Marriage is seen as involving a commitment which cannot be shaken off simply because the commitment becomes unpalatable or unpleasant to discharge. Modern thinking on divorce takes a somewhat different approach. It is more concerned with responding, in a non-judgmental way, to the *fact* of disruption in personal relationships: the *fact* of marriage breakdown is the basis of a decree for divorce. Is there a danger that in 'burying a dead marriage', the law may be tempted to bury at least some of the responsibilities that attach to marriage? Dr. Kevin Gray, speaking of the change in England in 1969 from fault-based divorce to no-fault divorce based on breakdown of marriage, has said:

> The idea that matrimonial innocence and blame could no longer serve as satisfactory tests of entitlement to divorce was expressed in statutory language which implies that the concept of responsibility is wholly *meaningless* in the context of marriage breakdown – an implication which is by no means justified. The old law had few merits, but it did at least recognise substance in that salutary principle of living which treats individuals as ultimately responsible for their actions. The notion of individual responsibility is an intrinsic, albeit inconvenient, feature of the human condition: we should be somewhat less than human, and our

existence less than purposive, if our decisions and actions were deprived of the dignity of being either right or wrong. To displace this principle of accountability is often to open a Pandora's Box of insoluble problems. *Reallocation of Property on Divorce*, 325–326 (1977).

Bernard Berkovits, also speaking of the position in England, has commented:

[T]he breakdown of marriage is viewed as a tragedy without fault. It seems strangely contradictory, therefore, to impose a continuous obligation on the husband to maintain his wife merely because of the 'accident' of having married her and the equal 'accident' of divorce . . . . [O]ne might note a peculiar dichotomy in social ideology. On the one hand we seem to have rejected, in matrimonial matters, the time-hallowed concept of individual responsibility for the consequences of one's behaviour, and consider marital breakdown to result from misfortune. Yet on the other hand we fail to provide, as a society, for such casualties of life, imposing instead a somewhat arbitrary, onerous and inefficient economic responsibility on the individual. Are we justified in placing the primary obligation on an unfortunate husband, himself a victim of harsh fate? *Towards a Reappraisal of Family Law Ideology*, 10 Family L. 164, at 171 (1980).

3. How is the proper balance to be struck? Cf. O'Donovan, *The Principles of Maintenance: An Alternative View*, 8 Family L. 180 (1978); Haverty, *Are Maintenance Judgments Outdated?*, Irish Times, 12 March 1982, p. 10; Harris, *The Value of a Wife*, 7 Family L. 5 (1977); Metcalf, *Divorce and the Right to Life-Long Maintenance*, 131 New L.J. 699 (1981).

S. v. S.

Unreported, June 1980, High Court, Ellis J., (1980–4SP)

Ellis J.:

The Plaintiff (aged 37) and the Defendant (aged 47) intermarried on 1st June, 1978. They are both citizens of this country and were married here. The Defendant is a farmer. The parties lived together in the farm residence as their matrimonial home until according to the Plaintiff in evidence she became unhappy about two or three months after the date of their marriage, and in July 1978 temporarily left the matrimonial home. She finally left it in February 1979, since when she has lived apart from the Defendant. Her evidence indicates that she is unlikely to return to live in the matrimonial home or that the parties will live together again. The Plaintiff alleges that she was obliged to leave the Defendant on account of his violence and cruelty to her. The Defendant denies the Plaintiff's allegations of violence and cruelty. There are no children of the marriage.

The Plaintiff has brought these proceedings claiming solely for an order for her maintenance by the Defendant on the ground that as from July 1978 the Defendant has failed and neglected to make a financial contribution towards her cost, upkeep and maintenance. Mr. O'Reilly, counsel for the Defendant, told the Court that he contests the Plaintiff's claim for maintenance on the ground that it is unsustainable, misconceived and unsupported by evidence, and also on the ground of desertion by the Plaintiff.

The Plaintiff was the only witness. At the conclusion of her evidence Mr. O'Reilly sought a direction and an order dismissing the Plaintiff's claim for maintenance on the grounds mentioned above (other than desertion), and also because he submitted that on the evidence the Court could not properly make a Maintenance Order against the Defendant within the meaning and application of the *Family Law (Maintenance of Spouses and Children) Act 1976*, or alternatively that there was no evidence on which such order could properly be made.

In her grounding affidavit filed on 18th February 1980 there is no averment by the Plaintiff directed or related to the financial circumstances or income of either party at any material time, or of any need or claim by her for financial support or maintenance by the Defendant.

The following evidence was given by the Plaintiff in support of her claim. Prior to their marriage in June 1978 the Plaintiff had been employed as a Clinical Teacher or Tutor . . . in [a] Hospital . . . at an annual salary of £4,289.00 gross with free accommodation. This post was permanent and pensionable and she had made contributions towards her pension. She possessed a house . . . which she was purchasing through a Building Society mortgage for £8,000.00, the mortgage instalments being £101.00 monthly which she is still paying. She had and has a nett income of £19.00 monthly on lettings to tenants in this house. On her marriage she resigned from her position . . . but subsequently applied for reinstatement about mid July 1978 at the time when she temporarily left the matrimonial home. After three unsuccessful applications she was reappointed to her old position in October 1978 but at a lower salary and loss of some pension rights. She remained in this position until October 1979 when she became employed in a similar position [at another] hospital . . . at an annual salary which is now £5,619.00 gross but without free accommodation. She did not give any evidence of the cost of such accommodation or of the value of her free accommodation in her earlier employment. . . . Neither did she give any evidence that she was unable to pay for her [new] accommodation . . . out of her own means. She still has her [first] house . . . but intends or hopes to sell it and purchase instead a house in [her new place of employment] which she estimated would cost now about £25,000.00 but which she says she can not afford at present. She did not give any evidence of the present or likely sale value of her [first] house . . . She expects that the Building Society will transfer the mortgage from it to the [new] house. She estimated that the cost of the sale of the [first] house and the purchase of the [new] house and the transfer from one to the other would cost about £5,000.00 including legal costs, the cost of furniture removal and the cost of other miscellaneous expenses. She stated her loss of salary altogether between the two positions was £1,871.72 in respect of which she supplied in evidence a written statement dated 9th May 1980 from the Staff Officer of the . . . Hospital [where she now works]. She estimated it would cost her about £500.00 to regain her full pension rights. She also stated she had to borrow £250.00 from her father, £415.00 from friends and £600.00 from the Bank as she was in need of money. She did not state why she was in need of money, or why she needed to borrow these monies, or how or for what purpose or purposes they were applied to or were to be applied. She estimated that her total financial loss including expenses and borrowings under the foregoing heads came to about £8,636.00. The Plaintiff also stated that on her marriage she sold her motor car, thereby implying financial loss, but as against this she agreed that the Defendant had later given her another motor car. No evidence of the respective values of these cars was given.

There was no evidence given by the Plaintiff of her other financial means or income or as to her needs or requirements in the nature of support or maintenance by the Defendant or to the financial position or means of the Defendant himself. It was not suggested by or on behalf of the Plaintiff whether or how the sum of £8,636.00 approximately claimed to have been 'lost' by her should be paid by the Defendant – whether as a lump sum or by periodical payments, and if the latter how the amounts of such payments should be determined.

On cross-examination the Plaintiff agreed that she was able to live on her salary and other means and income and to pay for her food, rent and other necessities and generally to make ends meet. The effect of her evidence was that she could support and maintain herself independently of the Defendant. There was no evidence of any request by her to him for financial assistance by way of maintenance and, except for the possible inference on account of her borrowings, there was no evidence given by the Plaintiff that after she had left the matrimonial home and the Defendant that she was dependent on him for support or maintenance.

As already mentioned, at the conclusion of the Plaintiff's evidence Counsel for the Defendant applied to have her claim dismissed. In addition to the reasons already given in support of his application he also submitted that even if the Plaintiff's claim for maintenance was legally sustainable there was no, or alternatively no sufficient, evidence for the Court to make any findings of the proper amounts of any payments for maintenance. He further submitted in this regard that the sums claimed for this purpose made no allowance for income tax or legitimate deductions therefrom, and were therefore incomplete as representing the Plaintiff's true or full financial position or needs if any. He also submitted that by analogy with alimony payments the Court in proceedings for maintenance under the *Family Law (Maintenance of Spouses and Children) Act 1976* had no power under such Act to order the Defendant to pay the Plaintiff a lump sum instead of or as well as periodical payments.

The case for the Plaintiff was that because of her marriage to and subsequent enforced separation from the Defendant, for which she claims he was legally responsible she was thereby caused to suffer the financial loss and expense of the nature and amounts claimed. It was submitted on her behalf that as from July 1978 the Plaintiff had been and is now and for the future will be obliged to live, provide for and maintain herself as an independent single person. She therefore claims and submits she is entitled to recover from the Defendant by way of maintenance the said financial losses which she claims she has lost on account of her failed marriage and separation from the Defendant on the basis that she would otherwise have had or would have the benefit of such monies for her support and maintenance since July 1978 and for which she says the Defendant was and is legally responsible.

Counsel for the Plaintiff sought permission to adduce if necessary additional evidence in relation to the Defendant's income and means as well as other matters to which the Court might have regard in determining the amount and duration of periodical maintenance payments if necessary until the amount of the Plaintiff's claim would be discharged.

I reserved my decision on this application on behalf of the Plaintiff until I had first decided on the main grounds of Mr. O'Reilly's submission that her claim was unsustainable and misconceived, and that the Plaintiff's alleged financial losses were not recoverable as 'maintenance' under the *Family Law (Maintenance of Spouses and Children) Act, 1976.*

This therefore is the immediate issue which I have to decide.

In my view Mr. O'Reilly is correct in this submission and I accede to his application to dismiss the Plaintiff's claim on the grounds:–

(a) that the financial losses which the Plaintiff claims to have sustained or will sustain for the reasons she alleges, (and apart from any question of desertion or the other grounds submitted by Mr. O'Reilly) are not financial losses properly recoverable from the Defendant by way of an order for maintenance under the *Family Law (Maintenance of Spouses and Children) Act, 1976* and
(b) that there was no evidence by or on behalf of the Plaintiff to support or justify the making of such Order under the relevant provisions of this Act. . . .

In the case of *H.D.* v. *P.S.* – Supreme Court – unreported [extracted *infra*, pp. 313–17] – in his judgment delivered on 8th May 1978 Walsh J. stated as follows:-

> It is clear from the whole structure of the Act that its purpose is to deal with the situation of the parties at the time the proceedings were brought under the Act (here 2nd January 1980), and that the primary function of the Act is to ensure that proper and adequate maintenance will be available in accordance with the provisions of the Act to spouses (and children) and that the basic question to be decided was whether at any given time there was a failure by one spouse to provide reasonable maintenance for the support of the other spouse and that the function of the Court under the Act is to determine whether or not there is a financial need justifying the making of the Order sought under the Act.

It appears to me that the real substance and purpose of the Plaintiff's claim is to recover by way of maintenance from the Defendant the past and apprehended financial losses or expenses which she claims to have sustained or may in the future sustain resulting from her marriage to and separation from the Defendant. However else she may devise a different cause of action for this purpose, in my opinion the nature of the losses or expenses alleged and of this form of claim to recover them do not come within the meaning purpose or application of the relevant provisions of the Act of 1976 quoted above in respect of which a maintenance order can properly be made. Neither in my opinion are such provisions, or indeed is the Act intended to provide a means or method to recover losses of this nature.

It is clear from her evidence that the nature and purpose of the Plaintiff's claim does not come within the purpose of the Act as stated by Walsh J. or in my own view of its purpose, nor has there been evidence given which would enable me to decide 'the basic question' relating to failure to provide reasonable maintenance for the support of the Plaintiff by the Defendant, or whether or not there has been or is a financial need to justify the making of the Order sought under the Act.

The matters on which Counsel for the Plaintiff has applied for liberty to adduce further evidence would not affect my decision even if evidence on such matters was given.

For these reasons I must dismiss the Plaintiff's claim.

Notes

1. Do you agree with the holding in this decision?
2. Does this decision hold that, where a spouse suffers financial loss as a result of marital separation, no order for maintenance may be made in respect of that loss under section 5 of the *Family Law (Maintenance of Spouses and Children) Act, 1976?* If this is what the case holds, is it a correct interpretation of the section?
3. Should the decision be interpreted merely as holding that the petitioner had not adduced sufficient *evidence* of failure to provide proper maintenance? Cf. *Shatter*, 270. The courts have often stressed the necessity for the petitioner to produce clear factual evidence supporting her (or his) case. Cf. *M.* v. *M.*, unreported, High Ct., McWilliam, J., 3 May, 1978 (1977–3378Sp.).
4. What light does the decision throw on the legitimacy of lump sum orders? Cf. *Shatter*, 272.
5. In every case where a wife separates from her husband without his agreement, must one or other of the spouses be held to be in desertion, actual or constructive? If not, what maintenance obligations (if any) may be imposed in such a case?
6. This decision raises the important issue of 'proper' sex roles in marriage. Section 5(4) of the 1976 Act is sex-neutral in its articulation of spousal obligations. There might be considered to be possible restraints on the judicial interpretation of these provisions as laying down sexually neutral criteria in so far as Article 41.2. 1° of the Irish Constitution provides that '. . . the State recognises that by her life within the home, woman gives to the State a support without which the common good cannot be achieved.' Moreover, Article 41.2. 2° of the Constitution provides that '[t]he State shall, therefore, endeavour to ensure that mothers shall not be obliged by economic necessity to engage in labour to the neglect of their duties in the home.' Similarly Article 45.2 provides as a directive principle of social policy for the guidance of the Oireachtas (and 'not [to] be cognisable by any court . . .') that '[t]he State shall, in particular, direct its policy towards securing that the citizens (all of whom, men and women equally, have the right to an adequate means of livelihood) may through their occupations find the means of making reasonable provision for their domestic needs. . . .' The purpose of this provision was interpreted by Kenny J. in *Murtagh Properties* v. *Cleary* [1972] I.R. 330, at 336, as being 'to emphasise that, in so far as the right to an adequate means of livelihood was involved, men and women were to be regarded as equal. It follows that a policy or general rule under which anyone seeks to prevent an employer from employing men or women on the grounds of sex only is prohibited by the Constitution.' However, it would appear that Kenny, J. would have been disposed to regard with less disfavour an exclusion of women from employment 'because the work is unsuitable for them or too difficult or too dangerous': *id*. (Cf. the much berated decision of *Goesaert* v. *Cleary*, 335 U.S. 464 (1948), cited by counsel in *Murtagh Properties*, but not mentioned by Kenny, J. in his judgment. See further B. Babcock *et al., Sex Discrimination and the Law: Causes and Remedies*, 93ff (1975).)

   The decision of *De Burca and Anderson* v. *Attorney-General,* [1976] I.R. 38 (1975), where the Supreme Court struck down an automatic exemption of women from jury service, would not appear to lend a great deal of support to the view that the courts are constitutionally required to apply 'sex roles' criteria in maintenance proceedings, in the face of the neutral language adopted by the legislative criteria. As Mr. Justice Walsh observed in *De Burca* (at 70):–

   > It is undoubtedly true that the Constitution, in dealing with the family draws attention to and stresses the importance of woman's life within the home and makes special provision for the economic protection of mothers who have home duties. . . . [W]omen fulfil many functions in society in addition to, or instead of, those mentioned in section 2 of article 41. . . . [W]omen [are] actively engaged in all of the professions, in most branches of business, in art and literature, and in virtually every human activity. . . .

But the following passage from Walsh, J.'s judgment (at 71) is of possible relevance to the question of 'proper' sex roles in relation to maintenance:

> There can be little doubt that the Oireachtas could validly enact statutory provisions which could have due regard, within the provisions of Article 40, to differences of capacity both physical and moral and of social function in so far as jury service is concerned. For example, it could provide that all mothers with young children could be exempt from jury service. On virtually the same consideration, it could provide that all widowers, husbands with invalid wives, and husbands deserted by the wives would be entitled to a similar exemption if they were looking after their young children. . . . However, the provision made in the Act of 1927 is undisguisedly discriminatory on the ground of sex only. It would not be competent for the Oireachtas to legislate on the basis that women, by reason only of their sex, are physically or morally incapable of serving and acting as jurors. The statutory provision does not seek to make any distinction between the different functions that women may fulfill and it does not seek to justify the discrimination on the basis of any social function. It simply lumps together half of the members of the adult population, most of whom have only one thing in common, namely, their sex. In my view, it is not open to the State to discriminate in its enactments between the persons who are subject to its laws solely upon the ground of the sex of those persons. If a reference is to be made to the sex of a person then the purpose of the law that makes such a discrimination should be to deal with some physical or moral capacity or social function that is related exclusively or very largely to that sex only.

The criterion espoused by Mr. Justice Walsh would appear to be somewhat less rigorous than that of total 'sex-neutrality'. The words 'very largely' would appear to permit legislation reinforcing concepts of 'proper' sex roles (as well, presumably, as differential judicial interpretation of legislative provisions drafted in neutral terms). The concept of 'social function', of which the Constitution speaks would appear to be capable of a very wide range of interpretation. The statement in Mr. Justice Walsh's judgment that legislation exempting '*all* mothers with young children' but fathers only in the circumstances specified by him would appear to suggest a tolerance of the concept of motherhood as a social function, in contrast to a sex-neutral concept of parenthood. See further, Binchy, *Family Law Reform in Ireland: Some Comparative Aspects*, 25 Int. & Comp. L.Q. 901, at 901–905 (1976); Binchy, *New Vistas in Irish Family Law*, 15 J. of Family L. 637, at 663–665 (1977); Forde, *Equality and the Constitution*, 17 Ir. Jur. (n.s.) 295, at 320ff (1982). See also *The State (D.P.P.)* v. *Walsh, supra*, p. 187.

7. In the United States the courts have gone some distance further in eliminating legal differences between spouses in relation to support obligations. The leading decision is *Orr* v. *Orr*, 440 U.S. 268 (1979). For consideration of broader aspects of the subject, see Dow, *Sexual Equality, the ERA and the Court – A Tale of Two Failures*, 13 N. Mexico L. Rev. 53 (1983). Judicial and legislative developments in relation to alimony are summarised by Freed & Foster, *Family Law in the Fifty States: An Overview*, 17 Family L.Q. 365, at 382–388 (1984). See also W. Weyrauch & S. Katz, *American Family Law in Transition*, 281–282 (1983), and *Friedlander* v. *Freidlander*, 80 Wash. 2d 293, 494 P. 2d 208 (Sup. Ct., En Banc. 1972).
8. It would be useful in this general context to read *Somjee* v. *Minister for Justice and the Attorney General, supra*, p. 179.
9. If the applicant in *S.* v. *S.* had children would the case have been decided on different lines? Of course the Court would have sought to ensure that the children were supported, but would the Court have considered that the wife was entitled to have the fact that she was a mother be taken into account in assessing her maintenance entitlement? Is the effect of the decision that, until childbirth (or pregnancy?) spouses do not normally owe each other maintenance obligations? Cf. *LeRoy-Lewis* v. *LeRoy-Lewis,* [1955] P. 1 (Barnard, J.).

C.P. v. D.P.

[1983] I.L.R.M. 380 (High Ct., Finlay, P., 1982)

The facts are set out *infra*, p. 347, in relation to the question of 'intention' as an element in the respondent's conduct, for the purposes of section 5(1) of the *Family Home Protection Act 1976*. On the question of maintenance, **Finlay, P.** stated:–

With regard to the wife's claim to maintenance, the husband does not dispute his total responsibility in accordance with his means to pay reasonable maintenance for his wife and children. She has in her affidavit set out a present schedule of expenditure which includes a sum of £40 per week rent and which comes to £230 with certain items not quantified. With regard to that amount, the husband asserts that it is exaggerated. The wife was cross-examined on it. It includes a sum of £30 in respect of school fees and outings and riding and swimming tuition for the children, a sum of £15 for recreation, riding lessons and contemporary dance lessons for the wife. It also includes a sum of £40 per week being total cost of maintaining a motor car. I was not satisfied that the individual items were significantly exaggerated in any instance, but the harsh and unpleasant fact is that the overall lifestyle of the children and wife, whilst in no sense extravagant nor irresponsible, exceeds what in my view under any circumstances the husband is able to pay.

In particular, a substantial amount of cross-examination was directed towards the earning capacity of the wife. In this regard, the facts are that she was 17 years of age when she married, had worked at unskilled work in the hotel industry, and has no professional or craft qualifications of any description. She is accepted by herself and asserted by her husband to be an extremely good, ordinary domestic cook and provided very high quality meals for the family at all times. She has together with the children a considerable interest in outdoor pursuits and hobbies and is good with animals. She herself has mentioned a number of projects, some of them being catering in people's houses, some of them being the keeping of dogs and maintenance of a kennel and possibly the breeding of pedigree dogs. Her capacity to take employment even if she could get it is obviously circumscribed by the obligations of looking after two children of the ages which I have mentioned.

The husband in his affidavit asserts a net income after tax of approximately £8,000 and sets out his present living expenditure exclusive of payment of maintenance to his wife and children and exclusive of the servicing of term loans and debts at something over £100. Under cross-examination and on oral evidence even in the direct evidence he conceded a slight increase in the net income which might bring it up to approximately £9,000 but denied the existence of any other source of income. I accept his evidence in this context.

The problem which therefore arises is that to maintain the wife and children at their present quite moderate standard of living probably would cost close to £200 per week, including an element of £40 for the rent of the premises in which they live and an element of approximately £40 for motor car expenses which are directly necessary by reason of the fact that they live outside a town and away from the schools which they attend. That figure probably exceeds the present disposable income of the husband, and to make payment for that amount would leave him out of his disposable net income with nothing on which to live.

Furthermore, into the future unless there is what would be on the evidence adduced before me a quite unexpected rise in the earning capacity of the husband of a very substantial kind, there cannot be any long term prospect of his wife and children maintaining even their present moderate standard of living out of the earnings of the husband even if he were prepared to make very substantial sacrifices with regard to his personal expenditure.

It seems to me clear that for this entire family what must happen is that the present family home must be sold, that a substantial portion of the debts of the husband must be paid out of the proceeds of that sale as so to reduce what is a crippling buurden of interest payment at present being experienced by him, that secure and stable accommodation must be found for the wife and children which is located notwithstanding both parents' ambitions for bringing the children up in the countryside in a particular atmosphere close to schools and close to real employment of which the wife is capable and that the husband must accept a limited standard of living and economic accommodation in order to try and meet the long term financial obligation of maintaining his wife and children. The wife must make, in my view, realistic if less pleasant plans towards obtaining worthwhile employment bearing in mind the limitations which are imposed upon that.

In the hope that the parties will see this problem on a long term basis in that light, and will make the necessary adjustments by agreement to secure such a future situation, I am making an order for maintenance at present which is not capable of being met out of the husband's income, but which must represent a charge on his capital assets, and in particular regretfully must possibly notwithstanding his proper sentimental attachment to them conceivably involve a charge on the family furniture and *objets d'art* which he has been hoping to keep for his children when they grow up. The minimum such figure on my calculation of the situation in this case is a payment of £150 per week maintenance. I emphasise, however, this is a short term provision in excess of what the ordinary income of the husband is or in my view is likely to bear for some time having regard to the necessity for him to keep himself, and that it will be subject to relatively early review when the other problems with regard to the property of the family have been disposed of either by agreement or as a result of further applications to the court.

Notes

1. This case highlights the fact that, where the spouses are living apart, extra costs will almost invariably result. Internationally, against a background of no-fault divorce, the pressure has been towards reducing the quantum and duration of maintenance entitlements of divorced women, accompanied by the view that women whose husbands do not support them should, in effect, be required to obtain employment outside the home. What advantages and disadvantages do you perceive in these developments? Contrast *E.D.* v. *F.D., supra*, p. 201.
2. The literature on this subject is enormous. See, e.g. Dewar, *Reforming Financial Provision: The Alternatives,* [1984] J. of Social Welfare L. 1; Jones, *Maintenance as the Aftermath of Divorce*, 12 Family L. 82 (1982); Blake, *Family Law or the Law of Relationships?* 11 Family L. 42 (1981); the English Law Commission's Discussion Paper, *The Financial Consequences of Divorce* (1980) and its Report, *The Financial Consequences of Divorce: The Response to the Law Commission's Discussion Paper and Recommendations on the Policy of the Law* (Law Com. No. 112, 1981); Deech, *The Principles of Maintenance*, 71 Family L. 229 (1977); O'Donovan, *The Principles of Maintenance: An Alternative View*, 8 Family L. 180 (1978); O'Donovan, *Should All Maintenance of Spouses be Abolished?*, 45 Modern L. Rev. 424 (1980); Eekelaar, *Law Commission Reports on the Financial Consequences of Divorce,* 45 Modern L. Rev. 420 (1982); Hayes, *Financial Provision and Property Adjustment Orders: The Statutory Guidelines*, 10 Family L.3 (1980); Barnett, *Financial Provision – A Compensatory Model?*, 13 Family 124 (1983); Aston, *Divorce – Women Get the Blame*, 137 Spare Rib 16 (Dec., 1983); Levin, *Aliment and Financial Provision: The Scottish Law Commission's Memorandum*, 6 Family L. 164 (1976); Payne, *Maintenance Rights and Obligations: A Search for Uniformity* Part I, 1 Family L. Rev. 1 (1978); De Sousa, *Maintenance on Divorce*, 8 Ottawa L. Rev. 349 (1976); Larson, *Equity and Economics: A Case for Spousal Support*, 8 Golden Gate U.L. Rev. 443 (1979); Hauserman, *Homemakers and Divorce: Problems of the Invisible Occupation*, 17 Family L.Q. 41 (1983); Glendon, *Modern Marriage Law and its Underlying Assumptions: The New Marriage and The New Property*, 13 Family L.Q. 441 (1980); Bruch, *Of Work, Family Wealth, and Equality*, 17 Family L.Q. 99 (1983); Weitzman & Dixon, *The Transformation of Marriage Through No-Fault Divorce: The Case of the United States*, ch.16 of J. Eekelaar & S. Katz eds., *Marriage and Cohabitation in Contemporary Societies* (1980); Espenshade, *The Economic Consequences of Divorce*, 41 J. of M. & Family 615 (1979); Olsen, *The Family and the Market: A Study of Ideology and Legal Reform,* 96 Harv. L. Rev. 1497 (1983).
3. Over the past fifteen years or so, the State has provided an increasing range of social welfare benefits and allowances to disadvantaged and disrupted families, notably through the Supplementary Welfare Allowance Scheme, the Deserted Wife's Allowance and the Deserted Wife's Benefit: see *Shatter*, 292–296, 300–303. This raises the question as to the appropriate relationship between public and private law so far as family support obligations are concerned. This issue has long been discussed in England. The *Report of the Committee on One-Parent Families* (Chairman: The Hon. Sir Morris Finer) (Cmnd. 5629, 1974) (analysed by Eekelaar, [1976] Public L. 64; Polak, 4 Family L. 140 (1974)) made proposals for the introduction of a non-contributory social security benefit, the 'guaranteed maintenance allowance', as a replacement (so far as the recipient was concerned) for maintenance payments, 'so that lone [parents] should be freed from the worry and distress which the inadequacy and uncertainty of these payments now produce'. Neither the Conservative nor Labour governments have yet implemented this proposal. For general analysis of the issues see B. Hoggett & D. Pearl, *The Family, Law and Society*, ch. 16 (1983); K. Gray, *Reallocation of Property on Divorce*, 329–333 (1977), Davis, MacLeod & Murch, *Divorce: Who Supports the Family?* 13 Family L. 217 (1983). From a more international perspective, see M. Glendon, *State, Law and Family: Family Law in Transition in the United States and Western Europe*, 272–279, 323–327 (1977); Krause, *Reflections on Child Support,* [1983] U. Illinois L. Rev. 99, at 113–117; Krause, *A Review of the Progress Made in Child Support, Paternity, Illegitimacy and Child Welfare*, 5 Fam. Advocate, No. 1, 13 (1982); Kloppenburg, *The Enforcement of Maintenance*, 40 Sask. L. Rev. 217 (1976); Agell, *Paying Maintenance in Sweden*, ch. 1 of *International Conference on Matrimonial and Child Support, May 1981: Conference Materials* (Alberta Institute of Law Research and Reform, 1982); Atkin, *The Effect of Social Security on the Payment of Maintenance – Some English Comparisons,* [1980] N.Z.L.J. 298. Reporting on the position in the United States, Professor Carol Bruch, of the University of California, Davis, expressed the view that:

In an era of constrained social programs, it seems unlikely that the financial privation of former wives and children will be lessened by public support systems. Rather, greater efforts to establish and enforce reasonable private responsibility for family-related dependency are already under serious consideration in several states. *Of Work, Family Wealth, and Equality*, 17 Family L.Q. 99, at 106 (1983).

4. Judicial decisions in England considering the question include *Kershaw* v. *Kershaw*, [1966] P. 13; *Ashley* v. *Ashley*, [1968] P. 582; *Barnes* v. *Barnes*, [1972] 3 All E.R. 872; *Reiterbund* v. *Reiterbund*, [1974] 2 All E.R. 455; *Tovey* v. *Tovey*, 8 Family L. 80 (1978); *Hulley* v. *Thompson*, [1981] 1 All E.R. 1128.
5. In New Zealand the *Social Security Amendment Act, 1980* effectively makes the determination of financial support by parents of their children a matter for an administrative decision made by officers of the Social Security Commission (with wide-ranging administrative powers of enforcement and investigation) rather than a question for judicial determination by the court: see Atkin, *Spousal Maintenance: A New Philosophy?* 9 N.Z.U.L. Rev. 336, at 338–340 (1981); Atkin, *Liable Parents: The New State Role in Ordering Maintenance*, 5 Otago L. Rev. 48 (1981); Atkin, *New Zealand Family Law – A Dramatic Year of Change*, 2 Oxford J. of Legal Studies 146, at 148–149 (1982). Apart from questions as to the Constitutionality of an administrative scheme exclusively assessing and determining family maintenance obligations, with no judicial 'long-stop', would it be desirable? Consider the observations of the Alberta Institute of Law Research, in its *Working Paper on Matrimonial Support*, 75–76 (1974):

   It may be said that the husband and wife should not have to incur the cost and undergo the bitterness of court proceedings; that they should not be subject to the economic effect of possible difference in the abilities of their respective lawyers; and that the tribunal should have a more uniform approach than can be expected from a system where judges spend only part of their time adjudicating upon support matters. Arguments such as these might lead to a conclusion that an administrative agency should be established with power to investigate and decide upon the amount to be paid. We are not persuaded by these arguments. The legal rights and obligations of the husband and wife are vitally affected, and each should have full right to make his own case. Each should know what evidence has been put forward by the other and should have a chance to test it and consider it. Where the financial position of the parties leaves room for negotiation, and the participation of lawyers tends more to equalize the positions of the parties than to enable one to obtain an unjustified advantage. The courts are the institutions which traditionally have adjudicated upon the rights of individuals and we do not see any reason to believe that administrative officials would do any better.

   In the Irish context, see the National Economic and Social Council's Report No. 47, *Alternative Strategies for Family Income Support* (1980), discussed by *Shatter*, 302–303.
6. From time to time there have been calls for a system of insurance as the solution to the financial problems of marriage disruption. Is this the answer? If so, why has it not yet been widely adopted? See Bradway, *Why Pay Alimony?* 32 Illinois L. Rev. 295, at 302ff (1937); Tompkins, *Report of the Subcommittee on the Family Law Process – Marriage Insurance*, extracted in J. Goldstein & S. Katz, *The Family and the Law*, 633 (1965); Bhardwaj, *An Outline of the Matrimonial and Child Law Insurance Plan: A New Law of Maintenance*, 28 R.F.L. 295 (1977); Sargisson, *Matrimonial Property Legislation – Its History, and Critique of the Present New Zealand Law*, 3 Auckland U.L. Rev. No. 1, 82, at 108–109 (1976); J. Giele, *Women and the Future: Changing Sex Roles in Modern America*, 226–227 (1978); Berkovits, *Towards a Reappraisal of Family Law Ideology*, 10 Family L. 164, at 171 (1980).
7. The taxation dimension is, of course, of considerable practical importance: see Gannon, *The Tax Implications of Marriage Breakdown*, 77 Incorp. L. Soc. Gazette 15 (1983).
8. Would it be a good reform to introduce a law requiring adult children to make reasonable efforts to support their aged parents, and to enable the parents to obtain a maintenance order against their children if they fail to do so? Cf. Garrett, *Filial Responsibility Laws*, 18 J. of Family L. 793 (1980).

L.B. v. H.B.

Unreported, High Court, Barrington, J., July 1980 (1979–449Sp.)

[The facts are set out in relation to the recognition of foreign divorces, *infra*, pp. 245–48. On the question of maintenance, **Barrington, J.** continued:]

Through the same Panamanian company Mr. B. owns the following properties in Ireland – 1. The family home which he values at £400,000. There is no mortgage on this property. 2. A castle . . . which he values at £50,000 but which is subject to a mortgage of about £20,000. 3. A house in Dublin which he values at £80,000. 4. Oyster bed rights on which he was unable to place a value.

In the United States of America Mr. B. owns some 200 acres of land situated about 50 miles from Washington D.C. with a water frontage of some 12,600 feet. The land is zoned for one acre homes and Mr. B has had it professionally valued at 9 million dollars. As the land is undeveloped Mr. B considered it more prudent to value it at 4 million dollars. It is subject to a mortgage of $475,000.

He is also involved in other business enterprises of lesser importance.

On the basis of the foregoing it is clear that Mr. B is a man of enormous wealth though he may have some difficulty in realising all his assets. He prefers not to draw a salary or director's fees from his companies but to operate largely on expense accounts. His wife said that he 'may be temporarily broke now' and he referred to difficulties in obtaining credit in Ireland. But I am quite satisfied that he is capable of surmounting any liquidity difficulties should he see fit to do so.

I am also satisfied that he has not maintained his wife in the style to which the wife of so wealthy a man may reasonably aspire and which she formerly enjoyed when the parties were living in France. I am satisfied therefore that the defendant has not maintained the plaintiff in the manner which is proper in the circumstances. I accept the evidence of the plaintiff that she cannot live, with any measure of comfort, in a house the size of the family home without, at least, the services of a housekeeper and a gardener. On the assumption that she pays the housekeeper and the gardener I will fix maintenance in the sum of £300 per week.

Notes

1. Precisely why should the wife of a very rich man be entitled to a large amount of maintenance?
2. Cf. *M.* v. *M.*, unreported, High Ct., McWilliam, J., 3 May 1978 (1977–3378 Sp.)

O'K v. O'K

Unreported, High Court, Barron, J., 16 November 1982 (1982–424Sp.)

Barron J.:

I propose now to turn to the question of maintenance. The plaintiff is at present living in her parents' home with her two children. However she has expressed the wish that she would prefer to return to the matrimonial home. This is vacant at present and there is no reason why she should not return there. The defendant . . . after tax and other deductions earned in the year ending the 5th April, 1982 an average of £122 per week. I have been given no figure for the current year and I am not prepared to assume any particular increase. The plaintiff is working in the family business and earns after tax etc £46 per week. In addition, she is in receipt of £22.50 a month children's allowances.

The defendant is living with a lady to whom he is not married in a three-bedroomed semi detached house. . . . She was called as a witness by the plaintiff to give evidence as to her earnings and the manner in which they were used. It is clear from her evidence that the entire of her take home pay apart from approximately £10 per week is used for the joint living expenses of the defendant and herself. The plaintiff has submitted that the earnings of this lady should be taken into account in assessing the defendant's means from which maintenance should be paid. No particular objection has been made to this approach to the matter. However, while I propose in the first instance to approach the question of maintenance on this basis, I wish to make it quite clear that I do so as a matter of practicality only. Neither the fact that the husband is living in an adulterous association nor the fact that the third party is earning or not earning is a consideration which should be taken into account. The wife should not be entitled to any greater maintenance from her husband because he has the benefit of earnings of a third party with whom he is living nor should the wife suffer because the third party with whom her husband is living is not earning and has to be supported by him.

In the present case the wife has £52 per week, £46 from her earnings and the balance from children's allowances. The husband has £112 per week and the third party has £78 per week. Out of this latter sum, she pays £5 per week for life insurance and approximately the same amount for bus fares. She can accordingly bring into a common pool with the defendant a sum of £68 per week. Out of these several earnings there are certain items which have to be paid. They are as follows:

> The defendant's union dues £3 per week. His life insurance £6 per week. Rent on the semidetached house . . . £38 per week. The mortgage on the [matrimonial home] £11 per week. School fees amounting to £20 per week.

The defendant says that on his earnings as a tradesman that there is no way in which he can pay for his two children. He says that the only reason that they were originally sent to fee paying schools was that the plaintiff's parents had agreed to assist in the fees. I accept this argument in part and feel that two thirds of the school fees should be paid out of the joint funds of the plaintiff and the defendant. I feel that the balance is something which the plaintiff's parents in effect promised to provide. Accordingly I will reduce the figure of £20 per week for school fees to £13 per week. This makes the total of these items to be £71 per week. Deducting this figure from the total amount available leaves a sum of £161 per week. It seems to me reasonable that this balance should be divided equally between the plaintiff and her two children and the defendant, having regard to the fact that part of it is being provided by the lady with whom he is now living. This would mean that out of the balance the plaintiff should get £80.50 per week together with the sums of £11 per week to pay the mortgage and the sum of £13 per week towards the school fees. This comes to a total of £104.50 per week. Since she already has £52 per week it means that the defendant should pay an additional £52.50 to the plaintiff to make up £104.50 per week. This is approximately half his take home pay. On the basis that there will have been some increase in his take home pay for this financial year, I would like to indicate that I would regard him as being obliged to pay one half of this increase to the plaintiff in addition to the sum of £52.50 which I have indicated.

If I am wrong in the approach which I have taken to the question of maintenance, then there is an alternative basis which is available. I must assume that the defendant has separated from his wife and children and that he has £112 per week to provide for them knowing that they have a further income of £52 per week and to provide also for himself. On this basis he would be required to pay £52.50 to his wife and to retain for himself £59.50. While this is more than half his available earnings it does not take into account the fact that he will have to pay rent for accommodation whereas his wife will not have to do so. On this basis also, it seems to me that the figure of £52.50 together with 50% of any increase in take home pay during this financial year would be a reasonable sum to require the defendant to pay. I will direct that the sum for maintenance shall be apportioned as to £20 per week to [one child] and as to £20 a week to [the other child] and as to the balance to the plaintiff.

Notes and Questions

1. Do you agree with Barron, J.'s disposition of the important question concerning the earnings or maintenance claim of a third party with whom the respondent is living? Is it right to ignore such earnings? Is it just to ignore a maintenance claim? There is, of course, a fundamental issue of social and legal policy at stake here. Can it be dealt with satisfactorily in a couple of sentences?
2. For a stimulating analysis of the decision, see O'Connor, *Support Obligations in the Family*, 1 Ir. L.T. (n.s.) 40 (1983). More generally, see Rosettenstein, *Cohabitation, Maintenance, and the Competition for Limited Resources – In Search of a New Perspective*, 12 Anglo-Amer. L. Rev. 181 (1983).

3. Section 6 of the *Family Law (Maintenance of Spouses and Children) Act, 1976* and section 12 of the *Courts Act, 1981* provide for the variation and discharge of maintenance orders in certain circumstances. There is no rule, however, that maintenance awards should be subject to *automatic* increase (or decrease) to take account of changes in the cost of living. Is this a correct policy, in your view? For an account of experience in the United States, see George, *Combatting the Effects of Inflation on Alimony and Child Support Orders*, 57 Conn. Bar J. 223 (1983). In England, the experience of divorced wives is alarming. The English Law Commission reported in 1980 that:

   > It seems that in practice, even in times of high inflation, an application for variation is more likely to result in a decrease rather than an increase in the sum ordered to be paid. *Discussion Paper, The Financial Consequences of Divorce: The Basic Policy*, para. 28 (1980).

   Why should this be so? What should be done?

4. For the purposes of measuring a person's income in assessing maintenance, is a husband entitled to arrange his financial affairs so that he diminishes his income at his wife's expense in order to increase his capital? Cf. *R.F.* v. *M.F.*, unreported, High Ct., D'Arcy J., December 1982 (1979–758 P).

DESERTION

R.K. v. M.K.

Unreported, High Court, Finlay, P., 24 October, 1978 (1978–330Sp.)

Finlay, P.:

. . . I am satisfied that the marriage between the parties has not for many years been a happy or successful marriage. From the very start the plaintiff was jealous and suspicious of her husband in relation to other women and certainly made at an early stage an unfounded accusation of infidelity on his part with a girl to whom he and a male companion had merely given a lift. The defendant was on the other hand extremely insensitive towards the plaintiff's difficulties as a wife and mother and demanding in his standards required from her. This situation culminated in short separations between the parties occurring on two occasions at least immediately after and immediately before the birth of one of the children. A lack of compassion and sensitivity on the part of the defendant had at these difficult times contributed to these separations and the reconciliations following them were accepted by him more as a convenience towards the running of his house rather than a genuine attempt to remake a marraige.

During one of these situations the defendant committed adultery as he admits with a married woman. Legally his wife has long since condoned it but it is doubtful if she ever forgave it. From then on this was a marriage of convenience. As such it continued in a tolerable fashion and with some increased material prosperity until the beginning of 1977 when the plaintiff was diagnosed as suffering from a motor neurone disease.

The plaintiff's reaction was one of depression and anxiety although she has shown considerable courage in the face of the progress of the disease. She became irritable and many of the unhappy aspects of the marriage became unbearable. The defendant's attitude was I regret to say most unfeeling and reflected his fundamental view of his wife as a housekeeper and minder of his children. Relations then rapidly deteriorated until the plaintiff left in November 1977.

The defendant has refused to rely upon desertion by the plaintiff and accepts a liability to pay maintenance. Even if this concession had not been made I would have rejected any contention that the plaintiff deserted the defendant. I am satisfied that in the civil law of this country as in the canon law of the Catholic Church in which this marriage took place the obligations of a husband or a wife are not obviated but may be heightened by the sickness of the spouse. From the diagnosis of the plaintiff's illness and her progressive incapacity caused by it the defendant showed a gross lack of attention to and sympathy with her real needs which amounted to cruelty justifying her departure from the home.

Many of the allegations of deprivation and abuse made by the plaintiff I cannot accept but the overall picture of an unfeeling attitude is well made out. This led the plaintiff to exaggerations before me and to attempt to create a worse picture of neglect than actually existed.

Before the departure of the plaintiff it is common case that S. was ordered out by his father. There is a conflict of evidence on the circumstances surrounding this dispute. I accept the defendant's account of this controversy and reject that given by S. and to an extent corroborated by his mother. Even on the defendant's account of the incident it constituted a severe approach by him to his responsibilities to his son and clearly was a particularly cruel blow to the plaintiff who had a particular affection for and reliance on her elder son.

Since the departure of the plaintiff from the house the defendant made no effort to effect a reconciliation or provide for her physical wellbeing. He made sporadic and inadequate attempts to maintain her though recently his attempts are regular and he has shown no other concern for her wellbeing. This total lack of compassion has been emulated by his son M. . . .

. . . [As to] the issue of maintenance[,] I am satisfied that the plaintiff, being by the conduct of the defendant, prevented from residing in the only family home is entitled as a first part of the maintenance against her husband to the cost of renting appropriate alternative accommodation. . . .

[For Finlay, P.'s consideration of the question of property entitlements, see pp. 267–68, *infra*.]

Notes and Questions

1. Do you agree with the proposition that 'the obligations of a husband or a wife are not obviated but may be heightened by the sickness of the spouse'? What about mental illness? In England, some proponents of more liberal divorce have argued that it is wrong for maintenance orders after divorce to have regard to any physical or mental disability of either spouse, on the basis that '. . . the afflicted spouse should be expected instead to turn to the state for assistance, just like any other disabled person who lack[s] private means of support . . .': Hayes, *Financial Provision and Property Adjustment Orders: The Statutory Guidelines*, 10 Family L. 3, at 9 (1980). See also Barnett, *Financial Provision on Divorce: Reforming s. 25*, 11 Family L. 299, at 230 (1981). Does this argument appeal to you?
2. How do you understand the bar of condonation in the light of Finlay, P.'s comment that '[l]egally [the defendant']s wife has long since condoned [the adultery] but it is doubtful if she ever forgave it.'?

P. v. P.

Unreported, High Court, Barrington, J., 12 March 1980 (1980–145P.)

Barrington, J.:

The parties to the present proceedings are a young married couple, the wife being now aged 28 and the husband 27.

They have one child who was born on the 22nd May 1979. . . .

I am satisfied that both parties worked very hard to raise the price of their house. Their savings were effected through an account in the wife's sole name.

At times the husband held down two jobs in an effort to raise more money. Though the account was in his then fiancée's sole name I am satisfied that by far the greater part of the savings came from him.

. . . At the time of their marriage the parties had an agreement that the wife would remain on a contraceptive pill for approximately two years after marriage. The purpose of this agreement was to enable them to pay off some of their debts and to furnish their house before they started a family.

Unfortunately difficulties arose in the marriage and the wife left the family home on a number of occasions. After her penultimate departure the wife had returned to her husband on certain conditions. These included that the wife should come off the pill, that the parties should try to have a baby and that the wife should then give up her job.

What happened thereafter is described by the wife in paragraph 12 of her affidavit as follows:–

> During the following weeks my husband and I barely spoke to one another. I continued to do domestic chores around the family home and prepare meals for my husband. The defendant lost his temper on a number of occasions and became extremely abusive towards me this deponent. I informed the defendant that I was frightened by his conduct towards me and that if our relationship did not improve I could not bear to remain in the family home with him. At this time I was three weeks pregnant.

The husband's version of what happened is that the parties had been reconciled to each other and were trying to have a baby and that he was totally shattered when the wife, quite unexpectedly, announced to him that she was leaving him. This was in November 1978. He admits that a scene then took place and that the wife left for the last time.

Soon after leaving, the wife discovered she was pregnant. She was asked in cross-examination if she was depressed at finding herself pregnant when her marriage had broken down. She denied being depressed about the pregnancy. She said that on the contrary she was delighted as that was what she got married for.

The wife stopped work on December the 15th 1978.

The baby was born on the 22nd May 1979. The birth was difficult. The baby was premature and was delivered by caesarean section. The child had convulsions and had to be kept in an incubator. The husband visited the wife in hospital and rather tactlessly revealed to her the fact that the child had had convulsions – a matter which the medical and nursing staff had withheld from her. On later visits to the hospital the husband found his wife cold and withdrawn. When the husband raised the question of what name the child should be called he was told to mind his own business and the wife refused to discuss the christening arrangements with him.

The husband was not, in fact, informed of the date of the christening which took place in his absence, and I am quite satisfied that the wife deliberately embarked on a course of excluding her husband from all contact with their child.

Both parties now admit that the marriage has irretrievably broken down. The husband, in evidence, conceded that the wife should have custody of the child. He said he would not like to see his son being brought up by anyone else. The wife, on the other hand, seemed reluctant to allow any access to the child by the husband. She felt that any access he had should take place in her presence. I can see no justification for excluding the husband from access to the child. Appropriate arrangements must therefore be made to grant him reasonable access.

I have mentioned the foregoing matters in some detail, not only because they are important in themselves, but also because they have influenced me in my approach to the more difficult questions which I have now to consider. These concern the reasons for the break-down of the marriage; whether the wife has been guilty of desertion; and whether she is or is not entitled to maintenance from her husband in her own right. There is no doubt about the husband's duty (or indeed his willingness) to maintain the child. He is at present paying £16 per week to the wife pursuant to an arrangement reached in the District Court.

When parties marry they marry for better or for worse. This, as I understand it, includes accepting quirks and difficulties in the character of the other marriage partner.

To establish 'just cause' for leaving the matrimonial home the partner who has left must establish some form of serious misconduct on the part of the other partner. Such conduct must, as Lord Asquith said:–

> . . . exceed in gravity such behaviour, vexatious and trying though it may be, as every spouse bargains to endure when accepting the other 'for better or worse'. The ordinary wear and tear of conjugal life does not in itself suffice. (*Buchler* v. *Buchler* [1947] 1 All E.R. 319, at 326).

The wife's case against her husband is that he is a violent and cruel man. She says he has beaten, insulted and humiliated her. The wife, who is a very attractive young woman, says her husband called her a 'fat pig' referring apparently to a minor weight problem about which she appears to be excessively sensitive. She says he attacked her with a knife and frequently threatened to beat her where it would hurt but would not show. She says he was a naturally violent and vicious man and that she was terrified of him.

While the husband does drink there is no allegation that he habitually drinks to excess. The wife's allegations amount to a much more serious allegation, to wit, that he is a naturally violent and cruel man.

Most of the incidents on which the wife relies are alleged to have taken place when she and her husband were alone together and there is no corroborative evidence to support either one story or the other. A number of incidents were, however, referred to in evidence in which third parties were, to some degree, involved and which may cast some light on the relationship between the parties.

Before the marriage the wife's father, Mr. M., overheard an argument between the engaged couple. He heard his prospective son-in-law saying to his daughter that the 'girl who wears my ring has to be worthy of it'. Mr. M. naturally resented this remark which he took to be highly offensive to his daughter.

The husband lost a week's wages during the week in which the parties were away on their honeymoon. On their return the bride's parents, as a gesture, sent the newly married couple a chicken and £20. The husband resented the gift of £20 and accepted it only on the basis that it was to be a loan and not a gift. He further resented the fact that the parents-in-law would not accept the £20 back at a later stage. The husband said he wished to establish himself as the main breadwinner in the house and that he did not consider that accepting gifts of money was a good way to start. I consider that his attitude on this point, while difficult, was not altogether discreditable.

A more serious incident took place on the 24th June 1979 at the home of the wife's parents. The husband arrived to see his son. The occasion was an emotive one as it was the first occasion on which the husband had seen his son since his wife had left hospital. It was also the second anniversary of the marriage. The child was, at this stage, still very young and delicate. The mother was, perhaps, overly protective to it. As the father arrived the mother was just finishing feeding the baby. The father asked to be allowed to help. The mother told him not to be silly and words apparently took place between the parties. The wife left the room and spoke to her mother. The mother went upstairs and woke the wife's father, who was having his afternoon nap. The father came down and asked the son-in-law to leave the house and when he declined to do so the police were sent for. Sergeant Fennessy who came on the scene found the husband being aggressive towards his wife and said that he 'put up his fist in a threatening manner'. Sergeant Fennessy says he was not impressed by the husband's manner. He said that the house was tense and that it was obvious that the husband was the cause of the tension. He thought he should have exercised more reasonable restraint. Sergeant Fennessy asked the husband to stay away from the house in the best interest of the family and the child.

Sergeant Fennessy was quite satisfied that the husband was to blame for this particular scene. Sergeant Fennessy may, however, have been conditioned, to some degree, by the account which he had received from the father-in-law before entering the room. The father-in-law himself had previously been conditioned by the mother-in-law who, in turn, had been conditioned by her daughter. Moreover, I do not think it extraordinary that the husband should have been tense and difficult on this particular occasion having regard to the background of the incident and having regard in particular to the fact that he had been excluded from his son's christening. I do not think that this incident supports a conclusion that the husband is a cruel and vicious man. For the same reasons I do not regard that incident or subsequent incidents where the husband accosted the wife when she had the baby out in a pram as decisive. These latter incidents are all to be regarded in the light of the fact that the husband was denied all formal access to his son from June of 1979 until February of 1980 when arrangements were made by this Court for him to have interim access.

Another significant incident in relation to which there is independent evidence is described by the wife in Paragraph 7 of her Affidavit as follows:-

> Some months later, the Defendant again returned home from work quite late, and started a row over his dinner, which was in the oven. The Defendant informed me that he was going out, and that I was not to be in the family home when he returned. As I feared that my husband would be violent towards me on his return, I, your deponent left the family home and went to stay with my mother-in-law, at the home of the Defendant's parents. The following day I returned to the family home accompanied by my father-in-law.

In evidence, the wife referred to this incident as having taken place in August, 1977. She said her husband was late home on that date, and that his dinner was waiting for him in the oven. He had apparently met his Best Man in town. The husband was abusive to her when he came home. He was not drunk. The husband's sister, P. and her boyfriend – a Mr. G. – were in the house at the time. According to the wife, P. said that if any person had spoken to her (P.) in the way the husband had spoken to his wife, she would have knocked him flat on the floor. The wife said the husband told her that he was going out, and that she was not to be there when he came back. She said she was too terrified to stay. Accordingly, she went to her mother-in-law's house.

The husband admitted in evidence that he was late home, on that particular evening. He said however, that he had warned his wife that he would be late. He said there was no dinner waiting for him when he got home. He said there was a pot of potatoes on the top of the stove. He said he inquired of his wife about his dinner, but that he was told to get it himself. He said he attempted to cook himself a steak, but that he had no skill in cooking and burnt the steak to a cinder. He then made himself a cup of tea and a sandwich.

He said that the group had earlier arranged to go for a drink to the local public house. He said that he and Mr. G. went ahead to the pub to keep seats for his wife and his sister. He denied that he had asked his wife to leave the house. He said that she did not arrive at the pub, and that when he returned home, she was gone.

P. and Mr. G. substantially bear out the husband's version of what happened.

P. says that her brother came home between 5.30 and 5.45 p.m. (As his job ended at 4 o'clock, he would normally have been expected home earlier). She said that she and the wife were sitting in the sitting-room. She said there was no dinner made. She said the wife asked why the husband was late, and where was he. She said the wife was annoyed and just sat in silence. She said the wife told the husband that his dinner was in the kitchen. She said the husband came back to say that the potatoes were raw and that the wife told him to cook them. She said there was a general atmosphere of coolness in the house. She said the husband later made a cup of tea and sandwiches and that the atmosphere then improved. She said that the party decided to go for a drink and that the men went ahead to keep places in the pub. She said that she and the wife were to follow, but, she said, the wife later came downstairs with a suitcase, and informed her that she was leaving. She later got a taxi.

Mr. G. is [a tradesman]. He was obliging by doing some job for the married couple in the house. He says that the husband arrived home between 5.30 and 6 p.m. Mr. G. was at his work outside in the back kitchen. He said that the husband came in and started cooking his dinner. He says that he took a steak out of the refrigerator and attempted to cook it, but that he burnt it and then threw it to the dog. He said that the husband made tea and brought in cups of tea for his sister and his wife. He said that an arrangement had been made earlier, to go out to the local pub for a drink. He said that he inquired when they were going for their drink, and that his sister, P., had said that he and the husband should go on first, and that she and the wife would follow. He said that he expected the girls to follow them down. He heard no scene or shouting in the house that night.

P. and Mr. G. cannot be regarded as totally independent witnesses, as P. is the husband's sister, and Mr. G. her boyfriend, but nevertheless, they struck me as sensible and credible people. Yet it seems impossible to reconcile their account of this incident with that of the wife. This causes me misgivings about other instances in which the wife's evidence conflicts with the husband's, and in relation to which there is no independent testimony.

In my own view, the husband is a hard-working, excitable and difficult man. His mother says of him that he has 'a bit of a temper', but that he is not one to bear a grudge. I am not satisfied that the wife has proved her case that he is a violent or vicious man. There is no medical evidence to suggest that he suffers from any kind of psychiatric disorder. In all the circumstances, I am not satisfied that the wife has made out her case that she had 'just cause' for leaving the matrimonial home. Accordingly, it appears to me that the wife has been guilty of desertion, and that the Court is debarred by Section 5, sub-section (2) of the *Family Law (Maintenance of Spouses and Children) Act, 1976*, from making a Maintenance Order for her separate support.

I have also reached the view that it would not be appropriate or proper for me to make an Order pursuant to Section 22 of the same Act, debarring the husband from the family home.

Both parties, however, appear agreed that the wife is the proper person to have custody of the child, and both parties are also agreed that this means that she cannot work for some years to come. This, in turn means that the maintenance for the child must include a sum sufficient to enable the mother to look after the child. I accordingly fix maintenance for the child, pending further Order, at the sum of £30 per week. . . .

Notes and Questions

1. As has been mentioned, *supra*, p. 200, section 3 of the *Family Law (Maintenance of Spouses and Children) Act, 1976* defines desertion as including 'conduct on the part of one spouse that results in the other spouse, with just cause, leaving and living separately and apart from him'. It makes no reference to an *intention* on the part of the spouse guilty of constructive desertion that cohabitation should end. Is proof of such an intention necessary? Cf. *Shatter*, 276–277. Can you distinguish with any certainty or confidence between an 'intention' and a 'wish'? Is this a matter of psychology, morality or law? As to the law before 1976, see *C.* v. *C.*, unreported, High Ct., Kenny, J., 27 July 1973 (1973–144Sp.)
2. The primary casualties of the rule denying entitlement to maintenance to spouses who are in desertion are wives. Is this fair? Is the financial imbalance between the sexes something which family law should seek to remove or merely reflect? Is the proper approach to attempt to ensure that dependent spouses are adequately maintained by their independent spouses, or should family law be seeking to make all spouses financially independent?
3. See also *P.G.* v. *C.G.* and *C.G.* v. *P.G.*, unreported, High Ct., Finlay, P., 12 March 1982 (wife's claim for maintenance rejected on the ground of her desertion; allegation of constructive desertion rejected on the evidence; husband admitted having assaulted the wife 'though not in a serious manner' on two or three occasions; Finlay, P. believed that '[d]ue largely to his immaturity . . . he was probably uncaring and insensitive during the marriage.')
4. If a spouse has 'just cause' for leaving but the dominant fact motivating the spouse to leave is something unrelated to the 'just cause', should that spouse be entitled to a maintenance order? Cf. *S.D.* v. *B.D.*, unreported, High Ct., Murphy, J., 19 March 1982 (1981–1945P.), and scrutinise carefully the text of section 3(1) of the Act.
5. When does excessive drinking constitute 'just cause' for a spouse's departure? Cf. *M.B.* v. *E.B.*, unreported, High Ct., Barrington, J., February 1980 (1979–566Sp.).
6. It should be noted that, irrespective of the question of the applicant spouse's entitlement to a maintenance order, the Court may make a maintenance order for the dependent children of the family: see sections 5(2), 5(3) and 6(5) of the *Family Law (Maintenance of Spouses and Children) Act, 1976*; see also *P.* v. *P.*, *supra*, p. 214, and cf. *Shatter*, 284.

ADULTERY

L. v. L.

Unreported, High Court, Finlay, P., 21 December 1979 (1979–378Sp.)

Finlay, P.:

. . .The material facts concerning the Plaintiff's claim for maintenance, as I have found to be on the evidence, are as follows. Up to March, 1978 the Defendant was consistently employed. At times, however, when he was self-employed, he was receiving very little remuneration. In March 1978 he was dismissed out of an employment which he had recently obtained in January of 1978 and for a period of some six months was completely unemployed. During that period he apparently formed an attachment with another woman and he commenced, what I am satisfied, was an adulterous relationship with her which was discovered by the Plaintiff shortly before the end of July, 1978. The Defendant denied his association or that it was an adulterous one but the Plaintiff being satisfied upon evidence which she herself discovered that that was the truth of the matter indicated that she was no longer prepared to live with the Defendant. Eventually the Defendant left the family home at the very end of August of 1978. The Defendant has, since that time, continued his adulterous relationship with the lady originally concerned.

The Plaintiff remained in the family home and resumed her employment as a secretary at the beginning of September, 1978 and subsequent to that time in the month of October, 1978 she formed an adulterous relationship with a man which lasted for possibly a month or so. Subsequently, in the month of November, 1978 she formed an adulterous relationship with another man which continues up to the present. This second person does not live with the Plaintiff though he from time to time stays over night in her house, which is the family home and he does not, I am satisfied on the evidence, regularly maintain her in any way though he does, undoubtedly, provide her with entertainment and the opportunity to avail of social occasions.

The Defendant obtained contractual employment as a consultant for a period of approximately six months between October, 1978 and March, 1979 at a salary of £350 per month. He was subsequently unemployed between April, 1979 and the middle of September, 1979 when he obtained another contractual post as a consultant in which he is presently paid £600 per month plus an allowance for expenses out of which he does not, I am satisfied, make any profit of £300 per month. This contract is due to expire in March of 1980 and being a particular task carried out by him for the company who are his employers, has not got any guarantee of renewal. The Defendant has not yet passed the final of his professional examinations as an accountant and, therefore, whilst he may claim to be a person with considerable accountancy experience, he cannot claim to be a qualified accountant. The Plaintiff has remained consistently in employment as a secretary since the beginning of September, 1978 and is presently earning at a rate which yields to her a net take home pay of £55 per week.

The Defendant disputes his liability to pay maintenance to the Plaintiff firstly and primarily on the grounds that she has been guilty of adultery and secondly upon the grounds that she is not in want having regard to her earning capacity and earnings. . . .

[Finlay, P. quoted Section 5, subsection (3), of the *Family Law (Maintenance of Spouses and Children) Act, 1976*. He continued:]

Counsel have been unable to refer me to any decision interpreting this subsection and I am unaware of any one.

Having considered the subsection and the submissions made to me by Counsel I am satisfied that it must be construed as follows. If the Court is satisfied that the spouse against whom maintenance is claimed has condoned or connived at or by wilful neglect or misconduct conduced to the adultery then it has no discretion and must order maintenance provided that the other conditions contained in the Act of 1976 with regard to maintenance are fulfilled, that is to say that the other spouse has failed to provide such maintenance for the applicant spouse as is proper in the circumstances including, *inter alia*, the earnings or capacity to earn of the applicant spouse.

If, on the other hand, the Court is not satisfied that the respondent spouse has condoned or connived at or by wilful neglect or misconduct conduced to the adultery then it has a discretion and may exercise that discretion having regard to all the circumstances. All the circumstances must in my view include the financial circumstances of the applicant spouse. It seems to me that if an applicant spouse who has been guilty of adultery not condoned, connived at or conduced to by the other spouse were notwithstanding that in a position of extreme want or considerable penury that the Court might have regard to that as a circumstance which would entitle it to exercise its discretion in favour of making an order for maintenance. Furthermore, it seems to me that if an applicant spouse had committed adultery but had ceased at the time of application that adulterous relationship that may well be a consideration which the Court should take into account. Furthermore, the express reference in the subsection to the conduct of the other spouse would seem to indicate that a spouse against whom maintenance was claimed who had not condoned, connived at or conduced to the adultery of the applicant spouse might by his own conduct, including presumably a subsequent adultery on his part, make himself liable where he otherwise would not be to the payment of maintenance. I do not intend that these should be considered an exhaustive list of the circumstances which the Court may take into consideration which must, of necessity, vary with every case but they are the sort of circumstances which it appears to me may be material to this situation. With regard to subclause (a) of subsection 3, I am firstly satisfied that it must be interpreted insofar as it refers to a condoning of the adultery as intended to carry the ordinary legal meaning of condonation, namely a co-habiting subsequent to the discovery of the adultery. There is no evidence in this case that any condonation in that form took place.

With regard to the word 'connived' contained in Section 3, subsection (a), I must interpret this as indicating conduct on the part of the other spouse consisting of a knowledge of the adultery and a failure to make any remonstrance concerning it or to take any steps to try and persuade his partner from continuing with it. Again in this case it is clear on the evidence that the parties had separated and, in my view, notwithstanding a contention made by the Defendant to the contrary, had probably separated on a more or less permanent basis before the applicant spouse committed adultery and I do not consider that there could, on my construction of the word 'connived' in the subsection, be said to be any evidence that the Defendant had connived at the adultery of his wife.

The issue, therefore, on the sub-clause (a) of subsection 3 must be confined in my view on the evidence to a question as to whether the Defendant has by wilful neglect or misconduct conduced to the adultery. I would have considerable doubt as to whether, properly interpreted, the facts of this case could suggest that there was a wilful neglect of the Plaintiff by the Defendant conducing to the adultery but I am satisfied as a matter of probability that wilful misconduct on the part of the Defendant has so done.

The evidence before me suggests that this was a normal and happy marriage relationship up to the Spring, or possibly even as far as the early Summer, of 1978. It is clear that the sudden loss of a lucrative job by the Defendant in March of 1978 put a strain on both the parties to the marriage. There is, however, not evidence which would satisfy me that that was an intolerable strain although the Defendant asserted that his marriage became entirely unsatisfactory from that time onwards due to the conduct, by way of coldness and non-communication, of his wife. There is no evidence to suggest that either of the parties to the marriage had prior to that time been in any way unfaithful to each other or had been in any way in the habit of building up relationships with people of the other sex, whether of an adulterous nature or not. The evidence does, however, suggest that the Defendant then commenced the adulterous relationship with the person with whom he has presently continued it and did so in what could be described as a flagrant and public fashion, still circulating amongst what had been the mutual friends of this young pair. By that which can only be described as wilful misconduct I am satisfied that the Defendant effectively destroyed this marriage. It is undoubtedly true that the Plaintiff's reaction to the discovery of her husband's infidelity was swift, and in a sense final, and it is also true that the Plaintiff's reaction to it was with very little delay indeed to commence herself a short-term adulterous relationship and subsequently with a different person a more long-term relationship of the same kind. On balance, however, I have come to the conclusion that it is improbable that the Plaintiff would have fallen into either of these two relationships had she not been left, in effect, as a deserted wife by her husband who by a constant denial of his new relationship gave little grounds for hoping that the marriage might be saved. In these circumstances I am driven to the conclusion that within the proper interpretation of subsection 3(a) of section 5 of the Act of 1976 the Defendant has, by wilful misconduct, conduced to the adultery of his wife. On my reading of the Section that leaves me with no discretion as to whether or not to make a maintenance order for the support of the Plaintiff other than the discretion arising from the capacity of the Defendant to pay, the question as to whether he had made proper provision for her and the earning capacity and other source of means of the applicant spouse. . . .

Notes

1. Does 'connivance' in section 5(3) of the *Family Law (Maintenance of Spouses and Children) Act, 1976*, as understood by Finlay, P., differ from the concept of connivance in proceedings for divorce *a mensa et thoro*?
2. In the United States the question of the effect of subsequent adultery or cohabitation on alimony decrees has recently come under increasing debate: see Wall, *Comment*, 66 Marquette L. Rev. 605 (1983); J. O. T. II, *Comment*, 33 Ala. L. Rev. 577 (1982); Balbirer, McLachlan & Ferro, *Survey of 1982 Developments in Connecticut Family Law*, 57 Conn. Bar J. 20, at 45–47 (1983).

O.C. v. T.C.

Unreported, High Ct., McMahon, J., 9 December 1981 (1981–81Sp)

McMahon, J.:

. . . The . . . wife [makes a] claim for a Maintenance Order under the *Family Law (Maintenance of Spouses and Children) Act, 1976* for the support of herself and her son D.

The wife claims that, notwithstanding her admitted adultery with X., she is entitled under Section 5(3)(a) or (b) to a Maintenance Order for herself and she also claims a Maintenance Order for the support of D. on the grounds that she is no longer able to support him out of her means.

The parties were married in 1952 and lived in Dublin. There were four children of the marriage, namely A [their only daughter], born October 1952, B, born April 1954, C, born April 1959 and D, born November 1964. In April 1967 the wife deserted the husband and . . . she cohabited with X and called herself Mrs. X. The husband brought proceedings for criminal conversation against X and the wife brought proceedings against the husband under the *Guardianship of [Infants] Act, 1964* claiming the custody of the four children. The proceedings were settled on terms that the husband discontinued the criminal conversation action and the husband and wife entered into a Consent and a Deed of Separation. The Consent gave the wife custody of A and the husband custody of B and provided for joint custody of C and D. It was agreed that neither parent should remove any child from the jurisdiction without the written consent of the other. The husband agreed to pay for the education and health bills of all the children and provide them with reasonable pocket money and suitable clothing until each attained the age of eighteen or in the case of a child attending a university or other institution until the completion of such education or the age of twenty-two whichever should be the earlier.

The Deed of Separation incorporated the Consent and provided that the husband and wife should live separately and apart and not molest one another and each renounced all rights under Part 9 [of the] *Succession Act 1965* to the estate of the other. The wife undertook to support and maintain A, C and D so long as she should have custody of them and not to visit the husband's home . . . or to interfere in any way with the husband in his person or manner of living and she waived all right to be maintained or supported by him and undertook to take no steps to compel him to pay any maintenance.

As a result of further disputes concerning the guardianship of the children the proceedings were re-entered for hearing and by Order dated the 14th May 1969 Mr. Justice Butler gave the wife custody of A and D. The husband appealed against that Order and before the Supreme Court the wife alleged that since the proceedings in the High Court she had discovered her husband having sexual intercourse with a Miss Y. The Supreme Court heard oral evidence in relation to this allegation and rejected the wife's evidence. The Supreme Court dismissed the husband's appeal but varied the Order of the High Court. The husband was given the custody of B and C. The wife was given the sole custody of A and D. Provision was made for the children living with the wife for certain periods. Finally the Order provided that neither party should take the children other than A out of the jurisdiction without the written consent of the other parent.

The Judgments make it clear that the Court gave the wife custody of A and, D relying on her evidence that she had terminated her association with X and intended to live with the children A and D in a home which she had acquired [in County Dublin].

The Order of the Supreme Court was made on the 14th May,1970. On her father's death in the year 1969 the wife had become entitled to a sum of £50,000 under a family trust. She never completed the purchase of the house [in County Dublin] and in 1970 she took A., C., and D. to England where she made the children Wards of Court. She lived in London together with the children with X. until 1972 using the name Mrs. X. The association with X ceased in 1972 and the wife continued to live in London until 1977. During that time A married and C returned to live with his father in Dublin. While living in England the wife bought and sold properties and embarked on different business ventures. She returned to Dublin in 1977 and lived there until she went to the United States in 1979. She opened a business in Dublin during the period she lived there. She went to the United States in 1979 taking D with her and has lived since then in [a] town . . . in Texas. D attended State High School and graduated in June 1981 and the wife gave evidence that she intended to send him to university to study script writing and film making for which he had discovered a talent in High School. The wife is not entitled to work in the United States because she has only a visitor's visa but she is studying to qualify as a real estate agent and when qualified she will be entitled to work in that capacity. It is her intention to remain permanently in the United States.

The wife returned to Ireland from the United States in June 1981 and while her husband was abroad on holidays she brought two furniture removal vans from England with a number of workmen and two men who appeared to be bodyguards to the husband's house. C was in the house . . . and was prevented by the two men from telephoning his brother B to warn him of what was taking place. The wife removed a considerable quantity of furniture in the vans and she also removed letters and photographs from the husband's bedroom. The police were alerted and prevented the furniture leaving the country and it was recovered by the husband. The wife retained the photographs and letters. They were tendered in evidence at this trial and I ruled that they were inadmissible because they had been obtained in flagrant violation of the husband's constitutional right to the inviolability of his home (*The People (A. G.)* v. *O'Brien* [1965] I.R. 142).

The wife gave evidence of her assets and liabilities. Her main asset is a house in the United States which she hopes to sell for about £48,000. The house is subject to a mortgage. Taking her liabilities including the mortgage into account she appears to have assets of a net value of £35,000. The husband lives in a valuable house [in] County Dublin and has a rental income of £4,000 from a letting of part of his home . . . and [other] property. . . . He has also some derelict sites in Dublin which he hopes to sell. He appears to be worth between £230,000 to £250,000. He has been living with Miss Y for some years and she is now expecting his child.

I am satisfied that Section 5 (3) (a) [of the] *Family Law (Maintenance of Spouses and Children) Act 1976* does not apply to the wife's claim for maintenance. There is no suggestion that the husband condoned or connived at the wife's adultery. She attributes her adultery with X to her husband's neglect and her belief that he was having affairs with other women. In my view the marriage was seriously deficient in affection and trust from an early stage but I do not think the wife's adultery with X was due to wilful neglect on the part of the husband. I attribute it to infatuation with X. The wife is a very determined personality. She had wealthy parents on whom she could have fallen back if she found her marriage no longer tolerable. Her attachment to X was too prolonged and persistent to be attributed to a reaction to neglect on the husband's part.

Under Section 5(3)(b) where the wife's adultery was not condoned or connived at by the husband or conduced to by his wilful neglect or misconduct the Court can still make a maintenance order for the support of the wife if it considers it proper to do so having regard to all the circumstances including the conduct of the husband. The wife's adultery with X, the terms of the Deed of Separation and her conduct since the separation amount to an unequivocal repudiation by her of any relationship with the husband. Her flagrant breaches of the terms of the separation deed and of the terms on which the Supreme Court awarded her custody of C and D damaged the husband in his relationship with these children. At the time the parties separated the wife became entitled to a large sum of money sufficient to make her financially independent for the remainder of her life. In these circumstances it would in my view clearly be unfair to the husband to revive the obligation to support his wife which was extinguished by her adultery. In view of her net asset position it does not appear to me that she is in need of support. She has chosen to live in the United States where she is not entitled to Social Welfare and is not entitled to work until she graduates as a real estate agent but she expects that she will then be able to earn a living and support herself. As she intends to live in the United States for the rest of her life she must expect that her means would be sufficient to bridge the gap until she commences to earn a living as an estate agent.

The husband's liability to support D is not affected by the wife's adultery. The wife's evidence did not indicate whether D had in fact started to attend the university I shall assume that he has and therefore is a dependent child of the husband's and will remain so until he attains the age of twenty-one years. In the Separation Deed the wife undertook to maintain D as long as she had custody of him and the husband undertook to pay for his education to the age of twenty-two if D should attend a university. This was on the basis that D remained in the joint custody of the husband and wife. It was never contemplated that the husband should be liable for fees and maintenance at an American university in the circumstances which now obtain. While he lives in the United States I do not consider that the discharge of D's university expenses or a contribution towards such expenses or to his maintenance is support which it is proper the husband should be liable for. The wife intends to continue to maintain D and to pay his university expenses and I assume she intends to live on her capital until she is able to earn enough as an estate agent. The claim for a maintenance order for the support of D therefore fails.

Notes and Questions

1. Do you agree with the present policy of the law in relation to adultery and maintenance? If you do not, what would you suggest in its place? In England, the *Divorce Reform Act, 1969* introduced a species of no-fault divorce, but the legislators at the time did not seriously address the obvious consequences likely to result with regard to maintenance. Courts found themselves awarding maintenance after divorce to adulterous wives. Husbands against whom orders for maintenance were made in such cases argued that this was unfair. This alleged injustice has frequently been invoked by those pressing for a general curtailment or abrogation of men's maintenance obligations to their divorced wives.
2. Would it ever (or always) be proper for the Court to make an order for custody or access in favour of a parent conditional on the payment of maintenance by that parent to the other parent or to the child or children? As to experience in the United States, see Folberg & Graham, *Joint Custody of Children Following Divorce*, 12 U. Cal. Davis L. Rev. 523, at 564 (1979); Cartwright, *Modification of Child Support Decrees in the 1980's: A Jurisprudential Model*, 21 J. of Family L. 327, at 339–340 (1983); Freed & Foster, *Family Law in the Fifty States: An Overview*, 17 Family L.Q. 365, at 371 (1984).

ENFORCEMENT OF MAINTENANCE ORDERS

A wide range of machinery for enforcement of maintenance orders exists, including applications under section 8 of *the Enforcement of Court Orders Act, 1940*, orders for attachment of earnings under Part III of the *Family Law (Maintenance of Spouses and Children) Act, 1976*, and orders under section 6 of *the Debtors (Ireland) Act, 1872*. For a detailed consideration of these approaches, see *Shatter*, 285–289. As to the reciprocal enforcement of maintenance orders, see *infra*, p. 255.

In *H.* v. *H.*, unreported (oral judgment), High Ct., 7 April 1982, O'Hanlon applied the *Mareva* principle, in a liberal fashion, in maintenance proceedings, to a voluntary redundancy payment. Summarising the effect of the decision, counsel for the plaintiff, Peter Charleton, B.L. states:

> This case may be persuasive authority for the proposition that where a maintenance order has been obtained, or is pending, and the husband takes steps to place his assets in such a position as would give rise to the inference that he intends to dispose of them or dissipate them immediately, or he has made known his express intention to flee the jurisdiction with them . . . an injunction may be obtained to restrain him from so doing, or to freeze his assets in such a way as to make them unobtainable pending his explanation of his behaviour. It must be emphasised that this case was particularly strong on the facts in this regard. *Family Law – Mareva Injunctions*, 4 Dublin U. L. J. (n.s.) 114, at 119 (1982).

On the subject of *Mareva* injunctions generally, see further *Fleming* v. *Ranks (Ireland) Ltd.*, [1983] I.L.R.M. 541 (High Ct., McWilliam, J.). It is worth noting that McWilliam J. refers to Mr. Charleton's article at pp. 545–546.

It has for long been widely considered that imprisoning spouses for failure to comply with maintenance orders is generally counter-productive since it will further deplete the financial resources of the family: see, e.g. the 19th Interim Report of the Committee on Court Practice and Procedure, *Desertion and Maintenance*, p. 12 (Prl. 3666, 1974); *Shatter*, 300; Hayes, *Maintenance Defaulters – Are Poor Men Wrongfully Sent to Prison?* 13 Family L. 243, at 248 (1983); Quenstedt, *The Disrupted Family as a Public Responsibility*, 1 Family L.Q. No. 3, 24, at 25 (1967); cf. Blank & Rone, *Enforcement of Interspousal Obligations: A Proposal*, 2 Women's Rts L. Rev. No. 4, 13, at 18 (1975) (recommending weekend gaol terms). Other commentators suspect that 'the ultimate sanction of imprisonment might well have a salutory effect upon defaulting spouses': Payne & Downs, *Permanent Alimony*, 9 W. Ont. L. Rev. 2, at 52 (1970).

Empirical research in the United States supports the view that imprisonment may, in

certain circumstances, have some deterrent efficacy: see Chambers, *Men Who Know They Are Watched: Some Benefits and Costs of Jailing for Nonpayment of Support*, 75 Mich. L. Rev. 900 (1977); Baldous, *Fathers in Jail*, 78 Mich. L. Rev. 750 (1980). Whether, in spite of this deterrent function, imprisonment is the most appropriate – or even *an* appropriate – response is a matter for debate: cf. Chambers, *Child Support Collections in Michigan – A Study of the Effects of Tenacity and Terror*, ch. 10 of I. Baxter & M. Eberts eds., *The Child and the Courts* (1978).

Chapter 6

DIVORCE

Introduction

Before 1922 divorce by Private Act of Parliament was permitted: see Duncan, *Desertion and Cruelty in Irish Matrimonial Law*, 7 Ir. Jur. (n.s.) 213, at 213–221 (1972), where the subject is analysed in detail. The 1922 Constitution contained no explicit prohibition against divorce legislation, but as a result of the alteration of Standing Orders in the Oireachtas in 1925, it became effectively impossible to introduce divorce legislation by Private Act: see *Shatter*, 144–145.

The 1937 Constitution contains an explicit prohibition on the introduction of divorce legislation. Article 41.3.2° provided simply that:–

> No law shall be enacted providing for the grant of a dissolution of marriage.

The question of foreign divorce decrees is the subject of a specific provision in the Constitution. Article 41.3.3 provides that:–

> No person whose marriage has been dissolved under the civil law of any other State but is a subsisting valid marriage under the law for the time being in force within the jurisdiction of the Government and Parliament established by this Constitution shall be capable of contracting a valid marriage within that jurisdiction during the lifetime of the other party to the marriage so dissolved.

In this chapter we shall examine first the scope of Article 41.3.3., and then look briefly at some of the social and legal issues involved in the divorce question.

RECOGNITION OF FOREIGN DIVORCES

MAYO-PERROTT v. MAYO-PERROTT

[1958] I.R. 336 (Supreme Court, 1958, aff'g Murnaghan, J., 1955)

Murnaghan, J.:

It would appear to be an established rule of private international law that a valid foreign judgment *in personam* may be enforced by an action for the amount due under it if the judgment is *i*, for a debt or definite sum of money, and *ii*, final and conclusive. To this rule it is said that there is an exception, if the cause of action in respect of which the judgment was obtained, was of such a character that it would not have supported judicial proceedings in this country.

Prima facie the judgment upon which the present proceedings are based would come within the terms of the rule above stated, but it is argued on behalf of the defendant that the case falls within the said alleged exception.

By the joint effect of a decree by a Special Commissioner on the 13th July, 1953, of a certificate of making a decree *nisi* absolute dated the 5th October, 1953, and of an order for the payment of costs made on the 26th October, 1953, all made in a proceeding entitled 'In the High Court of Justice Probate Divorce and Admiralty Division (Divorce) Between Helen Joan Mayo-Perrott, Petitioner, and John Frederick Mayo-Perrott, Respondent,' the defendant was ordered to pay to the plaintiff the sum of £328 17s. 0d. the costs of the said proceedings. By the joint effect of two further orders dated respectively the 12th November, 1953, and the 14th January, 1954, had and made in the said proceeding the defendant was ordered to pay to the plaintiff the further sum of £50 4s. 0d. for costs. The said two sums are unpaid except as to the sum of £39 19s. 7d. for which sum the plaintiff must give credit to the defendant.

The said proceedings were instituted in the English Court by the plaintiff, seeking a divorce from the defendant, who was subject to, and who also submitted to, the jurisdiction of that Court. Similar proceedings could not have been maintained in this country.

. . . . The plaintiff's counsel relied on the provisions of Article 41.3.3°, in support of his argument that the public policy of this country gives at least sufficient recognition to decrees of dissolution of marriage by foreign courts as to take this case out of the scope of the said exception contended for on behalf of the defendant. This paragraph does not lend itself to easy interpretation, but for the purposes of this judgment it is sufficient for me to say that looking at the said sub article 3 as a whole I am of the opinion that the public policy of this country is clear in regard to divorce and is incompatible with the prevailing law in England in that regard.

A Court in Ireland can scarcely be expected to lend its active support to the enforcement of a law which it regards as repugnant to the Republic's own distinctive policy, and to this extent at least the said exception is in my opinion established.

It follows, therefore, that if the several orders for costs on which the present proceedings are based are part and parcel of the decree in the divorce proceeding and are not severable therefrom the plaintiff cannot succeed. The only authority cited to me in support of a submission that the said orders for costs were severable was *Raulin* v. *Fischer* [1911] 2 K. B. 93, but this case is, in my opinion, clearly distinguishable on the facts. I have, on consideration, come to the conclusion that the said orders for costs are not severable from the substantive order of divorce, and cannot be enforced by action in Ireland as creating a separate and independent cause of action *in personam.*

From this judgment the plaintiff appealed to the Supreme Court.

Maguire, C.J.:

At the outset it must be emphasised that the only question with which the Court is concerned is whether a judgment and decree of divorce *a vinculo matrimonii* in the High Court of Justice in England in so far as it awarded costs to the plaintiff may be enforced by an action in this country.

It is an established rule of private international law that a valid foreign judgment *in personam* may be enforced here if the judgment is (*i*), for a debt or definite sum of money; and (*ii*), final and conclusive, but not otherwise. To this rule there are exceptions, the first of which is:– An action cannot be maintained on a valid foreign judgment if the cause of action in respect of which the judgment was obtained was of such a character that it would not have supported an action in this country.

Article 41.3.2°, of the Constitution provides as follows:– 'No law may be enacted providing for the grant of a dissolution of marriage.'

In view of this provision it seems clear that the cause of action in respect of which this judgment was obtained would not have supported an action in this country. Accordingly if this provision stood alone this judgment would appear to be within the exception to the rule quoted and to be unenforceable here. The appellant, however, contends that Article 41.3.3°, qualifies the provision of Article 41.3.2°, in such a way that this judgment is not within the exception. [Maguire, C.J. quoted Article 41.3.3°. He continued:]

The sub-section is not easy to construe. The appellant contends that its effect is that a divorce *a vinculo matrimonii* which is valid according to the domicile of the parties would be recognised as valid by our Courts and that the marriage so dissolved would be no longer a subsisting valid marriage under our law within the meaning of the sub-section. Consequently, it is submitted that either of the parties to the divorce proceedings could validly re-marry within this jurisdiction. If this view be correct it follows – or so it is submitted – that the decree of divorce being valid here the judgment for costs may be enforced by an order of the High Court.

In view of the declared object of the Article to protect the institution of marriage and the explicit provision of sub-s. 2, already referred to, that no law providing for the grant of a dissolution of marriage may be enacted by our legislature this seems to be a somewhat startling conclusion. The argument in support of it is firstly that the Article is only a re-enactment of the law here before 1922, and secondly that sub-s. 3 of the Article is designed to achieve this result. The position before 1922 appears to have been that although the Courts in Ireland could not grant a divorce *a vinculo* a petitioner who had obtained a decree *a mensa et thoro* in Ireland might apply to the High Court of Parliament in England for an act annulling his marriage. A divorce *a vinculo* thus obtained would no doubt be valid here in Ireland. On the other hand, it would seem that a divorce *a vinculo* obtained in England would only be valid here if the parties were domiciled there. This question was left undecided in *Sinclair* v. *Sinclair* [1896] 1 I. R. 603. Such a divorce would of course be valid in England. No prosecution for bigamy could be maintained there against one of the parties who remarried during the lifetime of the other, nor would the children of the second marriage be regarded there as bastards. It may well have been, however, that it would be otherwise if the party who so remarried returned to Ireland. Earl Russell who obtained a divorce in America which was not recognised as valid in England was convicted of bigamy in England – *The Trial of Earl Russell* [1908] A. C. 446.

Article 41.3.3°, seems to me clearly to be designed to double-bar the door closed in sub-s. 2. Far from recognising the validity of a divorce obtained outside the country it seems to me expressly to deny to such a divorce any recognition for it prohibits the contracting of a valid marriage by a party who has obtained a divorce elsewhere. The sub-section says as plainly as it could be said that a valid marriage which is dissolved under the law of another State remains in the eyes of our law a subsisting valid marriage. It may be that the Constitution recognises that a decree of dissolution of marriage elsewhere may be valid in the country where it has been obtained, but to my mind as I have said it denies it any validity here. As already stated, it would seem sufficient to dispose of the appellant's case that sub-s. 2 prevents the cause of action in respect of which the decree sued upon was obtained from being made the basis of proceedings in this country. I have, however, considered the argument which has been so pressed that the Article as a whole merely intended to state the law as it was before 1922. I am not convinced that even if this were so it would assist the appellant.

In my opinion, however, the contention that sub-s. 3 of Article 41 qualifies the very clear earlier provisions of the Article in the way suggested is entirely unsustainable. The interpretation which the appellant seeks to place upon the sub-section is almost the exact opposite of what the Article to my mind plainly means.

I would dismiss this appeal.

Lavery, J.:

I agree with the judgment of Mr. Justice O'Daly.

Kingsmill Moore, J.:

Apart from the difficulties involved in the correct construction of Article 41.3 of our Constitution the law appears to be well settled. Until 1858 neither in England or Ireland could divorce *a vinculo* be granted by the ordinary Courts. It could, however, be granted by private Act of Parliament '. . . with a regularity in the procedure for obtaining it which, in the opinion of the best authorities, caused it to rank among legal remedies.' Westlake's

Private International Law, 6th ed., at p. 83. In *Shaw* v. *Gould* L. R. 3 H. L. 55, Lord Colonsay says at p. 91, 'The procedure, though Parliamentary, was substantially judicial – the allegations were investigated, and, if substantiated, the relief sought was granted as matter of right and justice. In short, Parliament was the tribunal for such cases, and was resorted to as matter of recognised procedure by those who sought relief on good grounds, and could afford to pay for it.' In 1858 by 20 and 21 Vict., c. 85, the procedure for divorce *a vinculo* was, in England, given to a regular divorce Court which could pronounce a final decree. The Act did not apply to Ireland, and the old procedure of petitioning for a private bill to the Imperial Parliament remained the only method available. When the Irish Free State was set up this method ceased to be available, and no standing orders were passed to enable similar bills to be presented to the Oireachtas. Finally by Article 41. 3. 2°, of our present Constitution it is provided expressly that 'No law shall be enacted providing for the grant of a dissolution of marriage.' Such a dissolution cannot now be obtained in our jurisdiction.

An entirely different question is the recognition which will be afforded by our Courts to the decrees of dissolution of marriage granted by foreign Courts to persons domiciled within the jurisdiction of those Courts. The law both of England and Ireland recognised, at least up to the adoption of our present Constitution, the validity of the change of status effected by such decrees. The law is stated by Lord Watson in *Le Mesurier* v. *Le Mesurier* [1895] A. C. 517 at p. 540. 'Their lordships have . . . come to the conclusion that, according to international law, the domicile for the time being of the married pair affords the only true test of jurisdiction to dissolve their marriage. They concur, without reservation, in the views expressed by Lord Penzance in *Wilson* v. *Wilson* L. R. 2 P. & D. 435 at p. 442, which were obviously meant to refer, not to questions arising in regard to the mutual rights of married persons, but to jurisdiction in the matter of divorce. "It is the strong inclination of my own opinion that the only fair and satisfactory rule to adopt on this matter of jurisdiction is to insist upon the parties in all cases referring their matrimonial differences to the Courts of the country in which they are domiciled. Different communities have different views and laws respecting matrimonial obligations, and a different estimate of the causes which should justify divorce. It is both just and reasonable, therefore, that the differences of married people should be adjusted in accordance with the laws of the community to which they belong, and dealt with by the tribunals which alone can administer those laws. An honest adherence to this principle, moreover, will preclude the scandal which arises when a man and woman are held to be man and wife in one country and strangers in another." ' The judgment of Lord Westbury in *Shaw* v. *Gould* L. R. 3 H. L. 55, at pp. 86–88, equally accepts this principle. Moreover, the Courts have accepted the validity of a divorce granted in the Court of the domicile of the parties even where the grounds for such divorce would not have been recognised as sufficient in the English Courts. *Harvey* v. *Farnie* 8 App. Cas. 43; *Pemberton* v. *Hughes* [1899] 1 Ch. 781. In *Bater* v. *Bater* [1906] P. 209, Sir Gorell Barnes said at p. 217, (This principle) 'is based upon the simple proposition that if this country recognises the right of a foreign tribunal to dissolve a marriage of two persons who were at the time domiciled in that foreign country, it must also recognise that their marriage may be dissolved according to the law of that foreign country, even though that law would dissolve a marriage for a lesser cause than would dissolve it in this country. Absurd results would follow if that were not so, because by the law of the domicile they would cease to be husband and wife, and yet if they returned to this country they would be husband and wife. That is not convenient, nor is it logic, and I think if they were *bona fide* and properly domiciled in the country where it takes place it is a good divorce.'

It is apparent from the judgment of Warren P. in the Irish case of *Sinclair* v. *Sinclair* [1896] 1 I. R. 603 that he accepted those principles. What he did question – and found unnecessary to decide – was the effect of a divorce judgment of a foreign Court where the parties were not domiciled in the jurisdiction of such Court. That such a judgment will not be recognised as affecting a valid divorce is now clear. *Green* v. *Green* [1893] P. 89: *The Trial of Earl Russell* [1904] A. C. 446. The subsequent proceedings in *Sinclair's Divorce Bill* [1897] A. C. 469 suggests that, if necessary, the House would have entertained the question of declaring the earlier decree of divorce made in the English Courts to be invalid, as the parties were not domiciled in the jurisdiction.

I can see no reason to suggest that there was in 1921 any difference between the law of England and of Ireland in the recognition which would be afforded to the change of status affected by a divorce decree of the Courts of a foreign country, where the parties to such divorce were at the date of the decree domiciled in the foreign country. From the view of jurisdiction England was a country foreign to Ireland. Politically and socially the two countries were closely interknit. Changes of domicile between the two countries were frequent, changes of residence even more frequent. A contrary view would lead to strange and perplexing results. If married persons domiciled in England were divorced and remarried the remarriages would be valid in England and the children of the remarriages legitimate; but if the remarried persons came to Ireland they would be subject to prosecution for bigamy and in Ireland their children would rank as illegitimate. Even more strange, if the original spouses deserted their spouses of the second marriage, came together again and had further children, those children would be legitimate in Ireland and illegitimate in England. There is certainly no support for such a view in any Irish decision, nor do I believe that in 1921 it would have occurred as correct to the mind of any Irish lawyer.

Has the law been altered by any provision of either the Constitution of the Irish Free State or our present Constitution? Article 73 of the Constitution of the Irish Free State ran as follows: 'Subject to this Constitution and to the extent to which they are not inconsistent therewith, the laws in force in the Irish Free State (Saorstát Éireann) at the date of the coming into operation of this Constitution shall continue to be of full force and effect until the same or any of them shall have been repealed or amended by enactment of the Oireachtas.' There is no provision of that Constitution which would make the pre-existing law as to the recognition of foreign divorces inconsistent with the Constitution, nor was such law repealed or amended by the Oireachtas of the Irish Free State. Article 50, 1, of our present Constitution runs: 'Subject to this Constitution and to the extent to which they are not inconsistent therewith, the laws in force in Saorstát Éireann immediately prior to the date of the coming into operation of this Constitution shall continue to be of full force and effect until the same or any of them shall have been repealed or amended by enactment of the Oireachtas.' It was contended that the Irish law in regard to the recognition of foreign divorces, as it existed in 1921 and up to the adoption of our present Constitution, is inconsistent with the provisions of Article 41, 3: that the effect of that Article is that our Courts no longer recognise the alteration of status effected by a decree of divorce of a foreign Court when the parties to the divorce suit were at the time of such suit domiciled in the foreign country; that they will not take any notice of such proceedings; and that as a corollary they will not entertain a suit for the costs of the divorce proceedings awarded by the foreign Court against one of the parties who is now resident in this country. This submission is based upon Article 41, 3, 3°. . . .

It is submitted that the effect of this Article is to refuse to recognise the validity of divorces *a vinculo* by a foreign Court in any circumstances, in as much as our law does not permit a dissolution of marriage and regards the marriage as valid and subsisting despite a decree purporting to dissolve it; and that the Article renders invalid any remarriage of persons so divorced, whenever such remarriage is contracted, so long as the first spouse is alive. First it must be noted that the prohibition is *not* applicable to all cases of dissolution of marriage, but only to cases where, under the law for the time being in force within our jurisdiction, the original marriage is regarded as valid and subsisting, or in other words where, by that law, the divorce is regarded as not being effectual to put an end to the original valid marriage. No doubt the Oireachtas could pass a law that no dissolution of marriage, wherever effected, even where the parties were domiciled in the country of the Court pronouncing the decree, was to be effective to annul the pre-existing valid marriage. If it did so, then, by the law for the time being in force, the first marriage would still be valid and subsisting within our jurisdiction. But the Oireachtas has not done so, and the law as existing when the Constitution was passed was that a divorce effected by a foreign Court of persons domiciled within its jurisdiction was regarded as valid in our jurisdiction. Such law was preserved unless inconsistent with the new Constitution and, in the absence of any statement in the Constitution altering such law, inconsistency cannot be spelled out from the words now being interpreted for they are perfectly consistent with the preservation of the pre-existing law which was the 'law for the time being in force.'

There were, indeed, divorces carried through under the law and by the Courts of a foreign state which were not regarded as effectual to put an end to the marriage. The most obvious instance was where the parties were not for the time being domiciled in the country whose Courts granted the divorce. *Keyes* v. *Keyes and Gray* [1921] P. 204 at p. 207.; *Green* v. *Green* [1893] P. 89; *Earl Russell's Case* 70 L. J. K. B. 998. But there may be other instances; *R.* v. *Hammersmith Superintendent Registrar of Marriages, Mir-Anwaruddin, Ex Parte* [1917] 1 K. B. 634; suggests that our law would not recognise as valid a dissolution effected in a foreign country by persons domiciled in such country, where by the law of that country, divorce could be brought about without recourse to the Courts; nor would it recognise as effective the dissolution of a marriage essentially monogamous by a form suitable only to the dissolution of a polygamous marriage. It is unnecessary to examine all possibilities. It is, however, legitimate to suggest that it is highly unlikely that the Constitution intended, without clear words, to reverse what is a practically universal rule of private international law, and to produce a state of affairs which was stigmatised by Lord Penzance and Lord Watson in the words already quoted, words which were also adopted by Warren P. in *Sinclair* v. *Sinclair* [1896] 1 I. R. 603. I cannot find anything in Article 41, 3, to suggest that the Courts (in the absence of further legislation) are entitled to do otherwise than regard as valid and effectual a divorce *a vinculo* granted by the Courts of a foreign country, where the parties at the time of the suit were domiciled in that country.

The remaining words of Article 41, 3, are not without difficulty. They apply only to persons whose divorce in a foreign country is not recognised as effectual by our Courts (e.g. where the divorced persons were not domiciled in that country), and where, therefore, the original marriage is considered to be still valid and subsisting. They say that a person whose marriage is thus considered by the law to be valid and subsisting 'shall not be capable of contracting a valid marriage within that jurisdiction (*i.e.* our jurisdiction) during the lifetime of the other party to the marriage so dissolved.' The words do not declare that such a person cannot *anywhere* contract 'a marriage valid within our jurisdiction,' but merely prohibit the contracting *within our jurisdiction* of a valid marriage. It is the contracting of the second marriage within the jurisdiction which is prohibited. There is nothing to make it invalid if contracted elsewhere.

The general policy of the Article seems to me clear. The Constitution does not favour dissolution of marriage. No laws can be enacted to provide for a grant of dissolution of marriage in this country. No person whose divorced status is not recognised by the law of this country for the time being can contract in this country a valid second marriage. But it does not purport to interfere with the present law that dissolutions of marriage by foreign Courts, where the parties are domiciled within the jurisdiction of those Courts, will be recognised as effective here. Nor does it in any way invalidate the remarriage of such persons. It avoids the anomalous, if not scandalous, state of affairs stigmatised in the passages which I have already cited whereby legitimacy and criminality could be decided by a flight over St. George's Channel.

But to hold that our law accepts the cardinal principle that questions as to married or unmarried status depends [*sic*] on the law of the domicile of the parties at the time when such status is created or dissolved is not to say that our law will give active assistance to facilitate in any way the effecting of a dissolution of marriage in another country where the parties are domiciled. It cannot be doubted that the public policy of this country as reflected in the Constitution does not favour divorce *a vinculo*, and though the law may recognise the change of status effected by it as an accomplished fact, it would fail to carry out public policy if, by a decree of its own Courts, it gave assistance to the process of divorce by entertaining a suit for the costs of such proceedings. The debt which it is sought to enforce is one created by proceedings of a nature which could not be instituted in this country, proceedings the institution of which our public policy disapproves. For these reasons I hold that the appeal fails and the suit cannot be entertained in our Courts.

O'Daly, J.:

. . . . The plaintiff's argument raises wide issues upon which, for the purpose of a decision in this case, it is unnecessary to offer any opinion. But assuming, in the plaintiff's favour, that our law, as it now stands, acknowledges the validity of the order of the English Courts and as a consequence recognises the plaintiff's status as a *femme sole* the problem of this case remains, viz., can the Court in view of the provision of Article 41. 3. 2°, of the Constitution give judgment for the costs of the English divorce proceedings?

Article 41. 3. 2°, interdicts the enactment of any law providing for the grant of a dissolution of marriage. Public policy on this subject could not be stated in a more categorical fashion. It follows that our Courts cannot in any circumstances grant dissolution of marriage.

What is being sued for here are the costs of a suit of a kind which these Courts could not entertain, and the plaintiff has not sought to show that there is in a case of this kind any principle of law upon which the costs can be severed from the substantive part of the judgment.

Cheshire, in his Private International Law, 5th ed. at p. 151, observes that the conception of public policy is, or should be, narrower and more limited in private international law than in internal law. A transaction that is valid by its *lex causae*, he says, should not be nullified on this ground unless its enforcement would offend some moral, social or economic principle so sacrosanct in English eyes as to require its maintenance at all costs and without exception.

Enforcement by our Courts of the costs of a decree of divorce would clearly offend against a moral principle which the Constitution asserts. The terms of sub-s. 2° are reinforced by the pledge which in sub-s. 1° the State gives to guard with special care the institution of marriage and to protect it against attack. If there is ever to be a case in which on grounds of repugnancy to public policy the Courts will decline to enforce a foreign judgment this is, it seems to me one.

The Courts will not aid divorce or, rather, the Courts, under the Constitution, may not aid it.

In my opinion the learned trial Judge was therefore right in dismissing the plaintiff's claim.

Maguire, J.:

. . . . The *Divorce and Matrimonial Causes Act, 185*[*7*], and the amending Acts never applied to Ireland. There never was at any time jurisdiction in the Civil Courts in Ireland to grant a divorce from the bonds of matrimony or to order payment of costs in such an action. There was no such cause of action. No such order or judgment has ever been made in the Courts of Ireland. The only way a dissolution of marriage could be obtained was by legislation *ad hoc*, by promoting a private Bill, in other words by an Act of Parliament of the United Kingdom. This procedure appears to have fallen into disuse between 1922 and 1937. No rules for this purpose were provided by the Oireachtas set up under the Constitution of 1922. During this period no legislation of this kind was enacted. Since 1937 it is no longer possible. [Maguire, J. quoted Article 41.3 of the Constitution. He continued:] This provision must be read and construed in conjunction with the other provisions of Article 41.

Article 41. 3. 2°, clearly provides that henceforth no law shall be enacted providing for the grant of a dissolution of marriage. This makes it now impossible to provide for divorce by Act of Parliament.

Clause 3° of sub-article 3 is relied upon. It seems to me that there are no facts in this case which call for the application of this sub-Article and that it is not relevant. The argument founded on it is of no assistance in solving the problem raised by this case.

The problem really is, can a person who cannot obtain a dissolution of marriage here, pursue by legal proceedings up to judgment and execution a person whom he or she has divorced in another country for the costs of the divorce proceedings abroad. It is clearly repugnant to the laws of Ireland that the decree of dissolution as a whole could be implemented by a judgment of the Courts of this country founded on a judgment of a foreign court. This seems to me so clear that it needs only to be stated. It is incapable of argument. It has not been sought to argue this. Can this judgment of the English Courts be split up and disintegrated so as to enable the plaintiff here to maintain an action founded on that part of the judgment which provides only for payment of costs ignoring the major part of such judgment. That is what it is sought to do in this case. In my opinion the Court which has before it an action founded on a foreign judgment must look at that judgment as a whole. If on doing so the Court finds that the gist of that judgment is for something that cannot be enforced here, and is not justiciable here, even though it is not sought to enforce it, then it is the duty of the Court so to determine, and to refuse to entertain a claim for relief which is merely ancillary and insignificant in itself when contrasted with the terms of the judgment as a whole. The terms of this judgment are not severable. To hold otherwise would be to invite and give effect to a serious intrusion, indeed a loophole, on the age-old divorce laws of this country. To implement that part of this English judgment for divorce which deals with costs is repugnant to the Constitution and to the laws of Ireland, and the public policy reflected in those laws over a long period of Irish history.

I would dismiss this appeal.

Notes

1. For academic analysis of the decision, see *Shatter*, 152–154, Webb, *Case Note*, 8 Int. & Comp. L. Q. 744 (1959); Davitt, *Some Aspects of the Constitution and the Law in Relation to Marriage*, 57 Studies 6 (1968); Grogan, *Comments on the Foregoing Article I*, 57 Studies 20 (1968); Clarke, *Comments on the Foregoing Article II*, 57 Studies 24 (1968); Jones, *The Non-Recognition of Foreign Divorces in Ireland*, 3 Ir. Jur. (n.s.) 299 (1968); J. Kelly, *Fundamental Rights in the Irish Law and Constitution*, 203, (2nd ed., 1967); Duncan, *The Future of Divorce Recognition in Ireland*, 2 Dublin U. L. Rev. (No. 1) 2 (1971); Lee, *Irish Matrimonial Laws and the Marital Status*, 16 N.I.L.Q. 387 (1965) (reprinted in 103 I.L.T. & Sol J. 151 (1969)); P. North, *The Private International Law of Matrimonial Causes in the British Isles and the Republic of Ireland*, 376–378 (1977); Kerr, *The Need for a Recognition of Divorces Act*, (1976) 1 Dublin U.L.J.11.
2. In the English decision of *Breen* v. *Breen*, [1964] P. 144 (1961), Karminski J. favoured Kingsmill Moore, J.'s interpretation of Article 41.3.3. For critical analysis of *Breen* v. *Breen*, see Unger, *Note: Capacity of Marry and the Lex Loci Celebrationis* 24 Modern L. Rev. 784 (1961). See also Kerr, *op. cit.*, at 14.
3. Which approach (if any) in *Mayo-Perrott* do you favour? Why? Do you agree with Kahn-Freund's contention

([1974] III Hague Receuil 139, at 231–232) that '[t]he Constitution elevates to the level of a constitutional norm the previously accepted rules on the recognition of foreign divorce'? Is this view consistent with later developments?

RE: CAFFIN DECEASED: BANK OF IRELAND v. CAFFIN
[1971] I.R. 123 (High Ct., Kenny, J.)

Proceedings were taken to determine which of two women was entitled to elect to take a legal right, as surviving spouse, of half the estate of a deceased testator, Haden Crawford Caffin. Mr. Caffin, who had been born in England married his first wife, Yvonne in England in 1928. The couple were domiciled in England at the time of the marriage. They were divorced in England in 1956. At that time both were also domiciled there. In the same year Mr. Caffin married his second wife, Kathleen, in Dublin. At the time of the marriage, Mrs. Kathleen Caffin was domiciled and resident in Ireland, while Mr Caffin was domiciled and resident in England. Thereafter, until Mr. Caffin's death in 1970, they lived in Ireland.

Kenny, J.:

. . . . As the marriage of Mr. Caffin and Mrs. Kathleen took place in Dublin, it would have been invalid if on the 10th July, 1956, Mr. Caffin's marriage to Mrs. Yvonne was a subsisting valid marriage under the law for the time being in force in the Republic of Ireland.

The history of the law relating to divorce *a vinculo* in Ireland, which is the background to parts of the Article, explains the prohibition on the grant of a dissolution of marriage. The Courts in Ireland never had jurisdiction to grant a divorce *a vinculo* and, until the year 1921, a husband or wife who was domiciled in Ireland and who had grounds for a divorce had to apply to the Imperial Parliament for an Act dissolving the marriage. . . . A passage in the speech of Lord Westbury in *Shaw* v. *Gould* (1868) L.R. 3 H.L. 55 is an accurate statement of the position in Ireland where, however, no legislation similar to the *Matrimonial Causes Act, 1857*, was ever in force. That passage, which appears at p. 84 of the report, is as follows:– 'In England, since the Reformation, marriage, being no longer a sacrament, has always, in theory of law, been dissoluble for adultery in the wife, and for incestuous adultery and other crimes by the husband; but until the recent Divorce Act [*the Matrimonial Causes Act*, 1857] this law was administered by Parliament alone, and, although the decision of Parliament was in the form of an Act of *privilegium*, and not of a judicial decree, yet the Act was granted upon evidence providing that the case came within the scope of certain established rules. This proceeding was in spirit a judicial, though in form a legislative act. The justice of divorce was recognised, but no forensic tribunal was entrusted with the power of applying the remedy. But the law and practice of Parliament was well known; and, in fact, this House acted as a Court of justice.' The practice of Parliament will be found described in *Sinclair's Divorce Bill* which was the hearing by the House of Lords of a bill presented after proceedings in the courts of Ireland: see *Sinclair* v. *Sinclair* [1906] 1 I. R. 603.

In 1921 the courts in Ireland and in England recognised the validity of a decree of divorce *a vinculo* made by the courts of the country where the husband and wife were domiciled. In the course of the speech of Lord Westbury, to which I have referred, he said at p. 85 of the report:– 'It cannot, therefore, be correctly said, that divorce *a vinculo matrimonii* was contrary to the principles and institutions of this country. It follows that the validity of a foreign decree of divorce must be ascertained in the same manner and on the same rules by which the conclusive effect of other foreign judgments have to be determined. The position that the tribunal of a foreign country having jurisdiction to dissolve the marriages of its own subjects, is competent to pronounce a similar decree between English subjects who were married in England, but who before and at the time of the suit are permanently domiciled within the jurisdiction of such foreign tribunal, such decree being made in a *bona fide* suit without collusion or concert, is a position consistent with all the English decisions . . .'.

Lord Watson expressed the same view, when giving the advice of the Privy Council in *Le Mesurier* v. *Le Mesurier* [1903] A. C. 517, in the following terms:– 'When the jurisdiction of the Court is exercised according to the rules of international law, as in the case where the parties have their domicil within its forum, its decree dissolving their marriage ought to be respected by the tribunals of every civilised country. . . . On the other hand, a decree of divorce a vinculo, pronounced by a Court whose jurisdiction is solely derived from some rule of municipal law peculiar to its forum, cannot, when it trenches upon the interests of any other country to whose tribunals the spouses were amenable, claim extra-territorial authority.'

The Oireachtas established by the Constitution of 1922 had power to pass legislation dissolving a marriage and to give jurisdiction to the courts to grant divorces *a vinculo.* Article 78 of that Constitution provided that, subject to it and to the extent to which they were not inconsistent therewith, the laws in force in the Irish Free State at the date of the coming into operation of the Constitution should continue to be of full force and effect until they were repealed or amended by enactment of the Oireachtas; and so the law giving recognition to decrees of divorce *a vinculo*, where the decrees were made by the courts of the country in which the husband and wife were domiciled, remained in force because there was nothing in the Constitution of 1922 which altered this.

This historical background explains the purpose of Article 41, s. 3, sub-s. 2, which was to deprive the National Parliament of its power to pass legislation dissolving a marriage or to give jurisdiction to the courts to grant a divorce. The recognition of orders of divorce made by the courts of another country where the husband and wife had their domicile has no logical connection with the power of the Oireachtas to dissolve a marriage; and the restrictions imposed on it by the Constitution do not involve a general principle that the Courts should not, or cannot, recognise orders for the dissolution of a marriage made by the courts of another country when the parties to the marriage were domiciled in that country at the time of the court proceedings. This gets support from the words 'under the law for the time being in force within the jurisdiction of the Government and Parliament established by this Constitution' for they give the National Parliament jurisdiction to decide by legislation that some decrees of dissolution made by the courts of other States are to be recognised by our courts. This was the interpretation adopted by Kingsmill Moore J., and by Ó Dálaigh J. (as he then was) with whose judgment Lavery J. agreed, in *Mayo-Perrott* v. *Mayo-Perrott.* [1958] I.R. 336. It is destructive of the view that the Article prohibits the recognition of any order for divorce *a vinculo* made by the courts of another country, and of the reasoning of Maguire C.J. in that case.

The National Parliament has not legislated on the matter and so the law for the time being in force under Article 78 of the Constitution of 1922 and Article 50 of the Constitution of 1937 is that the Courts recognise a dissolution of marriage granted by the courts of the country where the parties were domiciled. I agree with the view of Kingsmill Moore J. which he expressed as follows in the *Mayo-Perrott Case* [1958] I.R. 336 at p. 348 of the report:– 'No doubt the Oireachtas could pass a law that no dissolution of marriage, wherever effected, even where the parties were domiciled in the country of the Court pronouncing the decree, was to be effective to annul the pre-existing valid marriage. If it did so, then by the law for the time being in force, the first marriage would still be valid and subsisting within our jurisdiction. But the Oireachtas has not done so, and the law as existing when the Constitution was passed was that a divorce effected by a foreign Court of persons domiciled within its jurisdiction was regarded as valid in our jurisdiction. Such law was preserved unless inconsistent with the new Constitution and, in the absence of any statement in the Constitution altering such law, inconsistency cannot be spelled out from the words now being interpreted for they are perfectly consistent with the preservation of the pre-existing law which was the "law for the time being in force."'

I do not accept the view of Maguire C.J., expressed at p. 344 of the report of that case, that Article 41, s. 3, sub-s. 3, was designed to 'double-bar the door closed in sub-s. 2'. The two sub-sections are dealing with different branches of the law and I do not agree with him that 'the sub-section says as plainly as it could be said that a valid marriage which is dissolved under the law of another State remains in the eyes of our law a subsisting valid marriage' – because the sub-section does not say this. If this was the meaning which it was intended to express, the sub-section would have read:– 'No person whose marriage has been dissolved under the civil law of any other State shall be capable of contracting a valid marriage within the jurisdiction of the Government and Parliament established by this Constitution during the lifetime of the other party to the marriage so dissolved.' What Maguire C.J. said ignores altogether the significance of the words 'under the law for the time being in force within the jurisdiction of the Government and Parliament established by this Constitution.'

I have considered the issue whether the Court should refuse to recognise the English divorce because it was given on the ground of desertion, which does not seem to have been a ground on which divorce *a vinculo* could have been granted to those domiciled in Ireland by the Imperial Parliament before 1921. As Mr. Caffin and Mrs. Yvonne were domiciled in England, the grounds upon which divorce *a vinculo* could be granted are to be determined by English law and not by reference to the law in Ireland in 1921.

This judgment is not a decision on the difficult questions (*a*) whether a divorce granted by the courts in Northern Ireland to a person domiciled there will be recognised by our law and (*b*) whether a divorce granted to a person who was resident, but not domiciled, in another State has any effect in the Republic of Ireland.

[Kenny, J. held accordingly that Mrs. Kathleen Caffin was the spouse of the deceased for the purposes of Part IX of the *Succession Act, 1965* and that she was entitled to a share by way of legal right under section III of the Act.]

Notes

1. For academic analysis of this decision, see O'Reilly, *Recognition of Foreign Divorce Decrees*, 6 Ir. Jur. (n.s.) 293 (1971); Duncan, *Desertion and Cruelty in Irish Matrimonial Law*, 7 Ir. Jur. (n.s.) 213, at 232–235 (1972). Mr. Duncan comments (at 234–235):–

   > The position now seems to be that Irish public policy is set against a foreign divorce decree where the question is one of helping to enforce it; but the same public policy is not against lending recognition to changes in status effected by the same decree. Thus, at present, it appears to be quite in accord with Irish public policy to recognise an English decree for the purpose of excluding the wife from her rights under the Succession Act (*Re Caffin Deceased*); but it is wholly repugnant to Irish public policy to allow the same wife to recover from her errant husband in Ireland the costs of her English divorce action (*Mayo-Perrott*). This is the kind of anomaly that is bound to follow if, in the conflict of laws, cases of enforcement are subjected to a more rigorous public policy test than cases of recognition.

2. Why, in your view, does Kenny J. regard as 'difficult' the question whether a divorce granted by the courts of Northern Ireland to a person domiciled there will be recognised by our law? Have Articles 2 and 3 of the Constitution any relevance?
3. Similarly, why do you think Kenny J. raises the possibility of recognition being afforded to divorces on the basis of residence rather than domicile? Cf. Kerr, *The Need for a Recognition of Divorce Act*, (1976) 1 Dublin U. L. J. 11.

C. v. C.

Unreported, High Court, Kenny, J., 27 July 1973 (1973–144Sp.)

Kenny, J.:
[The parties] were married [in] 1954 in Dublin. Both of them were citizens of Ireland and the husband was and has at all times since the marriage been domiciled in the Republic of Ireland. . . .

[Kenny, J., recounted the history of the marriage from 1954 to 1968: the spouses had during this time spent periods living apart. Kenny, J. continued:]

In 1968 the wife went to England to get employment and resided there. In October 1971 she brought proceedings in the High Court in England for a divorce *a vinculo* and obtained an Order that the marriage between the husband and her was dissolved unless he showed cause within a certain period. No cause was shown and the Order dissolving the marriage was made absolute in January 1972. The petition seeking the divorce contained a statement that the husband and wife were domiciled in England or alternatively that the husband was not domiciled in the United Kingdom or in the Channel Islands or in the Isle of Man and that the wife had been ordinarily resident in England for three years immediately preceding the presentation of the petition. The statements in the petition were verified by an affidavit made by the wife.

The wife has now brought these proceedings for maintenance under the *Married Women (Maintenance in case of Desertion) Act, 1886* ('the Act of 1886'). The wife swore an affidavit in these proceedings and has given oral evidence and, at the end of her case, the husband's counsel submitted on a number of grounds that no case against his client had been established. He said that the husband had not deserted his wife because she had told him to leave and he asked for a dismissal of the proceedings.

The first matter which arises for decision relates to the effect of the divorce obtained by the wife in England. The domicile of a wife is that of her husband until their marriage is validly terminated by a divorce *a vinculo* and as the husband was at all times domiciled in the Republic of Ireland, the Courts in this country do not recognise the divorce in England as having the effect of dissolving the marriage. While a divorce given by the Courts of the country in which the husband and wife are domiciled will be recognised (*Re Caffin Deceased: Bank of Ireland* v. *Caffin* [1971] I.R. 123) a divorce granted to a wife who was resident in England against a husband who is domiciled in the Republic of Ireland does not have the effect, so far as the Courts in Ireland are concerned, of dissolving the marriage. I know that the Courts in England now have jurisdiction under legislation to grant divorces to wives who have been resident for three years in England but this jurisdiction did not exist in 1921 and the doctrine of the comity of Courts does not require that the Courts in the Republic of Ireland should recognise this divorce. No legislation has been passed by the National Parliament giving recognition to divorces granted to a wife resident in England who is domiciled in the Republic of Ireland and, in my opinion, the husband and wife are under our law, married.

Counsel for the husband said that the divorce was evidence that the wife had repudiated the marriage bond. If this meant that she was prevented from asserting in the Courts in Ireland that she was the wife of the husband, I do not accept the argument. For the reasons which I gave in *Gaffney* v. *Gaffney* [subsequently appealed to the Supreme Court, and reported, [1975] I.R. 133–ed.] there can be no estoppel between husband and wife as to the existence of a valid marriage between them. The wife's application to the High Court in England for a divorce *a vinculo* does not prevent her claiming to be the husband's wife in the Republic of Ireland. . . .

Note

If the Oireachtas were to enact legislation giving recognition to divorces granted to a wife resident in England but domiciled in the Republic of Ireland, would Kenny, J. recognise it, on the basis of *C.* v. *C.*? Would such legislation be constitutional? Would legislation giving recognition to foreign divorces on the basis of one week's residence be constitutional, on the basis of this decision? Does anything hinge on the fact that the wife, rather than the husband, was petitioner? Cf. Duncan, *Foreign Divorces Obtained on the Basis of Residence, and the Doctrine of Estoppel*, 9 Ir, Jur. (n.s.) 59, at 65 (1975).

GAFFNEY v. GAFFNEY

[1975] I.R. 133 (Supreme Court, 1975, aff'g. Kenny, J., 1973)

Walsh, J.:

The plaintiff married the late Henry Gaffney in Dublin in December, 1940; at the date of the marriage they were both resident and domiciled in the State and they had been resident and domiciled within the State since the dates of their respective births. The husband died in a swimming accident in Spain on the 1st April, 1972, intestate. On the 10th April, 1959, the husband had gone through a form of marriage with the defendant, then Lydia Klemm, in the register office in Blackburn, Lancashire, in England; each of the parties gave their place of residence as No. 22 Derby Street, Blackburn. After the marriage the husband and the defendant came to Dublin where they resided as man and wife. On the 21st July, 1958, the High Court of Justice (Probate, Divorce and Admiralty Division), Manchester District Registry, made an order purporting to dissolve the marriage between the husband and the plaintiff on the grounds of desertion of the plaintiff by the husband without cause for a period of three years immediately preceding the presentation of the petition, unless cause was shown to the said court within six weeks why the decree should not be made absolute. An order absolute was subsequently made on the 7th January, 1959.

The divorce proceedings had been instituted by a petition in the name of the plaintiff as petitioner and annexed to it was a statement, sworn by the petitioner and signed by her, to the effect that the statements contained in the petition were true. Paragraph 4 of the petition stated that the husband then resided at No. 22 Edward Street, Blackburn, and paragraph 5 stated that both the husband and the plaintiff were domiciled in England. The petition also stated that the husband deserted the plaintiff without cause for a period of at least three years immediately preceding the presentation of the petition, and that such desertion had begun by the husband leaving the matrimonial home in Blackrock in the County of Dublin one day in December, 1953, after which he did not return to cohabit with the plaintiff. The petition also claimed that it was not presented or prosecuted in collusion with the husband, who was named as the respondent therein, and prayed that the marriage of the husband and the plaintiff be dissolved.

After the death of the husband the defendant entered a caveat in the Probate Office. As a consequence of this the plaintiff issued the present proceedings on the 9th February, 1973, claiming a declaration that she was the lawful widow of the husband and a declaration that within the meaning of s. 120 of the *Succession Act, 1965*, the husband was guilty of desertion of the plaintiff which continued up to the date of his death. The plaintiff also sought a declaration that the husband was a spouse who was guilty of conduct which justified the plaintiff in living separate and apart from him, and a declaration that the purported divorce granted in England did not in law validly dissolve the marriage of the husband with the plaintiff and was of no effect. An order was also sought declaring the plaintiff to be entitled to obtain a grant of letters of administration to the estate of the husband, and that the caveat entered by the defendant be set aside.

The matter came for hearing before Mr. Justice Kenny on the 21st June, 1973. Having given judgment in the matter, the learned judge made an order declaring that the plaintiff was the lawful widow of the husband, that the purported divorce did not validly dissolve the marriage of the plaintiff and the husband, that the plaintiff was entitled to apply for a grant of letters of administration to the estate of the husband, and directing that the caveat entered by the defendant should be set aside. In the course of the hearing the learned judge had heard evidence from both the plaintiff and the defendant, and also from four other witnesses. The evidence which the learned trial judge heard dealt, among other matters, with the circumstances which led up to the presentation of the petition for divorce in England, and the part which both the plaintiff and the husband played in that. Stated briefly, the evidence presented on behalf of the plaintiff was to the effect that, while the petition was in her name, she was coerced into presenting it and signing it; and that she did not wish to obtain a divorce and that the coercion which caused her to sign the petition was exercised by her husband who did want a divorce, and that the husband was at all material times up to the date of his death resident and domiciled within this State. Therefore, the jurisdiction of the English Court to grant the divorce was put in question.

The defendant appealed against the order of Mr. Justice Kenny upon the grounds that he was wrong in holding that the divorce did not validly dissolve the marriage in question, that he was wrong in law in holding that the plaintiff was entitled to apply for a grant of letters of administration, and that he was wrong in ordering that the caveat entered by the defendant should be set aside. The real point of the defendant's appeal, which does not appear in so many words in the notice of appeal, is that the evidence tendered by and on behalf of the plaintiff in support of the allegation that the divorce was improperly obtained, and in support of the claim that the plaintiff and the husband were not at any time domiciled in England, should not have been received by the judge on the grounds that the plaintiff was estopped from giving such evidence. The basis of the claim of the estoppel was that, as she was the petitioner in the divorce proceedings and on the face of it had invoked the jurisdiction of the English court, the plaintiff should not now be heard to say that the English court did not have jurisdiction; it was further submitted that, having obtained a dissolution of the marriage on foot of the said petition, the plaintiff should not now be heard to say that the purported dissolution was invalid for want of jurisdiction in the court which granted it.

The net question to be decided in the case is whether the marriage between the plaintiff and the husband was a valid subsisting marriage in Irish law at the date of the death of the husband. Nothing in the case has been raised to throw any doubt upon the validity of the marriage, so it comes down to a question of whether it was still subsisting at the date of the death of the husband. If it was a subsisting marriage, then the plaintiff is clearly entitled to the declarations sought in the present case.

Judicial dissolution of marriage was not available in any part of Ireland until 1939. In that year the courts of Northern Ireland were given power by statute to dissolve marriages. In this State no such judicial process is available. Notwithstanding the absence of this particular jurisdiction in Irish courts, it was a principle of the system of private international law recognised by the Irish courts that they would recognise decrees of dissolution of marriage granted by the courts of another country where the parties were domiciled at the time. Domicile was recognised and accepted as the foundation of the jurisdiction to dissolve marriage. In *In re Lyons* (1937) 72 I.L.T.R. 87 the Court of Appeal in Northern Ireland refused to recognise a decree of divorce granted in the United States because, at the time of the commencement of those proceedings which led to the dissolution of marriage, the parties were not domiciled within the jurisdiction of the court which pronounced the decree. In the course of his judgment in *Mayo-Perrott* v. *Mayo-Perrott* [1958] I.R. 336, Kingsmill Moore J. stated the Irish law to have been that the recognition of foreign divorces in Irish courts depended upon establishing that the domicile of the parties was within the jurisdiction of the court pronouncing the decree. Recognition and application of this principle of private international law was part of the common law in Ireland and, like Kingsmill Moore J. in the *Mayo-Perrott Case* [1958] I.R. 336 and Mr. Justice Kenny in this case, I am satisfied that it is still part of our law. It follows, therefore, that the Courts here do not recognise decrees of dissolution of marriage pronounced by foreign courts unless the parties were domiciled within the jurisdiction of the foreign court in question. In so far as the Courts of this country are concerned, the marriage remains as valid and as subsisting in this country as it would have been but for the intervention of the purported decree of dissolution.

It is correct, however, to draw attention to the provisions of Article 41, s. 3, sub-s. 3, of the Constitution which, as Ó Dálaigh J. pointed out in his judgment in the *Mayo-Perrott Case* [1958] I.R. 336, appear to empower the Oireachtas to define from time to time that marriages dissolved by foreign civil tribunals are to be regarded as valid subsisting marriages under the law of this country. That appears to mean that the Oirachtas would have power by legislation to define what foreign judicial decrees of dissolution of marriage shall or shall not be recognised in our Courts as legally changing the status of the parties.

Contrary to what appears to have been the view of Kingsmill Moore J., I do not think that Article 50 of the Constitution refers to any law other than statute law, and in my view the text of Article 50 makes that clear. The reference is not to 'law' or to 'the law' but to 'the laws' in a context which deals with repeal or amendment by enactment of the Oirachtas. It will be noted that Article 40 of the Constitution in s. 4, sub-s. 1, uses the phrase 'in accordance with law,' and sub-s. 2 of that section speaks of somebody being detained 'in accordance with the law.' Our law contains a great deal more than statute law; many of the doctrines by judges and in due course came to be modified, if not entirely abandoned, by judges. Neither Article 73 of the Constitution of Saorstát Éireann nor Article 50 of the present Constitution could be construed as freezing our common law, or other non-statutory law, in the condition in which it was found at the coming into force of the Constitution of 1922 so that it could never be departed from save by enactment of the Oireachtas. The common law exists independently of statute law save to the extent to which it is modified by statute, subject always to the qualification that common-law practices or doctrines cannot qualify or dilute the provisions of the Constitution: see *The State (Browne)* v. *Feran* [1967] I.R. 147.

It is not suggested in the present case that the approach of our Courts to decrees of dissolution of marriage made by foreign courts is in any way inconsistent with, repugnant to, or incompatible with the provisions of the Constitution. In fact, counsel for the defendant submitted in this Court that, if at the time a petition for dissolution of marriage was presented in the High Court in England the parties were not domiciled in England, the decree purporting to dissolve the marriage could not be recognised in the Courts here.

There is no dispute about the fact that the husband's domicile of origin was Irish, and it is well settled that such domicile persists until it is shown to have been abandoned and that another domicile has been acquired. It must be proved to have been intentionally and voluntarily abandoned and supplanted by another: see *In re Joyce, Corbet* v. *Fagan* [1946] I.R. 277 where the dictum of Black J. to that effect was assented to by Sullivan C.J. and by Murnaghan J., and see the decisions of Mr. Justice Budd in *In re Sillar, Hurley* v. *Wimbush* [1956] I.R. 344 and *In re Adams* [1967] I.R. 424. So far as the plaintiff was concerned, it was not suggested that her domicile during the subsistence of her marriage was different from that of her husband. The law has been that during the subsistence of a marriage the wife's domicile remains the same as, and changes with, that of her husband. For the purpose of this case it is proper to adopt this view, although it is possible that some day it may be challenged on constitutional grounds in a case where the wife has never physically left her domicile of origin while her deserting husband may have established a domicile in another jurisdiction.

As the plaintiff set out in this case to establish that the husband's domicile had never changed, she has undertaken that burden of proof. By reason of the fact that she was the petitioner and that she swore in the petition that her husband's domicile was in England, it is claimed by the defendant that the plaintiff is now estopped from setting up the contrary.

The paramount issue in the present case is the status of the plaintiff and her husband at the date of his death. The plaintiff was either his wife or she was not. Apart from other legal incidents in this country, certain constitutional rights may accrue to a woman by virtue of being a wife which would not be available to her if she were not. The matter cannot, therefore, by any rules of evidence be left in a position of doubt nor could the Courts countenance a doctrine of estoppel, if such existed, which had the effect that a person would be estopped from saying that he or she is the husband or wife, as the case may be, of another party when in law the person making the claim has that status. In law it would have been quite open to the husband to have denied at any time after his marriage to the defendant that he was in law her husband. If during the currency of that marriage the plaintiff had claimed that she was his wife, she might have been met with the answer which is being offered on behalf of the defendant in this case – that the plaintiff was estopped from doing so because she had submitted to a jurisdiction which purported to change that status. Consent cannot confer jurisdiction to dissolve a marriage where that jurisdiction does not already exist. The evidence which the plaintiff sought to offer in the present case was directed towards showing that the court in question did not have jurisdiction. In my view, the learned trial judge was quite correct in admitting that evidence.

In brief, the evidence which the judge admitted and accepted in the present case established a number of facts. The plaintiff's husband after he had left her (which was before the date of the purported divorce) set up residence in another part of Dublin and never resided in England. He went to England on occasional visits when he stayed with his mother who did live in Blackburn in a house which he had bought for her. The husband had said to the plaintiff on a number of occasions that he wanted to get a divorce, but she had not consented to this. Notwithstanding that, in 1957 he instructed a firm of solicitors in Manchester to prepare a petition by the plaintiff seeking dissolution of the marriage without any instructions given by her to the solicitors that they were to act for her or to apply for dissolution of the marriage in her name. A petition was prepared (with the plaintiff's named as petitioner) containing statements as to the husband's residence and domicile which the husband knew to be false. The petition, which was received by the husband from her solicitors in Manchester, was brought by him to the plaintiff at her residence in Dublin where he threatened her with physical violence if she did not swear the necessary verifying affidavit. She was then in a poor state of health and was unable to resist the threats and duress of her husband; in consequence of that she signed the document and swore the necessary affidavit. She went to England in 1958 to give evidence in proceedings which were apparently remarkable for their brevity. Prior to appearing in the court, she and her husband were coached by someone as to how to give their evidence; the gist of the advice apparently being to answer 'yes' or 'no' to every question the judge asked. The person who gave this instruction was apparently the solicitor acting in the case. On the morning of the hearing both the plaintiff and her husband and their eldest daugher left Dublin by air for Manchester.

It is quite clear from the evidence that the husband never had an English domicile and was not in fact resident in England. There is little doubt that, if the true facts had been made known to the court in England, no decree for dissolution of marriage would have been pronounced; it is very probable that even now, if the true facts were made known to the appropriate authority in England, the decree of dissolution of marriage would be set aside. That, however, does not affect the jurisdiction of the Courts here to deal with the situation. The Court here is charged with the task of determining the status of the plaintiff at the date of the death of the husband and it is beyond doubt that she was the wife of the husband, Henry Gaffney, at the date of his death. Therefore, even if there was only the question of jurisdiction of the English court involved, the dissolution of marriage which is pronounced could not be recognised in this country because of the want of jurisdiction in that court.

It is unnecessary to deal with what would be the position if there had been jurisdiction and the facts as to coercion and duress found by the judge had to be considered in that context. It might well be that in such a situation it would be incumbent upon the plaintiff to have the decree of dissolution, made by the court having jurisdiction, set aside before she could successfully assert the status of wife.

For the reasons given, I am of opinion that the purported dissolution of marriage is of no effect in Irish law as it was made without jurisdiction and that, in consequence, the plaintiff is the person entitled to claim as wife under the provisions of the *Succession Act, 1965.* I would uphold the order made by the trial judge and dismiss this appeal.

Henchy, J.:

Counsel for the defendant limits his argument in support of this appeal to one point: he contends that the evidence heard *de bene esse* at the trial as to the circumstances of the divorce was inadmissible. He concedes, in as many words, that, if that evidence was admissible, this appeal would be unsustainable for there would then be uncontroverted evidence to support the judge's finding that, as neither the husband nor the wife was resident or domiciled in England, the English court had no jurisdiction to make the divorce decree and that, accordingly, it should not be recognised here.

The argument against the reception of the evidence is that the wife, being the moving party as the petitioner for the divorce, is estopped by the record from impunging the correctness of what she put on record in getting the divorce decree; in other words she is estopped from denying that she and the husband were domiciled in England. This was a falsehood that misled the English court into assuming a divorce jurisdiction which the absence of residence or domicile of the parties withheld from it. Estoppel, it is said, arises because the divorce decree was a judgment *in rem* which determined in a final manner the status of the parties; and the parties to that decree should not be heard to attempt to repudiate the change of marital status necessarily and substantively brought about by the decree.

The flaw in this argument is that the divorce decree could be a judgment *in rem*, carrying with it the rule of estoppel by record, only if it had been given within jurisdiction: see Halsbury's Laws of England (3rd ed.), vol. 15, p. 168, para 336, and p. 178, para. 351. If it be shown that the English court had no jurisdictional competence to make the order, such order is a nullity and is incapable of supporting an estoppel of record. If the absence of jurisdiction had appeared on the face of the decree, there would have been no doubt about its worthlessness as a foundation for estoppel. I fail to see why, although the decree seems good on its face, evidence should not be received to show that its facade conceals a lack of jurisdiction no less detrimental to its validity than if it had been written into the order. To hold otherwise would be to close one's eyes to the available truth and to give effect instead to a spurious divorce which the English court was deluded by sworn misrepresentations into making.

The position is not affected by the fact that it is a foreign decree. The comity of courts under private international law does not require or permit recognition of decisions given, intentionally or unintentionally, in disregard of jurisdictional competence. Counsel for the defendant is unable to point to any authority showing that a party to a foreign divorce which was given without jurisdiction was debarred from giving evidence pointing out the want to jurisdiction. On the contrary, a number of the authorities cited in the High Court (or cases referred to in those authorities) exemplify or support the reception of such evidence: see, for example, *Bonaparte* v. *Bonaparte* [1892] P. 402; *Shaw* v. *Gould* (1868) L.R. 3 H.L. 55; *Middleton* v. *Middleton* [1966] 2 W.L.R. 512. I am satisfied that there can be no estoppel by record when the record arose in proceedings, domestic or foreign, upon which the court in question had no jurisdiction to adjudicate.

Counsel for the defendant further questioned the admissibility of the evidence heard *de bene esse* by urging that the plaintiff was also estopped from giving evidence in condemnation of the English divorce decree when, by her conduct, she had adopted and acted on it by executing, with the husband, an indenture in 1964 whereby she commuted the alimony payable to her under the divorce decree. There might be force in this submission if the deed of 1964 was the genuine act of the plaintiff. However, it has been held in the High Court that this deed was procured by duress on the part of the husband, and there has been no appeal against the finding. It is impossible therefore, to hold that the plaintiff approbated the divorce decree when the act of approbation relied on was not her free voluntary act. I would dismiss the appeal.

Griffin, J. delivered a concurring judgment in which he said:–

. . . The domicile of a wife is that of her husband and it was not contended either in High Court or on the hearing of this appeal that the plaintiff was not at all material times domiciled in Ireland. In these circumstances, it is in my view beyond question that the English court had no jurisdiction to grant a decree of divorce *a vinculo* in any proceedings between the plaintiff and her husband: see *Shaw* v. *Gould*, (1868) L.R.3 H.L.55. . . .

O'Higgins, C.J. concurred with **Walsh, J.'s** judgment.
Parke, J. concurred 'with the judgments that have been delivered'.

Notes

1. For analysis of the decision, see *Shatter*, 155–159; Duncan, *Foreign Divorces Obtained on the Basis of Residence, and the Doctrine of Estoppel*, 9 Ir. Jur. (n.s.) 59 (1975); Clare Canton, *Note: Duress and Estoppel in Matrimonial Causes*, 94 L.Q. Rev. 15 (1978); Webb, *Shotgun Divorces*, [1976] N.Z.L.J. 411.
2. In the light of this decision, attempt to state the present law relating to the domicile of dependency of married women.
3. For an interesting consideration of the question of estoppel in the context of a disputed marriage where no problems of conflicts of law arose see *Hodgens* v. *Hodgens*, I.R. 10 Eq. 4 (Ch. App., 1875).

M.T.T. v. N.T.

[1982] I.L.R.M. 217 (Sup. Ct., 1982, rev'g High Ct., D'Arcy, J., 1981)

Henchy, J.:

MTT ('the wife') was a natural-born Irish citizen when she validly married NT ('the husband'), a natural-born British citizen, in London in 1966. They set up home in England and the four children of the marriage were born there.

In 1974 the family moved to Co. Cork, which was the wife's native place. There the husband got a permanent and pensionable local-authority post and the family home was set up in a house at Fountainstown, Co. Cork. This was their only place of residence from 1974 until 1976 when the marriage broke down. Towards the end of 1976 the husband moved into a rented flat in Cork City, leaving the wife and four children in the family home at Fountainstown. He continued to pay the outgoings of the family home and to give the wife a monthly sum by way of maintenance for herself and the children.

In June 1977 the wife brought proceedings in the Cork District Court under the *Family Law (Maintenance of Spouses and Children) Act, 1976*, seeking an order for increased maintenance payments for herself and the children. She got such an order in 1977. It was varied by another order in 1978, under which the payments were increased. About this time the wife left the family home with the four children and went to reside elsewhere in Ireland. The husband then returned to the family home in Fountainstown.

Before that the husband had taken steps to bring the marriage to an end. In February 1977 he filed (and served on the wife), a petition in London for the dissolution of the marriage on the ground that it had broken down irretrievably. The petition was not defended. A decree *nisi* absolute issued in August 1978.

The husband then applied in the Cork District Court for a variation of the existing maintenance order, contending that the absolute decree of divorce absolving him from any liability to continue to make maintenance payments to the wife. The District Justice accepted that proposition, holding that the English divorce was one that required to be recognised in this State.

The wife, being dissatisfied with the latter decision, appealed to the High Court by way of case stated. Her contention in the High Court was that the English divorce did not qualify for recognition in this State, because at the relevant time (i.e. the time of the service of the divorce petition) the husband was not domiciled in England. The High Court judge referred the matter back to the District Justice (an unpermitted expedient, in view of the fact that this was an appeal by case stated and that the District Justice was then *functus officio*) for a finding as to the husband's domicile at the relevant date. In reply, the District Justice made additional findings from which he deduced that the husband's domicile was Irish. Having considered those further findings, the High Court judge allowed the appeal, holding that the divorce could not be given judicial recognition here because the husband's domicile was Irish at the relevant time. From that decision the husband has now appealed to this Court.

The net point is still the same: at the time of the divorce was the husband's domicile Irish or British? If it was British, the divorce qualifies for recognition in our courts; if it was Irish, the divorce was given without jurisdiction and cannot be acted on here: see the decision of this Court in *Gaffney v Gaffney* [1975] I.R. 133.

Before the husband's domicile could be held to be Irish, it would have to be established that he had abandoned his British domicile of origin and had opted instead for an Irish domicile of choice. This is a mixed question of law and fact, an affirmative answer to which depends on whether it appears from the husband's conduct and the general course of events that he had cast off his British domicile of origin and had chosen to take on in its place an Irish domicile. The rebuttable presumption is that a person retains his domicile of origin.

In this case I think both the District Justice and the High Court judge misdirected themselves in law in holding that the husband had acquired an Irish domicile of choice. I consider that they wrongly allowed employment and residence to be the decisive factors. Undoubtedly the husband left England with his wife and children, set up a family home in Cork and took up permanent employment there. In doing so he did no more than what tens of thousands of people are doing throughout the EEC, where freedom of movement and mobility of employment are the order of the day under the Treaty. He spent but two years in Cork with his family before he brought his petition for divorce in London. He had gone to Cork, presumably because there was permanent employment available there and because it was his wife's native place. From these meagre facts or inferences, and they are all we have, it would be an unwarranted deduction to say that, by his will and act, he had of his own volition stripped himself of his British domicile and chosen to take on in its place an Irish domicile. From the facts as found by the District Justice, I am satisfied that the husband put the position correctly in the divorce petition when he averred that, while he was then residing in Cork, his domicile was British. A man's sojourn abroad with his wife and children for two years, even in a position of permanent employment, is not, without more, capable of displacing the presumption that the domicile of origin has been retained. The period lived abroad may be no more than the external manifestation of the temporary compulsion of circumstances. Such bare facts as we have in this case as to the husband's foreign residence do not show the volitional and factual transition which is a *sine qua non* for shedding a domicile of origin and acquiring a domicile of choice.

I would allow this appeal, thus restoring the finding of the District Justice that the English divorce was valid – a finding which he made on the erroneous ground that, because the marriage was validly contracted in England, the English court had, for that reason, jurisdiction to dissolve it.

Griffin, J. (concurring):

. . . . As to domicile, it is not contested that the defendant's domicile of origin is British. The plaintiff alleges that the defendant had changed his domicile. It is well settled that the burden of proving a change of domicile from a domicile of origin to a domicile of choice is on those who assert it. As Black J said in *In re Joyce: Corbet v Fagan,* [1946] I.R. 277:

> Whatever difference of view may be possible on any other aspect of the law of domicile, one principle at least is beyond doubt, namely, that the domicile of origin persists until it is proved to have been intentionally and voluntarily abandoned and supplanted by another.

See also *In re Siller, Hurley v Wimbush and Anor* [1956] I.R. 344 per Budd, J. in *In Re Adams Deceased*, [1967] I.R. 424. Unless therefore the plaintiff can show that the proper inference to be drawn from the established facts in the case is that the defendant has shown unmistakably by his conduct that he had formed the settled purpose of residing indefinitely in Cork and that he had an intention to abandon his former domicile, the plaintiff will not have discharged the onus of proof on her. I agree with Henchy J that the established facts in this case fall short of what would be required to discharge the onus of proof, and that the defendant had at all material times retained his British domicile. The decree for divorce obtained by the defendant in the Divorce Registry in London on 23 August 1978 is, therefore, one which will be recognised in our courts. I would accordingly allow the appeal.

O'Higgins, C.J. concurred with **Henchy, J.'s** judgment.

Notes

1. For analysis of the decision see Buckley & O'Mahony, *Recognition of Foreign Divorces – a Further Gloss*, 76 Inc. L. Soc. of Ireland Gazette 211 (1982).
2. Do you agree with the decision? What do you understand by the concept of 'British domicile'?
3. Did the evidence establish that Mr. T. had 'sojourned abroad' for two years or for longer? Does the duration matter?
4. Would you agree with the proposition that what makes this a difficult case is the paucity of relevant evidence?

L.B. v. H.B.

Unreported, High Court, Barrington J., July 1980 (1979–449 Sp.)

Barrington, J.:

This is, to say the least, an unusual case.

The plaintiff and the defendant were married in Paris on the 4th of June, 1947. The plaintiff is a British subject. She had been working during the War in the American

Embassy in London and, after the liberation of Paris, was transferred to that city. There she met the defendant, who was an officer in the American Army.

The defendant's parents lived in Maryland, United States of America. But, on his discharge from the Army in April 1946, the defendant, instead of returning to the United State, went into business in Paris. He acted as an agent dealing in surplus American war goods. One of his major successes was, in association with a partner, to negotiate the sale of some 300 surplus American locomotives to the Hungarian Government. On this transaction alone he made a profit of some three hundred thousand dollars. The defendant and his partner also dealt with medical supplies and aircraft. The defendant sold the first Comet aircraft sold outside the British Commonwealth. Later the defendant became a worldwide agent for the Fouga Company which was then starting to manufacture a Jet trainer aircraft called the Fouga Magister. The defendant later became a shareholder in that company and sold 700 Jet trainers. This agency business appears to have petered out sometime in or around 1960 and since then the defendant appears to have interested himself in property and owns extensive properties in Ireland and in the United States of America. The defendant, on his own admission, now has assets worth more than a million pounds.

The parties were married on the 4th of June 1947. In October 1947 the defendant bought a splendid house, 'M', which stood on some 70 acres about fifteen miles outside Paris. There he and his wife lived in style with a staff of seven servants to look after them. He was a member of the local Agricultural Co-Operative Society at Versailles and himself and his wife were members of local golf clubs. He said it was his intention to settle permanently in France.

The parties had one child – A. – who was born on the 14th of March 1950. The mother had gynaecological problems and went to London where she was attended by an English gynaecologist on her confinement. The fact that A. was born in London appears to have no significance for this case.

Some years later unhappy differences arose between husband and wife. The wife had a nervous upset or breakdown. I am satisfied, that, of the two, the husband was and is the dominant and by far the more forcible personality. He also had and has much greater knowledge of business affairs. I am also satisfied that he was the person principally responsible for the breakdown of the marriage.

Be that as it may by 1957 both parties had decided that they wanted a divorce. They accordingly consulted two French lawyers or avoués. There is conflict as to how the wife was put in touch with her lawyer. The wife says the husband procured the two avoués. The husband says he advised his wife to go to an avoué of her own choice and that this avoué in turn selected an avoué for him. He says he was particularly careful about this because he knew his wife had had a nervous breakdown and he did not want any divorce to be questioned afterwards. Be that as it may the husband paid the costs of both parties.

The avoués were retained to obtain the divorce and to make appropriate arrangements concerning the custody of A. and the division of communal or family assets between husband and wife.

A decree of divorce was obtained from the French Courts, on the petition of the husband and cross-petition of the wife, on the 25th of April 1958. Some time about 1954 the parties had sold their house outside Paris and subsequently lived at various fashionable addresses in Paris. At the time of the divorce they were still occupying the same house at Marne La Coquette, but no longer living as husband and wife.

In the previous July the couple had entered into an agreement under which the wife agreed to give the husband custody of her seven year old son and agreed to accept a sum of £500 in respect of her share of the family assets. The husband agreed to pay her alimony at the rate of £520 per annum. He also agreed to provide, for her use for life, a house in England and to be responsible for all outgoings on it other than tenant's repairs.

The husband says that this settlement was decided on by the two legal advisers after he had made full disclosure to them of his financial affairs. The wife however says that the husband was always secretive about his financial affairs and that she entered into this settlement because she despaired at being able to prove that her husband had substantial assets. Her principal confidant and adviser at this stage appears to have been – not her avoué – but the President of her local golf club and he appears to have advised her to take whatever she could get, on the basis that she would not be able to prove that her husband had any assets.

Many years later the wife came across a letter to her husband from Lloyds Bank (Foreign) Limited in Geneva dated the 3rd of July 1957 for which it appears that on that date they held shares to the value of $223,726.98 dollars in safe keeping for him.

I find it hard to accept that a responsible lawyer, apprised of this information, could have advised a wife against whom no impropriety had been alleged to enter into a settlement of the kind which the Plaintiff entered into in July 1957. In any event I am satisfied that the financial provision made for the wife in this settlement was grossly inadequate.

The French divorce did not mark a final break between the parties. At the time of the divorce the parties were living in the same house but not as husband and wife. This pattern of living was not changed by the divorce. According to the husband he and his wife found it convenient to preserve the semblance of a marriage for the sake of their son.

In 1960 the husband, who was interested in shooting and fishing, bought . . . a stately home in the West of Ireland. He provided town accommodation for his wife at various addresses in Dublin. In 1968, by agreement, he bought a house in Dublin for his wife in substitution for the house promised to her under the French settlement. This house was in need of substantial repair and renovation. The repair work was began but never completed. There is a controversy between the parties as to whether the wife ever slept in this house. But I am satisfied that the renovation work was never completed and that this house was not at any material time, and is not now, a fit or suitable place for her or anyone else, to live in. The defendant says that Mrs. B. never made up her mind on what property she wanted. He might be right in this.

The wife spent short periods in other properties owned or rented by the defendant in Dublin, but eventually she moved to the defendant's home in the West of Ireland. According to the defendant she did this to make access to her son more easy. According to the plaintiff she did it because she had no where else to go. Both stories may very well be true.

The plaintiff has remained living in the defendant's home in the West of Ireland since sometime in the 1960s. I am satisfied that the defendant introduces her to friends, neighbours and business associates as 'Mrs B'. The defendant regards his house in the West of Ireland as being his home. He spends a considerable part of the year there. Neither the plaintiff nor the defendant ever remarried but the defendant spends a considerable amount of time in the United States of America where he has substantial business interests and where he also has an ongoing relationship with another lady.

Over the years the plaintiff's alimony or allowance has been raised from £10 a week to £50 a week. She also has the right to buy groceries, pharmaceuticals etc. in various shops where the defendant operates credit accounts. Each year she is given her ticket to fly to London for the spring or autumn sales and last year was given £250 to pay for her hotel and other expenses. She lives in a splendid house with 36 acres of garden. But she has no domestic staff. She says she had to let the housekeeper go because she could not afford to pay her. She says the kitchen in the house has never been converted and that conditions there are 'like Siberia'. She complained that she has no iron and no hot water. She is often alone in an enormous house which is in such poor repair that there is no lock on the back door. She says that she had no money and therefore no freedom. She complains that the defendant is a 'very mean man'.

Procedure

On the 19th of January, 1968 the plaintiff through her solicitors Messrs T.F. O'Connell Rooney & Co. wrote to the defendant's solicitors Messrs T.G. McVeagh & Co. suggesting that the defendant purchase for her the house already mentioned in Dublin and also suggesting an upward review of the plaintiff's alimony 'if only for the question of devaluation of the pound over the period since the agreement'. Messrs O'Connell Rooney continued: 'Mrs. B, wishes to do this by amicable arrangement with Mr. B but finds it difficult to discuss the proposition with Mr. B. directly and for this purpose has requested us to write to you.'

On the 3rd of May 1979 the plaintiff's French lawyers Messrs Theodore Goddard wrote to the defendant saying that they had been instructed 'by your former wife' in connection with her financial rights under the French divorce. They went on to say that they had made an arrangement to have a notary appointed to assess the financial rights of husband and wife under the French divorce decree in the light of information they had received as to the husband's real wealth at the time of the divorce.

They continued – 'nevertheless and entirely without prejudice to our client's rights, we have instructions to seek a voluntary settlement with you upon terms which obviously will be substantially less onerous than those which, from the documentary evidence we hold, our client will obtain under execution of the relevant Court Orders'.

The defendant replied to this letter by letter dated the 18th of July 1979 referring Messrs Theodore Goddard to the two avoués who had represented the defendant and the plaintiff respectively at the time of the divorce proceedings.

No further step appears to have been taken before the French Courts. I am satisfied that the reason for this was that the defendant has no assets within the jurisdiction of the French Courts and that any relief the French Courts might offer the plaintiff would therefore be valueless.

On the 25th of July 1979 the plaintiff issued the present proceedings by way of special summons in which the plaintiff formulated her claim as wife of the defendant for maintenance under the *Family Law (Maintenance of Spouses and Children) Act, 1976* and for a declaration as to the extent of her beneficial interest in the defendant's house in the west which was claimed to be a family home. The grounding affidavit did not refer expressly to the French divorce but referred to 'unhappy differences' and to 'certain arrangements' made in or around 1958 under which the defendant was to pay the plaintiff regular maintenance.

The defendant filed a replying affidavit in which he raised the French divorce as a defence and denied that the plaintiff is his wife.

The plaintiff then sought to challenge the validity of the divorce and the Master ordered that a statement of claim be delivered.

A statement of claim was delivered on the 3rd of June 1980 and contains, at paragraph 4, the following plea – 'the plaintiff contends that the said purported divorce is null and void, or, alternatively, is one the validity of which should not be recognised by this Honourable Court on the grounds that the parties were not domiciled in France at the time thereof and on the further grounds that the defendant obtained the said divorce and subsequent order of the French Court dated the 30th day of November 1957, by fraud, which amounted to a substantial denial of justice to the plaintiff herein'.

At the hearing Mr. Blayney, who appeared for the plaintiff, abandoned the plea of fraud but sought leave to amend this pleading by substituting a plea of collusion. I allowed him to amend his statement of claim accordingly.

Mr. Gill, on behalf of the defendant, submitted that the plaintiff had been uncandid with the Court in that she had been prepared to approbate or reprobate the divorce decree as suited her convenience and in that there was no express reference to the divorce decree in her grounding affidavit for the present proceedings. I am quite satisfied that the plantiff's primary concern in the present proceedings is to obtain proper financial provision for herself and that she was prepared to approbate or to reprobate the French divorce depending upon which course was to her economic advantage. I do not however think that there was any lack of candour or impropriety on her part in her approach to the present proceedings. She simply placed herself in the hands of her lawyers and their approach to the case was influenced by their understanding of the law in their respective jurisdictions and by the inherent difficulties of the case.

The case as presented and argued, raises four major questions. These are as follows:–

1. Were the parties domiciled in France at the date of the granting of the French divorce on the 25th of April 1958?
2. Was the French divorce of the 25th of April 1953 obtained by collusion and if so, what are the implications of this?
3. Is the defendant's house in the west of Ireland a family home within the meaning of the *Family Home Protection Act, 1976.*
4. What maintenance, if any, should the husband pay to the wife? These questions raise complex issues of French and Irish law.

French law

On the issue of French law I am fortunate in having had the assistance of Mr. John Sell who is in practice as a professional lawyer in France and is also qualified as a solicitor in England.

On the basis of his evidence it would appear that in 1957 French law forbade a property settlement between husband and wife who were parties to a divorce suit until the final decree of divorce had been pronounced. It would therefore appear that the agreement entered into between the plaintiff and the defendant in July 1957, was and is now, null and void in French law. It is accordingly null and void in Ireland.

It would also appear that in 1957 there were only three grounds on which a French Court could pronounce a decree of divorce. The first ground was based on adultery and the second ground was based on husband or wife having been found guilty of certain criminal offences. The Court had no option but to grant a decree of divorce to a petitioner who established one of these grounds. The third ground related to the 'behaviour' of one of the parties to the marriage. In relation to this matter the Court had a discretion on whether or not to grant a decree of divorce. The behaviour referred to must be behaviour which the Court considered sufficiently serious to entitle the other party to a decree of divorce. It had to be genuine behaviour in the sense that it was quite forbidden for the parties to manufacture 'behaviour' for the purposes of obtaining a divorce. For lawyers to be parties to manufacturing evidence for the purposes of obtaining a divorce was considered to be professionally reprehensible. Notwithstanding this the practice of manufacturing such evidence was common among certain lawyers in France. If the Court became aware that the parties or their lawyers had been in collusion to manufacture evidence for the purposes of a divorce petition it would certainly reject the petition. However once the decree of divorce was made final and absolute it could not be upset even though it had been obtained by collusion. Mr. Sell offered the opinion on the basis of the evidence before him, that a French Court would regard the present case as one of collusion. Notwithstanding this he stated that the decree could not now be set aside by any Court in France.

In relation to property Mr. Sell said, at the relevant time, subject to certain exceptions, all movables and immovables acquired by a married couple during marriage became the communal property of both and on the pronouncement of the final decree of divorce, husband and wife were entitled to an equal division of these communal assets. An example of an exception would be a gift expressly stated by the donor to be for the benefit of the wife to the exclusion of the husband or vice versa. The parties could, of course, agree on a different division of the communal assets but no such agreement could validly be entered into until the final decree of divorce had been made.

In the present case accordingly – the agreement of July 1957 between husband and wife being null and void – Mrs. B. was entitled on the pronouncement of the absolute decree of divorce on the 25th of April 1958 to one half of the communal assets as they existed on that date. There was no time bar on the winding up or division of the family assets. This was the significance of the letter from Messrs Theodore Goddard to the defendant of the 3rd of May 1979. There having been no valid agreement as to the division of the communal assets it was open to either husband and wife to have a notary appointed to enquire into the extent of the family assets. The practice was for the notary to write to both parties asking them to furnish him with an inventory of the communal assets. If one party failed to assist the notary the party not in default could obtain from the notary a 'minute' of difficulties. The party not in default then brought this minute before the divorce Court which was entitled to divide the family assets equally between the parties on the basis of whatever evidence the party not in default was able to furnish to the Court. This was the procedure which Messrs Theodore Goddard were threatening in their letter of the 3rd of May 1979. In the circumstances of the present case the procedure was however of no avail to Mrs. B. because Mr. B. has no assets within the jurisdiction of the French Court against which execution could be levied.

For this reason it seemed pointless to pursue the matter any further in France. Instead proceedings were instituted in Ireland by Irish lawyers who took a different approach to the problem.

Domicile

Mr. Blayney's first submission was that the Irish Court should not recognise the validity of the French divorce because the parties were not domiciled in France at the time the French divorce proceedings were commenced in 1957. Mr. Blayney conceded that, apart from the question of collusion discussed below, if the parties were domiciled in France at the commencement of the divorce proceedings that the Court should recognise the decree as valid.

He relied on the law as laid down in the Judgment of Mr. Justice Kingsmill Moore in *Mayo-Perrott* v. *Mayo-Perrott* [1958] I.R. 336; and in the Judgment of Mr. Justice Kenny in *Re Caffin Deceased: Bank of Ireland* v. *Caffin*, [1971] I.R. 123 and by the Supreme Court in the case of *Gaffney* v. *Gaffney* [1975] I.R. 133. Mr. Gill accepted that Mr. Blayney's submissions on this branch of the law were correct and I accept that that is the law which I have to apply.

A major issue in the case therefore is whether the defendant was or was not domiciled in France in 1957.

[After a review of the evidence, Barrington, J. continued:]

Under the circumstances I think that I must approach the case on the basis that Mr. B. was domiciled in France in 1957 and that the French Courts had, accordingly, jurisdiction to deal with the divorce matter.

Collusion

I now turn to deal with the question of alleged collusion.

I have already noted that in 1957 both parties wished to have a divorce. Mr. B. submitted a petition for divorce and Mrs. B. submitted a cross petition. I am satisfied that Mrs. B. had, at that time, what would in Ireland be regarded as sufficient grounds for a judicial separation. So far there is no question of collusion.

But some time in or about July 1957, while the divorce proceedings were pending the parties and their respective avoués met and entered into a property settlement which was null and void in French law as being made prior to the final decree of divorce.

It is clear from the decree of divorce that the divorce was based not upon any real ground of complaint which Mrs. B. may have had against her husband but upon certain letters which she is alleged to have written to him and he to her. The divorce decree recites a formal call by the husband to the wife to resume conjugal life and a letter alleged to have been written by her in which she replied:–

> I have already informed my husband on several occasions of my express wish not to live with him any longer. I intend to retain my independence and moreover I have organised my life without him. . . .

It also recites a letter alleged to have been written by him to her on the 10th September 1957 in which he says:–

> Over a number of years I have not felt for you any of the love or the affection which would have enabled us to live happily together. . . .

and a further letter dated the 16th September 1957 in which he is alleged to have written:

> Whatever you may do is of no further interest to me and I only wish for one thing, to rebuild my life as soon as possible.

The court then proceeds to accede to the petition and the counter-petition on the basis of these letters. It goes on to provide that both parties are to pay their own costs.

At the time this alleged correspondence is supposed to have taken place the husband and wife were living together in the same house. There was no necessity for them to write letters to each other. The wife says she never saw the letters that were supposed to have been written to her by her husband and that the entire matter was arranged between the avoués.

Mr. B. agrees that his letters were drafted by his avoué. He may have made some changes in them. He was not clear on this. But he says that the letters expressed his feelings. He could not recall if the letters were actually sent to his wife. He agreed that there was a 'rapport' between the two avoués. He did not seriously dispute his wife's version of what had happened but he said that at the time, that was the only way under French law of obtaining a divorce on terms equal to both parties. Of the avoués he said 'they knew their job'.

On the basis of the foregoing I have no doubt whatsoever that the divorce was a collusive divorce. In many ways it represented the worst form of collusion as the evidence on which the Court decided the case was manufactured to achieve that precise result. I am satisfied on the basis of Mr. Sell's evidence that had the Court known the truth of the matter it would have dismissed the petition and cross-petition. I also have Mr. Sell's uncontested evidence of the view which the legal profession in France took of organising a collusive suit of this nature. I also have his uncontested evidence that despite the collusive nature of the suit, the decree of divorce cannot now be set aside in France.

In considering the question of collusion the dates at which the various steps were taken in the divorce suit may be of importance. According to Mr. B. the parties and their avoués met some time in 1957 and worked out a property settlement which, according to Mr. B. the two avoués considered fair. This is the property settlement contained in the invalid agreement of July 1957 which also gives custody of the only child of the marriage to Mr. B. and provides that Mr. B. is to pay all the costs of the proceedings.

Next a formal demand is made to Mrs. B. on the 6th September calling upon her to resume conjugal life with her husband. She replies declining to do so, says she intends to retain her independence and adds 'moreover I have organised my life without him'. On the

10th of September the husband writes to the wife telling her he no longer loves her and on the 16th of September he writes saying 'whatever you may do is of no further interest to me'.

On the 30th of November 1957 the Court pronounced a provisional decree of divorce. In this decree Mrs. B. is referred to as temporarily residing at N__________. The decree authorises each party to deny the other access to his or her residence and if necessary to call on a police officer or even the armed forces to expel the other.

The final decree of divorce comes through on the 25th of April 1958. In this decree Mr. B. is referred to as living at R__________ while Mrs. B. is referred to as living at G__________.

All along the two parties had been living together in the one house though not as husband and wife. The decree, having granted a divorce, provides that the costs are to be borne equally by the parties although as previously indicated, by the agreement of July 1957 it was provided that Mr. B. should bear the entire costs of the proceedings. I can only conclude that the parties first met and agreed on a form of divorce; that they then manufacturered evidence to produce the agreed result; and that they did not reveal to the court that they were living in the same house and that Mr. B. was paying the costs of both parties as those facts might have proved embarrassing.

In these circumstances I have to enquire as to what the status of this decree is in Irish law. In doing so I must regard it as a decree of divorce granted by a Court of competent jurisdiction to people domiciled within its jurisdiction.

Under the principles of private international law, approved by our Courts in *Re Caffin deceased: Bank of Ireland* v. *Caffin* and in *Gaffney* v. *Gaffney* the decrees of such a Court are entitled to recognition and respect from the Courts of all other civilised nations.

In the present case however I am satisfied that there was such a measure of collusion between the parties in the proceedings before the French Court as to amount to a fraud upon that Court. I am also satisfied that if the French Court had known of the collusion it would have rejected the petition and the cross-petition. One is not here dealing with the kind of fraud or collusion which occurs when one or both parties pretend to be domiciled within the jurisdiction of a particular Court. Clearly a decree made by a foreign Tribunal under such circumstances is not entitled to recognition because one cannot confer jurisdiction on a tribunal by falsely pretending that it has jurisdiction: see Dicey's *Conflict of Laws*, 7th ed., p.306 (1958).

Neither is one dealing with cases where one of the parties has committed a fraud, or suppressed the truth, or where there has been collusion between the parties about peripheral matters. Clearly matters which have been fully heard and determined before a competent Tribunal should not lightly be reopened (see *Bater* v. *Bater* [1906] P. 209 and *Crowe* v. *Crowe* 157 L.T. 557).

In the present case there can be no doubt as to the jurisdiction of the French Courts to deal with the matter. But this Court has become aware of certain matters of which the French Court was ignorant. From these it appears that the entire suit was manufactured and conducted in such a way that it amounted to a fraud upon the French Court as a result of which the French Court was led unwittingly to a conclusion which the parties and their lawyers had prearranged.

A similar issue, but in the domestic context, arose for consideration in the House of Lords in the case of *Shedden* v. *Patrick* 1 Macq. 356 (1854). The issue in that case was whether an earlier decision of the House of Lords could be treated as a nullity by inferior tribunals, or by the House itself, if proved to have been obtained by fraud and collusion.

The House ultimately held that the allegations of fraud and collusion were not made out on the facts, so that it did not become necessary to decide the point of law which was, nevertheless, extensively discussed. Lord Brougham in his speech referred to the *Duchess of Kingston's Case*, 20 Howard State Tr.619 (1776) where a Court, trying a charge of bigamy against the Duchess, ignored a decree of nullity purporting to dissolve her first marriage on proof that the decree had been obtained by fraud and collusion. Lord Brougham's speech contains the following passage:–

> . . . The sentence of the Consistorial Court was the sentence of a Court of competent and exclusive jurisdiction. This House had no right to interfere with the sentence of that Court any more than that Court had to interfere with any sentence pronounced in this House. But it had a right to disregard it, and it did disregard it upon proof that it was a nullity.

. . . It also seems clear from modern English cases that the English Courts do not regard the fact that a divorce is recognised in the State where the parties are domiciled as entitling the decree of divorce to recognition in England in all circumstances. In the case of *Macalpine* v. *Macalpine,* [1958] P. 35, the husband was domiciled in the State of Colorado in the United States of America. His wife was resident in England. He obtained a divorce in the State of Wyoming and, according to expert opinion called at the trial in England before Sachs J, such a divorce would be regarded as valid in Colorado.

It appeared, however, that in the course of the divorce proceedings the husband had sworn that he did not know the residence of his wife and that he could not ascertain it by reasonable diligence. This was totally untrue as the husband had been in communication both with his wife and with her mother and was perfectly well aware of his wife's address.

The Suit was advertised in local newspapers in Wyoming but the wife in fact received no notice of the proceedings.

Sachs J. refused to recognise the divorce because of the husband's fraud and because of failure of natural justice. At page 140 of his judgment he stated:–

> Failure of natural justice in the course of proceedings with a foreign Court may thus be said to go to the root of its competence in a manner similar to absence of jurisdiction over the subject matter before it.

The rule of English law that where a decree of divorce has been pronounced in the Court of a foreign place where the parties are not domiciled, the English Courts will treat it as valid, provided it would be recognised as valid by the Court of the place where they were domiciled at the relevant time, was further considered in the case of *Middleton* v. *Middleton* [1966] 1 All E.R. 168. In that case the husband, in order to pretend that the Courts of Illinois had jurisdiction to grant him a divorce, had falsely sworn that he had been resident in the State of Illinois for more than one year. In fact he had been resident there for only three or four months. In that respect therefore the case was a comparatively straightforward one in that the Courts of Illinois had no jurisdiction to grant him a divorce. However, in the course of his judgment Cairns J., the trial Judge, identifies (at p. 172) five rules governing the approach of English Courts to foreign decrees of divorce recognised in the countries where the parties are domiciled. These are as follows:–

1. If a decree of divorce has been pronounced in the Court of a foreign place where the parties were not domiciled, the English Court will treat it as valid provided it would be recognised as valid by the Courts of the place where they were domiciled.
2. If a decree of divorce has been obtained in a foreign Court by false evidence about the matrimonial offence relied on, it will not on that ground be treated by the English Court as invalid provided it has not been set aside in the foreign Court.
3. If a decree has been obtained in a foreign Court contrary to natural justice the English Court will treat it as invalid.
4. The English Court has a discretion to refuse to recognise a foreign decree which offends against English ideas of substantial justice.
5. If a petitioner has obtained a decree in a foreign Court, which had no jurisdiction to pronounce it, by deceiving the Court into believing that it had jurisdiction, the English Court will treat it as invalid.

As Cairns, J. recognises these rules may occasionally be in conflict. Rule 4 concerning the discretion of the English Court to refuse to recognise a foreign decree which offends against English ideas of substantial justice would appear to apply also to decrees of the Courts of countries where the parties were actually domiciled. The rule derives from a *dictum* of Lindley, M.R., in *Pemberton* v. *Hughes* [1899] 1 Ch. 790. . . .
This Rule was applied by the English Court of Appeal in 1962 in the case of *Gray* v. *Formosa* [1963] P. 259. In that case the husband was Maltese and a Roman Catholic. He settled in England and married an English woman by whom he had three children. He subsequently returned to Malta and resumed his domicile of origin. He then refused to support his wife and two of his children on the basis that the English marriage was not valid because he, as a Maltese Catholic, could not validly contract a marriage outside the Roman Catholic Church. He did support his son but only as an illegitimate child. Later he successfully petitioned the Maltese Courts which granted him a decree of nullity. The English Court of Appeal refused to recognise the decree of nullity on the basis that the proceedings offended English ideas of substantial justice. The case is important as it illustrates that the English Courts, at any rate, claim a residual discretion to refuse to recognise a decree made by the Courts of the country of domicile in a matrimonial matter if the decree offends English ideas of substantial justice. It would appear indeed that in the case of *Gray* v. *Formosa* considerable play was made by both the Maltese Court and the English Court of Appeal with the question of where the wife was domiciled. The question, however, appears irrelevant. There was no doubt but that the husband was domiciled in Malta. Therefore, if the marriage was valid the wife was domiciled in Malta also and if the marriage was invalid the domicile of the wife was irrelevant. But a court entering on a consideration of a nullity suit would presumably consider the marriage valid till the contrary was shown.

It may be significant that paragraph 4 of the Statement of Claim in the present case originally pleaded that the defendant had obtained the French divorce 'by fraud, which amounted to a substantial denial of justice to the plaintiff'. It is clear that this original plea could not succeed as there was no fraud or no substantial denial of justice *inter partes.* The collusion however, between the parties was such that the entire proceedings became a charade and the French Court was unwittingly led to a conclusion which had been predetermined by the parties. There was a substantial defeat of justice for which the parties, and not the Court, bear the responsibility. The case therefore presents problems similar to those considered in *Shedden* v. *Patrick* discussed above. This Court is fixed with knowledge of matters of which the French Court had no knowledge. It is accordingly no disrespect to the French Court if it refuses to recognise a divorce obtained in such circumstances. Indeed, once this Court has been fixed with knowledge of what happened in the French divorce proceedings it is hard to see how it could recognise the validity of the divorce and at the same time observe the constitutional duty of the State to uphold the institution of marriage.

The husband had not raised any plea of estoppel against the wife in this case. I myself raised the question of estoppel in the course of the hearing but Mr. Blayney submitted on the basis of the decision of the Supreme Court in *Gaffney* v. *Gaffney*, that a plea of estoppel would not lie. The situation which has arisen in thise case is not the same as that in *Gaffney* v. *Gaffney*, but, nevertheless, the case raises issues of public policy and the status of individuals so that it would appear that a plea of estoppel would not lie. Even if such a plea did lie I do not think it could be successful in view of the conclusion which I have reached as to the dominant role which the husband played in what happened.

It appears to me therefore that I must approach the balance of the case on the basis that the plaintiff is the defendant's wife . . .

[Barrington, J. went on to consider questions relating to maintenance (*supra*, pp. 210–11) and the family home (*infra*, pp. 325–26.]

Notes

1. Commenting on this decision, *Shatter*, 161 states that:

   a considerable degree of uncertainty has been introduced into this area of the law by the denial of recognition to the French divorce decree on the ground that recognition of the divorce would have constituted 'a substantial defeat of justice', a concept that was at no stage fully defined in the judgment delivered by the court.

   Do you agree with this criticism?
2. Is the decision consistent with the authorities cited and discussed?
3. Is the case decided on Constitutional grounds?
4. For analysis of the decision, see Duncan, *Collusive Foreign Divorces – How To Have Your Cake and Eat It*, [1981] Dublin U.L.J. (n.s.) 29 (1983).

N.M. v. E.F.M.

Unreported, High Court, Hamilton J., July 1978 (1977 No. 87 EMO)

Hamilton, J.:

This is an appeal brought by the defendant from an Order made by the Master of the High Court on the 8th day of December, 1977 by which it was ordered that the Maintenance Order made by Liverpool County Court on the 23rd day of July, 1973 whereby the defendant was ordered to pay the sum of £70 per month for the maintenance of the above named complainant until such date as she should remarry or further Order.

The Order of the Master of the High Court was made pursuant to a request dated the 6th day of October, 1977 from the Secretary of State, Home Office, Whitehall, London.

Accompanying the said request was a certified copy of the said Maintenance Order made on the 23rd day of July, 1973, a certificate that the said Order was enforceable in the United Kingdom, a certificate that established that notice of the institution of proceedings was served on the defendant, a certificate that notice of said Order was served on the defendant and a certificate that the complainant was in receipt of Legal Aid for the purpose of raising and proceeding with this Action.

From the said Order the defendant appealed to this Court on the grounds that:–

1. Recognition or enforcement of the Maintenance Order would be contrary to public policy on the grounds that the complainant obtained a decree of dissolution of marriage on the 7th day of August, 1967 against the respondent and the Maintenance Order is for alimony consequent on the said divorce.
2. The complainant deserted the defendant.
3. Complainant was refused maintenance by the Court in Liverpool in 1977 when she applied to enforce the the Order of the 23rd day of July, 1973 and the same is not enforceable in England.

The defendant herein, having been served with the Enforcement Order made by the Master of the High Court, appealed to this Court in accordance with the provisions of Section 7 (1) of the *Maintenance Orders Act, 1974.*

A maintenance order is defined in the said Act as:

> An order (including an affiliation order or an order consequent thereon which provides for the periodical payment of sums of money towards the maintenance of any person, being a person whom the person liable to make payments under the order is, in accordance with the law of the jurisdiction in which the order was made, liable to maintain.

'Reciprocating jurisdiction' means Northern Ireland, England and Wales or Scotland. Section 6(1) of the Act provides that:–

> Subject to and in accordance with this Act, a maintenance order made in a reciprocating jurisdiction and enforceable therein shall be recognised and enforceable in the State when, on receipt by the Master of the High Court, from an appropriate authority for the enforcement of the order, an order is made under sub-section 4.

Section 6(4) of the Act provides that:–

> The Master shall consider the request privately and shall make an order (in this Act referred to as an enforcement order) for the enforcement of the maintenance order to which the request relates unless it appears to him from the documents before him or from his own knowledge that its recognition and enforcement is prohibited by Section 9.

Section 9 of the Act provides that:–

> A maintenance order made in a reciprocating jurisdiction shall not be recognised or enforceable if, but only if:
> (a) Recognition of enforcement would be contrary to public policy,
> (b) Where it was made in default of appearance, the person in default was not served with notice of the institution of the proceedings in sufficient time to enable him to arrange for his defence, or
> (c) It is irreconcilable with the judgment given in a dispute between the same parties in the State.

It is not contested in this appeal that the statutory requirements necessary for the Master of the High Court to adjudicate in this matter, were not complied with.

It is agreed by both parties that:–

> (a) both parties are Irish citizens;
> (b) they were married in . . . Dublin [in] October, 1944;
> (c) they emigrated to England in 1946;
> (d) a decree of dissolution of their marriage was obtained in the High Court of Justice, Probate, Divorce and Admiralty Division (Divorce) Liverpool District Registry on the 20th day of January 1967, which decree was made absolute in the 7th day of August, 1967;
> (e) the complainant returned to Ireland where she resides . . . in . . . County X.
> (f) the defendant/respondent remarried in January 1972 and having suffered a heart attack returned to Ireland in 1974 and lives [in County Y].

With regard to the submission made on behalf of the defendant that the maintenance order was not enforceable in England as both parties are now resident in Ireland, there has been submitted in evidence a Certificate of the Registrar of her Majesty's High Court of Justice District Registry Liverpool dated the 14th day of April, 1979, which certifies that:–

> (1) [The complainant] is entitled to enforce payment of the attached certified order in the United Kingdom against [the defendant].
> (2) The arrears due up to and including the 23rd day of February 1977 amount to £1,960.

I consider that I am bound by the terms of the said certificate and the Appeal on this ground must be dismissed.

It is however submitted on behalf of the defendant that the maintenance order obtained by the complainant was an order made in proceedings for a dissolution of marriage and was consequent to a decree of dissolution of marriage and that it would be contrary to public policy to recognise or enforce the said maintenance order.

Counsel on behalf of the respondent relied in support of the submission on *Mayo-Perrott* v. *Mayo-Perrott* [1958] I.R. 306, *Re Caffin Deceased: Bank of Ireland* v. *Caffin* [1971] I.R. 123 and *Gaffney* v. *Gaffney* [1975] I.R. 133.

[Hamilton, J. quoted passages from the judgments of Kingsmill Moore and Maguire JJ. in *Mayo-Perrott* v. *Mayo-Perrott*. He continued:]

[*Mayo-Perrott* v. *Mayo-Perrott*] related to the costs of divorce proceedings and it was held that the order for costs was not severable from the substantive Order for divorce and could not be enforced in Ireland as creating a separate and independent cause of action *in personam*.

What is sought to be enforced here is a maintenance order admittedly made in divorce proceedings and consequent to a grant of dissolution of marriage and the question for determination by me is whether the enforcement of such a maintenance order would be contrary to public policy.

I accept unreservedly that if the recognition or enforcement of a maintenance order would have the effect of giving active assistance to facilitate in any way the effecting of a dissolution of marriage or to give assistance to the process of divorce that such recognition or enforcement would be contrary to public policy.

In the case of *Mayo-Perrott*, the Supreme Court decided that the terms of the judgment which was sought to be enforced were not severable.

In this particular case the maintenance order sought to be enforced was made on the 23rd day of July, 1973 and though made in and consequent to proceedings for a decree of dissolution of marriage, such decree had been granted and made absolute on the 7th day of August, 1967.

In enforcing and recognising this maintenance order made on the 23rd day of July, 1973 it can not be said that such enforcement or recognition is giving active or any assistance to facilitate in any way the effecting of a dissolution of marriage or is giving assistance to the process of divorce. It is merely providing for the maintenance of spouses and as such can not be regarded as contrary to public policy.

For these reasons I must dismiss the defendant's appeal herein.

Notes

1. Does this decision uphold the principle that *any* foreign decree for alimony following a divorce will be enforceable in the State? The general international trend is for reduced maintenance awards after divorce, and for a reduction in the period during which maintenance is to be paid. If a foreign court were to award a divorced wife £10 per week for 26 weeks, after which no maintenance could be claimed, would this really be 'providing for the maintenance of spouses'?
2. For a consideration of the subject from a broader international perspective, see Cavers, *International Enforcement of Family Support*, 81 Colum. L. Rev. 994 (1981).
3. Is the holding in the decision that because the order for maintenance, as a matter of historical fact, came after rather than before the granting of the divorce decree, enforcing that order here could not be regarded as giving assistance to the process of divorce? If this is a correct interpretation of the holding, some interesting questions follow. First, does it imply that alimony *pendente lite* or any other form of interim maintenance granted *before* a divorce decree might not be enforceable here since to do so could, in at least some cases, be regarded as giving assistance to the process of divorce? Could such a temporal distinction be defended? More importantly, is it not too simple to argue that, where maintenance is awarded after the decree of divorce, enforcing the award does not assist the process of divorce or 'facilitate the effecting of a dissolution of marriage'?
4. In section 9 of the General Scheme of Legislation included in their *Report on Domicile and Habitual Residence as Connecting Factors in the Conflict of Laws* (LRC 7–1983), the Law Reform Commission propose that:–

   > a spouse's right to maintenance shall not be affected by the fact that the other spouse has obtained by default a decree of divorce, legal separation, nullity of annulment in a State in which the defaulting spouse did not have her residence.

   Do you agree with this recommendation? What are the policy considerations? In the United States, the issue arose against a social background of migratory divorce: see Jacobs, *The Enforcement of Foreign Decrees for Alimony*, 6 L. & Contemporary Problems 251 (1939); Sayre, *Recognition by Other States of Decrees for Judicial Separation and Decrees for Alimony*, 28 Iowa L. Rev. 321 (1943); Lorenzen, *Haddock* v. *Haddock Overruled*, 52 Yale L. J. 341 (1943); Cook, *Is Haddock* v. *Haddock Overruled*?, 18 Indiana L. J. 165 (1943); Holt, *The Bones of Haddock* v. *Haddock*, 41 Mich. L. Rev. 1013 (1943); Foster, *For Better or Worse? Decisions Since Haddock* v. *Haddock*, 47 Amer. Bar Assoc. J. 963 (1961). See also the English Law Commission's Report, *Family Law: Financial Relief After Foreign Divorce* (Law Com. No. 117, 1982).

DALTON v. DALTON

[1982] I.L.R.M. 418 (High Court, O'Hanlon, J., 1981)

O'Hanlon, J.:

The application now before the court is for an order pursuant to s. 8 of the *Family Law (Maintenance of Spouses and Children) Act, 1976* that the separation agreement concluded between the plaintiff and the defendant on 6 April 1981, be made a rule of court.

Such order, if made, would be deemed (by virtue of the provisions of s. 8 of the Act) to be a maintenance order for the purpose of s. 9 and Part III of the Act, and the enforcement machinery provided for in those provisions would thereupon come into play. There is, accordingly, a significant benefit for the plaintiff in having the agreement made a rule of court, if the court thinks fit to exercise its jurisdiction to do so under s. 8 of the Act.

The agreement in question appears to be, in all respects 'a fair and reasonable one which in all the circumstances adequately protects the interests of both spouses and the dependent children if any) of the family', the expression used in s. 8 of the Act, subject to the comments hereinafter made about clause 11 of the agreement.

This clause provides as follows

11. The husband and the wife hereby agree to obtain a decree of divorce a vinculo and the husband further agrees not to contest any divorce proceedings issued by the wife and husband and wife further acknowledge that they have been living apart since 1 August 1976.

The address given in the agreement for each of the parties is in County Dublin, and there is no indication in the agreement or in any of the other documents before the court that the parties or either of them are domiciled elsewhere than in Ireland or intend to adopt a domicile outside Ireland in the future.

It appears to me that considerations of public policy require that the court shall not lend its support to an agreement providing for the obtaining of a divorce *a vinculo* by a husband and wife, and this may well be the position even if the parties are domiciled elsewhere than in Ireland when the application is made or propose to take up such foreign domicile in the future.

I reach this conclusion principally by reference to passages in the judgments delivered in the case of *Mayo-Perrott* v *Mayo-Perrott* [1958] I.R. 336.
Kingsmill-Moore J states at 350:

But to hold that our law accepts the cardinal principle that questions as to married or unmarried status depends on the law of the domicile of the parties at the time when such status is created or dissolved is not to say that our law will give active assistance to facilitate in any way the effecting of a dissolution of marriage in another country where the parties are domiciled. It cannot be doubted that the public policy of this country as reflected in the Constitution does not favour divorce *a vinculo* and though the law may recognise the change of status effected by it as an accomplished fact, it would fail to carry out public policy if, by a decree of its own courts, it gave assistance to the process of divorce by entertaining a suit for the costs of such proceedings. The debt which it is sought to enforce is one created by proceedings of a nature which could not be instituted in this country, proceedings the institution of which our public policy disapproves. For these reasons I hold that the appeal fails and the suit cannot be entertained in our courts.

Similar views were expressed by O'Daly J. (with whose judgment Lavery J concurred) at 351–352; by Maguire J at 353–354 and by the judge of first instance, Murnaghan J at 339 of the report.

I am of opinion that to ask the court to make the agreement which has been concluded between the parties in the present case a rule of court is to ask the court to lend its support to a course of conduct which is contrary to public policy within this jurisdiction. For this reason I have decided that I should refuse the application.

[On the final hearing of the case there was an appearance for the defendant. By consent of the parties, the offending clause of the agreement was deleted and the agreement was made a rule of court.]

Notes

1. What would have been the outcome of the decision if clause 11 had read as follows:

   The husband and wife acknowledge that they have been living apart since 1 August 1976. In the event of the wife issuing divorce proceedings, the husband agrees not to contest such proceedings?

2. Cf. *Cohane* v. *Cohane*, [1968] I.R. 176 (Sup. Ct.).
3. For analysis of the policy considerations, see Moore, *The Enforceability of Premarital Agreements Contingent Upon Divorce*, 10 Ohio N. U. L. Rev. (1983).

4. The *Hague Convention on Recognition of Divorces and Legal Separations* (1970) introduced wide grounds for the recognition of foreign divorces and separations. Article 2 of the Convention *requires* recognition (subject to the remaining terms of the Convention) if, when the proceedings were issued in the State of the divorce or separation ('the State of origin'):
(1) the respondent had his habitual residence there; or
(2) the petitioner had his habitual residence there and one of the following further conditions was fulfilled–
 (a) such habitual residence had continued for not less than one year immediately prior to the institution of proceedings;
 (b) the spouses last habitually resided there together; or
(3) both spouses were nationals of that State: or
(4) the petitioner was a national of that State and one of the following conditions was fulfilled–
 (a) the petitioner had his habitual residence there; or
 (b) he had habitually resided there for a continuous period of one year falling, at least in part, within the two years preceding the institution of the proceedings; or
(5) the petitioner for divorce was a national of that State and both the following further conditions were fulfilled–
 (a) the petitioner was present in that State at the date of institution of the proceedings, and
 (b) the spouses last habitually resided together in a State whose law at the date of institution of the proceedings did not provide for divorce.

Article 7 permits (but does not require) Contracting States to refuse to recognise a divorce, when, at the time it was obtained, both the spouses were nationals of States which did not provide for divorce and of no other State. Article 10 enables Contracting States to refuse to recognise a divorce or legal separation 'if such recognition is manifestly incompatible with their public policy ("ordre public").'

Two other Articles are of particular relevance in the Irish context. Article 19 permits Contracting States to reserve the right—
(1) to refuse to recognise a divorce or legal separation between two spouses who, at the time of the divorce or legal separation, were nationals of the State in which recognition is sought, and no other State, and a law other than that indicated by the rules of private international law of the State of recognition was applied, unless the result reached is the same as that which would have been reached by applying the law indicated by those rules;
(2) to refuse to recognise a divorce when, at the time it was obtained, both parties habitually resided in States which did not provide for divorce. A State which utilises the reservation stated in this paragraph may not refuse recognition by the application of Article 7.

Article 20 permits Contracting States whose law does not provide for divorce to reserve the right not to recognise a divorce if, at the date it was obtained, one of the spouses was a national of a State whose law did not provide for divorce. For analysis of the Convention, see Anton, *Commission I: The Recognition of Divorces and Legal Separations*, 18 Int. & Comp. L. Q. 618, at 620–643, 658–664 (1969); Juenger, *Recognition of Foreign Divorces, British and American Perspectives* 20 Amer. J. of Comp. L. 1 (1972); Karsten, *The Recognition of Divorces and Legal Separations Act, 1971*, 35 Modern L. Rev. 299 (1972); Mann, *The Hague Convention Recognition of Divorces and Legal Separations*, 120 New L. J. 925 (1970); von Mehren & Nadelmann, *The Hague Conference: Convention of June 1, 1970 on Recognition of Foreign Decrees*, 5 Family L. Q. 303 (1971); Nadelmann, *Habitual Residence and Nationality as Tests as The Hague: The 1968 Convention on Recognition of Divorces*, 47 Tex. L. Rev. 766 (1969); Duncan, *The Future for Divorce Recognition in Ireland*, 2 Dublin U. L. Rev. 2, at 8ff (1969) Batiffol, *La Onzième session de la Conférence de la Haye de droit international privé*, 58 Rev. Crit. de Droit Internat. Privé 215, at 216–226 (1969). In Britain the *Recognition of Divorces and Legal Separations Act 1971* introduced rules of recognition even wider than those set out in Article 3 of the Hague Convention, following the English and Scottish Law Commissions' Report, *Hague Convention on Recognition of Divorces and Legal Separations* (Cmnd, 4542, 1970) (Law Com. No. 34; Scot. Law Com. No. 16).

The question whether Ireland should ratify the Hague Convention and introduce its recognition rules into our law raises some interesting issues of policy. At the outset it may perhaps be asked why, if our Constitution prohibits divorce, the State should adopt a Convention which gives effect to the principle of *favor divortii*: cf Siehr, *Domestic Relations in Europe: European Equivalents to American Evolutions*, 30 Am. J. of Comp. L. 37, at 50 (1982). Divorce recognition rules cannot be viewed in isolation: a broader social perspective is required. Quite clearly, to the extent that our recognition rules become progressively wider, the case relating to a divorce jurisdiction *within* the State is transformed. If it were considered desirable for Ireland to ratify the Convention, what reservation, if any, should we make? What should our policy be regarding Article 7? Few of these questions have yet been publicly canvassed. For a helpful analysis on the general theme, see Garfield, *The Transitory Divorce Act: Jurisdiction in the No-Fault Era*, 58 Texas L. Rev. 501 (1980).

DIVORCE: THE SOCIAL ARGUMENT

Since legislation providing for the grant of a dissolution of marriage is prohibited by Article 41.3.2° of the Constitution, the Irish judicial decisions are concerned with questions of *recognition* of foreign divorces rather than the issue of whether divorce is socially desirable or necessary. The judges have been circumspect in their treatment of related aspects of family law (cf. e.g. *O'B.* v. *O'B.*, unreported, Sup. Ct., 18 June 1983 (181/1982), extracted *infra*, pp. 306–11) and have not been drawn into debating this social question in the courts.

So far in Ireland the issue of divorce has generated relatively little detailed analysis. In its Report published in 1967 the Dáil Committee on the Constitution proposed the replacement of the present Constitutional prohibition of divorce by a provision to the effect that:

> In the case of a person who was married in accordance with the rite of a religion no law shall be enacted providing for the grant of a dissolution of that marriage on grounds other than those acceptable to that religion.

This proposal met with a mixed reception from the leaders of the various denominations: see *Shatter*, 148–149. At present a Joint Committee of the Oireachtas is examining the subject of marriage breakdown.

The case in favour of divorce based on breakdown of marriages has more recently been made by Mr. William Duncan, Senior Lecturer in Law at Trinity College Dublin, in *The Case for Divorce in the Irish Republic* (I.C.C.L. Report No. 5 – 1979), revised edition with postscript was published in 1982. For critical analysis of Mr. Duncan's arguments, see Judge Gerard Clarke, 2 Ir. L. T. (n.s.) 105 (1983); Coulter, [1979–80] Dublin U.L.J. 115; Mannix, 73 Inc. L. Soc. of Ireland Gazette 215 (1979); Binchy, 15 Ir. Jur. (n.s.) 361 (1980). See also Mr. Duncan's reply to Binchy, 16 Ir. Jur. (n.s.) 186 (1981).

The Divorce Action Group has also published a 25 page booklet, *Social Reform of Marriage in Ireland: Practical Steps for Legal Change*, edited by its Chairman, Mr. John O'Connor. The booklet, published in 1983, includes a *Draft Family Proceedings Bill*, and explanatory notes.

The divorce question is also analysed by W. Binchy, *Is Divorce the Answer?* (1984), who concludes that, on balance, divorce is not the answer to the problems of marital disruption. Binchy argues that other social and legal remedies are urgently required to meet the problems flowing from marriage disruption. To similar effect is the Life Education and Research Network's *Marriage Breakdown* (1984), incorporating that organisation's recommendations to the Oireachtas Joint Committee on Marriage Breakdown.

Chapter 7

FAMILY PROPERTY

Introduction

In Ireland there is no law of 'family property', in the sense that the property of husband and wife are treated as part of a common pool, to which both spouses have a shared entitlement. Of course, such a common pool can always be created by specific settlement, but in the absence of a settlement the courts have been reluctant to hold that property is held in joint or common ownership. Certain old doctrines, developed long ago at a time when married women had a precarious legal status, still play a part in protecting the property interests of wives.

The courts have used the trust concept to ensure that wives who have contributed to the purchase or improvement of property have the beneficial interest of their contribution duly recognised. Whether sufficient allowance is given to this contribution, especially when it is of an indirect nature, must be considered when analysing the decisions set out below.

HEAVEY v. HEAVEY

111 I.L.T.R. 1 (High Court, Kenny, J., 1974)

Kenny J.:

The plaintiff married the defendant on 30th August, 1954. After their marriage they lived for some years in a house in Dublin which had been purchased by him in his name for £2,300. The plaintiff, who owned a business in Thurles where a grocery and confectionery trade was carried on, sold it in 1956 for £3,105 and this together with arrears of rent and £1,130 received on the sale of the fittings and stock were given by her to him and he lodged it in her name in the Educational Building Society. Between 1958 and 1961 three endowment policies, which she had taken out on her life, matured and she paid the £1,173 which she got from the insurance companies to him. She also had some saving certificates and when they became payable she gave the £402 which she got to him. She was also the owner of a one-seventh interest in a cinema in Thurles which yielded an annual income of £550 which she gave to him each year until 1968. From the time they were married until 1968, he gave her a generous housekeeping allowance, paid all the bills in connection with the household and the expenses of the education of the children. He opened a joint bank account in their names and lodged most of the money he got from her in it. Each could draw cheques on this account.

In 1957 the husband bought two houses in Haddington Road, Dublin, in his name and converted the two houses into flats. In 1959 he bought a house in Northumberland Road ('house A'), Dublin for £2,450 in his name and converted it in the same way. The family home in North Circular Road, which had been bought for £2,300, was sold in 1959 for £7,500 and with this he bought a fine house in Merrion Road, which was conveyed to him for £5,000 and he then spent about £12,000 in altering and decorating it. He and she and their children went to live in the house in Merrion Road where she still resides.

In 1967 another house in Northumberland Road ('house B') was purchased by him for £15,500 and on the 7th July, 1967, he had it conveyed into her name. Most of the purchase money came from the joint account. In an affidavit sworn on the 23rd April, 1974, the husband gave his reasons for having this property conveyed into the sole name of the wife:

'I purchased the premises . . . in June 1967: I put the said premises in the plaintiff's (the wife's) name (a) to help avoid death duties after my death (b) to invest the plaintiff's money given to me over the previous years. When I purchased the said premises it was in three flats, unfurnished, undecorated, letting value about £20 per week. That is what I put in the plaintiff's name, a big empty house with no income from the same. When I put the said premises in the plaintiff's name it never occurred to me that the plaintiff would ever claim the said premises until after my death. I most definitely would not have put the said premises in the plaintiff's name if it ever entered my mind at that time that the plaintiff would claim the said premises or rents therefrom. The reason why I spent so much money converting the said premises into luxury flatlets was to give the plaintiff and our children a troublefree property after my death.'

The total cost of the purchase of that house including auctioneers' fees and solicitors' fees, was £16,904. The cost of converting the premises into luxury flats was £16,560 and this was financed by an overdraft given by the Bank of Ireland to the husband. He has a very prosperous business and the bank were prepared to advance this sum to him on the security of the title deeds of the two houses in Haddington Road and the other house he owned in Northumberland Road. The husband used this account for his business also and in April 1972, shortly after the banks in this country had decided to convert overdrafts into term loans, part of this overdraft became a term loan of £17,000 at interest of 16%. He received most of the rents from house B in Northumberland Road until the 19th May, 1973, when the wife began to collect them. The conversion of the premises was done on such an elaborate scale that the annual gross income from them was £6,380 in 1969 and £6,747 in 1970.

In 1972 the wife began proceedings against him for a judicial separation, for custody of the children and for a declaration under the *Married Women's Status Act*, that she was the owner of the house in her name as from the date of purchase of it and of the other four houses. The three proceedings were heard together and I made an order for judicial separation because of his cruelty, awarded the custody of the children to her and fixed alimony at £75 per week. Subsequently, when I had heard further evidence, I found that she was beneficially entitled to the entire interest of the lessee in house B in Northumberland Road as from the date of purchase and that he was beneficially entitled to the other four houses and an order giving effect to this was made on 16th May, 1973. By it the husband was also restrained until further order from selling the house in Merrion Road until he provided such alternative suitable accommodation for the wife as might be sanctioned by the Court.

She subsequently applied for an account of the rents and profits of the house in Northumberland Road received by him from the 7th July, 1967, to the 19th May, 1973. On the 4th February, 1974, I directed the following accounts to be taken before the Examiner:

1. An account of the rents and profits of the premises in Northumberland Road in the City of Dublin received by the defendant (the husband) from the 7th July, 1967, to the 19th May, 1973.
2. An account of the amounts expended by the defendant in converting the said premises into flats between June, 1967, and May, 1973.
3. An account of the amount due by the defendant to the Bank of Ireland in connection with the purchase of the said premises by the defendant in the name of the plaintiff.

The Examiner made up his certificate on the 12th June, 1974. He found that the husband had received £30,514.11 of the rents and profits of the premises from the 7th July, 1967, to the 19th May, 1973, and that he had paid £7,472.39 on account thereof leaving a balance of £23,041.72 on that account. Bank interest paid by the husband on the amounts expended on the purchase and conversion of the premises was not included in this account. On the second account the Examiner found that the husband had expended £16,560 in converting the premises into flats between June, 1967, and May, 1973, and on the third account he found that on the 22nd October, 1973, £7,385 was due by the husband to the Bank of Ireland in connection with the purchase by him of the premises in the name of the wife. This was the proportionate part relative to the purchase price of the amount due by the husband to the bank.

Counsel for the wife have argued that she is entitled to be paid the £23,041.72 because the husband is not entitled to credit for the amounts expended by him in converting the premises into flats and so cannot claim that this should be paid out of the rents. It has also been submitted that he the husband is not entitled to credit for the sum which he owes the bank in respect of the purchase or conversion. The husband, who has appeared in person, did not direct his argument to any of the interesting legal questions which arise but abused his wife for her greed.

It is a presumption of law that when a husband makes a purchase of property or transfers money or securities into the name of his wife solely, it is intended as a gift to her absolutely at once and there is no resulting trust in his favour. (See: *In re Eykyn's Trusts* (1877) 6 Ch. D. 115; *In re Condrin, Colohan* v. *Condrin* [1914] 1 I.R. 89 and *McCabe* v. *The Ulster Bank Limited* [1939] I.R. 1, 14. The same principle applies when a husband expends his own money on the property of his wife even if that property has been transferred by him to her. It is, however, not an absolute rule of law that the wife gets the benefit of the expenditure; it is a presumption only which may be rebutted by evidence so that if the wife leads the husband to believe that money which he spends on improving her property will be repaid to him out of the rents of the property when improved, he has a valid claim to be reimbursed out of the rents. I agree with the statement of the law in the speech of Lord Upjohn in *Pettitt* v. *Pettitt* [1969] 2 All E.R. 385, at p. 409:

> It has been well settled in Your Lordship's house (*Ramsden* v. *Dyson* (1866) L.R. 1 H.L. 129) that if A expends money on the property of B, *prima facie* he has no claim on such property. And this, as Sir William Grant M.R. held as long ago as 1810 in *Campion* v. *Cotton* (1810) 17 Ves. 263, is equally applicable as between husband and wife. If by reason of estoppel or because the expenditure was incurred by the encouragement of the owner that such expenditure would be rewarded, the person expending the money may have some claim for monetary reimbursement in a purely monetary sense from the owner, or even, if explicitly promised to him by the owner, an interest in the land . . .

It seems to me that it is unreal to approach the question of the ownership of or claims for shares in or reimbursement of expenditure on property as between husband and wife when each has made contributions to its purchase or improvement by trying to ascertain what the agreement between them was or what agreement can be implied from their behaviour. Husband and wife do not contemplate disputes or the break up of their marriage when they are getting married or when they are living happily together and the arrangements about domestic expenditure and their dealings in property are very informal and are not the result of negotiations between them which result in legal agreements. I am fortified in this conclusion by the judgments of the Lord Chief Justice of Northern Ireland, Lord MacDermott, and of Mr. Justice Lowry (as he then was) in *McFarlane* v. *McFarlane* [1972] N.I. 59, from which I have got considerable assistance. When there is an express agreement, the Courts must give effect to it but, in the absence of a proved contract, I think that the question whether a husband has a claim for improvements carried out to his wife's property should be solved by the application of the flexible concept of a resulting or constructive trust (see the speech of Lord Pearson in *Gissing* v. *Gissing* [1970] 2 All E.R. 780). When this concept is adopted, the guiding principle is that stated by Lord Diplock in the same case:

> A resulting, implied or constructive trust – and it is unnecessary for present purposes to distinguish between these three classes of trust – is created by a transaction between the trustee and the cestui que trust in connection with the acquisition by the trustee of a legal estate in land, whenever the trustee has so conducted himself that it would

be inequitable to allow him to deny to the cestui que trust a beneficial interest in the land acquired. And he will be held so to have conducted himself if by his words or conduct he has induced the cestui que trust to act to his own detriment in the reasonable belief that by so acting he was acquiring a beneficial interest in the land.

This principle should, I think, be applied to a transfer of property by a husband to a wife and to expenditure on improvements carried out by him on her property. If he expended his money in improving his wife's property, particularly property which he has transferred to her, he has in my view, no claim to be repaid the amount which he spent even if he thought that the amount would be repaid out of the rents unless she led him to believe that it would be refunded.

This principle, however, does not apply when the husband has borrowed the money to purchase the property or to carry out the improvements. If the wife is aware that the husband is borrowing the money for either of these purposes, it would, in my view, be inequitable for her, when a dispute arises between them, to retain the rents for herself and to refuse to have the outstanding debt incurred by the husband paid out of them. In this case the wife was keeping the husband's books and knew that part of the cost of purchasing house B in Northumberland Road and the entire cost of converting them were being financed by a bank loan given to the husband.

The accounts, which were directed by the order of the 4th February, 1974, do not include an account of the amount due by the husband to the Bank of Ireland in connection with the conversion of the premises into flats between June, 1967, and May, 1973.

Subject to the result of this account, the financial position of the parties seems to me to be that the husband is entitled to credit against the rents which he collected for the amount which he owes the Bank of Ireland in connection with the purchase and conversion of the premises by him in the name of the wife together with the probable amount of interest which he will have to pay. The amount which he owes the bank in connection with the purchase is £7,385; the amount of interest which he will have to pay is not proved in evidence. At 16% the annual interest on £7,385 is £1,168 and the best estimate I can make of the interest which he will pay on the term loan is to allow five years at £1,168 and four years at £584 (which is half the original sum of interest) on the assumption that the husband will be repaying capital and interest each year. The total amount of interest is therefore £8,176 and when this is added to the principal, the total is £15,561. The husband is entitled to credit for this sum against the amount of the rents which he received. He will also be entitled to credit for the amount which may be found to be due by him to the Bank of Ireland for principal and interest in connection with the conversion of the premises into flats.

I regret the necessity of sending the case back to the Examiner for another account. If the husband had retained a legal adviser to conduct this case on his behalf, it would not have been necessary but the claim that part of the expenses of conversion had been financed out of a bank overdraft on which money is still due was not made until after the Examiner had made up his certificate.

There will accordingly be an account before the examiner of the amount due by the defendant to the Bank of Ireland for principal and interest in connection with the conversion of the premises house B in Northumberland Road by the defendant. When the result of this is known, it will be possible to dispose of the matter.

[The Supreme Court, in an oral judgment, dismissed the husband's appeal in July, 1976: see *Shatter*, 316.]

Notes

1. To what extent does *McFarlane* diverge from *Gissing*? Cf. Gibson, *A Wife's Right in the Matrimonial Home*, 27 N.I.L.Q. 333, at 334ff (1976). For a penetrating analysis of the subject generally see Cooney, *Wives, Mistresses and Beneficial Ownership*, 14 Ir. Jur. (n.s.) 1 (1979). See also Maudsley, *Constructive Trusts*, 28 N.I.L.Q. 123

(1977). For a more recent analysis of the English cases, see W. Murphy & H. Clark, *The Family Home*, ch. 3 (1983).

2. An interesting insight into Kenny, J.'s thinking on the subject of property relationships between spouses may be gained from his analysis of the English property decisions, in a lecture delivered four years before *Heavey* v. *Heavey*: see *Some Aspects of Family Law*, 22 March 1970, Lecture No. 46 of the Society of Young Solicitors, pp. 6–7.
3. See also *N.D.* v. *A.D.*, unreported, High Ct., O'Hanlon, J., 10 December 1982 (1980–470Sp.).
4. The presumption of advancement may catch persons involved in legal evasion. In *P.* v. *P.*, unreported, High Ct., Costello, J., July 1980 (1978 No. 641P) a transfer of property was taken in the name of the wife, who was Irish, rather than her husband, who was British, to avoid the necessity of applying to the Land Commission for its consent to the transfer, under section 45 of the *Land Act 1965*. The transfer contained a certificate to the effect that the wife, 'becoming entitled to the entire beneficial interest in the property' was an Irish citizen. In later proceedings the husband, who had provided the consideration, sought to establish that he had not intended to benefit his wife. Costello, J. rejected this claim, saying:

> Mr. P. is in [an] inescapable dilemma: . . . if he acted honestly, and the certificate was a true one, then the property belongs to his wife; if he acted dishonestly, and the certificate was a false one, the Court will not allow him to take advantage of his own dishonesty. What the Defendant asks is that the Court should apply its equitable principles and hold that a resulting trust exists and that the Plaintiff holds the land in trust for him. But the very equitable principles which the defendant calls in aid prevents the Court making a declaration in his favour. The estate must lie where it falls. . .

C. v. C.
[1976] I.R. 254 (High Ct., Kenny, J., 1975)

Kenny, J.:

The defendant husband and the plaintiff wife were married on the 3rd April, 1961. After their marriage they lived for some time in a flat and then, in October, 1963, the husband purchased a house for £2,200. A deposit of £220 was paid on the signing of the contract. The husband, who was a barman at the time of the marriage, was earning about £7 a week and had no savings. The wife had inherited £242 on the death of her father, and her mother provided her with some more money. She gave these sums to the husband so that he could pay the deposit and the expenses of the purchase of the house. He had obtained an advance from the Irish Permanent Building Society of £2,005 and this, together with the sums paid to him by the wife, made it possible for him to close the sale. She knew that the house was to be purchased in his name only and, although she had paid the moneys for the deposit and the expenses of the sale, she did not object to its transfer to him because, in her own words, 'it was our home and I thought we jointly owned it.'

The mortgage for £2,005 was repayable over a period of 30 years by monthly instalments of £13.65. The husband was unable to pay the instalments on a number of occasions and the pass-book shows that payments of varying amounts were made irregularly. As the husband was unable to make the monthly payments, the wife got seven sums of £100 each at different times from her mother and brother to pay the instalments due to the Society. These sums were given by the wife to the husband so that he could pay the instalments: the total amount contributed by her to the purchase price of the house and the repayment of the mortgage was £1,027.

There are four children of the marriage, the oldest being 12 years old and the youngest 4 years old.

The husband remained at work as a barman until 1968 when he began to work as a self-employed electrician earning about £35 per week. In February, 1972, he was employed as an electrician and received a gross salary of £39 per week together with expenses which varied from week to week. His net salary in the first week of his employment in May, 1973, was £35.66 and in the last week of his employment with this firm in May, 1974, was £37.81. In addition he worked part-time as a barman during the evenings . . . and from the 3rd

May, 1973, to the 7th November, 1974, he earned £1,306 from this work. This was an average weekly sum of about £18. His employment as an electrician ended in May, 1974. He registered for unemployment benefit in June, 1974, and continued to draw this at the rate of £30.85 until November when he obtained employment again.

The marriage was a happy one until 1967 when the husband began to insult and assault the wife. On many occasions he came back to the house late in the evening or early in the morning in a drunken condition. The relations between them became so bad that in 1971 she went with her children to reside with her mother where she remained for 10 months and returned only when the husband had promised that he would treat her well.

When she returned, he behaved towards her with some consideration for a short time but the former pattern of conduct soon appeared again. Although he was earning about £50 per week at this time he gave her £13 per week only to run the house and clothe the children. There are three bedrooms in the house and, at some time in 1973, he began to lock the large room when he was going out and took the key with him so that the wife was compelled to sleep with her children in one of the other rooms. In July, 1973, he turned off the electricity to the house and disconnected the telephone; in that month a most distressing episode occurred when he returned home late at night with his sister and began to play a guitar which he owned. The noise was deafening and the wife and the children were frightened, particularly as he and his sister were very drunk. There were many other assaults and quarrels and the Guards were sent for on a number of occasions. The husband continued to live in the house until October, 1974, when he left and went to live elsewhere. Since then the wife has been drawing home assistance. Though the husband paid the mortgage instalments and electricity bills for some time after he left, he has now ceased to do this.

In July, 1973, the wife brought proceedings against the husband under the *Married Women's Status Act, 1957*, claiming that she was entitled to the house in equal shares with him. She also brought proceedings claiming custody of the children and payment for their maintenance. The proceedings were adjourned on many occasions at the request of the parties and ultimately the two actions were heard together in November, 1974.

When the matrimonial home is purchased in the name of a husband, either before or after a marriage, the wife does not become entitled, as wife, to any share in its ownership either because she occupies the status of wife or because she carries out household duties. In many cases, however, the wife contributes to the purchase price or mortgage instalments. Her contributions may be either by payment to the husband of moneys which she has inherited or earned, or by paying the expenses of the household so that he has the money which makes it possible for him to pay the mortgage instalments. Domestic arrangements in relation to the payment of debts or the sharing of expenses are almost always informal and the parties do not make agreements which have that precision which is necessary to make them enforceable as contracts in a court of law. When there is an agreement between them as to the ownership of the house which is in the husband's name only, the Court will enforce it; but the number of cases in which this happens is small. The principles derived from the last century (when married women did not earn and when any property they had was usually settled) are of little assistance in determining the ownership of the matrimonial home when the wife has made contributions towards its purchase or towards the repayment of the mortgage instalments. Trying to infer what was the implied agreement which arose when payments were made or expenses paid by a wife is a futile task because, when the spouses are living happily together, they do not think of stipulating that payments by one of them are made to acquire a share in the matrimonial home or furniture.

I think that the correct and most useful approach to these difficult cases is to apply the concept of a trust to the legal relationship which arises when a wife makes payments towards the purchase of a house, or the repayment of the mortgage instalments, when the house is in the sole name of the husband. When this is done, he becomes a trustee for her of a share in the house and the size of the share depends upon the amount of the contributions which she has made towards the purchase or the repayment of the mortgage. I think that this view is supported by the decisions in *Pettitt* v. *Pettitt* [1970] A.C. 777; *Gissing* v. *Gissing* [1971] A.C. 886; *McFarlane* v. *McFarlane* [1972] N.I. 59; *Hazell* v. *Hazell* [1972] 1 W.L.R. 301; *Kowalczuk* v. *Kowalczuk* [1973] 1 W.L.R. 930; *Heavey* v. *Heavey* (1974) 111 I.L.T.R. 1. This approach also has the advantage that it gives that flexibility which is essential in dealing with domestic matters.

In this case the original cost of the house was £2,200. There was no evidence of its present value but I do not think that this is relevant to the ascertainment of the interest to which the wife is entitled because the sums contributed by her, towards the original purchase at least, were paid in 1962 and her beneficial interest in the house arose not when her dispute with her husband started but when she made the payments. As the cost of the house was £2,200 plus the interest element in the mortgage repayments, and as she paid £1,027, I propose to hold that she is entitled to one half of the beneficial interest in the matrimonial home. Accordingly, there will be a declaration that the husband holds the premises, as to one half the beneficial interest therein, in trust for the wife. . . .

[Kenny, J.'s consideration of the plaintiff's action for an injunction evicting the defendant from the house is set out *infra*, p. 299]

Notes

1. Commenting on Kenny, J.'s reference to the 'futile task' of attempting to infer what was the implied agreement between spouses living together, Mr. Paul O'Connor submits that:

   these remarks . . . provide a measure of support for the view that the trust concept, specifically the constructive trust, does not depend for its existence on a finding of intention. If a spouse makes indirect significant contributions, thereby benefiting the legal owning spouse, what compelling reasons are there for holding that a constructive trust should not be applied? In such a situation one spouse would have been enriched, in a quite tangible manner, by the other spouse. It is submitted, on this basis, that the spouse who has no legal interest in the property ought nonetheless to be recompensed. *Indirect Contributions and the Acquisition of a Beneficial Interest in Property*, 2 Ir. L.T. 40, at 41 (1984).

2. For a comparative analysis of the law in England, Canada, Australia and New Zealand, see Hodkinson, *Constructive Trusts: Palm Trees in the Commonwealth*, [1983] Conv. 420.
3. See also *M.* v. *M.*, 114 I.L.T.R. 46 (High Ct., Finlay, P., 1978) and *K.* v. *K.*, 114 I.L.T.R. 50 (High Ct., Finlay, P., 1978).

R.K. v. M.K.

Unreported High Court, Finlay, P., 24 October 1978 (1978–330 Sp.)

[The facts of the case have already been set out at pp. 213–14 *supra* in relation to the issue of maintenance. On the question of the plaintiff's asserted beneficial interest in the family home, **Finlay P.** stated:]

I am not satisfied that the plaintiff is entitled to any beneficial interest in the house and lands at S________. On the legal principles I am confined to an examination of a direct or indirect contribution on her part to the acquisition of the property. It is conceded that no direct contribution in money was made by the plaintiff. S__________ was purchased by the defendant in his own name approximately 17 years ago and it was purchased for cash, that is to say without raising a mortgage on it. The only work alleged by the plaintiff to have been done by her prior to the purchase of S__________ was that each week she did what I will describe in a neutral phrase as the family banking. This consisted of making certain calculations and making out a cheque for signature by the defendant to cover (a) wages, (b) household or housekeeping expenses (c) spending money by the defendant and on some occasions cash for invoices which were going to be paid in cash and associated with the business. On some of the occasions when the plaintiff was carrying out this banking transaction of cashing the cheque so drawn and signed by her husband she probably also carried out interviews on his part with the bank manager. I am not satisfied that any other work was done by the plaintiff though I am speaking of course in the context of work connected with the business of building.

The extent of her work in the household and in the care of her children was very considerable but our law does not recognise so far at least a right arising from that type of work to a part ownership of any family or marriage property. The task I have described is not in my view a task which could attract remuneration nor constitute an identifiable taking part in the defendant's business. It is from the proceeds of that business that the cost of acquiring the property came. The claim therefore under the *Married Women's Status Act, 1957* must in my view fail.

Notes

1. Does the law as stated in this decision give effect to a sound legal policy in your view? Is it constitutional? Cf. O'Connor, *Indirect Contributions and the Acquisition of a Beneficial Interest in Property*, 2 Ir. L.T. 40, at 41 (1984).
2. Cf. O'Donovan, *Legal Recognition of the Value of Housework*, 8 Family L. 215 (1978).
3. In *L.* v. *L.*, unreported, High Ct., Finlay, P., 21 December 1979 (1979–378Sp.) there were no children and for the first two years after the marriage, both spouses had been employed, each contributing to a joint family fund, but 'living up to the limit of it, neither acquiring by mortgage repayments any premises nor accumulating any savings.' A house was then bought in the husband's name. Finlay, P. held that there was no evidence that contributions made by the wife from her earnings during the two years, 'either directly or indirectly, contributed to the acquisition of the family home.'

R. v. R.

Unreported, McMahon, J., 12 January 1979 (1978–243Sp.)

McMahon, J.:

These proceedings are brought by the wife who is the Plaintiff by a Special Summons claiming an Order under Section 12 [of the] *Married Women's Status Act, 1957* declaring that she is entitled to the sole beneficial interest in the family home or alternatively determining the extent of her beneficial interest in the premises.

The parties were married in March 1968. They had been going together for some years before marriage. The husband is a machine operator in a Dublin firm. The wife was aged eighteen on marriage and the husband was some years older than his wife.

For the first year of their marriage the parties lived in a mobile home which the husband had acquired. He then bought a home in a County Dublin village by means of a mortgage. He obtained some of the money for the deposit of £500 by the sale of the mobile home and some by borrowing from a Credit Union. The House was purchased in the husband's name.

There were no children of the marriage. The parties separated and the marriage broke up in September 1973. The family home has been sold with the wife's consent and the nett proceeds are held by the husband's solicitor pending the outcome of these proceedings. The wife has resumed employment and has not made any claim on the husband for maintenance.

Before the marriage the wife held various jobs and she continued to work after marriage. The records of the Department of Social Welfare which have been proved show that between July 1968 and July 1973 the wife was employed for a total of 166 weeks, that is, an average of 33 weeks per year. The wife claims that the money she earned was spent on her own necessaries and on meeting the expenses of the household and in that way her earnings helped her husband to meet the mortgage repayments on the house and she is therefore entitled to a beneficial interest in the proceeds of the sale. The husband swore an affidavit in which he said that after they were married his wife worked for short periods only and all the money which she earned was spent on herself on make-up, buying clothes and having her hair done. Faced with the records of the wife's employment from the Department of Social Welfare the husband retreated somewhat from this extreme position but still alleged that most of the wife's earnings were spent on herself. The wife's evidence was given with moderation and carefully and in general I accept it. The husband is clearly mistaken in his recollection of the periods for which the wife was employed and I do not think that his allegations of extravagance on her part were substantiated.

The family home cost £3,500. It is situated in a new housing estate adjoining a County Dublin village which would in estate agents' language be described as a dormitory suburb. The husband's job involved night work and he therefore required a car to get to work. The wife's earnings helped the husband to live in this County Dublin village and to run the car and at the same time the couple were able to enjoy a reasonable but not extravagant standard of living. Had the wife not been earning the husband would not have been able to keep up the mortgage repayments and run a car and maintain their standard of living. The wife spent some of her earnings on providing food and other requisites for the household and some was spent on herself for clothes and having her hair done but so far as the money was spent on the wife's needs it seems to me that these were expenses which the husband would have been bound to meet if she was not able to pay for them herself. I can see no distinction between money paid for necessaries for herself and in my view both kinds of expenditure come within the principle enunciated by Mr. Justice Kenny in *C.* v. *C.* [*supra*, p. 266] namely, that the wife's contribution which will give her a claim to a beneficial interest in the matrimonial home may take the form of paying the expenses of the household so that her husband has the money which makes it possible for him to pay the mortgage instalments. In either case there is a saving to the husband and if that enables him *pro tanto* to meet the mortgage repayments the wife should be regarded as contributing towards those repayments.

The husband got the benefit of the appropriate tax reliefs as a married man in his assessment to income tax and the wife's earnings were subject to deduction of tax at the rate of 35p in the pound. The fairest approach in my view is to assume that their respective contributions to the family purse and therefore to the mortgage repayments were in the same proportion as their respective gross earnings before tax. On that basis I calculate the husband's gross earnings during the period the parties lived together at £10,000 and the wife's gross earnings £1,800. I therefore hold that the nett proceeds of the sale of the house should belong to the husband and the wife in the proportion of 100 to 18.

Notes

1. Does this decision hold that the *general rule* on which a Court should proceed is that, where a married woman works in paid employment outside the home, then the respective contributions of the spouses to the acquisition of the home are to be apportioned in the same proportion as their respective gross earnings before tax? Or does the case depend on the fact that the wife's contribution was indirect? Or is the decision based on its special facts? Cf. *E.R.* v. *M.R.*, unreported, High Ct., Carroll, J., 26 January 1981 (1977–653Sp.).
2. Why did the Court not consider the personal expenditure patterns of the husband? Presumably he had his hair cut during the five years the parties lived together. Assume for a moment that a husband has extravagant interests, not shared by his wife: should his expenditure on these interests be subtracted when calculating his beneficial interest in the home?

M.B. v. E.B.

Unreported, High Court, Barrington, J., February 1980 (1979 566SP)

Barrington, J.: . . . [T]he purchase price of the house was £11,250. The husband raised the entire purchase price other than a sum of £4,500 which was financed by a County Council loan. Mr. Connolly, on behalf of the wife, has admitted that the wife has no claim to the interest in the house, represented by the cash raised by the husband. The house is in the husband's name and Mr. Connolly confines his claim to a beneficial interest in an undivided 2/5ths of the house, the purchase of which was financed by the mortgage of £4,500.

The wife's claim is brought under Section 12 of the *Married Women's Status Act, 1957.* This Section provides a machinery for determining any question arising between husband and wife as to the title to, or possession of, any property. It does not, however (despite the wording of sub-section 2), confer any jurisdiction on the Court to divide property between husband and wife in a manner which the Court considers equitable. It is merely a jurisdiction to determine in whom the title to the property in dispute, resides. . . . [Barrington, J. then referred to the judgments of Kenny, J. in *C.* v. *C., supra*, pp. 265–66 and of MacMahon, J. in *R.* v. *R., supra*, pp. 268–69. He continued:]

The present case is not quite on all fours with *C.* v. *C.* and *R.* v. *R.* In the present case the husband paid the greater part of the purchase money . . ., and the balance was raised by the mortgage. I am satisfied that the wife made a very substantial contribution towards the setting up of the matrimonial home, but she made no direct contribution towards the repayment of the mortgage and, as the parties lived together in the matrimonial home for just over two years, the effect of the indirect contribution (which I am satisfied she made) on reducing the capital sum outstanding on foot of the mortgage, must have been minimal.

As previously stated, the wife's take-home pay at the time of her marriage was £43.00p subsequently reduced to £32.00p to meet a tax liability of her husband's. While the wife raised none of the cash to purchase the house, she paid a sum of £150 being approximately one half of the legal fees due to the purchasers' and the mortgagee's solicitors. At the time of the marriage, the husband's weekly wage was only £35.00p. The wife says (and I accept), that there was 'a kind of an agreement' between the parties under which the husband paid the mortgage repayments and the E.S.B. bills, and the wife bought virtually everything else that was needed for the house. No doubt this agreement was not rigidly adhered to, and each party made occasional purchases as convenience dictated. I am quite satisfied however, that the wife bore the main financial burden of running the house.

In July, 1978, the wife, who was then 5 months pregnant, resigned her job in the Civil Service and received a gratuity of £1,550. She also received a sum of £250.00 compensation in respect of a motor car accident in which she had been involved. All this money, with the exception of a sum of less than £400, was spent by her on buying furniture and equipment for the house. Among the items she bought from her own monies were furniture, curtains and accessories, lampshades, wallpaper and paint, carpets, a vacuum cleaner, a tumble dryer, towels, bed linen, blankets, etc., delph, pots, baking utensils, cutlery, tea-towels, sewing machine, baby's pram, clothes, etc., roof rack for car, electric food mixer, groceries from July, 1977 to July, 1978. Besides, the parties shared equally the cost of the following:– Cooker, washing machine, 2 wardrobes, dressing-table, 3-piece suite, television table, kitchen table and chairs.

The wife estimates the monetary value of her contribution to the joint household expenses at more than £3,400. I have no doubt that but for the wife's willingness to make the contribution which she did make to the joint household expenses, the husband could not have repaid the mortgage repayments, run the car which both parties considered necessary to get to and from work, or enjoyed the lifestyle which he did enjoy.

There may be circumstances in which articles brought to, or bought for, the matrimonial home by one marriage partner, clearly are intended to remain the property of that marriage partner. Other property – such as a watch or jewellery – may clearly be personal to one partner rather than to the other. The *Married Women's Status Act* provides a machinery for ascertaining the title to such property.

But when, as in the present case, the property was clearly bought 'for the house', the circumstances appear to me to be different. It would be absurd to conclude that the wife owned all of the tumbledryer but only one-half of the washing machine.

What the husband and wife were doing in the present case was establishing a home. As Mr. Justice Kenny has pointed out, marriage partners seldom enter into formal agreements when the marriage is going well. But, the understanding between them may, at times, be seen in their actions or course of conduct. If they appear to be acting on the principle that all things are common between friends, then, it appears to me, that a Court can readily infer that that principle gives the basis of the understanding between them.

In the present case the parties were not in the business of buying and selling furniture and household goods. They were buying goods for a particular house which was their house, and utensils to suit the needs of a particular household which was their household. It appears to me that the logical inference from this is that the furniture and goods purchased, unless personal to one of the parties (as, for instance in the present case, clothes for the husband) are the joint property of both parties.

Mr. Connolly put his claim to the furniture and to a share in the beneficial interest in the house, in the alternative. I find it hard to see, how the purchase of the furniture can, in itself, affect the wife's claim to an interest in the house.

But the subsequent conduct of both parties does, however, cast light on what the basic understanding or 'kind of agreement' between them was and on the nature and interest of the trust which they created for each other. It appears to me to be quite clear on the facts of this case, that the understanding between them was by their joint efforts to buy and furnish a home. As Lord Denning said in *Hazell* v. *Hazell* [1972] 1 All E.R. 923, at 926:

> It is sufficient if the contributions made by the wife are such as to relieve the husband from expenditure which he would otherwise have had to bear. By so doing the wife helps him indirectly with the mortgage instalments because he has more money in his pocket with which to pay them. It may be that he strictly does not need her help – he may have enough money of his own without it – *but if he accepts it* (and thus is enabled to save more of his own money), she becomes entitled to a share. [Barrington, J.'s emphasis – ed.]

The husband had the financial resources to pay immediately for a 3/5ths interest in the home. The wife's claim is made only in respect of the remaining 2/5ths interest. The most favourable interpretation, from the husband's point of view, seems to be to confine the joint effort to the acquisition of the remaining 2/5ths interest in the house and the furniture.

I accordingly reach the conclusion that the wife is entitled to an undivided 5th share in the beneficial interest of the equity of redemption, subsequent upon the re-payment of the mortgage, and an undivided one half share in the household goods and furniture, other than such items as are personal to one or other of the parties.

So far as the house is concerned an account should be taken, between husband and wife, as of the 28th day of July 1979 (the date on which he left the matrimonial home). As and from that date the husband is, as against the wife, entitled to a three fifths interest in the house free of the mortgage. The balance outstanding on foot of the mortgage as of that date is apportioned to the remaining two fifths. The wife is entitled to one of these two fifth shares after deduction from them of (1) the balance outstanding on foot of the mortgage as of the 28th day of July 1979, and (2) in the event of a sale of the house, the costs and expenses of the sale.

The husband gets credit for one half of the interest element in mortgage repayments made by him since the 28th day of July 1979. But both parties are entitled to any increase in value of their respective shares in the house.

Notes

1. If the wife had not testified that there was 'a kind of an agreement' between the spouses, do you think the case would have been decided differently? Cf. *Shatter*, 314.
2. Section 21 of the *Family Law (Maintenance of Spouses and Children) Act, 1976* implements a recommendation of the Commission on the Status of Women in its Report in 1972. It provides that:

> Any allowance made by one spouse to the other spouse after the commencement of this Act for the purpose of meeting household expenses, and any property or interest in property acquired out of such allowance, shall, in the absence of any agreement, whether express or implied, between them to the contrary, belong to the spouses as joint owners.

Is this a useful reform? Is it drafted in too general terms? Cf. *Shatter*, 340–341. Are spouses in general aware of this provision? In England a similar, but more restrictive, reform introduced by section 1 of the *Married Women's Property Act, 1964* was not widely known, and, so far as it was known, was largely misunderstood by the general public eight years later: see B. Hoggett & D. Pearl, *The Family, Law and Society: Cases and Materials*, 85–86 (1983).

M.G. v. R.D.

Unreported, High Ct., Keane, J., 28 April 1981 (1980–No.423)

Keane, J.:

The parties were married [i]n . . . October, 1973. The plaintiff was an air hostess and the defendant was a bank official. The plaintiff continued to work after the marriage. There are no children of the marriage. The parties separated in March, 1977, and have not lived together since then.

The matrimonial home, which is the subject matter of the present proceedings, was a house in a Dublin suburb which was purchased in June, 1973. It was purchased in the name of the defendant, the total cost being £9,500. The purchase was financed by a staff loan of £8,000 from the defendant's employers, a term loan of £1,000 from another bank and a loan of £1,000 from the defendant's mother. The staff loan was at a fixed low rate of interest, i.e. 4%. It is agreed that there are 33 years of the mortgage term still unexpired and there is a substantial sum owing under the mortgage.

After her marriage, the plaintiff continued to pay her salary into a separate bank account. She regularly spent part of this money on housekeeping items, principally food. She also bought – by means of a personal loan – a car which was used by both parties. The monthly repayments of £32 to his employers in respect of the staff loan were made by the defendant, as were the monthly instalments of £30 in respect of the loan of £1,000 from another bank. He also paid the other normal outgoings, including such items directly referable to the house as the rates, ground rent and insurance. There was no evidence to suggest that the payments made by the plaintiff were on foot of any agreement or arrangement, even of the loosest character. The defendant gave evidence, which I accept, that he urged the plaintiff on a number of occasions to agree to operate a joint bank account, but that she refused.

The plaintiff agreed that the amount of her weekly contributions to the housekeeping during the period from April 1975 to June 1976 – in respect of which her bank statements and paid cheques were available – was probably £10 or £11. The defendant's net income in 1975/1976 was £2,627.83. Some of this would probably have been spent on personal items not attributable to the marriage. As against this, the plaintiff's net earnings for that period were higher than her earnings for the previous two years, substantially higher in the case of the first year. This suggests that the plaintiff's weekly contributions to the housekeeping expenses may have been higher in 1975/6 than in the previous years. The plaintiff, of course, also paid for a car which was used by both parties. Moreover, because the plaintiff was an air hostess, the cost of some overseas holidays which they took together was substantially reduced.

While it is difficult to be exact in these matters, I think it is probable that the plaintiff's contributions to the joint expenses of the household over the four years of the marriage amounted, on average, to one-fifth of those expenses. It is also clear that, although her contributions enabled the parties to maintain a particular standard of living while ensuring that the house repayments were met, the defendant would have been in a position to make those repayments even if the plaintiff had made no financial contribution to the household expenses.

The case made on behalf of the plaintiff is that these contributions helped the defendant indirectly with the house repayments because he had more money with which to pay them; and that, the contributions having been accepted by the defendant, the plaintiff became entitled to a beneficial interest in the house.

There is undoubtedly authority to support this proposition. . . .

[Keane, J. quoted from Kenny, J.'s judgment in *C.* v. *C., supra*, p. 265. He continued:]

In that case, the wife paid the deposit on the house and also paid a number of the mortgage instalments. It was not a case in which the beneficial interest of the wife arose because of indirect contributions such as are relied on in the present case. While Kenny J. refers, in the passage which I have quoted, to the possibility that financial contributions by the wife to the household expenses may make it possible for a husband to pay the mortgage instalments, he does not say in so many words that such a state of affairs will, without more, raise the inference of a resulting trust which is necessary to give the wife a beneficial interest in the house. Indeed, one of the authorities to which he refers, *McFarlane* v. *McFarlane* [1972] N.I. 59, a judgment of the Northern Ireland Court of Appeal, is authority for the contrary proposition. It might appear therefore that Kenny J. did not intend, in this passage, to lay down any general principle of the nature contended for by the plaintiff in the present case.

However, in *R.* v. *R.* [*supra*, p. 268] McMahon J. took the view that Kenny J.'s observations did in fact support such a proposition. The facts in that case were more closely akin to those in the present case: there was no suggestion that the wife had made any direct contribution either to the deposit or the mortgage repayments, but she had met other household expenses. . . .

[Keane, J. quoted McMahon, J.'s conclusion in *R.* v. *R.* He continued:]

A different view, however, was taken by Gannon J. in *McGill* v. *S.* [*supra*, p. 166]. . . .

[Keane, J. summarised the facts of this case, and quoted a passage from Gannon, J.'s judgment. He noted that it did not appear that *R.* v. *R.* had been cited in the course of the argument in that case. Keane, J. also referred in some detail to the decision of Barrington, J., in *M.B.* v. *E.B., supra*, p. 270. He continued:]

Finally, I should refer to the three reported judgments of the President, *M.* v. *M.*, 114 I.L.T.R. 46 (1978), *K.* v. *K.*, 114 I.L.T.R. 50 (1978) and *L.* v. *L.* (judgment delivered 21st December, 1979). In the first, certain indirect contributions by the wife were taken into account, but she had also made a substantial contribution to the purchase price. In the second, there appear to have been indirect contributions by the wife to the mortgage repayments. Neither of these decisions is, accordingly, of assistance in a case such as the present. In *L.* v. *L.* the wife contributed most of her earnings towards defraying the couple's joint living expenses, including the mortgage repayments, although the monthly instalments were actually paid over to the building society by the husband. The President held that she was entitled to a beneficial interest in the property. It does not appear, however, from the judgment that the question as to what extent, if at all, indirect contributions may be taken into account was actually argued in that case.

I think it is clear from this summary of the authorities that there is some divergence of view as to the extent to which indirect contributions of the nature relied on in the present case can generate a beneficial interest in the matrimonial home; and the difficulty is increased by the existence of conflicting decisions in England and Northern Ireland on the same topic. In *Gissing* v. *Gissing* [1971] A.C. 886, Lord Diplock said (in a passage which was cited by Gannon J. in *McGill* v. *S.*):–

> Difficult as they are to solve, however, these problems as to the amount of the share of a spouse in the beneficial interest in a matrimonial home where the legal estate is vested solely in the other spouse, only arise in cases where the Court is satisfied by the words or conduct of the parties that it was their common intention that the beneficial interest was not to belong solely to the spouse in whom the legal estate was vested but was to be shared between them in some proportion or other.
>
> Where the wife has made no initial contribution to the cash deposit and legal charges and no direct contribution to the mortgage instalments nor any adjustment to her contribution to other expenses of the household which it can be inferred was referable to the acquisition of the house, there is in the absence of evidence of an express agreement between the parties no material to justify the Court in inferring that it was the common intention of the parties that she should have any beneficial interest in a matrimonial home conveyed into the sole name of the husband, merely because she continued to contribute out of her own earnings or private income to other expenses of the household. For such conduct is no less consistent with a common intention to share the day-to-day expenses of the household, while each spouse retains a separate interest in capital assets acquired with their own monies or obtained by inheritance or gift.

In the same case, however, Lord Reid said at p. 896:

> As I understand it, the competing view is that, when the wife makes direct contributions to the purchase by paying something either to the vendor or to the building society which is financing the purchase, she gets a beneficial interest in the house although nothing was ever said or agreed about this at the time: but that, when her contributions are only indirect by way of paying sums which the husband would otherwise have had to pay, she gets nothing unless at the time of the acquisition there was some agreement that she should get a share. I can see no good reason for this distinction and I think that in many cases it would be unworkable.

When the matter came before the Northern Ireland Court of Appeal in *McFarlane* v. *McFarlane*, Lord McDermott, L.C.J., having said that it seemed open to doubt whether Lord Reid's opinion had gained general acceptance, and having referred to Lord Pearson's opinion in *Gissing* v. *Gissing* as indicating that some kind of 'arrangement' was necessary before one could derive a beneficial interest from indirect contributions, went on to summarise his own view as follows:–

> The conclusion I have reached on this important and difficult question is that there is a relevant distinction between the two kinds of contribution and that the indirect contribution, if it is to earn a beneficial interest in the property acquired, must be the subject of agreement or arrangement between the spouses. Here I do not refer to a contractual relationship solely, but would include any understanding between the spouses which shows a mutual intention that the indirect contributions of one or the other will go to create a beneficial proprietary interest in the contributor.

Sir Robert Lowry in the same case said (at p. 75):–

> It is now being made clear that indirect contributions serve the purpose of direct contributions only where there is a mutual intention that they should do so.

The Court of Appeal in England, however, have taken a different view. In *Falconer* v. *Falconer* [1970] 3 All E.R. 449, Lord Denning, M.R., said that notwithstanding *Gissing* v. *Gissing*, the inference of a trust is to be readily drawn when each party has made a financial contribution to the purchase price or the mortgage instalments, even though the financial contribution is indirect and takes the form of payments for housekeeping expenses. This view was reiterated by the Court of Appeal, again presided over by Lord Denning, M.R., in *Hargrave* v. *Newton* [1971] 3 All E.R. 866, *Hazell* v. *Hazell* [1972] 1 All E.R. 923; and *Kowalczuk* v. *Kowalczuk* [1973] 2 All E.R. 1042.

The conflict of authority in England appears to flow from a divergence of view as to how the constructive trust, as a result of which the contributing spouse becomes entitled to a beneficial share, comes into being. The view taken in *Gissing* v. *Gissing* by Viscount Dilhorne, Lord Diplock and possibly Lord Pearson appears to be that it can only come into being as the result of a actual intention formed by both parties that the contributing spouse should have such a beneficial interest. It appears to be the clear inference from at least two of these speeches that, while such an intention may be inferred from the acts of the parties without its being expressed in words by either of them, it must exist. The contrary view is that, where the indirect contributions are sufficiently substantial, such an intention may be imputed to the parties, without any other evidence from which the Court could infer its existence.

I share the doubts expressed by Gannon J. in *McGill* v. *S.* as to the validity of the proposition that the making of indirect contributions, of itself and without any other evidence, can constitute sufficient evidence to justify the inference of a resulting or constructive trust. The strongest argument in favour of that proposition appears to be that to hold otherwise would be to create an unreal and arbitrary distinction between the direct payment by the contributing spouse of mortgage instalments and an indirect contribution by way of payment of other household expenses. It seems to me, however, that the distinction is a real one and supported by principle: in the absence of special circumstances, the payment on a regular basis by one spouse of the mortgage instalments is clearly capable of supporting the inference that it was intended that the payor should be entitled to a beneficial interest in the property in respect of which the instalments were paid. Different considerations may well apply, however, to the discharge by one spouse of liabilities which are the responsibility of the other, but which are not related in any way to the acquisition of the property in question: as Lord McDermott points out in *McFarlane* v. *McFarlane*, in most cases such payments are made without any thought of building up a beneficial interest in any form of property and as part of 'a joint and unselfish adventure'. It seems to me entirely reasonable in such circumstances that the Court should require at least some evidence to indicate that they were in fact made in pursuance of a common intention that the contributing spouse should be entitled to some beneficial interest in the property.

The suggestion has also been made that, since a resulting trust arises by operation of law, it is not appropriate to test its existence by reference to anything in the nature of a consensus between the trustee and the *cestui que trust*. This is hardly convincing: Lord Diplock, in his detailed analysis of the problem in *Gissing* v. *Gissing* has pointed out that the resulting trust arises because of the inequity of permitting a purchaser to accept contributions to the purchase price and at the same time deny the existence of any beneficial interest in the contributor, when it was the common if unexpressed intention of the parties that the contributor should have such an interest. Manifestly, in the case of indirect expenditure by a spouse which benefits the other spouse, the intentions both of the contributing spouse and the recipient spouse as to whether such contributions were to give the contributing spouse a beneficial interest in any property, whether those intentions are articulated in words or not, must be relevant, in a court of equity, in determining whether a resulting trust has come into operation. The test to be applied in determining whether such a common intention existed is doubtless an objective one: it depends on the inferences as to the intentions of the parties which a reasonable man would draw from their words or conduct. The fact remains that it is the existence or non-existence of such a common intention, whether actually expressed or reasonably to be inferred from words or conduct, which is critical in determining whether the resulting trust has come into operation.

It is also of interest to note that, in each of the Court of Appeal decisions in England to which I have referred, the conclusion might very well have been the same, even had the principles laid down by Lord Diplock in *Gissing* v. *Gissing* been applied. *In Falconer* v. *Falconer*, there were in fact direct contributions by the wife. In *Hargrave* v. *Newton* there had been a finding of fact that the wife had made an adjustment to her contribution which it could be inferred was referable to the acquisition of the house. (See the judgment of Lord Denning at p. 868). In *Hazell* v. *Hazell*, Megaw, L.J., (at p. 928 (c)) interpreted the findings of the trial judge as meaning that:-

> The conduct of the wife in going out to work was in order to bring in a contribution to the expenses which were going to be incurred because of, and in connection with, the acquisition of the matrimonial home.

In *Kowalczuk* v. *Kowalczuk*, the wife's claim under the corresponding English Act was disallowed.

In the present case, the parties lived together for less than four years. The plaintiff was working before her marriage and continued to work after it. She maintained an independent bank account. There is nothing in the evidence to suggest that either she or the defendant thought for a moment that the fact that she was regularly using her own income to defray expenses for which he was responsible meant that she was acquiring a part ownership of the house in which they were living. Both the plaintiff and the defendant were obviously used to a reasonable standard of living before the marriage. The plaintiff, by making the payments that she did, helped to ensure that something approximating to the same standard of living was enjoyed by both of them after the marriage. That is all perfectly understandable; but the fact remains that there was nothing in the evidence to suggest that, prior to the break up of the marriage, it crossed the mind of either party that any change in the legal ownership of the property would result. Yet the contributions, amounting, as I have found, to approximately one-fifth of the joint household expenses, can hardly be regarded as insignificant. It follows that, if the law in this country were that substantial contributions by a wife to household expenses which were the responsibility of the husband and which left him with more money to repay the mortgage instalments automatically entitled the wife to a beneficial interest in the relevant property, the plaintiff in the present case would succeed. For the reasons I have given, I am satisfied that this proposition does not correctly state the law; and I must accordingly dismiss the plaintiff's claim.

Notes

1. If the spouses had lived together for twenty years rather than four, with the wife continuing to contribute in the same proportion, but with no further evidence as to the spouse's intentions, would she still have been entitled to nothing? On the general question of duration of marriage as a factor in the determination of property entitlements, see Oldham, *Is the Concept of Marital Property Outdated?*, 22 J. of Family L. 263 (1984).
2. In *S.D.* v. *B.D.*, unreported, High Ct., 19 March 1982 (1981–194Sp.) Murphy, J. followed and applied *M.G.* v. *R.D.*, expressing the opinion (at p. 19) that the law had been 'correctly stated by Mr. Justice Keane. . . .'

W. v. W.

[1981] I.L.R.M. 202 (High Court, Finlay, P.)

The parties were married in 1966 at which time a farm was transferred to the defendant husband subject to encumbrances. Both parties applied their savings to stocking and improving the farm. The plaintiff wife brought horses to the lands and indulged in successful bloodstock activities. The plaintiff took an active part in the work on the lands and paid a further £1800 into the farm bank account. Many improvements were made to the farm. A modern milking parlour was erected and equipped the finance for which came from a mortgage on the lands. The mortgage was later redeemed. The plaintiff claimed to be entitled to a beneficial interest in the farm and based her claim on the following (1) her industrial, financial and bloodstock contributions which made income for the farm out of which all encumbrances were discharged; (2) her work on the farm which added to farm income out of which improvements were made. The plaintiff was unable to give precise details concerning the encumbrances and the defendant did not give evidence.

Finlay, P.:

. . . The issue with which this judgment is concerned is solely confined to a claim made by the wife to be entitled to a beneficial interest in a farm of land registered on a folio in the name of the husband.

Upon this issue evidence was given by the wife and by an agricultural expert on her behalf but no evidence was given by or on behalf of the husband. [At this point the Judge recited the facts of the case and then continued] . . . I am solely concerned with the claim of the wife for an interest in the main holdings of land.

This claim was presented to me by counsel on behalf of the wife in two alternative and in a sense concurrent forms. It is firstly submitted that insofar as the transfer of the lands originally made to the husband was subject to encumbrances that on the evidence I should hold that the wife had contributed over the years both by her industry, by the bringing into the farm of her own personal savings on marriage and her share in the monies received by way of gift on the wedding; by bringing in her original bloodstock and working with them thus making income for the farm and by her actual work at the ordinary dairy portion of the farm to the general farm income out of which I should assume on the evidence those encumbrances were discharged and that those facts gave her an interest arising from that transaction in the farm. A similar submission was made in regard to the evidence adduced by the wife that upon the building of the modern milk-parlour a further mortgage was raised on the farm and subsequently discharged and the sums of money brought in by her.

In addition and as I have said not only as an alternative but as a concurrent submission it is claimed on behalf of the wife that since she consistently worked on the farm both in relation to the dairying end of it and in relation to the bloodstock end of it that that work added to the general fund or income from the farm in each year and that insofar as that was used for the purpose of making improvements to the farm in particular represented by improvements in the buildings and yards etc., that was a contribution by her towards the acquisition of the entity which now constitutes the farm as improved and that as such would give her a claim to an equitable interest in the farm.

In considering this claim on the facts as I have found them I have in particular been referred to and carefully considered the following decisions.

C. v. *C.* [*supra*, pp. 265–66] *Heavey* v. *Heavey* [*supra*, pp. 261–64] *McGill* v. *S.* [*supra*, pp. 166–70].

From these three decisions . . . and from the judicial decisions quoted with approval in them, I am satisfied that the following broad propositions of law arise which are applicable to the facts of this case.

1. Where a wife contributes by money to the purchase of a property by her husband in his sole name in the absence of evidence of some inconsistent agreement or arrangement the court will decide that the wife is entitled to an equitable interest in that property approximately proportionate to the extent of her contribution as against the total value of the property at the time the contribution was made.

2. Where a husband makes a contribution to the purchase of property in his wife's sole name he will be presumed by a rebuttable presumption to have intended to advance his wife and will have no claim to an equitable estate in the property unless that presumption is rebutted. If it is, he would have a claim similar to that indicated in respect of the wife with which I have already dealt.

3. Where a wife contributes either directly towards the repayment of mortgage instalments or contributes to a general family fund thus releasing her husband from an obligation which he otherwise would have to discharge liabilities out of that fund and permitting him to repay mortgage instalments she will in the absence of proof of an inconsistent agreement or arrangement be entitled to an equitable share in the property which had been mortgaged and in respect of which the mortgage was redeemed approximately proportionate to her contribution to the mortgage repayments: to the value of the mortgage thus redeemed and to the total value of the property at the relevant time. It is not expressly stated in the decisions to which I have referred but I assume that the fundamental principle underlying this rule of law is that the redemption of any form of charge or mortgage on property in truth consists of the acquisition by the owner or mortgagor of an estate in the property with which he had parted at the time of the creating of the mortgage or charge and that there can be no distinction in principle between a contribution made to the acquisition of that interest and a contribution made to the acquisition of an interest in property by an original purchase.

4. Where a husband contributes either directly or indirectly in the manner which I have already outlined to the repayment of mortgage charges on property which is in the legal ownership of his wife subject to the presumption of advancement and in the event of a rebuttal of that presumption he would have a like claim to an equitable estate in the property.

5. Where a wife expends monies or carries out work in the improvement of a property which has been originally acquired by and the legal ownership in which is solely vested in her husband she will have no claim in respect of such contribution unless she established by evidence that from the circumstances surrounding the making of it she was led to believe (or of course that it was specifically agreed) that she would be recompensed for it. Even where such a right to recompense is established either by an expressed agreement or by circumstance in which the wife making the contribution was led to such belief it is a right to recompense in monies only and cannot and does not constitute a right to claim [an] equitable share in the estate of the property concerned.

6. A husband making contributions in like manner to property originally acquired by and solely owned as to the legal estate by his wife may again subject to a rebuttal of a presumption of advancement which would arise have a like claim to compensation in similar circumstances but would not have a claim to any equitable estate in the property.

Applying these principles of law which I believe to be the relevant principles to be derived from the decisions to which I have referred to the facts as so far found by me in this case I am satisfied that the following conclusions and consequences arise.

Whilst the evidence of the wife concerning the encumbrances affecting the property when it was first transferred to her husband, was explicably without detail, it has not been contradicted by any evidence adduced on behalf of her husband nor was she in fact cross-examined about it. I must therefore conclude that such encumbrances did exist and were discharged after the transfer of the farm to the husband. A precisely similar conclusion arises with regard to her evidence as to the raising of a charge and its subsequent redemption at the time of the construction of the modern milking-parlour.

I will therefore direct that a further issue be tried before me as to: (1) the extent of the encumbrances subject to which the lands were transferred to the husband and the time at which they were finally redeemed together with the value of the lands at the date of transfer and at the date of the eventual redemption of these charges; (2) the amount of the charges raised by way of mortgage on the lands at the time of the construction of the milking parlour; the value of the lands at the time that mortgage was created; the date on which they were eventually redeemed and the method by which they were redeemed and the value of the lands at the date at which they were redeemed.

In this context I intend of course to deal not only with legal mortgages but with any form of charge raised on the land whether secured by the equitable deposit of title deeds or otherwise.

Since the husband did not give evidence before me on the issues so far tried and since he did not produce, at this or any other stage in the proceedings, any documentary evidence other than certain farm accounts which are irrelevant to this question I will direct that he make discovery of all documents relevant to the issue now still to be tried and I will give liberty to the wife if she is so advised to serve interrogatories on the husband concerning the transactions to which I have referred.

I am, needless to say, concerned with the cost of the proceedings which have already been maintained between the husband and wife in this case and with the thought of imposing upon the parties further expense and costs. It seems to me that both discovery and interrogatories should be capable of being properly achieved without formality and that it might be possible for the parties upon full examination of the documentary proofs available to reach agreement on the extent of the share to which as a consequence the wife is entitled in these lands. If such an agreement cannot be reached I will, of course, re-enter the matter for further hearing at a suitable time.

To assist the parties in reaching an agreement which might avoid expense I feel I should indicate that it would be my intention from the evidence I have already heard to hold that the contribution of the wife during the two relevant periods in which prima facie charges on these lands were being redeemed would be approximately 50% which takes into account both her work, the monies brought in by her and in particular the results of her dealing in bloodstock. The proportion or share to which she should be entitled to be declared an equitable owner in these lands would therefore be half of the proportion represented by the amount of the charge redeemed and the value of the lands at the relevant time which would in effect be a combination of the value of the lands at the time of the raising of a mortgage and the value of the lands at the time when it was finally redeemed. This statement of my intention on the evidence already heard by me may assist the parties to reach an agreement as to a share in respect of which the wife is entitled to claim in these lands. Insofar as the wife has claimed an equitable estate in these lands solely derived from her contribution to improvements I must on the authorities hold that it is not sustainable in law.

Notes

1. Do you consider that the three *Irish* cases cited by Finlay, P. fully sustain his six propositions of law? If not, on which of 'the judicial decisions quoted with approval in them' has Finlay, P. relied?
2. Are you clear on how propositions 4 and 6 would work in practice?
3. See also *B.* v. *B.*, unreported, High Ct., Finlay, P., 27 February 1981 (1979–569Sp.).

F.G. v. P.G.

[1982] I.L.R.M. 155 (High Court, Finlay, P., 1981)

Finlay, P.:

This is a claim brought on plenary summons by the plaintiff who is the wife against the defendant who is the husband seeking a declaration that she is entitled to a share in certain premises consisting of a house situate in the County of Dublin (which I will hereinafter refer to as the Dublin house) which is held in the sole name of the defendant.

The facts out of which the claim arises I find after hearing oral evidence to be as follows.

The parties were married in the year 1958, neither of them having at that time any relevant capital assets. After the marriage they lived in various rented accommodation for some years and during this period the plaintiff was wholly occupied with her duties as a housewife and also as a mother and did not earn in any outside occupation. There were three children of the marriage.

In the year 1964 the defendant purchased in his sole name the Dublin house for the sum of £2,450. The purchase price was provided in the following manner. The defendant was at that time employed by a firm with a pension scheme to which he had contributed. By terminating his employment he became entitled to a refund of a sum of £150 out of that pension fund. This together with a sum of £50 which notwithstanding a conflict on the evidence I am satisfied he borrowed from a bank against his security he used as a deposit on the house of £200. The balance of the price of the house of £2,250 was raised by him as a mortgage from the Irish Permanent Building Society.

Shortly after the purchase of this house, the defendant emigrated to America leaving the plaintiff and the three children of the marriage living in the Dublin house.

The plaintiff and their three children joined the defendant in America in early 1966.

During the intervening period the mortgage repayments on the house were met out of funds contributed by the defendant from his earnings in America and during this period the plaintiff again was wholly occupied with her duties as a mother and a housewife.

After the plaintiff and her children went to America the house was let and for all practical purposes has from then until now been let to a number of successive tenants, the arrangements and the organisation of the letting and the collection of the rents being organised by the plaintiff's sister who is in Ireland. From the income derived from such lettings, firstly, the mortgage repayments had been met, secondly, the maintenance and other outgoings on the house had been met and in later years, I am satisfied, the house was used for the purpose of raising a loan in a Dublin bank the servicing of which was also provided from the rental income.

Approximately a year after the arrival of the plaintiff in America she obtained employment and with minor interruptions continued to earn in outside employment and to contribute to a joint family fund until 1978 when the parties separated and obtained a civil divorce under American law.

I had been informed by counsel that amongst the property provisions made in those proceedings the plaintiff was declared entitled to the Dublin house but it has been conceded on her behalf that this order cannot properly be proved before me and that no submission is being made to me that I am in any way bound by it.

In the years 1967 to 1978 the plaintiff and the defendant out of the joint family fund and with the aid of borrowings which included, I am satisfied, borrowings from the bank in Ireland to which I have already referred, indulged in a series of property purchases and sales some of which were for the purpose of providing accommodation for the family and some of which were plainly speculative and with a view to investment. All of these properties were apparently purchased in the joint names of the plaintiff and the defendant and were of course situated in America.

During those years, the parties were not, I am satisfied, at any time affluent and considerable difficulty was consistently encountered in meeting the overall family expenses and the cost of the upbringing and education of the children.

In the evidence adduced before me, there was a serious conflict as to the extent to which each of the parties contributed to the family finances. The plaintiff strenuously asserted that the defendant due to a drink problem was an erratic and inadequate earner and had a consistently high level of personal expenditure.

The defendant denied this and contended on the other hand that the plaintiff was over-stating her earnings and significantly under-stating the extent to which she expended those earnings on her personal wants as distinct from contributing them to a general family fund.

I received in evidence a number of accounts prepared by accountants on behalf of both parties for income tax purposes between the years 1971 and 1978. Having considered these accounts and having considered all the other evidence I heard concerning the earnings of both the parties, I have come to the conclusion that in the years 1967 to 1978 taking them together and averaging out the different years the plaintiff contributed approximately 40% to the general family pool of finance by her earnings and the defendant contributed approximately 60%.

On these facts, the submissions made on behalf of the parties may thus be summarised.

On behalf of the plaintiff it is contended that notwithstanding that the Dublin house was in a sense largely self-servicing as to mortgage repayments that it could never have been retained having regard to the general family finances were it not for the contributions made by her to the family fund. She had given evidence which I accepted that the overall family plan prior to the unfortunate break-up of this marriage was that the entire family would eventually return to Ireland and that for this purpose the retention of the Dublin house was an integral part of that plan. Relying upon the decision in *Nixon v Nixon* [1969] 3 All E.R. 1133, counsel on behalf of the plaintiff contended that the fact that no monies were ever remitted from the family pool to which the plaintiff by her earnings contributed for the purpose of discharging the mortgage repayments on the Dublin house was irrelevant and that, I must consider, the Dublin house and the various American properties as all being part of family assets the retention and acquisition of which was achieved by the joint family fund created by the earnings of both the plaintiff and the defendant.

On behalf of the defendant, on the other hand, it was contended that since at no stage was any money provided or earned by the plaintiff ever directly or indirectly used to purchase the house in Dublin and since the original deposit and first year's mortgage repayments were provided by the defendant alone and all subsequent repayments were provided from the letting of the house itself that the plaintiff could not have any conceivable interest in the house. It was also submitted that the plaintiff had already received a share of the jointly owned property in America and therefore had no claim to the Dublin house.

After careful consideration, I am satisfied that the principles laid down in *Nixon v Nixon* constitute a persuasive precedent which I should follow and that applying them to the facts of this case as I find them that in general the contention made on behalf of the plaintiff is correct.

I have no doubt that had the plaintiff not earned in the years 1967 to 1978 and had she not contributed her earnings to the extent that she did to the general family pool that there was no way in which the defendant could during those years have avoided disposing of the Dublin house so as to service and finance the general expenses of the family and the property deals in which he was engaged in America. She has, therefore, in my view contributed to the acquisition of the equity of redemption in the Dublin house just as clearly as if the monies earned by her had been remitted to discharge the mortgage repayments.

Bearing in mind, the earlier sole contribution by the defendant towards the acquisition of that equity of redemption which lasted up to 1967 and relating that to my finding that from 1967 to 1978 the plaintiff contributed 40% of the general family pool, I have reached a conclusion that the beneficial share to which the plaintiff is entitled in this house is 30%. I accordingly so declare and grant an ancillary injunction restraining the defendant from disposing of the Dublin house otherwise than by agreement with the plaintiff or with the liberty of the court.

Note

See also *H.D.* v. *J.D.*, unreported, High Ct., Finlay, P. (1980–1120Sp.) decided on 31 July 1981 (the same day as *F.G.* v. *P.G.*) and expressly following *W.* v. *W.*

J.C. v. J.H.C.

Unreported, High Ct., Keane, J., 4 August 1982

The case involved, *inter alia*, a dispute between a wife and her husband about the ownership of a dwellinghouse in County Dublin.

Keane, J.:

. . . The Plaintiff is Australian. The Defendant is English by birth but resided for many years in Australia, where he met the Plaintiff. The Defendant had been previously married, but that marriage was dissolved by a decree of the Family Court of Australia on 25th March, 1978. The Plaintiff and the Defendant were married in a Registry Office in England on 6th May, 1978. . . .

The parties having spent some time travelling eventually settled down in this country where the Defendant set up a business of a model photographic agency and hairdressing salon, the Plaintiff also participating in the running of it. This venture ultimately proved unsuccessful and it is clear that disagreements as to its management contributed significantly to the deterioration in the relationship between the Plaintiff and the Defendant, which culminated in the former's leaving the matrimonial home in March, 1982. There was no child of the marriage.

. . . Th[e dwellinghouse] was bought in October 1977 for £38,380. It is agreed that it was purchased entirely out of monies provided by the Defendant. I was told that it was conveyed to the Plaintiff and the Defendant as joint tenants, although the actual conveyance was not produced.

The Plaintiff said that she understood at the time that the property would belong to the Defendant and herself in equal shares and that he thereby intended to give her some security in the event of his pre-deceasing her. (The Plaintiff at the time the parties met was twenty-one and the Defendant thirty-seven). The Defendant said that his object in having the property conveyed into their joint names was to ensure that if he died before the Plaintiff, she would be the sole beneficiary of his estate.

Where property is taken in the joint names of two or more persons, but the purchase money is advanced by one of them alone, the law presumes a resulting trust in favour of the person who advanced the purchase money. This presumption may however be rebutted; and in particular the circumstance of the person into whose name the property is conveyed being the wife of the person advancing the money may be sufficient to rebut the presumption under the doctrine of advancement. However, it has been said in one English decision (*Pettit* v. *Pettit* [1970] A.C. 777) that these presumptions are inappropriate to transactions between husbands and wives today and are readily rebuttable by comparatively slight evidence.

In the present case, the evidence of the Plaintiff and the Defendant overwhelmingly reinforces the presumption of advancement which would arise if there were no other evidence pointing to the intention of the parties. It is clear that the Defendant intended the property to be jointly occupied by the Plaintiff and himself during their lifetimes but also intended the legal ownership to devolve upon her if he predeceased her. It is quite plain that he intended to give it to her; and that accordingly the property has been held from the beginning and is held now by the Plaintiff and the Defendant on a joint beneficial tenancy. There will be a declaration accordingly. . . .'

Notes

1. Could it be argued that Keane, J. understates the force of the doctrine of advancement?
2. In *R.F.* v. *M.F.*, unreported, High Ct., D'Arcy, J., 1 December 1982 (1979–7580P), D'Arcy, J. said:

   [T]he presumption [of advancement] is based on the fact that the Courts presume the husbands to have natural love and affection for their wives. But it is a presumption and it is rebuttable. In fact nowadays 'across the water' it is so easily rebutted it has ceased to exist altogether, except in exceptional circumstances. The House of Lords based their decision on the changed nature of social conditions. I don't think social conditions here have changed yet to justify the view of the House of Lords, I think the law of presumption of advancement still exists, but it has been whittled down in this country.
3. For consideration of developments in the United States, in relation to the presumption of a resulting trust in favour of wives, see Wright, *Note*, 61 N.C.L. Rev. 576 (1983).
4. In *G.N.R.* v. *K.A.R.*, unreported, High Ct., Carroll, J., 25 March 1981 (1980–882Sp.), Miss Justice Carroll, after a detailed analysis of the respective contributions of the spouses to the acquisition of the family home, held that the wife was entitled to 51.87% and the husband 48.13%. However, she rounded the figures off to 51% and 49%, respectively, because she considered it 'almost impossible' in her calculation 'to be sure that they are accurate to two decimal points'. Would you have anything approaching the same confidence about any degree of accuracy for calculations in respect of a marriage extending over thirty years, in times of inflation?

McC. v. McC.

Unreported, Supreme Court, 29 March 1984 (1981–357Sp., 1982–52)

Henchy, J.:

In these proceedings the wife as plaintiff is claiming against the husband as defendant that she is entitled to a share in the family home in Cork. The marriage has broken down and the wife has instituted these proceedings for the purpose of asserting a number of claims. In this appeal, however, the only question is whether Costello J. was correct in holding that the wife's claim to a share in the family home in Cork was unfounded.

In 1972 the husband and wife were living in Dublin. He was employed by an insurance company. In that year he was transferred to Cork. That meant that he had to sell the family home in Dublin. This he did. It realised £5,000, but out of that sum there had to be paid £3,200 in discharge of a mortgage on the house. That left £1,800. It seems to be agreed that because the wife had in effect contributed one-third of the purchase price of that house, she was entitled to one-third of the £1,800. However, she never got any part of the £600 she was entitled to. She allowed her husband to use it.

The husband proceeded to buy a family home in Cork. It cost £9,000. Because he was in the employment of an insurance company, he was able to get his employers to take a mortgage for the full amount of the purchase money. Thus he did not have to lay out any part of the purchase money. He merely had to pay the instalments due under the mortgage.

As to the £1,800 left over from the sale of the Dublin home, the wife allowed the husband to use it in full. He spent it in furnishing and fitting out the Cork home. Costello J. held that, because the wife was entitled to one-third of the £1,800, she became entitled to a one-third share in the furniture and fittings (including carpets) in the Cork home. Counsel for the wife contends that that was not a correct conclusion. He says that the proper conclusion to be drawn from the use of the wife's money in furnishing and fitting out the Cork home is that it gave her a one-third share in the house itself.

Since the decision of Kenny J. in *C.* v. *C.* [1976] I.R. 254, it has been judicially accepted that where the matrimonial home has been purchased in the name of the husband, and the wife has, either directly or indirectly, made contributions towards the purchase price or towards the discharge of mortgage instalments, the husband will be held to be a trustee for the wife of a share in the house roughly corresponding with the proportion of the purchase money represented by the wife's total contribution. Such a trust will be inferred when the wife's contribution is of such a size and kind as will justify the conclusion that the acquisition of the house was achieved by the joint efforts of the spouses.

When the wife's contribution has been indirect (such as by contributing, by means of her earnings, to a general family fund) the courts will, in the absence of any express or implied agreement to the contrary, infer a trust in favour of the wife, on the ground that she has to that extent relieved the husband of the financial burden he incurred in purchasing the house.

In the present case it has been contended on behalf of the wife that, in allowing the husband to use her one-third of the £1,800, which he spent on furniture and fittings for the house in Cork, he should be held to be a trustee for her of a one-eighteenth share in the house (one-eighteenth being the proportion between the wife's £600 and the £10,800 spent by the husband on acquiring the house and furnishing it). This contention rests on the submission that the wife's £600 went into a family fund and that to that extent it eased the financial liability incurred by the husband in purchasing the house.

I am unable to accede to this proposition. The wife's £600 was in no way applied to the purchase of the house. The full purchase price was provided by the husband's employers, who got a mortgage on the house. The employers collected the mortgage payments by means of deductions from his salary. So it could not be said that the £600 or any part of it relieved the husband of any share of the financial burden he incurred in purchasing the house.

The true position, it seems to me, was that found by Costello J., namely that the £600 was applied by the husband, not in acquiring the house, but as part of the £1,800 he spent on furniture and fittings. The expenditure thus by the husband of the £600 could not be said to have given the wife any beneficial interest in the house. All she got was, as was held in the High Court, a one-third share in the furniture and fittings (including carpets).

I would accordingly dismiss this appeal.

Griffin and **Hederman JJ.** concurred.

Notes

1. To what extent is this decision in harmony with earlier High Court decisions?
2. Does the decision take into full account the substance of the wife's claim? Having mentioned that the mortgage was for the full purchase price and that the husband's employers collected the mortgage payments by means of deductions from his salary, the judgment concludes: 'So it could not be said that the £600 or any part of it relieved the husband of any share of the financial burden he incurred in purchasing the house'. But do the premises support this conclusion? Could it not be argued that the extra six hundred pounds must inevitably have relieved the husband's burden? The fact that he received his salary with the mortgage payments already deducted would not make this relief any less effective. The judgment appears to imply that the husband was not a free agent in that the deduction of his payments was an integral aspect of his employment but nonetheless, viewed from a broader perspective, he was free, and the wife's money facilitated his choice. He could perhaps have chosen to finance the purchase of the house by other means: since he elected to go for the 100% mortgage linked to his employment, using the £600 for ancillary necessary expenditure, it may be argued that he was clearly relieved of the financial burden to the extent of this contribution.
3. See also *B.* v. *B.*, unreported, High Ct., Finlay, P., July 1978 (1977–500Sp.). Does that decision hold that, however poor the prospects of success for a marriage, and however likely it may be that the spouses will separate or divorce, this factor may not be taken into consideration in determining the terms of the resulting trust which may arise?
4. See also *O'K.* v. *O'K.*, unreported, High Ct., Barron, J., 16 November 1982 (1982–424Sp.), *C.* v. *C. & A.C. Bamlett (Ireland) Ltd.* v. *Curran*, unreported, High Ct., McWilliam, J., 10 March 1981 (1979–580Sp. and 1979–453Sp.).

5. The Law Reform Commission in their *First Report on Family Law*, pp. 19–20 (LRC 1–1981), have recommended that, where a spouse, whether directly or indirectly, makes a contribution in money or money's worth to the acquisition, improvement or maintenance of the family home, then, subject to any agreement, arrangement or understanding between the parties, he or she is to acquire a beneficial interest (or an enlarged share in the beneficial interest) of such an extent as appears just and equitable to the Court. In this regard a 'contribution in money or money's worth' should include, *inter alia*, the contribution made by each spouse to the welfare of the family including any contribution made by looking after the home or caring for the family.

NORTHERN BANK LTD. v. HENRY

[1981] I.R. 1 (Sup. Ct., 1980, aff'g High Ct., McWilliam, J., 1978)

Henchy J.:

The contest in this case is between the plaintiff bank and the wife of one of its customers. The wife is the first defendant. The husband, who was the customer, is the second defendant; in 1969 he granted a legal mortgage of the family home to the third defendant.

In 1974 the husband's account with the plaintiff bank was heavily overdrawn and his finances were in disarray generally. It was a source of urgent worry to the plaintiffs, who badly needed a collateral security for their debt. The plaintiffs needed that security quickly, for there were other creditors of the husband and cheques drawn by him in favour of some of those creditors had been dishonoured by the plaintiffs. The only substantial item of property that he appeared to have was the family home, and it was mortgaged to the third defendant. However, as a security it was better than nothing in the eyes of the plaintiffs; they required the husband to give a second mortgage on it and he agreed to do so.

The plaintiffs doubtless felt that they had to carry through the transaction swiftly. Advised by their legal department in Belfast, the plaintiffs took up the documents of title and saw the investigation of title that had been carried out when the mortgage to the third defendant was executed in 1969; the plaintiffs made no further investigation of the title, other than to get a Dublin firm of solicitors to have a negative search carried out in the Registry of Deeds. Having thereby established that no dealing with the property had been registered since 1969, the plaintiffs did not investigate the title further, although they knew that the property was the family home and that the husband had ceased to use it as his address in his correspondence with them. A competent solicitor, acting for a normal purchaser of the property, would not have been content to take the title on such a cursory investigation. But all the plaintiffs wanted was a second mortgage, and their advisers probably felt that if they took time to investigate the title fully they might lose priority to another creditor. For that reason I do not wish to criticise them for telescoping the investigation in the interests of business expediency. So, with the title thus looked at summarily, the plaintiffs got the second mortgage executed.

As was later proved, the husband had no title whatsoever to the property. If the plaintiffs had pursued the matter by means of appropriate requisitions on title, they would have discovered not only that it was the wife who was in occupation of the house but that she was in the process of formulating against the husband a claim that she was beneficially entitled to it. The High Court has made a declaration to that effect and that decision stands unchallenged. What the plaintiffs seek primarily to establish in these proceedings is that, as purchasers for value without notice of the wife's title, they should have priority over her.

Section 3, sub-s. 1, of the *Conveyancing Act, 1882*, deprives the plaintiffs of that priority if the wife's entitlement 'would have come to [*the plaintiffs'*] knowledge if such inquiries and inspections had been made as ought reasonably to have been made . . .' Counsel for the wife argues that the plaintiffs ought reasonably to have inquired as to who was in occupation and as to whether there was any litigation threatened or pending affecting the property and that, if they had done so, they would have learned of the wife's claim. Accordingly, the argument goes, the plaintiffs should not be allowed to dislodge the wife from the property (which she admittedly owned at the time the plaintiffs got the second mortgage of it) because their abstention from making the suggested inquiries fixed them with constructive notice of the wife's claim. The answer depends on the scope or meaning that should be given to the expression 'such inquiries and inspections . . . as ought reasonably to have been made' in s. 3, sub.-s. 1, of the Act of 1882.

In my judgment, the test of what inquiries and inspections ought reasonably to have been made by the plaintiffs is an objective test which depends not on what the particular purchaser thought proper to do in the particular circumstances but on what a purchaser of the particular property ought reasonably to have done in order to acquire title to it. The words 'purchaser' and 'purchase' in this context have the meanings ascribed to them by s. 1 of the Act of 1882 and thus include 'mortgagee' and 'mortgage.' In a particular case a purchaser, looking only at his own interests, may justifiably and reasonably consider that in the circumstances some of the normal inquiries and inspections may or should be dispensed with. The special circumstances, thus narrowly viewed, may justify the short-cut taken, or the purchaser may consider that they do so. In either event, such a purchaser is not the purchaser envisaged by s. 3, sub-s-. 1, of the Act of 1882. That provision, because it is laying down the circumstances in which a purchaser is not to be prejudicially affected by notice of any instrument, fact or thing, is setting as a standard of conduct that which is to be expected from a reasonable purchaser. Reasonableness in this context must be judged by reference to what should be done to acquire the estate or interest being purchased, rather than by the motive for or the purpose of the particular purchase.

A purchaser cannot be held to be empowered to set his own standard of reasonableness for the purpose of the sub-section. He must expect to be judged by what an ordinary purchaser, advised by a competent lawyer, would reasonably inquire about or inspect for the purpose of getting a good title. If his personal preference, or the exigencies of the situation, impel him to lower the level of investigation of title below that standard, he is entitled to do so; but, if he does so, he cannot claim the immunity which s. 3, sub-s. 1, reserves for a reasonable purchaser. A reasonable purchaser is one who not only consults his own needs or preferences but also has regard to whether the purchase may affect, prejudicially and unfairly, the rights of third parties in the property. In particular, a reasonable purchaser would be expected to make such inquiries and inspections as would normally disclose whether the purchase will trench, fraudulently or unconscionably, on the rights of such third parties in the property.

In this case, the plaintiffs made no inquiry as to who was in occupation of the property. I consider that a reasonable purchaser would have done so. A minimum requirement for the proper investigation of a title is to see that the purchaser will either get vacant possession on completion or, if the contract or the needs of the purchaser do not so permit or require, get evidence of any estate or interest that will stand between him and vacant possession. Considering the many ways, both at common law and under statute, in which a person in occupation may have an estate or interest adverse to that of a vendor, and which would not appear on an investigation of the vendor's paper title, I consider that the plaintiffs, as purchasers, ought reasonably to have investigated this aspect of the title. Had the plaintiffs done so, the fact of the wife's possession of the property would have come to light, as well as her wellfounded claim to the beneficial ownership of it.

Nor did the plaintiffs make any inquiry as to whether any litigation was threatened or pending in respect of the property. I consider that this also was an inquiry which a purchaser ought reasonably to have made. The plaintiffs knew that this was a 'purchase' from the husband of the family home. Even if it had not been a family home, it was foolhardy for a purchaser not to inquire about pending or threatened litigation, particularly litigation stemming from statutory notices served under statutes such as the Housing Acts or the Planning Acts, which might fatally flaw the title. This property was known to the plaintiffs to be the family home. Notwithstanding that this purchase took place before the passing of the *Family Home Protection Act, 1976* (which makes a transaction of this kind void for want of the prior written consent of the wife), the plaintiffs, as purchasers, ought reasonably to have adverted to the fact that there were decisions showing that a wife who had made payments towards the acquisition of the home, or towards the payment of the mortgage instalments on it, acquired a corresponding share in the beneficial ownership. As a matter of ordinary care, therefore, an inquiry as to threatened or pending claims was called for. In fact there was such an impending claim by the wife. By not inquiring about its existence the plaintiffs became an unwitting party to an unconscionable, if not an actually fraudulent, effort by the husband to mortgage the family home behind his wife's back at a time when he had no beneficial title to it. The plaintiffs, by not making the normal inquiry as to threatened or impending litigation affecting the property (indeed, by making no requisitions on title whatsoever), facilitated the husband in nefariously concealing his wife's wellfounded claim to the ownership of the property. Because of that, the plaintiffs cannot be said to have shown the care to be expected from a reasonable purchaser. It must be held, therefore, that knowledge of the wife's claim would have been acquired by the plaintiffs if they had made the inquiries that ought reasonably to have been made.

The interpretation given in this judgment to s. 3, sub-s. 1, of the Act of 1882 does not amount to the imposition of any novel or unfair duty of investigation of title on purchasers. Well before the enactment of the Act of 1882, which aimed at setting statutory bounds to the existing doctrine of constructive notice, the Chancery judges had evolved this same test for determining whether a purchaser or mortgagee should have constructive notice attributed to him. Sir Edward Sugden (later Lord St. Leonards), in his Law of Vendors and Purchasers (14th ed. 1862), summed up the pre-1882 approach of the Chancery judges to the question of constructive notice as follows, at p. 755:–

> The question upon constructive notice is not whether the purchaser had the means of obtaining, and might, by prudent caution, have obtained the knowledge in question, but whether the not obtaining it was an act of gross or culpable negligence.'

Nineteenth century judges were prone to stigmatising actionable negligence as 'gross' or 'culpable.' Indeed, Rolfe B. at pp. 115–6 of the report of *Wilson* v. *Brett* 11 M. & W. 113 (1843) said that he 'could see no difference between *negligence* and *gross* negligence – that it was the same thing, with the addition of a vituperative epithet'; this incisive view was approved by Willes J. in *Grill* v. *General Iron Screw Collier Co.* L.R. 1 C.P. 600 (1866). When, therefore, the pre-1882 Chancery judges applied the test of negligence to determine whether a purchaser should be fixed with constructive notice, they were doing no more than asking whether the purchaser's lack of knowledge was consistent with the conduct to be expected from a reasonable man in the circumstances.

Section 3, sub-s. 1, of the Act of 1882, in providing that a purchaser is not to be prejudicially affected by notice of any instrument, fact, or thing unless 'it is within his own knowledge, or would have come to his knowledge if such inquiries and inspections had been made as ought reasonably to have been made by him,' gave statutory stress to the existing judicial insistence that constructive notice could be found only when the lack of knowledge was due to such careless inactivity as would not be expected in the circumstances from a reasonable man. The default of a reasonable man is to be distinguished from the default of a prudent man. The prudence of the worldly wise may justifiably persuade a purchaser that it would be unbusinesslike to stop and look more deeply into certain aspects of the title. But the reasonable man, in the eyes of the law, will be expected to look beyond the impact of his decisions on his own affairs, and to consider whether they may unfairly and prejudicially affect his 'neighbour,' in the sense in which that word has been given juristic currency by Lord Atkin in *Donoghue* v. *Stevenson* [1932] A.C. 562.

In the present case, the plaintiffs may have been justified as a matter of business prudence in taking the second mortgage from the husband, hurriedly and without any proper investigation of the title. But it would be impossible to hold that a purchaser in this situation, given competent legal advice and having due regard to the prejudicial consequences to persons in proximity to him (such as the wife) that could result from a skimped investigation of the title, would have acted reasonably in thus taking a conveyance of the family home. The test for constructive notice is legal reasonableness, not business prudence.

I would reject this appeal by the plaintiffs, thus affirming the decision of Mr. Justice McWilliam which dismissed, on the ground of their constructive notice of the wife's title, the plaintiff's claim to be given priority over her.

Kenny and **Parke, JJ.** delivered concurring judgments.

Notes

1. The discussion of negligence in this case raises the question whether a wife dispossessed as a result of careless investigation of title might have a right of action in the tort of negligence against the negligent purchaser or mortgagee (or the solicitor).
2. Cf. *K.* v. *K. (No. 2)*, unreported, High Ct., Barrington, J., 17 October 1980 (1978–113Sp.).

Chapter 8

DIVORCE A MENSA ET THORO

Introduction

In Chapter 6, consideration was given to Article 41.3.2° of the Constitution, which specifies that no legislation may be enacted providing for the grant of a dissolution of marriage. The High Court has, however, inherited from the Ecclesiastical Courts jurisdiction to grant a decree of divorce *a mensa et thoro*. The decree does not dissolve the marriage or entitle either party to remarry: it simply relieves the spouses from the obligation to cohabit with one another. The law relating to divorce *a mensa et thoro* is analysed by Shatter, ch. 8, and by Hayes, *The Matrimonial Jurisdiction of the High Court*, 8 Ir. Jur. (n.s.) 55, at 55–60 (1973). There are several older textbooks, which analyse the subject in some detail. They include *Kisbey*, chs. 1–3; *Geary*, chs. 8, 11–12, pp. 566–567; *Browne*, 276–280; *Shelford*, ch. 5; *Burn*, vol. 2, 495c–500a, 501L–503a, 503d–508a.

A decree may be granted on one or more of three grounds: adultery, cruelty and unnatural practices. There are at least four bars to a decree. These are recrimination, condonation, connivance and collusion. (A possible fifth bar, based on a principle of natural justice, arises where the petitioner conduced to the adultery of the respondent.)

The essence of recrimination is that the petitioner is himself or herself guilty of the conduct alleged or proved against the respondent. Condonation consists of 'forgiveness legally releasing the injury' resulting from the respondent's conduct. To be effective as a bar, the forgiveness must be voluntary and made with knowledge of the respondent's wrongful behaviour. This forgiveness is subject to an implied condition that the respondent will in future treat the innocent spouse with 'conjugal kindness'. Connivance, as the name implies, arises where the petitioner has behaved in such a way as to induce the respondent to commit adultery. Mere neglect or inattention will not suffice: the petitioner's conduct may range from some active procurement to corruptly failing to take the necessary steps to remove the other spouse from a situation of gross temptation: *Forster* v. *Forster*, 1 Hag. Con. 144, 161 E.R. 504 (1790); *Lovering* v. *Lovering*, 3 Hag. Ecc. 85, 162 E.R. 1089 (1792). Collusion involves as agreement between the spouses for one to commit, or appear to commit, adultery, so that the other may obtain a decree. This bar is of no practical importance today: *Shatter*, 139.

These four bars are absolute: if any one of them is established a decree of divorce a mensa et thoro *must* be refused. A possible other bar, discretionary rather than absolute, was canvassed in *Scovell* v. *Scovell,* [1897] 1 I.R. 162 (Mat., 1895). This would arise in cases where the petitioner has, by reckless conduct and wilful neglect, conduced to the respondent's adultery. Whether the scope of the bar is wider than this has not been tested in litigation.

GROUNDS FOR A DECREE

(i) *Adultery*

Adultery consists of the voluntary act of sexual intercourse between one of the spouses during marriage and any other person who is not the other spouse. Thus, where a wife is raped, she does not commit adultery. For the commission of adultery, it would appear that in England an act falling short of complete sexual intercourse but involving at least some penetration is required (*Dennis* v. *Dennis,* [1955] P. 153 (C.A.) and *Sapsford* v. *Sapsford,* [1954] P. 394. Cf. (Karminski, J.) *Hamerton* v. *Hamerton*, 2 Hag. Ecc. 8, at 14, 162 E.R. 767, at 769–770 (1828)). There is no known Irish decision on this point.

The type of evidence that is necessary to establish adultery cannot be stated in specific terms, since the circumstances 'may be infinitely diversified. . . .' (*Loveden* v. *Loveden*, 2 Hag. Con. 1, at 3 and 161 E.R. 648, at 648. See also *Lyons* v. *Lyons,* [1950] N.I. 181 (K.B.D. (Mat., Andrews, J.).) It has been stated that:–

> The only general rule that can be laid down upon the subject is that the circumstances must be such as would lead the guarded discretion of a reasonable and just man to the conclusion [that adultery has been committed]; for it is not to lead a rash and intemperate judgment, moving upon appearances that are equally capable of two interpretations, neither is it to be a matter of artificial reasoning, judging upon such things differently from what would strike the careful and cautious consideration of a discreet man. *Loveden* v. *Loveden, supra*, at 3 and 648–649, respectively. See also *Shelford*, 405ff., *Burn*, 503iff.

(ii) *Cruelty*

D. v. D.

Unreported, High Ct., Butler, J., 20 December 1966
(1965–5M, 1966–2M)

Butler, J.:

These proceedings comprise the husband's petition for restoration of conjugal rights dated 21st January 1965 and the wife's petition dated 31st January 1966 for divorce *a mensa et thoro* on the grounds of the husband's cruelty; both suits having been consolidated by an order of Murnaghan J. made on consent of the parties on 21st October 1966. The facts of the marriage between the parties, their subsequent cohabitation and their present separation have been proved before me without contradiction and the only issues I have to decide are first whether the husband has been guilty of conduct towards the wife which amounts to cruelty entitling her to a divorce, and secondly, whether the husband is entitled to a decree for the restitution of conjugal rights.

The husband is now aged 53 and is a [professional person]. The wife is aged 36 and was formerly a nurse. In 1960 the husband was a widower living alone in . . . the family home [which] had been made over to him by his father in 1945 when he was just married. His wife had died the previous year, 1959, in tragic circumstances. He was concerned about his future and to some extent about his health and was anxious to marry again. Early in November of 1960 he placed an advertisement in a weekly newspaper. The wife who was then working in [a] Hospital replied. The parties met and within a short period of the first meeting on the husband's proposal had agreed to marry. The marriage took place [in] January 1961. The early date of the marriage was again at the husband's insistance. It is clear that the husband had suffered from a condition of nerves from his student days. He himself is and was aware of this and is I think constantly worried about it. However, I think he is not disposed to admit even to himself that it is a condition that requires regular attention and treatment. In evidence he was inclined to make comparatively light of any attacks he had in the past and is disinclined to take medical advice for fear, I suspect, that he may be told that he is worse than he feels he is. He had some form of breakdown in his student days which caused him to postpone his final examination for a year. He had a further serious attack in 1957 when he was in St. Patrick's under the care of Dr. Moore for a period of 5 months after which he says himself he was 'completely cured.' It did not appear in evidence whether he had any attacks in the interval. His former housekeeper who has known him for many years says that he had periodic attacks of depression which took the form of sitting alone staring in front of him and not talking.

He told the wife nothing of this before the marriage, and although he did say that his first wife had died suddenly he did not reveal that she had died in circumstances which raised a probability of suicide. I am inclined to think that this was not deliberate concealment on his part but is rather a manifestation of his reluctance to face unpleasant realities.

The wife for her part was also anxious for the marriage. She had originally answered the advertisement, as she says herself 'as a kind of joke' but was impressed by his letter in reply in which he had revealed that he was a [professional person] without family ties or commitments and that he had a house of his own. Within a week of the first meeting she had visited the house and had accepted his proposal. A very short time afterwards she had agreed to the early date for the wedding.

The marriage did not get off to a very good start. Surprisingly the husband was somewhat ignorant of sexual techniques. The marriage was not consummated during the honeymoon and for some time afterwards – when the wife had provided him with literature on the subject and the husband had seen his doctor and received advice. During this difficulty he admits that the wife's attitude was helpful. About the same time the wife learned of the first wife's tragic death and also – through finding hospital accounts and receipts – of the husband's nervous condition and his sojourn in St. Patrick's. It is not surprising that she should have been disappointed or even that she should have felt that she had been deceived. Neither is it surprising that the husband should have had one of his bouts of nervous depression. This was exacerbated by the death of his father [in] February. All this led to an unpleasant and uncomfortable atmosphere in the house. The wife was worried and thought, naturally enough, that her husband needed and should seek medical treatment. On his part he did not want anyone to talk to him about his nerves. He steadfastly refused to consider going back to Dr. Moore and accused the wife of making his nerves worse by what he considered nagging on the subject. She no doubt was confirmed in her view that she had been deceived. Nevertheless the parties did get on together after a fashion. She was free to see her sisters and friends regularly and even have them visit her. She says that her husband did not welcome visitors and made some of them, including her sister, so uncomfortable that they did not return. I accept this. Apart altogether from the husband's mental state I think he is of a quiet and withdrawn temperament which is not helped by his religious turn of mind, introspective and meditative. I find he was demanding and difficult to live with and not indeed the ideal or even a suitable partner for a young wife in her early thirties who had been used to communal life with a hospital nursing staff of similar age and temperament. I have no doubt that she was bitterly disappointed in her marriage and genuinely worried about her husband's mental health. It would be natural for her to refer to this and, given his reaction to suggestions that there was anything wrong with him, equally natural that he should react in recriminations that she was making matters worse and was not helping the marriage to draw together, to use his own phrase. This I think was the climate and background to their lives together – punctuated by periods of relative happiness and tolerance as when they went on holidays together or when the wife returned having spent some nights with her sister or [her family's home] in January 1962 and other occasions. On the other hand by times the husband's depression and worry and his disappointment got the better of him and he undoubtedly reproached his wife with making his nerves worse and being cold and indifferent. There is no evidence – except perhaps on the night the wife fled to [the X family] that he was ever violent or to support the other allegations in the wife's petition that he is a man of violent and uncontrollable temper; that he frequently abused his wife in gross terms; that he swore at her or struck her. Again apart from the [X] incident there is no evidence that Mrs. D. was in fear of her husband, although she was constantly anxious not to upset him. He undoubtedly did cause her to leave the house on three occasions – one when she went to her sister; when she fled to the [X family] and when he asked her and her mother to leave at Easter 1962. I find it unnecessary to review the evidence of these incidents at length. Suffice is to say that allowing for Mrs. D.'s interests in this suit I am prepared in general to accept her version of what occurred. It is, however, very relevant that shortly after each incident the husband was anxious for reconciliation and to make amends and that – apart from the first occasion – was rebuffed by the wife. Even on the first occasion during which she was away at most three nights she had consulted a solicitor with a view to separation. I do not find in the evidence foundation for the allegations of cruelty made in the wife's petition nor do I find established cruelty as interpreted and applied by the Ecclesiastical Courts as explained and applied in a long series of cases down to the present day. I accept almost all of what Mr. D'Arcy [counsel for Mrs. D.] submitted as to the forms and kinds and degrees of cruelty that have been held sufficient for relief. However, the courts have never allowed a divorce on the grounds that a party has repented of his bargain and found life with his partner unpleasant or even intolerable. The conduct complained of in its effect on the petitioning spouse must have been such as to render the continued performance of the obligations of marriage impossible. Insofar as the grounds relied on are cruelty this must be of such a nature as to have caused actual bodily harm or its reasonable and probable apprehension or, if short of that, must have excited such 'feelings of horror and even loathing' as is said by the Court of Appeal in *Russell* v. *Russell* [1895] P. 315 as to show the absolute impossibility that the duties of married life could be discharged. I do not find this type or degree of conduct on the part of the husband in this case. The most serious incident relied on and where the husband came nearest to violence and arousing terror in the wife was the night she fled to [the X family] but even here, far from being in the state that she could not tolerate any further contact with her husband, she rang him up the next morning and met him to obtain the relatively trifling sum she needed to pay her fare home to [her family's home] instead of borrowing it from one of her sisters or the neighbour to whom she had fled.

It is I think also significant that after each parting, it was the husband who was most upset and that the wife was cool and self-possessed and able to look after her own interests by consulting a solicitor and seeking provision for her future.

Thus far I have been dealing with incidents prior to the reconciliation at the beginning of 1964. Even if I am wrong and that prior to that the husband had been guilty of cruelty there is here evidence of the most complete reconciliation. He made an attempt at a completely new start. He bought Mrs. D. a gold watch; they went to the pictures together: he agreed to make the fresh start in new surroundings in a flat: he agreed to Mrs. D's keeping on her job and ultimately, whether the suggestion came from him or her, he sold his childhood home and bought a new house as a matrimonial home and put it in the wife's name. They were happy together for six months and conceived a child.

There is much I have left out of this account but of which I am not unmindful – Mrs. D's mother's visits; that Mr. D. visited Mrs. D. regularly when she was in hospital prior to the birth of her stillborn child and, on the other hand the extreme concern caused to Mrs. D by her husband's sitting up in bed at night staring in front of him and refusing help or comfort from her. Nor am I unmindful of the fact that simple treatment by a specialist had on one occasion cleared up his neurosis but that nevertheless he shunned and avoided further treatment.

The events that led up to the final parting in late May or early June 1964 have been fully dealt with in the evidence which I do not propose to review. There was no violence or any suggestion of such. Accepting Mrs. D's account of what happened and judging it by its effect on the wife as shown in her immediately subsequent actions, I am not prepared to hold that it amounted either to such cruelty as would entitle her to a divorce or even to such conduct as would suffice to revive cruelty previously condoned, had there been such. Mrs. D was immediately able to write to her husband for money, which on her own evidence she did not really need. She again consulted a solicitor with a view to arranging a separation. She refused all attempts at reconciliation. She obtained an agreement from her husband not to seek reconciliation until the birth of her child. When the child was born she rebuffed her husband when he visited her in hospital – she refused to allow him to attend the child's christening and afterwards refused all contact with him or to discuss any advances by intermediaries. During this time the husband, as was his duty, contributed a fixed and agreed sum to her support and paid, as the correspondence shows, such reasonable accounts as were presented to him.

I am satisfied that the case for the relief claimed by the wife has not been made out. . . .

[**Butler, J.** went on to consider Mr. D's petition for conjugal rights. This part of his judgment is set out *supra*, pp. 184–85]

Notes

1. Other relevant decisions include *Carpenter* v. *Carpenter*, Milw. 159 (1827) and *M'Keever* v. *M'Keever*, I.R. 11 Eq. 26 (Warren, J., 1876). See also *Murphy* v. *Murphy*, [1962–1963] Ir. Jur. Rep. 77 (High Ct., Davitt, P., 1962) (cruelty, followed by condonation, followed by a revival of the acts of cruelty by repetition); and see *L.* v. *L.*, unreported, High Ct., Murphy, J., 7 December: 1982 (1980–749Sp.). Another decision that is of interest in the present context, although the case concerned proceedings for restitution of conjugal rights, is *Ruxton* v. *Ruxton*, 5 L.R. Ir. 455 (C.A.).
2. Is the bar of condonation based on a sound policy? Many commentators have argued that it is not. See, e.g., Fox, *Condonation: An Obstacle to Reconciliation*, 2 Family L.Q. 259 (1968).
3. It has long been recognised that women who are the victims of violence or other misconduct by their husbands may in some cases be obliged, through economic necessity, to remain in the home. This element of economic coercion should be taken into account by the Court in determining whether condonation has been established: see the Law Reform Commission's *Report on Divorce a Mensa et Thoro and Related Matters*, pp. 17–18 (LRC 8–1983. A recent empirical study in the United States is reported by Strube & Barbour, *The Decision to have an Abusive Relationship: Economic Dependence and Psychological Commitment*, 45 J. of Marriage & Family 785 (1983).

B. v. B.

Unreported, High Court, Murnaghan, J. with Jury, 10 December 1970, reported in the *Irish Times*, 11 December 1970, p. 11.

Mr Justice Murnaghan, addressing the jury, said that the case for each of the parties had been opened on a far higher scale than the evidence substantiated. In deciding this case they were exercising a jurisdiction which was originally vested in the ecclesiastical courts. The law had generally remained the same, modified to some degree, but not to any great degree. The ecclesiastical courts recognised no middle course between renewed cohabitation [and] separation from bed and board – *a mensa et thoro*. That was the order the petitioner sought here. That did not break a marriage as such; it merely allowed people to live apart without the obligations which spouses normally had to each other under the bond of marriage.

Mr. Justice Murnaghan said that no definition of cruelty had been laid down and he was not going to venture on ground which many eminent judges had declined to venture on. It was much easier to say what was not cruelty than to define it. It was sufficient for the purpose of this case for him to say that the cruelty alleged was not of itself sufficient unless the result of that cruelty was to cause the petitioner actual ill health, mental or physical, or both.

McA. v. McA.

[1981] I.L.R.M. 361 (High Court, Costello, J.)

The petitioner sought several remedies, including a decree of divorce *a mensa et thoro*.

Costello, J.:

. . . In exercising its jurisdiction to grant a decree of judicial separation the court applies the principles on which the ecclesiastical court referred to in the *Matrimonial Causes and Marriage Law Ireland Amendment Act, 1870* acted, (see s. 13 of the 1870 Act). The petitioner here seeks a decree on the grounds of cruelty, but does not allege that the respondent has been guilty of physical violence towards her. It is clear that in the ecclesiastical courts a decree could be granted on the ground of the cruelty of the respondent even in the absence of proof of physical violence, the test being conduct which renders the co-habitation unsafe or which makes it likely that co-habitation will be attended by injury to the person or health of the party. (See *Carpenter v Carpenter* (1827) Milw. 159, at 160). This principle was adopted and applied at an early stage in the exercise of a similar jurisdiction in the civil courts in England. In *Kelly v Kelly* (L.R.2 P.&D.58) the court expressly pointed out that it was concerned with a case in which there was no proof of physical violence; nonetheless it granted a decree of judicial separation. Channell B. pointed out:

> It would be difficult to frame a definition of legal cruelty which would be applicable to all cases which may arise. The object of the Matrimonial Court in exercising its jurisdiction in decreeing judicial separation for cruelty is to free the injured consort from a co-habitation which has been rendered, or which there is imminent reason to believe will be rendered, unsafe by the ill-usage of the party complained of. It is obvious that the modes by which one of two married persons may make the life or the health of the other insecure are infinitely various but as often a perverse ingenuity may invent a new manner of producing the result the Court must supply the remedy by separating the parties. The most frequent form of ill-usage which amounts to cruelty is that of personal violence but the courts have never limited their jurisdiction to such cases alone. (See pages 60 and 61.)

There are many cases in the English Reports in which decrees of judicial separation have been made on the ground of what is somewhat loosely called 'mental cruelty', that is to say, acts not involving physical violence. Following the principle which I have just quoted from *Kelly v Kelly* it has been pointed out that 'to establish cruelty it must be shown that the defaulting spouse has been guilty of deliberate behaviour the effect of which either has been or must be in the ordinary course to injure the health, bodily or mental, of the other spouse'. (See Judgment of Henn-Collins J in *Atkins v Atkins* [1942] 2 All E.R. 637, at 638). In applying this principle the court in *Atkins Case* granted a decree where the evidence was that of constant nagging by the respondent wife. The difficulty in laying down anything but the broadest general principle is however illustrated by the fact in a later case where a somewhat similar allegation was made the court refused to order a decree. (See *King v King* [1953] A.C.124.)

In the present case I am satisfied that the defendant's conduct has, in fact, injured the plaintiff's health. That conduct has been deliberate in the sense that it was consciously adopted by him. I should make clear however that the defendant, I am satisfied, has not set out deliberately to injure his wife's health. But this does not disentitle the petitioner to relief as it has been established in *Kelly v Kelly* and confirmed in the House of Lords in a more recent case (see *Gollins v Gollins* [1964] A.C.644) that cruelty in matrimonial cases can exist in the absence of intention to injure. The conduct which has injured the petitioner's health in the present case was a deliberate refusal by the defendant to communicate with his wife except when absolutely necessary and then in the most formal way. He has persisted in this conduct over a considerable period of time. He has deliberately withdrawn himself emotionally from her. He has sought protection from the strain in the family home in the practice of transcendental meditation but this has only aggravated the situation by making him appear emotionally cold and insensitive to his wife's needs. He has refused to co-operate with his wife in trying to find a solution to their marital difficulties and has declined to see their family doctor, a consultant psychiatrist, a marriage counsellor or a social worker, all of whom at different times had offered at the request of the plaintiff their expert assistance. Sometimes he communicates to his wife through their three-year-old daughter, sometimes by means of notes. Conversation between them has been reduced to a minimum and relates, it would appear, to the necessities of living together and nothing more. The marriage has clearly broken down. There has been no sexual intercourse between the parties for about three years and the defendant no longer sleeps in his wife's bedroom. This is not a case in which the breakdown can be attributed equally to both spouses or in which fault cannot be apportioned. The wife has candidly admitted to her faults and has accepted that she has not been an easy person at times to live with. But I am satisfied from the evidence that the major blame for what has happened to this marriage must lie on the conduct of the defendant which I have just outlined. This conduct has had, as I have said, adverse effects on the wife's health. These effects have been serious and could very easily become much more serious. It is true that before the marriage the plaintiff, whilst attending university, had to seek psychiatric help due to the strain of her final year's examination, but I am satisfied that although she is a person who perhaps suffers anxiety more easily than others and although she may be more prone to depression than others she is by no means a neurotic person. However, conditions in the home were such that in July of 1977 she was forced to seek assistance from her local doctor who placed her on anti-depressants. Again she sought medical help in December 1978 and her condition of anxiety and depression was such that her local doctor although himself trained in psychiatry felt it desirable to obtain the assistance of a consultant psychiatrist. She attended a consultant psychiatrist in January of 1979 and since then has seen him regularly. She has been on anti-depressants now for over 2½ years. She also has had to avail of the assistance of a social worker. The medical evidence satisfies me that her condition of anxiety and depression has been caused by the conduct of the respondent to which I have referred and that evidence also satisfies me that if the order which the plaintiff seeks in these proceedings is not made and if the parties continue to live together that this may well result in her developing a chronic neurotic depression. In all the circumstances of the case therefore, it seems to me that the acts which I have outlined amount to legal cruelty and entitle the plaintiff to a divorce a mensa et thoro and I will so order.

Notes

1. See Neville Brown, *Cruelty Without Culpability or Divorce Without Fault*, 26 Modern L. Rev. 625 (1963).
2. See also *L.* v. *L.*, unreported, High Ct., Murphy, J., 7 December 1982 (1980–749Sp.).
3. Cf. *Ward* v. *Ward*, [1948] N.I. 60 (K.B.Div. (Mat.) Porter, L.J.).
4. In the light of *McA.* v. *McA.*, would *D.* v. *D.*, *supra*, p. 290 be decided differently today?

(iii) *Unnatural Practices*

A third ground for the granting of a decree of divorce *a mensa et thoro* is that of unnatural practices indulged in by the husband. The scope of this ground is uncertain, since there are very few reported decisions and those that have been reported are somewhat unclear. See the Law Reform Commission's *Report on Divorce a Mensa et Thoro and Related Matters*, pp. 12–14 (LRC 8–1983).

Notes

1. The Statistics for petitions for divorce *a mensa et thoro* presented to, and granted by High Court over the past decade are as follows:

	Petitions	*Decrees*
1973:	26	2
1974:	51	10
1975:	43	4
1976:	37	3
1977:	29	5
1978:	39	1
1979:	34	2
1980:	27	2
1981:	25	2
1982:	20	6

These statistics give some indication of the relevance of the remedy of divorce *a mensa et thoro* to family relationships and, in particular, maintenance obligations today. So far as maintenance is concerned, the *Family Law (Maintenance of Spouses and Children) Act, 1976* provides flexible protection to dependent spouses. Under this Act there is no need to establish that the respondent spouse is guilty of any wrongdoing: all that need be proved to the satisfaction of the Court is that the respondent has failed to provide such maintenance for the family as is proper in the circumstances. See further chapter 5.

2. The Law Reform Commission have recently made radical proposals for reform, in their *Report on Divorce a Mensa et Thoro and Related Matters* (LRC 8 – 1983). The Commission propose the retention, with minor modifications, of the grounds of adultery and cruelty and abolition of unnatural practices as a specific ground. The Commission, also recommend the introduction of the following new grounds.

(1) 'That the respondent has behaved in such a way that the petitioner cannot reasonably be expected to live with the respondent.'
(2) Desertion, actual or constructive.
(3) Breakdown of marriage.
(4) One year's separation, where the respondent consents to a decree being granted.
(5) Five years' separation (whether or not the respondent consents).

The Commission also propose that the Court be empowered to 'convert' a separation agreement into a decree for legal separation, provided it is satisfied that the agreement is a fair and reasonable one.

Regarding the existing bars to a decree, the Commission recommend that connivance should be retained, that recrimination and collusion be abolished that condonation be made a discretionary bar and that conduct conducing to adultery should constitute a substantive (rather than discretionary) bar.

The Report also contains important recommendation's relating to children. The Commission recommend that the Court should have duty to protect the children of judicially separated spouses; that a decree of legal separation should not be granted unless there are no children of the marriage under 18 or, where there are children under 18, proper arrangements (whether by Court order or Otherwise) have been made for their welfare (including custody and education of, and financial provision for, the children). Also the Commission recommend that the Court in separation proceedings should have power to make orders for the custody and education of the children.

3. In *Airey* v. *Ireland*, Series A, No. 32; 2 E.H.R.R. 305 (1979), the European Court of Human Rights held that Ireland was in breach of Articles 6(1) and 8 of the European Convention for the Protection of Human Rights and Fundamental Freedoms, by reason of its failure to provide free legal aid to the plaintiff, a married woman who wished to take proceedings for divorce *a mensa et thoro* against her husband. Article 6(1) provides in part that:

> In the determination of his civil rights and obligations . . . everyone is entitled to a fair and public hearing within a reasonable time by an independent and impartial tribunal established by law. . . .

Article 8 provides as follows:

1. Everyone has the right to respect of his private and family life, his home and his correspondence.
2. There shall be no interference by a public authority with the exercise of this right except such as is in accordance with the law and is necessary in a democratic society in the interests of national security, public safety or the economic wellbeing of the country, for the prevention of disorder or crime, for the protection of health or morals or for the protection of the rights and freedom of others.

Since many aspects of private or family life are regulated by law in Ireland and since protection of the private or family life of spouses might sometimes necessitate their being relieved from the duty to live together, effective respect for private or family life "oblige[d] Ireland to make this means of protection effectively accessible, when appropriate, to anyone who m[ight] wish to have recourse thereto". Having regard to the complexities of law and practice, it was not realistic to argue (as the Government had done) that Mrs Airey was free to take proceedings without legal assistance. For consideration of the decision, see *Shatter*, 24–25; Maidment, *The Airey Case*, 10 Family L. 69 (1980); Forde, *Equality and the Constitution*, 17 Ir. Jur. (n.s.) 295, at 308–309 (1982). More broadly, see Evrigenis, *Recent Case-Law of the European Court of Human Rights on Articles 8 and 10 of the European Convention on Human Rights*, 3 Human Rights L.J. 121 (1982).

A scheme of civil legal aid was subsequently introduced. For consideration of the scheme, see *Shatter*, 25–26.

Chapter 9

THE FAMILY HOME: INJUNCTIONS AND BARRING ORDERS

Introduction

In this chapter we will examine the common law injunction excluding a spouse from the family home, and then consider the statutory provisions relating to barring orders, introduced in 1976, and strengthened by legislation in 1981. Leading analyses of this subject include Horgan, *Legal Protection for the Victim of Marital Violence*, 13 Ir. Jur. (n.s.) 233, at 234 ff (1978); Charleton, *The Scope of the Remedy of the Barring Order*, 1 Ir. L. Times (n.s.) 79 (1983); O'Connor, *Barring Orders*, 1 Ir. L. Times (n.s.) 96 (1983) and McNally, *Barring Orders and Ouster Orders – Judicial Change of Attitude?*, 77 Incorp. L. Soc. of Ireland Gazette 279 (1983); Duncan, *He Stepped Out and He Stepped In Again: The Function of a Barring Order,* [1983] Dublin U.L.J. 155.

THE COMMON LAW INJUNCTION

GAYNOR v. GAYNOR
[1901] 2 I.R. 217 (Porter, M.R.)

This was an application by summons under section 17 of the Married Woman's Property Act, 1882, by the plaintiff Judith Gaynor, against her husband the defendant Patrick Gaynor, for an order that the premises and property specified in the schedule thereto should be declared to be the separate estate and property of the plaintiff, and that the plaintiff was accordingly entitled to the title and possession of the said premises and property, and that the defendant be restrained from entering into the said premises and from interfering with the said property, and for the costs of the application.

The property comprised in the schedule was as follows:–

1. Premises in the town of Kingscourt, in the county of Cavan, held under lease for lives renewable for ever, dated the 28th May, 1776, subject to the yearly rent of £1 2*s.* 9*d.* late Irish currency.
2. A seven day retail licence for the sale of beer, wine, spirits, &c., to be consumed on the premises, now in the name of Judith Gaynor the plaintiff.
3. The stock in trade, furniture, fittings, and chattels in the said premises.
4. The receipts or earnings received and to be received by the plaintiff from the retail trade of publican, carried on by the plaintiff on the said premises.
5. Any other property of the plaintiff forming part of her separate estate.

The material facts as stated in the affidavit of the plaintiff were as follows:–

John Courtney, father of the plaintiff, was assignee of the lease mentioned in the schedule, and carried on therein the business of a publican, with a retail publican's seven-day licence. By deed of October 12, 1886, the said John Courtney conveyed the lessee's interest in the premises to the plaintiff, who was then unmarried, as her absolute property, and transferred the licence into her then name of Judith Courtney, and made over to her by way of gift all the stock in trade, furniture, goods, chattels, and effects then upon the premises; and the plaintiff carried on the said licensed business in her own name from the date of the said assignment.

The plaintiff was married to the defendant in September, 1893; and by an agreement in writing made between her and the defendant the said premises, licence, stock in trade, furniture, and effects were to be and remain her sole and separate property, and the defendant was not to have any interest therein. This agreement was not forthcoming, and the plaintiff believed that it was in the possession of the defendant, and stated that she believed the effect of it was as above stated. The defendant had no property of his own, and went to reside with the plaintiff on the premises. There were no children of the marriage. Disagreements took place shortly after the marriage by reason of the plaintiff refusing to transfer the licence into the name of the defendant, which he requested her to do. At various times from October, 1894, down to December, 1900, the defendant assaulted and beat the plaintiff, for which he was summoned before the magistrates and fined and imprisoned. When in the house he systematically interfered with the plaintiff's business, and acted as if he was owner of it. He was constantly drunk, and took money out of the till. He used to serve customers, and keep the money received from them. The result of his interference and misconduct was that the business was seriously injured. At the time of the application the defendant was not living in the house, but the plaintiff was in daily fear of his returning to the house and illtreating her again and interfering with the business as before.

In support of her application under section 17, the plaintiff's counsel mentioned that she could not afford the expenses of taking 'proceedings for divorce' by which, the context suggests, he meant proceedings for divorce *a mensa et thoro*.

Porter, M.R.:

This application is brought for a purpose which is quite justifiable, but the question is, how far I have jurisdiction to make as order under section 17 of the *Married Woman's Property Act, 1882*. I have before me the official record of the conviction of the defendant, and I am satisfied that he has treated the plaintiff very badly, and has used the premises in a way inconsistent with her right to carry on her business therein without molestation. I am also satisfied that the business is her separate property, and I think that the case comes within section 17 of the *Married Woman's Property Act, 1882*, and that I have jurisdiction to decide as to the property being the separate estate of the wife. The section says, 'In any question between husband and wife, as to the title to, or possession of property.' I think that there has been a question between husband and wife, as his conduct amounts to a claim by him on the property.

But it is another matter how far the order should go. I have a great objection to do indirectly that which could be done directly by proper proceedings, viz. to grant a judicial separation. I do not know if the plaintiff has any remedy by an application to a magistrate, but I am asked to make an order, which would amount to a judicial separation, that not only is the husband to be kept out of the premises, but that she is to continue in them, as she must do, if she is to carry on the business there. What order then should I make? It appears that the plaintiff was married to the defendant in 1893, and that in 1886 her father made the property over to her, and that there was an agreement in writing on her marriage with the defendant, which is not forthcoming, but which she says provided that the premises, licence, stock in trade, furniture and effects on the premises were to remain her separate property. I think that the plaintiff has established her right to the property mentioned in the schedule to the summons, omitting the last paragraph (5) thereof, and that she should be declared entitled to the same and the possession thereof, as between herself and her husband. But now comes the point, the summons asks that the defendent be restrained from entering into the said premises and from interfering with the said property. I do not see my way to go so far as that. I can make an order that he be restrained from interfering with the property and the business, and for costs.

In *Wood* v. *Wood* 19 W.R. 1049 an order was made by Malins, V.-C., restraining the husband from in any way interfering with the conduct of the business of a private hotel keeper, and from continuing in possession of the private hotel and premises, or any part thereof. The husband there had by post-nuptial settlement entered into a contract with his wife, by which she was to conduct a hotel for the benefit of herself and children, and to occupy it as a *feme sole*. Malins, V.-C., held that the husband had violated the contract by entering into possession of the hotel, and that, therefore, the plaintiff was entitled to an injunction in the terms of the prayer of the bill. That injunction was very nearly equivalent to a judicial separation. The decision was on the ground that the husband had contracted that he should not interfere with the possession of the wife, and that a Court of Equity would enforce such a contract. *Symonds* v. *Hallett* 24 Ch. D. 346, where *Wood* v. *Wood* 19

W.R. 1049 and other cases were discussed, does not go so far, though there the Court of Appeal held that the wife was entitled to an interim injunction restraining the husband from entering the house, because he claimed the right to go to and use the house, not as a husband to enjoy the society of his wife, but for his own purposes, and in *Weldon* v. *De Bathe* 14 Q. B. D. 339, the Court of Appeal intimated that though a husband is entitled to enter his wife's house against her will in order to enforce his marital rights, he is not entitled to do so for any other purpose, but no decision was given on the point, as it was not necessary.

I am, therefore, only justified in making an order, declaring the right of the plaintiff to the property, and restraining the defendant from interfering with it. If the defendant persists in coming into the premises and ill treating the plaintiff, she ought to take proceedings for a judicial separation.

The following order was made:–

THE Judge doth declare that the premises and property specified in the schedule hereto are the separate estate and property of the plaintiff, and that the said plaintiff is accordingly entitled as between herself and the defendant, to the possession of the said premises and property; and the Judge doth order that the defendant be and he is hereby restrained from in any way interfering with the said property or with the business and trade of a licensed publican, carried on by the said plaintiff in the said premises held under the lease in the said schedule mentioned. . . .

[SCHEDULE.]

Notes

1. See also *O'Malley* v. *O'Malley*, 85 I.L.T.R. 43 (Sup. Ct., 1950 aff'g High Ct., Gavan Duffy, J., 1950). For a general discussion of some of the principal issues raised in cases such as *Gaynor* v. *Gaynor* and *O'Malley* v. *O'Malley*, see Ellis, *The Right of Occupation of the Matrimonial Home and its Enforcement by the Courts*, 4 Anglo-Amer. L. Rev. 59 (1975). See also Lowe, *Evicting the Recalcitrant Spouse*, [1979] Conv. 337; Samuels, *The Matrimonial Injunction*, 125 New L.J. 365 (1975).
2. Cf. *Kelley* v. *Kelley*, 51 R.I. 173, 153 Atl. 314, 74 A.L.R. 135 (1931), critically analysed by McCurdy, *Property Torts Between Spouses and Use During Marriage of the Matrimonial Home Owned By the Other*, 2 Villanova L. Rev. 447, at 467–471 (1957).

C. v. C.

[1976] I.R. 254 (High Court, Kenny, J., 1975)

[The facts of the case are set out *supra* p. 265. On the question of granting an injunction, **Kenny, J.** said:]

. . . The husband's behaviour has been so outrageous and has such a bad effect on the children that I propose to grant an injunction restraining him from entering the matrimonial home although he is the owner of a half share in it: see *Gurasz* v. *Gurasz*. [1969] 3 W.L.R. 482. There was no discussion about access and the husband made no request for this. If he wishes to have some provision for it, an application for this can be made later.

Notes

1. Should the fact that a violent spouse has a proprietary interest in the family home have *any* relevance to the question whether or not an injunction should be made ordering the spouse out of the home?
2. In *F.* v. *F.*, unreported, High Ct., 20 May 1982 (1982–94Sp.), Murphy J. said that an injunction at common law restraining a spouse from entering the matrimonial home 'should be granted or withheld on the same grounds as those specified in Section 22 of the *Family Home (Maintenance of Spouses and Children) Act, 1976*'. Do you agree? Cf. *Richards* v. *Richards*, [1983] 2 W.L.R. 633 (H.L. (Eng.)), considered *infra*, p. 306, note 4.
3. A victim of marital violence may, of course, seek to have the spouse prosecuted for assault, grievous bodily harm or breach of the peace. See *Shatter*, 110–111; Horgan, *Legal Protection for the Victim of Marital Violence*, 13 Ir. Jur. (n.s.) 233, at 234 (1978). To what extent do you regard the criminal law as an appropriate or effective

response to marital violence? See Parnas, *Individual Response to Intrafamily Violence*, 54 Minn. L. Rev. 585 (1970); Parnas, *The Relevance of Criminal Law to Inter-Spousal Violence*, ch. 8 of J. Eekelaar & S. Katz ed., *Family Violence: An International and Interdisciplinary Study* (1978); Maidment, *The Law's Response to Marital Violence: A Comparison Between England and the U.S.A., id.*, ch. 6, at 111–115; Freeman, *The Phenomenon of Marital Violence and the Legal and Social Response in England, id.*, ch. 5, at 80–86; Berk & Loseke, *'Handling' Family Violence: Situational Determinants of Police Arrest in Domestic Disturbances*, 15 L. & Society Rev. 317 (1980); Cannings, *Myths and Stereotypes-Obstacles to Effective Intervention in Domestic Disputes Involving a Battered Woman*, 57 Police J. 43 (1984); Worden & Pollitz, *Police Arrests in Domestic Disturbances: A Further Look*, 18 L. & Society Rev. 105 (1984). Are the rules of evidence relating to the competence and compellability of spouses adequate in this context?

4. Should the prosecuting and investigative authorities adopt the same approach towards spousal assault, so far as discretion to arrest and prosecute is concerned, as they do towards street muggings? Cf. Woods, *Litigation on Behalf of Battered Women*, 7 Women's Rts. L. Reptr. 39 (1981).
5. Where a spouse who has been subjected to violence or the threat of violence leaves the home, she (or he) may have a good defence in proceedings for restitution of conjugal rights (*Ruxton* v. *Ruxton*, 5 L.R. Ir. 455 (C.A., 1880); she (or he) may also take proceedings for divorce *a mensa et thoro* on the ground of cruelty (cf. *supra*, pp. 290–95); moreover, in proceedings for maintenance against the violent spouse under the *Family Law (Maintenance of Spouses and Children) Act, 1976*, the violent spouse may be held to be guilty of constructive desertion – a holding which is far from inevitable, however, and which depends greatly on the *quantum* of violence and the likelihood of its taking place in the future: see *P.* v. *P., supra*, p. 214, *P.G.* v. *C.G.* and *C.G.* v. *P.G.*, unreported, High Ct., Finlay, P., 12 March 1982.
6. The law of torts should not be ignored. Apart from actions for damages for battery, assault and infliction of emotional suffering, whether intentional or negligent, it appears that a spouse may obtain an injunction against assault and batter (cf. *Egan* v. *Egan*, [1975] Ch. 218 (Oliver, J.) (injunction against apprehended violence by 19-year-old son on mother); an injunction against trespass to land or chattels could also be appropriate in some cases, although the courts have shown themselves reluctant to use the 'heavy artillery of Court orders' (*Cullen* v. *Cullen*, [1962] I.R. 268, at 290) in this context.
7. The relationship between spousal assault and the question of child custody may present the Court with intractable problems. Cf. *B.H.* v. *A.H.*, unreported, High Ct., Barrington, J., 11 January 1982 (1980–683Sp.). Problems may also arise in relation to the exercise by a parent of his or her right of access to the child: cf. *O'C.* v. *O'C.*, unreported, High Ct., McMahon, J., 16 December 1976 (1975–1056P.). See also *O'B.* v. *O'B.*, unreported, High Ct., Kenny, J., 5 January 1971 (1965–207Sp.), where, although the father was granted access to his children, an injunction was also granted restraining him from telephoning the mother or calling at the house except for the purpose of exercising his right of access.
8. The subject of child care policy is beyond the scope of this book. For a bibliography of recent Irish literature critically analysing the present child care system, see *Shatter*, 262, fn. 97. The position of tort law is considered by B. McMahon & W. Binchy, *Irish Law of Torts*, 145 (1981). In 1979, Sweden became the first country to ban corporal punishment within the home: see Ziegert, *The Swedish Prohibition of Corporal Punishment: A Preliminary Report*, 45 J. of Marriage & the Family 917 (1983). Cf. *X, Y & Z* v. *Sweden*, 5 E.H.R.R. 147 (European Commission of Human Rts, 1982).
9. A recent study of the social and psychological factors of child abuse is Felthous, *Psychosocial Dynamics of Child Abuse*, 29 J. of Forensic Sciences 219 (1984).

BARRING ORDERS

Section 22 of the *Family Law (Maintenance of Spouses and Children) Act, 1976* gave the Court power to order a spouse to leave the home if the Court was of opinion that there were reasonable grounds for believing that the safety or welfare of the applicant spouse or any dependent child of the family required it. This statutory procedure for barring orders was improved by the *Family Law (Protection of Spouses and Children) Act, 1981*. Section 2 of the 1981 Act provides as follows:

> (1) On application to it by a spouse (in this Act called the 'applicant spouse'), the Court may, if it is of opinion that there are reasonable grounds for believing that the safety or welfare of that spouse or of any child so requires, by order (in this Act called a 'barring order')–
>
> (*a*) direct the other spouse (in this Act called the 'respondent spouse'), if residing at a place where the applicant spouse or the child resides, to leave that place, and
>
> (*b*) whether the respondent spouse is or is not residing at that place, prohibit that spouse from entering that place until further order by the Court or until such other time as the Court shall specify.

(2) A barring order may, if the Court thinks fit, prohibit the respondent spouse from using or threatening to use violence against molesting or putting in fear the applicant spouse or any child and may be made subject to such exceptions and conditions as the Court may specify.
(3) A barring order may be varied by the Court on the application of either spouse.
(4) A barring order, if made by the District Court or by the Circuit Court on appeal from the District Court, shall, subject to *section 11* of this Act, expire twelve months after the date of its making.
(5) On or before the expiration of a barring order a further barring order may be made with effect from the expiration of the first-mentioned barring order.
(6) For the purposes of *subsection (1)* of this section an applicant spouse or a child who would, but for the conduct of the respondent spouse, be residing at a place shall be treated as residing at that place.

For consideration of section 22, see McGann, *The Domestic Violence Jurisdiction of the District Court and the Magistrates' Courts*, 73 Incorp. L. Soc. of Ireland Gazette 137 (1979).

The 1981 Act introduced a new order, the 'Protection order', designed to give protection to the spouse and children, pending the determination of the application for a barring order. Section 3 provides as follows:

(1) If, between the making of an application for a barring order and its determination, the Court is of opinion that there are reasonable grounds for believing that the safety or welfare of the applicant spouse or of any child so requires, the Court may make an order (in this Act called a 'protection order') that the respondent spouse shall not use or threaten to use violence against, molest or put in fear the applicant spouse or the child.
(2) A protection order may be made notwithstanding that the summons in relation to the application for a barring order has not been served on the respondent spouse.
(3) A protection order shall cease to have effect on the determination by the Court of the application for a barring order.

The 1981 Act also deals with difficulties of notification and enforcement experienced under the 1976 legislation. Section 4 of the 1981 Act provides:

(1) A barring order or a protection order shall take effect on notification of its making being given to the respondent spouse.
(2) Oral communication to the respondent spouse by or on behalf of the applicant spouse of the fact that a barring order or a protection order has been made, together with production of a copy of the order, shall, without prejudice to the sufficiency of any other form of notification, be taken to be sufficient notification of the respondent spouse of the making of the order.
(3) If the respondent spouse is present at the sitting of the Court at which the barring order or protection order is made, that spouse shall be taken, for the purposes of *subsection (1)* of this section, to have been notified of its making.
(4) An order varying a barring order shall take effect on notification of its making being given to the spouse other than the spouse who applied for the variation, and for this purpose *subsections (2)* and *(3)* of this section shall apply with the necessary modifications.

And section 5 provides:–

(1) The Court, on making, varying or discharging a barring order or on making or discharging a protection order, shall cause a copy of the order in question to be given or sent as soon as practicable to the applicant spouse, the respondent spouse and the member of the Garda Síochána in charge of the Garda Síochána station for the area in which is situate the place in relation to which the application for the barring order was made.
(2) Non-compliance with *subsection (1)* of this section shall not affect the validity of the order.

Section 6 provides:–

(1) A respondent spouse who contravenes a barring order or a protection order or, while a barring order is in force, refuses to permit the applicant spouse or any child to enter and remain in the place to which the order relates or does any act for the purpose of preventing that spouse or child from doing so shall be guilty of an offence and shall be liable on summary conviction to a fine not exceeding £200 or, at the discretion of the court, to imprisonment for a term not exceeding six months, or to both.
(2) *Subsection (1)* of this section is without prejudice to the law as to contempt of court or any other liability, whether civil or criminal, that may be incurred by the respondent spouse.

Section 7 empowers a member of the Garda Síochána, on complaint being made to him by or on behalf of the applicant spouse, to arrest the respondent spouse without warrant where the Garda has reasonable cause for believing that the respondent spouse is committing or has committed an offence under section 6 of the Act.

Section 8(1) provides that, where a person charged with an offence under section 6 of the Act is released on bail and commits an offence under that section while so released, any sentences of imprisonment passed on that person for offences under that section are to be consecutive.

Section 11 deals with the discharge of orders. It provides as follows:–

(1) Either spouse may apply for the discharge of a barring order or a protection order to the court that made the order and thereupon the court shall discharge the order if it is satisfied that the safety or welfare of the spouse of child for whose protection the order was made does not require that the order should continue in force.

(2) On the determination of any matrimonial cause or matter between the spouses or of any proceedings between them under the *Guardianship of Infants Act, 1964*, the court determining any such cause, matter or proceedings may, if it thinks fit, discharge any barring order or protection order directed against one of them.

Proceedings under the Act are heard otherwise than in public: section 14(1). See generally Charleton, *The Scope of the Remedy of the Barring Order*, 1 Ir. L. Times (n.s.) 79 (1983).

In the decisions extracted below which deal with section 22of the 1976 Act, it should be noted that the central criterion against which the Court is to determine whether a barring order should be made is the same in both section 22 of the 1976 Act and section 2 of the 1981 Act. Accordingly these decisions throw light on the scope of the present law.

McA. v. McA.

[1981] I.L.R.M. 361 (High Court, Costello, J.)

[The facts of the case have been set out *supra*, pp. 293–95 in relation to divorce *a mensa et thoro*. On the question of a barring order, **Costello, J.** stated:]

. . . I am satisfied that the defendant's conduct has seriously affected the plaintiff's welfare and that that conduct justifies the court making an order barring the defendant from the family home. I am also satisfied from the evidence of the plaintiff herself and from the medical evidence that the barring order is necessary for the welfare of the infant. . . . That evidence satisfies me that this little girl (who is only three years of age) is, in fact, affected by the very serious strain which presently exists in the family home and that her welfare requires that the order be made. . . .

IN THE MATTER OF G.C. AND K.C. INFANTS, D.C. v. A.C.

High Ct., May 1981 (1980–693Sp.) Reported in part, [1981] I.L.R.M. 357

The plaintiff took proceedings for, *inter alia*, a barring order against the husband. The couple had married in 1973. Their first child was born in 1975. According to the wife, the marriage deteriorated from the birth of their child. The husband did not help with the care of the baby or doing housework. He was, moreover, extravagant in spending money on himself.

Carroll, J.:

. . . Another cause of difficulties in this marriage has been violence by the husband to the wife. He had a habit of switching on T.V. very loudly when he came home. When the wife attempted to turn this off or down, he forceably removed her on several occasions from the room. He claims he did nothing else and intended no violence. She claims when she tried to resist he slapped her, banged her head on occasions against the wall and on one occasion gave her a black eye. I am satisfied that there was violence as described by the wife on at least three or four of these occasions.

On another occasion, when she came in at 5 a.m. in the morning, he dragged her off the bed by her ankles and down two steps of the stairs to the half landing at which stage the wife agreed to leave the house. On that occasion I am satisfied the reason he did so was because she told him that it was none of his business where she was and was not because she came in at 5 a.m. (not that that would justify his actions). He did not object to her going out with her friends at any time and did not allege that anything improper had then or ever taken place. This incident took place in November 1979 when relations were strained.

On another occasion just before Christmas 1980 the husband had a disagreement with the wife as to whether she should accompany the children to his family home on Christmas Day or not. On impulse he locked her in the bathroom on the first floor about 8 o'clock in the evening and took the children intending to keep them until Christmas Day, a period of about three days. He found the following day that he could not do so because of work and he returned the children. In the meantime the wife had to climb out of the window on the first floor on to a sloping roof and then across a glass roof on to the garage roof from where she had to be assisted down by a neighbour. As she was then locked out of the house, she had to go to her parents' home that evening. She said she did not have a good head for heights. His explanation was that he forgot to come back and let her out. This incident did not involve violence but showed an irresponsibility on the husband's part which placed the wife in a situation which was inherently dangerous. . . . The wife did make some attempt to patch up their difficulties. She went to marriage guidance counselling over a period of three months in the summer of 1979 but the husband only attended two or three times.

In or about November 1979 the wife tried to persuade the husband to move out of the house for a trial separation. Around the same time (December 1979/January 1980) the family business out of which the couple received financial support, got into financial difficulties and the support stopped. The wife succeeded in persuading the husband to move out of the house in early February 1980 and in this she was helped by her brother-in-law who offered the husband a temporary place to stay. Some time later he went to stay at his parents' house. After he had moved out, the wife instituted these proceedings seeking a barring order and maintenance for herself and the children. The husband has not sought to move back into the house and says he would not do so without the wife's agreement but he disputes her entitlement to a barring order. . . .

The fathers of both parties also gave evidence. The husband's father said that he had never grown up and the wife's father described him as being incompetent to manage money. I agree with the judgment of these men, both of whom are responsible people anxious to do their best for their respective children and their two grandchildren.

The couple were young and immature when they got married. The wife has achieved a degree of responsibility and maturity, no doubt due partly to motherhood. She is supporting the children entirely on her earnings. She has sold her car because she cannot afford to run it and uses a bicycle to go to school. She is paying off one of the debts incurred as part of their joint financing but which is in her sole name. The husband, on the other hand, has paid nothing towards the maintenance of the children since he left the family home in February of 1980 and has paid nothing off the debts which they accumulated during their marriage, but he did go on a holiday to France in the Summer of 1980. He has at the moment a net income of £68 per week out of which he pays his mother £15 for board. In the past few months he has been sent down the country on a weekly basis (Monday to Friday) in connection with [an assignment] which is likely to last for two years and is receiving both subsistance and travelling expenses so that he has £53 over and above his day to day living expenses each week. He has saved nothing out of this.

The wife is also seeking an order that the family home which is in their joint names be transferred into her sole name. The building society have obtained an order of possession but have delayed execution pending the outcome of these proceedings. Her father has offered to pay all arrears amounting to £7,000 and the future mortgage instalments, provided the property is transferred to her with clear title. The house is very suitable for the children in that it is near to the wife's place of work. The road is a cul-de-sac with plenty of companionship of their own age for the children. There is, however, the possibility of a valuable equity of redemption. While no expert evidence was given as to the value of the house, it has been accepted by both parties that the house has appreciated in value since it was bought and if it were now sold and the mortgage paid off, there would be a considerable balance available. No feasible alternative has been put forward by the husband to save the house from being sold. He disputes the wife's entitlement to have the house transferred into her name.

It is clear from the evidence that the children and in particular the elder one, have improved since their parents separated. The elder child, from being quite a disturbed boy, has settled down to a remarkable degree. The wife has become calmer and is a better and more relaxed mother to the children. Prior to the separation she could not sleep at night and could not stand the TV blaring during the day.

The first issue is whether a barring order should be made. Under s. 22 of the *Family Law (Maintenance of Spouses and Children) Act, 1976* the court may make such order if it is of opinion that there are reasonable grounds for believing that the safety or welfare of the spouse applying for it or of any dependant child requires it.

The violence which the husband has shown in this case may have been due to his frustration coupled with his immaturity. I am satisfied on the evidence that there are reasonable grounds for believing that incidents of physical force possibly coupled with violence might occur again unless he achieves some degree of maturity. I do not think that he is by nature a violent man but the evidence shows that he lacks self control at times.

Quite apart from the question of safety, which would be an issue where violence was involved, the court is also entitled to make a barring order if the welfare of the spouse or children requires it. I am satisfied on the evidence because there has been such an improvement in the well-being of the wife and children since the husband left the family home that the welfare of the wife and children require his absence at least for a certain period.

In the circumstances I propose to grant a barring order on the grounds of both safety and welfare barring the husband from the family home for a period of two years. In that time it is possible that he may qualify [in his profession] and achieve some degree of maturity which he is lacking at the moment. . . .

Notes

1. Is the holding in this case consistent with *O'B.* v. *O'B. infra*, p. 306?
2. Cf. *P.* v. *P.*, unreported, High Ct., Barrington, J., 12 March 1980 (1980–14Sp.)(barring order refused).
3. In the United States, legislators were in some respects slower to respond to the problem of spousal violence than their Irish counterparts: see Sacco, *Comment: Wife Abuse: The Failure of Legal Remedies*, 11 John Marshall J. of Practice & Procedure 549 (1978). In recent years, the position there has improved: see Schechter, *The Violent Family and the Ambivalent State: Developing a Coherent Policy for State Aid to Victims of Family Violence*, 20 J. of Family L. 1 (1981); Combo, *Comment: Wife Beating: Law and Society Confront the Castle Door*, 15 Gonzaga L. Rev. 171 (1979); Cook, *Domestic Abuse Legislation in Illinois and Other States: A Survey and Suggestions for Reform,* [1983] U. Illinois L. Rev. 261; Mouton, *Note: Wife Abuse Legislation in California, Pennsylvania and Texas*, 7 Thurgood Marshall L. Rev. 282 (1982). The courts and commentators in the United States have investigated the constitutionality of aspects of state legislation providing for exclusion orders in cases of

domestic violence: see, e.g. *State ex rel. Williams* v. *March*, 626 S.W. 2d 223 (Mo. Sup. Ct. En Banc, 1982); Taub, *Ex Parte Proceedings in Domestic Violence Situations: Alternative Frameworks for Constitutional Scrutiny*, 9 Hofstra L. Rev. 95 (1980); Grim, *Domestic Relations: Legal Responses to Wife Beating: Theory and Practice in Ohio*, 16 Akron L. Rev. 705, at 717–719 (1983).

C. v. C.

Unreported, High Court, O'Hanlon, J., 16 December 1982
(1980–897 Sp. and 1982–1022SP.)

O'Hanlon, J.:

The jurisdiction created by Section 22 of the *Family Law (Maintenance of Spouses and Children) Act, 1976* enabling the Court to make an Order barring a spouse from the family home where the safety or welfare of the other spouse or any dependent child requires it, is a very beneficial one and has been widely availed of since the Act was passed. In a sense the jurisdiction thereby conferred goes even further than the traditional decree for a judicial separation of the parties *a mensa et thoro*, since the conventional follow-up to such an Order was the award of alimony in favour of the wife, but divorce proceedings did not and do not involve the making of an Order compelling either spouse to leave the family home and go and live elsewhere. If the wife had to do so by reason of the conduct of the husband her claim for alimony took into account the need to provide a new home for her elsewhere.

By reason of the very drastic and far-reaching nature of the remedy provided by Section 22 of the Act, I take the view that such relief should not be granted unless it can be shown that the spouse against whom the Order is sought has been guilty of serious violence or other cruelty, whether mental or physical, or other serious misconduct, which has jeopardised the safety or welfare of the other spouse, and has earned the penalty and stigma of exclusion from the family home by such misconduct.

In the present case, having listened carefully to the evidence given on both sides, I do not think that a sufficient case has been made out against the husband to warrant the making of such an Order against him. I am satisfied that he has caused the wife considerable distress and upset at different periods throughout the married life by insensitive behaviour and language and by failure or inability to demonstrate his affection for her in the manner she needed. I do not, however, regard the wife as a person of a timid or submissive character who would be easily overborne by a stronger personality and I feel that many of the difficulties that have marred the parties' married relationship have been caused by a constant clash of personalities and a certain incompatibility of temperament which neither party strove hard enough to eliminate. I think it is very likely that the husband is a well-organised person, and the wife a badly-organised person, and that each of them was caused a good deal of frustration and aggravation by taking up entrenched positions and refusing to depart from them. This is exemplified by their disputes and difficulties when it came to managing the household finances. The husband was able to see the overall picture of the annual budgetary needs of the family and may have been somewhat rigid in consequence in allotting money for daily needs, while the wife could only see that there were large sums of money coming in and going out every year and that a disproportionately small amount seemed to be made available for her side of the household economy.

One outcome of a situation of fairly constant friction was that the wife eventually sought solace, if not in the arms, then at least in the company of another man, whereupon the husband also lapsed into a period of unfaithfulness to the marriage tie which extended over a fairly lengthy period. Neither episode seems to have continued into the recent past and my impression from the evidence is that in the past two years the parties have settled down to a state of co-existence under the one roof, with few outbreaks of raised voices and open discord, but without the atmosphere of a home where parents and children are living in a state of mutual harmony and affection.

I am not convinced that it would be better for the children that this less-than-desirable home life should be exchanged for another arrangement under which they would live apart from their father and be subjected to the deplorable regime of rights of access exercised at particular times each week, interspersed with periodical visits to Court to deal with holidays or changed arrangements for weekly contact with their parent. I think children are very sensitive indeed about having to reveal to their school-friends and others that their father and mother are separated, and that there is something abnormal about their home and family life, and I think it very probable that the children, if given the choice, would opt for the continuance of life at home with both parents even though the parents were not getting on well together and found each other's company difficult to tolerate.

For the time being I propose to deal with the case by refusing the wife's claim to have her husband barred from the family home. . . .

Notes

1. Do you agree with the holding in the decision? Was O'Hanlon, J., right to emphasise the interests of the children, as he did? Would you agree with his view as to how best their needs could be served? Cf. O'Connor, *Barring Orders*, 1 Ir. L. Times (n.s.) 96 (1983).
2. Can *C.* v. *C.* and *In the Matter of G.C. and K.C., Infants, D.C.* v. *A.C., supra*, p. 302, be reconciled? Is *C.* v. *C.* consistent with *O'B.* v. *O'B., infra.*
3. O'Hanlon, J.'s approach appears to find support in the empirical studies on children's response to parental discord: see Cochran and Vitz, *Child Protective Divorce Laws: A Response to the Effects of Parental Separation on Children*, 17 Family L.Q. 327 (1983).
4. The question of the extent to which the interests of children should be considered as a factor in barring orders came before the House of Lords in *Richards* v. *Richards*, [1983] 2 W.L.R. 633. In a decision which changed the practice in some Court of Appeal decisions and which surprised a number of the commentators, the House of Lords held that children's interests should not be given priority over other factors. For commentary on the decision, see Khan, *Ouster Applications and Children's Needs*, 14 Family L. 30 (1984); Hall, *Comment: Eviction of a Husband,* [1984] Camb. L.J. 38, J.M.T., *Note*, 100 L.Q. Rev. 4 (1984). See also McNally, *Barring Orders and Ouster Orders – Judicial Change of Attitude?*, 77 Incorp. L. Soc. of Ireland Gazette 279 (1983). Lord Scarman's dissenting judgment is worthy of note, since it raises the question of the relevance of the welfare criterion in guardianship proceedings. Would it be possible (or proper) for a court to make an order evicting a spouse from the home, under section 11 of the *Guardianship of Infants Act, 1964*? (In considering the question, ignore the technical problems regarding enforceability which could arise under subsection (3) of section 11.) Alternatively could the wardship jurisdiction be involved for the same purpose? Cf. J.M.T., *Note*, 100 L.Q. Rev., at 6–7 (1984).
5. Unmarried couples who are living together do not fall within terms of the 1981 legislation. Should they? Contrast the position in England, analysed by McCann, *The Domestic Violence Jurisdiction of the District Court and the Magistrates' Court*, 73 Gazette of the Incorp. L. Soc. of Ireland 137 (1979); see also Rutherford, *Domestic Violence and Cohabitees*, 128 New L.J. 379 (1978).
6. In 1979 the number of District Court applications for barring orders was 1,493. This had risen to 2,428 in 1982. In 1982 there were also 56 applications for protection orders (in the Dublin Metropolitan District).

O'B. v. O'B.

[1984] I.L.R.M. 1 (Sup. Ct., 1983)

O'Higgins, C.J.:

This appeal has been brought by the defendant, who is the husband of the plaintiff, against the making by Costello J in the High Court, of a barring order, on the application of the plaintiff, prohibiting him from entering the family home. . . .

The order was made on 23 June 1982 and was associated with other orders providing for custody of and access to the two infant children of the marriage and also for maintenance.

The ground of appeal on which most reliance was placed by counsel on behalf of the defendant was to the effect that neither the evidence before the learned trial judge nor the facts as found by him, constituted proper or sufficient ground for the making of a barring order. In addition it was argued that the evidence before the learned trial judge established that an application by the plaintiff (the wife) for a barring order based on similar grounds had been fully considered and adjudicated upon by Judge Clarke in the Circuit Court, on appeal from the District Court, and had been rejected by him. On this account it was submitted that this issue was *res judicata* and that the wife as plaintiff could not renew her application in the High Court and that such should not have been entertained by the learned trial judge.

Before considering these grounds of appeal it is necessary to refer to the statutory basis for the making of barring orders and to recent changes in the exercise of the jurisdiction. Having done so it will, I think, appear that this appeal probably constitutes the last occasion upon which this Court can consider the proper application of the statutory provisions to the making of such orders. On the basis that this is so, this appeal is of particular importance.

The jurisdiction to make a barring order, excluding one spouse from the family home at the instance of the other, was conferred by s. 22 of the *Family Law (Maintenance of Spouses and Children) Act, 1976* (the 1976 Act). This is a comprehensive statute concerned with many of the problems which arise from a broken or disturbed marriage. S. 22 is contained in Part IV, under the heading: 'Miscellaneous'. The power of barring a spouse which it confers is not expressly contemplated by the long title, and, as it is the only section which deals with the matter, the basis upon which the power is to be exercised must be gathered from the words of the section only, without reference to any general intent of the statute. [**O'Higgins, C.J.** quoted section 22(1) and stated the effect of section 22(4). He continued:] Under sub-s. (1) for the court to act it was necessary to establish 'that there are reasonable grounds for believing that the safety or welfare of that spouse (the applicant) or of any dependant child of the family requires it' [the making of the barring order]. The use of the word 'safety' probably postulated a necessity to protect from actual or threatened physical violence emanating from the other spouse. The word 'welfare' is not so easy to construe. I incline to the view that it was intended to provide for cases of neglect or fear or nervous injury brought about by the other spouse. In both situations, it seems to me, that it is the conduct of the accused spouse and its effect upon the other, or the children, which the court had to consider. In his report to this Court, Costello J has indicated that it has been the practice to accord to the section a very wide ambit, particularly in considering what is meant by 'welfare'. I am sure this has been a correct practice provided that what endangers the 'welfare' being considered can be attributed to the conduct of the other spouse, whether that conduct consists of positive action or attitude or mere neglect. In other words, under s. 22 of the 1976 Act, in my view, the courts were required to look not only to the endangered safety or welfare of the applicant spouse or children, but also to the conduct of the other spouse, in order to see if such conduct caused the danger. It seems to me from his report that this also was the sense in which the learned trial judge felt that the section had to be interpreted and applied.

I have, of necessity, been referring to s. 22 of the 1976 Act and to the manner of its application, in the past tense. I have done so because this section has been repealed by s. 17 of the *Family Law (Protection of Spouses and Children) Act, 1981* (the 1981 Act). Under this '1981 Act' the jurisdiction to make barring orders is confined to the Circuit and District Courts, with the District Court order having an initial duration of twelve months and the Circuit Court order, in the exercise of that court's initial jurisdiction, being open as to duration. In repealing s. 22 of the 1976 Act, s. 17 of the 1981 Act provided in sub-s. (3) as follows:

(3) An application made to the High Court under the said section 22 and not determined before the commencement of this Act, may be dealt with by that court under this Act.

The 1981 Act came into operation on 24 July 1981. The application for the order sought in these proceedings was then pending before the High Court and was in fact heard by Costello J on 23 June 1982. The application was, therefore, made during the period of transition, but fell to be considered and dealt with by the High Court, as provided for in s. 17(3) 'under this Act', i.e. under the 1981 Act.

I note from his report to this Court that Costello J regarded the application which he had to deal with in these proceedings, as one to be dealt with under the 1976 Act. While in this respect he was incorrect, this fact does not seem to me to be material because the principles which he sought to apply were those which, in my view, ought to be applied under the 1981 Act. S. 2 of the 1981 Act provides in the same terms as s. 22 of the 1976 Act for the making of a barring order by the court 'if it is of opinion that there are reasonable grounds for believing that the safety or welfare of that (applicant) spouse or of any child so requires.' In this Act, however, the long title indicates expressly that the cause of the trouble must be the conduct of the other spouse. This long title is in the following terms:

An Act to make further provision for the protection of a spouse and any children whose safety or welfare requires it, because of the conduct of the other spouse, and to provide for other connected matters.

It is clear, therefore, that in order to justify the making of a barring order under the 1981 Act there must be something in the conduct of the spouse concerned which endangers the safety or welfare of the other members of the family. Once a barring order is made the barred spouse commits an offence and may be imprisoned for six months if he or she contravenes its terms. Further, a barring order, if made by the Circuit Court or by the High Court in pursuance of its transitional jurisdiction, can be without limit as to duration (subject to an application to discharge the order when the necessity for its continuance no longer exists – see s. 11). These consequences indicate that the making of such an order requires serious misconduct on the part of the offending spouse – something wilful and avoidable which causes, or is likely to cause, hurt or harm, not as a single occurrence but as something which is continuing or repetitive in its nature. Violence or threats of violence may clearly invoke the jurisdiction. However, when one enters the area of tension or of mere disharmony in the home, even if clear incompatibility between the two spouses is established, can the existence of such a situation justify one spouse in barring the other merely because the situation would be much easier if only one spouse lived in the house? Or can the fact that the marriage has broken down – even irretrievably – justify the removal from the home of one of the spouses because it is difficult for both to live in the same house? In my view, none of these situations, taken alone, justify the making of a barring order. It must be remembered that a judicial separation could not be decreed on such grounds. In my view, neither should a barring order. I am fortified in this view by a consideration of s. 11 of the 1981 Act which envisages the court discharging a barring order when satisfied that the safety or welfare of the 'spouse or child for whose protection the order was made does not require that the order should continue in force.' It seems to me that this section indicates that the barring order, which is contemplated by the Act, is intended to deal with a situation which is changeable and remedial by the act of the parties or one of them but not with a situation of complete marital breakdown which may be beyond the competence of either to remedy. Such a situation probably can only be dealt with by the spouses agreeing to differ and to live apart.

Taking this view of the 1981 Act and how it is to be construed and applied in relation to the making of a barring order, as I do, I now turn to this present appeal. I have, of course, read with care the learned trial judge's note of the evidence which he had to consider and also his report as to the reasons for his decision. It is apparent from the evidence, both on affidavit and given orally, that strains began to appear in this marriage some years ago. These strains culminated in the defendant leaving the family home in April 1979 by his own choice. Apart from a weekly visit to see his two children he lived apart from his family until September 1980, when he returned. It is clear that this return revived the strains and tensions which formerly existed and caused the plaintiff to apply in the District Court for a barring order which she obtained in February 1981. This order was set aside by the Circuit Court Judge (Judge Clarke) in June 1981 and in the following months the defendant returned to the family home. Once again tensions, strains and difficulties were apparent in the home. These led to this renewed application for a barring order. The evidence of the plaintiff indicates that various incidents occurred – rudeness by the husband in front of the children, a lack of sensitivity in his manner to her and efforts by him at dominance in running the house – none of which, in themselves, could be regarded as amounting to serious misconduct, and all of which would probably have been tolerated, overlooked and forgiven, if the marriage were viable. There was, as the learned trial judge found, no case of violence to be made against the defendant. While it is clear that the plaintiff suffered severe nervous strain as a result of the defendant residing in the same house, it is equally clear that this did not stem from any particular conduct on his part, but rather because he was there. Again, while the children were exposed to tension and a disagreeable atmosphere in their home, this appears to have been due to the situation which existed between their parents. It seems to me that this was the view which the learned trial judge took of the evidence which he considered and I think this is borne out from the following passage in his report: (I quote)

> In 1977 there was talk of a separation. The defendant left the plaintiff in the circumstances outlined by the plaintiff in her evidence. They lived apart. As far as Mrs. O'B was concerned, this was a much better situation for her. It is clear that this marriage is irretrievably broken down. This evidence is not contradicted. Judge Clarke obviously thought, and rightly thought, that the parties should be given a chance to try to see as to whether this young marriage could be saved. Mrs. O'B tried to work this out without sexual relations with her husband. There has been very serious tension and matrimonial strain. I am satisfied that this led to her collapse in the [named] Hotel. I am satisfied that she re-entered the case for this reason. A very serious situation has developed. It was very undesirable for the children.

It seems to me that the learned trial judge in expressing this view was indicating that he felt that a barring order should be made in this case simply because the marriage had irretrievably broken down. He did not attribute, as a reason or ground for making this barring order, any particular conduct on the part of the defendant. For the reasons I have already given I do not think that this approach to the making of the order is correct or justified under the 1981 Act. For this reason I feel that, on the evidence before him, the learned trial judge was not justified in making the order which he made.

Having come to this conclusion I do not find it necessary to deal with the second ground of appeal which has been argued before this Court.

It follows that, in my view, this appeal ought to be allowed. If my view is accepted by this Court, it means that the parties to these proceedings will be confronted by a situation in which, in all probability, a barring order is no longer open to either party. This will mean that they will have to accommodate themselves either to living together or agreeing to separate. It is not permissible for any member of this Court to advice on what ought to be done. I merely express the hope that each of the parties, out of the love which they clearly bear for their children, will seek a way to make the achievement of happiness for their children their paramount consideration. Happiness for their children requires some form of collaboration and partnership by their parents in the home. It also requires an adequate and proper religious upbringing and the support of both parents in the provision thereof. I do hope that if the parties to these proceedings recognise that, so far as a barring order is concerned, this is the end of the road, that they will also recognise the necessity of composing their differences and making a way in life which will, at least, remove avoidable tensions from their children's upbringing.

I would allow this appeal.

McCarthy, J.:

. . . As I understand them, the arguments advanced on behalf of the husband appellant are, broadly, that the order should not have been made and, narrowly, that the principle of *res judicata* governs the matter, the issue having already been determined by the decision of Judge Clarke on 24 June 1981 – that, essentially, there was no difference in the facts as they appeared before Costello J and that he, Costello J accordingly, was bound by the Circuit Court decision. I may dispose of this latter ground of appeal forthwith. It may well be that in many instances the facts before a Circuit Court Judge trying a District Court appeal are essentially the same as those that might, in those limited number of cases in the High Court that will survive the 1981 Act, found the decision of the Circuit Court on the hearing of a District Court appeal; such is not the case here. The outstanding difference is that, after Judge Clarke's order, the husband returned to the family home and there remained until the order made by Costello J on 24 June 1982 – a period of almost 12 months. Whilst I appreciate the force of the arguments advanced by counsel for the husband, I reject this ground of appeal.

In propounding the broader ground, Mrs. Robinson has drawn attention to those sections of the 1981 Act, as I have cited above. As I understand it, in general terms, she founds her argument on three bases:

(a) There must be grave apprehension in the court that the safety and welfare of the family is at risk.
(b) Subsidiary to (a), such is not the appropriate view in a case where the break up of the marriage is, essentially, due to incompatibility.
(c) These two propositions are supported by the terms of the relevant sections of the 1981 Act with particular emphasis being laid upon s. 11 (the discharge of a barring order).

The contention is a simple one – s. 11 must be read as contemplating a change in circumstance such as will warrant an application being made for the discharge of a barring order; the gravity of the circumstances warranting the making of a barring order are borne out by ss. 5, 6 and 7; the Gardai must be notified 'as soon as practicable' of the making of the order; a spouse who contravenes the order is liable to a term of imprisonment; and, perhaps most critically important, such spouse is liable to arrest without warrant when there is reasonable cause for believing that such spouse is committing an offence under s. 6. The breadth of these provisions, bringing within the range of the criminal law with all its dire consequences what might well be innocent or, at least, trivial acts or omissions, emphasize in the most positive way the gravity of the circumstances necessary to warrant the making of a barring order. Indeed, s. 2 subs. 2, itself, emphasises the type of situation that would, ordinarily, be in contemplation. There may be circumstances – for example, mental disturbance of an aggravated kind or, even, infection with some highly contagious disorder, in which a spouse, innocent of any serious misconduct towards the other spouse or any member of the family, may be subjected to a barring order; ordinarily, however, in my view, the statute clearly contemplates positive action or conduct on the part of the guilty spouse, be it by way of physical or mental violence or the like, which is of such a nature that the safety or welfare of the innocent spouse or of any child of the marriage requires the making of the order. Mr. Shanley, on behalf of the wife, has contended that if the court has reasonable grounds for being of opinion that the safety and welfare of the spouse and children required the making of the order, then that is sufficient. In his argument, which in no way suffered from its brevity, he accepted, initially, the basis of the appellant's submission there being no allocation of fault between the parties, whilst retaining a fall back argument to the effect that if fault required to be proved, it was proved. As to the latter part, it seems to me clear that the learned trial judge founded his decision on the basis that the parties were incompatible. [**McCarthy, J.** read the extract from **Costello, J.'s** judgment, already quoted by **O'Higgins, C.J. McCarthy, J.** continued:] Earlier, in his judgment, Costello J had excluded any question of physical violence.

In dealing with Mrs. Robinson's argument, Mr. Shanley has suggested that the construction she seeks to place upon the statute, a construction which I hold to be correct, involves a rewriting of s. 2. I do not agree; it seems to me merely giving appropriate meaning to the wording of subs. 1 of 2, recognising the fundamental nature of the marriage contract as constitutionally recognised and, as indeed expressed in the words of the marriage service 'in sickness and in health'. In cases such as this, it may well be inevitable that some form of judicial separation or separation by deed will follow what is called the irretrievable break-down of the marriage; in my view, however, the provisions of the Act of 1981, with the criminal consequences that follow from certain breaches of it, were not intended to and do not cover the circumstances of cases such as this. It follows that I would allow this appeal. . . .

Griffin J. dissented. He agreed that under section 2(1) of the 1981 Act a barring order ought not be made unless the safety or welfare of the applicant spouse or child is at risk 'by reason of the conduct of the other spouse', but, on the evidence, he could not accept that the husband's conduct had been 'no more than what might be expected in the ordinary wear and tear of married life as I understand it.' Griffin, J. referred to several matters, including the husband's financial irresponsibility; his failure to provide adequate funds for the purchase of food for the family; his constant abuse and humiliation of his wife in front of their children and his undermining of her authority.

Questions

1. Do you agree with this decision? Why?
2. If one spouse wants to continue living with the other but the other does not want this, does this decision give any assistance to the couple as to how they are to resolve the problem?
3. O'Higgins C.J. interpreted section 11 of the 1981 Act as 'fortif[ying]' him in his view that the respondent's *conduct* has to be taken into consideration by the Court before granting a barring order. Yet section 11 nowhere mentions conduct. Is section 11 intended *only* 'to deal with a situation which is changeable and remedia[ble] *by the act of the parties or one of them*. . . .' (emphasis added)? What about a case where the medical evidence shows that because of a change in the health of the children, for example, their welfare no longer requires that the order should continue in force? Surely the order could be discharged in such circumstances, without reference to any 'act' of the parties or one of them?
4. McCarthy, J. regards the power of arrest without warrant under section 6 of the 1981 Act as 'perhaps most critically important', in bearing out 'the gravity of the circumstances warranting the making of a barring order'. Do you agree? Do all the other offences for which there is a power to arrest without warrant permit such an inference? Cf. E. Ryan & P. Magee, *The Irish Criminal Process*, 525–533 (1983).
5. Can it be argued that the Court should have made *no* inference as to the tacit limitation regarding the defendant's conduct from the fact that *defiance* of a barring order constitutes an offence? Could not the Oireachtas have simply been conscious of the evidence that evicted husbands sometimes return to the home, in breach of an exclusion order, and then injure or threaten to injure their wives? Would that not have been a sufficient reason for making defiance of a barring order an offence?
6. For analysis of the decision, see Charleton, *The Scope of the Remedy of the Barring Order* 1 Ir. L. Times (n.s.) 79 (1983); McNally, *Barring Orders and Ouster Orders – Judicial Change of Attitude?*, 77 Incorp. L. Soc. of Ireland Gazette 279 (1983); Duncan, *He Stepped Out and He Stepped in Again: The Function of a Barring Order*, [1983] Dublin U.L.J. 155. The general problem analysed in *O'B* v. *O'B* was noted and discussed six years ago by Horgan, *Legal Protection for the Victim of Marital Violence*, 13 Ir. Jur. (n.s.) 233, at 242–243 (1978).
7. May a person who is the victim of persistent harassment by his or her spouse falling short of physical violence sue in tort? If so, which tort? Assault? Intentional infliction or mental suffering? Nuisance? Cf. *Motherwell* v. *Motherwell*, 73 D.L.R. (3d) 62 (Alta. Sup. Ct., App. Div., 1976). Invasion of privacy? Cf. *Capan* v. *Capan*, 14 C.C. L.T. 191 (Ont. High Ct., Osler, J. 1980). Would there be any remedy under the Constitution in such circumstances?
8. Where the home is also used as a business premises, special problems may arise: cf. *R.K.* v. *M.K.*, unreported, High Ct., Finlay, P., 24 October 1978 (1978–330Sp.).

Chapter 10
SEPARATION AGREEMENTS

Until early in the last century, courts were slow to recognise the validity of agreements between spouses to live separate and apart. They were concerned lest, in giving legal effect to such arrangements, they might damage the resolution of spouses generally to try to make a success of their marriage. Since then the trend has been to give legal recognition to separation agreements (cf. *M'Donnell* v. *Murphy*, 2 Fox & Sm. 279, at 305 (1824)), but subject to a different restraint: the courts have been conscious that women and children may not receive adequate protection in such agreements since in many cases the husband will have greater financial power. Accordingly they have looked with some suspicion at provisions in separation agreements that involve limitations on the amount of maintenance or on the right to apply to the Court for maintenance. The legislature has evinced a similar degree of caution. *The Family Law (Maintenance of Spouses and Children) Act, 1976* introduced provisions facilitating the enforcement of maintenance obligations in certain separation (and other) agreements, as well as seeking to protect spouses from signing away their rights to maintenance. It is interesting to contrast this approach, which stresses the policy of *protecting* economically vulnerable spouses, with a contrary policy, gaining international support in the past decade, which seeks to endorse *contractual liberty* between spouses on the assumption that the spouses can look after themselves so far as maintenance rights and obligations are concerned. Recent international trends on these lines are discussed by Weitzman, *The Legal Regulation of Marriage: Tradition and Change – A Proposal for Individual Contracts and Contracts in Lieu of Marriage*, 62 Calif. L. Rev. 1169 (1974); Weyrauch, *The Metamorphosis of Marriage*, 13 Family L.Q. 415 (1980); Shultz, *The Contractual Order of Marriage: a New Model for State Policy*, 70 Calif. L. Rev. 204 (1982); Bartke, *Marital Sharing – Why Not Do It by Contract?*, 67 Geo. L. J. 1131 (1979); Note, *Marriage Contracts for Support and Services: Constitutionality Begins at Home*, 49 N.Y.U.L. Rev. 1161 (1979); Note, *Marriage as Contract: Towards a Functional Redefinition of the Marital Status*, 9 Columbia J. of L. & Social Problems 607 (1977); Hunter, *An Essay on Contract and Status: Race, Marriage, and the Meretricious Spouse*, 64 Va. L. Rev. 1039 (1978). A collection of essays on the subject is included in J. Krauskopf ed., *Marital and Non-Marital Contracts: Preventive Law for the Family* (1979). For a more cautious approach see Gipson Wells, *A Critical Look at Personal Marriage Contracts*, 25 Family Coordinator 33 (1976).

The subject of *dum casta* clauses in separation agreements has given rise to litigation: see *Lewis* v. *Lewis*, [1940] I.R. 42 (High Ct., Hanna, J., 1939); *Ormsby* v. *Ormsby*, 79 I.L.T.R. 97 (Sup. Ct., 1945). The decisions are analysed by *Shatter*, 127–128. For consideration of the issue from the perspective of the United States, see Foster & Freed, *Alimony: Dum Casta and Smart Women*, 1 Family l. Rev. 26 (1978).

The Family Law (Maintenance of Spouses and Children) Act, 1976

The *Family Law (Maintenance of Spouses and Children) Act, 1976* introduced important changes in relation to separation agreements. Perhaps the most important is contained in Section 5, which enables a spouse to obtain an order for maintenance where the other spouse has failed to provide 'such maintenance . . . as is aproper in the circumstances'. This provision applies whether or not the spouses have entered into a separation agreement (or other agreement providing for maintenance). Of course, where the spouses have entered into such an agreement, this may be a very significant, if not conclusive, reason for the Court to refuse to make and order for maintenance under section 5, particularly where the agreement is a fair one, adequately protecting the interests of the applicant spouse and the children. But this would not always be the case. For example, a destitute mother of six children may have signed an agreement with her husband four years previously whereby the husband, who was in good employment, agreed to pay the family £20 a week maintenance; if she were to apply for a maintenance order today under section 5, the court would be very likely to make an order for maintenance over and above the sum contractually agreed upon.

Two other important provisions in the 1976 Act should be noted. Section 8 provides that:

> Where–
> (*a*) the parties to a marriage enter into an agreement in writing (including a separation agreement) after the commencement of this Act that includes either or both of the following provisions, that is to say–
> (i) a provision whereby one spouse undertakes to make periodical payments towards the maintenance of the other spouse or of any dependent children of the family or of both that other spouse and any dependent children of the family,
> (ii) a provision governing the rights and liabilities of the spouses towards one another in respect of the making or securing of payments (other than payments specified in paragraph (*a*) (i) of this section), or the disposition or use of any property, and
> (*b*) an application is made by one or both of the spouses to the High Court of the Circuit Court for an order making the agreement a rule of court,
> the Court may make such an order if it is satisfied that the agreement is a fair and reasonable one which in all the circumstances adequately protects the interests of both spouses and the dependent children (if any) of the family, and such order shall, in so far as as it relates to a provision specified in paragraph (*a*) (i) of this section, be deemed, for the purpose of section 9 and Part III of this Act, to be a maintenance order.

And section 27 provides that:

> An agreement shall be void in so far as it would have the effect of excluding or limiting the operation of any provision of thi Act (other than section 21).

(Section 21 deals with property in household allowances. It is briefly mentioned, *supra*, p. 272.

H.D. v. P.D.

Unreported, Supreme Court, 8 May 1978 (20–1978)

Walsh, J. (for the Court):

The applicant and respondent intermarried on January 26th 1952 in . . . London. . . . The applicant at present resides in . . . England and the respondent resides in County X. At the date of the marriage each of them resided in England. Their domicile at the time of their marriage is of no relevance to this case and the Court has had no evidence offered to it on this subject.

There were four children born of the marriage: the first in November 1952, the second in September 1955, the third in April 1957 and the fourth in January 1960. All of the children were girls. Following the marriage, the parties first resided in England and then later in Zambia from 1954 to 1963 and from 1963 to 1966 in Ireland and from 1966 to 1969 again in Zambia. On their return to Ireland the applicant and the children resided firstly in a house . . . in the Country of X, and from about May 1971 until October 1971 in an annex to the same house. It would appear that the respondent resided with them in the same house and continued to reside in it with his mother for the several months the applicant and her children resided in the annex.

From October 1971 until August 1974 the applicant resided with her children, except when they were attending school and when two of them were working in Dublin, in County Y and then moved to County Z in June 1973 and finally to [South East] England, in August 1974. During the years of marriage there were several differences between the parties and in December 1971 when the applicant was residing in County Y she filed a petition in the High Court for a divorce *a mensa et thoro* against the respondent. She also sought an order for the award of the custody of the children of the marriage to herself.

On the 28th November 1972, a motion was brought in the High Court on behalf of the applicant for an order for the payment of alimony *pendente lite.* On the 12th February 1973, the motion was listed for hearing before Mr. Justice Finlay and it was announced in Court by counsel for the parties that a settlement of the petition had been reached on the basis of a written consent signed by the parties and their respective solicitors and the settlement was handed into court. By the consent of the parties the Court ordered that the said consent should be received and filed with and deemed to be part of the order of the Court and also by consent directed that all further proceedings on the petition and on foot of the motion for alimony *pendente lite* be stayed on the terms set out in the consent with liberty to either party to apply to the Court at a later date.

The document referred to as the consent was handed into the Court and is one which was signed by the applicant and the respondent and by the respective solicitors of the parties. It provided that the parties had agreed that the petition should stand dismissed and that the motion for alimony should be adjourned *sine die* upon the following terms. These terms were that the respondent should pay to the applicant 'in full satisfaction of all claims in the petition' the sum of £10,000 which was to be payable as to £5,000 immediately and as to the balance being the sum of £5,000 on or before the 12th February 1974. The respondent further agreed to pay interest on the outstanding sum of £5,000 or any part that might remain outstanding at the rate of 10% per annum. With regard to the children, the parties agreed to act as joint guardians of the children and the custody of the children was until further order granted to the applicant provided that the respondent should be given reasonable access to the children and that if the children, or any of them, desired to spend half of the school holidays with the respondent he would be entitled to have them or each of them at his own expense during such holidays. The respondent further agreed and undertook to pay for the education of the third child at a named school until she attained the age of 18 years and to pay for the education of the fourth child at a named school until she also attained the age of 18 years. The respondent agreed and undertook to indemnify and help to keep indemnified the applicants against all charges in respect of the education of the said two children. The respondent also undertook to enter into a legal mortgage for the purpose of securing the payment of the said sum of £5,000 and interest already referred to and to secure the indemnities already referred to by way of legal mortgage on the respondent's lands and premises in County X. The applicant on her part undertook to 'indemify and to keep indemnified the respondent against all claims of whatever nature whether arising either before or after the execution of the consent for which he might otherwise be liable as husband of the petitioner.' The remaining portion of the consent dealt with the payment of the costs. The consent also reserved the liberty to either party to apply to the Court.

Following reception by the Court of the consent, the £10,000 referred to was paid in accordance with the terms of the consent and the applicant provided a home for herself and her children. The home was a cottage which she brought in. . . . England, some of the purchase money for which was secured by way of mortgage. She also had to bear the cost of the maintenance of the children, save in so far as their education was provided for in the terms of the consent. It is unnecessary to go into the details of the expenditure of the £10,000 and the upbringing of the children by the applicant in view of the particular point which arises for determination in this case.

On the 24th March 1977 a special summons was issued in the High Court by the applicant against the respondent by which the applicant claimed relief pursuant to section 11 of the *Guardianship of Infants Act, 1964* and an order 'giving directions regarding the welfare of the two younger children and directing the respondent to pay towards the maintenance of these two children such weekly or other periodical sums as having regard to the means of the respondent and/or the applicant as the Court considered reasonable.' The applicant also claimed, pursuant to section 5 of the *Family Law (Maintenance of Spouses and Children) Act, 1976* an order 'directing the respondent to make to her periodical payments in support of the applicant and of each of the dependent children of the applicant of such amount and at such times as the Court might consider proper.' The applicant claimed further, pursuant to section 5 subsection (2) of the *Family Home Protection Act, 1976* an order directing the respondent to pay the applicant such amount as the Court considered proper to compensate the applicant and the two younger children who were claimed to be dependent children for their loss arising from the deprivation of their residence in the family home [in] Co. X. It was alleged that the respondent had by his conduct rendered this unsuitable for habitation as a family home. The *Family Law (Maintenance of Spouses and Children) Act, 1976* and the *Family Home Protection Act, 1976*, which, as their dates indicate, were enacted only after the court proceedings and the consent in question, together form a very comprehensive and far-reaching code of law designed especially to protect spouses and children both as to the cost of their maintenance and as to their shelter. The net point which arises for decision in this case is the validity of the respondent's claim that the applicant is in effect estopped from pursuing whatever rights she may be entitled to under the Acts in question by reason of the consent and that the matters in issue may be regarded as *res judicata.* During the argument in the case in this Court the word estoppel was not used but the net effect of the submissions on behalf of the respondent amounts to a claim of estoppel by reason of the order of the High Court embodying the consent already referred to. The consent which was entered into in the present case was in effect a separation agreement though not in the ordinary form of a separation agreement and it did not purport expressly to release each of the parties from the duty of cohabiting with the other. Neither did it contain any of the other features which frequently appear in formal separation agreements.

In my view, the claim by the applicant in this case falls within the provisions of section 5 of the *Family Law (Maintenance of Spouses and Children) Act, 1976.* As the parties are living apart by agreement there is no question of desertion by the applicant. There is no question whatever of the applicant having been guilty of adultery, a matter which may be taken into account by a court when asked to make a maintenance order. As each of the two younger children has already attained the age of 16 years, each of the children can only be considered to be a dependent child if she is or will be receiving full-time education or instruction at a university, college, school or other educational establishment and is under the age of 21. Each of these two younger children is under the age of 21 and the question of whether or not they are receiving full-time education of the type prescribed is not a matter which needs concern this Court. It is essentially one for the court which deals with the facts of the case. Counsel for the respondent laid great stress upon the fact that the consent entered into by the parties in the matrimonial proceedings was made part of the order of the court that therefore there had been an adjudication and a final settlement of all these matters concerning the maintenance of the wife and children. I do not accept this submission having regard to the provisions of the *Family Law (Maintenance of Spouses and Children) Act, 1976.* It is somewhat difficult to say, and unnecessary at the moment to decide, what is the legal effect of making the consent part of the order of the court when one essential part of the consent was that the petition for divorce should stand dismissed. It is undoubtedly a record of what was agreed between the parties but whether in the event of the parties failing to live up to the agreement the remedy would be to sue upon foot of the agreement or to seek direct intervention of the High Court on foot of the order is a matter which I need not now decide though I very much doubt if the latter course would be available. I am supported in this view by the fact that the order of the Court was to stay further proceedings upon the petition and in the motion for alimony. It would thus appear at first sight that the proper remedy in the event of a breach was to go back to court to continue the proceedings or to have them reentered. Section 8 of the *Family Law (Maintenance of Spouses and Children) Act, 1976* makes express provision for the position of an agreement in writing (including a separation agreement) entered into after the commencement of the Act. The types of agreement referred to would include the consent in the present case if it had been entered into after the commencement of the Act. In such a case the Court may, if it is satisfied the agreement is a fair and reasonable one adequately protecting the interests of both spouses and dependent children of the family, deem it, for the purposes of section 9 of the Act, to be a maintenance order. It is clear from the section that a separation agreement entered into after the date of the coming into force of the Act of 1976 does not amount to an election, even if that were possible, to forego the benefit of the provisions of the Act but effectively constitutes no more than a factor to be taken into account by the Court in determining an application brought before it under the Act. *A fortiori*, the operation of the Act cannot be affected by a separation agreement or other document in the nature of the consent in this case entered into before the passing of the Act unless there is an express provision to the contrary in the Act. It is clear from the whole structure of the Act that its purpose is to deal with the situation of the parties at the time the proceedings were brought under the Act and that the primary function of the Act is to ensure that proper and adequate maintenance will be available in accordance with the provisions of the Act to spouses and children. The basic question to be decided is whether at any given time there is a failure by one spouse to provide reasonable maintenance for the support of the other spouse and for any dependent children of the family of the spouses. In my view it is not possible to contract out of the Act by an agreement made after the Act came into force or by an agreement entered into before the legislation was enacted. While in the present case it is not necessary to decide what would have been the effect on these proceedings if the petition for divorce had been successful and alimony was being paid pursuant to that nevertheless one may express the view that if the Oireachtas in enacting the *Family Law (Maintenance of Spouses and Children) Act, 1976* had intended that an order for the payment of alimony in a divorce *a mensa et thoro* decree or *pendente lite* should be a final determination of the amount to be paid by one spouse to the other, the Act would obviously have said so. In the case of separation agreements entered into after the commencement of the Act and made rules of court under section 8, a provision in any such agreement for periodical maintenance payment is *not* final and there is nothing to prevent the spouse receiving the payments from subsequently applying for a maintenance order if the circumstances have changed. This appears to be clear from section 5 of the Act. Moreover, an order making the separation agreement a rule of court is not a maintenance order except for the purpose of payments through the District Court Clerk and attachment of earnings. It is also to be noted that section 3 at paragraph (i) of the Act includes an order for the payment of alimony pending suit or permanent alimony within the definition of an antecedent order which by virtue of section 10 of the Act is one of the payments for which attachment of earnings may be ordered.

In this whole connection it is interesting to note that section 116 of the *Succession Act, 1965* provides that where a testator, during his lifetime, has made permanent provision for his spouse all property which is the subject of such provision (other than periodical payments made for her maintenance during his lifetime) is to be taken as being given in or towards satisfaction of the share as a legal right of the surviving spouse. The section applies *only* to a provision made before 1 January, 1967 – the date of the commencement of the 1965 Act. It seems clearly to have been the intention of the legislature that, in the case of a permanent provision made after the date, the right – section 113 of the 1965 Act – to renounce his or her legal right by the spouse being provided for would be taken into account in the framing of any such provision. Furthermore, the legislature in enacting the 1965 Act did not consider that 'periodical payments made for her maintenance during his lifetime' constituted 'permanent provision' for a man's wife. I draw attention to this because one should not overlook that the responsible Minister in the case of both the *Succession Act, 1965* and the *Family Law (Maintenance of Spouses and Children) Act, 1976* was the Minister for Justice and it would not be unreasonable to assume that certain of the provisions in the 1976 Act were framed with the relevant provisions of the 1965 Act in mind.

It appears to me that in a case such as the present one the function of the Court under the Act of 1976 is to determine whether or not there is a financial need justifying the making of the order sought under the Act. Therefore, if by reason of a previous arrangement between the parties, either in the form of a separation agreement or in some less formal type of agreement, one spouse makes payments to the other spouse or may have already made a lump sum payment, the income of which or other use of which may be sufficient to alleviate in whole or in part the financial need complained of, the Court shall have regard to such payments in deciding what order should be made in a claim for maintenance pursuant to section 5 of the Act.

Maintenance will include the cost of providing adequate housing or shelter and if, as in the present case, a settlement already made in matrimonial proceedings has gone some way towards providing that part of the maintenance then it is a matter which the judge shall take into account. Similarly, if any income is derived from the money which was paid under the consent between the parties he may also take that into account. Such items fall within the income and financial resources of the spouse as is set out in section 5 subsection (4) paragraph (a) of the Act of 1976 and that effectively prevents any type of fraud being sought to be achieved by a spouse who is already in receipt of payments under a contract of separation or otherwise going behind it to seek to lay a claim for maintenance as if such other periodical payments or financial resources did not exist. It is also to be borne in mind that all maintenance orders granted under section 5 of the Act of 1976 are subject to variation in the appropriate circumstances.

As this appeal was brought on the judgment of Mr. Justice Doyle upon the net issue already referred to it is unnecessary to rule upon any other matter and in my view the proper order would be to dismiss the present appeal and to indicate that the applicant's claim for maintenance is maintainable under the Act but that the judge may take into account the income or other maintenance, if any, which the applicant receives by reason of or arising out of the moneys paid under the consent entered into between the applicant and the respondent in the matrimonial proceedings.

Notes

1. The decision is analysed by McGann, *Maintenance Agreements and the Family Law (Maintenance of Spouses and Children) Act, 1976*, 72 Incorp. L. Soc. of Ireland Gazette 115 (1978).
2. Why should a husband enter *any* separation agreement if his wife may at some later stage apply for maintenance under section 5 of the *Family Law (Maintenance of Spouses and Children) Act, 1976*? Cf. *Shatter*, 130, recommending amending legislation which 'should provide that if a permanent financial settlement is concluded between spouses, under the terms of which a lump sum payment is to be made and/or property is to be transferred to the dependent spouse and (a) both spouses extinguish their rights to future maintenance, and (b) such settlement is approved by the High Court as properly protecting the interests of all the parties to it and their dependent children, and (c) is made a rule of court, such settlement is binding on the parties to it and is an

absolute bar on either party applying for maintenance for his or her support at any future date'. Mr. Shatter recommends, however, that 'in order to properly fulfill the first objective, this provision should only apply to spouses' maintenance and should not extend to children's maintenance'. This is because '[t]he overriding public interest in protecting the welfare of children requires that the courts be in a position to vary all orders and agreements made in relation to children when circumstances change. . . .' Do you agree with these recommendations?

3. It is perhaps worth noting the role of section 8 of the *Married Women's Status Act, 1957.* This section provides in subsection (1) that, where a contract (other than one relating to certain categories of life assurance or endowment) 'is expressed to be for the benefit, or by its express terms purports to confer a benefit upon', a third person who is the spouse or child of one of the contracting parties, it may be enforced by the third person in his or her name as if he or she were a party to it. 'Child' is defined, in subsection 5, as including 'step-child, illegitimate child, adopted person (within the meaning of the Adoption Act, 1952) and a person to whom the contracting party is in *loco parentis'*.

   The right conferred on a third person to enforce the contract is subject to any defence that would have been valid between the parties to the contract (subsection (2)); moreover, unless the contract provides otherwise, it may be rescinded by agreement of the contracting parties 'at any time before the third person has adopted it either expressly or by conduct.'

   What is the effect of this section? Does it mean, for example, that a child may enforce all or part of the terms of a separation agreement which contains a provision whereby a spouse undertakes to provide a specified amount of maintenance for the benefit of the child? Could an agreement as to custody or access similarly be enforced by the child? (Presumably in at least some cases the child would have little difficulty in showing that the opportunity to have an active relationship with a parent was a 'benefit', for the purposes of subsection (1).) As regards the right of the parents to rescind the contract, could it be argued that subsection (2) precludes rescission after the child has adopted the contract? Such an interpretation could involve considerable difficulties for parents although in some cases might work to the child's advantage. When could it be said that a child adopted a contract either expressly or by conduct? Is there a minimum age below which a child has not the capacity to adopt a contract?

4. As to the circumstances in which family arrangements may constitute legally building contracts, see Binchy *Family Arrangements and the Intentions to Create Legal Relations*, 105 I.L.T. & Sol. J. 215 (1971). See also *Smith* v. *Rogers*, unreported, Supreme Court, 16 July 1970 (196–1969).
5. On the general question of duress in this context, see Picher, *The Separation Agreement as an Unconscionable Transaction: A Study in Equitable Fraud*, [1972] Queens L. J. 441, and the Law Reform Commission's *Report on Divorce a Mensa et Thoro and Related Matters*, pp. 49–50 (LRC 8–1983).
6. See also Robilliard, *Undue Influence Between Husband and Wife*, 13 Family L. 108 (1983), analysing *Tommey* v. *Tommey,* [1982] 3 All E.R. 385 (Balcombe, J.). More generally, see Samuels, *Consent to Divorce at a Price*, 13 Family L. 105 (1983).
7. On the question of drunkenness, see *V.W.* v. *J.W.*, unreported High Ct., Costello, J., April 1978 (1977–2684P.); Cope, *The Review of Unconscionable Bargains in Equity*, 57 Austr. L. J. 279, at 292 (1983).

J.H. v. C.H.

Unreported, July 1979, High Court, Keane, J., (1978 181)

Keane, J.:

This matter comes before me by way of a Notice of Motion, in which the first relief claimed is an order receiving a settlement dated the 11th October, 1978, and making it a rule of court. . . . [**Keane J.** stated the effect of Section 8 of the *Family Law (Maintenance of Spouses and Children) Act, 1976.* He continued:]

In the present case, the parties entered into an Agreement dated the 11th October, 1978, under which the family home of the parties was to be sold and the proceeds used to discharge certain debts of the defendant. The balance together with the proceeds of the sale of certain other items was to be used as to £2,500 thereof in establishing a fund for the payment of the sum of £40 initially per week to the Plaintiff to be subsequently increased to £50. The balance of the proceeds of sale were to be employed in the purchase of a house in the names of the Plaintiff and Defendant or at the option of the Plaintiff was to be invested jointly in the names of the children. Any sum in excess of £42,000 realised from the sale was to be paid to the Defendant.

I am satisfied that the settlement thus arrived at is a fair and reasonable one and adequately protects the interests of both spouses and the dependent children. It was, however, urged on behalf of the defendant that since the agreement provided that the Plaintiff should have sole custody of the children and one of the children was now in the custody of the Defendant the basis of the agreement was gone and that it should not be made a rule of court. I do not think that is a sufficient ground for declining to make the Order sought: if the Defendant considers that the maintenance provisions are excessive, having regard to the fact that the Plaintiff has ceased to maintain one of the dependent children, he is perfectly entitled to apply to the court for an Order varying the amount of the maintenance payments under Section 6 of the Act. It was also urged that the agreement was not a final one, that there were matters left unresolved and that it was not intended to become binding on the parties until a formal separation deed was executed. Having heard the evidence of both the Plaintiff and the Defendant, I am satisfied that at the time the agreement was entered into it was intended to impose immediate legal obligations on both parties and that it was not intended to postpone the imposition of those obligations until a separation deed was executed. The fact that negotiations to vary the agreement were subsequently initiated but did not come to any finality does not affect this conclusion.

The agreement is plainly one that includes provision for the making of periodical maintenance payments and accordingly may be made a rule of court on the application of either party. I am not satisfied, however, that I am entitled to make anything in the nature of a decree of Specific Performance of an Agreement for the sale of property when there are no proceedings before the court in which that relief is claimed and the question as to whether such a degree can be made has not been fully argued. The object of Section 8 of the Act is clearly to ensure that a party to an agreement providing for maintenance payments has a swift an effective means of securing the enforcement of the provisions for such maintenance payments. It is not to enable a decree for Specific Performance of an agreement for the sale of property to be made where no proceedings are in being claiming any such relief. Accordingly, I will order that the Agreement of October 11th, 1978, be made a rule of court; and in the event of non-compliance by the Defendant with the provisions as to the sale of the property, it will be for the Plaintiff to take such steps as she may be advised, whether by way of substantive proceedings or a Notice of Motion in the present proceedings, to obtain such relief as may be appropriate. I have already made a Order for the payment of the arrears of maintenance amounting to £2,750 and given the Plaintiff liberty to amend the Special Summons to include a claim for a declaration under Section 12 of the *Married Woman's Status Act, 1957*, of the respective interests of the Plaintiff and the Defendant in the family home. . . .

Questions

Do you agree with Keane J.'s statement that if the defendant considered the maintenance provisions excessive he was 'perfectly entitled to apply to the court for an Order varying the amount of maintenance payments under Section 6 of the Act'? Cf. *Shatter*, 123. If you do not agree, what steps, in your view, would be open to a defendant in such circumstances who sought to pay less than the amount he had undertaken to pay in the separation agreement?

M.C. v. J.C.

[1982] I.L.R.M. 562 (High Court, Costello, J.)

Costello, J.:

The respondent is the husband of the petitioner and he says that he cannot now afford to pay the alimony which he agreed to pay his wife on 4 October 1979. So he has brought a motion asking the court for an order 'varying and reducing the maintenance order made herein by consent on 4 October 1979'. His wife resists thus application and I have been asked to make a preliminary ruling on a point of law which has been raised on her behalf. It is submitted that the respondent settled his wife's matrimonial proceedings by agreeing, *inter alia*, to pay her alimony at an agreed rate and he cannot now be heard to claim that his contractual obligation should be varied. I have to decide on the validity of this submission.

The respondent's case is based on order 70 rule 55 of the 1962 Rules of the Superior Courts. This provides as follows:

> A wife may at any time after alimony has been allotted to her, whether alimony pending suit or permanent alimony, apply by motion for an increase of the alimony allotted by reason of the increased faculties of the husband or by the reduction of her own faculties, or a husband may apply by motion for a diminution of the alimony allotted by reason of reduced faculties or of the wife's increased faculties, and the course of proceedings in such cases shall be the same as required by this order in respect of the original application for alimony and the allotment thereof so far as the same are applicable.

It will be noted that the right of a wife to apply for an increase in alimony and the right of a husband to apply for a diminution in alimony arises at any time 'after alimony has been allotted' to the wife. It seems to me that the issue I have to consider will be determined by the construction of these words and their application to the facts of this case.

Before examining the rule in greater detail I should explain exactly how the respondent's present obligation to the petitioner has arisen. The petitioner instituted proceedings in the High Court for an order of judicial separation and alimony. No hearing of the claim, however, took place as it was settled on agreed terms. An order of the court was made on 4 October 1979. Having recited that the cause was listed for hearing on 4 October and that it appeared to the court 'that a settlement had been reached herein in the terms set out in the schedule hereto which have been agreed between the parties' the order then went on to provide:

> By consent the judge by his final decree pronounced and decreed that the petitioner be divorced and separated from bed board and mutual co-habitation with the respondent by reason of the cruelty of the said respondent.

Following the signature of the registrar there appeared a schedule to the order which reads as follows:

1. The respondent will pay to the petitioner the sum of £10,000 within two months which sum includes the petitioner's costs.
2. The respondent will pay to the petitioner alimony at the rate of £100 per week from 5 October 1979 with annual increases in accordance with the consumer price index, the first base period to date from 21 August 1979 and increased payments to be made from the first Friday in October 1980.
3. Whereas the petitioner is not residing in the matrimonial home this order shall not constitute a waiver by her to the furniture in the said home which was purchased by her and for which she has receipts.

It will be observed that the only order made by the court was an order for judicial separation. The court made no order that the respondent would pay the sum of £10,000 or the agreed alimony – it merely recorded the parties' agreement on these points, receiving the consent but not making it a rule of court either under its general jurisdiction to do so or under the particular jurisdiction given by s. 8 of the *Family Law (Maintenance of Spouses and Children) Act, 1976*. So, if the respondent failed to pay the lump sum of £10,000 or failed to pay any of the weekly sums provided in the agreement (as in fact has happened) the petitioner's remedy, it seems to me, is to sue on the agreement and she cannot rely on the order and claim its enforcement by, for example, committal proceedings.

When considering a husband's right to seek a reduction in a periodic payment he is making to his wife it is relevant to bear in mind the circumstances which have given rise to his obligation to make them. An obligation could arise in one of six different ways:

1. The wife could have applied under the *Family Law (Maintenance of Spouses and Children) Act, 1976* for a maintenance order. If such an order had been made then the husband has a statutory right to apply to vary it (s. 6). In this case, however, the wife has made no application under the 1976 Act and no 'maintenance order' under it has been made. It is therefore not quite accurate to refer, as the respondent has referred in his notice of motion of 21 May 1982, to the order of 4 October 1979 as a 'maintenance order'.
2. The wife may have applied under the provisions of legislation repealed by the 1976 Act and obtained an order which is deemed (by s. 3 of the 1976 Act) to be a 'maintenance order'. This did not happen in the present case.
3. The wife may have applied to the High Court for a decree of judicial separation and for alimony and the court after hearing may have granted a decree of divorce and subsequently allotted permanent alimony under order 70 rule 54 of the Rules of the Superior Courts. The husband in such circumstances has a right to apply under order 70 rule 55 for a diminution in the alimony so ordered. But such circumstances did not occur in this case.
4. The wife may have applied to the High Court for a decree of judicial separation and may have intended to apply for permanent alimony under the rule. Her claim may have been settled and by agreement the court might have ordered the respondent to pay alimony on a periodic basis or the agreement may have been made a rule of court under s. 8 of the 1976 Act. But no order by the court was made directing the respondent to pay alimony and the consent was not made a rule of court under s. 8 of the 1976 Act.
5. The wife may have applied to the High Court for a decree of judicial separation and may have intended to apply for permanent alimony under the rule but her claim may have been settled and instead of an order for the payment of alimony the court may have recorded the husband's agreement to make a periodic payment at a stated sum. This is what happened in the present case.
6. The wife may have made no application to the court but the parties may have entered into a separation agreement by which the husband agreed to make her agreed periodic payments. This did not happen in the present case and so I need express no opinion as to the husband's right to apply under s. 6 of the 1976 Act or under order 70 rule 55 for a diminution order in such circumstances.

As I have already pointed out the respondent's right to claim that the alimony payment to his wife should be diminished and the court's jurisdiction to make such an order depends on whether there has, on the fact of this case, been an 'allotment' of alimony to her within the meaning of order 70 rule 55. It will be noted that this rule is preceded by one which provides that a wife who has obtained a final decree *a mensa et thoro* may apply to the court by motion for an 'allotment of permanent alimony' provided that she shall, eight days at least before making such application, give notice thereof to the husband or his solicitor. Should I read order 70 rule 55 as meaning that a wife has only a right to apply for an increase in maintenance and a husband for its diminution in cases where an order is made after a motion under order 70 rule 54 has been brought? I do not think so. It seems to me that the Rules Committee must have been well aware when this rule was adopted in 1962 that many matrimonial proceedings are settled without a hearing and before a motion under order 70 rule 54 is rendered necessary and it could not have intended to limit the review procedures permitted by order 70 rule 55 to cases in which motions under the preceding rule had been brought. So, it seems to me, an 'allotment of alimony' within the meaning of the rule I am now considering occurs when, by consent, an *order* is made by the court *directing* payment of alimony at an agreed sum. I am also of the view that an 'allotment of alimony' is made within the meaning of the rule if the wife's claim is settled on the basis that the husband will pay an agreed sum in alimony and that his agreement will be received by the court and scheduled to the court's order, as has happened in this case. It is true that the wife's entitlement to alimony does not arise from an order of the court but from her husband's agreement, but none the less she has, it seems to me, been allotted alimony within the meaning of the rule. It would place a very restrictive meaning on the rule and impose an unjustified and unnecessary restriction on the court's power to review alimony payments on the application of the wife or the husband as the case may be if the review procedures could only take place when an agreement to pay alimony had been made a rule of court and not when it had been received and scheduled to the court's order.

In my judgment, therefore, the respondent is not barred by his agreement or by the order of 4 October 1979 from bringing this application. Whether or not it will succeed is a matter of evidence and the exercise of the court's dicretion under the rules, on which aspects of the case I express no opinion today.

In reaching the conclusion I have just announced I did not lose sight of the authorities to which I was referred in the course of the helpful submissions made on the parties' behalf. *H.D. v P.D.* (*supra, p–*) was a case in which the High Court and later the Supreme Court considered its jurisdiction to make an order under s. 5 of the *Family Law (Maintenance of Spouses and Children) Act, 1976*. . . . But that case is quite clearly different to the present one. Here I am not concerned with an application to fix maintenance under s. 5 of the Act or to make a variation order under s. 6. This is an application under order 70 rule 55 of the High Court Rules and completely different considerations arise on it.

I was also referred to *Lewis v Lewis* [1940] I.R. 42 and *Ormsby v Ormsby* 79 I.L.T.R. 92 [**Costello, J.** summarised the facts and holdings in these decisions. He continued:]

It will be clear from the summary I have given of these two cases that they do not assist in elucidating the problem which I had to consider. The respondent in the present case does not seek to imply a term in the agreement he entered into on 4 October 1979 which would permit him to apply to the court for a variation order nor does he seek to suggest that the agreement of 4 October is contrary to public policy. His case is fairly and squarely based on the rule which I have already quoted and this rule did not fall for consideration in any of the cases to which I have been referred. Nor did they establish or illustrate any principle which, by analogy, I can apply to the issue raised in the proceedings before me.

Chapter 11

THE FAMILY HOME PROTECTION ACT, 1976

Before 1976, the law provided inadequate protection against the sale or other disposition of the family home by a vindictive spouse. There was considerable concern in the community about the position that might arise whereby a spouse (usually the husband) could sell the home over the head of the other spouse and the children, without seeking their consent and, in some cases, without even letting them know what he was doing. Of course, where the spouses owned the property jointly there was no such problem.

The English solution, adopted in the *Matrimonial Homes Act, 1967*, was to give protection against third parties, so far as occupation of the home was concerned, to a 'non-owner' spouse who registered a charge on the husband's estate or interest in the property. Clearly this type of approach would not afford adequate protection to those spouses who, perhaps lulled into a false sense of security or unwilling to antagonise the other spouse, did not take the active step of registering a charge.

In Ireland, the *Family Home Protection Act, 1976* has taken a different approach. This is a controversial piece of legislation, which has given rise to fairly widespread unhappiness among conveyancers. In the wake of some important judicial decisions and (minor) statutory reforms in 1981 some of these uncertainties (centring on sections 1 to 4) have been removed. It seems fair to say that so far, against the background of a separate-property regime, the Act appears to have succeeded in its policy goals. It is interesting to note the increasing judicial disposition to interpret and apply section 5 of the Act in a creative and humane manner.

For consideration of the 1976 Act, see *Shatter*, 317–334; *Wylie*, 198–217; Macken, *The Family Home Protection Act, 1976*, 111 I.L.T. & Sol. J. 52 (1977); Ussher, *The Position of a Purchaser under the Family Home Protection Act, 1976*, 71 Gazette of Inc. L. Soc. of Ir. 3 (1977); Daly, *The Effect on Conveyancing Practice of the New Law Society Contract for Sale and the Family Home Protection Act, 1976*, (S.Y.S. Lecture No.79, November, 1976); Carroll, *The Family Home Protection Act, 1976* (S.Y.S. Lecture No. 124, April 1980).

The central provisions of the Act are the following:–

1. – (1) In this Act, except where the context otherwise requires –

'conduct' includes an act and a default or other omission:

'conveyance' includes a mortgage, lease, assent, transfer, disclaimer, release and any other disposition of property otherwise than by a will or a *donatio mortis causa* and also includes an enforceable agreement (whether conditional or unconditional) to make any such conveyance, and 'convey' shall be construed accordingly;

'family home' has the meaning assigned by section 2;

'household chattels' has the meaning assigned by section 9 (7);

'interest' means any estate, right, title or other interest, legal or equitable;

'mortgage' includes an equitable mortgage, a charge on registered land and a chattel mortgage, and cognate words shall be construed accordingly;

'rent' includes a conventional rent, a rentcharge within the meaning of section 2 (1) of the *Statute of Limitations, 1957*, and a terminable annuity payable in respect of a loan for the purchase of a family home.

2. – (1) In this Act 'family home' means, primarily, a dwelling in which a married couple ordinarily reside. The expression comprises, in addition, a dwelling in which a spouse whose protection is an issue ordinarily resides or, if that spouse has left the other spouse, ordinarily resided before so leaving.

(2) In subsection (1) 'dwelling' means –

(*a*) any building, or

(*b*) any structure, vehicle or vessel (whether mobile or not).

or part thereof, occupied as a separate dwelling and includes any garden or portion of ground attached to and usually occupied with the dwelling or otherwise required for the amenity or convenience of the dwelling.

3. – (1) Where a spouse, without the prior consent in writing of the other spouse, purports to convey any interest in the family home to any person except the other spouse, then, subject to subsections (2) and (3) and section 4, the purported conveyance shall be void.

(2) Subsection (1) does not apply to a conveyance if it is made by a spouse in pursuance of an enforceable agreement made before the marriage of the spouses.

(3) No conveyance shall be void by reason only of subsection (1) –

(*a*) if it is made to a purchaser for full value.

(*b*) if it is made, by a person other than the spouse making the purported conveyance referred to in subsection (1), to a purchaser for value, or

(*c*) if its validity depends on the validity of a conveyance in respect of which any of the conditions mentioned in subsection (2) or paragraph (*a*) or (*b*) is satisfied.

(4) If any question arises in any proceedings as to whether a conveyance is valid by reason of subsection (2) or (3), the burden of proving that validity shall be on the person alleging it.

(5) In subsection (3), 'full value' means such value as amounts or approximates to the value of that for which it is given.

(6) In this section, 'purchaser' means a grantee, lessee, assignee, mortgagee, chargeant or other person who in good faith acquires an estate or interest in property.

(7) For the purposes of this section, section 3 of the *Conveyancing Act, 1882*, shall be read as if the words 'as such' wherever they appear in paragraph (ii) of subsection (1) of that section were omitted.

4. – (1) Where the spouse whose consent is required under section 3 (1) omits or refuses to consent, the court may, subject to the provisions of this section, dispense with the consent.

(2) The court shall not dispense with the consent of a spouse unless the court considers that it is unreasonable for the spouse to withhold consent, taking into account all the circumstances, including: –

(*a*) the respective needs and resources of the spouses and of the dependent children (if any) of the family, and

(*b*) in a case where the spouse whose consent is required is offered alternative accommodation, the suitability of that accommodation having regard to the respective degrees of security of tenure in the family home and in the alternative accommodation.

(3) Where the spouse whose consent is required under section 3 (1) has deserted and continues to desert the other spouse, the court shall dispense with the consent. For this purpose, desertion includes conduct on the part of the former spouse that results in the other spouse, with just cause, leaving and living separately and apart from him.

(4) Where the spouse whose consent is required under section 3 (1) is incapable of consenting by reason of unsoundness of mind or other mental disability or has not after reasonable inquiries been found, the court may give the consent on behalf of that spouse, if it appears to the court to be reasonable to do so.

5. – (1) Where it appears to the court, on the application of a spouse, that the other spouse is engaging in such conduct as may lead to the loss of any interest in the family home or may render it unsuitable for habitation as a family home with the intention of depriving the applicant spouse or a dependent child of the family of his residence in the family home, the court may make such order as it considers proper, directed to the other spouse or to any other person, for the protection of the family home in the interest of the applicant spouse or such child.

(2) Where it appears to the court, on the application of a spouse, that the other spouse has deprived the applicant spouse or a dependent child of the family of his residence in the family home by conduct that resulted in the loss of any interest therein or rendered it unsuitable for habitation as a family home, the court may order the other spouse or any other person to pay to the applicant spouse such amount as the court considers proper to compensate the applicant spouse and any such child for their loss or make such other order directed to the other spouse or to any other person as may appear to the court to be just and equitable.

6. – (1) Any payment or tender made or any other thing done by one spouse in or towards satisfaction of any liability of the other spouse in respect of rent, rates, mortgage payments or other outgoings affecting the family home shall be as good as if made or done by the other spouse, and shall be treated by the person to whom such payment is made or such thing is done as though it were made or done by the other spouse.
(2) Nothing in subsection (1) shall affect any claim by the first-mentioned spouse against the other to an interest in the family home by virtue of such payment or thing made or done by the first-mentioned spouse.

7. – (1) Where a mortgagee or lesser of the family home brings an action against a spouse in which he claims possession or sale of the home by virtue of the mortgage or lease in relation to the non-payment by that spouse of sums due thereunder, and it appears to the court –

(*a*) that the other spouse is capable of paying to the mortgagee or lesser the arrears (other than arrears of principal or interest or rent that do not constitute part of the periodical payments due under the mortgage or lease) of money due under the mortgage or lease within a reasonable time, and future periodical payments falling due under the mortgage or lease, and that the other spouse desires to pay such arrears and periodical payments; and

(*b*) that it would in all the circumstances, having regard to the terms of the mortgage or lease, the interests of the mortgage or lessor and the respective interests of the spouses, be just and equitable to do so, the court may adjourn the proceedings for such period and on such terms as appear to the court to be just and equitable.

(2) In considering whether to adjourn the proceedings under this section and, if so, for what period and on what terms they should be adjourned, the court shall have regard in particular to whether the spouse of the mortgagor or lessee has been informed (by or on behalf of the mortgagee or lessor or otherwise) of the non-payment of the sums in question or of any of them.

8. – (1) Where, on an application by a spouse, after proceedings have been adjourned under section 7, it appears to the court that –

(*a*) all arrears (other than arrears of principal or interest or rent that do not constitute part of the periodical payments due under the mortgage or lease) of money due under the mortgage or lease, and

(*b*) all the periodical payments due to date under the mortgage or lease,

have been paid off and that the periodical payments subsequently falling due will continue to be paid, the court may by order declare accordingly.

(2) If the court makes an order under subsection (1), any term in a mortgage or lease whereby the default in payment that gave rise to the proceedings under section 7 has, at any time before or after the initial hearing of such proceedings, resulted or would have resulted in the capital sum advanced thereunder (or part of such sum or interest thereon) or any sum other than the periodical payments, as the case may be, becoming due, shall be of no effect for the purpose of such proceedings or any subsequent proceedings in respect of the sum so becoming due. . . .

12. – (1) A spouse may register in the Registry of Deeds pursuant to the *Registration of Deeds Act, 1707* (in the case of unregistered property) or under the *Registration of Title Act, 1964* (in the case of registered land) a notice stating that he is married to any person, being a person having an interest in such property or land.

(2) The fact that notice of a marriage has not been registered under subsection (1) shall not give rise to any inference as to the nonexistence of a marriage.

(3) No stamp duty. Registry of Deeds fee or land registration fee shall be payable in respect of any such notice.

13. – Section 59 (2) of the *Registration of Title Act, 1964* (which refers to noting upon the register provisions of any enactment restricting dealings in land) shall not apply to the provisions of this Act.

14. – No stamp duty, land registration fee, Registry of Deeds fee or court fee shall be payable on any transaction creating a joint tenancy between spouses in respect of a family home where the home was immediately prior to such transaction owned by either spouse or by both spouses otherwise than as joint tenants.

15. – Where any person having an interest in any premises, on being required in writing by or on behalf of any other person proposing to acquire that interest to give any information necessary to establish if the conveyance of that interest requires a consent under section 3 (1), knowingly gives information which is false or misleading in any material particular, he shall be guilty of an offence and shall be liable –

(*a*) on summary conviction, to a fine not exceeding £200 or to imprisonment for a term not exceeding twelve months or to both, or

(*b*) on conviction on indictment, to imprisonment for a term not exceeding five years,

without prejudice to any other liability, civil or criminal. . . .

What Is a Family Home?

L.B. v. H.B.

Unreported, High Court, Barrington, J., July 1980 (1979–449Sp.)

[The facts have already been set out in relation to the recognition of foreign divorces, *supra*, pp. 245–48. On the question of the *Family Home Protection Act, 1976,* **Barrington J.** continued:]

At one stage Mrs. B, referring to the divorce proceedings, said, 'I was green – an idiot'. She added bitterly, 'He even took my son'. This is not correct, for, even though the husband may have been the dominant party in the divorce arrangements she, at least formally, agreed to giving him custody of her son. I am satisfied, however, that the fact that the husband had custody of the son had an important influence on her life. The parties worked out a modus vivendi under which they shared a common house, attended social events as husband and wife and preserved the facade of the marriage for the sake of their son. The son is now aged 30 and launched on his own life. But the parties still continue to occupy the same house. It is this strange aspect of the case which caused Mr. Blayney to argue that not only the legal but also the real relationship between the parties was that of husband and wife.

At the same time I am satisfied that the wife has no economic independence and no security. She says, and I accept, that she had to go to the husband's bank manager to borrow money to come to Court for the purpose of this case.

Section 2 of the *Family Home Protection Act, 1976* provides that the term 'family home' means primarily, 'a dwelling in which a married couple ordinarily reside'.

The husband has said that the house where the parties now reside is his home. The wife has no other home. It would accordingly appear that the house is a family home within the meaning of the *Family Home Protection Act, 1976*. I am accordingly prepared to make the declaration sought at paragraph 8(b) of the Statement of Claim.

I am aware that the house is not owned directly by Mr. B. It is owned by a company called Movie News Limited which in turn is controlled by a company incorporated in Panama in which Mr. B. owns what he describes as the 'vast majority' of the shares although some are also owned by his son. I do not think that this affects the issue that the house is a family home within the meaning of the Act.

C. v. C.

Unreported, High Ct., O'Hanlon, J., 12 May 1983 (1979–413Sp.)

O'Hanlon, J.:

In the Special Summons herein dated the 11th July, 1979, the Plaintiff claims relief under several different headings and under the provisions of a number of different statutes, against her husband, Y.C.

Orders have already been made by the Court in respect of custody of, and access to, the children of the marriage and in respect of the Plaintiff's claim for payment of maintenance for the support of herself and of the two children of the marriage. The Defendant has now applied to the Court in the same proceedings to deal with the claims made by the Plaintiff in Paragraphs 3, 4 and 5 of the Special Summons relating the lands comprised in Folio X of the Register of Freeholders, . . . with the dwellinghouse situate thereon, in respect of which the Plaintiff claimed a declaration that the said lands and premises constituted the family home, within the meaning of the *Family Home Protection Act, 1976*. She further claimed that the Defendant should be restrained from disposing of the property by sale or mortgage or otherwise howsoever, and claimed a declaration that she was entitled to the entire beneficial interest or alternatively some share in the beneficial interest in the said property.

Subsequent to the institution of these proceedings the Plaintiff caused a *lis pendens* to be registered against the said property, and also a notice pursuant to Sec. 12(1) of the *Family Home Protection Act, 1976*. As a result, the Lombard and Ulster Banking Company, which has obtained an order for possession against the said lands in its capacity as mortgagee, has been unable to exercise the power of sale which it claims to possess over the property, and it is largely to solve this impasse that the present application has been made to the Court on behalf of the Defendant.

An examination of the Folio reveals that the registered owner of the lands is not the Defendant, but a limited company Y.C. Limited, which became registered as full owner [i]n . . . May, 1979. An extract from the Register in the Companies Office, [in] November, 1978, gives the names of the Directors of the Company as O.C. (brother of the Defendant) and X.C. (wife of O.C.), while the Defendant is described as Secretary of the Company. A Special Resolution was passed [in] November, 1978 to include in the Objects Clause of the Company a provision entitling it to purchase lands and premises, including dwelling-houses, for the use of the directors, officers or employees of the Company, and the said O.C. and X.C. are therein described as the holders of all the shares then issued of the said Company. The date of incorporation of the Company was given by the Defendant as . . . July, 1978. The agreement to purchase the house . . . was made between the Vendor and the Defendant in or about the month of February, 1978, before the Company was incorporated, but when the time came to close the sale the assignment was taken in the name of the Company.

The documents relating to the sale were not produced in evidence (other than a certified copy of the Folio). The Defendant gave evidence to the effect that the purchase price was in the region of £26,000/£26,500. He said that his brother, O., provided the deposit, amounting to about £6,000/£6,500, and that the balance was provided by a loan made by the Lombard and Ulster Bank to the Company of £20,000 on foot of which a charge was registered in their favour on the Folio.

When the time came to insure the building, however, the proposal submitted to the Norwich Union Insurance Company was in the name of Y.C. and the policy was issued in favour of 'Y.C. and Others', the interest of the Lombard and Ulster Bank having been noted by the insurers. The house was destroyed by fire on the 22nd May, 1981. From the time the house was purchased it was used as a family home by the Plaintiff and the Defendant, until the Plaintiff left in or about the month of March, 1979, claiming that the Defendant had made it impossible for her to continue living with him.

Having considered all the evidence given by the Plaintiff and the Defendant I am satisfied that the Plaintiff made no financial contribution to the purchase of the house, either in respect of the provision of the deposit or in contributing to payment of the mortgage liability, and accordingly I commence by dismissing the claim brought by her to be entitled to the said lands and premises or to some share in the beneficial interest in the said property.

I now have to consider whether she is entitled to prevent a sale taking place of what was *de facto* the family home during the period immediately preceding the break-up of her marriage with the Defendant.

The Lombard and Ulster Banking Company having made an advance of £20,000 to the limited company, Y.C. Limited, and having obtained a charge on the property referred to in these proceedings, later obtained an Order for possession against the Company and wish to exercise their power of sale as mortgagees over the property. The amount now outstanding on foot of the mortgage is in the region of £30,000 and the property with the burnt-out house thereon was sold by auction on the 5th October, 1982, for £15,900. The completion of this sale is held up by the Plaintiff's action in causing a *lis pendens* to be registered against the property, and also a notice under Sec. 12(1) of the *Family Home Protection Act, 1976*.

The Plaintiff is highly suspicious concerning the entire transaction whereby the dwelling-house . . . was purchased in the name of a limited company, in which the Defendant was neither a director nor a shareholder, and believes this was merely a device to ensure that the provisions of the *Family Home Protection Act, 1976*, would have no application in the event of the property being subsequently put up for sale. Her suspicions may indeed be well-founded. The hearing of the case was adjourned to enable O.C. and X.C. to attend court and confirm that the property was purchased *bona fide* for a limited company owned and controlled by them, but they elected not to come to court and, as they reside [north of the border], their attendance could not be compelled by *subpoena*. There is the further circumstance that the proposal for insurance of the property was made in the name of the Defendant and the policy issued in his name, and although it was stated that a letter was subsequently sent to the insurance company seeking to have the insurance changed into the name of the limited company, the insurers have no record of ever having received such a letter.

Mere suspicion is not enough, however, to support a finding that the property was, in fact, purchased in trust for the Defendant, although registered in the name of the limited company and assigned to it. The mortgage moneys were advanced to the limited company and provided the greater part of the purchase moneys. The Defendant claimed in evidence that he and his wife and children were allowed to have the use and occupation of the property by leave and licence of the limited company owned and controlled by his brother and sister-in-law. Even if it could be shown by affirmative evidence that the transaction was a mere subterfuge designed to defeat the purposes of the Act of 1976, and that the Defendant should be regarded as having acquired the entire beneficial interest, or some share and interest therein, I cannot see how such a finding would now benefit the Plaintiff, since the property is no longer habitable, and the proceeds of sale of the derelict site will not suffice to meet the claims of the mortgagees.

On the evidence which has been produced before me, I must hold that the Defendant has not been shown to have an interest in the property . . . within the meaning of that expression as defined in Sec. 1 of the *Family Home Protection Act, 1976*, that is to say, 'any estate, right, title or other interest, legal or equitable'. This being so, the Plaintiff was not entitled to register the notice referred to in Sec. 12 of the Act in relation to this property; neither is she entitled to have the registration of the *lis pendens* continued on the Folio.

In these circumstances, I propose to make the Orders sought by the Defendant – (1) declaring that the Plaintiff is not entitled to any part or share of the beneficial interest in the said property; (2) directing that the notice she has caused to be registered under Sec. 12 of the *Family Home Protection Act, 1976*, should be removed from the Folio, and (3) directing that the *lis pendens* registered against the property be vacated.

The Plaintiff is left with such rights as are given her under the *Family Law (Maintenance of Spouses and Children) Act, 1976*, (as amended), for the maintenance of herself and the children of the marriage. It is useless pursuing a claim in respect of a home which has become derelict and uninhabitable. The Defendant is a guarantor of the liability of the company which is the registered owner of that property. It is in the Plaintiff's interest that that property should be sold as quickly as possible to clear off the mortgagee's claim, in so far as it is possible to do so, as otherwise interest will continue to accumulate and the Defendant's financial liabilities will continue to increase. When the property has been sold, and the insurance claim has been disposed of, a clearer picture should emerge as to the Defendant's ability to provide adequately for the needs of his wife and children. If there is a valid claim for maintenance under the provisions of the relevant Act of 1976 (as amended) then the Defendant carries the obligation to provide a home for his wife and children in substitution for the home which they previously occupied . . . in addition to providing for their other daily needs. This is a claim which can best be dealt with in the context of the claim for support under the Act of 1976 rather than by pursuing a claim which I have found to be unenforceable in any event, in respect of the derelict and burnt-out property. . . .

Notes

1. Should the law be amended to afford greater protection to dependent spouses and children in circumstances similar to those in this case?
2. Can *L.B.* v. *H.B.* and *C.* v. *C.* be reconciled?
3. See also *H. & L.* v. *S.*, unreported, High Ct., McWilliam, J., 10 July 1979 (1978–No. 312Sp.), holding that a home is a 'family home' even in cases where the spouse left the home before the passage of the *Family Home Protection Act, 1976*.

What is a Conveyance?

MURRAY v. DIAMOND

[1982] I.L.R.M. 113 (High Court, Barrington, J. 1981)

Barrington, J.:

This judgment deals with a net point of law raised as an issue between the plaintiff Denis Murray and the defendent David Diamond and his wife Jean Diamond by Carroll, J. in her order herein made on 6 July 1981.

The issue is set out in the schedule to that order and is as follows:

> Whether the judgment mortgage in favour of Denis Murray constitutes a purported conveyance by David Diamond of his interest in his family home such as would be rendered void by s. 3(1) of the *Family Home Protection Act, 1976* by reason of the absence of the prior written consent thereto by his spouse.

The point raised is clearly one of great practical importance raising, as it does, the question of the validity of judgment mortgages registered against the husband's interest in the matrimonial home without the consent of the wife.

The answer to the question raised turns, it appears to me, on the nature of a judgment mortgage itself. *The Judgment Mortgage Act, 1850* provides a means whereby a judgment creditor, who complies with the appropriate formalities, can convert his judgment into a judgment mortgage. One of the things he must do is to swear and register an affidavit giving particulars of his debt and particulars of the lands sought to be affected. It is this affidavit which, when registered, becomes the judgment mortgage (see *Madden on Deeds* (2nd Ed. p. 117).

'What is a judgment mortgage?' Lord Chancellor Brady asked in *Re Flood's Estate* 17 Ir. Ch. R. 116, 125 and answered:–
'It is, in fact, the affidavit made for the purpose of registering a judgment as a mortgage'.

S. 6 of the *Judgment Mortgage Act, 1850* sets out what such affidavit must contain, and goes on to provide that it will be lawful for the creditor making such affidavit to register same in the Registry of Deeds by depositing an office copy of such affidavit there. It then goes on to provide that:

> Such copy shall be numbered and transcribed and shall be entered in the books and indexes kept in the said office, in like manner as if the same were a memorial of a deed; and for the purpose of such entries the creditor under such judgment, decree, order or rule shall be deemed the grantee, and the debtor thereunder shall be deemed the grantor; and the amount of the debt, damages, costs or monies recovered or ordered to be paid thereby shall be deemed the consideration . . .

It seems clear from this that it is the registration of the office copy of the affidavit which converts the judgment into a judgment mortgage. But while the section says that for the purpose of the entries made in the register the judgment creditor is to be deemed the grantee and the judgment debtor to be deemed the grantor it is clear that the judgment mortgage comes into existence by operation of the statute and not by virtue of any positive act of the judgment debtor.

S. 3(1) of the *Family Home Protection Act, 1976* provides that, subject as therein, the purported conveyance is to be void where 'a spouse, without the prior consent in writing of the other spouse, purports to convey any interest in the family home to any person except the other spouse'.

In my opinion when a judgment mortgage is created the spouse against whom it is registered, does not convey any interest in the family home. *A fortiori* he does not 'purport' to convey any interest in the family home. The spouse against whom the judgment mortgage is registered is merely a patient. The judgment creditor is the agent and the mortgage comes into existence by operation of law.

Needless to say I am not here dealing with a case of fraud or with a case of connivance between one spouse and his or her judgment creditor to defeat the rights of the other spouse.

Apart from fraud or connivance I do not think that the mere fact that a man has, irresponsibily, allowed himself to get into debt, or allowed a judgment to be obtained against him and thereby allowed a situation to develop in which his creditor registers a judgment mortgage against his interest in the family home, would justify a court in saying that he has conveyed or purported to convey his interest in the family home to the judgment mortgagee. This appears to me to be the correct interpretation of the statute. The fact that the *Family Home Protection Act, 1976* may afford less protection to the innocent or unsuspecting spouse than some people may have considered does not mean that the purposes of that Act are defeated. I do not think that the principle in *Nestor v Murphy* [1979] IR326, on which the plaintiffs in the issue relied, has any application in the circumstances of the present case.

The above conclusion appears to dispose of the issue in the present case but, as some other points were argued before me, it may be proper to refer to them.

Counsel for the wife relied upon the reference in s. 6 of the *Judgment Mortgage Act* to the fact that the judgment creditor must know or believe that the judgment debtor 'is seized or possessed at law or in equity in any lands, tenements, or hereditaments, of any nature or tenure, or has any disposing power over any such lands, tenements or hereditaments, which he may without the assent of any other person exercise for his own benefit'.

Counsel submitted that as, under the provisions of *the Family Home Protection Act, 1976*, the husband can no longer dispose of the family home without the consent of the wife, the husband's interest in the family home is not an interest against which a judgment mortgage can be registered. It seems clear however from a careful reading of the section that the words 'which he may without the assent of any other person exercise for his own benefit' govern the words 'has any disposing power over any such lands, tenements, or hereditaments' and do not govern the words 'seized or possessed at law or in equity of any lands, tenements or hereditaments of any nature or tenure.' In other words the effect of this section is to allow the judgment creditor to register a mortgage not only against the judgment debtor's interests in lands but also to enable the judgment creditor to register a mortgage against certain 'disposing powers' provided only that the judgment creditor can exercise that disposing power for his own benefit without the consent of any other person (on this see Wylie, *Irish Land Law* p. 609).

Counsel for the wife, in the present case, also pointed to the provisions of s. 71(4) and s. 52 of the *Registration of Title Act 1964* as affecting family homes which are registered lands. S. 71(4) provides that, in the case of registered lands, registration of the affidavit of the judgment mortgagee operates to charge the interest of the judgment debtor in the land, subject to registered burdens, if any, and burdens to which, though not registered, that interest is subject by virtue of s. 72 and 'all unregistered rights subject to which the judgment debtor held that interest at the time of registration of the affidavit.' S. 52(1) of the same Act provides as follows:

1. On the registration of a transferee of freehold land as full owner with an absolute title, the instrument of transfer shall operate as a conveyance by deed within the meaning of the Conveyancing Acts, and there shall be vested in the registered transferee an estate in fee simple in the land transferred, together with all implied or express rights, privileges and appurtenances belonging or appurtenant thereto, subject to–
   a. the burdens, if any, registered as affecting the land, and
   b. the burdens to which though not so registered, the land is subject by virtue of s. 72,

   but shall be free from all other rights, including rights of the state.

The submission is that, in the case of the family home, the judgment mortgagee or transferee takes his charge of his estate from one spouse but subject to the rights of the other spouse if that other spouse is not a party to the transaction. It appears to me that this would be so only if the rights of the other spouse were property rights of the kind contemplated by the provisions of the *Registration of Title Act, 1964*. But I do not think they are. I prefer to follow the reasoning of Gannon J in *Guckian v Brennan* [*infra*, p. 338] where Gannon, J. held that the rights of the spouse who does not own the family home are valuable rights but not an estate or interest in lands. This reasoning was accepted by McWilliam J in *Lloyd v Sullivan* H.C. 6 March 1981 No. 39 Sp. 1981. See also *National Provincial Bank Ltd v Ainsworth* [1965] A.C. 1175.

Under these circumstances I think that the answer to the question raised in the issue should be that the judgment mortgage in question does not constitute a purported conveyance by David Diamond such as is rendered void by Section 3(1) of the *Family Home Protection Act, 1976*.

Notes

1. *Murray* v. *Diamond* was decided by Barrington, J. on 7 December 1981. Twelve days previously, in *Containercare (Ireland) Ltd.* v. *W.*, (1981–341Sp.) Carroll, J. had decided the same issue the same way, saying (at pp. 10–11, 18–19 of her judgment):

> A judgment mortgage, if registered against a family home, is not a disposition by a spouse purporting to convey an interest in the family home. It is a unilateral act by a judgment creditor and the creation of the judgment mortgage is effected by the registration in the Registry of Deeds, in the case of unregistered land, of the affidavit of judgment which has already been filed in Court.
>
> The [1976] Act does not require that the disposition affected by the Act be in writing. This is evident from the fact that equitable mortgages are captured under the definition of 'mortgage'. But the Act does require that the disposition should be by the spouse of the person whose consent is required.
>
> Therefore I am of opinion that section 3(1) of the Act cannot refer to a judgment mortgage because it cannot be construed as a conveyance by a spouse. . . .
>
> . . . I am of opinion that the Act does not confer on the spouse whose consent is required, any right or interest in the land where the land is unregistered. Neither does it limit in any way the estate or interest vested in the spouse who owns the property, an estate which automatically vests in the judgment mortgagee on the creation of the judgment mortgage.
>
> The effect of the Act is to impose 'a sanction of voidness' on a disposition by which a spouse alienates the property without consent. But where the estate or interest of a spouse is vested by operation of law in a judgment mortgagee, that judgment mortgagee takes free from the obligation to obtain the consent of the other spouse to a disposition by him.

2. For consideration of the existing English law, and proposals for change, see Hand, *Bankruptcy and the Family Home,* [1983] Conv. 219. See also Palley, *Wives, Creditors and the Matrimonial Home*, 20 N.I.L.Q. 132 (1969).

Does section 3 apply where both spouses are parties to the conveyance?

NESTOR v. MURPHY

[1979] I.R. 326 (Supreme Court)

Henchy J.:

The two defendants are a married couple. Their family home is in Lucan in the county of Dublin. It is held by them under a long lease and they are joint tenants of the leasehold interest. In July, 1978, they agreed to sell their interest to the plaintiff. They each signed a contract to sell to the plaintiff for £18,500. In form it is a binding and enforceable contract. However, they refuse to complete the sale. The reason they give is that the contract is void under s. 3, sub-s. 1, of the *Family Home Protection Act, 1976*, because the wife did not consent in writing to the sale before the contract was signed. That is the net point in this claim by the plaintiff for the specific performance of the contract.

A surface, or literal, appraisal of s. 3, sub-s. 1, might be thought to give support to the defendants' objection to the contract. That sub-section states:– 'Where a spouse, without the prior consent in writing of the other spouse, purports to convey any interest in the family home to any person except the other spouse, then, subject to subsections (2) and (3) and section 4, the purported conveyance shall be void.' Sub-sections 2 and 3 of s. 3, and s. 4, are not applicable to this case. By reason of the definition in s. 1, sub-s. 1, the contract signed by the defendants is a 'conveyance'. Therefore, the argument runs, the provisions of s. 3, sub-s. 1, make the contract void because a spouse (the husband), without the prior consent in writing of the other spouse, 'conveyed' an interest in the family home to the plaintiff.

The flaw in this interpretation of s. 3, sub-s. 1, is that it assumes that it was intended to apply when both spouses are parties to the 'conveyance.' That, however, is not so. The basic purpose of the sub-section is to protect the family home by giving a right of avoidance to the spouse who was not a party to the transaction. It ensures that protection by requiring, for the validity of the contract to dispose and of the actual disposition, that the non-disposing spouse should have given a prior consent in writing. The point and purpose of imposing the sanction of voidness is to enforce the right of the non-disposing spouse to veto the disposition by the other spouse of an interest in the family home. The sub-section cannot have been intended by Parliament to apply when both spouses join in the 'conveyance.' In such event no protection is needed for one spouse against an unfair and unnotified alienation by the other of an interest in the family home. The provisions of s. 3, sub-s. 1, are directed against unilateral alienation by one spouse. When both spouses join in the 'conveyance,' the evil at which the sub-section is directed does not exist.

To construe the sub-section in the way proposed on behalf of the defendants would lead to a pointless absurdity. As is conceded by counsel for the defendants, if their construction of s. 3, sub-s. 1, is correct then either the husband or the wife could have the contract declared void because the other did not give a prior consent in writing. Such an avoidance of an otherwise enforceable obligation would not be required for the protection of the family home when both spouses have entered into a contract to sell it. Therefore, it would be outside the spirit and purpose of the Act.

In such circumstances we must adopt what has been called a schematic or teleological approach. This means that s. 3, sub-s. 1, must be given a construction which does not overstep the limits of the operative range that must be ascribed to it, having regard to the legislative scheme as expressed in the Act of 1976 as a whole. Therefore, the words of s. 3, sub-s. 1, must be given no wider meaning than is necessary to effectuate the right of avoidance given when the non-participating spouse has not consented in advance in writing to the alienation of any interest in the family home. Such a departure from the literal in favour of a restricted meaning was given this justification by Lord Reid in *Luke* v. *Inland Revenue Commissioners* [1963] A.C. 557, when he said at p. 577 of the report:–

> To apply the words literally is to defeat the obvious intention of the legislation and to produce a wholly unreasonable result. To achieve the obvious intention and produce a reasonable result we must do some violence to the words. This is not a new problem, though our standard of drafting is such that it rarely emerges. The general principle is well settled. It is only where the words are absolutely incapable of a construction which will accord with the apparent intention of the provision and will avoid a wholly unreasonable result, that the words of the enactment must prevail.

Because it is evident from the pattern and purpose of the Act of 1976 that the primary aim of s. 3, sub-s. 1, is to enable a spouse who was not a party to a 'conveyance' of the family home, and did not give a prior consent in writing to it, to have it declared void, and because an extension of that right of avoidance to spouses who have entered into a joint 'conveyance' would not only be unnecessary for the attainment of that aim but would enable contracts to be unfairly or dishonestly repudiated by parties who entered into them freely, willingly and with full knowledge, I would hold that the spouse whose 'conveyance' is avoided by the provisions of s. 3, sub-s. 1, is a spouse who has unilaterally (*i.e.*, without the other spouse joining) purported to 'convey' an interest in the family home without having obtained the prior consent in writing of the other spouse. It is only by thus confining the reach of the sub-section that its operation can be kept within what must have been the legislative intent.

I would dismiss this appeal and affirm the order for specific performance made by Mr. Justice Butler.

Kenny and **Parke JJ.** concurred.

Notes

1. As to the meaning of 'conveyance', see also *Somers* v. *W.*, [1979] I.R. 94 (Supreme Ct., 1979, rev'g High Ct., Doyle, J., 1978).
2. In *Mulhall* v. *Haren* [1981] I.R. 364 (High Ct., Keane, J., 1979), a house jointly owned by the defendants, a husband and wife, was sold after negotiations carried on through an auctioneer. Proceedings for specific performance of the contract were later resisted by the defendants on several grounds. One, unsuccessful, ground was that the wife has not given her prior consent in writing to the agreement. Having quoted from Henchy, J.'s judgment in *Nestor* v. *Murphy*, Keane, J. said (at 373):

   I do not regard it as in any sense material that, on the assumptions I have made, the wife in the present case did not sign the contract, although she was party to it. The judgment of the Supreme Court is plainly based on the principle that a transaction to which both spouses are parties is not captured at all by the Act of 1976; and in this context it is manifestly immaterial whether the spouse on whose behalf protection is claimed signs the contract herself or authorises someone to sign it on her behalf. If, for example, the evidence in *Nestor* v. *Murphy* had established that the wife's solicitor had signed the contract as agent on her behalf with her full authority because she was away at the time, I do not believe that the decision would have been any different. It follows that this ground of defence fails.

3. In *Kyne* v. *T.*, unreported, High Ct., 15 July 1980 (1978–685P.), McWilliam J. said (at pp. 9–10):

   . . . I suppose it could be said, on a strict interpretation of section 3 of the Act, that there must be a consent in writing to each conveyance, that is to say, both to the contract and to the final conveyance to the purchaser, but I cannot imagine that it could have been the intention of the legislature to require two consents for the completion of one transaction, namely, the sale of the house, and thus leave a purchaser in the position of conducting all the work and incurring all the expense necessary for the completion of a purchase only to find that a spouse had changed his or her mind about giving consent and require the whole transaction to be abandoned.

4. On the question of a minor's consent to the disposal of the family home see section 10 of the *Family Law Act, 1981* and *Lloyd* v. *Sullivan*, unreported, High Ct., McWilliam, J., 6 March 1981 (1981–395).
5. On the question whether the 1976 Act applies to agreements to sell or to instruments of conveyance entered into before the Act came into operation, see *Hamilton* v. *Hamilton,* [1982] I.R. 466 (Sup. Ct.). Costello, J.'s strong dissent should be noted. On Henchy J's consideration of the relevance of Article 43.1 of the Constitution, see J. Kelly, *The Irish Constitution*, 232 (2nd ed., 1984).

What obligations are on the purchaser?
May the Courts dispense with a spouse's consent after a conveyance has been executed?

SOMERS v. W.

[1979] I.R. 94 (Supreme Court, 1979, rev'g High Court, Doyle, J., 1978)

Henchy, J.:

This case raises an important conveyancing point under the *Family Home Protection Act, 1976*. One of the primary objects of this Act is to limit the power of a spouse to alienate the family home without the prior consent in writing of the other spouse. . . .

Section 3 provides that where a spouse, without the prior consent in writing of the other spouse, purports to convey any interest in the family home to any person other than the other spouse then, subject to four specified exceptions, the purported conveyance shall be void. The only one of those exceptions that we are here concerned with is the proviso in s. 3, sub-s. 3, that the prohibition is not to apply if the conveyance is made to 'a purchaser for full value.' That exception gives rise to the issue in this case which is whether the plaintiff, who was the purchaser of the leasehold interest of the defendant's husband in the family home, was a purchaser for full value within the meaning of the Act of 1976.

The dwelling in question was called 'the contract premises' in the judgment of Mr. Justice Doyle, and I shall also employ that description. Before the marriage, the defendant's husband took a lease of the contract premises in his own name in March, 1961. When the husband and the defendant married in July, 1961, those premises became the family home. There were children of the marriage. Unfortunately it turned out an unhappy marriage. The husband is not a party to these proceedings, so we do not know his side of the story. The defendant says that, for stated reasons, she was compelled to leave the contract premises with her children in October, 1973. After she left, she got a tenancy from the Dublin Corporation, first in other premises and then, in June, 1976, at her present address where she has been living since then with her children. She never resumed marital relations with her husband.

On leaving the family home, the defendant went for advice to the centre at Coolock run by F.L.A.C. (*i.e.*, Free Legal Aid Centres), which is the group which supplies free legal aid for those who are in need of legal aid and cannot afford to pay a solicitor. She wished to have custody of the children and to be free to interference by the husband. On the 20th November, 1974, a written separation agreement was executed whereby it was agreed that the defendant and her husband would live separately without interference from each other; that the defendant would have custody of the children subject to stated access by her husband; and that the defendant would keep her husband indemnified against all debts and liabilities which she would contract or incur. The agreement made no provision for any payments by the husband for the maintenance of the defendant and her children; and it was silent as to the family home.

As a result, the defendant's husband retained the family home while incurring no financial commitments to the defendant or his children whereas the defendant, who had to go out to work as a cleaner in a factory, had to struggle to pay the rent of her Corporation house and bring up her children out of her slender wages and the sums she received in the way of social security payments. Whatever the rights or wrongs of the collapse of the marriage, the defendant finished up unfairly and excessively burdened with the problems of life.

On the 2nd August, 1976, the defendant's husband entered into a written agreement to sell his leasehold interest in the contract premises for £6,400 to the plaintiff. The *Family Home Protection Act, 1976*, had come into operation only a few weeks earlier (12th July, 1976). Both the husband's solicitor and the plaintiff's solicitor were aware that the Act of 1976 had come into force.

[**Henchy, J.** here referred to two letters. The first was written by the plaintiff's solicitor on the 10th August to the solicitor for the defendant's husband in the following terms:–

> I enclose herewith engrossed (*sic*) assignment with approved draft thereof for execution by your client and memorial. The spouse's consent to the assignment must be endorsed on it unless there is an official separation deed in which case we require a copy of same.

The second letter was from the husband's solicitor, on 11th August, replying to the plaintiff's solicitor's letter. The material portions were as follows:–

> Our client and his wife have been separated for some years. Our client's wife has been housed by Dublin Corporation and is therefore no longer relying on [*the contract premises*] as her family home. We understand that a separation agreement has been entered into but we did not act for either party at the time and do not have a

copy of the agreement. We understand from our client that he has never had a copy of the agreement and that same was with F.L.A.C. We understand that Mr. Paul Murphy of this organisation was dealing with the matter.

We did in fact try to make contact with the branch of F.L.A.C. for the purpose of obtaining a copy of the agreement but this we understand is at present closed for holidays. We do not have the address or telephone number of any other branch and cannot trace any in the telephone directory.

In view of the fact that the premises are not now a family home and your client is the purchaser for full value we cannot see how your client is concerned with the matrimonial situation.

Henchy, J. continued:]

At this time the husband was abroad temporarily so just then his solicitor could not get the defendant's address from him – but he was back in Dublin by the 16th August, 1976. The plaintiff's solicitor did not wait for the husband to return from abroad or for the F.L.A.C. centre to reopen after the summer holidays. Instead, he prepared a statutory declaration, to be made by the husband, stating that the defendant had not relied on the contract premises as her family home since the execution of the separation agreement and that she 'by virtue of said separation agreement has now no interest therein.' Considering that the plaintiff's solicitor had never seen the separation agreement, which made no reference to the contract premises, this averment was a wild and inaccurate leap in the dark. Without any real inquiry as to the facts and without any inspection of the separation agreement, words which expressed the opposite of the truth were put into the husband's mouth. The defendant's husband executed the statutory declaration thus prepared by the purchaser's solicitor, and the sale was closed on the 17th August, 1976, with the execution of the assignment on that date. The husband had a balance of some £3,400 out of the purchase price after paying off the mortgage and discharging the costs of the sale.

There the matter might have rested, with the husband walking off with the proceeds of the sale, were it not for the fact that the plaintiff, having spent some money on improving the contract premises, agreed to resell those premises in April, 1977, for £10,800. The new purchaser (or, rather, the building society which was financing the new purchaser) required proof that the provisions of s. 3 of the *Family Home Protection Act, 1976*, had not been breached. The plaintiff's solicitor discovered the defendant's address and wrote to her asking her to give her retrospective consent in writing to the assignment of the 17th August, 1976. The defendant refused, claiming that she was entitled to a proprietary interest in the contract premises. It was in that impasse that the plaintiff instituted the present proceedings in which she seeks an order under s. 4 of the Act of 1976 dispensing with the defendant's consent in writing to the assignment of the 17th August, 1976. In the High Court the judge, holding that the wife's consent was not necessary to that assignment, granted the order sought. It is against that decision that this appeal has been taken.

Section 3, sub-s. 3(*a*), of the Act of 1976 allows a conveyance to escape being void under that section if it is made to a purchaser for full value. It is common ground that the plaintiff paid the full value for the contract premises in 1976: but was she 'a purchaser' as defined by s. 3, sub-s. 6, that is to say, was she an assignee 'who in good faith acquires an estate or interest in property'? This is the nub of the case; for the contest is whether she, through her solicitor, acted in good faith in taking the assignment without the prior consent of the defendant. On that issue, the onus of proof rests on the plaintiff: see sub-s. 4 of section 3.

The question whether a purchaser has acted in good faith necessarily depends on the extent of his knowledge of the relevant circumstances. In earlier times the tendency was to judge a purchaser solely by the facts that had actually come to his knowledge. In the course of time it came to be held in the Court of Chancery that it would be unconscionable for the purchaser to take his stand on the facts that had come to his notice to the exclusion of those which ordinary prudence or circumspection or skill should have called to his attention. When the facts at his command beckoned him to look and inquire further, and he refrained from doing so, equity fixed him with constructive notice of what he would have ascertained if he had pursued the further investigation which a person of reasonable care and skill would have felt proper to make in the circumstances. He would not be allowed to say 'I acted in good faith, in ignorance of those facts, of which I learned only after I took the conveyance,' if those facts were such as a reasonable man in the circumstances would have brought within his knowledge.

When the *Supreme Court of Judicature Act (Ireland), 1877*, brought the rules of equity into play in all courts, the equitable doctrine of notice was given supremacy. Further, it was given statutory expression in s. 3 of the *Conveyancing Act, 1882*. For the purposes of this case the relevant parts of that section are contained in sub-s. 1 which states:–

> (1) A purchaser shall not be prejudicially affected by notice of any instrument, fact, or thing unless –
> (i) It is within his own knowledge, or would have come to his knowledge if such inquiries and inspections had been made as ought reasonably to have been made by him; or
> (ii) In the same transaction with respect to which a question of notice to the purchaser arises, it has come to the knowledge of his counsel, *as such*, or of his solicitor, or other agent, *as such*, or would have come to the knowledge of his solicitor, or other agent, *as such*, if such inquiries and inspections had been made as ought reasonably to have been made by the solicitor or other agent.

That s. 3 of the Act of 1976 is to be operated within this doctrine of notice is emphasised by the fact that sub-s. 7 of that section amends s. 3 of the Act of 1882 by deleting from it the above italicised words, thus extending the reach of constructive notice.

It is not in contention that the plaintiff did not know, personally or through her solicitor, that the defendant had a prima facie valid proprietary interest in the contract premises which the husband was selling. But ought the plaintiff reasonably, through her solicitor, to have ascertained that fact? If she ought, the position is the same as if she actually knew of the claim, in which case she could not be said to have purchased in good faith and the assignment would have to be declared void.

Let us first see what was the extent of the plaintiff's actual knowledge. Through her solicitor (for his knowledge is to be imputed to her) she knew (or was told) that the contract premises were the family home, that the defendant's husband was the vendor, that his marriage had broken up, that there had been a separation agreement, that the vendor's wife was living in a Dublin Corporation house and was no longer claiming that the contract premises were the family home. It was further stated by the vendor's solicitor that the vendor, at the time the title was being investigated, was abroad and that his wife's address was not available. It was against the background of that information that the plaintiff's solicitor decided to close the sale on getting a statutory declaration from the vendor. This statutory declaration, which was drafted by the plaintiff's solicitor, was inaccurate in fact and unfounded in law. It declared that the separation agreement had been entered into in or about October, 1973 (it was executed in November, 1974) and that by virtue of it the defendant had no interest in the contract premises although the separation agreement did not make any reference whatsoever to those premises.

Furthermore, as we know from the defendant's evidence in the High Court, she has a valid prima facie claim to a proprietary interest in the contract premises on the ground that she made an initial down-payment of £25 for them; that for the first five months of the marriage, when she was still working, she pooled her wages with her husband's; and that at one stage she obtained from her mother and made available to the husband £150 which he used to pay off arrears of rent.

In those circumstances should the plaintiff, as purchaser, be fixed with constructive notice of the contents of the separation agreement and of the existence of the defendant's claim? The answer must be 'Yes.' The contract for sale was executed on the 2nd August and the title had been investigated and the sale completed by the 17th August, 1976.

Expedition of that order is to be commended, but not at the expense of due investigation of title. When the plaintiff's solicitor asked to be supplied with the separation agreement and was told that it could not be supplied because the F.L.A.C. centre was closed for the annual holidays, he should not have allowed himself to be fobbed off with that excuse. It is not unusual for sales to be held up for reasons such as this in the month of August at the peak of the holiday season. Considering the dire risk of a void conveyance, it was foolhardy to close the sale without seeing the separation agreement. Had it come to hand it would have shown itself to be worthless as a document of title, and to be no basis for the statutory declaration on which the sale was completed; but it would have given the defendant's then address as a Dublin Corporation tenant so that it would have been possible, through the Corporation, to have traced her to her address at the time of the sale.

In any event, there was never any real difficulty in ascertaining the defendant's address, and discovering whether she was prepared to give her prior consent in writing to the sale. The defendant's husband may have been abroad at some stage, but he was back in Dublin by the 16th August, 1978 (when he executed the statutory declaration) and he well knew the defendant's address. It was folly to close the sale in those circumstances without insisting on the prior consent in writing of the defendant. No sooner was the sale closed than her husband went to the defendant and offered to give her the proceeds of the sale if she would take him back; feeling that she was well rid of him, she refused. But she should have been given the opportunity, before the sale, of withholding her consent unless her claim to an interest in the contract premises was satisfied. If the plaintiff's solicitor had insisted on compliance with his requisition that the defendant's consent should be endorsed on the assignment, the defendant's husband would have had no valid reason for refusing to ask her to do so. The inescapable conclusion is that the true facts, both as to the contents of the separation agreement and as to the existence and nature of the defendant's claim, would have come to the plaintiff's knowledge if (to use the words of the Act of 1882) 'such inquiries and inspections have been made as ought reasonably to have been made.' Therefore, the plaintiff must be held to have purchased with notice of those facts, so that the property she acquired (or purported to acquire) was not acquired in good faith.

The trial judge considered that to hold that the inquiries made by the plaintiff's solicitor were inadequate would add a new dimension to the practice of conveyancing; but that new dimension has been added by s. 3 of the Act of 1976. As a result of that section, a purchaser investigating title must now scrutinise matters that hitherto were not matters of title at all. He must ascertain if the property, because of its present or past use, is a family home within the meaning of the Act of 1976. If it is, he must find out if it is a sale by a spouse and, if so, whether the conveyance should be preceded by the consent in writing of the other spouse so as to prevent its being rendered void under section 3. If that other spouse omits or refuses to consent, the purchaser should require the vendor to apply to the court for an order under s. 4 of the Act of 1976 dispensing with the consent. Where a family home is being purchased from a husband (the converse will be the case if the wife is the vendor), it may, by virtue of the Act, be subject to an inhibition enabling the wife to block a valid sale unless her prior consent in writing is obtained. This inhibition arises for enforcement not only when the wife has acquired (*e.g.* by payment of rent, rates, mortgage payments or other outgoings) a proprietary interest in the family home but also when the needs of the wife and of the dependent children (as defined) so require in the circumstances.

If the purchaser takes a conveyance without compliance with the requirement as to consent, he carries the onus of proving that the conveyance comes under one of the exemptions in sub-sections 2 and 3. If, as in the present instance, the purchaser's case is that the wife's prior consent did not arise because he was a purchaser for full value without notice, he must show that the consideration amounted or approximated to the full value of the property and also that he, or his agent, made such inquiries or inspections as ought reasonably to have been made. If such inquiries or inspections have not been made but would, if made, have disclosed that the vendor should have obtained either his wife's prior consent in writing or a court order dispensing with that consent, the conveyance will be no less void than if the purchaser had actual knowledge that the wife's prior consent in writing required to be sought and he had taken the conveyance in disregard of that requirement.

In this case, the inquiries and inspections which ought reasonably to have been made as a matter of common prudence were not made. Instead, a statement which was unwarranted by any document and which falsely swept aside the defendant's rights was presented to her husband for execution as a statutory declaration and, on the basis of that statutory declaration, the sale by him went through behind his wife's back. It was a transaction of the precise kind that s. 3 of the Act of 1976 was designed to make void. Unfamiliarity with the Act of 1976 seems to have misled both the solicitor for the plaintiff and the solicitor for the defendant's husband.

Finally, a word as to the form of the present proceedings. The plaintiff moved by a special summons in which she asked for an order under s. 4 of the Act of 1976 dispensing with the defendant's prior consent to the sale. This, in my opinion, was not the correct order to seek. If the plaintiff could be said to have been 'a purchaser for full value,' the proper order to seek would have been an order declaring the validity of the assignment which had been made without the defendant's prior consent in writing. An order under s. 4 of the Act of 1976 is intended to cover the position *before conveyance* when the spouse omits or refuses to consent. When the conveyance has been executed without the consent, it is either valid without that consent or it is void *ab initio*; in either event an order under s. 4 would be inappropriate.

I would allow this appeal and rule that the assignment to the plaintiff is void.

Griffin, J. delivered a concurring judgment. **Parke, J.** concurred with both judgments.

Note

See also *H. & L.* v. *S.*, unreported, High Ct., McWilliam, J., 10 July 1979 (1978–312Sp.)

What duties of investigation are on the purchaser of registered land?

GUCKIAN v. BRENNAN

[1981] I.R. 478 (High Court, Gannon, J., 1980)

Gannon, J.:

The plaintiffs are a husband and wife who are joint owners of a dwellinghouse at No. 251 Grangemore, Raheny, Dublin 5, comprising a plot of ground of 9 perches in the townland of Grange and Barony of Coolock. That property is the subject matter of folio 19851 of the register of leasehold interests for the county of Dublin. The leasehold interest was created by a lease dated the 28th April, 1972, by which Merchant Banking Ltd. demised the property to Edward Parsons for the term of 250 years from the 29th September, 1969, at the yearly rent of £20. Edward Parsons was registered as full owner on the 21st August, 1972, subject to a charge (since released) and to the provisions of ss. 12 and 45 of the *Land Act, 1965*. Those provisions prohibit or restrict the alienation of land, or of any part of it. On the 18th August, 1978, the plaintiffs became registered as full owners of the property (subject to those statutory provisions and to a charge in favour of First National Building Society) by virtue of a transfer from Edward Parsons. On the 7th

December, 1979, the plaintiffs entered into an agreement to sell the property to the defendants.

In the course of an investigation of the title the defendants required the plaintiffs to furnish evidence that the assignment to them by Edward Parsons, the registered owner and original lessee, was unaffected by s. 3 of the *Family Home Protection Act, 1976*. That, I understand, was the purport of requisition 63(7) of the requisitions on title – as submitted in lieu of a more precise additional sub-paragraph in requisition No. 52. The plaintiffs' reply to requisition 63 (7) was:– 'Not necessary. The vendor has been registered as full owner of the property in the Land Registry and the register is conclusive.' The defendants are dissatisfied with that reply. On this issue the plaintiffs applied to the Court by a special summons under the provisions of s. 9 of the *Vendor and Purchaser Act, 1874*, for a declaration that requisition 63 (7) has been sufficiently answered and that a good title can be shown.

The necessity for a requisition of this nature is a consequence of the passing on the 12th July, 1976, of the Act of 1976. As the plaintiffs are joint owners, the defendants are not concerned with the possible effect of the Act of 1976 on their contract with the plaintiffs, or on the intended instrument of transfer to them. But the defendants apprehend that the plaintiffs could not make good title on this sale if the assurance by Parsons to the plaintiffs was affected by the Act of 1976 so as to have been avoided or invalidated under s. 3 of that Act. Because their title is registered under the provisions of the *Registration of Title Act, 1964*, the plaintiffs consider that the defendants' enquiry is unnecessary and that it is precluded by ss. 31 and 55 of the Act of 1964.

Section 5 of the Act of 1964 repealed the *Local Registration of Title (Ireland) Act, 1891*, and the *Registration of Title Act, 1942*. However, the Act of 1964 did not depart from the purpose or scheme of those Acts but reenacted their basic sections. Section 31, sub-s. 1, of the Act of 1964 (which corresponds to s. 34 of the Act of 1891) provides:–

> (1) The register shall be conclusive evidence of the title of the owner to the land as appearing on the register and of any right, privilege, appurtenance or burden as appearing thereon; and such title shall not, in the absence of actual fraud, be in any way affected in consequence of such owner having notice of any deed, document, or matter relating to the land; but nothing in this Act shall interfere with the jurisdiction of any court of competent jurisdiction based on the ground of actual fraud or mistake, and the court may upon such ground make an order directing the register to be rectified in such manner and on such terms as it thinks just.

Sub-section 2 of s. 31 is not pertinent to these proceedings. Section 51 of the Act of 1964 provides for the mode of transfer of ownership and states when the transfer shall take effect.

Section 55, sub-s. 1, of that Act states:–

> (1) On the registration of a transferee of a leasehold interest as full owner with an absolute title, the instrument of transfer shall operate as a conveyance by deed within the meaning of the Conveyancing Acts, and there shall vest in the registered transferee the leasehold interest so transferred, together with all implied or express rights, privileges and appurtenances attached to it, subject to–
> (*a*) the burdens, if any, registered as affecting the interest,
> (*b*) the burdens to which, though not registered, the interest is subject by virtue of section 72, and
> (*c*) all implied and express covenants, obligations and liabilities incident to the interest transferred, but free from all other rights, including rights of the State.

The question which concerns both the plaintiffs and the defendants is whether such interest of a spouse (who is not an owner) as may arise under the *Family Home Protection Act, 1976*, is a burden which comes within s. 55, sub-s. 1 (*b*), of the Act of 1964 or falls within the phrase 'all other rights,' free from which the full ownership with an absolute title may be registered. Such last-mentioned rights may affect the registered ownership by virtue of s. 55, sub-s. 2, in any case in which the registration is effected pursuant to a transfer made without valuable consideration.

The unregistered burdens which affect the registered transferee of a leasehold interest are set out in s. 72, sub-s. 1, of the Act of 1964, which states:– '(1) Subject to subsection (2), all registered land shall be subject to such of the following burdens as for the time being affect the land, whether those burdens are or are not registered, namely . . .' Of the 17 classifications which follow only those at paragraphs (*j*) and (*q*) were referred to in the course of this hearing. These read as follows:–

(*j*) the rights of every person in actual occupation of the land or in receipt of the rents and profits thereof, save where, upon enquiry made of such person, the rights are not disclosed . . .
(*q*) burdens to which section 59 or 73 applies.

Section 72, sub-s. 3, provides:– '(3) Where the existence of any such burdens is proved to the satisfaction of the Registrar, he may, with the consent of the registered owner or applicant for registration, or in pursuance of an order of the court, enter notice thereof on the register.' As s. 72, sub-s. 2, deals only with paragraphs (*a*), (*b*) and (*c*) of sub-s. 1 of that section, it is unnecessary to consider it. As s. 73 deals with mines and minerals it is not pertinent in these proceedings.

However, s. 59 is of importance, as it provides:–

(1) Nothing in this Act shall affect the provisions of any enactment by which the alienation, assignment, subdivision or sub-letting of any land is prohibited or in any way restricted.
(2) It shall be the duty of the Registrar to note upon the register in the prescribed manner the prohibitive or restrictive provisions of any such enactment; but such provisions shall be, though not registered, burdens on the land under section 72.

Section 3 of the *Family Home Protection Act, 1976* (in cases to which that Act applies) contains provisions by which the alienation of any land is restricted and may be prohibited.

[**Gannon, J.** quoted sections 2(1) and 3(1) of the 1976 Act. He continued:]

The word 'dwelling' is defined in s. 2, sub-s. 2, in terms which include any portion of ground 'attached to and usually occupied with' the dwelling. Having occupation of the property as a dwelling is, therefore, an essential qualification for a spouse who seeks to rely on the provisions in the Act in 1976 which restrict alienation of the property.

Section 13 of the Act of 1976 states:–

Section 59 (2) of the Registration of Title Act, 1964 (which refers to noting upon the register provisions of any enactment restricting dealings in land) shall not apply to the provisions of this Act.

The reason why the defendants consider that the reply to their requisition is inadequate is that the property is now a family home within the meaning of the Act of 1976, and may have been a family home at the time of the transfer to the plaintiffs and their registration as owners on the 18th August, 1978. The defendants apprehend that Parsons may have been a married man so that, if the previous written consent of his wife had not been obtained, the transfer by him to the plaintiffs would have been in contravention of s. 3, sub-s. 1, of the Act of 1976 and, therefore, void as a conveyance. The defendants say that s. 31 of the Act of 1964 affords no protection in those circumstances. The plaintiffs claim that they were purchasers for valuable consideration and that they paid the full value of the property to Parsons and that, as there was no fraud involved, they were under no obligation to make enquiry of Parsons; and they rely on s. 3, sub-s. 3, of the Act of 1976. For the plaintiffs, Mr. Garland submits that such right as a spouse (who is not an owner) may have by virtue of the Act of 1976 is in the nature of a personal right only, that it is founded upon occupation, and that it is only enforceable against the spouse in whom title is vested and remains so enforceable in the event of s. 3 of the Act of 1976 applying to a purported transfer. He argues that, where one spouse is in occupation of property of which the other spouse is sole owner, the spouse without title has not the sort of right which constitutes a burden under s. 72, sub-s. 1 (*j*), of the Act of 1964. He further contends that s. 13 of the Act of 1976 expressly precludes s. 59 of the Act of 1964 from applying in a manner which would bring the provisions of the Act of 1976 within s. 72, sub-s. 1 (*q*), of the Act of 1964.

For the defendants, Mr. Brady submits that the registered owner can not transfer the property free from the burdens mentioned in s. 55, sub-s. 1 (*a*) and (*b*), of the Act of 1964 – nor from the terms of the lease, as indicated in paragraph (*c*) of that sub-section. He says that the registration of ownership is subject to those burdens and that the conclusiveness of the register as evidence of title, as provided in s. 31 of the Act of 1964, is also subject to those burdens. Paragraph (*b*) of s. 55, sub-s. 1, of that Act refers to s. 72 as specifying the burdens to which the interest of the owner is subject, whether they be registered or not, and paragraph (*q*) of s. 72, sub-s. 1, includes the burdens to which s. 59 applies. Mr. Brady submits that, whether the right of a spouse, not being an owner, to occupation of leasehold registered land be a personal right or not, the restrictions on alienation in protection of that right contained in s. 3, sub-s. 1, of the Act of 1976 are a burden within s. 59 of the Act of 1964. He argues that s. 13 of the Act of 1976 merely relieves the Registrar of Titles of the duty of noting on the register the restrictive provisions of that Act, but that, nevertheless, that section brings them to his attention. He also contends that upon the transfer from Parsons the plaintiffs, in relation to s. 3 of the Act of 1976, were obliged to make enquiry as to whether or not Parsons had a spouse whose consent would be required; and he says that the definitions in the Act of 1976 and the provisions in s. 3, sub-ss. 5, 6, and 7, thereof preclude them from relying on the absence of notice.

These arguments raise far-reaching questions of increasing significance in conveyancing practice and counsel have been unable to find precedents in reported Irish cases. Whether a wife residing with her husband could be said to be in actual occupation of the house in which they live was considered in the House of Lords in *National Provincial Bank Ltd.* v. *Ainsworth*. [1965] A.C. 1175. That was a case under s. 70, sub-s. 1, of the Land Registration Act, 1925, of which paragraph (*g*) corresponds with paragraph (*j*) of s. 72, sub-s. 1, of the Act of 1964. The reasoning in the opinions delivered in that case is compelling in support of the view that the right is a non-transmissible personal one and that it is not a proprietary one. The following is an extract from the opinion of Lord Cohen at p. 1228 of the report; it refers to s. 70, sub-s. 1 (*g*), of the Act of 1925 but it is equally appropriate to s. 72, sub-s. 1 (*j*), of the Act of 1964:–

> As Russell L.J. in the court below pointed out it is the rights of a person in occupation which constitute the over-riding interest not the mere fact of occupation, and I agree with Russell L.J. that section 70 is dealing in all its parts with rights in reference to land which have the quality of being capable of enduring through different ownerships of the land according to normal conceptions of title to real property. The right on which the respondent must rely is a personal right as against her husband and is not of the quality to which Russell L.J. refers. In my opinion, therefore, it does not constitute an over-riding interest within section 70(1) (*g*).

The definitions in s. 2 of the Act of 1976 may well have been drawn to confer on a spouse a more acceptable legal concept of interest in the family property than that to be found in the opinion of Lord Hodson in *Ainsworth's Case* [1965] A.C. 1175, at p. 1220 of the report. But the Act of 1976 does not create, nor invest a married person with, any right affecting land or property in the nature of an interest in land which could fall within any of the classification of burdens within s. 72, sub-s. 1, of the Act of 1964. Such right as is conferred is a right which affects the instrument of transfer and its validity. If that instrument is invalid, the transfer is ineffective; but the spouse for whose benefit the transfer is rendered ineffective obtains no estate or interest which can affect the ownership or title to the property described in the transfer. If the instrument of transfer be invalid, there can be no transmission of ownership. The purpose of the Act of 1976, and the nature of the right conferred on a non-consenting spouse who is not the owner of the property intended to be alienated, have been set out in the recent judgment of the Supreme Court in *Nestor* v. *Murphy.* [1979] I.R. 326.

[**Gannon, J.** quoted from Henchy, J.'s judgment in *Nestor* v *Murphy.* [1979] I.R. 326, *supra*, p. He continued:]

From this it is clear that a purported instrument of transfer to which s. 3, sub-s. 1, of the Act of 1976 applies is incapable of conferring any title to or interest in a property which is, or had been, a family home. But it is also clear from this statement that the circumstances which cause s. 3, sub-s. 1, of the Act of 1976 to apply depend on factors which do not relate to title, ownership, or conveyancing practices, and may arise in relation to some periods of ownership and not to others. The registered property may be a family home only if and when a married couple ordinarily reside in it, and it is then only that the restrictive provisions of s. 3 of the Act of 1976 would apply. These circumstances may change during the course of differing periods of registered ownership; over successive periods some registered owners may not be married, some may be married couples who may be joint owners. The right of a spouse under s. 3 of the Act of 1976 is not a burden within s. 72, sub-s. 1 (*j*), of the Act of 1964.

It should be noted that s. 72 of the Act of 1964 does not create burdens: it merely classifies burdens which are created *aliunde.* This is of importance in relation to paragraph (*q*) of s. 72, sub-s. 1, of the Act of 1964. That paragraph includes within s. 72, sub-s. 1, as burdens which though unregistered will affect the registered ownership, those burdens which are created by s. 59 or by section 73. In s. 59 the creation of the burden is effected in sub-s. 2, and in s. 73 the creation of the burden is effected in sub-section 3. Sub-section 1 of s. 59 of the Act of 1964 takes in the provisions of s. 3, sub-s. 1, of the Act of 1976 in all cases where that Act applies and, but for sub-s. 2 of s. 59, those provisions would not fall within either paragraph (*a*) or paragraph (*b*) of s. 55, sub-s. 1, of the Act of 1964. Likewise, the restrictions and prohibitions contained in the *Land Acts* of 1923, 1939, 1946 and 1965 come within the ambit of sub-s. 1 of s. 59 and are created burdens within s. 72, sub-s. 1 (*q*), by s. 59, sub-s. 2, of the Act of 1964 without the aid of any specific sections in the Land Acts.

But the Act of 1976 has a specific section which appears to have misled the defendants; that section is s. 13 of the Act of 1976. Notwithstanding the parenthesis contained in s. 13 of the Act of 1976, the non-application of s. 59, sub-s. 2, of the Act of 1964 there expressed comprises the entire of that sub-section. Sub-section 2 of s. 59 has two distinct provisions and s. 13 of the Act of 1976 does not state that it excludes only one of them. Sub-section 2 of s. 59 imposes a duty on the registrar and it creates burdens; if it were intended that s. 13 of the Act of 1976 should do no more than relieve the registrar of the duty, then s. 13 would have said so in clear terms.

That s. 13 of the Act of 1976 was intended to take the provisions of that Act out of the scope of s. 59, sub-s. 2, and s. 72 of the Act of 1964 is understandable when the provisions of s. 3, sub-ss. 3 and 5–7, of the Act of 1976 are considered. In *Somers* v. *W.* [1979] I.R. 94 the effect of these sub-sections has been pointed out by the Supreme Court as increasing the burden of imputed notice to a purchaser. . . .

When the *Supreme Court of Judicature Act (Ireland) 1877*, brought the rules of equity into play in all courts, the equitable doctrine of notice was given supremacy. Further, it was given statutory expression in s. 3 of the *Conveyancing Act, 1882*. . . .

That s. 3 of the Act of 1976 is to be operated within this doctrine of notice is emphasised by the fact that sub-s. 7 of that section amends s. 3 of the Act of 1882 by deleting from it the above italicised words, thus extending the reach of constructive notice.

But the purpose of the registration of title under the scheme formerly provided by the Acts of 1891 and 1942, and now by the Act of 1964, is to avoid the application of the equitable doctrine of constructive or imputed notice: see *In re Walsh* [1916] 1 I.R. 40. It is provided at s. 31, sub-s. 1, of the Act of 1964 (which I have already quoted) that the register shall be conclusive evidence of the title of the owner to the land as appearing on the register and of any burden on it as appearing thereon and that, in the absence of fraud, that title shall not be affected in any way in consequence of the owner having notice of any deed, document, or matter relating to the land. Sections 55 and 72 of the Act of 1964 prescribe the manner of giving notice of interests adversely affecting ownership of the property transmitted to new ownership. There are provisions for rectification of the register and s. 97, sub-s. 1, of the Act of 1964 enables any person entitled to any right in, to, or over registered land or a registered charge, on producing an affidavit in a prescribed form of his right, to lodge a caution with the registrar to the effect that no dealing with the land or charge is to be had on the part of the registered owner until notice has been served on that person.

If s. 13 of the Act of 1976 had been omitted from that Act, the provisions of s. 59, sub-s. 2, of the Act of 1964 would apply to each transfer of registered land when the circumstances required the application of ss. 2 and 3 of the Act of 1976, and would cease to apply to the same lands when such circumstances ceased to exist. In that situation the doctrine of constructive notice, in its strictest application under s. 3, sub-ss. 3, 6 and 7, of the Act of 1976, would apply in some circumstances, but not in others, to the same registered title. That would defeat the purpose of the Act of 1964 and make its provisions highly impractical. In my opinion s. 13 of the Act of 1976 says and means that in relation to registered land the provisions of that Act which are restrictive of alienation are not burdens created by s. 59 of the Act of 1964 and do not come within s. 72, sub-s. 1 (*q*), of that Act.

In the result I am of opinion that on every sale of registered land where circumstances may indicate that it would be prudent for an intending purchaser to make enquiries such as are indicated in the *Family Home Protection Act, 1976*, those enquiries should be made in relation to the particular intended contract of sale and the intended instrument of transfer to the intending purchaser; but it is my opinion that beyond that the intending purchaser need not and should not go. That is to say, the provisions of s. 31, sub-s. 1, of the *Registration of Title Act, 1964*, afford a sufficient protection of the vendor and the intending purchaser in relation to all prior transactions affecting the registered ownership as appearing on the title. The duty of ensuring that any instrument of transfer is valid and effective, so as to enable a transmission of ownership to be duly registered, falls upon the registar at the time of the registration. Thereafter, in the absence of fraud, the register affords conclusive evidence of the validity of the title.

Accordingly, I think it appropriate in this case to make the order sought and to declare that the requisition referred to has been sufficiently answered by the plaintiffs as vendors.

Note
The decision is analysed by Brady in [1981] Dublin U.L.J. 86.

When is a refusal by a spouse to consent to a disposition unreasonable?

R. v. R.

Unreported, High Court, McMahon, J., 8 December 1978 (1978–574Sp.)

McMahon J.:

. . . The husband has brought a Special Summons pursuant to Section 4 [of the] *Family Home Protection Act, 1976* for an Order dispensing with the wife's consent to mortgaging the husband's interest in the family home. The parties were married in 1960 and they have lived since their marriage in a Dublin suburb. There are three daughters, the only children in the marriage, aged seventeen, sixteen and thirteen. The husband has a position as personnel services manager in a large organisation. The marriage has not been a happy one for several years and for the past year the husband has occupied a separate bedroom in the family home. These proceedings have been commenced because the husband intends to leave the family home and to live separately leaving his wife and children to occupy the family home. The husband has formed an attachment with another woman. It is quite clear from my observa[tion] of the parties in giving evidence that any affection which existed between them has ceased and the wife regards the husband's departure with indifference provided she and the children are adequately provided for. The purpose of the husband's application is to raise sufficient money by a mortgage of the family home to enable him to pay off some pressing Bank debts and to have some funds available to start up in a flat or other dwelling. The husband's finances are such that it is doubtful whether any arrangement will enable him to maintain himself separately from the family. His net income, after deduction of income tax and social welfare contributions is £6,116 per annum. He owes a sum of £4,100 on short term bank loans repayable over the next two years at the rate of £2,184 per annum. There is an existing mortgage on the family home and the amount outstanding is £2,184 and it is repayable at the rate of £436 per annum. The husband's proposal is that he should be permitted to raise a sum of £8,500 by a mortgage of the family home and that sum would be applied to the repayment of the outstanding bank loans and of the existing mortgage which would absorb a sum of £6,477. The husband proposes that he should have the balance of the £8,500 for his own use.

The wife's objection to this proposal is that the house is the husband's only asset and he is not entitled to any pension on retirement at the age of 65 except a Contributory Social Welfare pension. The wife therefore is concerned that the only source for her support and maintenance when the husband ceases to earn should not be diminished. She alleges that the husband has always been extravagant and has no idea of the value of money. The husband agrees that he has spent a disproportionate amount of his income on entertainment and dining out, but he claims that the organisation for which he works makes this necessary as a matter of preserving his contacts and status. The husband says that his proposal for a mortgage has been worked out on the advice of his bank manager and that the Building Society is prepared to advance the money which will be repayable over a period of ten years at the rate of £1,200 per year.

Under Section 4 of the *Family Home Protection Act, 1976* the Court cannot dispense with the wife's consent to the husband raising a mortgage on the family home unless the Court considers that it is unreasonable for the wife to withhold consent taking into account all the circumstances including the needs and resources of the wife and the dependent children. I propose to deal first with the wife's claim for maintenance because until the amount of weekly maintenance is fixed it cannot be seen whether the husband will have sufficient income left to support himself living separately from the family and to pay off the mortgage instalments.

The wife's evidence on what she required for maintenance of herself and her family struck me as being reasonable. She said she could manage on £50.00 per week though she might be in some trouble if emergencies arose such as illness of the children. This is on the basis that the husband paid all outgoings of the family home, but the wife says that if she were paid the amount which the husband reckons is required for paying for central heating oil, gas and electricity, that she could save money on that. That expenditure amounts to £450 per annum according to the husband's reckoning. I have come to the conclusion that the husband has over-estimated these amounts and that the proper sum to allow for maintenance of the wife and three children is £55 per week on the basis that the husband pays all outgoings of the family home except the cost of central heating oil, gas and electricity and any other fuel. This will leave the husband liable for mortgage repayments, and maintenance and repairs of the home, the ground rent, fire and householder's insurance and the rental of the television set, the television licence and the charges for piped television service. Excluding maintenance and repairs and mortgage repayments, these sums amount to £140 in round figures. The family home is a relatively new house and I take £60 per annum as a reasonable sum to allow for repairs. The husband should also continue to pay V.H.I. subscription which is at present £187. That means that the husband will have to find a sum of about £3,200 a year over and above any mortgage repayments in order to provide for the support and maintenance of his wife and children. If the mortgage repayments amount to £1,200 per year this leaves the husband, out of his net income, a sum of £1,700 for his own support which includes accommodation. Having regard to the standard of living which the husband's position requires him to maintain. I do not think that this sum would be sufficient for the husband's support and it would involve a substantial risk that he would not be able to keep up with the mortgage repayments. I have taken into account the prospect that the husband's earnings may increase as a result of inflation but I think it would be entirely speculation to assume that the increase would be sufficient materially to improve his prospect of paying off the mortgage repayments. I have also considered what his position would be if the Court were to sanction the mortgage for a smaller amount sufficient merely to repay the short-term bank loans but I do not think his ability to repay the mortgage would be appreciably improved. I have therefore come to the conclusion that the husband's financial liabilities are of such an amount that if funded by way of a mortgage repayable over a period of ten years he would not have sufficient income to live on himself and to give a reasonable prospect of keeping up the mortgage repayments. If he succeeds in paying off the short-term bank loans over the next two years the situation may well be different but I must deal with the situation as it is. In the circumstances I cannot hold that the wife's refusal to consent to the husband's proposal for a mortgage is unreasonable.

Notes

1. Do you agree with the judgment in this case?
2. Where does the decision leave the husband, so far as it concerns his ability to maintain himself separate from the family? Would you have wished to know more about the financial implications of the husband's attachment with another woman? How does this decision compare with *O'K.* v. *O'K.*, unreported, High Court, Barron, J., 16 November 1982 (1982–424Sp.).
3. See also Costello, J.'s dissenting judgment in *Hamilton* v. *Hamilton,* [1982] I.R. 466, at 488ff.

Section 5 Proceedings

E.D. v. F.D.

Unreported, High Ct., Costello, J., 23 October 1980 (1979–26Sp.)

[The facts have already been set out *supra*, p. 201 in relation to maintenance. On the subject of the *Family Home Protection Act, 1976*, **Costello, J.** said:]

The plaintiff is very apprehensive as to what may happen to her family home and I have been asked to make an order under Section 5 of the *Family Home Protection Act, 1976* transferring the family home into her name. The Defendant owes a considerable sum of money in this country. He owes £4,186 to [one b]lank; £1,400 approximately to [another b]ank; £2,300 to [an insurance company], £200 to [a travel agency]. He has been sued in the past and the sheriff has come to his home to enforce the judgments. He has allowed ejectment proceedings to be instituted for possession by the mortgagors of his family home. He has paid no Irish income tax since 1973. A visitor called recently to the Plaintiff enquiring about his whereabouts in respect of his income tax liability. He has been assessed in the sum of £10,000 in respect of back tax, but he claims, that the Revenue Official with whom he has been in touch has accepted that he has little or no liability to tax. He has paid no British tax, notwithstanding the high earnings to which I have referred over the past couple of years. He has an overdraft with his [English] Bank of cover £12,000, but he claims that the Bank is not pressing that it be reduced.

It was urged on his behalf that the court has no power to make the transfer order which the Plaintiff seeks. I cannot agree as I think that the section gives a very wide discretion to the court. But it can only be exercised when the Court is satisfied that the spouse is acting with the intention of depriving the applicant spouse or a dependent child of the family of her or his residence in the family home. It has to be said that the Defendant has for sometime acted in an improvident way. He has leased until recently an extremely expensive car; he stays on holidays in the most expensive hotels; he runs accounts in one of the most expensive mens shops in Regent Street; he entertains on a considerable scale. At the same time he allows his mortgage payments to fall into arrears so that ejectment proceedings are instituted against the family home, and he makes no effort to pay off the very substantial debts he has incurred, and runs up further ones. But I do not think that he has acted with the intention referred to in the section, and so I do not propose now to make an order under it.

The situation is, however, a serious one and the Plaintiff has every right to feel apprehensive for herself and her children. Section 11 of the Guardianship of Infants Act, 1964 confers wide powers to protect the infant's welfare and I propose to order that the Defendant should enter into negotiations with his creditors with a view to arranging a means of re-paying the sums due; that he enters into negotiations with the Revenue authorities of this country and the United Kingdom with a view to ascertaining his tax liabilities; and discharging them; that on request he informs the Plaintiff's solicitors of the progress of the negotiations and makes available on request correspondence in relation to them and particulars of his current earnings and copies of his Bank statements. There will be liberty to renew the application under section 5 if thought fit.

As to the committal motion, I accept the Plaintiff's evidence that the Defendant had threatened to reduce deliberately his income, but he has sworn that he did not in fact carry out his threat when he gave up [part of his work] contract with [employer A] and his . . . contract [with employer B] in June of this year and I am prepared to accept his word. As it appears that somewhat belatedly he is taking steps to adopt a more realistic life-style and face up to his family responsibilities I do not propose to make any order on the motion, other than one for costs. The Defendant must also pay the cost of the action, including costs which may have been reserved by any previous order.

Notes

1. In subsequent proceedings over a year later, on 16 December 1981, Costello, J. made an order under section 5 of the *Family Home Protection Act, 1976*, directing the husband to execute a conveyance to the wife of the family home. It appears that 'none of [Costello, J.'s] directions [had been] complied with during the . . . year [following the first hearing;] the judge then held that the intention required by . . . subsection (1) [of section 5] had been established . . .': *S.* v. *S.*, [1983] I.L.R.M. 387, at 389–390 (High Ct., McWilliam, J.). See also *C.P.* v. *D.P.*, [1983] I.L.R.M., 380, at 384–385 (High Ct., Finlay, P., 1982).
2. It is interesting that in dealing with the family home, Costello, J. should have stressed the needs of the children rather than the deserted spouse. Some groups supporting divorced men and the parties to second marriages tend to oppose the policy of actively protecting the wife and children's occupation of the family home. In England, the Campaign for Justice in Divorce have criticised the courts for placing:

> an exaggerated and unfair emphasis on the needs of children when decisions are made on the disposal of assets, particularly the matrimonial home and contents . . . *An Even Better Way Out*, para. 29 (May 1979).

This philosophy appears to have found some favour with the Scottish Law Commission. In a strikingly similar passage in its Report on maintenance (*Family Law: Report on Aliment and Financial Provision*, para. 3.83 (Scot. Law Com. No. 67, 1981)), the Commission expresses the view that:

> There is a danger that the supposed needs of children (who, after all, often have to move house and suffer a drop in living standards even in unbroken families) could be used to justify results which would be unfair to one of the spouses.

C.P. v. D.P.

[1983] I.L.R.M. 380 (High Ct., Finlay, P., 1982)

Finlay, P.:

. . . The parties married in 1970 and there are two children of the marriage, a daughter born in February 1971 and a son born in January 1974. Differences arose in the marriage and the parties agreed to separate and entered into an agreement in March 1980 under which it was agreed that the wife should have custody of the children subject to reasonable access by the husband; that the family home which was situated in Co. Wicklow should be sold by the husband as soon as a reasonable price could be obtained; that he should move out of it on 1 April 1980; that the wife should continue to reside there with the children, and should eventually consent to the sale of the family home; that in the meantime she should be paid reasonable maintenance, and that the husband should continue to discharge the outgoings that he had been discharging in respect of the family home. It was also provided that a further agreement would be entered into prior to the sale of the property concerning the division between the husband and the wife of the proceeds of the family home but that in the event of the agreement as to the application of those proceeds not being made that that agreement of March 1980 should terminate. Subsequent to that agreement, the husband did leave the family home and the wife continued with the two children to reside there for some time.

In January 1981, the parties entered into a further agreement. This recited that it was supplemental to the agreement already made and should be read with it. It was further recited that the wife had agreed to leave the family home pending its sale and reside in rented accommodation elsewhere and that the husband had agreed to reside in the family home pending its sale. It further provided that the husband should pay to the wife the sum of £139.00 per week, payment to commence on 20 October 1980 and to be reviewed on or about 20 April 1981. This agreement did not provide for any arrangement concerning the application of the proceeds of the sale of the family home. Upon the execution of that agreement, the wife left the family home with the two children and resided in rented accommodation successively in two different locations in Co. Wicklow. The husband returned to the family home and the position at the time the action came before me for hearing was that the wife was residing in rented accommodation in Wicklow with the children and the husband residing in the family home. . . .

The plaintiff offered no evidence which would entitle me to reach any conconclusion that she was entitled to any beneficial interest in the family home. She has not since the marriage worked or earned outside the family home nor did she subscribe out of any separate monies or income any sum towards the erection of the family home which was built by the defendant nor towards the acquisition of it or any property in it. The claim under that Act must therefore be dismissed.

It is necessary first to determine the claim of the wife to a transfer pursuant to the Family Home Protection Act of the family home since obviously depending upon that issue different considerations may apply to the appropriate amount of maintenance to be paid by the husband to the wife. The husband and wife have not agreed on any application of the proceeds of the sale of the family home nor has any sale of the family home been negotiated or provided for. There is not at present before me any application by the husband to dispense with the consent of the wife to the sale of the family home.

The claim of the wife to transfer of ownership of the family home pursuant to the Family Home Protection Act is based on the following facts and submissions. It is alleged by the wife that the husband has deposited the title deeds of the family home with a bank to secure overdrafts obtained by him, both apparently a personal overdraft and the overdraft of his professional firm of architects of which he was up to recently a partner and is now the sole proprietor. It is also alleged that he has other substantial unsecured debts including debts in relation to arrears of income tax, arrears of VAT tax arising out of the architectural practice and other miscellaneous debts, and it was submitted on behalf of the wife that the husband is engaging in such conduct as may lead to the loss of the family home with the intention of depriving the wife and the dependent children of their residence in it; that therefore the provisions of s. 5 sub-s. 1 of the *Family Home Protection Act, 1976* become operative, and that the order which I should make under the discretion vested in me by that sub-section should be to direct the husband for the protection of the family home in the interest of the wife and of the children to transfer the legal ownership in it to her.

On the evidence I find the facts concerning this issue to be as follows. The defendant has been at all times an architect who though not professionally qualified has carried on a relatively successful business as an architect for many years in X. Up to very recently he did so in partnership with one other person. The general nature of his business largely consisted of residential building work. I am satisfied on the evidence that the recession in the building trade recently experienced all over the country has affected the extent of his business. I am also satisfied that disputes between himself and his partner which have led to a recent dissolution of the partnership have probably also adversely affected the extent of his earnings. As a result of that and, as the inevitable result as so often happens of a separation and the necessity to maintain two households, the husband, I am satisfied, is now substantially in debt. It is not necessary for the purpose of the decision on this issue to ascertain with precision the total extent of his indebtedness, but broadly speaking he has a liability to discharge the overdraft of the former partnership which is probably in a sum in excess of £6,000, he probably has a tax liability for arrears in the region of £5,000 and he owes a total of £11,000 on two separate personal bank overdrafts. It appears to me improbable on the evidence that the extent of his other miscellaneous liabilities is less than £2,000.

The case made on behalf of the wife was that the accrual of these debts and in particular the lodging which recently took place by the husband of the deeds of the family home as security for the bank overdrafts constituted a course of conduct on his part which would lead to the loss of the family home, and that I should presume that he so intended. In part, this submission was based on an allegation that the defendant in asserting the figures and creating the debts which I have broadly outlined was concealing substantial earnings, and must have assets other than the family home in a sense secreted and acquired out of greater earnings than his expenditure over the last two or three years would indicate. I have very carefully considered and investigated this allegation and I am satisfied that the defendant and the accountant called on his behalf have between them given me a truthful and substantially complete account of both the husband's earnings and the extent of his indebtedness and of his total assets. The husband admits that in addition to the family home he has got furniture other than the general furnishings of a normal home consisting of antique furniture and *objets d'art* which he inherited, which he says, he considers to be in trust for his children though no express or legal trust appears to apply to them, and which are valued at approximately £12,000. Apart from that, he asserts that he has no other assets, investments, deposit accounts or other property other than the family home. This evidence, I accept. It would appear to me that since there is clear evidence that the wife did not consent in writing to the deposit of the title deeds by way of equitable mortgage against the bank indebtedness that, having regard to the provisions of the *Family Home Protection Act, 1976*, that equitable mortgage was a void conveyance within the meaning of those terms as set out in the Act, and that accordingly the bank could not immediately lawfully realise their interest as mortgagee. Having regard to the judgment of Carroll J in *Containercare v W. and Another* 1981 No. 341 Sp, 25 November 1981 however this is a distinctly academic point as the bank can with expedition if it so wishe[s] sue for the recovery of the monies due to it and register such judgment as a judgment mortgage against the defendant's interest in the premises.

There can be no doubt, therefore, that the present state of the husband's finances leads to a significant danger of the loss of the present family home though since the estimates of the value of those premises range between £60,000 and £70,000 it would not be a total loss but merely the sale of it and the realisation of a substantially reduced net proceeds.

The question which must arise, however, is as to whether there is evidence before me on which I would be entitled to hold in the words of s. 5 sub-s. 1 of the Family Home Protection Act, 1976 that the husband was:–

> engaging in such conduct as may lead to the loss of any interest in the family home . . . with the intention of depriving the applicant spouse or a dependent child of the family of his residence in the family home.

It has been submitted to me that I should construe the word 'intention' in this sub-section as not being equivalent with motive, but rather with the 'intention' which may be imputed to any person as to the natural and probable consequences of their conduct. As part of this submission and as part of the general submission on behalf of the wife on this issue, I have been referred to a judgment delivered by Costello J on 16 December 1981 in *E.D. v F.D.* in which he made an order under s. 5 of the Act of 1976 directing the husband to execute a conveyance to the wife of a family home which was in his sole name.

After careful consideration, I am satisfied that I cannot construe the word 'intention' in s. 5 sub-s. 1 of the Act of 1976 as being equivalent to the implied or imputed intention which can arise from the natural and probable consequences of an act or omission. There must, in my view, as was found as a fact in the case of *E.D. v F.D.* by Costello J be an element of deliberate conduct. I have come to this view as to the interpretation of s. 5 sub-s. 1 largely by comparing the terms of that section with s. 5 sub-s. 2 of the same Act. The latter sub-section which applies to the situation where a family home has been lost reads as follows:

> where it appears to the court, on the application of a spouse, that the other spouse has deprived the applicant spouse or a dependent child of the family of his residence in the family home by conduct that resulted in the loss of any interest therein or rendered it unsuitable for habitation as a family home, the court may order the other spouse or any other person to pay to the applicant spouse such amount as the court considers proper to compensate the applicant spouse . . .

It seems clear to me that if the Legislature had intended by the use of the words 'with the intention of depriving the applicant spouse' in s. 5 sub-s. 1 to involve only conduct the natural and probable consequences of which would be to deprive the applicant spouse that having regard to the terms of sub-s. 2 where the conduct that has actually resulted in the loss of a family home gives rise to the discretion of the court, that the word 'intention' would also have been used in that sub-section. To put the matter in another way, having regard to the terms of s. 5 sub-s. 2 if 'intention' were to mean only a conscious or deliberate act the natural and probable consequences of which would be the loss of the family home in sub-s. 1 of s. 5 it would be quite an unnecessary proviso and quite an unnecessary phrase.

On the evidence in this case, I am not satisfied that there is any deliberateness in the sense of that word which I think must be equated with the concept of intention in the sub-section referred to on the part of the husband, in the acts and omissions which have occurred in the last few years and which do present a risk to the loss of an interest in the family home. I believe he has been struggling though possibly unsuccessfully with a difficult professional situation and with mounting debts arising in the way which I have outlined already in this judgment. I am therefore not satisfied that I would be entitled to make at this time any order under s. 5 of the Family Home Protection Act, 1976 in favour of the wife, and I must refuse at present at least to make any such order.

Quite clearly the future financial interests of this family necessitate the earliest possible sale of the present family home which is unsuitable for the housing of either the wife and children or of the husband by reason of its size and the cost of its maintenance and upkeep. By far the most desirable thing is that they should agree upon effecting such a sale with the necessary agreement as to the application of the proceeds of the sale, hopefully using those for the purpose of providing a stable and secure family home for the wife and children and proper accommodation separately for the husband. If they cannot agree upon that, and if the husband, as it seems to me he must, seeks to sell the family home otherwise than by agreement this is clearly a case in which conditions as to the provision of alternative suitable accommodation for the wife and children will seriously arise for the court to consider as a requirement for granting any order dispensing with the wife's consent. . . .

Notes

1. For Finlay, P.'s consideration of the issue of maintenance, see *supra*, pp. 207–8.
2. See also *In the Matter of G.C. & K.C. Infants: D.C.* v. *A.C.*, High Ct., Carroll, J., 7 May 1981 (1980–693Sp.) (reported [1981] I.L.R.M. 357 on a separate issue – see *supra*, p. 302). The husband was extravagant in spending money on himself and failed to make the mortgage repayments, after the first two payments. The wife found out about this seven months later. She persuaded her husband to leave the home shortly afterwards. The husband made no further repayments on the mortgage. The wife sought an order under section 5(1) that the family home, which was in the joint names of the spouses, be transferred into her sole name. Miss Justice Carroll declined to make the order under section 5(1) considering that to do so 'would have the effect of divesting the husband of a valuable asset (i.e. his joint interest in the surplus moneys realised on sale) at a time when both he and his wife have considerable debts incurred in the course of their marriage for their living expenses.' She was however, satisfied that:–

   > the phrase 'engaging in such conduct' covers inactivity as well as activity. The Act does not specify that the spouse must have 'done such acts'. In my opinion the husband's failure to pay the mortgage instalments can be described as engaging in such conduct as may lead to the loss of and interest in the family home.

   Miss Justice Carroll made no reference to the question of intention. An interesting aspect of the decision is that Miss Justice Carroll said that she was prepared to make an order under section 5(2) if the family home was in fact sold, as seemed likely. She indicated in some detail the type of order she would make.
3. Would a *Mareva* injunction be a useful supplement to an application under section 5(1)? Cf. Charleton, *Family Law – Mareva Injunctions*, 4 Dublin U.L.J. 114 (1982). A more general, wider ranging injunctive power was asserted in respect of marital property in the New York decision of *Froelich-Switzer* v. *Switzer*, 107 Misc. 2d 814, 436 N.Y.S. 2d 123 (Sup. Ct., N.Y.Co., 1980). This approach has proved controversial: see Bronstein, *Family Law*, 34 Syracuse L. Rev. 299, at 316–318 (1983).

S. v. S.

[1983] I.L.R.M. 387 (High Ct., McWilliam, J.)

McWilliam, J.:

The plaintiff seeks an order under s. 5 sub-s. 1, of the *Family Home Protection Act, 1976,* protecting the interests of the plaintiff and her two young children in the family home in Co. X.

The summons, dated 8 October 1982, contained several other claims relating to the family home, including a claim that the plaintiff is entitled to an interest in the family home, but the only claim pursued on the hearing before me was for an order transferring the family home to the plaintiff.

The plaintiff and the defendant were married in July, 1977, and their two children are now aged two and a half years and eight months respectively. The family home was purchased in 1977, and, on the only evidence before me, that of the plaintiff, the deposit was paid jointly by the parties and the conveyance was taken in the joint names. I have not seen the relevant conveyance.

A firm owned and controlled by the defendant and a friend of his collapsed in 1980 and the plaintiff is unable to say what occupations were taken up by the defendant from that time onwards although he went out each day as though going to work and, at the weekends, provided money for the upkeep of the household. The plaintiff believes that he became involved with a night club in some capacity and also with some form of travel agency. She states that he refused at all times to discuss his financial affairs with her and that any questions by her on the subject gave rise to unpleasant scenes, but she also states that violence was not a feature of the marriage.

It appears that, in June, 1982, a representative of Allied Irish Banks Ltd called to the family home and stated, that because of the defendant's severe financial difficulties, the family home would have to be sold. Almost immediately afterwards the family left the family home to stay for a few days with the defendant's family in Co. Y. The defendant left Co. Y. after a few days stating that he was going to Dublin to meet a friend. From that time the plaintiff has not seen or heard from the defendant and she has been informed that his parents have not heard from him either. When the plaintiff returned to the family home she found that all the defendant's belongings and his passport had been removed and she believes that he has left the country.

As the plaintiff did not receive any post after her return to the family home she made inquiries at the post office and was informed that the post office had received written notification that all post should be sent to an address in Collins Avenue. An order for substituted service at this address was made by the court and the summons was served at that address. There has not been any appearance by or on behalf of the defendant.

Subsequently the plaintiff ascertained that there were and still are very considerable sums of money being claimed from the defendant by various creditors and that an investigation has been under way with regard to possible criminal offences.

[**McWilliam, J.** quoted section 5(1) of the Act. He continued:]

I was referred to the case of *E.D. v F.D.* in which Costello J considered the application of this subsection. He said, at page 8 of his judgment delivered on 23 October 1980,

> It was urged on his (the defendant's) behalf that the court has no power to make the transfer order which the plaintiff seeks. I cannot agree as I think that the section gives a very wide discretion to the court. But it can only be exercised when the court is satisfied that the spouse is acting with the intention of depriving the applicant spouse or a dependent child of the family of her or his residence in the family home. It has to be said that the defendant has for some time acted in a very improvident way. He has leased until recently an extremely expensive car; he runs accounts in one of the most expensive men's shops in Regent Street; he entertains on a considerable scale. At the same time he allows his mortgage payments to fall into arrears so that ejectment proceedings are instituted against the family home, and he makes no effort to pay off the very substantial debts he has incurred, and runs up further ones. But I do not think he has acted with the intention referred to in the section, and so I do not propose now to make an order under it.

In that case the defendant had very considerable earnings and the judge gave certain directions with regard to the steps to be taken by the defendant and, as none of these directions were complied with during the following year, the judge then held that the intention required by the subsection had been established and directed that a conveyance of the family home be made to the plaintiff.

I was also referred to the judgment of the President of the High Court delivered on 21 December 1981, in the case of *O'M. v O'M.* He said, at page 5,

> I must come to the conclusion therefore that the defendant's failure to work, failure to make any income and his consequent failure which has gone on now for a number of years to make any mortgage repayments on the house in Lucan which leaves it in a relatively immediate peril of being sold by the mortgagees who are the First National Building Society is a conscious and deliberate act intended to deprive his wife and children of the use of that house or of any alternative house which might result from selling it and purchasing another. In these circumstances, I am satisfied that s. 5 does become operable and that under the terms of it I have a wide discretion as to the order I can make.

In that case there was an application by the husband for an order dispensing with the consent of the wife to the sale of the family home and the President set out terms upon which this consent would be dispensed with.

I have also considered the judgment of the President of the High Court delivered on 27 May 1982, in a case of *C.P. v D.P.* in which, having considered the judgment of Costello, J., to which I have referred, he said:–

> After careful consideration, I am satisfied that I cannot construe the word 'intention' in s. 5 sub-s. 1 of the Act as being equivalent to the implied or imputed intention which can arise from the natural and probable consequences of an act or omission. There must, in my view, as was found as a fact in the case of *E.D. v F.D.* by Costello, J. be an element of deliberate conduct. I have come to this view as to the interpretation of s. 5 sub-s. 1 largely by comparing the terms of that subsection with s. 5 sub-s. 2 of the same Act.

In the present case the defendant appears to have looked after his wife and children to the best of his ability, possibly to a large extent with borrowed money. Although he may have acted improvidently and, possibly, dishonestly, and the natural and probable consequences of his actions may have been that the family home would be a target for his various creditors, it appears to me that it is unlikely that he formed any intention of depriving his wife and children of their residence in the family home and that it is much more likely that he left the country to escape the attentions of his creditors and other more distressing pursuers.

Accordingly, I must refuse to make the order sought.

Incidentally, if the statement in the plaintiff's affidavit is correct and she is the joint owner of one moiety of the family home, the order sought could only relate to the other moiety.

Notes

1. Cf. O'Connor, *Section 5 of the Family Home Protection Act*, 1 Ir. L.T. (n.s.) 132, at 133 (1983):

> Is there not a basis for arguing that a court should be able to intervene and make such order as it thinks proper when the conduct complained of, when objectively viewed, might lead to the loss of the family home (or any interest therein)? A husband, for example, may not, himself, have formed the intention of depriving his family of their residence in the family home. Yet his conduct, from the financial point of view, might be foolhardy and irresponsible and be such as to constitute a substantial risk to the security of the family home. He may, for example, wish to borrow money in order to satisfy a desire to gamble or be able to borrow in order to invest in some risky enterprise. It is submitted, given the social interest in seeing that a family be secure in the matrimonial home, that an objective determination of intention is preferable.

Do you agree? Could it be argued that it would be wrong to impose on the courts the task of assessing prospectively the wisdom or otherwise of business ventures?

2. Cf. *C.M.C.B.* v. *S.B.*, unreported, High Ct., Barron, J. 17 May 1983 (1980–247Sp.). Section 5(1) was held to apply where husband had:

> gone from one financial folly to another and regrettably . . . put his obligations to his wife and children at the bottom of his list of priorities, so much so that he . . . actively indulged in conduct which could only have been calculated to achieve the end of paying her nothing and ultimately of losing his interest in the family home.

Barron, J. stressed that one financial transaction by the husband 'was ill-advised'. As to his failure to continue his building business, '[t]he reality, painful though it may be lies in his own character, he is just unable to organise his own affairs.'

It may be argued that in spite of the word 'calculated' and a later reference to allegations that the husband was taking steps to 'endanger deliberately' his interest in the family home, the picture presented by the evidence was of incompetence or perhaps recklessness rather than of an intention to deprive the wife and children of their occupation of the home.

A.C. v. D.D. & IRISH NATIONWIDE BUILDING SOCIETY

Unreported, High Ct., McWilliam, J., 8 June 1983 (1980–994Sp.)

McWilliam, J.:

The Plaintiff and D.D., the Husband, were married on 29th May, 1974. There were three children of the marriage. Until 1979, the family lived in premises owned by a company of which the Husband was one of the directors. At the beginning of 1979 the Husband and members of his family purchased for the sum of £98,000 a holding of 32 acres approximately which included a house which became the family home of the parties to this proceeding. This family home and eight acres were conveyed to the Husband who was registered in the Land Registry as full owner on 20th February, 1980, but it appears that the family had moved into the family home in or about January, 1979. The details of the transaction are not clear to me, but it appears that the Husband was to contribute a sum of £45,000 for the purchase of the family home, of which £30,000 was to be borrowed from the Defendant Building Society and £15,000 was borrowed from his mother. The sum of £30,000 was borrowed from the Building Society and a mortgage dated 6th February, 1980, was executed by the Husband and the Plaintiff endorsed her consent on it. This mortgage provided for monthly repayments of £481.00. No repayments were made at any time.

The Plaintiff and the Husband separated in March, 1980, when the Plaintiff left the family home and has since been living in Dublin in a house owned by her brother. These proceedings were commenced by special summons issued against the Husband alone on 12th November, 1980. By this summons claims were made for custody of the children, for maintenance, for a barring order against the Husband, for a declaration that the Plaintiff was entitled to the beneficial ownership of the entire of the family home or of such percentage as the Court might determine, and for an order for the sale of the family home.

On 4th May, 1981, the parties entered into a consent which was received and filed in Court and the action was adjourned generally with liberty to re-enter. One of the terms of the consent was that the Husband would expedite the sale of the family home and pay the balance of the purchase price remaining, after the discharge of the amount due to the Building Society, to the solicitor for the Plaintiff to be invested in a house for the use of the Plaintiff and her children during her lifetime with remainder to the children absolutely.

As no repayments were made at any time on foot of the mortgage and the premises were not sold by the Husband, the Building Society issued proceedings against him by summons dated 5th July, 1982, an Order for possession was made in those proceedings on 26th July, 1982, and the premises were subsequently sold for £48,000, which was less than the sum then due to the Building Society, so that there was no surplus to be applied to the purchase of a house for the Plaintiff. It appears that there was some confusion at the hearing of the application for the order for possession in that the Plaintiff was represented before the Master of the High Court and an objection to an order was made on her behalf although the Husband consented to the order being made. The matter then came into the Judge's list and was heard at the end of a very long list in the absence of the solicitor for the Plaintiff and the order was made on the consent of the Husband.

On 3rd September, 1982, on an application on behalf of the Plaintiff, the Building Society was joined as a Defendant in these proceedings and an interim injunction was granted restraining the Building Society from selling the family home. This was followed by an application on notice to the Defendants for Orders giving the Plaintiff liberty to amend the special summons by including a claim under section 5 of the *Family Home Protection Act, 1976,* for the protection of the family home, requiring the Husband to discharge all arrears due on foot of the mortgage, joining the Building Society as a Defendant and preventing the Building Society from taking any steps on foot of the Order for Possession obtained on 26th July, 1982. On 29th September, 1982, the application for an order restraining the Building Society from selling the family home was refused and the other matters were adjourned. Further applications were made on behalf of the Plaintiff and the summons, as it now appears before me, was amended to include a claim against the Husband under the provisions of the Act of 1976, for compensation for the loss of the family home, a claim against both Defendants for damages for the sale of the family home, and a declaration that the Order of 26th July, 1982, was obtained co[l]lusively by the Defendants in breach of the Plaintiff's rights and is null and void and of no effect.

As I understand the arguments advanced on behalf of the Plaintiff, they are as follows:–

1. The Plaintiff's consent to the mortgage was invalid. This appears to be based on the fact that the Husband was then an agent for the Building Society and on an allegation that the Plaintiff gave her consent to the mortgage in his office and signed it a year before it was dated and after it had been signed by him. Presumably reliance is placed on the provisions of section 3(1) of the Act of 1976, although this section was not opened to me.
2. The Order for possession was obtained by collusion.
3. The Agreement of 4th May, 1981, to the compromise of the proceedings was entered into by the Plaintiff because of a misrepresentation by the Husband as to the value of the property.
4. The Husband's failure to pay the instalments when they became due and his failure to sell the property promptly deprived the Plaintiff of the difference between the amount of the loan and the value of the family home.

Counsel on behalf of the Building Society objected that the amended indorsement of claim did not make any allegation with regard to the invalidity of the mortgage. I consider that there was some justification for this objection, but he also met this ground of claim by submitting that, under section 3 of the 1976 Act, a purported conveyance by a spouse is expressed to be void only if the prior consent of the other spouse was not obtained, that there could be no conveyance until delivery of the deed and that delivery of the mortgage in this case was not effected until after the consent of the Plaintiff had been obtained. Counsel for the Plaintiff did not contest this submission. I am of opinion that the submission is correct but, even if it were not, I would be very slow to hold that a spouse could contest the validity of a mortgage after entering into a settlement, with the advantage of legal advice, in which she clearly acknowledges its validity.

I do not accept that the allegation of collusion in obtaining the Order for possession is sustainable. The Husband had no defence to the proceeding and the only right given to the Plaintiff is under section 7 of the 1976 Act whereby the Court may decide that, if the Plaintiff were capable of paying the arrears due and the future payments, it would be just and equitable to adjourn the proceedings, presumably to enable the Plaintiff to discharge the payments due and to become due. It has not been suggested that the Plaintiff was in a position to pay the arrears so that, if her legal advisers had been in Court when the order was sought, no ground could have been advanced for opposing it.

Although I am not clear what importance is attached to the allegation that the mortgage was executed by the Husband and her consent indorsed by the Plaintiff in January, 1979, I am satisfied from the evidence of the solicitor for the Husband that the deed could not have been executed until the following January.

On application being made on behalf of the Building Society, I dismissed the Plaintiff's claim against it at the close of the Plaintiff's case, the other two submissions relating solely to the claim against the Husband.

With regard to the compromise of 4th May, 1981, I am satisfied that the Husband over-estimated the value of the family home. His solicitor stated in evidence that, in 1979, the land would have been valued at somewhere between £1,500 and £2,000 per acre. At £2,000 per acre, the 26 acres taken by the Husband's family would have been valued at £52,000. At £1,500 per acre, the value would have been £39,000. In the one case the family home would then have been worth approximately £46,000 and, in the other, it would have been worth approximately £59,000 assuming that the total price of £98,000 was a proper one. These figures suggest that the price the Husband paid was probably the full value of the family home. It is clear, however, that, at the time of the compromise, the parties considered that, after discharge of the mortgage debt out of the proceeds of the sale of the family home, there would be a considerable balance to enable the Plaintiff to purchase a house for herself and her children. Although it has not been contested that the Husband represented the value of the family home to be £70,000 I do not accept that the Plaintiff has a good ground for her claim for £40,000, the amount which she estimates she should have had available for the new house had the Husband's valuation been correct and he had sold the property expeditiously. The Plaintiff was represented at the hearing and on the settlement and the consent makes it clear that it was appreciated that money was due on the mortgage. It must be assumed that the figures were investigated on behalf of the Plaintiff and it is not suggested that there was any misrepresentation as to the amount due on foot of the mortgage. As the matter comes before me, there is no claim for breach of the agreement contained in the consent and there is no claim to have this agreement set aside on the ground of fraud or misrepresentation. The claims being made are made under the provisions of the Act of 1976, and, in particular, the provisions contained in subsection (2) of section 5 of that Act.

[McWilliam, J. quoted the subsection. He continued:]

On behalf of the Husband it was argued that no claim can lie under this subsection where the spouse has left the family home. I do not accept that this argument, in this form, is valid because one spouse might, by his or her conduct, compel the other spouse to leave, but this is not an issue which I have to decide on the present application.

As I understand the argument on behalf of the Plaintiff in respect of the misrepresentation by the Husband as to the value of the family home, it is that it deprived the Plaintiff and the children of a home which would have been purchased with the surplus of the sale price remaining after the discharge of the mortgage and, therefore, that the representation constituted conduct depriving the Plaintiff of her residence in the family home within the meaning of the subsection. There appear to me to be several answers to this argument. In the first place, it seems to me that there is only one family home in this case, that is, the one sold on foot of the mortgage. Secondly, once it has been established that the mortgage was validly created with the consent of the Plaintiff, as I am of opinion that it was, the conduct of the Husband relied upon must consist in his failure to pay the instalments. Although there is no reference in subsection (2) of section 5 to 'an intention' to deprive a spouse of her residence in the family home as there is in subsection (1), I am of opinion that a failure to pay instalments due on a mortgage would not be conduct resulting in the loss of an interest in the family home sufficient to entitle a spouse to compensation under the subsection unless it were established that the other spouse was financially able to pay the instalments. The only figures before me indicate that the Husband did not have an income sufficient to meet the instalments, which amounted to £5,372 per annum. Finally, as the amount due on foot of the mortgage at the time of the compromise was dealt with under the terms of the consent, it cannot, in my opinion, now be made the basis of a claim under subsection (2).

Undoubtedly, the Husband did not carry out the terms of the agreement with regard to expediting the sale and, therefore, as no instalments were paid, the debt to the Building Society was substantially increased. This might support a claim under the agreement for the difference between the amount due to the Building Society at the time when the sale should have been effected and the time when it was effected, but no such argument was advanced before me and does not appear to be open on the form in which the matter comes before me. For the reasons I have stated above, I am of opinion that these defaults on the part of the Husband subsequent to the date of the compromise are not such as can support a claim under subsection (2).

Although the Plaintiff has been left in a most unfortunate situation, particularly as the Husband sustained a serious head injury in an accident in February, 1982, and is not yet able to engage fully in business, with a consequent loss of income, I must dismiss her claim on this application.

Notes and Questions

1. Do you agree with the holding? Are you surprised to find that a husband who made *no* mortgage repayments on the family home was found not to have 'deprived' his wife of her residence in the family home by conduct that resulted in the loss of an interest in the home?
2. McWilliam, J. expressed the opinion that, although there is no reference in section 5(2) to 'an intention' to deprive a spouse of her residence in the family home, as there is in section 5(1), nevertheless:

   > a failure to pay instalments due on a mortgage would not be conduct resulting in the loss of an interest in the family home sufficient to entitle a spouse to compensation under the subsection unless it were established that the other spouse was financially able to pay the instalments.

   This raises some obvious questions:
   (i) If admittedly a husband were not able to pay the instalments because *earlier* he had intentionally dissipated his assets or deprived himself of his earning capacity, would section 5(2) be inapplicable, on McWilliam, J.'s analysis?
   (ii) If a husband, through weakness or foolishness rather than malice, brings about a situation whereby he loses his ability to repay the mortgage, is section 5(2) inapplicable?
   (iii) What about the case where a husband undertakes a mortgage commitment which from day one he is unable to discharge?
3. Although it might be argued convincingly that it would be wrong to read into section 5(2) the requirement that the defendant spouse should have *intentionally* deprived the family of their residence in the home, it is not unreasonable to interpret the subsection as giving the Court some function in limiting the absolute scope of the words 'has deprived'. For example, where a husband acted properly in disposing of the home – because it constituted a serious health hazard for this children, for example – clearly the Court would be empowered to hold that no order should be made against him. Perhaps it might have been safer for McWilliam, J. to have concentrated on the broad discretion which the subsection clearly allows the court (cf. '. . . the court *may* order the other spouse . . . to pay . . . *such amount as the court considers proper* . . .'), rather than to express a general principle regarding financial inability to pay mortgage instalments – when this principle may well itself have to be qualified in future cases.
4. Wide-ranging protection is given by section 9 of the *Family Home Protection Act, 1976* (as amended by section of the *Courts Act, 1981*) against the unreasonable or vindictive disposal of household chattels by a spouse. See also *K.* v. *K.*, 114 I.L.T.R. 50 (High Ct., Finlay, P., 1978).

Chapter 12

PROCREATION AND SEXUALITY

A. *Contraception*

McGEE v. ATTORNEY GENERAL

[1974] I.R. 284 (Supreme Court, 1973, reversing High Court, O'Keefe, P., 1972)

Walsh, J.:

The facts of this case are not in dispute and I do not find it necessary to recite them in any detail. The central facts are that the plaintiff is a young married woman and that the case is concerned with the impact of the provisions of s. 17 of the Criminal Law Amendment Act, 1935, upon the sexual relations between the plaintiff and her husband.

The effect of the statutory provision in question is to make it a criminal offence for any person to sell or expose, offer, advertise, or keep for sale or to import or to attempt to import into the State any contraceptive. Section 17 of the Act of 1935 invokes s. 42 of the Customs Consolidation Act, 1876, and thereby includes contraceptives among the list of prohibited imports with the result that an importation of such an article could lead to the person importing the article being prosecuted and convicted under s. 186 of the Act of 1876. For the purpose of s. 17 of the Act of 1935 the word 'contraceptive' means 'any appliance, instrument, drug, preparation or thing, designed, prepared, or intended to prevent pregnancy resulting from sexual intercourse between human beings.' I thought it necessary to give this definition in the detail in which it appears in the Act of 1935 so as to make clear that this case is not in any way concerned with instruments, preparations, drugs or appliances, etc., which take effect after conception, whether or not they are described as or purport to be contraceptives. Whether any such article is designed to or in fact takes effect after conception is a question which in each particular case can be decided only as one of fact based on the best available scientific evidence.

The event which led immediately to the present proceedings was the refusal of the second defendants to permit the importation by the plaintiff of a contraceptive jelly for use by her in her sexual relations with her husband, with the consent of her husband, and which had been prescribed for her by her medical adviser. It does not appear to be in dispute that the article in question is a contraceptive within the statutory definition to which I have already referred.

There is no law in force in the State which prohibits the use of contraceptives within the State. It appears to be the accepted fact that at present there are no contraceptives manufactured within the State and, therefore, that any contraceptives presently available within the State must necessarily have been imported in breach of the statutory provisions; although if innocently imported it would not attract a penalty to the importer. Such importation, however, would leave the goods liable to seizure.

The plaintiff seeks a declaration that s. 17 of the Act of 1935 is inconsistent with the Constitution and was not carried forward by Article 50 of the Constitution and no longer forms part of the law of the State. She also seeks a declaration that the seizure by the second defendants of the commodity in question was unauthorised by law and was illegal. In consequence she also seeks damages for detinue or conversion.

[**Walsh, J.** quoted section 1 of Article 50. He continued:]

I have referred to the wording of s. 1 of Article 50 because, apart from being the foundation of the present proceedings, one of the submissions made on behalf of the

Attorney General was to the effect that a statutory provision in force prior to the Constitution could continue to be in force and to be carried over by Article 50 even though its provisions were such as could not now be validly enacted by the Oireachtas because of the provisions of the Constitution. Stated as a general proposition, I find that this is in direct conflict with the very provisions of Article 50 and is quite unsustainable. However, in my opinion, there are circumstances in which the proposition could be partially correct.

If a pre-Constitution statute was such that it was not in conflict with the Constitution when taken in conjunction with other statutory provisions then in existence and with a particular state of facts then existing, and if such other statutory provisions continued in effect after the coming into force of the Constitution and the particular state of facts remained unaltered, the provisions of the first statute might not in any way be inconsistent with the provisions of the Constitution. If, however, subsequent to the coming into force of the Constitution the other statutory provisions were repealed and the state of facts was altered to a point where the joint effect of the repeal of the other statutes and the alteration of the facts was to give the original statute a completely different effect, then the question would arise of its continuing to be part of the law. In my view, Article 50, by its very terms (both in its Irish and English texts), makes it clear that laws in force in Saorstát Éireann shall continue to be in force only to the extent to which they are not inconsistent with the Constitution; and that if the inconsistency arises for the first time after the coming into force of the Constitution, the law carried forward thereupon ceases to be in force.

The relevance of this to the present case is clear. There is no evidence in the case to indicate what was the state of facts existing at the time of the passing of the Act of 1935 and the years subsequent to it up to the coming into force of the Constitution, and even for a period after that. It appears to have been assumed, though there is no evidence upon which to base the assumption, that contraceptives were not manufactured within the State at that time or were not readily available otherwise than by sale. The validity or otherwise of a law may depend upon an existing state of facts or upon the facts as established in litigation, as was clearly indicated by this Court in *Ryan* v. *The Attorney General* [1965] I.R. 294. To control the sale of contraceptives is not necessarily unconstitutional *per se*; nor is a control on the importation of contraceptives necessarily unconstitutional. There may be many reasons, grounded on considerations of public health or public morality, or even fiscal or protectionist reasons, why there should be a control on the importation of such articles. There may also be many good reasons, grounded on public morality or public health, why their sale should be controlled. I use the term 'controlled' to include total prohibition. What is challenged here is the constitutionality of making these articles unavailable. Therefore, the decision in this appeal must rest upon the present state of the law and the present state of the facts relating to the issues in dispute. Therefore, even if it were established that in 1935, 1936 or 1937, or even 1940, contraceptives were reasonably available without infringement of the law, that would not necessarily determine that s. 17 of the Act of 1935 now continues to be in full force and effect.

The relevant facts, which are not in dispute in this case, are that at the present time the effect of s. 17 of the Act of 1935, if it is still in force, is effectively to make contraceptives unavailable to persons within the State without an infringement of the law and the possibility of a criminal prosecution and conviction.

The plaintiff claims that s. 17 of the Act of 1935 is inconsistent with ss. 1 and 3 of Article 40 of the Constitution. In respect of s. 1 of Article 40, it is claimed that s. 17 of the Act of 1935 discriminates unfairly against the plaintiff and fails to hold her, as a human person, equal before the law in that it fails to have due regard to her physical capacity, her moral capacity and her social function in the situation in which she now finds herself. The latter reference is to the plaintiff's particular condition of health. So far as s. 3 of Article 40 is concerned, it is claimed that, by reason of s. 17 of the Act of 1935, the State has failed to guarantee in its laws to respect and as far as practicable by its laws to vindicate her personal rights or to protect them from unjust attack, and has failed to vindicate her life, her person and her good name and her property rights. It is also claimed that s. 17 of the Act of 1935 is inconsistent with Article 41 of the Constitution in that it violates the inalienable and imprescriptible rights of the family in a matter which the plaintiff claims is peculiarly within the province of the family itself, in that the section attempts to frustrate a decision made by the plaintiff and her husband for the benefit of their family as a whole and thereby attacks and fails to protect the family in its constitution and authority: that claim was based on s. 1 of Article 41. Section 2 of Article 41 is invoked by the plaintiff in her claim that s. 17 of the Act of 1935 fails to recognise and give due weight to a private family decision of the plaintiff and her husband touching her life within the home and by attempting to frustrate that decision endangers the plaintiff's life and refuses to allow her to live her life within her home as she and her husband think best in the interests of the family.

The plaintiff has also invoked the provisions of s. 1 of Article 42 of the Constitution by relating the decision taken by herself and her husband to practise contraception as being partly motivated by their desire to provide for the better education of their existing children; and she submits that s. 17 of the Act of 1935 attempts to frustrate that decision. The plaintiff also says that her decision to practise contraception is in accordance with the dictates of her own conscience, and she invokes s. 2 of Article 44 of the Constitution which guarantees to every citizen freedom of conscience and the free profession and practice of religion, subject to public order and morality. The plaintiff claims that s. 17 of the Act of 1935 prevents her from leading her private life in accordance with the dictates of her own conscience. Article 45 of the Constitution, which is the Article which deals with the directive principles of social policy, is also invoked by the plaintiff. She relies on s. 1 of that Article wherein it is stated that the State shall strive to promote the welfare of the whole people by securing and protecting, as effectively as it may, a social order in which justice and charity shall inform all the institutions of the national life. In the same vein, the plaintiff also invoked that portion of the preamble to the Constitution in which the people, in giving themselves the Constitution, express the intention to seek 'to promote the common good, with due observance of Prudence, Justice and Charity, so that the dignity and freedom of the individual may be assured . . .'

Articles 40, 41, 42 and 44 of the Constitution all fall within that section of the Constitution which is titled 'Fundamental Rights.' Articles 41, 42 and 43 emphatically reject the theory that there are no rights without laws, no rights contrary to the law and no rights anterior to the law. They indicate that justice is placed above the law and acknowledge that natural rights, or human rights, are not created by law but that the Constitution confirms their existence and gives them protection. The individual has natural and human rights over which the State has no authority; and the family, as the natural primary and fundamental unit group of society, has rights as such which the State cannot control. However, at the same it is true, as the Constitution acknowledges and claims, that the State is the guardian of the common good and that the individual, as a member of society, and the family, as a unit of society, have duties and obligations to consider and respect the common good of that society. It is important to recall that under the Constitution the State's powers of government are exercised in their respective spheres by the legislative, executive and judicial organs established under the Constitution. I agree with the view expressed by O'Byrne, J. in *Buckley and Others (Sinn Féin)* v. *The Attorney General* [1950] I.R. 67, 83 that the power of the State to act for the protection of the common good or to decide what are the exigencies of the common good is not one which is peculiarly reserved for the legislative organ of government, in that the decision of the legislative organ is not absolute and is subject to and capable of being reviewed by the

Courts. In concrete terms that means that the legislature is not free to encroach unjustifiably upon the fundamental rights of individuals or of the family in the name of the common good, or by act or omission to abandon or to neglect the common good or the protection or enforcement of the rights of individual citizens.

Turning to the particular submissions made on behalf of the plaintiff, I shall deal first with the submission made in relation to the provisions of Article 41 of the Constitution which deals with the family. On the particular facts of this case, I think this is the most important submission because the plaintiff's claim is based upon her status as a married woman and is made in relation to the conduct of her sexual life with her husband within that marriage. For the purpose of this Article I am of opinion that the state of the plaintiff's health is immaterial to the consideration of the rights she claims are infringed in relation to Article 41. In this Article the State, while recognising the family as the natural primary and fundamental unit group of society and as a moral institution possessing inalienable and imprescriptible rights antecedent and superior to all positive law, guarantees to protect the family in its constitution and authority as the necessary basis of social order and as indispensable to the welfare of the nation and the State. The article recognises the special position of woman, meaning the wife, within that unit; the article also offers special protection for mothers in that they shall not be obliged by economic necessity to engage in labour to the neglect of their duties in the home. The Article also recognises the institution of marriage as the foundation of the family and undertakes to protect it against attack. By this and the following Article, the State recognises the parents as the natural guardians of the children of the family and as those in whom the authority of the family is vested and those who shall have the right to determine how the family life shall be conducted, having due regard to the rights of the children not merely as members of that family but as individuals.

It is a matter exclusively for the husband and wife to decide how many children they wish to have; it would be quite outside the competence of the State to dictate or prescribe the number of children which they might have or should have. In my view, the husband and wife have a correlative right to agree to have no children. That is not to say that the State, when the common good requires it, may not actively encourage married couples either to have larger families or smaller families. If it is a question of having smaller families then, whether it be a decision of the husband and wife or the intervention of the State, the means employed to achieve this objective would have to be examined. What may be permissible to the husband and wife is not necessarily permissible to the State. For example, the husband and wife may mutually agree to practise either total or partial abstinence in their sexual relations. If the State were to attempt to intervene to compel such abstinence, it would be an intolerable and unjustifiable intrusion into the privacy of the matrimonial bedroom. On the other hand, any action on the part of either the husband and wife or of the State to limit family sizes by endangering or destroying human life must necessarily not only be an offence against the common good but also against the guaranteed personal rights of the human life in question.

The sexual life of a husband and wife is of necessity and by its nature an area of particular privacy. If the husband and wife decide to limit their family or to avoid having children by use of contraceptives, it is a matter peculiarly within the joint decision of the husband and wife and one into which the State cannot intrude unless its intrusion can be justified by the exigencies of the common good. The question of whether the use of contraceptives by married couples within their marriage is or is not contrary to the moral code or codes to which they profess to subscribe, or is or is not regarded by them as being against their conscience, could not justify State intervention. Similarly the fact that the use of contraceptives may offend against the moral code of the majority of the citizens of the State would not *per se* justify an intervention by the State to prohibit their use within

marriage. The private morality of its citizens does not justify intervention by the State into the activities of those citizens unless and until the common good requires it. Counsel for the Attorney General did not seek to argue that the State would have any right to seek to prevent the use of contraceptives within marriage. He did argue, however, that it did not follow from this that the State was under any obligation to make contraceptives available to married couples. Counsel for the second defendants put the matter somewhat further by stating that, if she had a right to use contraceptives within the privacy of her marriage, it was a matter for the plaintiff to prove from whence the right sprang. In effect he was saying that, if she was appealing to a right anterior to positive law, the burden was on her to show the source of that right. At first sight this may appear to be a reasonable and logical proposition. However, it does appear to ignore a fundamental point, namely, that the rights of a married couple to decide how many children, if any, they will have are matters outside the reach of positive law where the means employed to implement such decisions do not impinge upon the common good or destroy or endanger human life. It is undoubtedly true that among those persons who are subject to a particular moral code no one has a right to be in breach of that moral code. But when this is a code governing private morality and where the breach of it is not one which injures the common good then it is not the State's business to intervene. It is outside the authority of the State to endeavour to intrude into the privacy of the husband and wife relationship for the sake of imposing a code of private morality upon that husband and wife which they do not desire.

In my view, Article 41 of the Constitution guarantees the husband and wife against any such invasion of their privacy by the State. It follows that the use of contraceptives by them within that marital privacy is equally guaranteed against such invasion and, as such, assumes the status of a right so guaranteed by the Constitution. If this right cannot be directly invaded by the State it follows that it cannot be frustrated by the State taking measures to ensure that the exercise of that right is rendered impossible. I do not exclude the possibility of the State being justified where the public good requires it (as, for example, in the case of a dangerous fall in population threatening the life or the essential welfare of the State) in taking such steps to ensure that in general, even if married couples could not be compelled to have children, they could at least be hindered in their endeavours to avoid having them where the common good required the maintenance or increase of the population. That, however, is not the present case and there is no evidence whatever in the case to justify State intervention on that ground. Similarly it is not impossible to envisage a situation where the availability of contraceptives to married people for use within marriage could be demonstrated to have led to or would probably lead to such an adverse effect on public morality so subversive of the common good as to justify State intervention by restricting or prohibiting the availability of contraceptives for use within marriage or at all. In such a case it would have to be demonstrated that all the other resources of the State had proved or were likely to prove incapable to avoid this subversion of the common good while contraceptives remained available for use within marriage.

In my opinion, s. 17 of the Act of 1935, in so far as it unreasonably restricts the availability of contraceptives for use within marriage, is inconsistent with the provisions of Article 41 of the Constitution for being an unjustified invasion of the privacy of husband and wife in their sexual relations with one another. The fundamental restriction is contained in the provisions of sub-s. 3 of s. 17 of the Act of 1935 which lists contraceptives among the prohibited articles which may not be imported for any purposes whatsoever. On the present state of facts, I am of opinion that this provision is inconsistent with the Constitution and is no longer in force.

For the reasons I gave earlier in this judgment, the prohibition of the importation of contraceptives could be justified on several grounds provided the effect was not to make contraceptives unavailable. For example, the law might very well prohibit for health reasons the importation of some if not all contraceptives from sources outside the country if, for example, there is a risk of infection from their use. No such reason has been offered in the present case and in any such instance, for the reasons already given, the law could not take other steps to see that contraceptives were not otherwise available for use in marriage.

As this particular case arose primarily out of the ban on importation, I think that, in so far as Article 41 is concerned, the declaration sought should only go in respect of sub-s. 3 of s. 17 of the Act of 1935. That does not necessarily mean that the provisions as to sale in sub-s. 1 of s. 17 cannot be impugned. If, in the result, notwithstanding the deletion of sub-s. 3, the prohibition on sale had the effect of leaving a position where contraceptives were not reasonably available for use within marriage, then that particular prohibition must also fall. However, for the moment I do not think it is necessary to make any declaration in respect of that.

So far I have considered the plaintiff's case only in relation to Article 41 of the Constitution; and I have done so on the basis that she is a married woman but without referring to her state of health. I now turn to the claim made under Article 40 of the Constitution. So far as this particular Article is concerned, and the submissions made thereunder, the state of health of the plaintiff is relevant. If, for the reasons I have already given, a prohibition on the availability of contraceptives for use in marriage generally could be justified on the grounds of the exigencies of the common good, the provisions of s. 1 of Article 40 (in particular, the proviso thereto) would justify and would permit the State to discriminate between some married persons and others in the sense that, where conception could more than ordinarily endanger the life of a particular person or persons or particular classes of persons within the married state, the law would have regard to this difference of physical capacity and make special exemptions in favour of such persons. I think that such an exemption could also be justified under the provisions of s. 3 of Article 40 on the grounds that one of the personal rights of a woman in the plaintiff's state of health would be a right to be assisted in her efforts to avoid putting her life in jeopardy. I am of opinion also that not only has the State the right to do so but, by virtue of the terms of the proviso to s. 1 and the terms of s. 3 of Article 40, the State has the positive obligation to ensure by its laws as far as is possible (and in the use of the word 'possible' I am relying on the Irish text of the Constitution) that there would be made available to a married woman in the condition of health of the plaintiff the means whereby a conception which was likely to put her life in jeopardy might be avoided when it is a risk over and above the ordinary risks inherent in pregnancy. It would, in the nature of things, be much more difficult to justify a refusal to do this on the grounds of the common good than in the case of married couples generally.

Next I turn to the submissions made on behalf of the plaintiff which relate to the provisions of s. 2 of Article 44 of the Constitution. In my view these submissions are based on a mistaken interpretation of the constitutional provision in question. In particular the reference to the decision of this Court in *Quinn's Supermarket* v. *The Attorney General* [1972] I.R. 1, 15 is misinterpreted. That particular case dealt with a situation where a law might be in such terms as to impose upon a member of a particular religion the choice of exercising his religion and thereby suffering some economic or other loss, or forgoing the practice of his religion to avoid the loss in question. It was held that any such law would be invalid having regard to the provisions of s. 2 of Article 44. In the present case the plaintiff says that, so far as her conscience is concerned, the use of contraceptives by her is in accordance with her conscience and that, in using them, she does not feel that she is acting against her conscience. It was submitted that social conscience, as distinct from religious conscience, falls within the ambit of Article 44. I do not think that is so. The whole context in which the question of conscience appears in Article 44 is one dealing with the exercise of religion and the free profession and practice of religion. Within that context, the meaning of s. 2, sub-s. 1, of Article 44 is that no person shall directly or indirectly be coerced or compelled to act contrary to his conscience in so far as the practice of religion is concerned and, subject to public order and morality, is free to profess and practise the religion of his choice in accordance with his conscience. Correlatively, he is free to have no religious beliefs or to abstain from the practice or profession of any religion. Because a person feels free, or even obliged, in conscience to pursue some particular activity which is not in itself a religious practice, it does not follow that such activity is guaranteed protection by Article 44. It is not correct to say, as was submitted, that the Article is a constitutional guarantee of a right to live in accordance with one's conscience subject to public order and morality. What the article guarantees is the right not to be compelled or coerced into living in a way which is contrary to one's conscience and, in the context of the Article, that means contrary to one's conscience so far as the exercise, practice or profession of religion is concerned.

However, the reference to *Quinn's Supermarket* v. *The Attorney General* [1972] I.R. 1 is relevant to this case in another way. The judgment in that case pointed out that the Constitution recognises and reflects a firm conviction that the people of this State are a religious people and that, as it then stood, the Constitution referred specifically to a number of religious denominations which coexisted within the State, thereby acknowledging the fact that while we are a religious people we also live in a pluralist society from the religious point of view. In my view, the subsequent deletion of sub-ss. 2 and 3 of s. 1 of Article 44 by the fifth amendment to the Constitution has done nothing to alter this acknowledgment that, religiously speaking, the society we live in is a pluralist one. It was also pointed out in that case that the guarantees of religious freedom and freedom of conscience were not confined to the different denominations of the Christian religion but extended to other religious denominations: see s. 2 of Article 44 which guarantees freedom of conscience and the free profession and practice of religion to every citizen, whether of the Christian religion or not.

Both in its preamble and in Article 6, the Constitution acknowledges God as the ultimate source of all authority. The natural or human rights to which I have referred earlier in this judgment are part of what is generally called the natural law. There are many to argue that natural law may be regarded only as an ethical concept and as such is a re-affirmation of the ethical content of law in its ideal of justice. The natural law as a theological concept is the law of God promulgated by reason and is the ultimate governor of all the laws of men. In view of the acknowledgment of Christianity in the preamble and in view of the reference to God in Article 6 of the Constitution, it must be accepted that the Constitution intended the natural human rights I have mentioned as being in the latter category rather than simply an acknowledgment of the ethical content of law in its ideal of justice. What exactly natural law is and what precisely it imports is a question which has exercised the minds of theologians for many centuries and on which they are not yet fully agreed. While the Constitution speaks of certain rights being imprescriptible or inalienable, or being antecedent and superior to all positive law, it does not specify them. Echoing the words of O'Byrne J. in *Buckley and others (Sinn Féin)* v. *The Attorney General* [1950] I.R. 67, 82, I do not feel it necessary to enter upon an inquiry as to their extent or, indeed, as to their nature. It is sufficient for the court to examine and to search for the rights which may be discoverable in the particular case before the court in which these rights are invoked.

In a pluralist society such as ours, the Courts cannot as a matter of constitutional law be asked to choose between the differing views, where they exist, of experts on the interpretation by the different religious denominations of either the nature or extent of these natural rights as they are to be found in the natural law. The same considerations apply also to the question of ascertaining the nature and extent of the duties which flow from natural law; the Constitution speaks of one of them when it refers to the inalienable duty of parents to provide according to their means for the religious, moral, intellectual, physical and social education of their children: see s. 1 of Article 42. In this country it falls finally upon the judges to interpret the Constitution and in doing so to determine, where necessary, the rights which are superior or antecedent to positive law or which are imprescriptible or inalienable. In the performance of this difficult duty there are certain guidelines laid down in the Constitution for the judge. The very structure and content of the Articles dealing with fundamental rights clearly indicate that justice is not subordinate to the law. In particular, the terms of s. 3 of Article 40 expressly subordinate the law to justice. Both Aristotle and the Christian philosophers have regarded justice as the highest human virtue. The virtue of prudence was also esteemed by Aristotle as by the philosophers of the Christian world. But the great additional virtue introduced by Christianity was that of charity – not the charity which consists of giving to the deserving, for that is justice, but the charity which is also called mercy. According to the preamble, the people gave themselves the Constitution to promote the common good with due observance of prudence, justice and charity so that the dignity and freedom of the individual might be assured. The judges must, therefore, as best they can from their training and their experience interpret these rights in accordance with their ideas of prudence, justice and charity. It is but natural that from time to time the prevailing ideas of these virtues may be conditioned by the passage of time; no interpretation of the Constitution is intended to be final for all time. It is given in the light of prevailing ideas and concepts. The development of the constitutional law of the United States of America is ample proof of this. There is a constitution which, while not professing to be governed by the precepts of Christianity, also in the Ninth Amendment recognises the existence of rights other than those referred to expressly in it and its amendments. The views of the United States Supreme Court, as reflected in the decisions interpreting that constitution and in the development of their constitutional law, also appear firmly to reject legal positivism as a jurisprudential guide.

Three United States Supreme Court decisions were relied upon in argument by the plaintiff: *Poe* v. *Ullman* (1961) 367 U.S. 497; *Griswold* v. *Connecticut* (1965) 381 U.S. 479; and *Eisenstadt* v. *Baird* (1972) 405 U.S. 438. My reason for not referring to them is not because I did not find them helpful or relevant, which indeed they were, but because I found it unnecessary to rely upon any of the dicta in those cases to support the views which I have expressed in this judgment.

Lastly, I wish to emphasise that I have given no consideration whatsoever to the question of the constitutionality or otherwise of laws which would withhold or restrict the availability of contraceptives for use outside of marriage; nothing in this judgment is intended to offer any opinion on that matter.

For the reasons I have given, I would grant the plaintiff a declaration that sub-s. 3 of s. 17 of the Criminal Law Amendment Act, 1935, is not, and was not at any time material to these proceedings, of full force and effect as part of the laws of the State.

Budd, J.:

. . . . The State guarantees as far as practicable by its laws to vindicate the personal rights of the citizen. What more important personal right could there be in a citizen than the right to determine in marriage his attitude and resolve his mode of life concerning the procreation of children? Whilst the 'personal rights' are not described specifically, it is scarcely to be doubted in our society that the right to privacy is universally recognised and accepted with possibly the rarest of exceptions, and that the matter of marital relationship must rank as one of the most important of matters in the realm of privacy. When the preamble to the Constitution speaks of seeking to promote the common good by the observance of prudence, justice and charity so that the dignity and freedom of the individual may be assured, it must surely inform those charged with its construction as to the mode of application of its Articles.

When I apply what I have stated about the principles of the Constitution to Article 40, I am driven to the conclusion that the Act of 1935 is in particular conflict with the personal rights of the citizen which the State in sub-s. 1 of s. 3 of Article 40 guarantees to respect, defend and vindicate as far as practicable. The other Articles which I have quoted from are in no way inconsistent with the construction I have placed on sub-s. 1 of s. 3 of Article 40. This Act does not defend or vindicate the personal rights of the citizen or his or her privacy relative to matters of the procreation of children and the privacy of married life and marital relations. Section 17, sub-s. 3, of the Act of 1935 is inconsistent with the Article already referred to and is therefore unconstitutional and invalid in law. I would allow this appeal.

Henchy, J.:

. . . . Because contraceptives are not manufactured in this State, the effect of s. 17 of the Act of 1935 as a whole is that, except for contraceptives that have been imported without the intention of evading the prohibition on importation, it is not legally possible to obtain a contraceptive in this State. It is doubtful if the legislature could have taken more effective steps by means of the criminal law to put an end to their use in the State. . . .

. . . . The dominant feature of the plaintiff's dilemma is that she is a young married woman who is living, with a slender income, in the cramped quarters of a mobile home with her husband and four infant children, and that she is faced with a considerable risk of death or crippling paralysis if she becomes pregnant. The net question is whether it is constitutionally permissible in the circumstances for the law to deny her access to the contraceptive method chosen for her by her doctor and which she and her husband wish to adopt. In other words, is the prohibition effected by s. 17 of the Act of 1935 an interference with the rights which the State guarantees in its laws to respect, as stated in sub-s. 1 of s. 3 of Article 40?

The answer lies primarily in the fact that the plaintiff is a wife and a mother. It is the informed and conscientious wish of the plaintiff and her husband to maintain full marital relations without incurring the risk of a pregnancy that may very well result in her death or in a crippling paralysis. Section 17 of the Act of 1935 frustrates that wish. It goes further; it brings the implementation of the wish within the range of the criminal law. Its effect, therefore, is to condemn the plaintiff and her husband to a way of life which, at best, will be fraught with worry, tension and uncertainty that cannot but adversely affect their lives and, at worst, will result in an unwanted pregnancy causing death or serious illness with the obvious tragic consequences to the lives of her husband and young children. And this in the context of a Constitution which in its preamble proclaims as one of its aims the dignity and freedom of the individual; which in sub-s. 2 of s. 3 of Article 40 casts on the State a duty to protect as best it may from unjust attack and, in the case of injustice done, to vindicate the life and person of every citizen; which in Article 41, after recognising the family as the natural primary and fundamental unit group of society, and as a moral institution possessing inalienable and imprescriptible rights antecedent and superior to all positive law, guarantees to protect it in its constitution and authority as the necessary basis of social order and as indispensable to the welfare of the nation and the State; and which, also in Article 41, pledges the State to guard with special care the institution of marriage, on which the family is founded, and to protect it against attack.

Section 17, in my judgment, so far from respecting the plaintiff's personal rights, violates them. If she observes this prohibition (which in practice she can scarcely avoid doing and which in law she is bound under penalty of fine and imprisonment to do), she will endanger the security and happiness of her marriage, she will imperil her health to the point of hazarding her life, and she will subject her family to the risk of distress and disruption. These are intrusions which she is entitled to say are incompatible with the safety of her life, the preservation of her health, her responsibility to her conscience, and the security and well-being of her marriage and family. If she fails to obey the prohibition in s. 17, the law, by prosecuting her, will reach into the privacy of her marital life in seeking to prove her guilt.

In *Griswold* v. *Connecticut* (1965) 381 U.S. 479 the American Supreme Court held that a Connecticut statute which forbade the use of contraceptives was unconstitutional because it violated a constitutional right of marital privacy which, while unexpressed in the American Constitution, was held to be within the penumbra of the specific guarantees of the Bill of Rights. In a judgment concurring in the opinion of the court, Goldberg, J. said at p. 498 of the report:– 'The State, at most, argues that there is some rational relation between this statute and what is admittedly a legitimate subject of state concern – the discouraging of extra-marital relations. It says that preventing the use of birth-control devices by married persons helps prevent the indulgence by some in such extra-marital relations. The rationality of this justification is dubious, particularly in light of the admitted widespread availability to all persons in the State of Connecticut, unmarried as well as married, of birth-control devices for the prevention of disease, as distinguished from the prevention of conception, see *Tileston* v. *Ullman* 129 Conn. 84, 26 A. 2d 582. But in any event, it is clear that the state interest in safeguarding marital fidelity can be served by a more discriminately tailored statute, which does not, like the present one, sweep unnecessarily broadly, reaching far beyond the evil sought to be dealt with and intruding upon the privacy of all married couples.' At p. 499 Goldberg J. cites with approval the words of Harlan J. in *Poe* v. *Ullman* (1961) 367 U.S. 497, 553:– '. . . the intimacy of husband and wife is necessarily an essential and accepted feature of the institution of marriage, an institution which the State not only must allow, but which always and in every age it has fostered and protected. It is one thing when the State exerts its power either to forbid extra-marital sexuality altogether, or to say who may marry, but it is quite another when, having acknowledged a marriage and the intimacies inherent in it, it undertakes to regulate by means of the criminal law the details of that intimacy.'

It has been argued that *Griswold's Case* (1965) 381 U.S. 479. is distinguishable because the statute in question there forbade the use of contraceptives, whereas s. 17 of the Act of 1935 only forbids their sale or importation. This submission was accepted in the High Court. However, I consider that the distinction sought to be drawn is one of form rather than substance. The purpose of the statute in both cases is the same: it is to apply the sanction of the criminal law in order to prevent the use of contraceptives. What the American Supreme Court found in *Griswold's Case* (1965) 381 U.S. 479 to be constitutionally objectionable was that the sweep of the statute was so wide that proof of an offence would involve physical intrusion into the intimacy of the marriage relationship, which the court held to be an area of constitutionally protected privacy. If the plaintiff were prosecuted for an offence arising under or by virtue of s. 17 of the Act of 1935, while there might not be the same degree of physical intrusion, there would necessarily be a violation of intimate aspects of her marital life which, in deference to her standing as a wife and mother, ought not to be brought out and condemned as criminal under a glare of publicity in a courtroom. Furthermore, if she were found guilty of such an offence, in order to have the penalty mitigated to fit the circumstances of her case, she would have to disclose particulars of her marital dilemma which she ought not to have to reveal.

In my opinion, s. 17 of the Act of 1935 violates the guarantee in sub-s. 1 of s. 3 of Article 40 by the State to protect the plaintiff's personal rights by its laws; it does so not only by violating her personal right to privacy in regard to her marital relations but, in a wider way, by frustrating and making criminal any efforts by her to effectuate the decision of her husband and herself, made responsibly, conscientiously and on medical advice, to avail themselves of a particular contraceptive method so as to ensure her life and health as well as the integrity, security and well-being of her marriage and her family. Because of the clear unconstitutionality of the section in this respect, I do not find it necessary to deal with the submissions made in support of the claim that the section violates other provisions of the Constitution.

What stands between the plaintiff and the exercise of any constitutional right claimed by her in this case is sub-s. 3 of s. 17 of the Act of 1935. With that sub-section out of the way, her cause of complaint would disappear because what she wishes to do (to import the required contraceptive by post) would then be legal as the importation, not being for sale, would not be forbidden by sub-section 1. Since s. 17 without sub-s. 3 can stand as a self-contained entity, independently operable and representing the legislative intent, sub-s. 3 is capable of being severed and declared unconstitutional. Therefore, I would allow the appeal to the extent of declaring that sub-s. 3 of s. 17 of the Act of 1935 is without validity as being inconsistent with the Constitution. In the particular circumstances of this case, I do not find it necessary to make any adjudication on the constitutionality of the remaining part of the section.

Griffin, J.:

. . . . One of the 'personal rights' claimed on behalf of the plaintiff is the right of privacy in her marital relations with her husband. . . .

The Courts have not attempted to define with exactitude or to make a list of the rights which may properly be included in the category of personal rights. But Mr. Justice Kenny [in *Ryan* v. *The Attorney General,* [1965] I.R. 294 instanced the right to bodily integrity and the right to marry. It seems to me that the right of married persons to establish a home and bring up children is inherent in the right to marry. In so far as the plaintiff is concerned, the questions of whether the right of privacy in relation to her intimate relations with her husband is one of the unspecified rights referred to in sub-s. 1 of s. 3 of Article 40 and, if so, whether such right has been violated by s. 17 of the Act of 1935 are essentially the matters for determination in this action.

In my opinion, the right of marital privacy is one of the personal rights guaranteed by sub-s. 1 of s. 3 of Article 40 and so the nature of that right possessed by the plaintiff must be considered. The plaintiff is without doubt in an unenviable situation. She has four very young children who live with her in a mobile home. We have no evidence of the size of this structure but it is to be assumed that space is at least limited. She and her husband are both young and they are anxious to have normal marital relations. This they cannot have because of the danger to the plaintiff's life or health in the event of another pregnancy and because of the unsuitability of oral contraceptives for her and her inability to use what are called the natural methods of birth control. It is in her interest and in the interests of her husband and small children that she should not take the risk of another pregnancy which might deprive the husband of his wife and the children of their mother. The plaintiff, her husband, and their children are a unit recognised by and given a special place in the Constitution. [*The judge referred to the provisions of s. 1 of Article 41 of the Constitution, and continued* . . .] The word 'family' is not defined in the Constitution but, without attempting a definition, it seems to me that in this case it must necessarily include the plaintiff, her husband and their children.

The nature of the right of privacy in marriage has been discussed by the Supreme Court of the United States of America in considering the constitutionality of a Connecticut statute which made the use of contraceptives a criminal offence. In *Poe* v. *Ullman* (1961)

367 U.S. 497 at p. 552 of the report Harlan J. said:– '"The family . . . is not beyond regulation," *Prince* v. *Massachusetts* (1944) 321 U.S. 158, . . . and it would be an absurdity to suggest either that offences may not be committed in the bosom of the family or that the home can be made a sanctuary for crime. The right of privacy most manifestly is not an absolute. Thus, I would not suggest that adultery, homosexuality, fornication and incest are immune from criminal enquiry, however privately practised. So much has been explicitly recognised in acknowledging the State's rightful concern for its people's moral welfare . . . Adultery, homosexuality and the like are sexual intimacies which the State forbids altogether, but the intimacy of husband and wife is necessarily an essential and accepted feature of the institution of marriage, an institution which the State not only must allow, but which always and in every age it has fostered and protected. It is one thing when the State exerts its power either to forbid extra-marital sexuality altogether, or to say who may marry, but it is quite another when, having acknowledged a marriage and the intimacies inherent in it, it undertakes to regulate by means of the criminal law the details of that intimacy.' Adultery and extra-marital sexuality are not, as such, crimes here.

To return to sub-s. 1 of s. 3 of Article 40, the guarantee of the State in its law to respect the personal rights of citizens is not subject to the limitation 'as far as practicable' nor is it circumscribed in any other way. The relevant portion of that sub-section in the Irish version, which prevails, is in the following terms:– 'Ráthaíonn an Stát gan cur isteach lena dhlithibh ar cheartaibh pearsanta aon tsaoránaigh.' The literal translation makes it a guarantee 'not to interfere with' rather than a guarantee to 'respect.' Does a law which effectively prevents the plaintiff and her husband in their particular circumstances from resorting to the use of contraceptives for the purpose of ensuring that the plaintiff will not have another pregnancy 'respect' or 'not interfere with' the right of family privacy of the plaintiff and her husband? In this context, I wish to emphasise that this judgment is confined to contraceptives as such; it is not intended to apply to abortifacients, though called contraceptives, as in the case of abortifacients entirely different considerations may arise. In my opinion, a statute which makes it a criminal offence for the plaintiff or her husband to import or to acquire possession of contraceptives for use within their marriage is an unjustifiable invasion of privacy in the conduct of the most intimate of all their personal relationships. . . . [Griffin, J. quoted a passage from the judgment of Douglas, J. in *Griswold* v. *Connecticut*, (1965) 381 U.S. 479, at 485. He continued:]

Although in s. 17 of the Act of 1935 the *use* of contraceptives is not prohibited, the section effectively prohibits the plaintiff from obtaining contraceptives and makes acquiring possession thereof a crime in the circumstances which I have already outlined; in my view the section achieves the same result as the Connecticut law.

It was submitted on behalf of the plaintiff that the entire of s. 17 is inconsistent with the Constitution and that sub-ss. 1 and 3 of s. 17 should stand or fall together. One of the grounds advanced in support of the argument that the entire section should fall was that contraception is a matter of private morality and not of public morality. In my view, in any ordered society the protection of morals through the deterrence of fornication and promiscuity is a legitimate legislative aim and a matter not of private but of public morality. For the purpose of this action, it is only necessary to deal with the plaintiff as a married woman in the light of her particular circumstances. In my opinion, by the inclusion of sub-s. 3, the provisions of s. 17 of the Act of 1935 in the words of Douglas J. do 'sweep unnecessarily broadly and thereby invade the area of protected freedoms.' In my judgment, this sub-section violates the personal rights of the plaintiff, in this case, her right of privacy in her marital relations with her husband under sub-s. 1 of s. 3 of Article 40. For the purposes of this action, it is not necessary that the entire of the section should be struck down.

For the reasons I have given, sub-s. 3 of s. 17 of the Act of 1935 is inconsistent with the Constitution and was not continued of full force and effect by Article 50 of the Constitution and, to the extent only of making a declaration accordingly, I would allow this appeal.
Fitzgerald, J. delivered a dissenting judgment.

Notes and Questions

1. Do you prefer the location of the right of marital privacy in Article 40.3 or in Article 41? Does it matter where it is located? Why? Cf. *Norris* v. *A.G., infra*, p. 374, and see J. Kelly, *The Irish Constitution*, 431–483 (2nd ed., 1984)
2. To what extent (if any) does Henchy, J.'s judgment rest on the particular condition of the plaintiff, so far as her health and the risks of pregnancy were concerned?
3. For analysis of *McGee* and related themes, see J. Kelly, *The Irish Constitution*, (2nd ed., 1984); Dooley, 3 Soc. Studies 186 (1974); O'Reilly, 65 Studies 8 (1977); Binchy, 65 Studies 330 (1977); Binchy, *Ethical Issues in Reproductive Medicine: A Legal Perspective*, ch. 9 of M. Reidy ed., *Ethical Issues in Reproductive Medicine*, at 95–98 (1982); McMahon *The Law Relating to Contraception in Ireland*, ch. 2 of D. Clarke ed., *Morality and the Law* (1982); Robinson, *The Protection of Human Rights in the Republic of Ireland*, ch. 6 of C. Campbell ed., *Do We Need a Bill of Rights?*, at 71–73 (1980); von Prondzynski, *Natural Law and the Constitution*, (1977) 1 Dublin U. L. J. 32; Stepan & Kellogg, *The World's Laws on Contraceptives*, 22 Amer. J. of Comp. L. 615 (1974); Clarke, *The Role of Natural Law in Irish Constitutional Law*, 17 Ir. Jur. 187 (1982).
4. Mr. Paul O'Connor has raised an interesting issue:

   If natural law is antecedent and superior to all positive law it suggests than an amendment purporting to alter the Constitution, in violation of the natural law, would not be valid. *'Kidnapping' and the Irish Courts*, 2 Ir. L. T. (n.s.) 4, at 4 (1984).
5. In *Eisenstadt* v. *Baird*, 405 U.S. 438 (1972), The United States Supreme Court converted the right to marital privacy first recognised in *Griswold* v. *Connecticut*, 381 U.S. 479 (1965) into a right of unmarried persons to have access to contraception. Speaking for the Court, Justice Brennan said:

   If under *Griswold* the distribution of contraceptives to married persons cannot be prohibited, a ban on distribution to unmarried persons would be equally impermissible. It is true that in *Griswold* the right of privacy in question inhered in the marital relationship. Yet the marital couple is not an independent entity with a mind and heart of its own, but an association of two individuals each with a separate intellectual and emotional make-up. If the right of privacy means anything, it is the right of the *individual*, married or single, to be free from unwarranted governmental intrusion into matters so fundamentally affecting a person as the decision whether to bear or beget a child.

   Do you agree with this argument? Is it logically sound? Or does the argument purport to depend on logic at all? Cf. Binchy, *The American Revolution in Family Law*, N.I.L.Q. 371, at 396 (1976).
6. In the wake of *McGee*, after a false start in 1975, legislation regulating contraception was eventually enacted in 1979. The *Health (Family Planning) Act, 1979* provides for a right of access to contraceptives primarily in the context of family planning. A registered medical practitioner may give a prescription or authorisation for a contraceptive to a person if he or she is satisfied that the person 'is seeking the contraceptive, *bona fide*, for family planning purposes or for adequate medical reasons and in appropriate circumstances'.

   The legislation has come under much public discussion; two principal issues as to its constitutionality arise. First, in (apparently) generally excluding unmarried persons from access to contraceptives, does the Act conflict with Article 40.1 or 40.3? Secondly, in limiting access of married persons to contraceptives by introducing the requirement relating to a subjective view of a medical practitioner, and in relieving persons from the obligation of giving prescriptions or selling contraceptives (section 11), is the Act in conflict with Article 40.1, 40.3 or 41? Both these questions are considered briefly by Binchy, *Ethical Issues in Reproductive Medicine: A Legal Perspective*, in M. Reidy ed., *Ethical Issues in Reproductive Medicine*, at 96–98 (1982).
7. If a spouse refuses to have sexual intercourse unless contraception is practised may the marriage be annulled? Cf. *S.* v. *S., supra*, pp. 76–78 and pp. 90–91. May the other spouse take proceedings for divorce *a mensa et thoro*? Is the spouse so refusing guilty of constructive desertion if the other spouse leaves him or her? Has the Constitution anything to say on this question? Could the other spouse claim interference with a Constitutional right to health or bodily integrity? Or would marital privacy cast its veil?
8. Mr. Justice Walsh has written on the general theme of privacy in *The Judicial Power and Privacy*, (1977) 1 Dublin U. L. J. 3.

THE UNBORN AND THE LAW OF TORT

WALKER v. GREAT NORTHERN RY. CO. OF IRELAND
28 L. R. Ir. 69 (Q. B. Div., 1891)

Action for personal injuries. Demurrer to the plaintiff's statement of claim, which was as follows:–

1. At the time of the happening of the injuries hereinafter complained of the defendants were and still are a railway company, having a railway from Armagh to Warrenpoint, in the country of Down, used by them for the carrying of passengers for hire from Armagh aforesaid to Warrenpoint aforesaid.

2. The mother of the plaintiff is Mrs. Annie Walker, of the city of Armagh, and on the date hereinafter mentioned was quick with child, namely, with the plaintiff, to whom she subsequently gave birth.

3. On the 12th day of June, 1880, the said Annie Walker, so quick with child as aforesaid, became and was received by the defendants as a passenger upon their said railway, to be by them carried on their said railway a journey from Armagh aforesaid to Warrenpoint aforesaid, for reward to the defendants, yet the defendants so negligently and unskilfully conducted themselves in carrying the said Annie Walker, and the plaintiff, then being *en ventre sa mere*, as aforesaid, and in managing the said railway and the carriage in which the said Annie Walker was a passenger upon the said railway on the journey aforesaid, that the plaintiff was thereby wounded and permanently injured and crippled and deformed. The plaintiff claimed £1000 damages.

O'Brien, C.J.:

This claim comes before us on demurrer to the statement of claim, which states – [His Lordship read the statement of claim]. Now, this is the statement of claim, which has been challenged by demurrer as disclosing no cause of action.

Counsel for the company say no such action lies; that at the time the injuries were inflicted the child was not a person *in rerum naturâ*; that it had no personality; that it was simply part of the mother, and that therefore no action can be maintained. In support of their contention they principally rely upon an undoubted proposition of criminal law, that under no circumstances is it held, at the present day, to be murder to destroy a child whilst in the womb. They quote from Russell on Crimes, page 645, where it is stated, on the authority of Lord Hale, 'that an infant in its mother's womb, *not being in rerum naturâ*, is not considered as a person who can be killed within the description of murder, and that therefore, if a woman being quick or great with child take any potion, or cause an abortion, or if another give her any such potion, or if a person strike her whereby the child within is killed, it is not murder or manslaughter.' And they also rely upon what seems clearly established in the case of descent at common law, that a child *en ventre sa mere* is considered not in existence; and, referring to *Richards* v. *Richards* Johns, 754, they show 'that the qualified heir was entitled to the rents and profits until the posthumous heir was born.'

To this contention on behalf of the defendants, counsel for the plaintiff reply that, as to the child *en ventre sa mere* not taking by descent at common law, this is an exception to the general rule, and that it arose from the rigour of the common law with regard to real estates requiring a tenant to the *prœcipe*, as pointed out by Sir Richard Arden, Master of the Rolls, in *Thelluson* v. *Woodford* 4 Ves. 335; and they rely upon the language of Mr. Justice Buller in the same case, who, when replying to the allegation that a child *en ventre sa mere* was a nonentity, sarcastically observed (p. 321): 'Let us see what this nonentity can do. He may be vouched in a recovery, though it is for the purpose of making him answer over in value. He may be even executor. He may take under the Statute of Distributions. He may take by devise. He may be entitled under a charge for raising portions. He may have an injunction, and he may have a guardian. Some other cases put this beyond all doubt. In *Wallis* v. *Hodson* 2 Atk. 117 Lord Hardwicke says, "The principal reason I go upon in the question is, that the plaintiff was *en ventre sa mere* at the time of her brother's death, and consequently a person *in rerum naturâ*, so that, by the rules of the common and civil law, she was to *all intents and purposes a child as much as if born in the father's lifetime.*"

In the same case Lord Hardwicke takes notice that the civil law confines the rules to cases where it is for the benefit of the child to be considered as born; but notwithstanding, he states *the rule to be that such child is to be considered living to all intents and purposes.*' And the plaintiff's counsel also reply upon a passage lower down (at the close of page 322) in Mr. Justice Buller's judgment, where he states – 'In *Doe* v. *Clarke* 2 H. Bl. 399 the words "that whenever such consideration would be for his benefit, a child *en ventre sa mere* shall be considered actually born" were used by me because I found them in the book from whence the passage was taken. Why should not children *en ventre sa mere* be considered *generally* as in existence? *They are entitled to all the privileges of other persons.*'

But counsel for the plaintiff join issue also as to the effect of the criminal law, and relying upon Coke (3 Inst., p. 50), they show that if a criminal act is done to the child when in the womb, and the child is born alive, and dies from the effect of that act, it is murder or manslaughter, according to the circumstances, and they rely especially upon the case of *Rex* v. *Senior* 1 Moody, C. C. 316 – a case considered by all the English Judges, except two, and in which it was unanimously decided that a doctor who, through culpable ignorance and want of skill, inflicted a wound on a child in the act of being born, and before it was born, and of which it died after it was born, was properly found guilty of manslaughter. The rules of the civil law are also appealed to – '*Qui in utero est perinde ac si in rebus humanis esset cusoditur, quoties de commodis ipsius partûs quæritur, quanquum alii antequam nascatur, nequaquam prosit.* And another expression of the same rule of the civil law is also referred to – '*Qui in utero sunt in toto poene jure civili intelliguntur in rerum naturâ esse.*' And again – '*Nascituri fictione tamen juris pro jam natis habentur quoties de ipsorum commodo agitur*': see *Blasson* v. *Blasson* 2 De G.J. & S. 670, where these rules are collected. And finally, counsel for the plaintiff refer to the decision of Sir Robert Phillimore in the case of *The George and Richard* L.R. 3 Ad. & Eccl. 466, where that learned Judge held that a child *en ventre sa mere* was a child within the meaning of Lord Campbell's Act, so as to be capable, when born, of maintaining an action in respect of the pecuniary loss sustained by the death of its father, owing to the wrongful act of others done whilst it was in the womb.

Now these are substantially the authorities referred to on behalf of the plaintiff; and having regard to these authorities, I wish it to be clearly understood that in deciding this case I do not intend to go this length, viz. that if a person knowing that a woman is *enceinte* wilfully inflicts injuries on her with a view to injuring the child, and the child is born a cripple, or after its birth becomes a cripple, owing to the injuries so wilfully inflicted, an action does not lie at the suit of the child so crippled. I am far from saying that such action would lie under such circumstances at the suit of the child when born; but before I would hold an action under such circumstances did not lie, I would desire to hear further discussion as to the limitations of the rule that a child *in utero* is considered as actually born when it is necessary for the benefit of such unborn child so to consider it.

I would like to have it further discussed whether that rule is limited to taking benefits by succession and bequest, or whether it would apply to a case where the child has been so wilfully injured in the womb that it is born a cripple, or becomes one after its birth, and is thereby permanently deprived of the ability to earn a livelihood. In the case I put it would be manifestly for the benefit of the child that it should be considered as born at the time the injuries were inflicted, and that an action could be maintained.

I would also wish to hear further discussion as to the generality of the language of Lord Hardwicke in the case in 2nd Atkins. No doubt that was a case of succession to personal property and as to whether a child *en ventre sa mere* could take under the Statute of Distributions, but the language of that great Judge is very general, as was observed by Mr. Justice Buller in *Thelluson* v. *Woodford* 4 Ves. 334. . . .

. . . . I decide the present case upon a single ground, namely, that there are no facts set out in the statement of claim which fix the defendants with liability for breach of duty as carriers of passengers. This is not a case of trespass. It is now settled law that railway companies do not warrant the absolute safety of passengers: all they undertake with regard to passengers is a duty to carry with due and reasonable care, and their liability is for negligence arising from a breach of that duty. . . .

It is . . . . an elementary rule of law, that if the action is one that can be maintained only in respect of a breach of duty, and the particular duty cannot be inferred from the facts stated, objection may be taken by demurrer.

Now, applying that rule to the present case, let us see what the statement of claim alleges, or rather does not allege. It does not allege that the mother made any contract in reference to the child – the contract was with the mother in respect of herself alone. It does not allege that any consideration was received by the company in respect of the child. It does not allege that the company, through its servants or otherwise, knew anything about the child or the condition of the mother.

It is quite plain, for aught that appears in this statement of claim, that however the child in the womb may be regarded, whether as part of the mother or having a distinct personality – whether an entity or a non-entity – it was, so far as any actual relation the company had with it, a non-entity; and, therefore, in my opinion, the existence of the duty, for the breach of which the defendants would be liable as carriers of passengers, cannot be inferred. To infer the existence of such a duty from the mere possibility that the mother was with child when she was received as a passenger by the defendants would be to act without the sanction of any judicial decision or, in my opinion, of any legal principle. The demurrer must therefore be allowed.

Harrison, O'Brien and **Johnson, J.J.** delivered concurring judgments.

Notes

1. To what extent was the court's opposition to the plaintiff's claim based on the absence of privity of contractual relationship rather than on the impropriety of awarding damages for injuries sustained before birth? Cf. B. McMahon & W. Binchy, *Irish Law of Torts*, 425 (1981); Robertson, *Toward Rational Boundaries of Tort Liability for Injury to the Unborn: Prenatal Injuries, Preconception Injuries and Wrongful Life*, [1978] Duke L. J. 1401, at 1406; Little, *Erosion of the No-Duty Negligence Rules in England, the United States, and Common Law Commonwealth Nations*, 20 Houston L. Rev. 959, at 1024ff. (1983); Murphy, *The Evolution of the Prenatal Duty Rule: Analysis by Inherent Determinants*, 7 U. Dayton L. Rev. 351, at 356ff (1982); Maledon, *Note*, 47 Notre Dame L. 349, at 355 (1971); H. Teff & C. Munro, *Thalidomide: The Legal Aftermath*, 40–41 (1976); Babin, *Comment: Preconception Negligence Reconciling an Emergency Tort*, 67 Geo. L. J. 1239, at 1242–1243 (1979).
2. Can any lessons be drawn about the *Walker* approach from the English decision of *Austin* v. *Great Western Ry.*, L.R. 2 Q.B. 442 (1867)?
3. *Walker*'s case has long been discredited. In *Irish Sugar Manufacturing Co.* v. *Flynn*, 64 I.L.T.R. 73 (Sup. Ct., 1929), the Court expressly reserved the question whether *Walker* had been correctly decided: see especially *per* Kennedy, C.J., at 78. Internationally the trend of decisions has been against *Walker*: see *Montreal Tramways Co.* v. *Leveille*, [1933] S.C.R. 456; *Duval* v. *Seguin*, 1 O.R. (2d) 482 (C.A., 1974); *Watt* v. *Rama*, [1972] V.R. 358, *Pinchin* v. *Santam Ins. Co.*, 1963 (2) S.A. 254. Cf. Binchy, *Torts*, 6 Ottawa L. Rev. 511, at 519–520 (1974); W. Morison *et al., Cases on Torts*, 382–386 (5th ed., 1981). In Ontario, section 4 of the *Family Law Reform Act, 1975* (St. Ont. 1975, c. 41), reflecting the advancing case-law, provided that:

> No person shall be disentitled from recovering damages in respect of injuries incurred for the reason only that the injuries were incurred before his birth.

4. The literature on the subject has been enormous. See, e.g., Winfield, *The Unborn Child*, 8 Camb. L.J. 76 (1942); Gordon, *The Unborn Plaintiff*, 63 Mich. L. Rev. 579 (1965); Lovell & Griffith Jones, *'The Sins of the Fathers' – Tort Liability for Pre-Natal Injuries*, 90 L.Q. Rev. 531 (1974); Veitch, *Delicta in Uterum*, 24 N.I.L.Q. 40 (1973); Matthews, *Quantitative Interference with the Right to Life: Abortion and Irish Law*, 22 Cath. L. 344 (1967); Campbell, *Abortion Law in Canada: A Need for Reform*, 42 Sask. L. Rev. 221, at 247–248 (1978); Morrison, *Torts Involving the Unborn – A Limited Cosmology*, 31 Baylor L. Rev. 131 (1979).
5. The common law position has since been supplemented by statute. Section 58 of the *Civil Liability Act, 1961* provides that:

   > For the avoidance of doubt it is hereby declared that the law relating to wrongs shall apply to an unborn child for his protection in like manner as if the child were born, provided the child is subsequently born alive.

   For consideration of this provision see B. McMahon & W. Binchy, *Irish Law of Torts*, 425 (1981).
6. In England, the English Law Commission's fear of encouraging domestic disharmony resulting from intra-family litigation based on ante-natal torts (*Report on Injuries to Unborn Children*, Law Com. No. 60, 1974) led to some curious compromises in the *Congenital Disabilities (Civil Liability) Act, 1976*: the child may sue his or her father but not his or her mother, unless the claim against the mother is for the negligent driving of a motor vehicle. See Pace, 40 Modern L. Rev. 141 (1977) and Stanton, 6 Family L. 206 (1976). The Pearson Commission, haunted even more by the spectre of family disharmony, recommended that no claim should be sustainable against *either* parent by the child save one arising from any activity for which insurance is compulsory: *Report of the Royal Commission on Civil Liability and Compensation for Personal Injury*, vol I, paras. 1471–1472 (Cmnd. 7054–1, 1978). Can you perceive why the policy of discouraging the 'disrupti[on] of family life' (para. 1471) is served by thus excluding claims for ante-natal injury while permitting children to retain full rights of action against both their parents in respect of all types of injury inflicted after birth?

ABORTION

The subject of abortion has given rise to much discussion in recent years. Internationally there has been a strong trend towards regarding abortion as a matter of choice for pregnant women and towards affording relatively little, or no, protection to the unborn life. There has been a general tendency in Europe and North America over the past twenty years to legalise abortion and to hold that Constitutional guarantees of privacy prevail over the right to life of the unborn. See Michel, *Abortion and International Law: The Status and Possible Extension of Women's Right to Privacy*, 20 J. of Family L. 241 (1981); Lyon & Bennett, *Abortion – A Question of Human Rights*, 12 Family L. 47 (1982); Glenn, *The Constitutional Validity of Abortion Legislation: A Comparative Note*, 21 McGill L. J. 673 (1975).

In Ireland the issue whether the Constitution, as originally promulgated, protected the unborn against abortion was unresolved. Some commentators took the view that the Constitution did protect the unborn against abortion; there were a few judicial *dicta*, of varying degrees of force and specificity, which lent some weight to this view. Other commentators were less sure that the Constitution afforded adequate protection to the unborn against abortion, since it expressly limited its guarantee of the right to life to 'every citizen' (a term which did not include the unborn) and since the Constitutional right of privacy might be invoked as a basis for legalised abortion. International experience showed that no Constitution or Convention, in the absence of explicit protection of the right to life of the unborn, had proved capable of withstanding argument in favour of legalised abortion. For consideration of these and related issues, see J. Kelly, *The Irish Constitution*, 374 (1st ed., 1980), 469–471 (2nd ed., 1984); Dooley, *Contraception and the Irish Constitution*, 3 Social Studies 186 (1974); O'Reilly, *Marital Privacy and Family Law*, 65 Studies 8 (1977); Binchy, *Marital Privacy and Family Law: A Reply to Mr. O'Reilly*, 65 Studies 330 (1977); Casey, *The Development of Constitutional Law under Chief Justice Ó Dálaigh,* [1978] Dublin U.L.J. 1, at 10; M. Arnold & P. Kirby eds., *'The Abortion Referendum': The Case Against* (1982); A Rynne, *Abortion: The Irish Question* (1982); Binchy, *Ethical Issues in Reproductive Medicine: A Legal Perspective*, ch. 9 of M. Reidy ed., *Ethical Issues in*

Reproductive Medicine, (1982); Life Education and Research Network, *Abortion Now* (1983); Binchy, *The Need for a Constitutional Amendment*, ch. 11 of A. Flannery ed., *Abortion and the Law* (1983); Treacy, *The Constitution and the Right to Life, id.*, ch. 7, (other commentators in this book also touch on the legal issues); de Bréadún, *Hard Words As Lawyers Takes Sides*, Irish Times 31 August 1983, p. 10; Kelly, *Voting Yes*, Sunday Tribune, 4 September 1983, p. 9; *Finn* v. *A.G.* [1983] I.R. 164.

On 7 September 1983, after extended public debate, the Constitution was amended by Referendum. The Eighth Amendment to the Constitution added a new subsection to section 3 of Article 40. The subsection provides as follows:

> 3° The State acknowledges the right to life of the unborn and, with due regard to the legal right to life of the mother, guarantees in its laws to respect, and, as far as practicable, by its laws to defend and vindicate that right.

The Irish language text, which prevails in case of conflict with the English text, provides:

> 3° Admhaíonn an Stát ceart na mbeo gan breith chun a mbeatha agus, ag féachaint go cuí do chomhcheart na máthar chun a beatha, ráthaíonn sé gan cur isteach lena dhlíthe ar an gceart sin agus ráthaíonn fós an ceart sin a choisaint is a shuiomh lena dhlíthe sa mhéid gur féidir é.

STERILIZATION

There has been very little discussion in Ireland on the question of the legality of sterilization. It seems clear that *therapeutic* sterilization is lawful: the Constitutional rights to bodily integrity and of health would appear to guarantee this, as well as common law principles. Moreover, sterilization within marriage for contraceptive purposes would seem not to be unlawful on the basis of the Constitutional right to marital privacy recognised in *McGee* v. *A.G., supra*, p. 357. Beyond this, the position becomes less clear. See Binchy, *Ethical Issues in Reproductive Medicine: A Legal Perspective*, ch. 9 of M. Reidy ed., *Ethical Issues in Reproductive Medicine*, at 109–111 (1982); K. Oldershaw, *Contraception, Abortion and Sterilization in General Practice*, 220 (1975); Rheingold, *The Law Relating to Birth Control*, in H. Rudel, F. Kincl & M. Henzl, *Birth Control: Contraception and Abortion*, 264–268 (1973).

B. *Sexual Conduct*

NORRIS v. ATTORNEY-GENERAL

as yet unreported, Supreme Court, 22 April 1983, affirming High Court, McWilliam, J., High Ct., 1980

The plaintiff, a male homosexual, sought a declaration that sections 61 and 62 of the *Offences Against the Penal Act, 1861* and section 11 of the *Criminal Law Amendment Act, 1885* were inconsistent with the Constitution. McWilliam, J, in the High Court, rejected the plaintiff's case. The plaintiff appealed to the Supreme Court.

O'Higgins, C.J. (with whom **Griffin, J.** and **Finlay P.** concurred):

. . . . In my view, [on the question of *locus standi*] the Defendant's objection in so far as it applies to that part of the Plaintiff's case which is based on marital privacy is well founded and should be upheld. The basis of the Plaintiff's case is that there exists in our society a significant number of male homosexual citizens, of whom he is one, for whom, sexually, the female offers no attraction, and who, desiring a stable relationship, must seek such amongst male companions of a similar outlook and disposition. For these, as the Plaintiff clearly implied in his evidence (see transcript, Book I, Q. 153) marriage is not open as an alternative either to promiscuity or a more permanent sexual relationship with a male person. This being so, it is *nihil ad rem* for the Plaintiff to suggest, as a reason for alleviating his own predicament, a possible impact of the impugned legislation on a situation which is not his, and to point to a possible injury or prejudice which he has neither suffered nor is in imminant danger of suffering within the principles laid down by this Court in *Cahill* v. *Sutton* [1980] I.R. 269.

I do not, however, agree with the Defendant's submission that merely because the Plaintiff has not been prosecuted nor his way of life disturbed as a result of the legislation when he challenges, he, on that account, lacks standing to complain. In my view, as long as the legislation stands and continues to proclaim as criminal the conduct which the Plaintiff asserts he has a right to engage in, such right, if it exists, is threatened, and the Plaintiff has standing to seek the protection of the Court.

Consideration of the Plaintiff's Case

At the core of the Plaintiff's challenge to the impugned legislation is the assertion that the State has no business in the field of private morality and has no right to legislate in relation to the private sexual conduct of consenting adults. It is the Plaintiff's case that for the State to attempt to do so, is to exceed the limits of permissible interference and to shatter that area of privacy which the dignity and liberty of human persons require to be kept apart as a haven for each citizen. Accordingly, the Plaintiff says, that any legislation which purports to do so is *de facto* inconsistent with the Constitution. Apart from this, however, the Plaintiff has advanced other grounds of alleged inconsistency which must be considered. I propose in the first place to deal with these other grounds and then to return to what appears to be the Plaintiff's main submission.

. . . . [T]he Plaintiff argues that the impugned legislation is inconsistent with Article 40.1 of the Constitution in that it discriminates against male citizens who are homosexual. I understand his complaint in this respect to be confined to the 1885 Act. In case I am incorrect in this respect, however, I would like to express the view that such an argument is scarcely entertainable in relation to the impugned Sections of the 1861 Act. Buggery as an act can only be committed by males. It is designated as a crime whether it is committed with a male or female. If follows that the prohibition applies to the act irrespective of whether it is committed by a homosexual irrespective of whether it is committed by a homosexual or heterosexual male. No discrimination could be involved.

As to gross indecency, however, the prohibition only applies to such conduct between males. Does the fact that it does not apply to gross indecency between females involve a discrimination which would be prohibited by Article 40.1? I do not think so. The legislature would be perfectly entitled to have regard to the difference between the sexes and to treat sexual conduct or gross indecency between males as requiring prohibition because of the social problem which it creates, while at the same time looking at sexual conduct between females as being not only different but as posing no such social problem. Furthermore, in alleging discrimination because the prohibition on the conduct which he claims he is entitled to engage in, is not extended to similar conduct by females, the Plaintiff is complaining of a situation which, if it did not exist or were remedied, would confer on him no benefit or vindicate no right of his which he claims to be breached. I do not think that such an argument should be entertained by this Court. For the same reasons, I would reject the Plaintiff's complaint that there is discrimination in the fact that the laws of the State do not apply criminal sanctions to heterosexual conduct outside marriage between consenting adults.

The Plaintiff has also submitted that the blanket prohibition of homosexual conduct effected by the legislation threatens his physical and mental health through frustration and disorientation arising from his congenital disposition. For this reason the Plaintiff asserts that his right to bodily integrity is endangered. In my opinion this submission is not a sound one. If the legislation is otherwise valid and within the competence of the legislature to enact, it cannot be rendered inoperative merely because compliance with it by the Plaintiff, due to his innate or congenital disposition, is difficult for or harmful to him. In this respect the exigencies of the common good must prevail. The Plaintiff also alleges that this legislation and, in particular, Section 11 of the 1885 Act, impairs his right of freedom of expression and freedom of association which are guaranteed by Article 40.6 of the Constitution. I do not accept this submission. Freedom of expression and freedom of association are not guaranteed as absolute rights. They are protected by the Constitution subject to public order and morality. Accordingly, if the impugned legislation is otherwise valid and consistent with the Constitution, the mere fact that it prohibits the Plaintiff from advocating conduct which it prohibits or from encouraging others to engage in such conduct or associating with others for the purpose of so doing, cannot constitute a breach of the Constitution.

I now turn to what I have described as the core of the Plaintiff's case. This is the claim that the impugned legislation constitutes an interference with his private life which is unwarranted and thereby infringes his right to privacy. This claim is based on the philosophical view attributed to John Stuart Mill, that the law should not concern itself in the realm of private morality except to the extent necessary for the protection of public order and the guarding of citizens against injury or exploitation. It is a view which received significant endorsement in the Report of the Wolfenden Committee on Homosexual Offences and Prostitution which reported to the British Parliament in 1957 and which contained the following statement in support of its recommendation for limited decriminalisation:

> There remains one additional counter argument which we believe to be decisive, namely, the importance which society and the law ought to give to individual freedom of choice in action in matters of private morality. Unless a deliberate attempt is to be made by society, acting through the agency of the law, to equate the sphere of crime with that of sin, there must remain a realm of private morality and immorality, which is, in brief and crude terms, not the law's business. To say this is not to condone or encourage private immorality.

. . .The caution shown by successive British Governments and Parliaments is understandable because what was proposed was a significant reversal of legislative policy in an area in which deep religious and moral beliefs were involved.

From the earliest days, organised religion regarded homosexual conduct, such as sodomy and associated acts, with a deep revulsion as being contrary to the order of nature, a perversion of the biological functions of the sexual organs and an affront both to society and to God. With the advent of Christianity this view found clear expression in the teachings of St. Paul, and has been repeated over the centuries by the doctors and leaders of the Church in every land in which the Gospel of Christ has been preached. Today, as appears from the evidence given in this case, this strict view is beginning to be questioned by individual Christian theologians but, nevertheless, as the learned trial Judge said in his judgment, it remains the teaching of all Christian Churches that homosexual acts are wrong.

In England, buggery was first treated as a crime by the Statute 25 Hen. VIII ch. 6, having been previously dealt with only in the ecclesiastical courts. In Ireland, it first received statutory condemnation in the Statute of the Irish Parliament 10 Car. I St. 2 ch. 60. Subject to statutory changes as to punishment, it continued to be prohibited and punished as a crime in accordance with the provisions of the 1861 Act which was complemented by the later provisions of the 1885 Act. While the statutory provisions have now been repealed in the entire of the United Kingdom, the question in this case is whether they ceased to operate in Ireland at a much earlier date – at the time of the enactment of the Constitution.

In the course of the trial of this action in the High Court, reference was, of course, made to the Wolfenden Report, to the Kinsey Survey on homosexual behaviour conducted in the United States and to a similar survey conducted in Sweden. No such survey has been conducted in Ireland, but the trial Judge, on the evidence he heard, was prepared to conclude that there is probably a large number of people in this country with homosexual tendencies. Of these, however, only a small number are exclusively homosexual in the sense that their orientation is congenital and irreversible. It is this small group (of those with homosexual tendencies) who must look to the others for the kind of relationship, stable or promiscuous, which they seek and desire. It follows that the efforts and activities of the congenital homosexual must tend towards involving the homosexually orientated in more and more deviant sexual acts to such an extent that such involvement may become habitual. The evidence, and the text-books produced as part thereof, in this case indicate how sad, lonely and harrowing the life of a person, who is or has become exclusively homosexual, is likely to be. Professor West in his work, *Homosexuality Re-examined*, states at p. 318:

> Exclusive homosexuality forces a person into a minority group; cuts off all prospect of fulfilment through a family life with children and hampers participation in mainstream social activities which are mostly geared to the needs of heterosexual couples.

He goes on to talk of those, whose life centres on short-term liaisons, as facing loneliness and frustration as they lose their sexual attractiveness with advancing age. Other authors, also referred to, indicate the instability of male homosexual relations, the high incidence of suicide attempts and the depressive reactions which frequently occur when a relationship ends (Harrison; Reid, Barrett & Hewer). These are some of the consequences which, experience has indicated, tend to follow on a lifestyle which is exclusively homosexual.

Apart from these sad consequences of exclusive homosexuality there are, unfortunately, other problems thereby created which constitute a threat to public health. Professor West in his work already mentioned and which was published in a revised form in England over ten years after the decriminalisation of homosexual conduct, says at p. 228:

> Far from being immune from venereal infection, as many used to like to believe, male homosexuals run a particularly high risk of acquiring sexually transmitted diseases.

The author goes on to show that in the post-decriminalisation decade in Britain many forms of venereal disease – syphilis, gonorrhoae, urethritis and intestinal infection – have shown an alarming increase in males, and that this is attributable directly to the increase in homosexual activity and conduct. In relation to syphilis, the author gives this serious warning:

> A promiscuous homosexual with such a reservoir of infection can transmit the disease, in all innocence, to a whole sequence of victims before the carrier is discovered. The diagnosis at this stage is not always obvious, even when suspected, since blood tests for this infection do not usually become positive until some weeks after the primarily chancre has appeared.

He might well have added that, in the case of the novice or the new entrant into homosexual activity, reticence or shame might well delay further the tracing and discovery of the carrier.

Apart from these known consequences of fairly widespread homosexual behaviour and conduct, one other matter of particular importance should be noted. This is the effect of homosexual activity on marriage. It has to be accepted that for the small percentage of males who are congenitally and irreversibly homosexual, marriage is not open or possible. They must seek such partnerships as they can amongst those whose orientation disposes them to homosexual overtures. But for those so disposed or orientated, but not yet committed, what effect will the acceptance of such overtures be likely to have on marriage? Again, precise information in relation to Ireland is not available. One can only look to what the Wolfenden Committee in its Report said, at paragraph 55, before the changes in the law occurred in the United States:

> The second contention, that homosexual behaviour between males has a damaging effect on family life, may well be true. Indeed we have had evidence that it often is: cases in which homosexual behaviour on the part of the husband has broken up a marriage are by no means rare, and there are also cases in which a man in whom the homosexual component is relatively weak, nevertheless, derives such satisfaction from homosexual outlets that he does not enter upon a marriage which might have been successfully and happily consummated. We deplore this damage to what we regard as the basic unit of society.

This view was, of course, based on the limited experience available to the Committee prior to any changes in the law. It indicates, however, that homosexual activity and its encouragement may not be consistent with respect and regard for marriage as an institution. I would not think it unreasonable to conclude that an open and general increase in homosexual activity in any society must have serious consequences of a harmful nature so far as marriage is concerned.

I have, of course, been speaking of homosexuality and of its possible consequences in accordance with what, in my view, can be gathered from the evidence in this case. What I have said can be summarised as follows.

(1) Homosexuality has always been condemned in Christian teaching as being morally wrong. It has equally been regarded by society for many centuries as an offence against nature and a very serious crime.

(2) Exclusive homosexuality, whether the condition be congenital or acquired, can result in great distress and unhappiness for the individual and can lead to depression, despair and suicide.

(3) The homosexually orientated can be importuned into a homosexual lifestyle which can become habitual.

(4) Male homosexual conduct has resulted, in other countries, in the spread of all forms of venereal disease and this has now become a significant public health problem in England.

(5) Homosexual conduct can be inimical to marriage and is *per se* harmful to it as an institution.

In the United Kingdom the decisive factor in bringing about decriminalisation of homosexuality was the acceptance of the view advocated by the Wolfenden Committee, and repeated in this case by the Plaintiff, that homosexuality was concerned only with private morality and that the law had no business in entering into that field. Whether such a view can be accepted in Ireland depends not on what was done by a sovereign parliament in the United Kingdom but on what our Constitution ordains and requires.

The Preamble proudly asserts the existence of God in the Most Holy Trinity and recites the People of Ireland as humbly acknowledging their obligation to 'Our Divine Lord Jesus Christ'. It cannot be doubted that a people, so asserting and acknowledging their obligations to Our Divine Lord Jesus Christ, were proclaiming a deep religious conviction and faith and an intention to adopt a Constitution consistent with that conviction and faith and with Christian beliefs. Yet it is suggested that in the very act of so doing the People rendered inoperative laws which had existed for hundreds of years prohibiting unnatural sexual conduct which Christian teaching held to be gravely sinful. It would require very clear and express provisions in the Constitution itself to convince me that such took place. When one considers that the conduct in question had been condemned consistently in the name of Christ for almost two thousand years, and, at the time of the enactment of the Constitution, was prohibited as criminal by the laws in force in England, Wales, Scotland and Northern Ireland, the suggestion becomes more incomprehensible and difficult of acceptance. But the Plaintiff says that the continued operation of such laws was inconsistent with a right of privacy which he enjoys. Here, he asserts a 'no go area' in so far as the law and the State is concerned in the field of private morality. I do not accept this view, either as a general philosophical proposition concerning the purpose of law, or as having particular reference to a right of privacy under our Constitution. I regard the State as having an interest in the general moral wellbeing of the community and being entitled, where it is practicable to do so, to discourage conduct which is morally wrong and harmful to a way of life and to values which the State wishes to protect. A right of privacy or, as it has been put, a right 'to be let alone', can never be absolute. There are many acts done in private which the State is entitled to condemn, whether such be done by an individual on his own or with another. The law has always condemned abortion, incest, suicide attempts, suicide pacts, euthanasia or mercy killing. These are prohibited simply because they are morally wrong and regardless of the fact, which may exist in some instances, that no harm or injury to others is involved. With homosexual conduct, the matter is not so simple or clear. Such conduct is, of course, morally wrong, and has been so regarded by mankind through the centuries. It cannot be said of it, however, as the Plaintiff seeks to say, that no harm is done if it is conducted in private by consenting males. Very serious harm may in fact be involved. Such conduct, although carried on with full consent, may lead a mildly homosexuality orientated person into a way of life from which he may never recover. As already indicated, known consequences are frustration, loneliness and even suicide. In addition it is clearly established that an increase in the practice of homosexuality amongst males increases the incidence of all forms of venereal diseases, including the incapacitating and often fatal disease of syphilis. Surely, in the light of such possible consequences, no one could regard with equanimity the freeing of such conduct from all legal restraints with the certain result that it would increase and its known devotees multiply. These, however, are not the only considerations. There is the effect of homosexuality on marriage. As long ago as 1957 the Wolfenden Committee acknowledged, in relation to Great Britain, the serious harm such conduct caused to marriage, not only in turning men away from it as a partnership in life, but also in breaking up marriages that had been entered into. This was the conclusion reached as to the state of facts before the criminal sanctions were removed. One can only suspect that with the removal of such sanctions and with the encouragement thereby given to homosexual conduct, considerably more harm must have been caused in Great Britain to marriage as an institution. In Ireland, in this respect, the State has a particular duty. By Article 41.3 'the State pledges itself to guard with special care the institution of Marriage, on which the family is founded, and to protect it against attack'. Surely, a law which prohibits acts and conduct by male citizens of a kind known to be particularly harmful to the institution of marriage cannot be regarded as inconsistent with a Constitution containing such a provision.

On the grounds of the Christian nature of our State, and on the grounds that the deliberate practice of homosexuality is morally wrong, that it is damaging to the health both of individuals and the public and, finally, that it is potentially harmful to the institution of marriage, I can find no inconsistency with the Constitution in the laws which make such conduct criminal. It follows, in my view, that no right of privacy, as claimed by the Plaintiff, can prevail against the operation of such criminal sanctions.

European Convention on Human Rights

One other argument has been advanced on behalf of the Plaintiff by Mrs. Robinson. This was based on the Convention for the Protection of Human Rights and Fundamental Freedoms which was signed at Rome on the 4th November 1950 and confirmed and ratified by the Government on the 18th February 1953. This Convention specifies rights and freedoms for the Citizens of subscribing countries, broadly similar to the rights and freedoms enjoyed by the citizens of Ireland under the laws and the Constitution. In particular, Article 8 of the Convention provides as follows:

> 1. Everyone has the right to respect for his private and family life, his home and his correspondence.
> 2. There shall be no interference by a public authority with the exercise of this right, except such as in accordance with the law and is necessary in a democratic society in the interests of national security, public safety or the economic wellbeing of the country, for the prevention of disorder or crime, for the protection of health or morals, or for the protection of the rights and freedoms of others.

Recently the European Court of Human Rights, which is the appropriate body to do so under the Convention, interpreted this Article on a complaint by one Jeffrey Dudgeon, a citizen of Nothern Ireland, that the legislation impugned in this action, which was then in force in Nothern Ireland, interfered with his rights as a homosexual. The Court by a majority verdict held that it did so, and that, accordingly, Sections 61 and 62 of the *Offences Against the Person Act, 1861* and Section 11 of the *Criminal Law (Amendment) Act, 1885* were inconsistent with the observance of Article 8 of the Convention. Mrs. Robinson has argued that this decision by the European Court of Human Rights should be regarded by this Court as something more than a persuasive precedent and should, in fact, be followed. She so contends because, she says, that since Ireland confirmed and ratified the Convention there arises a presumption that the Constitution is compatible with the Convention and that in considering a question as to inconsistency under Article 50 of the Constitution regard should be had to whether the laws being considered are consistent with the Convention itself. While I appreciate the clarity of her submission, I must reject it. Acceptance of Mrs. Robinson's submission would, in my view, be contrary to the provisions of the Constitution itself and would be according to the Government, by an executive act, the power to change both the Constitution and the law. The Convention is an international agreement to which Ireland is a subscribing party. As such, however, it does not and cannot form part of our domestic law, nor affect in any way, questions which arise thereunder. This is made quite clear by Article 29.6 of the Constitution which declares as follows:

> No international agreement shall be part of the domestic law of the State, save as may be determined by the Oireachtas.

A similar contention was put before the former Supreme Court in *In re O Laighleis* [1960] I.R. 93 and was rejected. In the course of his judgment in that case, Maguire C.J. said, at 125:

> The Oireachtas has not determined that the Convention of Human Rights and Fundamental Freedoms is to be part of the domestic law of the State, and, accordingly, this Court cannot give effect to the Convention if it be contrary to the domestic law or purports to grant rights or impose obligations additional to those of domestic law.
>
> No argument can prevail against the express command of Section 6 of Article 29 of the Constitution before judges whose declared duty is to uphold the Constitution and the laws.
>
> The Court, accordingly, cannot accept the idea that the primacy of domestic legislation is displaced by the State becoming a party to the Convention for the Protection of Human Rights and Fundamental Freedoms. Nor can the Court accede to the view that in the domestic forum the Executive is in any way estopped from relying on the domestic law. It may be that such estoppel might operate as between the High Contracting Parties to the Convention, or in the court contemplated by Section 4 of the Convention, if it comes into existence, but it cannot operate in a domestic court administering domestic law. Nor can the Court accept the contention that the Act of 1940 is to be construed in the light of, and so as to produce conformity with, a Convention entered into ten years afterwards.

I agree with these views expressed by Chief Justice Maguire.

For these reasons, I cannot accept Mrs. Robinson's argument that either the Convention on Human Rights or the decision of the European Court in the *Dudgeon* case are in any way relevant to the question which we have to consider in this case.

For the reasons set out in this judgment I have come to the conclusion that the Plaintiff is not entitled to the relief he claims and that this appeal should be dismissed.

Henchy, J. (Dissenting):

[Having held that the plaintiff had *locus standi*, to the extent recognised by the Chief Justice, and having considered other aspects of the case, Henchy, J. continued:]

. . . . I am unable to accept th[e plaintiff's] argument [in relation to Article 40.1] I think it implies an over-wide interpretation of the scope of that constitutional guarantee. It would be a different matter if an unwarranted discrimination had been made between males in respect of the offences dealt with by the impugned sections. But such is not the case. What the sections have done is to make certain conduct between males criminal, while leaving unaffected by the criminal law comparable conduct when not committed exclusively by males. Therein lies the reason why in my view unconstitutional discrimination under Art. 40, s. 1, has not been shown. The sexual acts left unaffected are for psychological, social and other reasons capable of being differentiated as to their nature, their context, the range of their possible consequences and the desirability of seeking to enforce their proscription as crimes. While individual opinions on the matter may differ, it was and is a matter of legislative policy to decide whether a compulsion of the common good is capable of justifying the distinction drawn. I would hold that the proviso contained in the second sentence of Art. 40, s. 1 makes constitutionally acceptable under that Article the line of demarcation between the acts made criminal and those here complained of for being left unproscribed by the criminal law.

The second, indeed the main ground on which it is submitted that the impugned statutory provisions are constitutional is that they violate an essential component of the plaintiff's right of privacy. That a right of privacy inheres in each citizen by virtue of his human personality, and that such right is constitutionally guaranteed as one of the unspecified personal rights comprehended by Art. 40, s. 3, are propositions that are well attested by previous decisions of this Court. What requires to be decided – and this seems to me to be the essence of this case – is whether that right of privacy, construed in the context of the Constitution as a whole and given its true evolution or standing in the hierarchy of constitutional priorities, excludes as constitutionally inconsistent the impugned statutory provisions

Having regard to the purposive Christian ethos of the Constitution, particularly as set out in the Preamble ('to promote the common good, with due observance of Prudence, Justice and Charity, so that the dignity and freedom of the individual may be assured, true social order attained, the unity of our country restored, and concord established with other nations'), the denomination of the State as 'sovereign, independent, democratic' (Art. 8), the recognition, expressly or by necessary implication, of particular personal rights, such recognition being frequently hedged in by overriding requirements such as 'public order and morality', 'the authority of the state', or 'the exigencies of the common good', there is necessarily given to the citizen, within the required social, political and moral framework, such a range of personal freedoms or immunities as are necessary to ensure his dignity and freedom as an individual in the type of society envisaged. The essence of those rights is that they inhere in the individual personality of the citizen in his capacity as a vital human component of the social, political and moral order posited by the Constitution.

Amongst those basic personal rights is a complex of rights, varying in nature, purpose and range, each necessarily a facet of the citizen's core of individuality within the constitutional order, and which may be compendiously referred to as the right of privacy. An express recognition of such a right is the guarantee in Art. 16, s. 1, subs. 4, that voting in elections for Dail Eireann shall be by secret ballot. A judicial recognition of such a constitutional right is the right to marital privacy which was given effect to in the decision of this Court in *McGee* v. *Attorney General* [1974] I.R. 284, the right there claimed and recognised being, in effect, for a married woman to use contraceptives – something which is at present declared to be morally wrong according to the official teaching of the Church to which about 95 per cent of the citizens belong. There are many other aspects of the right of privacy, some yet to be given judicial recognition. It is unnecessary for the purpose of this case to explore them. It is sufficient to say that they would all appear to fall within a secluded area of activity or non-activity which may be claimed as necessary for the expression of an individual personality, for purposes not always necessarily moral or commendable, but meriting recognition in circumstances which do not endanger considerations such as state security, public order or morality, or other essential components of the common good.

Put in specific terms, the central issue in this case is whether the Plaintiff's claim to be entitled to engage in private in homosexual acts must give way to the right and duty of the State to uphold considerations of public order and morality. In my opinion the legal test by which that issue should be determined is this: where, as in this case, a pre-constitutional legislature has condemned as criminal all homosexual acts between males (ranging from acts of 'gross indency', the commission of which does not require even physical contact, to acts of sodomy) and thereby blights and thwarts in a variety of ways the life of a person who is by nature incapable of giving expression to his sexuality except by homosexual acts, and who wishes to be entitled to do so consensually in private, the onus lies on the Attorney General, representing the State, if he is to defeat the individual's claim, to show that to allow him that degree of privacy would be inconsistent with the maintenance of public order and morality.

In my judgment the Attorney General has signally failed to discharge that onus. In the High Court, ten witnesses were called, all on behalf of the plaintiff. Although homosexual acts in private between consenting adults had largely ceased to be criminal in England and Wales since 1967; although in most European countries for many years the legal position has been no less liberal; although a similar degree of decriminalisation has been in force for varying periods in different jurisdictions throughout the world, including some twenty or so States in the U.S.A.; and although there have been many studies by experts of the social, religious and other effects of such decriminalisation; not a single witness was called by the Attorney General to rebut the plaintiff's case that the degree of decriminalisation contended for by him posed no real threat to public order or morality. On the contrary, the consensus of the evidence given was that the beneficial effects, both in terms of individual fulfilment of personality and of the social, political and religious mores of the community, that would flow from a relaxation of the impugned provisions, would outweigh any possible ill-effects on society as a whole.

I hope to support that conclusion, not by eclectic excerpts from the evidence, but by answers which epitomise the general tenor of the particular witnesses. . . . [Henchy, J. reviewed the evidence of some of these witnesses. He continued:]

The foregoing summary is no doubt an over-compressed version of the evidence given, and to that extent it probably does not reproduce many of the nuances and subtleties of the opinions expressed. But it is an indisputable fact that the evidence of all ten witnesses condemned, in one degree or another, and for a variety of reasons, the impugned sections for being repugnant to the essential human needs of compulsive or obligatory homosexuals and as not being required by – indeed as being inconsistent with – public order and morality or any of the other attributes comprehended by the constitutional concept of the common good.

In response to this massive and virtually unanimous volume of evidence, given almost entirely by experts in sociology, theology and psychiatry, the Attorney General adduced no oral evidence whatsoever. If the matters pleaded by him in his defence were susceptible of proof, at least to the extent of disproving or casting doubt on the conclusions expressed by the plaintiff and his witnesses, it would have been well within the resources and competence of the State to adduce such evidence. But the hearing in the High Court is notable for the total absence of contraverting evidence. True, efforts was made in cross-examination to get witnesses to accept contrary opinions said to have been expressed in the writings or pronouncements of other experts or authorities. But a close study of the evidence shows that the largely unanimous conclusions expressed on oath were essentially as I have summarised them and that they stood uncontroverted at the end of the hearing of the evidence.

What choice, then, was open to the trial judge? In my opinion, since this was an oral hearing on oath carried out under our adversary system (which is based on the determination, from sworn testimony, according to the required onus and level of proof, of the relevant issues), where the outcome of the case depended on a judicial conclusion as to the actual or potential effect of our society of specified statutory provisions or of their alternatives, when the conclusions expressed overwhelmingly supported the plaintiff's case, the trial judge was bound in law to reject the Attorney General's defence and to uphold, at least in part, the plaintiff's case. The decision of this Court in *Northern Bank Finance* v. *Charlton* [1979] I.R. 149, shows that if the judge had found the factual conclusions in accordance with the plaintiff's uncontroverted evidence, his findings could not be overturned on an appeal to this Court. . . .

As was made clear by the decision of this Court in *Ryan* v. *Attorney General* [1965] I.R. 294, where a constitutional challenge depends on expert opinion as to the actual or potential effect of questioned statutory provisions, the constitutional point must be ruled on the basis of the facts or opinions as admitted to be correct or as duly found by the judge from the evidence given. Where the evidence given is entirely to one effect, it cannot be rejected.

The learned judge (who dealt with this difficult case with commendable thoroughness), in substituting his own conclusions as to the personal and societal effects of the questioned provisions, seems to have laid undue stress on the fact that the prohibited acts, especially sodomy, are contrary to the standards of morality advocated by the Christian Churches in this State. With respect, I do not think that should be treated as a guiding consideration. What are known as the seven deadly sins are anathematised as immoral by all the Christian Churches, and it would have to be conceded that they are capable, in different degrees and in certain contexts, of undermining vital aspects of the common good. Yet it would be neither constitutionally permissible nor otherwise desirable to seek by criminal sanctions to legislate their commission out of existence in all possible circumstances. To do so would upset the necessary balance which the Constitution posits between the common good and the dignity and freedom of the individual. What is deemed necessary to his dignity and freedom by one man may be abhorred by another as an exercise in immorality. The pluralism necessary for the preservation of constitutional requirements in the Christian, democratic State envisaged by the Constitution means that the sanctions of the criminal law may be attached to immoral acts only when the common good requires their proscription as crimes. As the most eminent theologians have conceded, the removal of the sanction of the criminal law from an immoral act does not necessarily imply an approval or condonation of that act. Here the consensus of the evidence was that the sweep of the criminal prohibition contained in the questioned provisions went beyond the requirements of the common good, indeed in the opinion of most of the witnesses was inimical to the common good. Consequently a finding of unconstitutionality was, on the evidence, inescapable.

Having given careful consideration to all the evidence, I find that the essence of the unconstitutionality claimed lies, not in the prohibition as a crime of homosexual acts between consenting adult males, but primarily in making that prohibition apply without qualification to consulting adult males who are exclusively and obligatorily homosexual. The combined effect of the questioned sections is to condemn such persons, who are destined by nature to being incapable of giving interpersonal outlet to their sexuality otherwise than by means of homosexual acts, to making the stark and (for them) inhumane choice of opting for total and unequivocal sexual continence (because guilt for gross indecency may result from equivocal acts) and yielding to their primal sexual urges and thereby either committing a serious crime or leaving themselves open to objectionable and harmful intrusion by those who would wish to prevent such acts, or to intolerance, harassment, blackmail and other forms of cruelty at the hands of those who would batten on the revulsion that such acts elicit in most heterosexuals.

One way or the other, the impugned provisions seem doomed to extinction. Whether they be struck down by this Court for being unconstitutional or whether they be deemed invalid elsewhere in accordance with the *Dudgeon* decision, for being in contravention of the European Convention for the Protection of Human Rights and fundamental Freedoms, they will require to be replaced with appropriate statutory provisions. It would not be constitutional to decriminalise all homosexual acts, any more than it would be constitutional to decriminalise all heterosexual acts. Public order and morality; the protection of the young, of the weak-willed, of those who may readily be subject to undue influence, and of others who should be deemed to be in need of protection; the maintenance inviolate of the family as the natural primary and fundamental unit of society; the upholding of the institution of marriage; the requirements of public health; these and other aspects of the common good require that homosexual acts be made criminal in many circumstances. The true and justifiable gravamen of the complaint against the sections under review is that they are in constitutional error for overreach or overbreadth. They lack necessary discrimination and precision as to when and how they are to apply.

The opinion expressed by some of the witnesses in the High Court that homosexual acts in private should be decriminalised must not be taken literally. Indeed it is likely that most, if not all, of the witnesses who gave that opinion would wish on mature consideration to qualify it. Even the liberalising Sexual Offences Act, 1967, which was passed in England in consequence of the Wolfenden Report, makes extensive exceptions (e.g. in respect of members of the armed services, in respect of acts committed on merchant ships, and because of limitations imposed by the nature of the statutory definitions) to the immunity from prosecution granted. Similar restricting limitations have been inserted in the *Homosexual Offences (Northern Ireland) Order, 1982*, which was enacted for the purpose of removing the incongruity in that jurisdiction between the now-impugned statutory provisions and the European Convention, as found in the *Dudgeon* decision.

I make reference to these matters to indicate that, despite my finding of unconstitutionality in the impugned sections on the ground that by their overreach and lack of precision and of due discrimination, they trench on an area of personal intimacy and seclusion which requires to be treated as inviolate for the expression of those primal urges, functions and aspirations which are integral to the human condition of certain kinds of homosexuals. Save in circumstances when the common good requires otherwise, the Constitution leaves a wide range of choice to the Oireachtas in framing a law in place of the questioned provisions. Not only will the Oireachtas be empowered to make homosexual acts criminal, but for the purpose of upholding the requirements of the common good in its full constitutional connotation, it will be necessary for such legislation to hedge in such immunity from criminal sanctions as it may think fit to confer on acts of a homosexual nature in private between consenting adults, with appropriate definitions as to adulthood, consent and privacy and with such exceptions as to prostitution, immoral exploitation, publicity, drug abuse, commercialisation, family relationships and such other matters or areas of exception as the Oireachtas may justifiably consider necessary for the preservation of public order and decency. . . .

McCarthy, J. (Dissenting):

. . . . In so far as the judgment of Kenny, J. in [*Ryan* v. *The Attorney General* [1965] I.R. 294] in referring to the Christian and democratic nature of the State, is a relative identification of source (cited by Finlay, P. in *The State (C)* v. *Frawley* [1976] I.R. 365, at 373, and *The State (M)* v. *Attorney General* [1979] I.R. 73, at 80). I respectfully dissent from such a proposition if it were to mean that, apart from the democratic nature of the State, the source of personal rights, unenumerated in the Constitution, is to be related to Christian theology, the subject of many diverse views and practices, rather than Christianity itself, the example of Christ and the great doctrine of charity which He preached. Jesus Christ proclaimed two great commandments – love of God and love of neighbour; St. Paul, the Apostle to the Gentiles, declared that of the great virtues, Faith, Hope and Charity, the greatest of these is Charity (1st letter to Corinthians Ch. 13 verse 13). I would uphold the view that the unenumerated rights derive from the human personality and that the actions of the State in respect of such rights must be informed by the proud objective of the people as declared in the Preamble 'seeking to promote the common good, with due observance of Prudence, Justice and Charity, so that the dignity and freedom of the individual may be assured, true social order attained, the unity of our country restored, and concord established with other nations'. The dignity and freedom of the individual occupy a prominent place in these objectives and are not declared to be subject to any particular exigencies but as forming part of the promotion of the common good.

The right of privacy

The Constitution does not guarantee or, in any way, expressly refer to a right of privacy – no more, indeed, than does the United States Constitution, with which our Constitution bears so many apparent similarities. In the United States Constitution the right to privacy of one form or another has been founded upon the first amendment (*Stanley* v. *Georgia* 394 U.S. 557); the fourth and fifth amendments – (*Terry* v. *Ohio* 394 U.S. 1); in the penumbras of the Bill of Rights (*Griswold* v. *Connecticut* 381 U.S. 479) the contraceptives case); in the ninth amendment (*Griswold* v. *Connecticut*, supra); in the concept of liberty guaranteed by the first section of the fourteenth amendment (*Meyer* v. *Nebraska* 262 U.S. 390). In our Constitution a right of privacy is not spelled out; as pointed out by Henchy, J. in his judgment, there is a guarantee of privacy in voting under Art. 16, s. 1, subs. 4 – the secret ballot; a limited right of privacy given to certain litigants under laws made under Art. 34; the limited freedom from arrest and detention under Art. 40, s. 4; the inviolability of the dwelling of every citizen under Art. 40, s. 5; the rights of the citizen to express freely their convictions and opinions.

i – To assemble peaceably and without arms

ii – To form associations and unions

all conferred by Art. 40, s. 6, subs. 1; the rights of the family under Art. 41; the rights of the family as to education under Art. 42; the right of private property under Art. 43; freedom of conscience and the free profession and practice of religion under Art. 44 – all these may properly be described as different facets of the right of privacy, but they are general in nature, as necessarily they must be in a Constitution, and do not sent bounds to the enumeration of the details of such a right of privacy when the occasion arises. In our jurisdiction, this is best exemplified in the *McGee* case where, whilst Walsh, J. rested his judgment upon the provisions of Art. 41, Budd, Henchy and Griffin, JJ. relied upon the guarantees of Art. 40, s. 3. I would respectfully share the latter view as to the true foundation for what the *McGee* case upheld – the right of privacy in marriage. Whilst the Constitution of the Irish Free State (Saorstát Éireann) did not, as it were, isolate the fundamental rights of citizens in a manner in which the Constitution has done, Articles 6, 7, 8, 9 and 10 of that Constitution indicate the manner in which certain rights were spelled out but, to a degree, highlight the absence of such guarantees as are contained in Art. 40, s. 3 and Art. 41 of the Constitution. There may well be historical reasons for these differences – a greater awareness of the need for the enunciation of fundamental rights was present during the 1930s than at the time of the negotiations for the Treaty that led to the enactment of the Constitution of the Irish Free State (Saorstát Éireann). At all events, since 1937, the concept of judicial dynamism in constitutional law has grown, thereby, indeed, identifying more readily the role of the courts and, in particular, this Court as the judicial organ of government, not merely by way of a supervisory jurisdiction on the actions of the legislative and executive branches of government, but, further, by way of legal interpretation, playing its part in 'seeking to promote the common good, with due observance of Prudence, Justice and Charity so that the dignity and freedom of the individual may be assured. . . .', as most strikingly evidenced by the decision in the *McGee* case.

How then, to identify the nature of the personal right of privacy? It is been called by Warren, C.J. and Brandeis, J. of the United States Federal Supreme Court as 'the right to be let alone' a quotation cited by the Chief Justice in the instant case and by Walsh, J. in his dissenting judgment as a member of the Court of Human Rights in the *Dudgeon* case. By way of definition it has brevity and clarity and I would respectfully adopt it as accurate and adequate for my purpose, but, to a degree, the very definition begs the question. The right to privacy is not in issue – it is the extent of that right – the extent of the right to be let alone. If a man wishes to maim himself in private, may he no do so? No, because he may become a charge upon the public purse; if a man wishes to masturbate alone and in private, may he not do so? Yes; if he and another male adult wish to do so in private, may they not do so? No, each commits an offence under s. 11 of the 1885 Act; if a woman wishes to masturbate in private does she commit an offence? No; if two women wish to do so in private does either of them commit an offence? No; if a man and a woman wish together to do so in private, not being married to each other, does either of them commit an offence? No. In such latter circumstances, the act committed by the woman upon the man may be identical with that which another man would commit upon him, save that his partner is a woman. I refer to these particular examples to seek to illustrate the problem that arises if a test is related to what may bc generalised as compelling State interest. The term 'compelling State interest' is commonly used, particularly in the United States, in cases depending on the claim to privacy. It is self evident that such interest is overwhelming in the protection of minors, persons under incapacity of one kind or another, public decency, discipline in the armed forces or the security forces and so on. But what is the test in circumstances where none of these obvious instances of compelling State interest apply? The Chief Justice has touched upon the alleged greater spread of venereal diseases but I do not accept that the State in this instance has discharged in any way a burden of proof of establishing that such a circumstance amounted to a compelling State interest. I join with Henchy, J. in the observations he has made in his judgment as to the failure of the Attorney General with all the resources at his disposal, to call any evidence whatever to displace the impressive body of evidence called on behalf of the plaintiff. In my opinion, in order to justify State interference, it itself of a most grievous kind – the policeman in the bedroom – in a claim to the right to perform sexual acts or give expression to sexual desires or needs, in private, between consenting adults male or female, subject to the matters such as I have already instanced, a very great burden lies upon those who would question such personal rights. The Act of 1861 and, indeed, that of 1885, were passed during the long reign of a British Monarch whose name is identified with many human virtues – those of duty, responsibility, love of family and country and so on – a less attractive quality of that Age was the gross hypocrisy that prevailed frequently, indeed, amongst the ranks of the legislators themselves. Certainly, male homosexuality was known to exist on a wide scale and the Act of 1861 provided a most terrible penalty for what might well be the natural expression of such a human condition. Again, can it be justified to remain on the statute book in 1983, as consistent with, or more correctly, as not inconsistent with the personal rights guaranteed by the Constitution[?] As Henchy, J. has done, so I, also, have read the evidence of the several distinguished witnesses who testified for the plaintiff; I have examined the cross-examination of these witnesses and the textbooks and reports to which they referred. . . .

[I]n my opinion, there was no evidence before the learned trial Judge upon which he could hold other than that the impugned sections were not consistent with the Constitution.

I cannot delimit the area in which the State may constitutionally intervene so as to restrict the right of privacy, nor can I overlook the present public debate concerning the criminal law, arising from the statute of 1861, as to abortion – the killing of an unborn child. It is not an issue that arises in the instant case, but it may be claimed that the right of privacy of a pregnant woman would extent to a right in her to terminate a pregnancy, an act which would involve depriving the unborn child of the most fundamental right of all – the right to life itself. I recognise that there has been no argument in the instant case relevant to such an issue, but nothing in this judgment, express or in any way implied, is to be taken as supporting a view that the provisions of s. 58 of the Act of 1861, making it a criminal offence to procure an abortion, are in any way inconsistent with the Constitution. There are but two judicial references to this question, if question be the appropriate word. . . .

[**McCarthy, J.** quoted relevant passages from Griffin, J.'s judgment in *McGee* v. *A.G.* [1974] I.R., at 335 and Walsh, J.'s judgment in *G.* v. *An Bord Uchtála* [1980] I.R., at 69. He continued:]

For myself I am content to say that the provisions of the Preamble which I have quoted earlier in this judgment would appear to lean heavily against any view other than that the right to life of the unborn child is a sacred trust to which all the organs of government must lend their support. The right of the adult male citizen *privately* to express his sexual orientation alone or with another such person free from State interference is an entirely different matter.

The plaintiff has, further, rested his case upon alleged breach of the Constitutional guarantee of equality contained in Art 40, s. 1; having reached the conclusion already expressed, I do not consider it necessary to examine the law in the light of that section; I am not to be taken, however, as agreeing with the view that the plaintiff's argument implies an over-wide interpretation of the scope of that constitutional guarantee. . . .

Notes

1. McWilliam, J.'s judgment is critically analysed by Tomkin, *Homosexuality and the Law,* ch. 5 of D. Clarke ed., *Morality and the Law* (1982). For analysis of the Supreme Court judgments, see Gearty, [1983] Dublin U.L.J. 264; Binchy, 17 Ir. Med. Times, No. 11, p. 20 (1984).
2. Which judgment do you prefer. Why?
3. To what extent does Chief Justice O'Higgins endorse Devlin's point of view as expressed in *The Enforcement of Morals?* To what extent do the minority judgments echo Hart's standpoint?

4. After this case, would a prosecution for buggery be successful if taken against (*a*) a married man in relation to conduct in private with his wife; (*b*) a married man in relation to conduct in public with his wife; (*c*) a man in relation to conduct in private with a woman who is not his wife; (*d*) a man in relation to conduct in public with a woman who is not his wife?
5. Does Henchy, J. uphold the constitutionality of legislation penalising homosexual conduct in private where the man involved is not entirely homosexual in orientation? Is this not precisely the category of person whom Chief Justice O'Higgins wants to protect? Can the apparent conflict be resolved?
6. What 'social problem' is posed by sexual conduct or gross indecency between males that is not posed by sexual conduct between females?
7. Is the plaintiff's argument based on unequal treatment adequately met by the reply that, if similar conduct by females (or heterosexuals outside marriage) were also rendered criminal this 'would confer on him no benefit or vindicate no right of his which he claims to be breached'? Cf. Forde, *Equality and the Constitution*, 17 Ir. Jur. (n.s.) 295, at 314 (1982).
8. Does O'Higgins, C.J. hold that the exigencies of the common good must prevail over harm caused to individuals? If so, what are the limits of this principle? If it could be shown that a small number of homosexuals committed suicide because of the existing law, would this 'harm' outweigh the common good? What calculus is to be applied in answering this question?
9. On Henchy, J.'s view that, in the absence of evidence adduced by the Attorney-General, the Court was obliged to hold in favour of the plaintiff, see J. Kelly, *The Irish Connection*, 276 (2nd ed., 1984).
10. To what extent does the decision recognise a right to *individual* privacy?
11. The constitutionality of legislation prohibiting sodomy has been litigated in the United States with varying results: see *Doe* v. *Commonwealth's Attorney*, 403 F. Supp. 1199 (E. D. Va. 1975), summarily affirmed, 425 U.S. 901 (1976); *People* v. *Onofre*, 51 N.Y. 2d 476, 415 N.E. 2d 936, 434 N.Y.S. 2d 947 (1980), cert, denied 451 U.S. 987 (1981); Wilkinson & White, *Constitutional Protection for Personal Lifestyles*, 62 Cornell L. Rev. 563, at 591–600 (1977); Rizzo, *Note: The Constitutionality of Sodomy Statutes*, 45 Fordham L. Rev. 553 (1976); *Anon., Note*, 77 Mich. L. Rev. 252, at 265–266, 292–293 (1978); Schwartz, 5 W. New England L. Rev. 75 (1982). More generally, see Karst, *The Freedom of Intimate Association*, 89 Yale L. J. 624 (1980).
12. For an article consider if the implications of the *Dudgeon* case, written before the Supreme Court's judgment in *Norris*, see Connelly, *Irish Law and the Judgment of the European Court of Human Rights in the Dudgeon Case*, [1982] Dublin U.L.J. 25.
13. What do you think of McCarthy, J.'s location of the right to life of the unborn child in the Preamble to the Constitution? What do you understand by this statement that 'the right to life of the unborn child is a sacred trust to which all the organs of government must lend their support'?

Chapter 13

THE LAW OF SUCCESSION

The *Succession Act, 1965* 'brought about a revolutionary change in the law of succession in this State': *Re Urquhart Deceased: Revenue Commissioners* v. *Allied Irish Banks Ltd.*, [1974] I.R. 197, at 208 (Sup. Ct., *per* Walsh, J.). Before then, the law of succession in respect of property that passed as personal property in the case of intestacy was determined by the provisions of the *Statute of Distributions, 1695* and the *Intestates Estates Act, 1954.* A person who died testate could dispose of his other property as he or she thought fit; where a married man died intestate and without issue, his widow had a first charge of £4,000 on his realty and personalty.

The *Succession Act, 1965* has radically improved the position of surviving spouses and children. Where a person dies intestate leaving a spouse and no issue, the surviving spouse inherits the entire estate. Where the intestate person leaves a spouse and issue, the spouse is entitled to two-thirds of the estate, and the issue are entitled to the rest. Where the intestate leaves issue but no surviving spouse, the estate is distributed among the issue.

In cases where a person dies testate, leaving a spouse and no children, the surviving spouse has what is called a 'legal right' to half the estate; if the testator leaves a spouse and children, the spouse has a 'legal right' to one third of the estate. This 'legal right' may be renounced by an antenuptial contract made in writing between the parties to an intended marriage or may be renounced by a spouse after the marriage and during the lifetime of the testator, if the renunciation is in writing: section 113. On the subject generally see *Wylie*, paras. 14.55ff (1975); *Shatter*, 347ff; Sherrin, *Disinheritance of a Spouse: A Comparative Study of the Law in the United Kingdom and the Republic of Ireland*, 31 N.I.L.Q. 21, at 25–26 (1980).

Where the estate of a deceased person includes a dwelling in which at the time of the deceased's death the surviving spouse was ordinarily resident, the surviving spouse may require the personal representatives to appropriate the dwelling in full or partial satisfaction of his or her share in the estate: section 56(1). See *Wylie*, paras. 14.60, 16.55; *Shatter*, 353–354; *Hamilton* v. *Armstrong*, unreported, High Ct., O'Hanlon, J., 2 May 1983 (1981–844P.)

There has been little public discussion in recent years of the policy of giving surviving spouses substantial entitlements in relation to the property of deceased spouses. It is interesting to speculate as to why the *Succession Act, 1965* so radically improved these entitlements when it did. For general consideration of some of the issues raised by succession law, see Volkmer, *Spousal Property Rights at Death: Re-Evaluation of the Proposed Uniform Marital Property Act*, 17 Creighton L. Rev. 95 (1983) and Prager, *Sharing Principles and the Future of Marital Property Law*, 25 U.C.L.A.L. Rev. 1 (1977). More specifically one may seek to discover the policy or policies which the 'legal right' provisions are designed to serve. Is *protection* of a financially vulnerable widow the real basis? If so, why does the law allow financially independent widows to benefit from the legal right? Is the goal to *compensate* widows for having chosen the financially unrewarding vocation of housewife? Is the purpose to thwart the testamentary plans of *malevolent husband*? If so, why does the 'legal right' apply to cases where the husband acted in no way malevolently? Issues such as these arising in respect of related legislation in other common law jurisdictions are provocatively analysed by Kulzer, *Property and the Family: Spousal Protection*, 4 Rutgers – Camden L. J. 195 (1973).

The question of children's entitlements in cases where their parent has died testate is the one that has caused the most judicial discussion. Section 117 of the *Succession Act, 1965* provides as follows:

(1) Where, on application by or on behalf of a child of a testator, the court is of opinion that the testator has failed in his moral duty to make proper provision for the child in accordance with his means, whether by his will or otherwise, the court may order that such provision shall be made for the child out of the estate as the court thinks just.
(2) The court shall consider the application from the point of view of a prudent and just parent, taking into account the position of each of the children of the testator and any other circumstances which the court may consider of assistance in arriving at a decision that will be as fair as possible to the child to whom the application relates and to the other children.
(3) An order under this section shall not affect the legal right of a surviving spouse or, if the surviving spouse is the mother or father of the child, any devise or bequest or any share to which the spouse is entitled on intestacy.

For detailed consideration of the section see Cooney, *Succession and Judicial Discretion in Ireland: The Section 117 Cases*, 15 Ir. Jur. (n.s.) 62 (1980); Fitzpatrick, *The Succession Act, 1965, Section 117*, 110 I.L.T. & Sol. J. 77, 83, 89, 95, 101 (1976); Bacon, *The Rights of Children and the Discretion of the Courts under Section 117 of the Succession Act, 1965*, 77 Incorp. L. Soc. of Ireland Gazette 223 (1983).

In the following decisions we can examine how the courts have interpreted and applied Section 117 in a wide variety of contexts.

IN THE GOODS OF G.M. DECEASED: F.M. v. T.A.M.

106 I.L.T.R. 82 (High Court, Kenny, J., 1970)

Kenny, J.:

G.E.M. ('the testator') was the owner of a large form in County Meath which he worked and of lands in England. On the 10th December, 1924, he married B.C. one of the defendants. They had no children and in 1941 she decided to adopt a boy called F.B., the plaintiff, who came to live with them. The informal adoption followed a conversation which she had with her sister and she did not consult the testator who knew nothing of it until she brought the boy to the farm. There was no system of legal adoption in the Republic of Ireland at that time.

The plaintiff attended the national school at A. until he was eight and then went to boarding schools until he was 17 years of age when he became a student at the School of Navigation attached to the University of Southampton for one year. He then joined the Merchant Navy in which he reached the position of first mate. He holds a Master's certificate and since May, 1969, has been working for the British and Irish Steamship Company. He is now 32, lives in Dublin, married and has two children. His basic salary is £1,200 but his total earnings will be about £1,700 this year.

On the 19th March, 1954, An Bord Uchtála made an adoption order under the *Adoption Act, 1952*, by which the plaintiff became the adopted child of the testator and his wife. The application for this must have been signed by the testator and validity of the Order has not been challenged. From the time it was made the plaintiff was called F.M. or F.B.M.

Mrs. M. who is a medical doctor, paid all the expenses of the plaintiff's education and provided him with clothes and pocket money. The testator and the plaintiff were on friendly terms, but the bond of affection which the relationship of father and son usually creates never existed between them. The testator told the plaintiff that he would never become the owner of the farm at F. and all the evidence suggests that the testator never wanted the adoption and signed the documents in connection with it to please his wife. The testator has two nephews, J.A.K. and M.K., the sons of his sister who was a medical doctor who now lives in Northern Ireland. Mrs. K. and one of her sons called on a few occasions to see the testator. Mrs. M. did not welcome their visits and there was not any personal affection or attachment between the testator and his nephews.

On the 3rd March, 1961, the testator made his will by which he appointed his brother, T.A.M. and A., the well known solicitor, to be his executors and trustees. He left all his property in the Republic of Ireland and his shares and securities to them upon trust for his wife for life and after her death for the two nephews I have mentioned, absolutely. He left his farm at P. in England to them upon trust for his brother-in-law G.A.C. who had been managing it for many years, for his life and after his death to his nephew, M.K. absolutely. The remarkable feature about this will is that the plaintiff is not mentioned in it. The effect of section 24 of the *Adoption Act, 1952*, was that the plaintiff was to be regarded as the child of the testator and of his wife born to them in what the Act calls 'lawful wedlock' and who for the purpose of property rights was to be treated as a child of the testator if the testator had died intestate.

The testator died on the 19th January, 1968, when he was 93 years of age. He was domiciled in the Republic of Ireland. His property consisted of (a) the farm in Co. Meath subsequently acquired by the Land Commission for £50,000 payable in 8% Land Bonds and which, for the purposes of this application, I intend to value at £45,000; (b) shares and securities in the Republic of Ireland, in England and Scotland, which had a market value of about £65,000; (c) livestock and furniture worth about £8,500 and (d) the farm in England which had a value of about £18,500. His debts and funeral expenses were £2,257 so that the gross value of his estate after deduction of debts, but before deduction of testamentary expenses was about £135,250. The testamentary expenses (excluding the costs of these proceedings which I estimate will be about £5,000) will be about £5,000 so that the testator had disposing power over assets worth about £130,000. The estate duty payable in the Republic of Ireland was £38,067 against which there is a credit of £12,061, the duty paid in England. His widow has elected to take the legal share of one-third of his estate instead of the benefits given to her by the will (see section 111 of the Succession Act, 1965.)

There was some discussion as to whether the estate for the purposes of Part IX of the Act of 1965 includes the farm in England, but it has now been conceded that it does not. Section 109(2) of the Act has not changed the judge-made rule that the succession to immoveables is governed by the law of the place where they are situate, while that to moveables is regulated by the law of the domicile of the deceased. Section 109(2) bears a striking similarity to section 66 which appears in Part VI which deals with distribution on intestacy. Both define the type of interest in property with which the two parts are dealing, an estate to which the deceased was beneficially entitled for an interest not ceasing on death.

Part IX of the Act made radical changes in the law relating to the privilege to dispose of all property by will in any manner. The widow is now given a right to choose between what is given her by the will and one-third of the estate when children of the marriage have survived the testator. Section 117 provides that when the court is of opinion that a testator has failed in his moral duty to make proper provision for a child of his in accordance with his means, whether by his will or otherwise, the court may order that such provision shall be made for the child out of the estate as the court thinks just and the effect of section 110 is that a child who has been adopted under an order made by An Bord Uchtála is in the same position as a child born of the marriage. Section 120 specifies a number of cases in which a person may be excluded from inheriting. It has not been suggested that the plaintiff has done anything which would justify his omission from benefit under the will of the testator.

Counsel have referred to the legislation in England, New Zealand and in New South Wales which limits the unrestricted power of disposition by will. The *Family Protection Act, 1908*, of New Zealand was the first legislation of this type in a common law country while a similar law was made in New South Wales by the *Testators (Family Maintenance and Guardianship of Infants) Act, 1916.* The legislation in England began with the *Inheritance (Family Provision) Act, 1938*, which has been amended by the *Intestates Estates Act, 1952*, and the *Family Provision Act, 1966.* I have considered many of the decisions on these Acts. *Allardice* v. *Allardice* [1911] A.C. 730; *Re Allen* [1922] N.Z.L.R. 218; *Bosch* v. *Perpetual Trustee Co. Ltd.* [1938] 2 All E.R. 14; *In re Pugh decd.* [1943] Ch. 387 and *In re Goodwin* [1968] 3 All E.R. 12.

The concept underlying the legislation in New Zealand, New South Wales and England is that a testator owes a duty to make reasonable provision for the maintenance of his widow and of his dependants. Our Succession Act, however, is based on the idea that a testator owes a duty to leave part of his estate to his widow (the legal right share) and to make proper provision for his children in accordance with his means. It is not based on a duty to provide maintenance for his widow nor is it limited in its application to children who were dependent on him. The cases decided on the New Zealand, New South Wales and English Act of Parliament are, therefore, of little assistance.

An analysis of section 117 shows that the duty which it creates is not absolute because it does not apply if the testator leaves all his property to his spouse (section 117(3)) not is it an obligation to each child to leave him something. The obligation to make proper provision may be fulfilled by will or otherwise and so gifts or settlements made during the lifetime of the testator in favour of a child or the provision of an expensive education for one child when the others have not received this may discharge the moral duty. It follows. I think, that the relationship of parent and child does not of itself and without regard to other circumstances create a moral duty to leave anything by will to the child. The duty is not one to make adequate provision but to make proper provision in accordance with the testator's means and in deciding whether this has been done, the court may have regard to immoveable property outside the Republic of Ireland owned by the testator. The court, therefore, when deciding whether the moral duty has been fulfilled, must take all the testator's property (including immoveable property outside the Republic of Ireland) into account, but if it decides that the duty has not been discharged, the provision for the child is to be made out of the estate excluding that immoveable property.

It seems to me that the existence of a moral duty to make proper provision by will for a child must be judged by the facts existing at the date of death and must depend upon (a) the amount left to the surviving spouse or the value of the legal right if the survivor selects [sic] to take this, (b) the number of the testator's children, their ages and their positions in life at the date of the testator's death, (c) the means of the testator, (d) the age of the child whose case is being considered and his or her financial position and prospects in life, (e) whether the testator has already in his lifetime made proper provision for the child. The existence of the duty must be decided by objective considerations. The court must decide whether the duty exists and the view of the testator that he did not owe any is no decisive.

The testator in this case never made any provision for the plaintiff except that he allowed him to live at F. The plaintiff was the testator's only child and his mother and he were the only persons to whom the testator owed a duty for there was no one else with any moral claim on him. The estate of the testator was worth about £135,250 before payment of testamentary expenses and estate duty. If I take £10,000 as an estimate of the amount of testamentary expenses and costs, the value of the mother's legal right will be about £36,200 (one-third of £108,500) so that the amount available to make proper provision for the plaintiff is about £89,000. The amount of estate duty payable is £38,000 but as Mrs. M's legal right and any provision made for the plaintiff under section 117 will have to bear their proportions of this duty (section 118) I exclude it from the calculation. This is another striking change made in the law because except in relation to real estate, estate duty was, before 1967, payable out of the residue.

In my opinion the circumstances which I have described created a moral duty binding on the testator to make proper provision by will for the plaintiff. He made no provision whatever and so he failed in his duty. The court must, therefore, order that proper provision is to be made out of the estate and must decide this difficult question from the point of view of a prudent and just parent.

I think that the provision which such a parent would have made in this case would have been to have given one half of the estate (excluding the immoveable property in England) to the plaintiff. The amounts of the testamentary expenses and the costs of the two sets of proceedings will be deducted from the gross amount of the estate to arrive at the figure on which the one half is calculated.

Notes

1. Are there difficulties involved in judging the question of moral duty 'by the facts existing at the date of the death'? Why should the Court not avail itself of the benefit of hindsight and have regard to subsequent realities? Cf. Cooney, *Succession and Judicial Discretion in Ireland: The Section 117 Cases*, 15 Ir. Jur. (n.s.) 62, at 66ff (1980); Fitzpatrick, *The Succession Act 1965, Section 117*, 110 I.L.T & Sol. J. 77, at 90 (1976); *Re McNally, Deceased: Jennings* v. *McClancy*, 108 I.L.T. & Sol. J. 227 (High Ct., Kenny J., 1972); *F.* v. *F.*, unreported, High Ct., Barron, J., 28 July 1983 (1981-62Sp.).
2. See also *In the Matter of N.S.M. Deceased: B.S.M.* v. *R.S.W.*, 107 I.L.T.R. 1 (High Ct., Kenny, J., 1971). In that case, Kenny, J. stated:

   > In some cases a testator may be under a duty to make proper provisions for a married daughter: in others he may not. If for example a member of our community whose wife had predeceased him had an estate of £25,000 [1971 values – ed.] and had sons under 18 and a married daughter, he would not, in my opinion, be under any moral duty to her.

   Do you agree?
3. In *N.S.M.*, the testator had been divorced by his first wife in England in circumstances rendering its recognition here uncertain. The testator had remarried. Litigation as to which woman was the testator's 'spouse' was compromised, by Kenny, J. observed that 'the testator was certainly under a moral obligation to make provision for [the second wife]'.

L. v. L.
[1978] I.R. 288 (High Ct., Costello, J., 1977)

Costello, J.:

The plaintiffs' mother married the deceased on the 5th August, 1939, in Dublin and the two plaintiffs were the only children of this marriage. The first plaintiff is now aged 37 years and his sister, the second plaintiff, is now aged 33 years. Their mother was the deceased's first wife. She applied to the High Court in Liverpool, England, for a divorce and on the 18th February, 1951, a decree nisi was granted; the decree nisi was made absolute on the 11th April 1951. The deceased remarried in the month of July, 1951, and his second wife is the defendant in these proceedings. There were two children of this second marriage, a son who was born on the 3rd July, 1953, and a second son who was born on the 14th June, 1956. The deceased first wife remarried in the month of June, 1952.

The deceased died on the 19th September, 1973, having made two wills. The first will was dated the 17th December, 1951, and in it he made certain limited provision for the plaintiffs, being the children of his first marriage. However, the first will was revoked by a will made by the deceased on the 23rd August, 1960, in which no provision was made either for his first wife or for the children of his first marriage. Under the provisions of his second will the deceased bequeathed his property to his second wife (the defendant) and his solicitor, Mr. Boyle, in trust for his second wife absolutely should she survive him for a period of six calendar months; if she did not so survive him, then in trust for the issue of his marriage with his second wife living at the date of his death or that of his second wife, whichever should be the later, as tenants in common in equal shares. As the defendant has survived the deceased by more than six months she became entitled to the entire of the deceased's estate under the terms of the second will.

The plaintiffs bring this present claim under the provisions of s. 117 of the *Succession Act, 1965*. . . .

In the course of opening the case on behalf of the plaintiffs, Mr. Morris made the following submissions. He stated that he proposed to call evidence which would establish that the deceased's first wife was forced to go through the divorce proceedings in England, and that neither she nor her husband was domiciled in England at the time of those proceedings or at any time. He said that the legal effect of that evidence is that the English court had no jurisdiction to grant the decree of divorce, that the decree was a nullity in the eyes of Irish law, and that recognition cannot be given to it: he referred to *Gaffney* v. *Gaffney* [1975] I.R. 133. As the second marriage of the deceased was not a valid one, he said that the two children of that marriage are illegitimate in the eyes of the law of this country. Therefore, he claimed that 'the children of the second marriage have not any legal rights under the Succession Act,' and that the wife of the second marriage (the defendant) has no rights under the Act of 1965, and that the second family should not be taken into account in considering the plaintiffs' application under s. 117 of that Act. As a further logical step in this argument it was claimed that the deceased's first wife is the 'spouse' for the purposes of Part IX of the Act of 1965 and that, accordingly, she became entitled to one-third of the deceased's estate as a legal right under the Act. See [1974] I.R. at p. 199. However, I was told that the wife of the first marriage has waived this claim. Based on these submissions, counsel for the plaintiffs stated that the Court should divide the entire of the estate equally between the two plaintiffs, being the children of the first marriage, or, if it considered that the suggested waiver should not be validly made, that the Court should divide two-thirds of the deceased's estate equally between them.

It is clear that the validity of the plaintiffs' submissions depends partly on a determination of certain questions of fact (*i.e.*, whether the first wife was coerced into the divorce proceedings, and the nature of the domicile of the parties at the time of those proceedings) and partly on how s. 117 of the Act of 1965 should be interpreted.

Mr. Butler, on behalf of the defendant, urged on me the undesirability of hearing evidence in relation to the validity of the divorce decree and of making a decision in relation to the validity of the second marriage, unless it was absolutely necessary for me to do so. He agreed with the view which I expressed that, if the section was interpreted contrary to the plaintiffs' submissions, the result might be that evidence in relation to the divorce and the validity of the second marriage would not be relevant.

Having heard counsel on the matter, I decided that in the particular circumstances of the present case I should adjourn the hearing of the summons to consider, in the light of the submissions made, how the section should be construed. To that task I now turn.

At the outset I should say that this is not a case in which a question is raised as to whether the claimant under s. 117 of the Act of 1965 is a legitimate child of the testator. Accordingly, I do not have to consider in these proceedings whether an illegitimate child is entitled to apply under the section for an order in its favour. The issue raised is a different one. Here, the claimants are legitimate but it is suggested that, in considering their claim, the position of the deceased two children of his second marriage should not be considered because they are illegitimate. Basically, there are two issues which may require to be determined in all proceedings under section 117. First, the Court must determine whether there has been a failure on the part of the testator of the moral duty mentioned in the section and which he owed to the applicants. The second question (which would only arise if the first question were answered affirmatively) concerns the provision which the Court should make out of the testator's estate. I will consider the plaintiffs' submissions as they affect the Court's inquiry under each of these separate questions.

The Court must make an order that is just. The Court is required by s. 117, sub-s. 2, to consider the application from the point of view of a prudent and just parent; it is required to take into account the position of each of the children of the testator and any other circumstances which the Court may consider of assistance in arriving at a decision that will be as fair as possible to the child or children who are claimants under the section and to the other children. A parent, in acting prudently and justly, must weigh up carefully all his moral obligations. In doing so, he may be required to make greater provision for one of his children than for others. For example, one child may have a long illness for which provision must be made; or one child may have an exceptional talent which it would be morally wrong not to foster. But a just parent, in considering what provision he should make for each of his children during his lifetime and by his will, must take into account not just his moral obligations to his children and to his wife but all his moral obligations. The father of a family may have many moral obligations. Again, to give an example, a father may have aged and infirm parents who are dependent on him and to whom he clearly owes a moral duty. When acting justly and prudently towards his own children and he would have to bear in mind his obligations to his own parents; the provision he makes for his children may have to be reduced because of these other obligations. Therefore, it follows that, if a child of the testator claims after his death that insufficient provision was made for such child, the Court, when considering whether this was so or not, must bear in mind all the moral duties which the testator may have had and all the claims on his resources thereby arising.

In considering the validity of the judgments which the testator made during his lifetime and by his will, and how he fulfilled his moral obligations, it is obviously not relevant to consider only those obligations which could be enforced under the Act of 1965. To return to the example which I gave a moment ago, the dependent parents of a testator to whom he owed a moral duty would have no right under the section to claim that provision be made for them out of their deceased son's estate. Nonetheless, when adjudicating on a child's claim under s. 117 of the Act of 1965, it would obviously be relevant for the Court to bear in mind that the testator may have been under a moral duty to make provision for his own parents. Whilst, therefore, it can be said that the parents in the example which I have given have no 'rights' under this section (in the sense that they can make no claim pursuant to the section to have their rights, under the moral obligation owed to them, fulfilled), the existence of the moral duty owed to them may be relevant to the claim made by a child of the testator.

If it is accepted (as I think it must be) that the Court, when considering an allegation by a testator's child of a breach of duty to them, should bear in mind all the moral duties which the testator may have had, then, if the testator had an illegitimate child, it would be necessary to consider whether the Court should regard the testator as having had a moral duty to that illegitimate child. I think the answer to that question must clearly be in the affirmative. Therefore, it follows that, in adjudicating on the claim of a legitimate child, the moral duty which the testator may have owed to any illegitimate child he may have had must also be borne in mind by the Court. This is so (for the reasons I have given) whether or not the illegitimate child is entitled to make a claim under sub-s. 1 of section 117.

In the present case, the allegation is that the deceased has two illegitimate children as his second marriage was an invalid one. However, it seems to me that it cannot be suggested that the deceased owed his children by his second marriage no moral duty: whether the deceased's second marriage was valid or not, such a duty existed. The nature and extent of that moral duty cannot be affected by a decision now by this Court that the second marriage should not be recognised. Therefore, it follows that, in considering the first question (*i.e.*, whether the deceased failed in his duty to the plaintiffs), the existence and fulfilment of the deceased's moral duty to the children of his second marriage is a matter which it is relevant for the Court to consider. As the validity of the second marriage is not of any relevance to this part of the case, evidence relating to the alleged invalidity of the divorce proceedings is likewise not relevant to it.

If the deceased failed in his moral duty to the plaintiffs or either of them, the next issue which the Court would be required to consider is the extent to which and the manner in which it should make proper provision for the successful plaintiffs out of the deceased's estate. I will now consider whether the validity of the second marriage and the status of the children of that marriage are in any way relevant to this part of the Court's functions under section 117.

If a testator by his will makes provision for his children or some of them, it is clear that such beneficiaries could be affected by an order made under s. 117 because, in making provision out of the testator's estate for the claimant, the bequest to the other children may be reduced or possibly eliminated. Therefore, it is obvious that the Court, in making an order under s. 117, is required to consider the position of children who are beneficiaries. Its decision must be as fair as possible to all children who are claimants under s. 117 or who are beneficiaries under the testator's will. But the situation is different when the testator has a child or children in respect of whom he makes no provision in his will and who make no claim under the section. In such circumstances no order which the Court may make can affect their interests in any way; they have no right to any share in the estate under the will, and they have made no claim to a share in the estate under the Act of 1965. The position of such children is not in any way relevant to the task which the Court must perform when making a just provision out of a testator's estate in favour of the claimants.

In the events that have happened, none of the deceased's children obtained any benefit under his will. The plaintiffs, being the children of his first marriage, have made claims under s. 117 of the Act of 1965 but no claims under that section have been made by the children of his second marriage. Therefore, the position of the children of the second marriage is irrelevant to the considerations which arise on the second question in these proceedings; this is so whether the children of the second marriage are legitimate or illegitimate. Accordingly, for the purposes of the second question with which the Court may be faced in these proceedings, the validity of the second marriage and evidence relating to the divorce is not in any way relevant.

It is now necessary to turn to examine the relevance of the evidence proposed to be given relating to the validity of the divorce in the light of the position of the second wife (the defendant) under section 117. Where, as in this case, a testator leaves children, his surviving spouse is entitled to one third of his estate as a legal right under ss. 111 and 112 of the Act of 1965. If the second marriage of the deceased was an invalid one, then his first wife is the deceased's 'spouse' for the purposes of the Act of 1965, and she is entitled to the legal right to which I have referred. However, I have been informed that the deceased's first wife has expressly waived any claim to this right under the Act of 1965. She is perfectly entitled to do this. Therefore, if the first wife is the 'spouse' for the purposes of the Act of 1965, I can approach my task under the Act and make provision for the plaintiffs (if I think it proper so to do) without regard to the position of the first wife. If, on the other hand, the deceased's second wife (the defendant) is the 'spouse' of the deceased, then she is entitled to a legal right under the Act of 1965 or to her bequest under the deceased's will, and she can elect to take the bequest or the legal right; in default of election she would take under the will. I have assumed that in the present case the defendant claims to be entitled to the deceased's entire estate under the will and not to a legal right under the Act of 1965.

Sub-section 3 of s. 117 places a restriction on the powers of the Court which are granted by sub-s. 1 of that section. If the surviving spouse is the mother or father of the applicant child, then sub-s. 3 of s. 117 provides that no order under the section can affect any bequest to the spouse. The defendant is not the mother of either of the plaintiffs and, therefore, it follows that an order under s. 117 can affect a bequest to her whether or not she is the spouse of the deceased. Therefore, it is unnecessary for the Court to consider who is the 'spouse' of the deceased for the purposes of sub-s. 3 of s. 117 as unrestricted provision can be made out of the estate whichever be the spouse. Therefore, for the purposes of the restrictions imposed by sub-s. 3 of s. 117, the validity of the second marriage and the evidence relating to the divorce are not relevant.

It is necessary now to revert to the plaintiffs' submission that the second family (including the second wife) of the deceased should not be taken into account in considering the plaintiffs' claim. I have already pointed out that, in considering the first question (*i.e.*, the alleged failure of a moral duty to the plaintiffs), the moral duty which the deceased owed to persons other than the plaintiffs is a relevant matter for the Court to consider.

By marrying one another, the deceased and his second wife (the defendant) undertook mutual obligations towards each other and, by living with her as her husband, the deceased undertook a moral obligation for her welfare. From what I have already been told, the Court which hears this case could well conclude that that duty lasted through his life. It could have evidence (which it might or might not accept) that the deceased had a moral duty to make provision for her in his will. Founded, as it is, on the fact of the marriage and the relationship which the deceased and his wife thereby created for themselves, this moral duty cannot, in my view, be affected by a decision of this Court that it will not recognise the validity of the second marriage. Even if the Court cannot properly recognise the second marriage, it must accept as a fact that moral duties were created by the parties to it; in this connection see the judgment of Mr. Justice Kenny at p. 7 of the report of *In re M Deceased: B.S.M.* v. *R.S.W.* 107 I.L.T.R. 1 (1970).

In considering the plaintiffs' claim that the deceased failed in his moral duty to them, the Court should bear in mind that he also had a moral duty to make provision for his second wife; this duty has to be borne in mind when deciding how a prudent and just parent would act towards the children of his first marriage. The Court's deliberations on this part of the case would be unaffected by a finding that it should not recognise the validity of the second marriage. Neither could the validity of the second marriage be relevant in relation to the second issue in these proceedings, should the Court decide the first one in the plaintiffs' favour. I have already pointed out that the restrictions in sub-s. 3 of s. 117 on the Court's powers to make provision for the plaintiffs do not apply in this case; it does not necessarily follow from this that the Court will make an order affecting the bequest to the deceased's second wife. Having heard all the evidence, it may or it may not do so. In deciding what provision should be made out of the deceased's estate (if any), the Court should have regard to all the deceased's moral obligations at the time of his death, including those he may have owed to his second wife. For the reasons I have already given, the nature and extent of that moral duty cannot be affected by a decision of the Court that it should not recognise the validity of the second marriage. Equally, then, on this aspect of the case, evidence relating to the English divorce is irrelevant.

Therefore, I conclude that evidence relating to the validity of the English divorce is not relevant to any of the issues that arise in these proceedings. I also conclude that the Court should bear in mind, for the purposes I have indicated, the moral duties which the deceased owed to the wife and children of the second marriage. I need only add that the construction which I have placed on s. 117 of the Act of 1965 is not affected by the provisions of s. 110 of the Act. These provisions apply, in the manner set out in the section, the provisions of the *Legitimacy Act, 1931*, and of s. 26 of the *Adoption Act, 1952*, when it is necessary to deduce any relationship of the purposes of Part IX of the Act of 1965. Section 110 has no relevance to the facts of this case and does not, in my view, alter the construction which I think s. 117 bears.

Notes

1. What is the policy basis of section 117(3)? Is it sound? Is the subsection Constitutional?
2. Should the Court always ignore evidence that would establish that the deceased's first wife had been forced to go through foreign divorce proceedings? Might not this evidence affect the Court's assessment of the existence or extent of the moral duty owed by the deceased to the second wife? Take the hypothetical case of a man disposing of his wife by intimidating her into obtaining a divorce, with the assistance of his prospective new wife: may we assume that the man will *necessarily* owe the new wife a moral duty to provide for her by his will?
3. What about the more simple case of straightforward bigamy with no prior divorce, valid or invalid? Does a man in such a case *always* owe a moral obligation to his second wife? If not, would the question of the second wife's *bona fides* be relevant? If a man does not necessarily owe a moral obligation to his second wife in the case of bigamy where no (invalid) divorce has preceded the second marriage, why should he *always* owe a moral obligation to the second wife where he has gone through a 'shotgun' divorce?
4. See also *In the Matter of the Estate of E.J.D. Deceased*, unreported, High Ct., Carroll, J., 19 February 1981 (1979–596Sp) a case where the deceased had left his wife and children and gone to live with another woman, with whom he had two more children. Miss Justice Carroll considered that

   > [p]roper provision by the deceased for his children by his wife should have ensured a reasonably equitable distribution of his property between his two families so that his children by her would not have to live in straitened circumstances when his children by the [woman with whom he later lived] could live to a higher standard due to a large extent to the provision he had made for them and th[is woman].

   On the evidence, Miss Justice Carroll held that the moral obligations of the deceased to the woman with whom he lived and to his two youngest children had been fully discharged by dispositions during his lifetime and in his will.
5. In *In re D. Deceased: W.* v. *Allied Irish Banks Ltd.*, unreported, High Ct., Hamilton, J. 2 March 1977 (1975–469Sp.), an elderly testator, a widower, who died in 1972, left only a small portion of his substantial estate to his only daughter. Hamilton, J. had:

   > no doubt that it would be regarded as adequate provision but the obligation on the testator is to make proper provision according to his means. Taking into account the value of the testator's estate, the fact that she has been separated from her husband since 1956, her age, her health, her financial position and lack of prospects in life and the assistance that she has been to the testator during his lifetime, I am of opinion that the testator failed to make proper provision for the plaintiff in accordance with his means.

   See Cooney, *Succession and Judicial Discretion in Ireland: The Section 117 Cases*, 15 Ir. Jur. (n.s.) 62, at 72–73 (1980).
6. See also *In the Estate of Walker Deceased: O'Brien* v. *S., supra* p. 153. Is there something curious about a law which may indirectly protect a *bequest* by a deceased testator to his illegitimate child but which affords the same child no right to claim against the testator's estate under section 117 if the testator leaves the child nothing? Is the notion of a moral duty to persons other than the child a helpful one? For a good analysis, see Cooney, *op. cit.*, at 79–80.
7. To how many other persons may a testator owe a moral obligation? His or her sister? Cf. *Re Looney Deceased: O'Connor* v. *O'Keefe*, unreported, High Ct., Kenny J., 2 November 1970 (1969–126Sp). His or her father? Cf. *McN* v. *C. & McE.* unreported, High Ct., Barrington, J., 15 February 1984 (1982–917Sp.). His nieces? Cf. *J.J. & C.D.H.* v. *Allied Irish Banks Ltd.*, unreported, High Ct., McWilliam, J., 17 November 1978 (1978–57Sp.). A person to whom the testator is *in loco parentis?* Cf. *L.* v. *L.*, High Ct., Murphy, J. (oral judgment), 22 May, 1984 (1982–649 Sp.). Does a testator owe a moral obligation to charities generally or to certain particular charities? Cf. Cooney, *op. cit.*, at 76, 79. Is there any difference between the moral duties of male and female testators, respectively, by reason of their sex alone? Similarly has a sister, niece or daughter, as the case may be, a stronger moral claim than a brother, nephew or son, by reason of her sex alone?
8. What range of orders is open to the Court when it considers that the testator has failed in his or her moral duty? Cf. *Re F.F. Deceased: H.L.* v. *Bank of Ireland*, unreported, High Ct., Costello, J., 27 July 1978 (1977–346Sp.) at pp. 10ff. See also Cooney, *op. cit.*, at 73–75.
9. Where a son or daughter has been convicted of an offence may a prudent and just parent be considered to be *relieved* of the obligation to make provision for the child by will or should the parent be under an obligation to help in the child's *rehabilitation*? Cf. *Re F.F. Deceased: H.L.* v. *Bank of Ireland, supra*, at p. 10 of Costello, J.'s judgment.
10. See also *J.R.* v. *J.R.*, unreported, High Ct., Keane, J., November 1979 (1978–611Sp.), *In the Estate of J.M. Deceased: E.M.* v. *S.M. & F.R.*, unreported, High Ct., O'Hanlon, J., 26 July 1983 (1981–837Sp.), *In the Matter of the Estate of R.G. Deceased: R.G.* v. *P.S.G. & J.R.G.*, unreported, High Ct., Carroll, J., 20 November 1980 (1979–621Sp.)

11. In *M.H. & N. McG.* v. *N.M. & C.M.*, [1983] I.L.R.M. 519, at 525 (High Ct.), Barron, J. said:

> The basis of the plaintiffs' case is really that it is fair that they, who have never received anything from either of their parents, should receive some part of their father's estate. Although a father has a moral obligation towards his child to make proper provision for him in accordance with his means, this does not mean that a father is obliged to leave something to his child or to share his estate among his children assuming he has no other moral responsibilities. If that were the position, then the effect of s. 117 of the *Succession Act, 1965* would be to preclude a testator from leaving his estate away from his children and would preclude him from choosing in effect how to dispose of his estate. What s. 117 does is to prevent a testator who can make proper provision for his children, in accordance with his means, from refusing to do so.

UNWORTHINESS TO SUCCEED AND DISINHERITANCE

It should be noted that certain persons are excluded from benefitting from a deceased's estate, under section 120 of the *Succession Act, 1965*. See further, *Wylie*, paras. 14.35, 14.63 and *Shatter*, 355. Section 121 of the *Succession Act, 1965* is directed towards the problem of a spouse or parent seeking to evade his or her obligations by disposing of his or her property before he or she dies. The section provides as follows:

121.—(1) This section applied to a disposition of property (other than a testamentary disposition or a disposition to a purchaser) under which the beneficial ownership of the property vests in possession in the donee within three years before the death of the person who made it or on his death or later.

(2) If the court is satisfied that a disposition to which this section applies was made for the purpose of defeating or substantially diminishing the share of the disponer's spouse, whether as a legal right or on intestacy, or the intestate share of any of his children, or of leaving any of his children insufficiently provided for, then, whether the disponer died testate or intestate, the court may order that the disposition shall, in whole or in part, be deemed, for the purposes of Parts VI and IX, to be a devise or bequest made by him by will and to form part of his estate, and to have had no other effect.

(3) To the extent to which the court so orders, the disposition shall be deemed never to have had effect as such and the donee of the property, or any person representing or deriving title under him, shall be a debtor of the estate for such amount as the court may direct accordingly.

(4) The court may make such further order in relation to the matter as may appear to the court to be just and equitable having regard to the provisions and the spirit of this Act and to all the circumstances.

(5) Subject to subsections (6) and (7), an order may be made under this section—

(*a*) in the respect of the spouse, on the application of the spouse or the personal representative of the deceased, made within one year from the first taking out of representation,

(*b*) in the interest of a child, on an application under section 117.

(6) In the case of a disposition made in favour of the spouse of the disponer, an order shall not be made under this section on an application by or on behalf of a child of the disponer who is also a child of the spouse.

(7) An order shall not be made under this section affecting a disposition made in favour of any child of the disponer, if -

(*a*) the spouse of the disponer was dead when the disposition was made, or

(*b*) the spouse was alive when the disposition was made but was a woman who, if the disponer had then died, would have been precluded under any of the provisions of section 120 from taking a share in his estate, or

(*c*) the spouse was alive when the disposition was made and consented in writing to it.

(8) If the donee disposes of the property to a purchaser, this section shall cease to apply to the property and shall apply instead to the consideration given by the purchaser.

(9) Accrual by survivorship on the death of a joint tenant of property shall, for the purposes of this section, be deemed to be a vesting of the beneficial ownership of the entire property in the survivor.

(10) In this section 'disposition' includes a *donatio mortis causa.*

For consideration of section 121, see Sherrin, *Disinheritance of a Spouse: A Comparative Study of the Law in the United Kingdom and the Republic of Ireland*, 31 N.I.L.Q. 21, at 33–34 (1980).

The courts have faced the problem of dispositions by a man to a woman with whom he was living and their children, where the man has left his wife and is living with the other woman. In *In the Matter of the Estate of E.J.D. Deceased*, unreported, High Ct., 19 February 1981 (1979–596Sp.) Miss Justice Carroll dismissed an application under section 121 in such circumstances by children of a man and his wife, on the grounds that there was 'no proof, either directly or by inference, that the dispositions were made by the deceased for the purpose of leaving his children by his wife insufficiently provided for.' It seemed to Miss Justice Carroll that the purpose of various transactions by the deceased man 'was to provide for [his] second family and was not necessarily intended to result in diminishing the provision for his children by his wife.'

This case raises an important issue of legal policy, echoing several analogous legal questions in other areas of the law. In criminal law, there has been much analysis of the concept of 'intention' and how is should be distinguished from 'motive'. A not dissimilar issue arises in relation to the torts of interference with contractual relations and conspiracy: cf. B. McMahon & Binchy, *Irish Law of Torts*, 434, 445–448 (1981).

Chapter 14

ADOPTION

Adoption in Irish law involves the irrevocable transfer of parental obligations and rights to a third party. As a legal institution adoption in various forms may be traced back of the Code of Hammurabi, two thousand years before the birth of Christ: Huard, *The Law of Adoption: Ancient and Modern*, 9 Vand. L. Rev. 743, at 744 (1956). In Ireland the basic piece of legislation is the *Adoption Act, 1952*. This Act has been amended three times, in 1964, 1974 and 1976, and the adoption process was the subject of a Constitutional Amendment in 1979. For a detailed consideration of the subject see *Shatter*, ch. 12. Radical proposals for changes in the law are contained in the Report of the Review Committee on Adoption Services, *Adoption* (Pl. 2467, 1984) (hereinafter cited as "the *Adoption Report*" of 1984). The *Adoption Report* recommends the replacement of an Bord Uchtála by a specialist Adoption Court.

A most important provision, so far as adoption policy is concerned, is section 24 of the *Adoption Act, 1952*, which provides that, on the making of an adoption order:

(a) the child shall be considered with regard to the rights and duties of parents and children in relation to each other as the child of the adopter or adopters born to him, her or them in lawful wedlock;
(b) the mother or guardian shall lose all parental rights and be freed from all parental duties with respect to the child.

This policy of completely extinguishing the legal ties between the child and his or her natural parents, which was widespread in common law jurisdictions this century, has recently come under critical discussion; one argument is that some form of less final and complete placement of their children might appeal to young single mothers: see Amadio & Deutsch, *Open Adoption: Allowing Adopted Children to 'Stay in Touch' with Blood Relatives*, 22 J. of Family L. 59, at 70–72 (1983). Cf. Katz, *Rewriting the Adoption Story*, 5 Family Advocate No. 1, p. 9 (1982).

The 1952 Act established the Adoption Board, An Bord Uchtála, which has the power to make adoption orders. Since 1974, the welfare of the child is 'the first and paramount consideration in deciding any matter, application or proceedings before the Board or any court relating to the arrangements for or the making of an adoption order': *Adoption Act, 1974*, section 2. For analysis of this section see the judgments of Walsh and Henchy, J.J., in *G.* v. *An Bord Uchtála, supra*, pp. 128–52.

WHO MAY BE ADOPTED?

An adoption order may be made only in respect of children resident in the State, between six weeks and twenty one years old, who are either:
(a) orphans;
(b) illegitimate, or
(c) who have been legitimated by the subsequent marriage of their parents, but whose birth has not been re-registered under the *Legitimacy Act, 1931*.

An interesting question may arise as to whether category (c) is consistent with the constitutional guarantee of equal protection under Article 40.1.

WHO MAY ADOPT?

An adoption order may be made only where:
(a) the applicants are a married couple living together; or

(b) the applicant is the mother or natural father or a relative of the child ('relative' being defined as meaning 'grandparent, brother, sister, uncle or aunt, whether of the whole blood, of the half-blood or by affinity, relationship to an illegitimate child being traced through the mother only'); or
(c) the applicant is a widow; or
(d) in the circumstances set out by section 5(1) of the *Adoption Act 1974*. Section 5(1) provides that:

> . . . in any case where –
> (*a*) a child is in the care of a married couple who have made an application for an adoption order in relation to that child, and
> (*b*) the wife dies before the making of the adoption order
> the Board may make an adoption order relating to that child on the application of the widower: Provided that –
> (i) the widower has, at the date of his application another child in his custody, and
> (ii) every person, who consent to the making of the adoption order is required by section 14 of the [1952] Act or by section 2 of the Act of 1964, knows, when he gives his consent, that the applicant is a widower.

This distinction between widows and widowers has been criticised by *Shatter*, 177–178, who argues that:

> the law is illogical and inhumane. There is no reason why the existence of another child should in such circumstances be of fundamental importance in determining whether the widower should be permitted to adopt. There is no valid reason for the existence of different requirements for a widower than for a widow. In all cases the question should be simply whether it is in the interests of the child's welfare that an adoption order be made.

The *Adoption Report* of 1984 has proposed that a single person should in exceptional circumstances be eligible for consideration as an adoptive parent: para. 4.12. However, couples living together who choose not to marry or who cannot marry under Irish law or whose marriage is not recognised should not be eligible for consideration as adoptive parents: paras. 4.18–4.19.

Section 11(2) of the *Adoption Act, 1952* provides that, save in the case of a married couple living together, an order is not to be made for the adoption of a child by more than one person.

As to age requirements for adoptive parents, see the *Adoption Act, 1952*, section 11 and the *Adoption Act, 1964*, section 5(1); see also *Shatter*, 178. Should there be *any* age requirements? If so, what is the criterion by which the question of age should be determined? Cf. the *Adoption Report* of 1984, paras. 4.23–4.25.

RELIGIOUS REQUIREMENTS

M. v. AN BORD UCHTÁLA

[1975] I.R. 81 (High Court, Pringle, J., 1974)

Pringle, J.: 13th May, 1974

The plaintiffs, who are husband and wife, seek a declaration that the provisions of s. 12 of the Adoption Act, 1952, as amended by s. 6 of the *Adoption Act, 1964*, are repugnant to the Constitution of Ireland, 1937, and are invalid and of no effect. The plaintiffs also claim a declaration that the decision and order of the first defendant dated the 1st May, 1973, in relation to the application of the plaintiffs for an adoption order relating to a male child, who was born out of wedlock to the second plaintiff, were made unlawfully and without jurisdiction and in excess of jurisdiction; and that they were ultra vires and failed to have due regard to the natural and constitutional rights of the plaintiffs, and each of them, and of the said child.

The facts are not in dispute and can be shortly stated. The plaintiffs were married on the

4th July, 1970. The first plaintiff is aged 27 years and he is a Roman Catholic. The second plaintiff is 26 years old and is a member of the Church of England. The child was born to the second plaintiff on the 8th June, 1967, when she was unmarried. While originally brought up as a member of the Church of England, the child is now, and was at the time of the application for an adoption order, being brought up as a Roman Catholic and he will shortly be making his first Communion in that Church. Since the marriage he has resided with the plaintiffs, who have two young sons. The first plaintiff is not the father of the child who was born to the second plaintiff.

On the 28th March, 1973, the plaintiffs applied to the first defendants for an adoption order under s. 9 of the Act of 1952 for the adoption of the child who had been born to the second plaintiff. By letter dated the 1st May, 1973, the plaintiffs were informed by the first defendants that, having considered the application at a sitting on that date, the first defendants had decided to reject the application on the sole ground that the provisions of s. 12, sub-s. 2, of the Act of 1952 were not satisfied. That sub-section provides as follows:– '(2) the applicant or applicants shall be of the same religion as the child and his parents or, if the child is illegitimate, his mother.' Under sub-section 5 of the same section it is provided that 'A child's religion shall be taken to be that in which he is being brought up.' It is quite clear that, if these sub-sections are valid, the child could not be adopted under the Act of 1952 by the plaintiffs as they are not of the same religion and, therefore, cannot be said to be of the same religion as the child or of the same religion as his mother. Similarly, the second plaintiff could not adopt her own child as she is not of the same religion as the child.

The constitutionality of the provisions of s. 12 of the Act of 1952 is contested by the plaintiffs on several grounds. Those provisions are alleged to be repugnant to the Constitution on the grounds (a) that they contravene the provisions and requirements of ss. 1 and 3 of Article 40 of the Constitution and (b) that they contravene the provisions and requirements of Articles 41 and 44 of the Constitution. I propose to deal first with the contention that sub-s. 2 of s. 12 of the Act of 1952 contravenes sub-s. 3 of s. 2 of Article 44 of the Constitution which provides as follows:– 'The State shall not impose any disabilities or make any discrimination on the ground of religious profession, belief or status.'

Mr. Conolly and Mr. Barrington submitted on behalf of the plaintiffs that the effect of sub-s. 2 of s. 12 of the Act of 1952 is both to impose a disability and to make a discrimination in respect of (a) the plaintiffs as a group, (b) the plaintiffs individually, and (c) the child, on the ground of religious profession or belief. In regard to the plaintiffs as a group, as husband and wife, it was contended that there is a disability imposed and a discrimination caused on the ground of their religious profession or belief between a husband and wife who are of the same religion and a husband and wife, like the plaintiffs, who are of different religions. In regard to the plaintiffs as individuals, it was submitted that each of the plaintiffs is under a disability and is discriminated against because they happen to have married a person of a different religion; in addition it was said that the second plaintiff is under a disability and is discriminated against as the mother of a child whom she cannot adopt because they are not of the same religion. As regards the child, the contention is that he is under a disability and is discriminated against because he is not of the same religion as both the plaintiffs and because he is not of the same religion as his mother.

It is conceded on behalf of the plaintiffs that the right to adopt legally and the right to be adopted legally are not natural rights but are rights which are created by the Act of 1952. However, the plaintiffs say that these rights should be equally available to all persons who satisfy the requirements of the Act in regard to residence, age, and otherwise – regardless of their particular religious profession or belief.

It is quite clear that the right to apply for and obtain an adoption order pursuant to the

Act of 1952 is a valuable right both for the adopters and for the child. Section 24 of the Act of 1952 provides:– 'Upon an adoption order being made – (*a*) the child shall be considered with regard to the rights and duties of parents and children in relation to each other as the child of the adopter or adopters born to him, her or them in lawful wedlock . . .' By s. 26 of the Act of 1952 valuable property rights are conferred on both the adopted child and on the adopter or adopters. Under s. 11 of the *Irish Nationality and Citizenship Act, 1956*, upon an adoption order being made in which the adopter or, where the adoption is by a married couple, either spouse is an Irish citizen, the adopted child, if not already an Irish citizen, shall be an Irish citizen.

As regards the meaning to be given to the word 'disabilities' and 'discrimination' in Article 44, s. 2, sub-s. 3, of the Constitution, I was referred by Mr. Conolly to the judgment of the Supreme Court in *Quinn's Supermarket* v. *The Attorney General* [1972] I.R. 1 in which, at p. 15 of the report, Mr. Justice Walsh said:– 'The plaintiffs' case is based upon sub-s. 3 of s. 2 of Article 44. The plaintiffs have certainly suffered a disability in the sense that they are legally disqualified from, and are deprived of the power of, carrying on the business of selling meat after the hours set out in the statutory instrument. This is a deprivation but in my view, where the provision speaks of disabilities, the disability must be one which is suffered and imposed on the ground of the religious profession, belief or status of the person so disabled. That the provision was aimed at preventing the imposition of a personal, or perhaps even a corporate, disability is quite clear from the Irish text, which is:– "*Ní cead don Stát neach du chur fá mhíchumas ar bith. . . .*" If an imposed disability is to be examined, and the grounds upon which it is imposed are to be examined, clearly the grounds must relate to the person or body upon whom the disability is imposed.'

Later on the same page he said:– 'That the correct approach is that the question of disability should be examined on a subjective basis is, in my view, amply borne out by the provisions with regard to discrimination. It was submitted on behalf of the defendants here that "discrimination" should be construed as if it read "discrimination against." In my view the learned High Court judge was quite correct in rejecting that submission. If the provision had read "discrimination against" – meaning distinguishing unfavourably on the grounds of religious profession, belief or status – it would also mean that the test would have been related to the religious profession, belief or status of the person discriminated against. It is the omission of the word "against" which confirms me in my view that this portion of the constitutional provision should be construed as meaning that the State shall not make any "distinction" on the ground of religious profession, belief or status. This is confirmed by the Irish text which says "*ná aon idirdhealú do dhéanamh. . .*" To discriminate, in that sense, is to create a difference between persons or bodies or to distinguish between them on the ground of religious profession, belief or status; it follows, therefore, that the religious profession, belief or status does not have to be that of the person who feels he has suffered by reason of the distinction created. Indeed it is wide enough to enable the person who might be thought to have profited from the distinction but who did not accept the validity of such distinction, to challenge it by showing that it was based upon the religious profession, belief or status of the suffering party. In such instance the suffering party could avail of the remedies open to him under the "disability" provision, as well as under the "discrimination" provision, if in fact he was suffering a disability.'

That judgment was relied upon by Mr. Justice Butler in *Mulloy* v. *The Minister for Education* [1975] I.R. 88 where he held that the provisions of a scheme, introduced by the Minister for Education in regard to incremental salaries for secondary teachers, infringed the provisions of Article 44, s. 2, sub-s. 3, of the Constitution because the scheme excluded clerics. The learned judge said:– 'It seems to me to be clear beyond argument that the terms of the scheme confining it to lay teachers do create a difference and do distinguish between them and teachers of a different religious status, namely, clerics such as the plaintiff. It is also clear that the ground of such discrimination is the difference in religious status.' *Mulloy's Case* is also an answer to the argument of Mr. Liston that the right infringed must be a natural right, as the right held to be infringed in that case was stated by the learned judge to be 'his right to be considered for such payment on the same footing as a lay teacher in a similar position.'

Mr. Liston submitted that the legislature, in conferring the right of legal adoption, was entitled to provide reasonable restrictions on this right and that the provision that the adopter or adopters should be of the same religion as the child and his parents, or if the child is illegitimate, his mother, was a reasonable restriction. I cannot accept this submission. I do not agree that the restriction was a reasonable one, and, even if it were, it could not be valid if it infringed the Constitution, as I am satisfied it did. One of the matters decided in *Quinn's Supermarket* v. *The Attorney General* [1972] I.R. 1 was that, as the primary object of Article 44, s. 2 (as stated in sub-s. 1) was to ensure and guarantee to every citizen freedom of conscience and the free profession and practice of religion, a discrimination within the meaning of sub-s. 3 was not invalid if the implementation of the primary object required the making of that discrimination. It has not been suggested that the primary object of Article 44 required the making of the discrimination relied on in this case.

I have approached this case, as I must, on the basis that the provisions of the Act of 1952 must be presumed to be constitutional and that, in the ordinary case, the onus would be on the plaintiffs to rebut this presumption. I agree, however, with the statement of Taft, C.J. in *Bailey* v. *Drexel Furniture Co.* 259 U.S. 20 (1922) at p. 37 of the report where he said:– 'But, in the act before us, the presumption of validity cannot prevail, because proof to the contrary is found on the very face of its provisions.' I consider that that is the position here. The provisions of s. 12, sub-s. 2, of the Act of 1952 on their face are clearly in contravention of Article 44, s. 2, sub-s. 3, of the Constitution for the reasons advanced by counsel for the plaintiffs. If this is not so, I hold that the plaintiffs have discharged the onus of rebutting the presumption of the constitutionality. In my opinion, sub-s. 2 of s. 12 clearly imposes disabilities and makes a discrimination (within the meaning put upon those words by the Supreme Court) on the ground of religious profession or belief and, therefore, the sub-section is invalid.

Having regard to the opinion which I have formed as to the invalidity of sub-s. 2 of s. 12 of the Act of 1952 by reason of Article 44, s. 2, sub-s. 3, of the Constitution, I do not consider it necessary to decide whether or not it is also invalid having regard to Article 40, ss. 1 or 3, or Article 41.

Therefore, I will make an order declaring (a) that the provisions of sub-s. 2 of s. 12 of the Adoption Act, 1952, are repugnant to the Constitution and are invalid and of no effect, and (b) that the decision and order of the first defendants made on the 1st May, 1973, in relation to the application of the plaintiffs for an adoption order for the child were unlawful and invalid. I will make no order on foot of the other claims of the plaintiffs, but I will give liberty to either party to apply.

Notes

1. Do you agree with this decision? Pringle, J. appears to lay some emphasis on the fact that adoption confers 'valuable property rights' on adopters. Having regard to the fact that our law permits adoption for the benefit of the child rather than the parents, should Pringle, J. have had regard to elements of parental benefit, in your view?
2. Section 4 of the *Adoption Act, 1974* was enacted in response to this decision. It provides that:

> An adoption order shall not be made in any case where the applicants, the child and his parents, or, if the child is illegitimate, his mother, are not all of the same religion, unless every person whose consent to the making of the order is required . . . knows the religion (if any) of each of the applicants when he gives his consent.

Commenting on this provision, *Shatter*, 179, states:

> Whether [it] will more readily facilitate or will hinder adoption by parties to a mixed marriage will depend to a great extent on the attitude of the various adoption societies. As practically all of them are denominationally based, the societies by restricting placements for adoption to coules of one religious denomination could, in effect, render the law irrelevant and the situation not very different in practice from that which existed prior to the above case.

The Adoption Report of 1984 recommends no change in the law, the Review Committee considering the present position to be 'fair': para. 4.21.

3. Do you consider that section 4 is Constitutional? Should those whose consent for adoption is required have a completely unqualified right of veto in this regard? What Articles of the Constitution come into play?

PROBLEMS OF CONSENT

M. v. AN BORD UCHTÁLA
[1977] I.R. 287 (Supreme Court, 1976)

O'Higgins, C.J.:
The plaintiffs are husband and wife, and were married on the 6th June, 1972. The first defendant is a board established by the *Adoption Act, 1952,* to fulfil and discharge the functions assigned to it by that Act. It will hereinafter be referred to as 'the Board.' On the 14th May, 1970, a child was born to the second plaintiff who was then unmarried. The first plaintiff is the father of the child. He will hereinafter be referred to as 'the father,' while his wife will be referred to as 'the mother.'

The child was born in a provincial town; the mother, who ordinarily resided in the Dublin area, went there prior to, and for the purposes of, the birth. Subsequent to the birth, the child was placed with foster parents and on the 12th June, 1970, the mother signified her desire to place the child for adoption through an adoption agency. She did so by signing an acknowledgment of the receipt of an explanatory memorandum from the society dealing with the effect of an adoption order and the statutory provisions as to consent. This memorandum and the attached acknowledgment are known together as form No. 10, and the issue and signing thereof constitute the first practical step in an adoption through an adoption society. The memorandum and acknowledgment were in the form prescribed by s. 39 of the Act of 1952.

The decision by the mother to take the initial steps towards the adoption of her child was arrived at after much heart-searching and anguish, and after a period in which various options were considered and discussed by the mother with people who came to her assistance. The sympathy and understanding which she received from these recognised no limits. In particular this decision was arrived at in direct opposition to the wishes of the father who throughout this period wanted to marry the mother and care for the child as his own. Indeed, it appears that the decision to place the child with foster parents and then for adoption was finally taken by the mother only because the father, believing that she had already taken steps towards adoption, had broken off all relations with her and had left the country to take up employment overseas. As she said in evidence, this left her with 'no alternative' except adoption.

On the 7th August, 1970, the adoption society placed the child with adopting parents for a probationary period. This probationary or trial adoption was supervised by the officers of the society and the Board and was intended, as part of the normal procedure, to ensure that the final decision would be taken in the true interests of the child. On the 7th December, 1970, the adopting parents made a formal application to the Board for an adoption order in respect of the child.

The mother, of course, knew that this preliminary decision with regard to placing the child for adoption was not a final one and that she could still change her mind. Subsequent to the 12th June, 1970, she continued to seek out a possible means of providing for the child's future in some manner other than by adoption, albeit without any real substance being attached to the alternatives considered. The father was still out of the country; he was not in communication with the mother, and the breach between them appeared to be final.

Had the adoption procedure progressed in the normal manner, the mother would have been expected to have given her final consent to the adoption of the child by about February, 1971. This would have been some six months after the commencement of the probationary period, and the adoption order might then have been expected to be made. This consent is dealt with in s. 14, sub-s. 5, of the Act of 1952 which provides that it shall be in writing in the prescribed form. The form prescribed is known as form No. 4A and is, in fact, an affidavit.

The mother received from the adoption society a letter dated the 18th December, 1970, enclosing form No. 4A for completion. However, she did not comply with the request therein contained to complete the form. Another letter dated the 15th January, 1971, was also ignored by her. On the 17th February, 1971, the adoption society wrote to the mother's mother asking for her co-operation in getting the form signed. Again this letter had no effect. On the 16th March, 1971, the social worker who had helped the mother wrote pressing for a final decision and referring to the position of the adopting parents. This letter also produced no result. On July 5th the mother was visited by a priest who was a close friend of the adopting parents, and a nun who had been one of those who had helped and advised her. The purpose of their visit was to assist and counsel the mother in coming to a decision. The visit apparently had the desired effect because the mother set out the following day, with her mother, for the offices of the Catholic Protection and Rescue Society of Ireland in order to sign and complete form No. 4A. However, when the mother arrived there she became very distressed and left without doing what she had intended to do.

On the 9th July, three days later, the mother came back to the offices of the Society and, having been brought to a solicitor's office nearby, signed and completed the consent form. Earlier on that day two events occurred, of which each must have had some bearing on her action. In the first place she received a letter from the adoption society informing her that, as she had not signed the consent, the child would be taken from the adopters and brought to her home on the following morning which was Saturday, the 10th July. In addition she also received a telephone call at her place of employment from the father who had returned the previous day from overseas, and who arranged to meet her for lunch. She met him as arranged but did not disclose to him that the child had not been finally adopted nor what her intentions were. At this stage the father was still under the impression that the child had already been adopted and he was renewing his relationship with the mother on this basis. She did nothing to change this impression, and went from her meeting with him to sign and complete the consent form.

The father and mother continued to meet over the next few days, and there is evidence that by the 13th July they had reached a tentative arrangement that they would get married. The application for the adoption of the child having been listed for hearing before the Board, it was dealt with on the 20th July and an adoption order was made. The only persons notified of the hearing were the applicants who were the adopting parents.

On the 13th May, 1974, the father and mother as plaintiffs commenced this action in which they sought against the Board and the Attorney General the following declarations:–

'(a) A declaration that the infant is the legitimate child of the plaintiffs.

(b) A declaration that the provisions of s. 29 of the *Adoption Act, 1952*, contravene the provisions of the Constitution and are null and void and have no effect.

(c) A declaration that the provisions of ss. 14 and 15 of the *Adoption Act, 1952*, were not complied with in relation to the making of the adoption order.

(d) A declaration that the adoption order is null and void and has no effect.

(e) An order directing the first-named defendant to disclose the names of the purported adopters of the said infant and their present address.

(f) An order directing that the custody of the infant should be given to the plaintiffs.'

The plaintiffs, having failed to obtain the declarations sought at the trial of their action before Mr. Justice Butler, have appealed to this Court. In seeking the declarations sought, the plaintiffs challenge on two distinct grounds the adoption order made by the Board. In the first place it is submitted that the relevant provisions of the Adoption Act, which is a statute of the Oireachtas, are invalid having regard to the provisions of the Constitution. In the second place it is submitted that the requirements laid down by the Act were not complied with and that the order is null and void on that account. This second submission assumes the validity of the relevant provisions of the Act.

Where the relief which a plaintiff seeks rests on two such distinct grounds, as a general rule the court should consider first whether the relief wought can be granted on the ground which does not raise a question of constitutional validity. If it can, then the court ought not to rule on the larger question of the constitutional validity of the law in question. Normally, such a law as a statute of the Oireachtas will enjoy a presumption of constitutionality which ought not to be put to the test unnecessarily. However, there may be circumstances of an exceptional nature where the requirement of justice and the protection of constitutional rights make the larger enquiry necessary. Such, in my view, do not exist in this case.

Therefore, I propose in the first instance to consider whether the plaintiffs were correct in their submission that the relevant provisions of the Act were not observed in the adoption of the child and, if so, whether this affects the order which was made.

Part II of the Act of 1952 establishes the Board and, on the application of a person desiring to adopt a child, the Board is given power by s. 9 to make an adoption order. Section 10 defines who may be adopted, and s. 11 specifies who may adopt. Both these sections have been amended in respects which are not relevant to the issues in this case. Section 13 lays down certain requirements as to the suitability of the adopters. Section 14 deals with consent; it provides that an order *shall* not be made without 'the consent of every person being the child's mother or guardian or having charge of or control over the child, unless the Board dispenses with any such consent in accordance with this section.' Sub-section 2 of s. 14 empowers the Board to dispense with consent in case of mental incapacity or if the person cannot be found, while sub-s. 5 provides that the consent shall be in writing in the prescribed form, and sub-s. 6 provides that the consent 'may be withdrawn at any time before the making of an adoption order.'

Sub-section 3 of s. 15 provides:–

> The Board shall satisfy itself that every person whose consent is necessary and had not been dispensed with has given consent and understands the nature and effect of the consent and of the adoption order.

In my opinion, the observance of these statutory provisions as to consent is a basic prerequisite to the exercise of the power given to the Board by s. 9 of the Act of 1952. Section 14 of the Act specifies those whose consent shall be necessary, and the form and nature of the consent; it is to be in writing in the prescribed form and may be withdrawn at any time up to the making of the order. Section 15, sub-s. 3, imposes a statutory obligation on the Board to be satisfied that not merely has the formality of a written consent been observed but that it is a genuine and real consent in the sense that its nature and effect are fully understood by the person consenting. A failure to observe these statutory requirements could not be treated as a mere procedural irregularity but must be regarded as being destructive of the power sought to be exercised. Section 16 of the Act specifies the persons who 'shall be entitled to be heard on an application for an adoption order.' Included amongst the persons so specified is 'the mother of the child.'

I have now to consider whether these statutory requirements (some of them essential to the exercise by the Board of its power to make an adoption order) have been observed in this particular case. In my opinion they have not been observed.

It cannot be disputed on the evidence given at the trial that adoption was the last situation which the mother wished for her child. The father was clearly against such a course and the mother took the initial step of placing her child with an adoption society only because of an apparent breach with the father. This must have been obvious to all those who at this stage were seeking to help and advise the mother. The mother's subsequent behaviour, her delay in giving her final consent, the fact that she ignored the various letters written to her, her change of mind at the moment of decision on the 6th July, 1971, should have put those who were concerned in the adoption process on notice that they were dealing in this case with a mother who was liable to change her mind at any time.

The consent upon which the Board acted was given in the prescribed form on the 9th July, 1971. The Board had, or ought to have had, available to it full information on the entire background of the case. Nevertheless, without further enquiry, the Board made the adoption order on the 20th July, 1971. In between these two dates, the father and mother had come to a tentative understanding that they would marry. This change in their relationship opened an entirely new possibility for the future of their child. Unfortunately, however, no one – certainly no officer of the Board – had explained to the mother the nature of the consent she had given or that it could be withdrawn at any time before the making of the adoption order. She was left under the impression that the consent she had given on the 9th July was final and irrevocable and that, even if she were to marry the father, what had been done could not be undone. In evidence at the trial the mother stated, in effect, that had she known she could get the child back before the making of the order she would have done so.

The Board all the time had the statutory obligation under s. 15, sub-s. 3, of the Act of 1952 to satisfy itself that the mother not only had given a consent in the prescribed form (as she undoubtedly had done on the 9th July) but also that she understood the nature and effect of this consent. Not only is there no evidence that the Board took any steps so to satisfy itself, but all the evidence indicates that once the written consent in the prescribed form was obtained by the Board no further action (not even notification to her of the date of the hearing of the application for adoption) was taken to involve the mother in the adoption process. This meant that this mother not only did not understand the true nature of the consent she had given but that the Board took no step whatsoever to inform her. It also means that the Board did not discharge the statutory obligation imposed upon it under the provisions of s. 15, sub-s. 3, of the Act to satisfy itself that the nature and effect of the consent was understood by her. This failure, in my view, deprived the Board of any power to make the order it purported to make on the 20th July, 1971, since one of the essential statutory prerequisites to the exercise of that power had not been observed.

It follows, in my view, that the adoption order made by the Board was without jurisdiction and, therefore, is null and void.

Having come to this conclusion, I must now consider the position of the plaintiffs, the child and the adopting parents. It has been argued by counsel for the Board that the plaintiffs' failure to take action earlier than they did, with the consequent effect on the child in relation to his surroundings, renders it unjust and contrary to the child's interests to remove him now from the care of the adopting parents. No one can be unmoved by such a plea or feel anything but compassion for all of those involved in this human drama. However, in coming to a just conclusion one must not allow compassion, or permit sympathy to conceal, fundamental rights. Delay was not pleaded as a defence to the plaintiffs' claim, nor was it raised in any way when evidence was given on the trial of this action in the High Court.

The evidence shows that the mother, having signed form No. 4A on the 9th July, 1971, was fully convinced that she had done something which was irrevocable. She and the father were married on the 6th June, 1972, and both of them went to reside overseas. They were resolved to do everything possible to recover the child even though the task appeared formidable in their state of knowledge at that time. On their first return to Ireland in 1973 they consulted their solicitors, and a preliminary letter was written on their behalf to the adoption society on the 28th June, 1973. One can well understand that, following this preliminary step, many enquiries and investigations were necessary. In particular the plaintiffs were entitled to have the benefit of legal advice as to whether the provisions of the Act of 1952 had been observed and to know what their rights were before an action of this nature was launched. In fact this action was commenced in May 1974. I cannot accept that in the circumstances there was any unreasonable delay. I feel bound, therefore, to regard this argument as being unsustainable and irrelevant in the circumstances of this case.

As the order made on the 20th July, 1971, was null and void, it cannot affect the status or rights of either the plaintiffs or the child in relation to each other. Since father and mother were married on the 6th June, 1972, the child became their legitimate child and, it follows, part of their family: see s. 1, sub-s. 1, of the *Legitimacy Act, 1931.* In my view, their rights and responsibilities and the child's rights and status must be considered in the light of this fact.

In my view the plaintiffs are entitled to the declarations sought at paragraphs 13 (a), (c), (d) and (f), of the statement of claim, and such other ancillary declarations and order as appear necessary.

I think it proper to add that in my view this case is exceptional and is concerned with particular and special facts. I see no grounds for suspecting that such particular and special facts could have occurred before . . . or are likely ever to reoccur.

Because of the view I have come to, I do not think it necessary or proper for the Court to express my opinion on the submission that certain provisions of the *Adoption Act, 1952*, are invalid having regard to the provisions of the Constitution.

Henchy, J. (dissenting):

. . . . When the adoptive parents agreed to adopt this child five years ago, the State, for its part, underwrote the confidentiality of the adoption and the sanctity and security of the family resulting from the adoption. The State, speaking through the legislature, stipulated to this effect in the *Adoption Act, 1952.* This solemn and far-reaching undertaking could, of course, be held by the Courts to be nugatory in a particular case if a valid challenge to the jurisdiction to make the adoption order followed hard on the adoption order – but not if years are allowed to pass. Otherwise, the familial stability and security aimed at by adoption would be defeated. Even an order of the District Court (which usually has much less sweeping consequences than an adoption order), regardless of its invalidity, will not normally be quashed unless the application for certiorari is made within six months: see Order 84, r. 10, of the Rules of the Superior Courts, 1962. In my view, not even natural parents who have married after the adoption, and irrespective of what fundamental rights they may invoke, will continue, without limit of time, to have a standing to assert the invalidity of an adoption order.

Because of this Court's conclusion that the statutory prerequisites of a valid adoption were not compiled with – thus differing from the trial judge – the exercise of discretion in that context now arises for the first time. The child, a boy now six years old, has been growing up in an Irish provincial setting. He has never known his parents. His father has never seen him. His mother last saw him when he was about five weeks old. For the whole of his sentient life he has been with the adoptive parents. The plaintiffs' case simply is that, because the adoption order was made without jurisdiction, the child should now be sundered from the adoptive parents and, regardless of how damaging it might be to the child or to the adoptive parents, be sent out to a foreign country to take his place in the plaintiffs' home as their legitimated child. If the plaintiffs' case is accepted, this would be done without hearing any representations on behalf of either the child or the adoptive parents. No account would be taken of the possible ill-effects of the sudden and drastic transfer of this six-year-old boy to strange parents in a strange home in a far-away country.

For my part, I am satisfied that the orders asked for in the statement of claim are discretionary orders and that, in the light of what has happened with the passage of time, the plaintiffs have now no standing to apply for those orders. In my opinion, the discretion of the Court should not be exercised in their favour for that reason and, more particularly, because it has not been shown that those orders would be compatible with the welfare of the child.

I would hold that the plaintiffs are disentitled from relying on the invalidity of the adoption order as found in the judgment of the Chief Justice.

Kenny, J.:

. . . . If the Board had considered the two documents signed by the mother, they could not have satisfied themselves that she understood the nature of the consent – and there was no other evidence of her consent before them. In my view none of the documents gave her any information about her right to withdraw her consent and, as she was not informed of the date when it was proposed to make the adoption order, she did not know that she would have withdrawn it at any time up to the 20th July, 1971. The adoption order was made without jurisdiction or power and, therefore, is a nullity.

It has been argued by counsel for the Board that the plaintiffs have delayed so long in bringing these proceedings that the Court should not now take the child from the adopting parents and give him to the plaintiffs who are unknown to him. Delay was not pleaded and was not investigated in the High Court. On the documents I do not think that the plaintiffs have unreasonably delayed in bringing this action. When the mother signed the consent on 9th July, 1971, she thought it was the final step and that she had no further rights to the child. She married in June, 1972, and went with her husband to a foreign country when he had a position. They then decided that they would do everything they could to recover the child. Their first return to Ireland was in 1973 and, until they had the benefit of legal advice in that year, they thought that the consent given by the mother was binding. A letter claiming the return of the child was written by the plaintiffs' solicitor on the 28th June, 1973. The proceedings were commenced in May, 1974, and so there was no unreasonable delay.

I would allow the appeal and make the declarations claimed in paragraph 13, sub-paragraphs (a), (c), (d) and (f) of the statement of claim.

Griffin and **Parke, JJ.** concurred with **O'Higgins, C.J.**

Notes

1. The outcome of the decision was stated by *Shatter*, 193, fn. 102:

Subsequent to the Supreme Court decision, the adopters commenced proceedings seeking a declaration that they were not bound by the Supreme Court order as they [had] not [been] afforded any opportunity to be heard, and sought an order that the child remain in their custody. The natural parents sought an order of Habeas Corpus requiring the adopters to return their child to them. On 6th Oct. 1976, it was announced to the President of the High Court that the actions had been settled. A consent was executed by the parties in which they agreed that the child be made a ward of court and remain in the custody and care of the adopters. See the *Irish Times*, 24th July and 7th Oct. 1976.

See also O'Reilly, *Custody Disputes in the Irish Republic: The Uncertain Search for the Child's Welfare?*, 12 Ir. Jur. (n.s.) 37, at 43 (1977).

2. The Supreme Court decision caused considerable public discussion and some degree of unease. The result was the enactment of the *Adoption Act, 1976*. Section 2 rendered valid all consents given and orders made before its enactment to the extent that they might be invalid by reason of the defects existing in *M.* v. *An Bord Uchtála: Shatter*, 181. Thus, e.g., an order would not be invalid because the person who gave the consent was not aware that it could have been withdrawn at any time before the making of the order. Section 3 provided that a person whose consent is necessary for the adoption of a child should be informed before or 'as soon as may be' after giving consent of his or her right to withdraw it at any time before the making of the adoption order, and of his or her right to be heard on the application for the order. The section also provided that, on giving consent, the person must be asked to indicate in writing whether he or her wishes to be informed of the date on which the Board will hear him or her, if the person wishes to be heard, or to be consulted otherwise in relation to the order. Where the person elects not to be heard by the Board or otherwise to be consulted again in relation to the order, the Board need not inform or consult him or her. See *Shatter*, 181–182.

Section 5 of the Act provided that an adoption order is not to be declared invalid if the Court is satisfied:

'(a) that it would not be in the interests of the child concerned to make such a declaration, and

(b) that it would be proper, having regard to those interests and to the rights under the Constitution of all persons concerned, not to make such a declaration.'

Section 6 of the Act provided as follows:

'(1) If, in any proceedings, an adoption order is declared invalid by a court and the child concerned is in the custody of the person or persons in whose favour the adoption order was made or any other person or persons not being the person or persons who sought the declaration of invalidity, the court shall not then make an order as to the custody of the child unless such an order is sought and the court is satisfied that, by reason of the fact that any person having custody of the child has been joined in the proceedings and by reason of all the other circumstances of the case, it would be in the interests of justice that the question of the custody of the child should be determined then rather than in separate proceedings; but if the court decides, in accordance with this subsection, to determine the question of the custody of the child it shall do so subject to the provisions of section 3 of the Guardianship of Infants Act, 1964.

(2) Notwithstanding anything in subsection (1) of this section, the person or persons in whose favour an adoption order is made (or any other person or persons having custody of the child who is the subject of the order) shall not be joined or otherwise heard in any proceedings in a court in which the validity of the order is an issue without the consent of the court, and the court, in deciding whether to give such consent, may take into account submissions made to it by the Board or any other interested person relating to the identification at that time of the person or persons concerned or to any other relevant matter.'

3. After *M.* v. *An Bord Uchtála*, it was far from clear whether the Adoption Board was exercising an administrative, rather than a judicial, function. The issue was so fundamental in its implications as to the constitutionality of all adoption orders, that it was considered prudent to amend the Constitution to put the matter beyond doubt. Accordingly, after a Referendum, a new provision was inserted into the Constitution, as Article 37.2:

> No adoption of a person taking effect or expressed to take effect at any time after the coming into operation of this Constitution under laws enacted by the Oireachtas and being an adoption pursuant to an order made or authorisation given by any person or body of persons designated by those laws to exercise such functions and powers was or shall be invalid by reason only of the fact that such person or body of persons was not a judge or court appointed or established as such under this Constitution.

Commenting on this Amendment to the Constitution Professor J. Kelly, *The* Irish Constitution 368 (2nd ed., 1984) says:

> Whether such a technique of adhoc amendment of Article 37 is advisable may be doubted. Over and above its immediate object it may have unsuspected constructional implications in the future. It may be argued in a context not foreseen in 1979, that the people, byt specifically protecting the function of making adoption orders from attack under Article 37, implicitly admit that this function is not a 'limited' one; that similarly some other function now in administrative hands, of importance comparable with the function of the Adoption Board, must be seemed illicit under Article 37.

Do you agree? Could it not be argued that the very great social and personal implications of a possible judicial decision striking down the Constitutional validity of the adoption process more than justifies the pre-emptive caution of a Constitutional Amendment? The Amendment was presumed, not on the fact that the function of making adoption orders '*is* not a "limited" one', but rather merely that the Court *might* hold that it is. If you were a litigant seeking to invite the Court to draw the inference suggested by Professor Kelly in relation to some other administrative function, how confident would you be in the probable efficiency of the argument?

DISPENSATION WITH CONSENT

Under the *Adoption Act, 1952* the Board could dispense with the consent of the person whose consent was required if it was satisfied that that person was incapable by reason of mental infirmity of giving consent or could not be found: section 14(2). This power of dispensation was criticised for being too narrow. Accordingly section 3 of the *Adoption Act, 1974* was enacted, providing as follows:

(1) In any case where a person has applied for an adoption order relating to a child and any person whose consent to the making of an adoption order relating to the child is necessary and who has agreed to the placing of the child for adoption either –
(*a*) fails, neglects or refuses to give his consent, or
(*b*) withdraws a consent already given,
the applicant for the adoption order may apply to the High Court for an order under this section.
(2) The High Court, if it is satisfied that it is in the best interests of the child so to do, may make an order under this section –
(*a*) giving custody of the child to the applicant for such period as the Court may determine, and
(*b*) authorising the Board to dispense with the consent of the other person referred to in subsection (1) of this section to the making of an adoption order in favour of the applicant during the period aforesaid.
(3) The consent of a ward of court shall not be dispensed with by virtue of a High Court order under this section except with the sanction of the Court.

This section was considered in *G.* v. *An Bord Uchtála*, set out *supra*, pp. 128–52, which should now be consulted. Another important decision is *S.* v. *Eastern Health Board.*

S. v. EASTERN HEALTH BOARD

Unreported, February 1979, High Court, Finlay P., (1978/537 SP)

Finlay, P.:

This is a claim brought by the plaintiff for an order returning to her the custody of her 20 month old daughter.

It was originally instituted by special summons pursuant to the *Guardianship of Infants Act, 1964* against the Eastern Health Board through whose agency the child had purported to be placed for adoption.

The prospective adoptive parents who are in actual custody of the child were added as notice parties and duly applied to the Court for an order under section 3 of the *Adoption Act, 1974* dispensing with the consent of the plaintiff to adoption and placing the child in their custody pending the decision of the Adoption Board on their application to adopt it.

The proceedings were heard by me in accordance with the procedures set out in my Judgment in *G.* v. *An Bord Uchtála* [*supra*, p. 128] and I reserved my decision.

I find the facts to be as follows.

The plaintiff is an unmarried girl of 23 years of age. She was reared and educated in rural Ireland and obtained a good honours Leaving Certificate about five years ago. She then took up a clerical position in the Public Service in Dublin in which she has since been employed. At all material times she has lived on her own in a flat in the city. She is a practising Catholic.

She became pregnant at the end of 1976 and gave birth to her daughter on the 3rd June 1977 in St. Patrick's Home in Dublin. She remained there with her child for about 10 days and then left to resume her employment. From that time until the month of August 1977 she regularly visited her daughter in St. Patrick's Home going there two and possibly three times each week. Prior to leaving St. Patrick's Home she had had a discussion and received advice from a member of the congregation in charge who is a trained social worker. There was a conflict of evidence before me with regard to what the nature of that advice was but I am quite satisfied that the advice she received was that she should make up her own mind as to what future arrangements to make for the care of her child and that she was not persuaded, or even advised towards any particular course but only towards the necessity of coming to a decision. It would appear that at that time her idea was that she would provide for caring for the child herself though not necessarily in her actual flat but by having it in a nursery and looking after it at the week-ends and during periods while she was not working. She did not intend to give up her employment and there was apparently no question at that time, nor has there been any question at any time since, that the child could be brought up in the house of her parents in the country.

As a result of further telephone conversations between the plaintiff and the sister-in-charge in St. Patrick's an arrangement was made that the child should be placed in a nursery for young children in Greystones and that the plaintiff would then be able to look after her at the week-end and see her regularly as much as was possible and consistent with her work in the city. An actual arrangement for the bringing of the child to Greystones was arranged and it was stated by the plaintiff that her parents were going to come up with a motor car and bring out the child. One such arrangement was cancelled and then subsequently a second one simply did not happen. Between these events which occurred at the commencement of September 1977 and the 1st December 1977 the plaintiff neither made any contact with, nor did she in any way visit, St. Patrick's Home nor make any enquiry or have any communication concerning her child.

During that period the social worker in St. Patrick's made a number of attempts to contact the plaintiff firstly by letter and subsequently by phoning her to her place of employment. She failed to contact the plaintiff and it is admitted that eventually the plaintiff persuaded one of her colleagues or superiors in her employment to say that she did not work there any longer. As a result the matter was put into the hands of a social worker attached to the Eastern Health Board. The reason for this undoubtedly was that St. Patrick's Home is not normally geared nor suitable for the keeping of infants beyond a very short period after their birth. It was necessary therefore for the mother of this child to make a decision with regard to its future. The social worker attached to the Health Board wrote on the 23rd November of 1977 to the plaintiff introducing herself and asking the plaintiff to contact her. The letter contained an emphasised plea for the plaintiff to contact the social worker concerned as she did not want to embarrass the plaintiff by calling into the place of her work. It is relied on by the plaintiff's counsel as a threatening letter but it is, when considered in detail, a letter showing significant compassion and understanding of the problems facing the plaintiff.

As a result of this letter a meeting took place on the 1st December between the plaintiff and the social worker concerned. There is a conflict of evidence again about what occurred at this meeting and the plaintiff contends that she was strongly persuaded by the social worker to place her child for adoption. The social worker, on the other hand, states that the plaintiff herself mentioned adoption as being her decision, expressed relief that she had been able to face up to a decision and that she was again in contact with the problem. I accept the account of the social worker of this meeting. After the parties had met they went to the Home and the plaintiff saw her daughter again and then, at her own request, on the evidence before me, signed a form agreeing to place the child in adoption. This was done on that occasion as a result of the plaintiff's having been information by the social worker concerned that a meeting of the Placement Committee of the Eastern Health Board would take place in a few days time and that if a form was signed on that day the question of the placement of the child be brought before that meeting.

By arrangement the plaintiff and her mother again visited St. Patrick's Home between that date and the 19th December and both again saw the child. This was done after the plaintiff had been informed that prospective adoptive parents had been chosen and that the child was soon to be placed in their custody with the intention that they might adopt it. I am satisfied that the plaintiff was, at that time, content with the decision she had made and satisfied with the arrangements that were being made.

The child was, in fact, placed for the purposes of adoption with the prospective adoptive parents, Mr. and Mrs. B., on the 19th December 1977.

Again, notwithstanding a conflict in the evidence, I am satisfied that the plaintiff kept in contact over the next few months with the social worker whom she had met on the 1st December 1977. At the beginning and for possibly a period of four or five weeks after the first meeting the plaintiff seemed content with the decision she had made and with the placing of her child for adoption. Subsequently she became depressed and in particular expressed sorrow at the fact that she would not see her child again. She did not propose to look after the child herself but did discuss with the social worker other methods of having the child looked after which would not, as would adoption, prevent her from seeing it again. The advice she received during this period was, I am satisfied, to the effect that she could request the return of her child but that it would be wise for her to have good concrete proposals for it to be looked after if it was to be returned to her.

By October of 1977 the plaintiff had commenced a friendship with a young man some years younger than herself who was not the father of this child and she informed the social worker of this friendship. In the month of February 1978 again, notwithstanding a conflict in the evidence, I am satisfied that the advice she got from the social worker was to tell her young man with whom she was now quite friendly about the existence of the child and about the steps she had taken concerning it but this she did not do.

In or about the month of February the social worker informed the plaintiff that the final consent to adoption was ready and asked her if she was prepared to sign it which she was not then prepared to do. She then ceased, to some extent, to communicate with the social worker.

As a result the social worker wrote to her as she was concerned with the extent of her depression and asked her to come and visit her again to discuss her problems with her. The plaintiff's boyfriend read this letter and apparently came to the conclusion that it indicated that the plaintiff was possibly receiving psychiatric treatment and asked the plaintiff for an explanation of it. The plaintiff then, for the first time, told him of the existence of the child and of the role that the social worker was playing in the entire matter. This occurred around the 1st April of 1978.

Subsequently, after discussion between the plaintiff and her boyfriend she came to the conclusion that she would take the child back and look after it herself. She then admittedly told to the social worker concerned a series of untrue accounts of the proposals she had in relation to looking after the child herself. Firstly she told her that she was to be married in the following June which was not true. Secondly she told her that she had provided arrangements with a day nursery and would be leaving the child to it each day whilst she continued at her work. This was not true either. Upon this request being made the social worker concerned contacted her colleague who was dealing with the prospective adoptive parents and after discussion they decided to agree to the child being returned to the plaintiff.

A further conflict on the evidence arose before me as to whether the child was then returned precipitately and without sufficient warning to the plaintiff but I am satisfied that this is not so and that the plaintiff herself urged the necessity for the transfer of the custody of the child to be done speedily.

The child was, in fact, transferred to the custody of the plaintiff through the arrangements made by the social worker on the 19th April. At that time the social worker offered to give assistance and support at the commencement of the caring of the child by the plaintiff and this offer was apparently accepted.

The plaintiff having obtained custody of the child brought it to her flat, took some days off work and commenced to look after it herself. This proved quite beyond her capacity. She did not have the assistance of any woman and remained all day with the child, her boyfriend coming after his work in the evenings to give her assistance. She avoided any contact with the social worker and gave her a false account of where she was alleging that she was staying at one period with her boyfriend's family. After three days the plaintiff, due to her inability to cope with the child and being, I have no doubt, in a very distressed condition brought the child to the nursery in Greystones to which she had previously been recommended and left the child there. She then, for the first time, got in touch herself with the social worker who had been dealing with her.

A series of discussions and meetings then took place over a period of the next week or so between the plaintiff, her boyfriend and the social worker. There is again a conflict of evidence with regard to what happened at these discussions. I am, however, satisfied that no pressure was then put by the social worker upon the plaintiff to agree to the adoption of the child but that she was urged carefully to consider her plans for the child for the future and it was indicated to her that the idea of leaving it as a permanent feature in a nursery in Greystones and working in the city of Dublin was not in the interests of the welfare of the child. The plaintiff was asked to give to the social worker a decision on this matter after discussing it with her boyfriend and anyone else who might help her by Monday the 1st May. On that date the plaintiff telephoned the social worker and said she had definitely decided to permit the child to be adopted provided it could be returned to the same prospective adoptive parents who previously had custody of it. They were willing to accept the child back and the plaintiff, I am satisfied, suggested that the transfer of the child should take place on the following day the 2nd May 1978.

The events of that day are of some importance. The plaintiff went out to Greystones to the nursery where the child was, having been visiting it on a number of occasions in the previous week with her boyfriend, accompanied by the social worker and by her secretary.

I had evidence from the proprietor of that nursing home, who is quite independent of all the matters in dispute in this case, to the effect that the plaintiff, on this occasion, informed her of her final decision to permit the child to be adopted and appeared considerably more relaxed and contented than she had been on previous visits during the week when she came to see the child. The child was then brought from the nursery in Greystones into the city of Dublin and the plaintiff attended with the social worker concerned before the solicitor to the Adoption Board and signed a final consent swearing the appropriate affidavit and also an affidavit setting out shortly the history of the child and the negotiations with regard to its adoption which was in a narrative form and not one of the prescribed forms for an adoption. This had been prepared that morning by the authorities of the Eastern Health Board and brought by the social worker to the plaintiff. Subsequent to the execution of these documents and the swearing of these affidavits the plaintiff was interviewed by a separate official of the Eastern Health Board who is a social worker and signed a further form acknowledging that she understood what she had done, that she was not being pressurised to do it and that what she was doing was of her own free will. This form was signed by her after an interview with this separate social worker which lasted for approximately half an hour.

A short time after these events the plaintiff again contacted the social worker concerned and told her that she now regretted her decision finally to consent to the adoption of the child and on the advice, I am satisfied, of that social worker she then wrote to the Adoption Board withdrawing her consent on the 18th May of 1978.

On this occasion the prospective adoptive parents were not prepared to give back custody of the child to the plaintiff and after further correspondence which is not particularly material these proceedings were then instituted.

That concludes the findings of fact on the events surrounding the placing of this child in the actual custody of the applicants for adoption. In addition to evidence from all the parties concerned with these matters I also have evidence from two psychiatrists with regard to the capacity and suitability and fitness of the plaintiff to care for and look after a young child, from a psychologist on the same topic and from a psychiatrist who had interviewed and examined the child with its present custodians and the other children in their family and I also had evidence from the applicants for adoption and from a social worker aware of their circumstances and surroundings.

Having regard to the decision of the Supreme Court in *G.* v. *An Bord Uchtála* [*supra*, p. 128] I am satisfied that the issues which must be tried by me on the facts before me and the order in which they must be determined by me are as follows.

1. Whether the signing on the 1st November 1977 by the plaintiff of the form consenting to place her child for adoption and the permitting by her of the child being placed in the custody of the applicants for adoption on the 19th December constituted an agreement to place the child for adoption within the meaning of section 3 of the *Adoption Act, 1974* and therefore brought into operation the provisions of that Act.
2. Whether the events occurring in April 1978 and, in particular the handing back by the prospective adoptive parents of the child to the plaintiff with the approval of the adoption society concerned constituted a rescission or cancellation of that agreement.
3. Whether the events of the 2nd May 1978 including the signing by the plaintiff of a final consent to adoption and the handing back by her of the child into the custody of the prospective adoptive parents constituted an agreement to place the child for adoption within the meaning of section 3 of the *Adoption Act, 1974.*
4. If either the events of the 1st December 1977 or those of the 2nd May 1978 constituted an agreement to place the child for adoption whether it is in the best interests of the child that she should now remain in the custody of the prospective adoptive parents for some period of time and consent to adoption by the plaintiff be dispensed with so as to enable An Bord Uchtála if they see fit to make an adoption order in respect of the child.

Having regard to the fact section 3 of the *Adoption Act, 1974* does not enable the Court to make an adoption order but merely enables the Court to create a situation in which An Bord Uchtála may, if it sees fit, do so, I take the view that irrespective of what my decision is on the four issues already enumerated by me it becomes necessary also to decide the following issues.

(a) Whether the plaintiff has abandoned or deserted the infant or has otherwise so conducted herself that I should refuse to enforce her right to custody of the infant within the meaning of section 14 of the *Guardianship of Infants Act, 1964* and, if I so find, whether I should in my discretion decline to make an order for the return of the custody of the infant to her.

(b) Whether the plaintiff has abandoned or deserted the infant or allowed the infant to be brought up by another person at that person's expense for such a length of time and under such circumstances as to satisfy me that she was unmindful of her parental duties within the meaning of the provisions of section 16 of the *Guardianship of Infants Act, 1964* and, if I so find, whether I am satisfied that she is a fit person to have custody of the infant.

I will deal separately with each of these issues as I see them and with the evidence on which I have reached a decision upon them.

In the Judgment of the Supreme Court in *G.* v. *An Bord Uchtála* [*supra*, p. 128] the majority of the members of the Court, namely the Chief Justice, Mr. Justice Walsh, and Mr. Justice Parke decided that the mother of an illegitimate child had an alienable constitutional right to its custody. Although the Chief Justice and Mr. Justice Parke dissented from the other members of the Court on the ultimate decision in that case that decision did not involve directly the question as to whether the undoubted *prima facie* right of the mother of an illegitimate child to its custody was constitutional or statutory in origin. I therefore feel bound by the view expressed by the majority of the members of the Supreme Court on this precise issue as to the constitutional origin of the mother's right to custody. If I am incorrect in this understanding of the binding nature of these decisions upon me as a precedent I should emphasise that were I freed from precedent I would adhere to the decision arrived at by me in *G.* v. *An Bord Uchtála* and others that the right to custody is constitutional in origin.

[Having quoted extracts from the judgments of O'Higgins, C.J., Walsh and Parke, JJ., in *G.* v. *An Bord Uchtála*, Finlay, P. continued:]

Having regard to these decisions I am satisfied that the test which I must apply to each of the separate alleged agreements to place for adoption are that they must have been made freely with full knowledge of their consequences and under circumstances where neither the advice of persons engaged in the transaction nor the surrounding circumstances deprived the mother of the capacity to make a fully informed free decision. I am not, however, satisfied that evidence that in any particular case a mother either soon or later after the making of such a decision changed her mind is of itself evidence of the invalidity of the agreement to place. Section 3 of the Act of 1974 necessarily involves in many cases a situation where an agreement to place has been followed by a change of mind. Neither does it seem to me possible to support a contention that a change of circumstances in the position of the mother after the full and free making of a decision would warrant a subsequent invalidation of it.

Applying these standards and these tests to the entire of the events of December 1977 as proved in evidence before me I am satisfied that they constituted an agreement on the part of the plaintiff to place her child for adoption within the meaning of section 3 of the *Adoption Act, 1974.*

I say the entire of the events because, in my view, the evidence of such a free informed and willing agreement to place the child for adoption consists not only of the signing of the form on the 1st December 1977 but of the subsequent events prior to the 19th December 1977.

I am quite satisfied on the evidence that the meaning and effect of the signature of a form agreeing to the placement of the child for adoption, including the right of the mother subsequently to withdraw that consent and the corresponding right, if the child was in fact placed for adoption, of the prospective adoptive parents to apply to the Court to dispense with consent were all fully explained to the plantiff on the 1st December of 1977. The plaintiff is, in my estimation, an intelligent girl. She has had a good education [and] her subsequent years of employment in the Public Service ha[ve] left her, I am satisfied, as a person with a clear understanding of such matters. She, herself, stated in evidence that at the time when she signed the form on the 1st December 1977 she had decided that this was the best thing in the interests of her child as she could not see any way in which she could bring it up herself. It is quite clear that at that time there was no possibility of the child being brought up in her parents home. It is equally clear that she could not see any way in which she was prepared, even if she were able, to give up her work in order to bring up the child and it is equally clear that the father of the child did not enter into the picture of the child's future in any way. Whilst as a general proposition one might be slow to uphold a decision to place for adoption arising from one single interview between the mother of an illegitimate child and a social worker, I am satisfied that in the period after the 1st December and in particular, having regard to the subsequent visit by the plaintiff and her own mother to the child in the home, the plaintiff had an ample opportunity fully to consider the decision which she was then making and it was one that met with her free and fully informed approval at the time the child was eventually,as a result of her agreement, placed with the prospective adoptive parents on the 19th December.

The words of section 3 of the *Adoption Act, 1974* material to the second issue before me are, 'has agreed to the placing of the child for adoption'. I am bound to give a meaning to the word 'agreed' in this section. It is to me of significance that the word 'consent' elsewhere used in the section is not used in this context and whilst it appears inappropriate to construe this with the full meaning, consequences and characteristics of a legal agreement it seems to me to incorporate the concept of an arrangement between at least two parties. Having regard to the provisions of the section which deal only with the situation where there are applicants for an adoption order in respect of the child it would seem to me to follow that the agreement concerned must be construed as an agreement between the mother of the child and the applicants for its adoption inevitably made through some agency acting as agents for an undisclosed principal. If I am correct in this view of the interpretation of the word 'agreed' it follows in my opinion that it is an agreement capable of mutual rescission. The consent of the applicants for adoption in this case to the return of the child to its mother and her willingness to accept back custody of the child both of which occurred in April of 1978 constitute, in my view, a mutual rescission of that agreement. If the agreement is to be construed not as an agreement between the mother and the prospective adoptive parents but rather an agreement in the facts of this case between the mother and the adoption society permitting that society to place the child at their discretion with any adoptive parent then the intervention of the society in those events through the social worker concerned would constitute a mutual rescission of that agreement between the mother and the adoption society. I therefore conclude that after the 19th April of 1978 when the child was returned to its mother she was no longer, within the meaning of section 3 a person who has agreed to the placing of the child for adoption.

By the 2nd May 1978 the plaintiff in this case was, on my view of the evidence, in a much stronger position to make a fully, free and informed decision with regard to the future of her child than she had been in December of 1977. Notwithstanding her denials of its usefulness I am satisfied on the evidence that she had received wise and kindly counselling from the social worker involved in this case over the entire period between December and May. A major problem which may have affected her mind in December namely, the building of a new relationship with a new boyfriend unaware of the existence of her child had been solved by May of 1978. She had by that time, in addition got the support of his parents on the evidence before me who were aware of her situation. Although the trial was unsatisfactory in its concept and not every likely to succeed she had had a period of actually caring for the child herself and she had had a longer period of the more realistic situation in which it had been placed in the nursery in Greystones. I am satisfied, on the evidence, that no pressure was put upon her by the social worker or by anybody else to agree finally to adoption and the extent of the clarity of her mind at this time is, to some extent, to be inferred from the fact that her agreement was not a general agreement to the placing of the child for adoption but rather an agreement to the replacing of the child with the people who previously had had it. In all these circumstances I have come to the conclusion that the events of the 2nd May 1978 consisting of the execution of a final consent and the affidavits surrounding it and equally importantly the actual transfer of the child back into the custody of the applicants for adoption before me constituted a clear agreement to place the child for adoption on the part of the plaintiff. It was strongly urged upon me on her behalf that it was incorrect and, in a sense, precipitate to have had a final consent signed on this occasion rather than a new agreement to place for adoption. The form of the consent does not, in my view, affect the question as to whether it constituted an agreement to place for adoption within the section or not. The final consent is, in effect, a misnomer for the Act provides and it was fully understood by the plaintiff at the time of these transactions that she could still, before final adoption, withdraw that consent. On reliance upon that knowledge she did so within about 17 days of the transaction concerned.

The next issue which therefore arises is as to whether it is in the best interests of this child that she should remain for the present, pursuant to an order by me, in the custody of the applicants for adoption and the consent of the mother to that adoption should be dispensed with so as to enable An Bord Uchtála to decide on whether a final order of adoption should be made or not. I have no doubt on the evidence adduced before me that it is clearly and strongly in the best interests of this child that an opportunity should be created whereby it would be given the opportunity of being adopted by the present applicants for adoption. I have come to this conclusion upon the evidence of the applicants for adoption themselves and my estimation of them, upon the evidence of the social worker involved with their side of the proposed adoption and upon the evidence of Dr. McCarthy.

The applicants for adoption are in all respects ideal parents. They manifestly have a stable relationship with each other and a good stable caring home. They already have two natural children one of whom is relatively close in age to the child concerned in this case. I accept that when this child was first placed with them in December 1977 after its period in St. Patrick's Home it was, whilst in general terms physically well, underdeveloped both physically and probably emotionally as well. I accept their evidence that it progressed extremely well between then and April of 1978 and became integrated into the family and stable in its infantile relationships with them. I also accept that the short period of separation between the 19th April and the 2nd May undoubtedly had an injurious effect on the development of this child which took some months to repair. I also accept their evidence that it is at present developing normally and well.

Dr. McCarthy's evidence satisfies me that this child is essentially a child who has significantly suffered in its emotional and psychiatric development by the first period of six months in which it remained in St. Patrick's Home. His account of his interview with and observation of the child in the environment of its present family indicates clearly to me that it has the badges of an institutional child and that there are very real dangers to its ultimate intellectual and emotional development unless a continuity of an existing caring custody is maintained. My view is not that the child would particularly suffer from now being transferred to the custody of its mother but rather that the child would be most likely seriously to suffer now from being transferred from the custody of the applicants for adoption.

My findings on these four issues in the narrow sense conclude the essential decision in this case for pursuant to them I must make the appropriate order under section 3 of the *Adoption Act, 1974* For the reasons already set out by me in this Judgment however, I conclude that it is necessary that I should also make findings on the other issues raised before me.

I am satisfied that in considering the provisions of both section 14 and section 16 of the *Guardianship of Infants Act, 1964* I am bound by section 3 of that Act to have regard to the welfare of the infant as being the first and paramount consideration.

Furthermore I am satisfied that on the facts of this case, at least, the issues arising on section 14 and section 16 are necessarily inter-related. The combined effect of these two sections must, in my view be as follows. First, if I am satisfied that the plaintiff in this case has abandoned or deserted the infant then under section 16 I cannot order the delivery of the infant to the plaintiff unless I am satisfied that she is a fit person to have custody of the infant and even if I were so satisfied I should not in my discretion make an order for the return of the infant, having regard to the provisions of section 14 if considering its welfare as the first and paramount consideration I concluded that it was not in the interests of its welfare so to do.

If I were satisfied pursuant to the provisions of section 16 that the plaintiff had allowed the infant to be brought up by another person at that person's expense in such circumstances that she was unmindful of her parental duties then, it seems to me, that two consequences would follow. Firstly, I could not order the return of the infant unless I were satisfied that she was a fit person to have custody of the infant and secondly, even if she were a fit person to have custody of the infant it seems to me that I must conduct a further enquiry and that is I must consider, having regard to the welfare of the infant as the first and paramount consideration, as to whether in my discretion I should make an order for its return to the plaintiff. I have reached this conclusion because I am satisfied that if a parent allowed her infant to be brought up at the expense of another person for such a length of time and under such circumstances as to satisfy me that she was unmindful of her parental duties and if I concluded that that having occurred it was not in the interest of the welfare of the infant that he should be returned to the custody of that parent I would be bound to hold that that parent had so conducted herself that I should refuse to enforce her right to the custody of the infant.

On these issues I have come to the following conclusions. I am not satisfied that the plaintiff has, within the meaning of either of these two sections, abandoned her infant. Abandonment in these two sections must, in my view, be considered as total neglect, the leaving of an infant with the knowledge that there is nobody to care for it or look after it. The classic abandonment of an infant is an infant who may be left literally on the steps of an orphanage. The plaintiff's child was born in St. Patrick's Home and it is a reasonable inference from the evidence that after the plaintiff had left that Home, leaving the child behind her, there was no possibility that the authorities of the Home, either in conjunction with the Eastern Health Board or with other appropriate societies or authorities, would ever permit this child to be left without some care and custody.

With some hesitation I have come to the conclusion that in law the plaintiff must be held to have deserted her infant. The period of that desertion, on the evidence before me, was between the beginning of September of 1977 and the beginning of December of 1977. Whilst as I have already held the plaintiff cannot be said to have abandoned her child at that time she took no steps of any description to ascertain its welfare, to provide for its welfare or to engage the services of others who would provide for its welfare. In particular during that period, it is clear on the evidence, that she refused to permit herself to be contacted by the authorities of St. Patrick's Home. Her refusal to communicate with those authorities and the devices which she operated to prevent them from communicating with her must be viewed in the light of the fact that some urgent question of the welfare of this child might have required to be dealt with by its mother. As far as the plaintiff was concerned during that period arrangements which were not appropriate and of which she would not have approved might have been in the course of being made in relation to this child.

My hesitation in reaching a conclusion that the plaintiff must be held to have deserted her child during this time is one stemming from compassion. I can understand the reasons which led the plaintiff in the situation in which she was at this particular time to seek to avoid contacting the authorities in the Home and in particular to seek to avoid reaching a decision about this matter. Her conduct was prompted to a large extent by an escapism and one which is understandable. Desertion however, does not necessarily mean heartless or wanton desertion. It seems to me that I am forced to conclude that these acts did constitute a desertion. I am satisfied that on the true construction of both these sections once a desertion has taken place these sections become operative even though it was followed in time by subsequent attempts to make provision for the welfare of the child.

Upon this finding the next enquiry must be as to whether the plaintiff is a fit person to have custody of the infant. On this issue I had the evidence of both Dr. Daly and of Dr. McCaffrey who, upon psychiatric examinations of the plaintiff, were satisfied that there was no emotional or psychiatric abnormality or want in the plaintiff which would make her incapable of looking after a young child. A somewhat different view was expressed by a psychologist who examined the plaintiff. The social worker who dealt with the plaintiff during the time when she had the child for three or four days expressed considerable reservations about the plaintiff's capacity to look after the child.

On the balance of probabilities I am satisfied that the plaintiff is a fit person to have custody of this child. That finding constitutes a finding only that there is nothing in her make-up arising from her personality or from any physical, emotional or psychiatric abnormality which would prevent her from being capable of caring for a young infant.

The final issue therefore to be decided on this aspect of the case is as to whether, in my discretion regarding the welfare of the child as of first and paramount importance, I should decline to make an order for the return of the child to the plaintiff in the event of the child not being the subject of a final adoption order made in favour of the present applicants for adoption.

The proposals now made by the plaintiff for the care and custody of this child were she returned to her may be summarised as follows. The plaintiff, I am satisfied, intends to marry her boyfriend on the 10th March. She would propose, were the child returned to her custody, that she, her husband as he then would be and the child should live in the first instance in a flat in Dublin and that her husband should continue in his work which is steady and good employment though not particularly well paid. The plaintiff would continue in her employment for a short period only so as to qualify for a substantial marriage grant and would then retire from her employment and devote her entire time to the upbringing of this child. There are elements of unreality in the proposals which the plaintiff is making though I was strongly impressed by her fiancé and in particular by his mother who would obviously take a substantial part in supporting and assisting these young people upon their marriage and in particular, if the child were returned to them. The plaintiff's approach to the problem of looking after this child, having regard to its history, is somewhat euphoric and it is doubtful if she fully realises the problems she may have. If, however for any reason the adoption of this child by the present applicant for adoption and in effect therefore its continued custody and care by them is not achieved, it seems to me that the next best chance the child would have for its welfare would be in the custody of its mother. I do not therefore feel that I would be bound in those circumstances to decline to make an order for the custody of the child to be returned to its mother.

Summarised therefore, my decision in this case and the orders which I intend to make are as follows.

1. An order pursuant to section 3 of the Adoption Act 1974 giving custody of the child to the applicants for adoption for a period of six months.
2. An order authorising the Adoption Board to dispense with the consent of the plaintiff to the making of an adoption order in favour of the applicants during the period of six months.
3. A declaration between the plaintiff and the Eastern Health Board that if, pursuant to the orders made herein, the Adoption Board does not within the period of six months make an adoption order in favour of the applicants that in the absence of a change of circumstances in relation to the plaintiff there are not any grounds for refusing to return to her the custody of her child.

Notes

1. The decision is analysed by O'Connor, *Consent and its Revocation in Adoption Proceedings*, 16 Ir. Jur. (n.s.) 275 (1981). See also *McC* v. *An Bord Uchtála and St. Louis Adoption Society,* [1982] I.L.R.M. 159 (High Ct., McWilliam, J., 1981).
2. In *McF.* v. *G. & G., The Sacred Heart Adoption Society & An Bord Uchtála*, [1983] I.L.R.M. 228 (High Ct., 1981), McWilliam, J. said:

   As regards . . . fear, anxiety, poverty or other deprivations, I am of opinion that these considerations must be considered from a practical point of view. The mere fact of having an illegitimate child causes stress and anxiety and, if there were plenty of money, arrangements could be made for care and accommodation without the necessity of involving the Adoption Board at an early stage. But in most cases, there is stress and anxiety and there is not sufficient money and there is not adequate accommodation, and if absolute rules as to fear, stress, anxiety or poverty were to be applied there would hardly be a case found in which one or other of them would not be present so that it could be argued that a consent was not valid. In the present case I am of opinion that, at the time she gave her consent to adoption, the plaintiff was made fully aware of the consequences of such consent and that what she wanted to do was to have the child adopted. The fact that she might have made a different decision had she come from a differently orientated family, been wealthy or proposing to marry the father of the child does not seem to me to alter the position that, under the circumstances in which she found herself, she gave her consent freely and fully appreciating what she was doing.

   Professor John Kelly regards this statement as 'a very important qualification': *The Irish Constitution*, 628 (2nd ed., 1984).
3. For further consideration of *McF* v. *G. & G., The Sacred Heart Adoption Society & an Bord Uchtála* and of *McC.* v. *An Bord Uchtála and St. Louis Adoption Society*, see O'Connor, *Recent Developments in the Law of Adoption*, 1 Ir. L. Times (n.s.) 22 (1983).
4. See also *N.B. and T.B.* v. *An Bord Uchtála, the Eastern Health Board and St. Louis Adoption Society,* unreported, High Ct., Barron, J., 18 February 1983 (1982–878Sp.) and *The State (M.G.)* v. *A.H. & M.H. and A.H. & M.H.* v. *An Bord Uchtála and the Western Health Board*, unreported, High Ct., McWilliam, J., 25 April 1983 (1983–23SS) and 1983–65Sp.)
5. Where a mother dies after she has agreed to placing the child for adoption but before the adoption order has been made, is it necessary for the Court to make an order under section 3? See *T.H. & N.H.* v. *An Bord Uchtála*, unreported, High Ct., McMahon, J., 20 November 1981 (1981–868).
6. The most important decision on the Constitutional and statutory position of the natural father in relation to adoption of his child is *The State (Nicolaou)* v. *An Bord Uchtála,* [1966] I.R. 379 (Sup. Ct.), which is set out *supra*, pp. 120–26. See also *P.C.* v. *B.H., an Bord Uchtála & A.G.*, unreported, High Ct., McWilliam, J., 25 April 1980, (1978–4931P.)
7. The *Adoption Report* of 1984 proposes radical changes in respect of consent and dispensing with consent to adoption. Consent to adoption would be irrevocable. Consent could be dispensed with in extreme cases where the parent-child relationship had already broken down, where repeated efforts to restore it had failed and rehabilitation of the child in his or her family was 'clearly not feasible': para. 6.8.

Chapter 15

GUARDIANSHIP OF CHILDREN

A great volume of litigation has built up on the subject of guardianship of children. The concept of 'guardianship' is nowhere defined in our legislation but it embraces an amalgam of the parental functions relating to the upbringing of children, including such matters as custody of the child, decisions as to how the child is to be reared and educated, and as to the religious dimensions (if any) of the child's life. See *Shatter*, 201; Eekelaar, *What Are Parental Rights?* 89 L.Q. Rev. 210 (1973); Hall, *The Waning of Parental Rights,* [1972B] Camb. L.J. 248; Dickens, *The Modern Function and Limits of Parental Rights,* 97 L.Q. Rev. 462 (1981); Hopkins, *Rights and Duties in Relation to Children*, 7 Family L. 169 (1977).

Two notable trends of the law relating to guardianship over the past century have been, first, towards equality between parents and secondly, towards placing somewhat less stress than formerly on parental claims relative to those of third parties. The Constitution casts its shadow over both these developments, but the precise effects of the Constitution have yet to be fully determined.

IN THE MATTER OF TILSON INFANTS; TILSON v. TILSON

[1951] I.R. 1 (Sup. Ct., 1950, aff'g High Ct., Gavan Duffy P., 1950)

Earnest Tilson married Mary Barnes in 1941 in a Catholic Church. He signed an ante-nuptial agreement that any issue of the marriage would be brought up as Catholics. The couple had four children (all boys). All were baptized and brought up as Catholics. In 1950 the husband left home unexpectedly, taking the three elder boys with him. Some time later he placed them in a Protestant orphanage and boarding school, called the 'Bird's Nest'. He indicated a clear desire that the children should be brought up as members of the Church of Ireland. Mrs. Tilson brought habeas corpus proceedings against the Board of Trustees of the School.

In the High Court, Gavan Duffy, P. granted an order for *habeas corpus.* The husband Ernest Tilson, appealed to the Supreme Court against this judgment and the order made thereunder.

Murnaghan J.:

. . . The point of law which was argued was whether under the Constitution the agreement of Ernest Tilson and Mary Josephine Tilson to bring up the children of the marriage as Roman Catholics had in law a binding force. In the law of England until 1882 a married woman, both as to property and in other respects, occupied in law a position of inferiority as respects her husband. By marriage her personal property – unless protected by the device of settlement to her separate use—passed to him, and he had also extensive rights over her real property. At common law the father had complete control over the children of the marriage and the wife had no voice against the wishes of the husband. In the Court of Chancery the absolute power of the father was in some respects subject to control, the King through this Court exercising a power as *parens patriae* and proceeding on the principle that the legal power of the father was in the nature of a trust which must not be abused. In the Court of Chancery the wishes of the mother in relation to a child were regarded only in so far as they affected the interest and well-being of the child. Even after the passing of the Guardianship of Infants Act, 1886, which many learned judges spoke of as a mothers' Act, the Courts respected the father's sole right to direct the religion of his children, and departed from this right only when the interests of the children required it or where the father by his conduct had abandoned his right or had relinquished it. The principles of the Court of Chancery as followed in the Chancery Division of the High Court of Justice were stated by the Court of Appeal in England in the *Agar-Ellis Case* 10 Ch. D. 49 which has been said to reach the high-water mark of the father's authority.

The position of married women was greatly improved in relation to property by the Married Women's Property Act, 1882; women were given a share in local government under the Local Government Act, 1898; subsequently they obtained the suffrage at parliamentary elections. The Constitution of 1922 recognised the equality of women (article 14), and article 16 of the Constitution gave the important rights dealt with by it to 'every citizen without distinction of sex.'

In the light of these facts I have to interpret the Constitution adopted by the people in 1937. The Constitution states fundamental principles, and, however these principles may have been reached, when they are enshrined in the Constitution they become, and are, the fundamental law of the State. Previously existing laws and principles are of no force in the State unless they derive efficacy from article 50 of the Constitution.

The Constitution, under the heading, 'Fundamental Rights,' includes an article 42 under the heading. 'Education'. . . .

[Murnaghan, J. read Article 42.1. He continued:]

This article includes among 'Fundamental Rights' the inalienable right and duty of parents to provide according to their means for the religious and moral, intellectual, physical, and social education of their children. Where the father and mother of children are alive this article recognises a joint right and duty in them to provide for the religious education of their children. The word, 'parents,' is in the plural and, naturally, should include both father and mother. Common sense and reason lead to the view that the mother is under the duty of educating the children as well as the father; and both must do so according to their means.

The Court was, however, asked to say that the word, 'parents,' was used in some generic sense that included only the father when he was living. The archaic law of England rapidly disintegrating under modern conditions need not be a guide for the fundamental principles of a modern state. It is not a proper method of construing a new constitution of a modern state to make an approach in the light of legal survivals of an earlier law. This Court in *In re Frost, Infants* [1947] I.R. 3 has already construed article 42 in the sense which I have indicated and has recognised that the mother, as well as the father, was a joint sharer of the right and duty. The point involved in *Frost's Case* [1947] I.R. 3, however, was this. A father and mother had made ante-nuptial engagements to bring the children of the marriage up in the Roman Catholic religion. Subsequently, the wife – the Catholic party- entered into a deed with the husband by which the children were to be brought up in the Protestant religion and they were educated as Protestants for several years. Notwithstanding this agreement of father and mother, the mother, after the father's death, claimed the right to depart from the agreement and to make of her own authority a new arrangement by which the children should be brought up as Roman Catholics. The Court rejected this contention and did not agree that the Constitution gave to the wife as surviving parent a right to prescribe the religious education. In the judgment delivered by Sullivan C.J. he deals with a case where there has been no agreement between the parents and approves of the rule that in general and apart from special circumstances the Court in such a case will determine the religion of the children according to the wishes of the father. The Court did not decide that where an agreement had been made by the father and mother and had been put into practice for years that the father alone could rescind it.

In the facts of *Frost's Case* there had been an ante-nuptial agreement to bring up the children as Roman Catholics, but the father and mother had made a solemn agreement to the contrary and this new agreement had been acted on for years. The Court, however, made this reservation:–

'It is not necessary in this case to consider the question whether the provisions of the Constitution affect what had been the established law as to the validity and effect of ante-nuptial agreements in respect of the religion of children, in view of the fact that subsequent to their marriage the parents agreed that their children should be educated in a different religion from that stated in the ante-nuptial agreement.'

Reference to an ante-nuptial agreement possibly having a binding force under the Constitution would have no meaning if the Constitution had not given to the mother in the opinion of the Court a right greater than she enjoyed before the Constitution, nor would Sullivan C.J. have said, at p. 28, that 'the Constitution does not define the respective rights of the parents during their lifetime,' if the mother had no rights during the lifetime of her husband. In the passage quoted, Sullivan C.J. treats it as established law that before the Constitution of 1937 an ante-nuptial agreement by the father to bring up his children in a particular religion was not binding in law. The cases in which this doctrine was laid down, *In re Browne, a Minor* 2 Ir. Ch. R. 151, *Hill* v. *Hill*, 31 L.J. Ch. 505. *In re Meades, Minors* I.R. 5 Eq. 98 and *Andrews* v. *Salt* 8 Ch. App. 622, were fully discussed in the argument. These cases were criticised either as based on no sound principle, or, if based on public policy, as based on a public policy which was contrary to the Constitution. I do think that there underlies these cases some principle that in Chancery the father was in the position of a trustee, and that being a trustee he could not predetermine how in all circumstances he would execute his trust. The Court in *Frost's Case* [1947] I.R. 3 does refer to the principle as an established one. On the other hand, if the principle was established on any view of public policy, the law in force so established becomes part of our law unless inconsistent with the Constitution or some provision thereof.

In my opinion the true principle under our Constitution is this. The parents – father and mother – have a joint power and duty in respect of the religious education of their children. If they together make a decision and put it into practice it is not in the power of the father – nor is it in the power of the mother – to revoke such decision against the will of the other party. Such an exercise of their power may be made after marriage when the occasion arises; but an agreement made before marriage dealing with matters which will arise during the marriage and put into force after the marriage is equally effective and of as binding force in law. It is a mere commonplace to say that the former rule of English law, whereby a husband could break a promise without which in many cases his wife would not have married him, enabled fathers to take a line of conduct which, if legal, was accounted by many persons as not honourable. This rule has no place, however, where the power which is a joint power has been exercised – such a joint power cannot be revoked by the action of one of the parties.

The Constitution, in article 42. 3. does deal with the case where the parents fail in their duty.

[Murnaghan, J. read Article 42.5 He continued:]

If a difference between father and mother leads to a situation in which the child is neglected the State, through the Courts, is to endeavour to supply the place of the parents. It is to a case of this kind that Sullivan C.J. refers in *Frost's Case* [1947] I.R. 3. I cannot accept the contention of counsel for the appellant that this Court in *Frost's Case* [1947] I.R. 3. decided that where a joint agreement has been made by a father and mother entitled under the Constitution to make it, the father at his mere wish can substitute an arrangement of his own.

Counsel for the respondent, while relying on article 42, 1 and 5, above referred to, sought to support the argument by reference to article 41 and article 44 of the Constitution, as well as to the Preamble. If the Court is able to arrive at a decision of the case upon the construction of article 42, and article 42, 5, alone and without reference to article 41 and article 44, nothing is to be gained by discussing these last-mentioned articles in the present case. It is right, however, to say that the Court, in arriving at its decision, is not now holding that these last-mentioned articles confer any privileged position before the law upon members of the Roman Catholic Church, and during the argument counsel for the respondent expressly disclaimed any such privileged position.

The affidavits disclose a state of affairs between husband and wife which has been unfortunate and there has been unhappiness, save for brief intervals. The husband appears to be, if not intemperate, fond of drinking and I do not think he has accepted his obligations as a husband to provide for his family. In December, 1949, he was summoned before a District Justice and the summons was dismissed under an undertaking by which he bound himself to pay £4 per week for the support of the family. I cannot help inferring that he thought out an ingenious way of relieving himself from the payment which he had been obliged to agree to. The manner in which he removed the children from the dwelling in which they were living with him and the mother and his representations that his wife had deserted the children lead to a very unfavourable impression. The children had been in fact well cared for and were living with the mother when Tilson took them away to get them supported and maintained at little or no expense. It may be that Tilson had cause for some recriminations, but when he comes to state them they are not very clear. Mrs. Tilson works in a laundry and earns £3 per week. Tilson objects to this, but without this money I fear the family would have to do without much which they have up to the present been enjoying.

Unless compelled to do so by strong reason the Court would, I think, be loath to allow children – especially children of tender years – who were being brought up well at home to be delivered to a home for necessitous children. These matters which I have briefly mentioned do not, however, call for any consideration in the present case. In my opinion the appeal can be, and ought to be, decided on the point of law that in the circumstances Tilson had no justification on the ground of religious upbringing or any other ground for taking the children from the family home. In my opinion they ought to be returned to the mother to be educated by her, if not by the parents jointly in the manner in which they had been taught pursuant to the ante-nuptial agreement.

Maguire, C.J., O'Byrne and **Lavery, JJ. concurred with Murnaghan, J.**
Black, J. delivered a dissenting judgment.

Notes

1. See also *In re May, minors,* [1959] I.R. 74 (High Ct., Davitt, P., 1957) where, in a marriage between two Catholics, a husband was held bound by an *implied* undertaking that the issue of the marriage should be brought up as Catholics. The husband had become a Jehovah's Witness ten years after the marriage and had sought to alter the faith of his children. Davitt, P. said:

   It is certainly unusual – it is perhaps a thing quite unheard of – that in the ordinary case of a marriage between Catholics any formal, or indeed any express, agreement is made by the parents. It is assumed and taken for granted as a matter of course that they will, in consonance with their duty as Catholics bring up their children in their own faith. Where we find, as will be found generally, that the parents have been married according to the rite of their Church; that their children are baptised according to its rites; that they are taught at home and at school the truths of their religion; that in due course they receive the Sacraments of Penance, the Holy Eucharist, and Confirmation; and that the members of the family as a unit profess and practise their faith according to the teaching of their Church, there is only one reasonable inference to be drawn, and that is that the parents have impliedly agreed that their children should be brought up and educated as Catholics.

   See also the important decision of *H.* v. *H.*, unreported, High Ct., Parke, J., 4 February 1976 (1975–450Sp.), *infra*, p. 454.

2. If the 'welfare' test were to be applied today under section 3 of the *Guardianship of Infants Act, 1964* to cases involving pre-marital undertakings to rear children in a particular religious denomination, would the outcome of the decisions be the same as in *Tilson* and *May*?
3. On the general eclipse of paternal supremacy, see J. Kelly, *The Irish Constitution*, 336–339 (2nd ed., 1984).
4. Cf. section 17(1) of the *Guardianship of Infants Act, 1964*. Is it Constitutional? To what extent does the 'legal right' referred to in the subsection qualify the application of the welfare criterion?
5. For analysis of the subject from the perspective of the United States, see Ernstoff, *Forcing Rites On Children*, 6 Family Advocate No. 3, p. 13 (1984).

The Guardianship of Infants Act, 1964

The *Guardianship of Infants Act, 1964* 'gives statutory expression to the equitable rule that all matters concerning guardianship and custody of children should be decided on the basis of the welfare of the child and to the constitutional principle that parents have equal rights to, and are the joint guardians of, their children': *Shatter*, 210.

Section 6 (1) provides that 'the father and mother of an infant shall be guardians of the infant jointly'.

Section 11 provides as follows:–

(1) Any person being a guardian of an infant may apply to the court for its direction on any question affecting the welfare of the infant and the court may make such order as it thinks proper.

(2) The court may by an order under this section –

(*a*) give such directions as it thinks proper regarding the custody of the infant and the right of access to the infant of his father or mother;

(*b*) order the father or mother to pay towards the maintenance of the infant such weekly or other periodical sum as, having regard to the means of the father or mother, the court considers reasonable.

(3) An order under this section may be made on the application of either parent notwithstanding that the parents are then residing together but an order made under subsection (2) shall not be enforceable and no liability thereunder shall accrue while they reside together, and the order shall cease to have effect if for a period of three months after it is made they continue to reside together.

(4) In the case of an illegitimate infant the right to make an application under this section regarding the custody of the infant and the right of access thereto of his father or mother shall extend to the natural father of the infant and for this purpose references in this section to the father or parent of an infant shall be construed as including him; but no order shall, on such application, be made under paragraph (*b*) of subsection (2).

Section 3 makes it clear that in guardianship proceedings the child's interests are paramount. It provides that:

Where in any proceedings before any court the custody, guardianship or upbringing of an infant, or the administration of any property belonging to or held on trust for an infant, or the application of the income thereof, is in question, the court, in deciding that question, shall regard the welfare of the infant as the first and paramount consideration.

Section 2 provides that:

. . . 'welfare', in relation to an infant, comprises the religious and moral, intellectual, physical and social welfare of the infant.

In several decisions the Courts have considered the welfare principle. The decisions extracted below indicate the ways they have done this.

J.J.W. v. B.M.W.

110 I.L.T.R. 45 (Supreme Court, reversing High Court, Kenny, J., 1971)

Kenny, J.:

This case relates to the custody of three children, C.A.W. born on the 17th April, 1962, S.W. born on the 25th June, 1964, and C.W. born on the 1st April 1968. The husband, J.W. and the wife formerly B.O'C., who were and are Roman Catholics, were married in Dublin on the 5th March, 1962, when the wife was seven months pregnant. . . . After the marriage they lived with the wife's parents for some time, then bought a house in north

Dublin and when the husband got a position in Liverpool, they went to live there. The two eldest children were born in Dublin and the youngest in Liverpool.

They became friendly with Mr. and Mrs. L., who lived near them and who had two children, one born in 1963 and the other in 1964. The wife had threatened to leave the husband on a number of occasions. She had a miscarriage in 1966 and her mother was so concerned about her health when she came to Dublin that she tried to persuade the husband to allow his wife to remain in Dublin to recuperate. The husband refused to allow this and said that if his wife remained in Dublin, she would never return to him. On the 24th March, 1969, the wife left the home at P. Avenue where they were living and took S. and C. with her. She wanted to take C.A. but the husband would not allow this. She left with Mr. L. who called to the house and took her away and they went to live in a hotel in Liverpool. The husband asked his wife's parents to come from Dublin and Mr. O'C., who strongly disapproved of his daughter's behaviour in leaving her husband and going away with another man who was married, came to Liverpool and by the use of threats of violence to Mr. L. and an assault on his daughter, got the two children from her. The three children were brought to Dublin where they stayed with the husband's parents. The husband kept his position in Liverpool where he worked until March, 1970, when he got employment in Dublin. He is now living with his parents and is earning £30 per week.

The husband's parents, who are elderly, found the task of looking after three children a heavy one and Mrs. W. succeeded in having the two eldest taken into a home run by the Poor Clare Sisters. There, the children attended the national school which is attached to the home, are taken out each week-end and have spent their holidays with the father and his parents. The youngest child has remained with the husband's parents.

The wife is now living with Mr. L. in a flat in Liverpool. This flat consists of the two upper floors of a building on the ground floor of which is a garage showroom where Mr. L. carries on business as a dealer in second hand cars. It is a spacious flat with a lounge, a drawingroom and three bedrooms. The whole building is held on a seven year lease by Mr. L. who was formerly employed as a car salesman but who now has formed a company in which the wife and he own the shares. Mr. L. has been divorced by his wife because of his adultery with Mrs. W. and now pays the former Mrs. L. £12 a week less tax for the maintenance of the two children. The house where his wife and he lived has been transferred to his wife and has, I infer, been sold by her as she now lives with her parents.

The wife did not know that the two eldest children were in the home in Dublin until this year. On the 25th April, 1971, she came to Dublin by arrangement with her father and the two elder children were removed from the home by her parents, who usually took them out on Sundays, and were brought to the wife who was waiting at the Dublin Airport and they were immediately brought to England. On that evening an application was made to me by the husband for an injunction to restrain the removal of the children from the Republic of Ireland and I made an order giving their custody to him and directing that when he had got them, he was to bring them before this Court. The wife then brought divorce proceedings in England against her husband charging him with various forms of sexual perversion and asked the Court in England to give her the custody. The Court in England, however, took the view that the custody of the children was a matter to be decided by the Courts in Ireland and directed her to give the children to the husband. The case has now been at hearing for two days.

The wife has said that she had to leave the husband because of the sexual perversions which he inflicted on her and because of the excessive demands for intercourse which he made. She has said that her nerves could not stand it any longer and that she did not have sexual relations with Mr. L. before she left her husband.

The question whether the husband compelled the wife to submit herself to these unnatural practices is directly in issue in the proceedings in England and has little relevance to these proceedings. I feel, therefore, that I should not express any finding on it. As the Court in England has recognised the right of this Court to deal with the custody of the children, I think I should not make any finding on a matter which is directly in issue in the case in England. I have no doubt that the husband is very highly sexed and that he boasted to his wife about his conquests before marriage. But whatever the husband did cannot excuse or justify the wife in going to live with Mr. L. He was married and what they have done is contrary to the basic moral law which all Christians accept.

All cases about the custody of children are difficult and a source of worry. The Court is making a decision which will affect the happiness and fate of human beings for, although the verdict is not final and can be reviewed in later years, an award of custody in most cases decides that issue during the child's minority. In this case, if the husband gets custody of the children they will grow up and stay in the Republic of Ireland and will inevitably drift away from the wife. If the wife gets them, they will grow up in England and the husband will see little of them and will have almost no contact with them.

The legal principles to be applied are the same in the Republic of Ireland (see the Guardianship of Infants Act, 1964, and the decision of the Supreme Court in *B.* v. *B.* [1975] I.R. 54 (affirming a judgment of mine in that case) and in England (the decision of the House of Lords in *J.* v. *C.* [1969] 1 All E.R. 788 in which Lord McDermott's speech contains an outstanding review of the Irish and English cases on the matter)). These establish the general rule that the paramount consideration is the welfare of the children which is defined so that it includes the religious, moral, intellectual, physical and social aspects. Neither the father nor the mother has any superior or special right of custody. An order is not final but may be reviewed at any time. Both the parents remain guardians so that each is entitled to be consulted in connection with any important decisions which have to be taken in relation to the children.

There are, however, other factors in addition to the legal rules. The aim of the parents, of the State and of the Courts exercising this jurisdiction is to have happy, stable, Christian citizens. The main need of children, if they are to be happy, is the sense of security which comes from a feeling that they are liked and loved for their own sakes. They are not pieces of furniture to be moved around from house to house: they are not to be treated as symbols of victory in a matrimonial contest. An award of custody is not a prize for good matrimonial behaviour. They must be given the chance to develop roots somewhere. The element of unity in a family which has been endangered by the separation of husband and wife should be fostered among the children and so they should grow up together. Unfortunately all these cases become a tiresome debate as to which of the parties was responsible for the breakdown of the marriage. The Court, however, must deal with the case on the basis that the marriage has broken down and that there is no chance of a reconciliation. The blame for this is irrelevant except in so far as it relates to the children's welfare. A hot tempered, emotional, difficult, incompetent wife may be a much more suitable person to have custody of young children than a cold, unsympathetic, self-righteous and very able husband.

What factors favour the wife? The ages of the children strongly favour her case because mothers are very much closer in sympathy and affection to young children than fathers are. His role becomes much more important when the children are over 12. As all the children are girls this also supports, the mother's case because fathers find it difficult to understand the minds and the physical and psychological needs of young girls. This intimate, instinctive relationship between mothers and young girls has assumed a particular importance today when there is a television in almost every household and on which matters in relation to sex (which would have been unmentionable twenty-five years ago) are discussed openly and without restraint of any kind. Although some of us may deplore it and indeed, find much of it in appalling taste, we have to educate children who live with it and who are profoundly shaped by it. Therefore children must be given sex education and this should be done primarily by a parent. Fathers and grandparents cannot give this instruction.

Two of the children are in an institution because the husband is out for five days in the week earning his living. Both his parents are over 60 and will find the children increasingly difficult. The wife will be able to provide a home for the children and will be there for most of the time. Even if the eldest child is sent to boarding school in the near future, there will be a period of at least six years during which C. will be at home. I think that the home which the wife can provide would be more suitable and sympathetic than that of the husband's parents. I do not, however, believe that what the children have said about their grandmother, Mrs. W. is true. I am convinced that she did not punish them and it is notorious that girls of C. A's. age are frequently untruthful and tend to exaggerate.

The main argument against the wife is the fact that she is living with a whom to whom she is not married and so, she is committing a serious sin judged by Christian standards. As he will take the place of the father, the children will have a deplorable example before them all the time. They will quickly learn that their mother is living in a way condemned by the Church to which she belongs and in which they are being brought up. Court orders for divorce will not alter this. It is difficult to imagine the children giving a great deal of attention to what they are taught about Christian marriage when they have this model before them, and example by parents is worth more than years of sermons, instruction and public piety.

A factor which supports the husband's case is that the children have been in Ireland since March, 1969, and have been at school here. It is not in their interest that they should be moved from school to school because such a change is always upsetting and is, indeed, a major problem in many households. If the wife is given custody, the children will be changing not only from one school to another but to another system of education with a different programme so that they will find themselves behind in some subjects in the class to which they should go at their ages. The school which the two eldest children are now attending is an excellent one and I am convinced that they will be very well looked after there if they stay. The wife's plans for the education of the children in England are vague. Mr. L. has said that he has been promised places for them in a school near where he is living. But the result of giving custody to the wife is that the two eldest children will be moved from the good school where they are well settled to one in England. Against the wife also is the factor that from March, 1969, until April, 1971, she allowed the husband to have the custody of the children and did not make any effort to get them. She thought that all the children were living with their grandparents and her parents appeared to her to support the view that the children should be in Dublin. She had, however, no one to help her in Ireland and though she could have brought proceedings here, she probably thought that the united opposition of the four grandparents and her relationship with Mr. L. would defeat her claim. I am convinced however that she did not abandon the children.

The financial position of Mr. L. compared to that of the husband is also against the wife's case. Mr. L. is in a notoriously competitive business, has no capital and is wholly dependent upon bank advances. He has to pay £15 a week rent, has to pay his former wife £12 a week less income tax, gives the wife £35 and takes £30 out of the business for himself. Thus, before he pays any wages, he spends about £90 a week. The wife and he, however, give signs of prosperity. In so far as it is relevant, both of them were expensively and well dressed and have been able to afford air trips for the children.

Mr. L., who has given evidence and who has said that he will be glad to have the children, has not shown a high sense of moral responsibility. He left his wife without cause and he may leave Mrs. W. I attach no significance to the wife's statement that she has a 49 per cent interest in his business; she cannot run it if Mr. L. leaves her and the leasehold interest and goodwill owned by the newly formed company are of little value.

The husband is now living with his parents and the youngest child. He has sold his house in England and has £600 available for the purchase price of one in Dublin. He says that he hopes to buy a home in Dublin where his children and he could live. This would involve finding a housekeeper who is prepared to look after them and I know from evidence in other cases that it is extremely difficult to get a suitable one and that the minimum wages will be about £10 per week. He would also have to pay the instalments on the loan which he would require to buy a house and the amount would not be less than £5 a week.

Another aspect of the case which, I think, favours the wife is that the four grandparents helped with the children when they were brought to Dublin in 1969. Unfortunately, this has now ceased and silly quarrels have broken out between them about some incident at the school sports when one grandmother did not recognise the other. The hurtful, vicious things which they have said about each other during this case have made any cooperation between them impossible. Why did Mrs. O'C. give the irrelevant evidence that the husband had told her that she looked after him better than his mother did? If he said this (and I doubt it), it must have been painful and humiliating for Mrs. W. to hear it given in evidence. Unpleasant, and for the children, upsetting quarrels between the grandparents seem to be certain from now on if the children remain in Dublin.

The religious, moral and intellectual welfare of all the children would be better promoted by leaving them with the father. They will get a good secular and religious education, they will not have the corrupting example of their mother living with a man to whom she is not married and the upset caused by moving them to another school will not occur. If therefore the religious, moral and intellectual aspects of welfare were the only ones to be considered, I would, without hesitation give the custody to the husband. But they are not the only elements. There is the age of the children, the fact that all of them are girls and that two of them have since 1970 been in a boarding school or institution. It is certainly unusual in the Republic of Ireland to have a child aged 6 in a boarding school or institution: the necessity for this illustrates the father's difficulty in bringing up girls.

In my view the ages of the children, their sex, the certainty that they would be happier if they were living at home rather than in a school and the necessity that they should grow up together (and the case for the mother having the custody of the youngest child is very strong) makes it so desirable that they should be with their mother that these elements should be held to outweigh the arguments based upon the moral, religious and intellectual aspects.

The two eldest children must stay at the school where they are now until the term there ends in July. When this happens, the three children should be given to their mother, if she undertakes on oath that she will bring the children back to the Republic of Ireland whenever required to do so by a Court order and that she will not leave or bring the children outside the Republic of Ireland and the United Kingdom of Britain and Northern Ireland without the permission of this Court. The husband will have the custody of the three children for one month in each year for holidays.

I do not propose to make any order for the payment of maintenance in respect of the children to the mother. She has made the case that Mr. L. and she are wealthy enough to support them. So long as she lives with Mr. L., she should not, in my opinion, be given any maintenance.

From the above judgment the plaintiff appealed to the Supreme Court.

Walsh J.:

. . . In the High Court the learned judge having heard the evidence on both sides came to the conclusion that the religious, moral and intellectual welfare of all three children would be better promoted by leaving them with their father. He arrived at that view largely, if not wholly, upon the consideration that the defendant was living with a man to whom she was not married and that to have the children brought up in that atmosphere would be, in the words of the judge, a 'corrupting example' and that they would quickly learn that their mother's home arrangements are condemned by the church to which she and they belong and would be something they could not possibly reconcile with the tenets of the religion in which they are to be brought up and in which the mother states she will bring them up. Even if the mother marries Mr. L. after her own divorce proceedings in the English court result in an absolute decree the position will not be any different in so far as these particular topics are concerned. I see no reason to disagree with the conclusion arrived at by the High Court judge on these topics.

The learned High Court judge did, however, come to the conclusion that the children would be happier if they were living at home by which, I presume, he means living as members of a family as distinct from being in a boarding school for part of the year as that would enable them to grow up together and he thought that these considerations made it so desirable that they should be with their mother that they should outweigh the view he had taken on the other topics. The three topics already discussed by the judge, namely, the religious, moral and intellectual aspects of the children's welfare are three of the five aspects referred to in the definition of welfare in section 2 of the Guardianship of Infants Act, 1964. I assume, therefore, that the learned judge in referring to the conditions in which he concluded the children would be happier if living with their mother fell under the remaining two aspects of welfare, namely, physical and social welfare of the infants.

While the financial position of the mother and the man she is living with appears to be better in terms of pounds per week than that of the plaintiff the learned trial judge did not attach any particular weight to this aspect of the matter because he took the view that the business in which the wife and Mr. L. are engaged, namely, the sale of second hand motor cars, was a notoriously speculative one and that the actual assets of the business offered no long term stability. His decision really turned upon the view that because of the father's present circumstances whereby he is compelled to keep two of the children for the greater part of the year in a boarding school and is therefore unable to let them all grow up together in one household the fact that the mother could do so was a decisive factor in favour of holding that the welfare of the children would on the whole be better served by giving them into her custody.

I find myself unable to agree with this conclusion. As matters stand at the moment the children are leading a stable existence. They see their father at least twice a week; they visit their grandparents and are visited by their grandparents; and they have their holidays and one day a week with their father. They are growing up in an environment which offers them a far more stable background than could be guaranteed in the case of custody with the mother. At the moment they are in the position they might have found themselves in if their mother had died instead of leaving as she did. An effort has been made to suggest that the father has simply done no more than give them the minimum of consideration by placing them in a boarding school which, for reasons which have not been explored or explained, is described in the yellow pages of the telephone directory as an orphanage and in which the fees are remarkably low. It is understood, however, that the school in question specialises in catering for children from broken homes and it may well be that it is not intended to be run as an economic proposition but that the primary concern of those running it is to assist the children and therefore to put it within the reach of as many children as possible who find themselves in the unfortunate condition of the children in this case. The father has sold his house in England and after repayment of mortgage etc. has about £600 in hand which he hopes in due time to use as a deposit or down-payment in the purchase of a house here. He hopes to set up family life again with the assistance of a housekeeper if he can get a suitable person but one must bear in mind that having regard to his income which is about £1,600 a year it will not be an easy task to secure all of this. However in the circumstances of the case the evidence does not disclose that the children are not happy and having regard to the melancholy events affecting their parents' marriage over the last few years it is very much in the interests of the children to be brought up, as they are being brought up, in close proximity to their four grandparents and their father, all of whom are to the children recognisably stable elements in their lives. The present position of their mother offers no such stability and there is nothing to suggest that in the immediate future any such stability will be available. In my view, the welfare of the children would be best served by leaving them in the custody of their father and I would allow this appeal.

In so far as the mother is concerned she should, of course, be given reasonable rights of access to her children towards whom she is obviously very affectionate but having regard to the previous history of her relationship with the children it should be made a condition that on no account are they to be taken out of the jurisdiction without the consent of the High Court or of this Court. It is scarcely necessary to remind the parties that the award of custody does not affect the rights which accrue to the parents as guardians of the children. If the parents cannot, as between themselves, agree upon the conditions and mode of access of the mother to the children then of course the matter will have to be reviewed again in Court. The mother is, of course, entitled as of right to state her views and to concern herself with the upbringing of her children and the husband must have due regard to them.

Fitzgerald, J. delivered a concurring judgment.
O'Dálaigh, C.J., McLoughlin and **Budd, JJ.,** concurred.

Notes

1. On the general question of the relevance of adultery in the determination of custody of children, see O'Reilly, *Custody Disputes in the Irish Republic: The Uncertain Search for the Child's Welfare?*, 12 Ir. Jur. (n.s.) 37 (1977) and O'Connor, *The Impact of Adulterous Relationships on the Outcome of Custody Disputes*, 2 Ir. L.T. (n.s.) 23 (1984). Mr. O'Connor submits (at 24) that:

   > Overall . . . a better approach to adopt would be to look at the welfare of the child in its totality without attaching different weights to the various elements which comprise welfare. The principle that the welfare of the child is to be regarded as the first and paramount consideration is one of great generality. A formidable task confronts those who would wish to make it more concrete. An attempt to provide more serviceable criteria by establishing some scale of priorities among the factors that constitute welfare is something which ought to be avoided. Such an attempt would seem to be doomed to failure. It would not result in the outcome of custody disputes becoming any more predictable. Nor would it diminish the often agonising difficulty confronting judges in determining which party is to have custody.

   See also *Re F.*, [1969] 2 Ch. 238, at 241–242 (*per* Megarry, J.). But accepting that each of the various elements of the welfare principle should not be given a fixed, pre-ordained, inflexible weight, can *no* case be made for giving broad, general, weightings to these elements? Otherwise could it be argued that the welfare principle may become too subjective and unpredictable?
2. The courts in Ireland are not, of course, unique in finding it difficult to decide upon what relevance, if any, adulterous conduct should be considered to have to the child's welfare. See B. Hoggett & D. Pearl, *The Family, Law and Society: Cases and Materials*, 339–347 (1983).
3. Do you agree with the view that a woman who divorces and remarries is in no better position, so far as moral example for her children is concerned, than if she continues in an adulterous relationship? Would your answer depend on whether the divorce, although valid in the country where it is granted, would not be recognised in Ireland? Would the position be different if the woman obtained a civil annulment in Ireland or in England? Or a religious annulment? Contrast the approach of McWilliam J., in *MacC.* v. *MacC.*, unreported, High Ct., January 1976 (1975–244Sp.) in respect of a foreign divorce. See also *H.* v. *H.*, *infra*, p. 454.
4. Do you agree with Kenny, J.'s statements:

   (a) that 'mothers are very much closer in sympathy and affection to young children than fathers are'?
   (b) that 'fathers find it difficult to understand the minds and physical and psychological needs of young girls'?

(c) that 'fathers cannot give . . . instruction' to their children in relation to sex education?

(d) that 'it is notorious that girls of [the] age [of nine years] are frequently untruthful and tend to exaggerate'? On this question generally, see Binchy, *The Sex of a Parent as a Factor in Custody Disputes*, 77 Inc. L. Soc. of Ireland Gazette 269 (1983); Robinson, *Joint Custody: An Idea Whose Time Has Come*, 21 J. of Family L. 640, at 657ff (1983).

5. See also *B.* v. *B.*, [1975] I.R. 54 (Sup. Ct., 1970, aff'g High Ct., Kenny, J., 1969). Do you agree with the statements in the judgments in *B.* v. *B.*, as to which parent is, by reason of his or her sex, more suitable to have custody of children of certain ages and of one sex or the other? Cf. Orthner & Lewis, *Evidence of Single-Father Competence in Childrearing*, 13 Family L.Q. 27 (1979). More generally, see Rypma, *The Biological Bases of the Paternal Responses*, 25 Family Coordinator 355 (1976)

6. On the policy of keeping children together, where this is possible, see further *O'B* v. *O'B*, unreported, High Ct., Kenny, J., 5 January 1971 (1965–207Sp.), p. 12.

M.B. O'S. v. P.O. O'S.

110 I.L.T.R. 57 (Sup. Ct., 1974, rev'g. High Ct., Kenny J.)

Kenny, J.:

P. O'S. and M.P. were married on the 6th of July, 1966, when she was pregnant. They had three children, J.T. born on the 19th January, 1967, K.R. born on the 11th of January, 1968, and J. born on the 7th March, 1969. They lived outside Ireland for some time and then returned to live in Cobh. The marriage became increasingly unhappy: the husband regretted that he had entered into it and the wife's relations with her mother-in-law were not good. The husband felt that the wife was neglecting the children and the marriage finally broke up on the 6th of April, 1970, when the husband left the wife and gave the three children to his sister, Mrs. O'F., who undertook to look after them. Correspondence between solicitors took place and the wife agreed that the husband should have custody of the three children. She did this because she hoped that it would contribute to a reconciliation and because she was in a highly nervous condition. The children were kept by Mrs. O'F., until September, 1971, when they were given to the husband's parents who kept them until April, 1972. In that month the husband took the children in Dublin where he was living with Mrs. F., who had taken the name of Mrs. O'S., and they have been there since then. After the husband left the wife, she took proceedings against him for maintenance and is now entitled to a weekly payment of £6. She has succeeded in getting a University degree at University College, Cork, and will be able to get work as a teacher. She has now brought these proceedings in which she seeks custody of the three children. If she succeeds, she proposes to live with her parents who have a large house in Cobh where there would be plenty of room for them. Her father is 59 and her mother is 55.

I accept the wife's evidence that when she agreed that the husband should have the custody in April, 1970, she did not intend this to be a permanent arrangement. The husband and wife are Roman Catholics: no evidence is given about the religious beliefs of the second Mrs. O'S., but her husband and she have brought the children to Mass on Sundays and they have family prayers. She is a perfectly suitable person in every way to have joint custody except that she is not married to the husband. The husband and she have one child who was born in November, 1971. Indeed I think that she is a more balanced person than the wife, who is emotional, slightly hysterical and tends to change her mind very often. The wife, however, has great determination and considerable intellectual ability: this is shown by her success in getting a degree from the National University of Ireland after her marriage had broken up.

In deciding the custody of children when the parents are not living together, the Court is to have regard to the welfare of the children as the first and paramount consideration and welfare is defined in the Guardianship of Infants Act, 1964, as comprising the religious and moral, intellectual, physical and social welfare of the child. In so far as the intellectual welfare of the children is involved I think that the balance is in favour of the husband. I think it probable that the schools to which the children will be sent in Dublin will be better than those in Cobh and the husband and the second Mrs. O'S., together will provide a better background for the children's upbringing. Similarly, the physical welfare of the children will be best secured by giving them to the husband. I have no doubt that the second Mrs. O'S., will look after the children as well as the first Mrs. O'S., would, and the husband and wife living together are obviously a better background for the children if the aim is to produce happy, well-integrated children. I have never been certain what social welfare in the Act means. If it means that the children are to be happy, I think it probable that they would be happier with the husband and the second Mrs. O'S., than they will be with the plaintiff. They have seen little of their mother since April, 1970, and her excuses for not visiting them more frequently lacked conviction. There is, moreover, the factor that it is undesirable to move young children around from parent to parent; these children now have their roots in the husband's household and so long as the husband and Mrs. O'S., continue to live together, the children would probably be happier with them. I think it probable that the husband will continue to live with the second Mrs. O'S., and that I can ignore the risk that she will leave him. Evidence was given that the husband was trying to get an ecclesiastical annulment of his marriage to the wife but I think his prospects of getting this are very remote. The second Mrs. O'S. has got a divorce from her first husband in England.

The moral welfare, however, of the children would not be promoted by the fact that their father is living with a lady to whom he is not married and by whom he has had one child. As the children grow up they will be taught the virtues of chastity and the importance of marriage and they will be living in a household where each of them will be aware that the lady with whom their father is living is not his wife. This will be an utterly deplorable example to them.

During the hearing I referred Counsel for the husband to the decision of the Supreme Court in *J.J.W.* v. *B.M.W., supra*, p. 428 and said that in my view it concluded this case. . . . This case seems to me to be a much stronger case than *J.J.W.* v. *B.M.W.*, because the mother proposes to keep custody of the children and bring them up herself. Counsel for the husband said that I should not follow the decision in *J.J.W.* v. *B.M.W.* but I believe it is my duty to do so. I realise there will be some suffering for the children in being uprooted from the household where they have lived since April, 1972, but children are adjustable and having regard to their ages, will quickly get used to living in Cobh. The moral factor is so much in favour of the wife that it out-weighs the advantages which the husband and the second Mrs. O'S, have and, in those circumstances and having regard to my obligation to follow the decision in *J.J.W.* v. *B.M.W.* I have no doubt whatever that I should award the custody of the three children to the wife. . . .

One of the matters alleged against Mrs. O'S was that she had had an affair some three and a half years ago when she was married. I accept her evidence that it has ended and that the man with whom she had it has married someone else. It is not relevant at all to the welfare of the children because it is over. She may be fond of social life and going out but I am satisfied that her father's house is perfectly suitable in every way and that she will have the advantage that her parents will be living there and will be able to help her with the children. Their ages are 59 and 55 and so they have an average expectation of life until they are about 77. If one applies that average, the children will have become adults when the grandparents die.

Orders under the Guardianship of Infants Act are not final and I wish to emphasise that this decision is given on the facts as disclosed in the evidence. If these change, the question of the custody of the children would have to be considered again.

From the Judgment of Kenny J., the defendant appealed to the Supreme Court.

Henchy J.:

It is now four years since these three children had their home with their mother. For the first two years – after the marriage had broken down, irretrievably, it would seem now, – they lived with a married sister of the father's in Cobh, so the mother then had access to them regularly and easily. For the last two years, however, they have been living in Dublin with their father, who has come to work in Dublin and who has set up house with the woman whom I shall refer to for convenience as the stepmother. She has got a divorce in England from her husband and there is one child of the father's union with her. This union looks like being permanent. The three children have settled contentedly into this domestic environment and are being affectionately and efficiently looked after by the father and stepmother. The question is, should they now be sundered from what they look on as their home and delivered into the custody of their mother in Cobh? The trial judge thought so, solely on the ground that the father's household is inimical to their moral welfare.

While all relevant matters must be given due consideration, the statute requires that the first and paramount consideration must be the religious and moral, intellectual, physical and social welfare of the children.

As to their intellectual welfare, the judge thought the present custody more likely to favour it. I would agree. Their formal education is being pursued in suitable schools, and the home atmosphere is conducive to study and intellectual development generally. I see no reason to think that their intellectual advancement would be bettered if they were transferred to the custody of their mother in Cobh. Rather do I think it would be retarded by the emotional disturbance that the change would cause and by the rupture of the continuity of their schooling.

Likewise I agree that their physical welfare would be better served if they remain with their father and stepmother. There they are in a comfortable suburban home where they enjoy unfaulted home comforts. Their health is being assiduously looked after. They are being well fed and clothed, and their personal hygiene and general physical activities seem to be above reproach. There is nothing in the evidence to suggest that a change to Cobh would be better for their physical welfare.

As to their social welfare, which I take to be their well-being as members of society, I agree that their present environment is to be favoured. They seem to relate well to the other members of the household and to their schoolmates. They are not unhappy. They lead an active, normal, well-integrated existence. In their young lives, this is the third home they have known. To sunder them from it and to thrust them in to a fourth, this time with their grandparents, who are probably strangers to them, in a large, old house, would be a change fraught with the problem of fitting into new schools and making new friends and settling into a new domestic and social environment. All this would be apt to inflict a trauma that might have permanent ill-effects on them. On this ground particularly, a change of custody would be ill-advised.

There remains the question of their religious and moral welfare. It is undeniable that the household in which they live is founded on a union between their father and a divorced woman. But it has the appearances of being a permanent union. So the children will have to come to terms with it, either at close quarters or from a distance. It is a tragic and regrettable fact, but they will have to live with it.

As to their religious welfare, the judge found no fault in the way the children are being trained in the knowledge and practice of their faith as Roman Catholics. They attend Roman Catholic schools, they attend Mass regularly, they are taught their prayers at home and they say family prayers together at night. So it could not be said that the father and stepmother are neglectful of the children's religious welfare. They seem to be doing so much as they could be expected to do in that respect in the circumstances.

It is the moral welfare of the children, in the present custody, that troubled the judge most. He considered that the bad example of the father and stepmother living together in their present relationship to be adverse to the children's moral welfare, so much so that he held that it outweighed all the other advantages of the present custody. Being of that opinion, he construed the decision of this Court in *J.J.W.* v. *B.M.W., supra*, p. 428 as binding him to award custody to the mother.

It seems to me that the considerations that led to the decision in *J.J.W.* v. *B.M.W.* are essentially different from the facts of the present case. There the mother had taken the two younger of three children and gone with them to live adulterously in England with a man who had left his wife and children. However, the father, with the help of the mother's parents, quickly recovered the two children and took them to live with him and the eldest child in his parents' house in Dublin. Subsequently the mother managed to get the children to England for a few weeks before an order of the County Court in England restored them to the father. When the case came to Court the father had custody of the children, but because of the grandparents' ill-health, the two elder children were in a boarding school. The children's home was with their father in the grandparents' house. There seems to have been no evidence that they were other than contented and well looked after. The High Court judge and the Supreme Court were agreed that the alternative home in England that was being offered by the mother would not be to the religious and moral welfare of the children. That conclusion is readily understandable. The wife and the divorced man for whom she had deserted her husband depended for their living on a second-hand car business. The domestic atmosphere they could provide for the children was looked on as morally ill-founded, precarious, unproven and potentially corrupting. Both Courts held that the moral benefit lay with the known and satisfactory environment of the father's custody rather than that of a doubtful *ménage* in a foreign country. Where the Supreme Court differed from the High Court judge was in holding that, in spite of the fact that the father had to keep two of the children in a boarding school, it was to their intellectual and social welfare that he should retain custody.

I find no enunciation of principle or analogy of circumstances in *J.J.W.* v. *B.M.W.* to help in the elucidation of the present case. Like most such cases, *J.J.W.* v. *B.M.W.* is a decision on its own facts. What primarily distinguishes the present case is that the custody sought to be changed is that with the father, in a household founded, no doubt, on an irregular union, but which for two years has operated to the intellectual, physical and social welfare of the children and has not been found to have militated against their religious and moral welfare. The judge, nevertheless, held that the bad example that the children will get in the household of the father and stepmother, as they grow up and are taught the importance of marriage and the virtue of chastity, will operate against their moral welfare, and that this disadvantage outweighs all the advantages of the father's custody. The core of this appeal, therefore, is whether that inference is justifiable on the evidence.

I am not persuaded that it is. It is undeniable that the father's irregular union with the stepmother is and will continue to be a bad example to the children. If I felt that this bad example would be obviated or substantially reduced by the removal of the children to their grandparents' house in Cobh, the mother's claim to the custody would be enhanced. But even under the High Court order now appealed from, the father *and the stepmother* will have access to the children for a whole day every week, and the father can have them for a full month during the summer holidays. The bad example, such as it is, will remain before the children's eyes. It is a tragic fact of life which the children will have to come to terms with. To state that is not to condone the conduct of the father and stepmother, but merely to recognize the inevitable. The question is, will the bad example be worse if the children continue to live with their father?

I incline to the opinion that the irregularity of the relationship between the father and the stepmother is less likely to scandalise or deprave the children if they continue to live together in the same household. At least, I think it no more likely to do so than if the children go to live with their mother and spend a whole day every week with the father and the stepmother. Beyond the mere fact that the father and stepmother are living together i[n] an unmarried state, there is nothing in the evidence to suggest that the children do not live in a healthy moral atmosphere. When asked in evidence how the children were looked after, a housewife who lives nextdoor replied:–

> They seemed to me just a normal family going to Mass, taking the children out on Sundays. They garden a lot and the children have dogs and cats like everyone else on the road and they seemed to me just a normal family. . . .

The lady who lives next-door on the other side was no less approving of the father and stepmother as custodians of the children:

> I always found them an ideal as I felt the children were very well looked after. They used to play with my nieces when they were in the house with me and appeared perfectly normal, natural children.

I have read the transcript of the evidence carefully and have failed to find a complaint from any quarter as to the way the children have been brought up for the past two years. The father and stepmother treat them with care for their needs, physical and moral, and the children have responded with feelings of affection and confidence. Against the tangled background of a broken marriage, the children have become habituated to a domestic regime which has a degree of order, discipline and stability normally associated with a two-parent family. In this their third home in four years, they have found, perhaps for the first time in their lives, emotional security. I do not think they should be severed from that home in the hope that their youth will enable them to pass unscathed through the suggested change of custody, particularly when the evidence is that they dread the prospect of being removed to Cobh to live with their mother. The wishes of these children, aged, 7, 6 and 5, should [not] be ignored in dealing with this belatedly asserted claim by the mother. Had this claim come to Court before the children had sent out such firm roots in their present environment, the considerations governing the case would be quite different.

In all the circumstances, I consider that the children's welfare as statutorily defined requires that they be left to the custody of their father. Accordingly, I would allow the appeal. Were the circumstances to change, the question of custody would, of course, be open to review.

Griffin, J. delivered a concurring judgment.

Walsh, J. (Dissenting):–

. . . The learned trial judge referred to the decision of this Court in *J.J.W.* v. *B.M.W..*, *supra*, p. 428. In my view, he did not correctly construe the decision in as much as he appeared to hold that the effect of the decision was that the moral welfare of the children would outweigh other considerations. That was not so. A study of the decision in that case makes clear that the opinion of this Court was based on considerations of intellectual and social welfare as well as moral and religious welfare.

In the present case the learned judge expresses the view that he has never been certain what social welfare in the Guardianship of Infants Act means. He took the view that if it meant that the children would be happier then he was of opinion that they would be happier with their father in his present household. I do not think it means happiness in the sense that the children are going to enjoy more pleasure or have greater material benefits or more interesting or stimulating company. In my view, social welfare in the context of the Act means the type of welfare which is to be judged by what is best calculated to make them better members of the society in which they live. The point has been made in this case that no appeal has been taken by the wife against the judge's opinion that the children's social, physical and intellectual welfare would be better served by leaving them with the husband than returning them to the wife. I do not think this a valid point because I think all the ingredients which the Act stipulates are to be considered; namely, the religious, moral, intellectual, physical and social welfare of the child are to be considered globally. This is not an appeal to be decided by the simple method of totting up the marks which may be awarded under each of the five headings. It is the totality of the picture presented which must be considered. The picture is to be viewed and judged as a whole and not as a sum of the values of each of the constituent parts of the picture because, unless together they all form one acceptable composition, the picture is a bad one. The word 'welfare' must be taken in its widest sense. The children who are the subject of this case are still at a very tender age and the decisive consideration ought to be what is best for the welfare of the children in these very critical years of their lives.

In Article 42 of the Constitution the State acknowledges that the primary and natural educator of the child is the family and it guarantees to respect the inalienable right and duty of parents to provide according to their means for the religious, moral, intellectual, physical and social education of their children. It has already been held in this Court in *The State (Nicolaou)* v. *An Bord Uchtála* [1966] I.R. 567 that in the provisions of the Constitution relating to the family, the family is one founded upon marriage. The Constitution recognises the family as the natural primary and fundamental unit group of society; that is the keystone of the social structure which the Constitution undertakes to maintain. The household in which these children now reside with their father is not a family in that sense.

If actions of this kind were to be determined on considerations such as I have mentioned, which would amount to no more than a sum of the different advantages which might be gained, then cases such as the present one could always be resolved in favour of the stronger or wealthier parent. These three children would, in my view, be far more of a family unit if they lived with their mother instead of residing with their father in the mixed ménage in which they now find themselves. So far as the physical and educational or intellectual aspects of their welfare are concerned the difference between what their mother can provide for them and what their father can provide is at best marginal. So far as the social, moral and religious aspects are concerned the present atmosphere in which they are found, in spite of every good intention on the part of their father and the woman he is living with, is one which is a manifest repudiation of the social and religious values with which they should be inculcated at this age of their lives. In addition, the relationship of a mother to her very young children is something that cannot be replaced or usurped by any other woman, however well intentioned, and could only be justified where the mother has been found to be so greatly wanting in her duty to her children that the situation would warrant the removal of the children from her. That is not the situation in the present case. The fact that the children's mother may not be as good a housekeeper or as efficient a housekeeper or as tidy or even as clean as another woman is beside the point. In my view, the welfare of the children requires that they should be returned to their mother to form the natural family unit from which, unfortunately, only the father is missing but in which there is no element alien or hostile to ordinary family life. It may very well cause some immediate grief to the children to be removed from their present home to be returned to their mother but I think that will be very quickly assuaged by the fact that they will be living with their mother and their grandparents. The house in which they find themselves at the moment is one which their father, after deserting his wife, elected to set up with another woman who is not his wife. In my view, this cannot in any way be a substitute for a proper family life which they can enjoy with their mother and taking all the elements into account I am of opinion that it is in the interests of the children in these tender and formative years that they should reside in a family unit presided over by their mother and in which there are not present the extraneous and harmful elements which exist in the household of which they are a part so long as their father retains their custody.

I would dismiss this appeal and direct that the children should be returned to the custody of their mother.

Notes

1. Can this decision be reconciled with *J.J.W.* v. *B.M.W.?* See generally O'Reilly, *Custody Disputes in the Irish Republic: The Uncertain Search for the Child's Welfare?*, 12 Ir. Jur (n.s.) 37, at 40–41 (1977).
2. In *A.H.S.* v. *M.S.*, unreported, High Ct., Barron, J., 12 November 1982 (1982–185Sp.), Barron, J. said:–

   Each case must be taken as a decision on its own facts. Nevertheless the judgments of the Supreme Court do indicate the weight to be given to various factors which arise in these cases. In the case cited and in other cases in which one of the parties was living in a permanent adulterous association, and *a fortiori* where the association was less than permanent, the Supreme Court has essentially regarded the moral danger to the child as being more important than its physical and social welfare unless it can be shown that it would be harmful to its latter welfare to remove it from a settled home.

   Is this also your interpretation of the Supreme Court's approach?
3. As to the position where an adulterous relationship has *ceased*, see *C.* v. *C.*, unreported, Supreme Court, 8 May 1970 (59–1969).
4. The relationship between moral and religious welfare merits reflection. In *McD.* v. *McD.*, unreported, High Ct., 19 February 1979 (1977–799Sp.), Finlay, P. stated (at pp. 22–23 of his judgment):

   The capacity of children to become good members of the society in which they live, their moral welfare as I have defined it and their religious welfare as I have defined it all depend on any given case upon the nature and standards of the society in which they live, its commonly accepted moral norms and the moral and ethical code of the religion in which they are being brought up.

   These children were, I am satisfied on the evidence before me, intended to live and grow up for the present at least in this country and to be brought up as practising members of the Catholic Church.

   As was pointed out by Mr. Justice Walsh in his judgment in *O'S.* v. *O'S.* society in Ireland accepts as a fundamental and integral unit the family and the Constitution therefore protects and safeguards the integrity of that unit. In addition I would consider the moral code of that Society as well as the moral and ethical code of the Catholic Church [which] considers as fundamental the sanctity of marriage and condemns and disapproves of adultery.

   What the mother in this case has already done and what she continues and intends to continue doing is a firm and clear repudiation both of the fundamental integrity of the family as a unit and of these moral standards with regard to the sanctity of marriage and condemnation of adultery.

   See further *H.* v. *H.*, *infra*, p. 454. Do you think that our law in relation to custody, as administered by the Courts, is pluralist, religiously neutral, or otherwise? 'Welfare' sounds like a social or psychological concept, but is it not really a value-laden notion? How can a psychiatrist or general practitioner give evidence as to a child's 'welfare', if the Court ultimately makes a value-judgment partly in accordance with moral rather than medical norms? Are not 'moral welfare' and (especially) 'religious welfare' totally different concepts from 'physical welfare' and 'emotional welfare'? What role, therefore, should psychological theory play in judicial decisionmaking in child custody cases? For a provocative analysis, see Okpaku, *Psychology: Impediment or Aid in Child Custody Cases?* 29 Rutgers L. Rev. 1117 (1976). See also Foster & Freed, *Child Custody and the Adversary Process: Forum Conveniens?* 17 Family L.Q. 133, at 139–141 (1983); Silberman-Abella, *Procedural Aspects of Arrangements for Children Upon Divorce in Canada*, 61 Can. Bar Rev. 443, at 458–462 (1983); Stone, *The Welfare of the Child*, ch. 15 of I. Baxter & M. Eberts eds., *The Child and the Courts*, at 243 (1978); Finlay, *1976 in Family Law*, in R. Baxt ed., *An Annual Survey of Law 1976*, 163, at 182–183 (1977); S. Maidment, *Child Custody and the Courts*, 81–82 (1984). Some sound practical advice is offered by Fernaud, *Puncturing the Pretensions of a Psychiatric Witness*, 3 Family Advocate No. 1, p. 18 (1980).

E.K. v. M.K.

Unreported, Supreme Ct., 31 July 1974 (86–1974), reversing High Ct., Kenny, J., 23 May 1974 (1973–172Sp.)

The plaintiff took proceedings under section 11 of the *Guardianship of Infants Act, 1964* against the defendant, her husband, in relation to the custody of their two children A, born in 1969, and B, born in 1970. The parties were both under thirty years old, being the children of wealthy parents, and having been accustomed to a high standard of living. The defendant objected to custody being awarded to the plaintiff on the basis that she had formed an association with another man (Mr. X.).

Kenny, J.:

. . . The judgments of the Supreme Court in *M.B. O'S* v. *P.O. O'S* [*supra*, p. 435] emphasise that welfare is to be looked at as a whole and that one is not to break up the elements mentioned in the Act of 1964 (religious, moral, intellectual, physical and social) and award marks to each of the parents for each of these elements. The religious and moral factors weigh heavily in favour of the husband. As far as the intellectual element is concerned there is no difference. The ages of the children give the wive a much stronger claim insofar as physical welfare is concerned. Physical certainly includes emotional and the damage that might be done to B by taking her away from her mother now could be very great. The social element of welfare in the sense that it means that the children will grow up to be good citizens is extremely difficult to decide in this case: they will have before them the deplorable example set by their mother but the emotional upset of separating them from her might be seriously disturbing.

After much anxious thought, I have come to the conclusion that the children are so young that their physical and emotional welfare outweighs the elements which favour the husband and that despite the mother's deplorable association with Mr. X, they should remain in her care and custody on the undertakings which she has given on oath and to which I have already referred. The husband's rights of access will continue to be governed by the consent made in December 1973.

The husband appealed to the Supreme Court, which delivered judgment on 31 July 1974.

Fitzgerald, C.J.:

. . . Having regard to the ages of the children, 5½ and 3½ years respectively, they should, normally, be put in the custody of their mother. The wife's claim must, however, be recognised for what it really is. It is a claim not only to the custody of the children, but a claim for a licence from this Court to have custody of the children while she carries on an adulterous intercourse with another man.

Her conduct has had the effect of breaking up the marriage, ruining her own life and that of her husband. If she persists in this conduct, it will, in my opinion, inevitably result in ruining the lives of the two children. That is the matter which is the primary concern of this Court. No allegation has been established against the husband, and Mr. Justice Kenny has found every material fact against the wife. I am unable to share his view that the tender ages of the children justifies their being placed in the custody of the plaintiff. In my opinion, the custody of the two children should forthwith be transferred to the father.

Walsh, J.:

. . . A little over a year before the wife's final departure from the home she had, in the home, committed adultery with one of her husband's employees, namely, a groom who was some years younger than herself. This act of adultery had been detected by her husband at the time when it occurred and the immediate result was that the wife left the home on the same night. She took the younger child with her. The father, on the same night, had already moved the elder child to his own relatives. In April 1973 the wife returned to resume residence in the matrimonial home together with the children but occupied a separate room from that of her husband. It was not apparently his wish that full matrimonial relations should be resumed between them. The husband's attitude was that it would take some time to restore normal domestic relations between them but he was perfectly willing to have her reside in the house with himself and the children. From the time of her return to the matrimonial home until her eventual departure three months later the wife appears to have led her own separate social life but there is not any suggestion of misconduct on her part in that period:

[Walsh J. analysed the subsequent events in detail. He added:]

The most serious aspect of the wife's association with Mr. X and his visits to her home was that it is admitted that sexual intercourse took place between them on many occasions in her home while the children were also in the home although the children may not have been aware of that. It is also to be noted that an assurance that the children would not come under 'the influence' of Mr. X is a somewhat qualified assurance and is not one which indicated that they would not be associating with him. . . .

. . . The evidence given at the hearing before Mr. Justice Kenny clearly indicated that the wife has a permanent adulterous relationship with Mr. X and that he was a constant visitor to her house and that acts of adultery took place in the house during his visits. It is true that there was no evidence to the effect that either of the children had ever witnessed any such act or was aware of such conduct but nevertheless the precautions taken to prevent the children stumbling upon such conduct by one of them waking during the night and coming into the mother's bedroom were, to say the least of it, inadequate. The mother also made quite clear that she had no intention of terminating her relationship with Mr. X and would not choose between him and the children. In effect what she wanted was custody of the children and at the same time that the fact of her having custody of the children should not impede or bring to an end her relationship with Mr. X. At the time of the hearing, she gave evidence to Mr. Justice Kenny to the effect that she had been seeking an annulment of her marriage in the Ecclesiastical Courts but was not in a position to say and apparently did not know what were the grounds and had apparently given no thought whatever to the position in the ordinary civil law. It now transpires that her effort to obtain an annulment of the marriage has been unsuccessful. It was her intention, as she expressed in the witness-box, to marry Mr. X in a religious ceremony if she obtained an annulment of her marriage. Whether or not this was also the intention of Mr. X was not disclosed to the Court as he did not give any evidence.

. . . In my view, this appeal should succeed and the children should be given into the custody of their father. . . . The ingredients of what makes up the welfare of the children are set out in the Act and have been referred to in other cases and most recently in the judgments delivered in this Court in the case of *M.B. O'S.* v. *P.O. O'S.* [*supra*, p. 435] I see no reason to depart from the view I expressed in my judgment in that case that the ingredients, namely, the religious, moral, intellectual, physical and social welfare of the child are to be considered globally. These children are at an age when their relationship with their mother is a very close one and if all other things were equal there could be no question that in a choice between a father and mother children of this age should be given into the custody of their mother. However, other things are not equal but even when they are not equal a removal of the children from the custody of their mother at such an age would be justified only when it has been found that the mother has been so greatly wanting in her duty to her children that the removal would be warranted.

In my view, the facts of the present case as they stand at the moment warrant the making of such an order. It is unnecessary at this stage to explore the origins of the differences between the husband and wife. To some extent, though not completely, the mother's adultery with the groom can also be discounted because so far as her influence on the children was concerned the husband did not appear to think that that made any material difference when he agreed to the return of the mother to the house even though he was not cohabiting with her as man and wife. To that extent at least it may be said that there was some form of condonation although obviously not forgiveness. It is now apparently accepted by both parties that the marriage has, to use their own phrase, 'irretrievably broken down.' I am not at all sure that this is necessarily a correct view of the situation though it may appear to be so at the moment. What is of immediate concern, however, is that the wife has quite openly and intentionally repudiated the matrimonial bond by her association with Mr. X and has for all practical purposes replaced her husband by Mr. X. I must emphasise, however, that the question of the custody of children is not to be decided as a method of punishing the mother for what could be regarded as wrongful conduct. The paramount consideration is the welfare of the children. A reference has been made in Mr. Justice Kenny's judgment, which appears also in one or two English cases, that the welfare of the children is not the only consideration. I find it difficult to conceive what other considerations there are in an Act which is expressly designed to look after the welfare of children. The question of doing 'justice' between the husband and wife is, in my view, an extraneous factor. Whether a particular result may or may not cause upset to one of the parents is not material unless the effects of that on the parent is in some way likely to affect the welfare of the child itself. Even if one were to assume in a given case that a wife who left home and set up a separate establishment and conducted an adulterous liaison with another man was even encouraged to do so by her husband or driven to it by her husband's misconduct the question of the welfare of the children would still arise to be considered as a separate matter.

It may well be true that this liaison can be conducted for a while at least in a way which will conceal it from the children but at best that can be but for a comparatively short time. If the children should learn of it, what is the effect likely to be? The first effect would be that a new element is introduced into their lives, namely, the existence of Mr. X who even to the children's eyes has supplanted their father in their mother's affections and has furthermore succeeded in replacing their father in their mother's bed. On the evidence it does not appear that so far as the educational, intellectual or physical aspects of their welfare is concerned there is any material difference between their position in the custody of their mother and the position arising from their being given into the custody of their father. There is, however, in my view, a very marked difference in so far as the question of the social, moral and religious aspects of their welfare is concerned. To repeat the words I used in *M.B.O'S* v. *P.O.O'S* the life which is being led by the mother in this case is a manifest repudiation of the social and religious values with which the children should be inculcated and which she believes she can teach them while at the same time clearly repudiating them herself in the sight of her own children. It is bad enough that the children even at the best of times should have to live in a situation where they go backwards and forwards between a father and mother who are living apart. But to do that in a situation where one or other of the parents is associating with a third party in a manner completely incompatible with the matrimonial state and with the family life in which children should be brought up is a very important and tragic addition to an already unfortunate situation. It has been submitted that because the children are so young at the moment that they are unlikely to be aware of the situation that they should be left where they are. But if they are left in the mother's custody for another couple of years then they will inevitably reach the stage where their mother's situation cannot be concealed from them and by then . . . the question of changing their custody is bound to cause greater concern to them and their removal would be a greater blow to them. So far as the previously agreed rights of access are concerned, they were reasonably generous to both sides and were such that both parents had frequent association with the children and the opportunity for such associaiton. However, I think it is important that the children should have a home which is regarded as their permanent home and on the facts of this case I think that should be the father's home. The mother's conduct both with Mr. X and her previous conduct with the groom indicate that she is to say the least somewhat restless and her conduct does not, for the moment in any event, indicate any assurance of a more stable existence in the immediate future. It is true that time is a great healer and that in future years, perhaps sooner than later, the situation may settle down and some form of reconciliation may be effected between the husband and wife which, apart from the benefit it would bring to themselves, would certainly be of undoubted benefit to the children. The husband is still willing to receive the wife back into his house although not willing to have her with him as husband and wife so that even on that basis, which is not acceptable to the wife, there would be complete and permanent access to the children by both parents. How the parents choose to arrange their private lives even in such a household is a matter for themselves provided it does not act contrary to the welfare of the children. However, the present situation is that the wife is unwilling to accept such an arrangement and is not willing to give up her present situation or change it in any way in which I would regard as material to the present case. During the hearing of this appeal she has offered an undertaking that there would be no visits of any kind by Mr. X to her house . . . if she has custody of the children. It is of course understood in this offer that her association and liaison with Mr. X will continue but that some way will be devised of continuing this association without the necessity for his coming to the house. It appears to me that if this association is pursued in the fashion in which it has been pursued up to date that this undertaking is going to create a situation in which it will make it very difficult to carry out this undertaking or alternatively will mean that the wife's absences from the house and her children, particularly at night-time, will be more frequent than hitherto. Coupled with this is the difficulty of obtaining domestic or suitable domestic help to look after the house while she is continuing her association with Mr. X away from the house. In my view, this suggestion is not really a practical or realistic one. The very fact that it is widely accepted, as I myself accept, that the best place for young children of this age is with their mother is based upon the understanding and assumption that the mother is constantly to hand to care for the children if they should wake at night or require the many small attentions which children of this very tender age require. On the other hand, it is said that the husband who at the moment only has a rather elderly housekeeper and whose continuation in his service is somewhat doubtful is really not in a position to provide adequately for the children. It is also mentioned that because the little girl suffers from a skin ailment which requires constant application of ointment that somebody should always be on hand to do this and that the mother does it effectively at the moment. So far as the medication or the application of medication is concerned it appears to me that the husband is sufficiently well-to-do to provide if necessary a properly trained children's nurse to look after his children. I think the same reasoning would apply to the provision of domestic help or the obtaining of domestic help. As he has not yet been given an opportunity to try to cater for the children, in my view no judgment can be passed on his alleged inability to do so. So far as the education of the children is concerned stress is laid upon the fact that the little girl is attending a kindergarten and that the boy is attending a convent school . . . and that the educational opportunities available at the husband's residence, which is only about twenty miles away, would be much less adequate. The husband's ultimate intentions, if he receives custody of the children, is to send them to [another s]chool . . . which caters for both boys and girls when they reach the appropriate age. No suggestion has been made that [this other s]chool would not be a suitable one and the husband appears to be willing to change house again if necessary to accomplish this. All things considered, I am of opinion that the most stable base and the most secure base which can be provided for these children is to have them placed in the custody of their father and that by so doing their welfare is best served. I think the rights of access which had been formally agreed should continue and they will give the wife ample opportunity of seeing the children and of caring for them and, of course, she is perfectly free to visit them as often as she likes. In the events which have happened, if any home can be called a family home it is the home kept up and run by the husband. It is the wife who has departed from the family and has taken the step of breaking it. This break may not be permanent and as I have already remarked the return of the husband and wife to the same habitation would be greatly in the interests of the children and this is more likely to be accomplished if the children are given into the custody of the father. In the present circumstances the way of life chosen by the mother is more likely to be harmful to the children's welfare than the husband's life and the home which the husband can provide is likely to provide a more stable and secure background for the children. In their mother's present unsettled condition there can be no guarantee that she will not move to reside elsewhere and if her liaison with Mr. X. should come to an end because of her inability to obtain an annulment of the marriage one cannot be assured that that will not produce a greater instability in her life. Not merely are the children very young but indeed the father and mother may be regarded as still being young and, in my view, whatever prospect may exist of an ultimate reconciliation of this family it is more likely to be advanced by stabilising the children's position than leaving them in the present more unstable and uncertain position.

For these reasons I would allow the appeal and I think an order should be made giving the custody of the children to the husband.

Budd, J. delivered a concurring judgment.

Henchy, J. (Dissenting):

. . . Of one thing I am quite certain. If the judge had held that the wife's extra-marital relationship with Mr. X was, viewed in itself at the end of the hearing, not compatible with the welfare of the children, he would not have deprived her of the custody without giving her an opportunity of adducing further evidence. Apart from what is to be gathered from the content of the hearing, counsel for the wife has told this court that he informed Kenny J. that he wished to tender the evidence of medical witnesses as to the deleterious effect a change of custody would have on the girl's health, that the judge said that if necessary he would adjourn the hearing to enable such evidence to be given, but that in the event, because the issue of custody was being decided in favour of the wife, the necessity for such evidence did not arise. It is obvious, therefore, that if the judge, at the end of the hearing in the High Court, found himself leaning towards taking the custody from the wife and giving it to the husband, he would have adjourned the matter to enable the medical evidence to be given. Counsel for the wife, finding himself bereft of that evidence for the purpose of this appeal, has applied to this court to hear it, but the application has been refused. The result is that the children's custody has now to be decided in the absence of what might be crucial evidence affecting the girl's welfare.

It may, of course, be said that the wife's misconduct is so irresponsible and so potentially harmful to the children that it outweighs any harm that might be indicated by such medical evidence. For my part, I should not be happy to leave the children in the wife's custody on the basis of the High Court order. It rests on an undertaking by the wife that Mr. X would not take the children on outings, that when the children are with the wife Mr. X will not come to the house before 8.30 p.m. and will leave not later than midnight, and that there will be no acts of sexual intercourse between the wife and Mr. X while the children are in the house. Making the order conditional on that undertaking was a well-intentioned but, I fear, ineffectual contrivance to save the innocence of the children from contamination by the wife's adulterous liaison with Mr. X. Life being what it is, I feel it would be only a matter of time, if Mr. X were to continue to be a regular visitor to the house, before, either by sight or sound within the house or gossip picked up outside, the children learned the unpalatable truth of the situation. The result of that could be disastrous for the children's moral welfare and emotional security.

However, a new factor has now entered into the case. At the eleventh hour, the wife has stated to this court through her counsel that she is willing to give an undertaking that Mr. X will not visit her home at any time and that she will not allow him to have any contact whatsoever with the children. If this undertaking is honoured, both in the spirit and the letter, it would substantially obviate the immediate risk of moral harm to the children from this association. But it does not wipe the slate clean in favour of the wife. Her past behaviour and her poor moral standards remain to cast a shadow over the children's welfare. If this case were governed solely by the test of the children's moral welfare, the evidence would seem to favour awarding custody to the father.

However, as I pointed out at the beginning of this judgment, the courts in determining the issue of custody are bound to give due weight to every available piece of evidence bearing on the religious and moral, intellectual, physical and social welfare of the children. I attempt no comparison of the respective merits of the husband and wife in terms of the intellectual, physical and social welfare of the children, for the reason that because of the confined scope of the hearing in the High Court those matters were not fully explored. As I read the evidence given in the High Court, it discloses no complaint against the wife's custody other than that arising from her association with Mr. X. Otherwise, the children appear to be happy and well looked after, the girl attending a preparatory school and the boy attending a convent school. . . . If custody were given to the husband, the children would go to live with him in a house he has had built . . . but in which he has yet to take up residence, there to be looked after by a housekeeper who has yet to be installed. There would be no preparatory school for the girl and the boy would have to adjust himself to starting at a new school. As to the respective merits of the two custodial regimes, I would merely comment that, as far as the evidence goes, if the father were given the custody it would be an exchange of the known for the unknown.

To my mind, one of the greatest and most disturbing uncertainties in this case arises in regard to the medical evidence which was offered to be given, but which was not received, in the High Court and again in this court. We are told that this evidence would show that it would be undesirable on medical grounds to change the present custody of the girl. This child, aged 3½, has been sickly from birth, has congenital eye trouble, and suffers from eczema. To make an order sundering her from her mother's custody and handing her over to the care of her father and an elderly housekeeper might prove to be disastrous for the child. It may, of course, be that a judge, having heard the medical evidence, might still hold, on measuring it against the moral and other relevant considerations, that custody should be given to the father. But I do not think such a drastic step should be taken without at least hearing that evidence. It is but a truism to say that the real casualties in matrimonial disputes such as the present are the children. It would be regrettable if their plight was compounded by procedural rigidity which would cause a court charged with determining their custody to avert its eyes from relevant and available considerations.

To this it may be answered that in the present case custody could be transferred to the husband, and if it did not prove to be in the best interests of the children's welfare they could be reinstated in the wife's custody. But what if the little girl pined and sickened when removed from her mother? The trauma of the change might do her serious harm which might not be easily put right by restoring her to her mother. Leaving aside the implications of the wife's affair with Mr. X, the uncontroverted evidence is that this child is happy and well cared for in the wife's custody. Prudence dictates that that custody should not be terminated in favour of custody with the father, in a household yet to be set up, until all available evidence is heard as to the risks as well as the merits of such a change. The wife wishes to give some such evidence. I would not disturb the present custody without giving her an opportunity of doing so. If this were a straight contest between the husband and wife there might be something to be said for ruling against the wife on the ground that she should have tendered, and not merely offered to tender, the medical evidence in the High Court. But it is the children's welfare we are concerned with, and they should not be put to the risk of a faulty ruling as to their custody through treating the High Court hearing as being based on all relevant evidence when in fact it was almost exclusively confined to evidence on only one aspect of the case.

If the undertaking now offered by the wife had been given when the husband first complained of the effect on the children of her association with Mr. X, this case might never have come to court. I would now favour acting on that undertaking, not out of any condonation of the wife's misconduct nor out of any conviction that she is necessarily the proper person to have custody in the future but, in the interests of the children, to preserve the present custody until, in case the husband wishes to pursue the matter further on the ground of a change of circumstances, the High Court has had an opportunity of determining the question of custody on the basis of all relevant evidence which the parties may wish to tender.

Accordingly, I would vary the order appealed against by substituting for the undertaking set out in that order the undertaking now given to this court by the wife through her counsel that she will not allow Mr. X. to visit her home or to have any contact with the children. To that extent only, I would allow the appeal.

Griffin J. (Dissenting):–

I agree with the judgment delivered by Mr. Justice Henchy.

I wish only to add that a further reason for not disturbing the present custody of the children with the mother without giving her an opportunity of producing medical evidence is that while such evidence might not persuade the High Court judge hearing the case to leave the children in her custody, it might be of paramount importance in deciding what rights of access should be accorded to her if custody is given to the father. In the matter of access the primary consideration is the children's welfare. If, as we are told, medical evidence is available as to the extent to which the little girl's health is likely to be affected if separated from her mother, I consider that a refusal to allow the mother to produce that evidence would amount to a refusal to have regard to a factor which may be vital to the children's welfare, from the point of view of both custody and access.

Notes

1. In the light of this decision and the previous two decisions would you feel confident giving legal advice to a woman living with a man other than her husband on the question of the likelihood of the Court awarding her custody of her children. Would your views change after reading the later decision of *MacD.* v. *MacD., infra*, p. 449?
2. On the question of proof of adultery, see *W.* v. *W.*, unreported, Supreme Court, 6 December 1974 (148–1974).
3. If a five-year-old child wakes in the middle of the night, should the law have any view on whether the mother or the father ought be the one to get up and tend to the child? Should it have regard to evidence that generally it is in fact the mother who does this work? Or should the practice of the particular spouses involved in the proceedings be determinative?
4. Formerly the courts were in some cases more disposed to give consideration of spousal misconduct precedence over the policy that young children should live with their mother: cf., e.g., *In re Mitchell,* [1937] I.R. 767 (Sup. Ct., 1937, aff'g High Ct., 1936).
5. It appears that the Court regards itself as having a legitimate function in determining, reflecting and arguably reinforcing 'proper' sex roles in the upbringing of children. Yet the *Guardianship of Infants Act, 1964* contains no express differentiation between the parents on the basis of their sex. See generally Binchy, *The Sex of a Parent as a Factor in Custody Disputes*, 77 Incorp. L. Soc. of Ireland Gazette 269 (1983). Should our law introduce a provision along the lines of subsection (1A) of section 23 of New Zealand's *Guardianship Act 1968*? The subsection (inserted in 1980) is to the effect that:

   > . . . regardless of the age of a child, there shall be no presumption that the placing of a child in the custody of a particular person will, because of the sex of that person, best serve the welfare of the child.

6. On the question of schooling, it is worth noting Kenny, J.'s statement in *B.* v. *B.*, unreported, High Ct., 4 July 1972 (1968–1465P.) that

> [a] boarding school is obviously a more suitable institution for a boy over 12 who is in his mother's custody.

Do you agree? Cf. *In re V. Minors*, unreported, High Ct., Teevan, J., 15 November 1968.

MacD. v. MacD.

Unreported, Supreme Court, 5 April 1979 (70–1979)

Henchy, J.:

As counsel have agreed in the course of the argument, the question of the custody of these estranged parents' two children reduces itself to this – to which is the greater weight to be given: the risk to the children's religious and moral welfare through their being in the custody of the mother, who is living with a man who is not her husband, or the risk to their emotional and psychological well-being through their being in the custody of their father, who is a busy executive employed by a large business organisation and is therefore required to leave home early every working day and be away from home all day, leaving the children in the care of a housekeeper?

The two children are a girl aged 6½ and a boy aged 4½. They are – as both parents agree they should be – being brought up as Catholics. The father, aged 46, is a Catholic; the mother, aged 35, is a Protestant. The marriage has failed, irretrievably it would seem. She has gone to live . . . with another man (whom I shall refer to as 'S.D.'). For some four years this liaison between the mother and S.D. has lasted, and it is their intention to get married as soon as she can get a divorce abroad. S.D., who is a Protestant, is already divorced.

If the custody of the children were to depend on the past conduct of the parents or on the merits of their claims, the father's case for getting custody would, in my judgment, certainly prevail. The immediate cause of the collapse of the marriage was the mother's decision to put her attachment to S.D. before the needs of her husband and children. If custody of children could be granted as a badge of moral approval, the father, who has been steadfast as a husband and a father, would come before the mother. But the right to custody may not be determined in that way. . . . [T]he conduct, wishes and needs of the parents are irrelevant except in so far such considerations bear on the welfare of the children.

In order to come to a decision as to where the welfare of these children lies, I must compare and contrast the two households in question.

The mother and S.D. live in a large house with spacious grounds . . . S.D., aged 40, is a man of some affluence, being a director of two property companies, and conducts his business largely from his residence. While the mother had custody of the children and they were living in that household, they were on mutually affectionate terms with S.D.; but he did not seek to oust the father in their affections. He and the mother provided a home in which the children were healthy and happy. The mother, by all accounts, has been a loving and attentive mother, and the children are as devoted to her as she is to them. In short, there has been only one criticism made of this household, and it is that made by the father: he finds it utterly repugnant that his children should live in a ménage presided over by S.D. He considers him – as a Protestant, a divorcee, a person who 'dabbles in property' and, above all, as his wife's paramour – to be a person with whom his children should have no association whatsoever. Those objections are substantial and understandable. Indeed, the President of the High Court, in awarding custody to the father, held that, from the point of view of the children's moral, social and religious welfare, the consistent and more stable environment of their father's custody would be far preferable to that of the mother's custody.

By way of comparison and contrast, let me turn and consider the father's household. He lives in a large house. . . . As a housekeeper he has a young woman of 26, who is satisfactory as a housekeeper but who will be leaving in a few months to get married. Then he will have to find another housekeeper. Even if he is successful in finding a suitable person, she will probably be a stranger to the children. Every day from Monday to Friday the father has to leave home early to get to his place of business.

. . . This means that, apart from weekends, the children would see their father only in the morning and in the evening – which in winter would hardly ever be in daylight – and their mother only during the limited periods of access. Even with a good housekeeper, it would be a lonely and empty life for these young children who are so attached to their mother. When they would come home from school in the early afternoon, they would have neither mother nor father to turn to. This could not be good for them. It is difficult to believe that they would not pine for their mother's care and attention, particularly in the long afternoon hours before their father's return from work. In the High Court a child psychiatrist gave it as his opinion that it would be undesirable, in the interests of the children's emotional security and having regard to the close bond of affection he found between the mother and the children, to change the custody from the father to the mother. However, the President, after carefully considering that and the other evidence, was not satisfied that there is a substantial risk of any real lasting and serious injury to the emotional and psychiatric make-up of the children in giving their custody to the father.

The problem for a court in a case such as this is to determine which custody – with the father or with the mother – is more likely to accord with the children's welfare, welfare being understood as a composite of its statutory elements. In considering the corresponding English statutory provision, which also requires that the court 'shall regard the welfare of the infant as the first and paramount consideration', Lord MacDermott said in *J. v. C.* [1970] A.C. 710, at 711:

> Reading these words in their ordinary significance, and relating them to the various classes of proceedings which the section has already mentioned, it seems to me that they must mean more than that the child's welfare is to be treated as the top item in a list of items relevant to the matter in question. I think they connote a process whereby, when all the relevant facts, relationships, claims and wishes of parents, risks, choices and other circumstances are taken into account and weighed, the course to be followed will be that which is most in the interests of the child's welfare as that term has now to be understood. That is the first consideration because it is of first importance and the paramount consideration because it rules on or determines the course to be followed.

In my opinion, that statement represents the correct approach. In the case of very young children, having regard to the ties of nature, the person *prima facie* entitled to their custody, where the parents are estranged, is the mother, for by reason of her motherhood she will usually be the person primarily and uniquely capable of ministering to their welfare. If the case is being made that by reason of her character, her conduct, or any other circumstances, she should be held to be disentitled to the custody, the onus of proof of that disentitlement should lie on the person making that case.

I look therefore to see if the father has discharged that onus in this case. An analogous situation had arisen in the case of *Re L. (infants)* [1962] 3 All E.R. 1. There the mother of two young children, girls aged four and six, had left home with the children and had gone to live near a man with whom she had an adulterous relationship. The father had retaken the children and they were being looked after in a house occupied by him, his unmarried sister and a maid. When the question of the children's custody came before the court Plowman J., holding in favour of the erring wife as against the blameless father, said (at p. 3):

> In my view, the care and affection that the children, I am quite sure, are getting now both from their father and their aunt, who is looking after them, is really no substitute for the love and affection which small girls of that age will get from their mother. While one must have the greatest sympathy for the father in a case of this sort, where it

was the mother who was the cause of breaking his home because she left him and took the children with her, and where I do not find anything in the father's conduct which compels me to call for a censure, it is my duty to put any considerations of that sort on one side and simply to look at this thing from the point of view of what is best for these two children; as I have already said, I take the view that what is best for them at present is to go back and live with the mother.

That approach did not find favour in that case with the Court of Appeal, who reversed Plowman J. and held that, because the father was blameless and had a good home for the children, he should therefore be given their custody, rather than the mother whose conduct merited disapproval. All three judges of the Court of Appeal rejected the emphasis placed by Plowman J. on what was best for the children as being the crucial test.

But that was before the decision of the House of Lords in *J.* v. *C.* [1970] A.C. 668. The approach of Plowman J., rather than that of the Court of Appeal, accords with that decision, particularly with the passage from the speech of Lord MacDermott which I have already quoted. Consequently when a comparable question of custody came before the Court of Appeal in *S (D.B)* v. *S (D.J.)* [1977] 1 All E.R. 656, the test propounded by Plowman, J. was held to be the correct one and it was ruled that 'cases such as *Re L. (infants)* are not now to be regarded as authoritative in any sense of the word'.

I would adopt the same attitude to our statutory provisions. I consider the conduct, past and present, of the parents to be relevant only to the extent that it bears on the welfare of the children as it is spelled out in its statutory definition. It is one of the melancholy features of cases such as this that a decision allocating the custody of the children to one of the parents may run counter to the merits of the other parent.

Accepting all the facts as found by the President of the High Court, I have to see if the obvious risks to the children's religious and moral welfare, if they are to live with the mother and S.D., are outweighed by the no less obvious risks to their emotional and psychological well-being if they are to live in the father's household, from which he will be absent every day from Monday to Friday from about 8.30 a.m. until 6 p.m. The President, having seen and heard the witnesses, expressed himself as not satisfied that there is a substantial risk of any real, lasting and serious injury to the emotional and psychiatric make-up of the children if their custody is given to the father. With great respect, I am unable, after carefully considering the facts as found, to share such a sanguine prognosis. If the father is given custody, the children will normally be left all day with strangers – by which I mean non-relatives – and they will have neither father nor mother to turn to. For young children to return home from school to a house where there is neither father nor mother, only a housekeeper, is a harsh and lonely prospect. Their father they could expect to see only when he comes home at night. They would be destitute of the love and attention, the sympathy and care, the soothing physical presence which their mother could give them, and which she did give them when they were in her custody. It would be strange if they did not pine for her and traumatically feel a need for her, particularly when ill, or hurt, or lonely, or frightened, or otherwise upset. No expert evidence was given as to the likely effect on them of the particular circumstances attaching to custody with their father, but I should be surprised if a child psychiatrist or psychologist would see such a situation other than as one calculated to produce in them feelings of rejection, alienation, loneliness, unwantedness and emotional frustration, such as to be capable of producing emotional and psychological disturbances, if not actual physical or psychosomatic ill-health. Even without such evidence, the situation is so fraught with deprivation for the children that the risk it poses to their well-being cannot be discounted. In short, they have a daily need for their parents, especially their mother, and in the absence of coercive reasons why that need should be overlooked, I feel it would be wrong to disregard it and say that it would be sufficient for their physical and emotional well-being if they have a housekeeper to look after them during the day, and their father at night. A true and balanced view of their welfare should not result in their being unnecessarily condemned to an unhappy childhood through being deprived for five days of the week of any normal contact with their father or mother.

The alternative custody, with their mother, would fill the children's basic need for motherly love and care. It would remove the fears, the loneliness and the emptiness involved in having to spend long and tedious hours in a large house in which there is only a housekeeper – a housekeeper who will have to be replaced on her marriage in a few months time, and the uncertainty as to whose successor adds a further peril to the situation. Custody with the mother is more likely to promote the physical and social welfare of the children; and because she could personally take them to and from school, and give them emotional security and motherly help in their problems, their intellectual welfare also might be better served if they are in her custody.

However, because the mother can provide custody only in a household presided over by S.D., the divorced man with whom she is living after deserting the father, creates a risk that the religious and moral welfare of the children will suffer if she is given custody. It is a very real risk, particularly as the children are Catholics and S.D. and the mother are both Protestants. The mother's relationship with S.D. will be a bad example and a cause of scandal to the children. But it will be that, whether or not the mother is given custody. The father's wish that the children should have no contact whatsoever with S.D. is not practicable. Even if the father were given custody, the mother would have to be allowed periods of access to them, and that access, in order to have any real value in terms of the children's welfare, would have to be in the mother's home, which is the house where S.D. lives and works. The mother's relationship with S.D. is already an accomplished fact in the children's lives. The intention of the mother and S.D. to get married as soon as she gets a divorce abroad has not been doubted. It will be impossible to screen off from the children the mother's life with S.D. As far as this case is concerned, the question is confined to making a prognosis as to the extent to which the religious and moral welfare of the children will be imperilled if they go to live with their mother and S.D., and to weighing in the balance that peril against the father's inability during most of the week to surround the children with any direct parental presence or help.

The mother has given evidence (which has not been doubted in cross-examination and which is supported by her conduct when she already had the custody) that she is prepared to bring up the children as Catholics, to see that they will get proper religious instruction, to ensure that they will say their prayers, and to take them to Mass on Sundays. In other words, she is prepared, so far as in her lies, to look after the religious and moral welfare of the children; and there is no suggestion that S.D. will seek to thwart her resolution to do so. The unfortunate extra-marital situation in which she finds herself, which cannot be regularised so as to acquire constitutional propriety, detracts considerably from her willingness and ability to satisfy the religious and moral welfae of the children. But so long as she is ready as a loving and caring mother to do her best to see to that welfare, the obvious need of these young children for her as a mother should weigh heavily in the balance in favour of her claim to be given custody, particularly when the alternative is custody with the father which would mean that every day from Monday to Friday the children would be starved of parental love and attention.

In the light of all those considerations, I consider that the mother's prima facie valid claim to the custody of the children should not be held to have been ousted. Looking at the situation, as I must, solely in terms of what is best calculated to promote the religious and moral, intellectual, physical and social welfare of the children, I am of opinion that so long as the circumstances and relations of the parties are as the evidence given in the High Court shows them to be, the mother, for all the shortcomings of her situation, has the better capacity to meet the amalgam of needs constituting the statutory definition of welfare. To the extent that she may be wanting in that capacity, it is to be hoped that the granting to the father of generous periods of access, particularly at weekends, will enable any necessary supplement or corrective to be supplied, especially in matters of religion and morals. In reaching this conclusion as to custody, I am swayed by the fact that the father, deserving as he is of sympathy on the collapse of his marriage without fault on his part and of respect for his willingness to do the best for his children in difficult circumstances, is unable to provide from day to day the basic parental attention necessary for the welfare of the children. . . .

Kenny, J.:

. . . After much anxious consideration I have come to the conclusion that the welfare of the two children would best be served by awarding custody of them to the mother. . . .

The principal matter which must govern the approach to this case is the youth of the children ($6\frac{1}{2}$ and $4\frac{1}{2}$). Young children have a much greater emotional need of their mother than they have of their father who, when they are young, seems to them to be a somewhat remote figure. A mother has an instinctive understanding of children's minds and needs. She provides warmth, visible signs of affection, love, a feeling of security a last refuge in times of trouble and patience in listening to their petty complaints. The feeling that their mother is always available at home is an important element in the emotional life of a young child: from this comes confidence and courage to face the trials which life presents to a young child.

In every case in which young children are involved, the factors I have mentioned create a strong *prima facie* case for giving them into the custody of their mother. That case may of course be rebutted if it is shown that the mother is an unfit person to have them in her custody. She may be promiscuous or addicted to alcohol or may be indifferent to the children (this last mentioned matter does occur in rare cases).

In this case there was coercive evidence that the wife was a loving mother, that the children were devoted to her and felt a need of her company, that she had always been careful to bring them up as Roman Catholics, that she brought them to Mass each Sunday and got them to say night prayers and that the children were happy and not frightened in her presence. It is lamentable that she is living with a man to whom she is not married and this will be a deplorable example to the children when they begin to realise the significance of it. But this does not outweigh the matters which are in the mother's favour. . . .

Since writing this judgment I have had the advantage of reading that of Mr. Justice Henchy and I wish to say that I agree with it.

Wisely, counsel did not refer us to the many decided cases on this matter. As all the members of this Court were judges either of this Court or of the High Court in most of the relevant cases, counsel rightly assumed that we were familiar with them. I expressly reserve for future consideration by a full Court the questions whether the decisions of this Court in *J.J.W.* v. *B.M.W.* and *E.K.* v. *M.K.* were correct.

Griffin, J., in a dissenting judgment, reviewed the evidence and concluded that, on the facts found by the President, his finding was justified.

Notes

1. An earlier unreported decision of the Supreme Court in which the adultery question arose should also be noted. In *M.T.* v. *R.T.*, 1 May 1978, the Supreme Court (Henchy, Kenny and Parke JJ.), reversing the trial Judge, granted custody of his three eldest children to a man living with a woman who was not his wife. No written judgments were delivered. For an account of the decision, see O'Reilly, *Custody Disputes in the Irish Republic: The Uncertain Search for the Child's Welfare?*, 12 Ir. Jur. (n.s.) 37, at 69–70 (1977).
2. It is interesting to note that as late as 1977 *Re L. (Infants)* was still being cited to the English Court of Appeals as being still of binding authority: see *Re K. (Minors)*, [1977] Fam. 179, at (*per* Stamp, L.J.).

3. (a) Has a mother 'an instinctive understanding of children's minds and needs', which a father lacks? Is it wise to speak, or think, in such general terms?
   (b) Is it true, generally or universally, that '[y]oung children have a much greater emotional need of their mother than their father who, when they are young, seems to them to be a somewhat remote figure'?
   (c) Is it a compliment to a mother to tell her that she provides 'a last refuge in times of trouble and patience in listening to [her children's] petty complaints'? Is there a suggestion that the father should not be troubled with such matters? Or merely that, as a social fact, fathers do not actually take the trouble? Should the Court, in making decisions as to custody, reflect or seek to change social attitudes?
4. Can you see any basis for Kenny, J.'s apparent uncertainty as to whether the decisions of the Supreme Court in *J.J.W.* v. *B.M.W.* and *E.K.* v. *M.K.* had been correctly decided?

H. v. H.

Unreported, High Court, Parke, J., 4 February 1976 (1975–450Sp.)

Parke, J.:

In this case the plaintiff and the defendant were married [in] 1971 in Dublin according to the rites of the Roman Catholic Church. Both were, and possibly still are, members of that Church although the degree to which either now practises religion is extremely doubtful. There is one child of the marriage, A, who is the subject matter of these proceedings and who was born [in] October 1973.

Although it is clear that there was no express agreement between the parents as to the religious upbringing of the child it is equally clear from the evidence of both of them that it was impliedly agreed that the children of the marriage would be brought up as Roman Catholics. To quote from the words of Davitt, P. in *Re May* 92 I.L.T.R. 1 at p. 5:

'It was taken as a matter of course that in accordance with their duty they would rear any children of the marriage as Catholics.'

This intention was put into effect by having A baptised as a Catholic although his youth has prevented any further steps being taken in that direction. It seems to me, therefore, that the only way in which the facts of this case differ from those in *Re May* is that in the latter case the parties had been married for upwards of ten years and had therefore an opportunity to further the religious education of their children. I do not think that this affects the principles to be applied in such cases.

Before considering these principles it is necessary to outline briefly the circumstances which give rise to the present proceedings. [Parke J. referred to allegations of drunkenness and assault made by the wife against her husband. He continued:]

In 1974 the wife went on a holiday to Tennerife unaccompanied by her husband and there she made the acquaintance of a Mr. X. He is an Englishman residing in a large English city where he holds a highly paid and responsible public position. He is an active member of the Jewish community in which he lives, adhering to the Reformed Branch of that religion. When he met the plaintiff he was married with one son but living apart from his wife with whom the son resided being regularly visited by his father. I am told that shortly before the hearing of these proceedings a decree *nisi* of divorce had been granted to Mrs. X in proceedings based on either desertion or separation for more than three years. No allegations of marital misconduct of any kind appears to have been made against either party. It is expected that the decree will shortly be made absolute.

I have had the benefit of seeing Mr. X in the witness box and hearing his evidence which was frankly and convincingly given. He impressed me as a man of integrity, of sincere and strongly felt religious convictions, deeply affectionate towards the plaintiff and able and anxious to make a permanent home for her and for A. I judge him to have the qualities which would make him a good father.

But, whatever qualities are possessed by Mr. X, his meeting with the plaintiff was disastrous for the marriage. The acquaintance progressed very rapidly. . . .

It is not difficult to imagine the defendant's state of mind when he made such a shattering discovery. At the best of times he was addicted to drink and to violence towards his wife who alleges that his conduct now became such that she was in real fear for her life. She says that he threatened to kill her and he admits that when she told him that she wanted to take A to England to live with her and Mr. X he said that he would 'shoot them both'. I am now satisfied that although there seemed to have been some confusion on this point in some people's minds that when he used the word 'both', he meant the plaintiff and Mr. X and that he never at any time threatened any kind of violence towards A. The plaintiff's brother-in-law to whom the defendant repeated the threat took it seriously. The defendant says that he only made it to frighten the plaintiff sufficiently to deter her from carrying out her intention. I am satisfied that the defendant would never have carried out such a threat if he was sober but, I cannot predict what he might have done if drunk.

However, given the defendant's character and temperament such a reaction appears entirely predictable and I am not disposed to attach as much importance to the episode as I am urged to do by Mr. Dempsey [on behalf of the plaintiff].

It must also be said in his favour that from the time the defendant was told by the plaintiff that she intended to make a permanent home with Mr. X in England he set about trying to make arrangements for the maintenance of A in his parent's home. The result of these efforts will be considered later.

In the result these proceedings were instituted on 7th October 1975 and on the same day a Notice of Motion was issued claiming an interim order for custody of the child [and] certain reliefs by way of injunction against the defendant. On the hearing of this motion on 9th October 1975 Kenny J. made an order giving sole custody of the child to the plaintiff until further order. At this hearing the defendant was represented and took the proper course of giving certain undertakings which were read on the order and accordingly no injunctions were granted.

The case made by the plaintiff is one which required no small degree of courage and is evidence of the depth and sincerity of her feelings towards A and Mr. X. On the other hand it evidences no consideration or concern whatsoever for the defendant or his feelings. It seems to be implicit in her case, that by reason of his conduct and the inadequacy of his financial resources he has forfeited the right to the custody of his child or to have any control whatsoever in his upbringing and education.

Her case can be stated very shortly. She asks for an order giving her custody of A so that she can take him out of the jurisdiction to live in the home which she and Mr. X intend to set up in England. She further states that she is anxious to adopt the Jewish faith and has already gone a considerable way towards attaining that object by study and other means. In consequence she says that it is her intention that A should be brought up in that religion. Given the foregoing premises I agree that this is a correct conclusion. Nothing could be more unsettling for a boy living in a wholly Jewish household and probably meeting many Jewish children of his own age, than to be brought up as a Christian.

Little or no attention seems to have been paid to the questions of how and when and where the defendant is to have access to his child. Even less does it appear to have been considered from the true basis namely, the right of the child to have access to his father. (See *M.* v. *M.* [1973] 2 All E.R. 81).

Stated thus, and I do not see how it can be stated otherwise, it is a novel claim particularly in the Courts of this country operating as they do under a Constitution which lays such a special emphasis on the institution of the family and which so clearly defines the family as a unit based upon marriage and parenthood.

In order that I shall not keep the parties in further suspense while I state the grounds for my decision I will say at once that I cannot accede to this claim and find myself bound to dismiss it.

Since the enactment of the *Guardianship of Infants Act, 1964* the paramount consideration which must guide the Court in deciding cases such as these is the welfare of the child. Welfare is defined as comprising the religious and moral, intellectual, physical and social welfare of the infant. The application of these principles has been considered by the Supreme Court in three cases, all as yet unreported. They are *J.J.W.* v. *B.M.W., supra*, p. 428, *M.B.O.'S* v. *P.O.O'S, supra*, p. 435 and *E.K.* v. *M.K., supra*, p. 447. In his dissenting judgment in *M.B.O'S* v. *P.O.O'S*. Walsh J. had this to say about the construction and application of the Act:

> . . . I think all the ingredients which the Act stipulates are to be considered; namely, the religious, moral, intellectual, physical and social welfare of the child are to be considered globally. This is not an appeal to be decided by the simple method of totting up the marks which may be awarded under each of the five headings. It is the totality of the picture presented which must be considered. The picture is to be viewed and judged as a whole and not as a sum of the values of each of the constituent parts of the picture because, unless together they all form one acceptable composition the picture is a bad one. The word 'welfare' must be taken in its widest sense.

The remaining members of the Court, Henchy and Griffin JJ. in no way dissented from this picture although they came to a different conclusion after reviewing the evidence.

Starting from the unchallengeable position that I must put out of my mind all considerations other than the welfare of A, Mr. Dempsey in his extremely able and thorough argument proceeds to another proposition for which there is ample judicial support namely, that a child of tender years should be entrusted to the custody of his mother unless she has so gravely failed in her duty as a mother as to forfeit such right because there is no real substitute for a loving mother's care. He says that although the plaintiff may have grievously failed in her duty as a wife she has never failed in her duty as a mother. He then argues that if, having given custody to the plaintiff I do not permit her to take A out of the jurisdiction and carry out her intention of making a permanent home with Mr. X she will be extremely unhappy and that this unhappiness will inevitably be sensed by A, may affect her treatment of [her child] and would in a number of ways be wholly inimical to his welfare. Mr. Dempsey relies upon an English case of *Poel* v. *Poel* [1970] 1 W.L.R. 1469 in support of this proposition which I accept as being of sound sense. It is, however, at this point that I believe that Mr. Dempsey's reasoning begins to go astray. What I am being pressed to do is first to decide the issue of custody without reference to where or in what home or establishment and then having decided that in favour of the plaintiff, I would be coerced in A's interest to allow her to carry out the rest of her plan. The point did not arise in *Poel* v. *Poel* or *M.* v. *M.* [1972] 2 All E.R. 81, because on previous applications custody had already been awarded and the only question was whether the order should be varied to allow the infant to be taken out of the jurisdiction. Where however the prime issue is that of custody it seems to me impossible to resolve that issue without taking into account the entire picture presented by the parties and the whole of their respective proposals for the future of the child. This is what the Supreme Court did in the three cases to which I have referred, balancing one proposition against another so as to determine after taking all factors into consideration, which of the proposals would be best for the child's welfare. I cannot therefore take the easier course of first deciding custody as it were in the abstract in favour of the plaintiff and following this up with an order permitting this custody to be out of the jurisdiction in the home to be provided by Mr. G. This appears to be entirely in accordance with the dictum of Lord MacDermott in *J.* v. *C.* [1970] A.C. 668 at pp. 711–712, quoted with approval by Henchy J. in *E.K.* v. *M.K.*

Although the requirements of the Act must be considered globally, in the words of Walsh J., each of them must be considered separately. The first requirement relates to religious welfare and on this an argument is advanced on behalf of the defendant which, if correct, is fatal to the plaintiff's case. In *re Tilson Infants* [1951] I.R. 1 the Supreme Court held that an express ante-nuptial agreement as to the religion in which the children, if any, of a marriage would be brought up is enforceable against a party seeking to repudiate it. In *In re May* 92 I.L.T.R. 1 (already referred to) Davitt P. held that the same principle applied to the agreement which is to be inferred on the marriage of two persons both practising the same religion that any children of the marriage would be brought up in that religion, there being no evidence of any contrary intention. Apart from the fact that I would consider myself bound by this decision I respectfully agree with it. If this be the present state of the law the plaintiff has no right to change A's religion against the wishes of the defendant and I should not make any order allowing her to do so. It is however, contended on behalf of the plaintiff that the principle has no application to these proceedings. The objection which I see to this proposition is that both the *Tilson* and the *May* cases appear to me to be in accordance with the provisions of Article 42, 1 of the Constitution which guarantees the inalienable right and duty of 'parents' to provide for the religious education of their children and this is the main basis of the judgments of Murnaghan and Black JJ. in *re Tilson Infants*. It is impossible to avoid observing the extraordinar[il]y close resemblance between the wording of Article 42, 1 and the definition of welfare in section 2 of the *Guardianship of Infants Act, 1964*. I do not think that the draughtsman of the Act had the slightest idea of attempting to upset the principles in these two cases but that even if he had the attempt would have been unconstitutional. I therefore propose to follow *In Re May* 92 I.L.T.R. 1 and on this ground alone would be prepared to dismiss the plaintiff's case. However this would appear to be a summary way of disposing of a case in which so many important issues were raised.

In hearing cases as to the custody of children the Court is not one of comparative religions. The Court is not to prefer one religion to another. The Jewish religion was one of those originally mentioned in Article 44, 1 (3). All believing Christians must believe that what they call the Old Testament is true because if it is not, Christianity is false and without any basis whatsoever. According to the law of this country there is no reason why a person's religious welfare should be the better or the worse for being either a Christian or a Jew. I do not propose to enter into any theological speculation as the result of a person baptised as a Christian being brought up in a religion which denies the divinity of Christ. Very probably no such arguments were addressed to me. All other things being equal, a change of religion of this sort might not affect a decision under the Act. One has, however, also to consider the social welfare of [A] which I take to mean making him a better member of the society in which he will live. Of all the great religions the Jewish faith is the most totally associated with race. I want to say as emphatically as possible that I do not use this expression in any critical or disparaging sense. I use it to state what is well known namely, that the number of persons professing the Jewish faith who are not also of the Jewish race in whole or in part, are comparatively few. I believe there is a serious danger that A might become 'an odd man out' in the Jewish society in which he would be reared in England and that the older he gets the more marked this would become. Again should he, in adult life, wish to return to his native country, here, again, there will be an anomaly. It is suggested of course that he might change his religion again and become a Christian but this does not seem to me to be a practical solution leading to his welfare. Leaving out any purely theological factors it seems to me that A's social welfare would not be advanced if his mother's proposal is carried into effect.

This Court is no more a Court of morals than one of comparative religions. A parent who has acted immorally is not to be punished by being deprived of a child. In *M.B.O'S.* v. *P.O.O'S.* the Courts awarded custody of children to a husband who was living with a woman who was not his wife and by whom he had children. The facts of this case were however exceptional in that the children had for more than four years lived in what on its face appeared to be a normal stable family, were exceptionally well educated both religiously and otherwise and were entirely happy. In general however, the Courts will not grant custody to a parent who has abandoned the matrimonial home and lives in an adulterous establishment. The reason for this is the extremely bad moral example which would be given to the child and this has been discussed in all the three Supreme Court cases to which I have referred. The circumstances present in *M.B.O'S.* v. *P.O.O'S.* do not apply in this case. [A] will be moving wholly into the unknown if he were to go to reside with the plaintiff and Mr. X. He would be living in a house with a man who was not his father and was not lawfully (in the Irish sense) married to his mother. The exact intentions of the plaintiff and Mr. X were not fully disclosed to me but they at all times spoke of a permanent arrangement. By this I infer that after Mr. X's divorce became absolute the plaintiff would contrive to get a divorce in England and would marry him. In both *Poel* v. *Poel* [1970] 1 W.L.R. 1469 and *M.* v. *M.* [1972] 2 All E.R. 81 this is what happened and the parent with custody was lawfully married. Under Irish law no lawful union can take place between the plaintiff and Mr. X. during the defendant's lifetime. All practising Christians know from the decalogue which they have inherited from the Jewish people that adultery is as much prohibited in that religion as it is in Christianity so that A, when he became aware of the facts as inevitably he would, would know that under the law of his native land his mother and Mr. X were living in adultery. Although a parent is not punished for acting immorally in these kind of cases the parent who deserts the parental home to live with another person has brought about the situation which led to the proceedings and is bound to take some of the consequences of this. It is significant that this fact is specifically referred to in the judgment of Budd and Henchy JJ. in *E.K.* v. *M.K.* [*supra*, p. 447].

As to the intellectual and physical welfare of A there is probably little doubt that it would be as good, and probably better, if he went to England instead of staying in the only household which the defendant can prepare. His education would be well provided for and I am sure that every medical care would be made available.

What then does the father offer? This case would have been a great deal easier to decide (apart from the question of religious education) had the father been either a more worthy person and better off financially. He drinks too much and becomes violent. He has at present £50 a week and no home of his own. When he heard of his wife's intention to take A to England he seems to have done his best to offer an alternative home. His parents and other members of his family live in a large house situate over his father's licensed premises. . . . There is certainly plenty of room for himself and A to live there and the family appear to have adequate means for the kind of life which they live. He has obtained the services of a young girl who will not be very well paid and cannot be very experienced, who will attend on ordinary week-days to look after A. One of the people living in the house is his mother who, in my judgment, is one of those many Dublin mothers who, for generations, have raised large families of which they have reason to be proud. She is, I believe, a simple and unpretentious woman. In the course of her evidence she said without I believe the remotest degree of schooling or knowledge of what learned Judges have said that she would try to give A good example. I believe that she would and be a very much better example than his mother. Again with perfect fairness she agreed that for a small child of little over two years of age there is no real substitute for a mother's care, but A has been deprived of a mother's care in the family's home by his mother herself. As always in these cases and no matter what order the Court may make it is the children who are inevitably the losers.

Taking everything into consideration which I am obliged to do under the Act and leaving out altogether the question of religious education, I propose to discharge the Interim Order made by Kenny, J. and to award custody of A. to the defendant. It is significant that in answer both to myself and to Counsel, the plaintiff did not state what she would do if her application was wholly refused. She should give thought to that. In cases such as this both parties may always apply to have any order varied and I will grant

such liberty. I will also consider any applications which may be made in respect of access, either now or on any future date.

Notes

1. Do you agree that the Court can, on the one hand, have regard to the child's religious welfare, and, on the other, commit itself to the proposition that it 'is not to prefer one religion to another'? If a new religion springs up claiming that Hitler was a divine messenger and that he will return in vengence to the earth in 1990, the Court will not remain neutral. How is this so? What are the limits of judicial neutrality? Cf. Bradley, *Religious Questions in Custody disputes*, 9 Family L. 139 (1979); Terrell, *Religious Considerations – Custody and Adoption*, 9 Family L. 198 (1979); S. Robilliard, *Religion and the Law*, 182–190 (1984); Bates, *Child Law and Religious Extremists: Some Recent Developments*, 10 Ottawa L. Rev. 299 (1978); Bates, *Comment: Child Law and Religious Extremists: Signs of a Changing Judicial Policy?* 11 Ottawa L. Rev. 681 (1979); Bates, *Religious Belief, Reasonableness and Child Custody*, 131 New L.J. 1139 (1981); Bissett-Johnson, *Recent Developments in Family Law*, 3 Fam. L. Rev. 244, at 252–253 (1980).
2. Mr. Justice Brian Walsh has stated extrajudicially (*Existence and Meaning of Fundamental Rights in the Field of Education in Ireland*, 2 Human Rights L.J. 319, at 324 (1981)) that:

   > . . . the religion in which a child should be brought up or educated is a matter in which both parents have equal rights. If they fail to agree, the matter has to be resolved by the courts having regard to what is in the best interests of the child itself. Furthermore, it is possible that parents may agree on a type of religion or other education that is positively harmful to the child. In that kind of case the courts may very well be asked to step in to set aside the parents' rights and to protect the rights of the child (which are also guaranteed).

3. Cf. *Elbaz* v. *Elbaz*, 29 O.R. (2d) 207, 114 D.L.R. (3d) 116 (High Ct., Pennell, J., 1980) and see Zemans, *The Issue of Cultural Diversity in Custody Disputes*, 32 R.F.L. (2d) 50 (1983).
4. May a custody order be made conditional on the partial curtailment of a parent's religious activities? Would this be Constitutional? The issue has arisen in the United States: see *Ex Parte Hilley*, 405 So. 2d 708 (Ala. Sup. Ct., 1981), discussed in *1980–1981 Survey of Developments in Alabama Law*, 33 Ala. L. Rev. 613, at 691–192 (1982): see also *Munoz* v. *Munoz*, 79 Wash. 2d 810, 489 P. 2d 1133 (Sup. Ct., 1971). For consideration of the issue in Canada, see *Brown* v. *Brown*, 3 D.L.R. (4th) 1983 (Bask. C.A., 1983).
5. Do you agree with the statement that '[u]nder Irish law no lawful union can take place between the plaintiff and Mr. X. during the defendant's lifetime'? Cf. *J.J.W.* v. *B.M.W., supra*, p. 428 and *MacC.* v. *MacC.*, unreported, High Ct., McWilliam, J., January 1976 (1975–244Sp.)
6. On the meaning of 'social welfare', see *Shatter*, 216–217. In *MacC.* v. *MacC., supra*, McWilliam, J. said:

   > Social welfare is a peculiar concept in the context. In this case, the social standing of each household appears to be the same and I will leave it at that.

   Is this your understanding of the concept?
7. On the question of access generally, see *Shatter*, 222–223, O'Reilly, *Custody Disputes in the Irish Republic: The Uncertain Search for the Child's Welfare?*, 12 Ir.Jur. (n.s.) 37, at 63–64 (1977). In *B.* v. *B.*, unreported, High Ct., Kenny, J., 14 December 1973 (1971–51Sp.), a mother who was pregnant and whose medical condition reduced her mobility sought more generous access than had been granted her originally. In acceding to this request, Kenny, J. expressed the view that:

   > it would be inhuman to compel the [mother] to choose between seeing her children and endangering her unborn child. . . . I do not see why [she] should have to endanger her health and the life of the child which she is carrying to see her children.

   Very few cases have been reported where breach of access orders by the parent granted custody has been alleged. Why should this be so? Cf. Platt, *Breach of Access Orders: The Futility of the Law*, 134 New L.J. 392 (1984). For an unsuccessful challenge to access provisions under the European Convention, see *Hendricks* v. *Netherlands*, 5 E.H.R. 223 (Eur. open Commission of Human Rights, 1982).
8. International aspects of custody disputes are considered further, *infra*, pp. 468–77.

The Child's Wishes

STATE (McP.) v. G.

Unreported, High Ct., 4 May 1965 (1965–22S.S.)

Davitt, P.:

The prosecutor in this matter, Mr. McP., parted with his daughter X when she was an infant of some few months old. He did so in circumstances which reflect no discredit whatever upon him. He has since then allowed her to remain with the respondent, Mrs. Guinan, her maternal Aunt, and to be brought up mainly at her expense. Again the circumstances were such that it would be harsh criticism to say that in doing so he was unconcerned about her welfare. The result, however, has been that father and daughter are comparative strangers to each other.

The jurisdiction which the prosecutor invokes in this matter is that conferred on this Court by Article 40 of the Constitution. That Article provides that the State shall guarantee in its laws to respect, and, as far as practicable by its laws to defend and vindicate the personal rights of the citizen. It also provides that no citizen shall be deprived of his personal liberty save in accordance with law. It imposes upon the Court the duty, upon complaint being made that a person is being unlawfully detained, to inquire into the said complaint, and provides that the Court may order the person in whose custody he is detained to produce his body in Court, and to certify in writing the grounds of his detention, so that this legality of his detention may be considered and his release order unless the Court is satisfied that he is being detained in accordance with law.

We have interviewed the girl and are quite satisfied that she wants to remain with her Aunt and does not wish to return to her father who is, unfortunately, a comparative stranger to her. She has come to look upon her aunt as a mother and in fact to refer to her as such. Except in an artificial and technical sense she is not being detained at all, and her right to personal liberty is not being infringed. She is, in reality, where she is by her own wish. She is nearly seventeen years of age. Before the enactment of the *Guardianship of Infants Act, 1964*, it was the practice of the Courts in matters of this kind to have regard to the wishes of a child, who had reached what was termed an age of discretion, as to where, and with whom, he or she was to reside. This practice was recognised in many reported cases, notably by the old Court of Queen's Bench in this country in *In re Connor* 16. I.C.L.R. 112; and more recently by this Court in *The State (Meagan)* v. *Meagan,* [1942] I.R. 180; and by the Supreme Court in *The People (Attorney General)* v. *Edge,* [1943] I.R. 115; and in *In re Frost Infants,* [1947] I.R. 4. It is clear from these cases that a boy was regarded as having reached an age of discretion at 14 years and a girl at 16 years. It could almost be said that in matters of this kind the Courts regarded such a child as having the personal right to choose where and with whom he or she was to reside. For instance in *In re O'Hara* [1900] 1 I.R. 232, at 258, Holmes L.J. observed: 'The law has fixed the age of sixteen as the period when a female minor can choose her own residence'.

It has been submitted on behalf of the prosecutor that the law has been altered by the *Guardianship of Infants Act, 1964*; and that in matters of this kind the Court can no longer have regard to the wishes of any person under the age of twenty-one as to where or with whom he will reside, notwithstanding the fact that he has passed, and long passed, the age of discretion. Having regard, however, to the opinion which I have formed of the matter generally I do not consider it necessary to decide whether this submission is well founded. Assuming, without so deciding, that it is; that the prosecutor as natural and statutory guardian of his daughter is *prima facie* entitled to her custody; that this Court has jurisdiction over her person to compel her, on her father's application and subject to the provisions of the Act, to return to live with him; then the position would appear to be as follows.

Part III of the Act deals with the enforcement of a parent's right to the custody of an infant – that is a child under the age of twenty-one years. By S. 14 it provides that where the parent of an infant applies to the Court for its production; and the Court is of the opinion that the parent has abandoned or deserted the infant; or that he has otherwise so conducted himself that the Court should decline to enforce his right to custody, the Court may, in its discretion refuse to make the order. I am quite satisfied that in this case the father has not abandoned or deserted his daughter or otherwise misconducted himself in such a way as to forfeit any right he might otherwise possess as to her custody. By S. 16 it is provided, *inter alia*, that where a parent has allowed an infant to be brought up by another person at that person's expense for such a length of time, and under such circumstances, as to satisfy the Court that the parent was unmindful of his parental duties, the Court shall not make an order for the delivery of the infant to the parent unless the parent has satisfied the Court that he is a fit person to have the custody of the infant. As I have already, I think, indicated I am not satisfied that the father in allowing his daughter to be brought up mainly at her aunt's expense was unmindful of his parental duties; and I am quite satisfied that he is a fit person to have her custody. By S. 3 of the Act, however, it is provided, inter alia, that where in any proceedings before any Court the custody, guardianship or upbringing of an infant is in question the Court in deciding the question shall regard the welfare of the infant as the first and paramount consideration. These present proceedings come, in my opinion, within the ambit of this section.

This girl is now nearly seventeen years of age. She has spent practically her whole life so far with her Aunt whom, as I have said, she regards as, and refers to, as a mother. She has grown up in the environment in which her Aunt lives, has gone to a local school, and doubtlessly made her own friends in school and otherwise. She has been well looked after. She is happy and content where she is and has no desire for any change. She has no dislike for her father; but is unable to regard him otherwise than as a comparative stranger. To take her out of her present surroundings and restore her to her father against her wish would be, to my mind, almost as unreasonable and contrary to her welfare as it would be to take a girl of her age, who had grown up normally with her parents and family, from the family circle and hand her over to the custody of strangers. As Holmes L.J. said in *In re O'Hara* [1900] 1 I.R. 232, at 253: 'No doubt the period during which a child has been in the care of a stranger is always an important element in considering what is best for the child's welfare. If a boy has been brought up from infancy by a person who has won his love and confidence, who is training him to earn his livelihood, and separation from whom would break up all the associations of his life, no Court ought to sanction in his case a charge of custody.' I entertain no doubt, after our interview with the girl, that if her welfare as defined in the Act is to be the first and paramount consideration in deciding the question of her custody she should be allowed to remain with her Aunt.

In my opinion the cause shewn should be allowed and the Conditional Order discharged.

McLoughlin and **Murnaghan, J.J.** concurred.

Notes

1. On the subject of the child's wishes, see further *Shatter*, 223–224. See also section 17(2) of the *Guardianship of Infants Act, 1964*, and cf. J. Kelly, *The Irish Constitution*, 635–636 (2nd ed., 1984). Mr. Shatter (at 223) considers it 'certainly arguable' that for the Court to uphold the wishes of a 14 year-old boy or 16 year-old girl today if it believed them totally contrary to the child's welfare and long-term interests would be contrary to section 3 of the *Guardianship of Infants Act, 1964*. In at least three states in the United States, the judge must honour the child's preferences (unless the chosen parent is not a fit and proper person to have custody: in Mississippi and Ohio at the age of 12, and in Georgia at the age of 14: Speca, *The Role of the Child in Selecting His or Her Custodian in Divorce*, 27 Drake L. Rev. 437, at 439–440 (1978). See also M. Freeman, *The Rights and Wrongs of Children*, 205–206 (1983). The trend of state legislatures seems to be away from expressing a specific age in favour of a more

discretionary approach: Speca, *supra*, at 440–443. A sensible analysis of the issue is presented by Mr. Freeman (at 206):

> There are undoubtedly problems with relying on the wishes of children. There are questions of competence. The[re are] dangers of the child having been coached. . . . The child may be responding to promises made by one parent. Older children may think that a particular parent cannot survive their loss, with the result that their decision may be influenced by what they see as a parent's welfare rather than their own. Children may reject the parent whom they see as responsible for the separation. There is also the danger that a child may, by expressing his preference for one parent, do untold damage to his relationship with the other parent. The view, therefore, expressed in one English case [*M.* v. *M.*, 7 Family L. 17 (1977)], that a child should have the right *not* to be asked to express any preference, has much to commend it. The older child faces an inevitable dilemma. If he fails to state a preference he invites the judge to make an undesired decision. If he states a preference he risks hurting one of his parents and damaging his relationship with that parent. The dilemma is difficult, if not impossible, to resolve in the context of adversary proceedings at the end of which one parent is to be awarded custody.

See further Genden, *Separate Legal Representation for Children: Protecting the Rights and Interests of Minors in Judicial Proceedings*, 11 Harv. Civil Rts. – Civil Libs. L. Rev. 545, at 573–574, 593 (1976); Bersoff, *Representation for Children in Custody Decisions: All that Glitters is Not Gault*, 15 J. of Family L. 27, at 42–43 (1976); Mlyniec, *The Child Advocate in Private Custody Disputes: A Role in Search of a Standard*, 16 J. of Family L. 1, at 6, 15–16 (1977); Siegal & Hurley, *The Role of the Child's Preference in Custody Proceedings*, 11 Family L.Q. 1 (1977). An important analysis, based on empirical research, is presented by Landsman & Minow, *Note: Lawyering for the Child: Principles of Representation in Custody and Visitation Disputes Arising from Divorce*, 87 Yale L.J. 1126, at 1163–1172 (1978); Coons & Mnookin, *Toward a Theory of Children's Rights*, ch. 22 of I. Baxter & M. Eberts eds., *The Child and the Courts*, (1978). Whether this crisis of loyalty in which the child finds himself or herself would be mitigated or removed if adversary proceedings were abolished is far from clear. It is doubtful whether the child's problem can be regarded merely in terms of legal proceedings. The empirical evidence suggests that, as a rule, the child's real wish is not to live with *one* parent rather than the other but to live in a united family with *both* of them: see J. Wallerstein & J. Kelly, *Surviving the Breakup: How Children Cope with Divorce*, 49 (1980 ed.); Futterman, *Child Psychiatry Perspectives: After the 'Civilized' Divorce*, 19 J. of Child Psychiat. 525 (1980); Steinman, *The Experience of Children in a Joint Custody Arrangement: A Report of a Study*, 51 Amer. J. of Orthopsychiat. 403 (1981); Westman & Cline, *Divorce Is A Family Affair*, 5 Family L.Q. 1, at 3–4 (1971); Awad & Parry, *Access Following Marital Separation*, 25 Canad. J. of Psychiat. 357, at 359 (1980).

2. For empirical confirmation of the danger of a parent encouraging a child to side with him or her against the other parent, see De Frain & Eirick, *Coping as Divorced Single Parents: A Comparative Study of Fathers and Mothers*, 30 Family Relations 265, at 272 (1981). See also Irving & Irving, *Conciliation Counselling in Divorce Litigation*, 16 R.F.L. 257, at 264–265 (1975).
3. For a brief comparative study of the judicial approach to the question of the child's wishes in common law jurisdictions, see Stone, *The Welfare of the Child*, ch. 15 of I. Baxter & M. Eberts eds., *The Child and the Courts*, at 241–243 (1978).
4. The question of the extent to which the Court should defer to the child's wishes in custody cases encapsulates a far larger philosophical question as to the extent to which legal autonomy is desirable for children in society generally. The issue has been debated in detail over the past fifteen years or so. For contrasting views, see Foster & Freed, *A Bill of Rights for Children*, 6 Family L.Q. 343 (1972); *Children and the Law – A Symposium*, 20 Cath. L. 85 (1974); Geiser, *The Rights of Children*, 28 Hastings L.J. 1027 (1977); Hafen, *Children's Liberation and the New Equalitarianism: Some Reservations About Abandoning Youth to Their 'Rights'*, [1976] Brigham Young U.L. Rev. 605; Schoeman, *Childhood Competence and Autonomy*, 12 J. of Legal Studies, 267 (1983).
5. In *The People (A.G.)* v. *Edge* [1943] I.R. 115, the Supreme Court held that the offence of kidnapping was not committed where a boy of 14 years of age consented to being taken by the defendant. The Court considered that the authorities established 14 as the age of discretion (at all events where the child was at that age 'capable of consenting or not consenting': [1943] I.R., at 141 (*per* Geoghegan, J.)). Until the age of discretion has been reached:

> there can be little, if any, doubt that a minor has not the capacity to consent; that consent can be given only by the guardian and consequently if there is not consent by the guardian the taking away is against the will of the minor. ([1943] I.R., at 138 (*per* Geoghegan, J.))

In *R.* v. *D.*, [1984] 1 All E.R. 574 (C.A. 1983), the English Court of Appeal took a different view. That case involved a prosecution for kidnapping by a father of his 2-year-old child. Watkins, L.J., having quoted from Geoghegan J.'s judgment in *Edge's* case on the question of minors under the age of fourteen years, said (at 581):–

> Whilst that would be a simple and convenient way of disposing of a difficult problem, it is not one which attracts itself to us. There are many children of well below that age who are mentally equipped to understand fully the implications of consenting to, for example, leave one parent and go away with the other. To put a parent in peril of being convicted of kidnapping when a child of, say, 12 years who fully understands what he or

she is doing when consenting to go away with that parent (because an age of discretion arbitrarily decided on by the court has not been reached) would, in our judgment, be wholly unjust. Moreover, we are strongly of the view that to leave to a jury the question of whether a young child has, or has not, consented to go away with a parent is undesirable and should not be done.

For one thing, it may, having regard to the age and disposition of the child, prove to be an impossible task and, for another, it would expose the child to the potentially harmful ordeal of giving evidence in a criminal trial when inevitably in a highly emotional state. The fact that children sometimes have to give evidence in sexual cases is no warrant for extending the need for this to be done. No judge who has had experience, in criminal and in family matters, of listening to children's evidence would, we believe, of his own volition countenance such a thing. The fact that a baby or a child of five years obviously cannot give any vestige of proper consent to being taken away is not a compelling reason, in our view, for introducing the notion that the will of a parent shall be regarded as the will of that child.

Lest it should be thought that we come to our conclusion with the problems arising out of matrimonial discord only in mind, we seek to make it clear that we regard our decision to be of general application. Accordingly, it will affect a person who is not a parent and who takes away a child.

This should dismay no one for, if the child is under 14 years of age, that person can be charged with child stealing contrary to S. 56 of the Offences against the Persons Act 1861, the maximum penalty for which is seven years imprisonment. If the child or youth is 14 years or over, it is unlikely that any harm would come to it by giving evidence on a charge of kidnapping and that a jury would find any extraordinary difficulty in evaluating that evidence.

For a penetrating critical analysis of *R.* v. *D.*, see Williams, *The Kidnapping of Children*, 134 New L.J. 276 (1984).

The question whether parents may (or must) provide a consent in relation to their children has arisen in connection with medical procedures: see B. McMahon & W. Binchy, *Irish Law of Torts*, 142–143 (1981), Skegg, *Consent to Medical Procedures on Minors*, 36 Modern L. Rev. 370 (1973), Wadlington, *Minors and Health Care: The Age of Consent*, 11 Osgoode Hall L.J. 115 (1973).

J. v. D.

Unreported, Supreme Court, 22 June 1977 (26–1977)

O'Higgins, C.J.:

In these proceedings the Plaintiff pursuant to the provisions of the *Guardianship of Infants Act, 1964* claims the sole custody of four infants. The Plaintiff is the father of these infants and in fact is the sole surviving parent. Two of the infants are at present living with the first-named Defendant. These are the two eldest who are girls. The youngest, another girl, lives with the second-named Defendant. The only boy who is the second youngest lives with the third-named Defendant. The three Defendants are sisters of the Plaintiff's late wife and are of course aunts of the infants. The Plaintiff's claim for custody having failed in the High Court before Mr. Justice Murnaghan, this appeal has been brought to this Court. It appears that the Plaintiff, who is English, married the late M, an Irish girl, on the 9th September 1961. The Plaintiff was a non-practising member of the Church of England, while M was a Catholic. The marriage took place in a Catholic church. The four infants the subject of these proceedings are the children of this marriage. The eldest [daughter], Y., was born [in] March 1963, [the next daughter] T, was born [in] June 1965 [the son] A, was born [in] September 1968 and [the youngest daughter] X, was born on the 20th June 1973. The children were baptised and brought up as Catholics. It appears that marital difficulties occurred between the Plaintiff and his wife in 1973 and in March of that year they had a month's separation by mutual consent. In July of the same year the Plaintiff's wife with the four children came to Ireland to her father's home. This was done with the consent of the Plaintiff who gave £140 to his wife to pay for the journey. While in Ireland the Plaintiff's wife decided not to return to England and wrote informing the Plaintiff of this decision. As a result he came to Ireland in September 1973. He appears to have met his wife's father but his wife was not willing to meet him. It is apparent that while in Ireland he regarded his relationship with his wife as at an end. On his return to England he went to live as a lodger with a Mr. and Mr. L. It appears that when he left the L house he had started a association with Mrs. L. who was the mother of four children. She left her home to follow him in December of 1973. She has in fact lived with him since. Mr. L, her husband, obtained a decree for divorce against her in 1974 citing the Plaintiff as co-respondent. Some time after going to live with the Plaintiff, Mrs. L. changed her name by deed poll to J. At this stage it appears from the evidence adduced before the learned trial Judge that the Plaintiff had accepted that his own marriage was at an end and he does not appear to have concerned himself in the slightest as to the welfare of his children or as to who would be caring for them. He lived with the former Mrs. L. and obviously was running an entirely new establishment of his own. On the 12th October 1975 the funeral. It appears that at the funeral he was not treated very civilly by his wife's family and that he felt badly about this. Whether on this account, or not, following his return to England he decided to institute these proceedings which were launched in July of 1976. On the 24th December of 1976 he married the former Mrs. L.

In these proceedings the Plaintiff claims the custody of his four infant children and, as already indicated, the claim is founded on the provisions of the *Guardianship of Infants Act, 1964*. Neither in this Court nor in the High Court, has any question been raised as to the validity of the *Guardianship of Infants Act* or any part thereof having regard to the provisions of the Constitution. It falls therefore to this Court to decide this appeal in accordance with the provisions of that Act and without regard to the difficult problems which could arise had its compatibility with the provisions of Article 41 of the Constitution been raised.

It is necessary, in my view, to note some of the provisions of the Act which appear to be relevant in the consideration of this appeal. Section 3 of the Act ordains that in proceedings such as these the Court must regard the welfare of the infant or infants concerned as the first and paramount consideration. Under Section 6 of the Act the Plaintiff as surviving parent is by the Section the guardian of these infants. However, by Section 8 sub-section (2) since the mother of the infants did not appoint a guardian to act jointly with him after her death the Court is empowered to do so. In the High Court the learned trial Judge exercised this power to appoint in respect of the infants in their care each of the Defendants. Each Defendant was accordingly appointed in respect of the infants for whom they accepted responsibility as joint guardian with the plaintiff. Under Section 11, on the application of a guardian of an infant, the Court is empowered to give such directions as it thinks proper with regard to the infant's custody and with regard to the right of access to the infant of either parent. Mr. Morris on behalf of the three Defendants, has asked that the Court, should it confirm the Defendants' appointments as joint guardians, to regard him as applying on their behalf for directions under Section 11. Section 14 provides, that where a parent of an infant applies to the Court for the custody of the infant and the Court is of opinion that he has abandoned the infant or has otherwise so conducted himself that the Court should refuse to enforce his right to custody the Court may decline in its discretion to make an order. Section 16 provides in very similar terms that where a parent has (a) abandoned an infant or (b) allowed an infant to be brought up by another or to be provided with assistance by a Health Authority for such length of time and under such circumstances as to satisfy the Court that the parent was unmindful of his duties, the Court shall not make an order, unless the parent satisfies the Court that he is a fit person to have custody. Under Section 14 there is a discretion. Under Section 16 there is none, if the Plaintiff fails to satisfy the Court that he is a fit person to have custody.

How do these provisions of the Act apply to the facts of this difficult case? Had there been no complicating factors the Plaintiff's rights as parent and surviving guardian of the infants to the custody of each of his children would as against everyone else, in my view, have been paramount and clear. In such circumstances no question could have arisen as to the welfare of the infants not being best served by being with their father. In this case however there are complicating factors. These factors are of such relevance and significance as drastically to alter the whole picture. In the first place there is the length of time that the infants have been living away from the Plaintiff in Ireland and in particular the time that has passed since each infant has found in effect a new home of its own. In addition, and very relevant on this claim under the *Guardianship of Infants Act*, is the conduct of the Plaintiff since he agreed to his infant children going to Ireland in 1973. I propose to examine each of these aspects of the case before expressing my view as to the manner in which the various provisions of the Act ought to be applied to the established facts.

Y is now aged 14, T is now aged 12. These two girls have been in Ireland since they were respectively 10 and 8 years of age. They have been living with the first-named Defendant and her husband since the 20th December 1973. The first-named Defendant has no family and both her husband and herself have provided for these two young girls a happy and a loving home. There is nothing to suggest that this will not continue and that these two girls if left where they are will not grow up in circumstances of domestic comfort and security. A is now aged 8½. He has been in Ireland since he was 4 years of age. Since the death of his mother he has been with the last-named Defendant who is married and who has three daughters. A suffers from asthma. He attends the local Christian Brothers' school. Again it is clear on the evidence that he is happy, is making progress in school, is treated by his aunt and her husband as if he were one of their own. Again it seems that the prospects are that A if left where he is will grow up in happy domestic surroundings. The youngest daughter X has been with the second-named Defendant and her husband since the 19th October 1975. This Defendant has no family. Again X is treated as if she were this Defendant's own daughter. She is happy and contented with her way of life, is at school and is getting on well. Again it does not seem open to question that X if left where she is will grow up in circumstances of domestic security and happiness.

As indicated, another complicating but relevant factor in this case is the conduct of the Plaintiff. It appears clear on the evidence that subsequent to his visit to Ireland in September 1973 the Plaintiff virtually abandoned his children to whatever fate would have in store for them. Initially he wrote and sent pocket money but this ceased probably as his affair with the then Mrs. L. developed around Christmas 1973. From that time on he ceased to bother or to enquire further for his children. This would appear to me to be a virtual declaration by him that his duty and responsibility for his children had ended when his relationship with his wife also came to an end. I do not think it unreasonable to regard this conduct or attitude by the Plaintiff as amounting to an abandonment of his infant children within the meaning of Section 14. Further, it seems to me that the Plaintiff prior to his first wife's death and subsequent thereto accepted a situation in which his children were being brought up by his wife's sisters and he did absolutely nothing to finance this operation or to defray even portion of the expenses. This seems to indicate that Section 16 of the Act can also apply.

In my opinion in this case the welfare of each infant is best served by refusing the order sought by the Plaintiff. For this reason alone in accordance with the provisions of Section 3 of the Act I would feel compelled to decide against the Plaintiff and to dismiss this appeal. I must add, however, that in my view the Plaintiff's claim ought to fail both under Section 14 and under Section 16 of the Act. In my view, the Plaintiff's conduct in relation to the infants would justify the Court in declining to make an order under each of these Sections. Accordingly, in my view, no order ought to be made on the Plaintiff's claim for custody and I agree with the view in this respect expressed by the learned trial Judge.

I think in addition that the learned trial Judge was correct when he exercised his powers under Section 8(2) of the Act to appoint each Defendant as joint guardian in respect of the infants under their respective care. I would approve and confirm the making of such orders. I would accept and act on Mr. Morris's indication that on behalf of each joint guardian so appointed he was applying for directions as to custody under Section 11 (2) (a) of the Act. I would direct that custody of Y and T be given to the first-named Defendant, of X to the second-named Defendant and of A to the third-named Defendant. I would in addition direct that appropriate facilities for access by the Plaintiff to his children be afforded by each Defendant. I would expect that the actual details with regard to such facilities can be worked out between the parties. However, if necessary this matter ought to be subject to further application to the High Court.

In my view this appeal ought to be dismissed.

Kenny, J.:

I have had the privilege of reading the judgment of the Chief Justice and I agree with him that the welfare of all the children to whom this case relates requires that they should remain where they now are. It would be monstrous to hand them over to their father: they have roots, a settled way of life and a feeling of security where they now are and unless I was compelled by the law to give them to their father, I would not do so. I have no doubt that giving them to their father would cause permanent psychological damage to them.

Counsel for the plaintiff relied strongly on the decision of the Irish Court of Appeal in *Re O'Hara* [1900] 2 I.R. 233 in support of his contention that there is a *prima facie* parental right to custody. I deny that there is any natural or *prima facie* right of a parent to custody of his children: there is a rule of prudence that in most cases the best place for a child is with its parent (*Reg.* v. *Gyngall* [1893] 2 Q.B. 243). It seems to me that *Re O'Hara* [1900] 2 I.R. 233 supports our decision in this case. The law on this matter was expressed by Lord Justice Holmes in his usual felicitous way:

> Previous to the passing of the Judicature Act a parent was held at Common Law to have as against strangers, an absolute right to the custody of his or her child of tender years, unless he or she had forfeited it by certain acts of misconduct. Accordingly in such case as the present, if the mother had before 1877, applied for a writ of habeas corpus, the only question to be considered would have been whether a right which prima facie belonged to her had been taken away by her own conduct, or by the provisions of an Act of Parliament. At the same time it did not follow that, although she might have succeeded at Common Law, she would be permitted to retain the possession of her daughter.
>
> The Court of Chancery, from time immemorial, has exercised another and distinguishable jurisdiction – a jurisdiction resting on the paternal authority of the Crown by virtue of which it can supersede the natural guardianship of a parent and can place a child in such custody as seems most calculated to promote the welfare.
>
> The Judicature Act introduced an important change in the principles upon which an application for a writ of habeas corpus in a case like the present is to be dealt with. Section 28 sub-s. 10 declares that in questions relating to the custody and education of infants the Rules of Equity shall prevail. The result of this is, that the Court to which the application is made must now place itself in the position in which the Lord Chancellor would be if the question of Harriet O'Hara's custody had arisen before him in a minor matter and decide (1) whether the mother by her conduct has disabled herself from making the application; and if she has not (2) whether it is more for the welfare of the child that she should remain in the home, and under the care, of the McMahons.

And in a later passage he says:

> A mother *prima facie* entitled as guardian by nurture, to the custody of her child may fail to make good her right to such custody, by 'reason of her own conduct or *where no valid objection can be taken thereto*, (italics mine) for reasons connected with the welfare of the child.

Substitute 'father' for 'mother' and these words apply to this case. The rule of prudence applies in the same way to a father as it does to a mother.

The Constitution has not in my opinion altered this. Article 41 deals with the Family: the children are part of that unit and the authority of the Family referred to Art. 41 [1.] 2[o] is that of the parents and children considered as a unit. It does not alter the principles stated by Lord Justice Holmes in disputes relating to custody. Counsel for the plaintiff when asked whether he wished to argue that s.3 of the *Guardianship of Infants Act, 1964* was repugnant to the Constitution, said that he did not.

Parke, J. concurred.

Notes

1. It would be desirable, in this context, to read *In re J., supra*, p. 110, *M.* v. *An Bord Uchtála, supra*, p. 406, and *G.* v. *An Bord Uchtála, supra*, p. 128. See also *Shatter*, 235ff.; Duncan, *Family Law – Custody of Children; Denial of Parental Rights*, [1978] Dublin U.L.J. 67; and the Irish Council for Civil Liberties Report No. 2 *Children's Rights Under the Constitution* (1977).
2. The question of the constitutionality of section 3 of the *Guardianship of Infants Act, 1964* was raised in the High Court decision of *P.W.* v. *A.W.*, unreported, Ellis, J., April 1980. Briefly the facts were as follows. In July, 1963 P.W. and his wife, A.W., were married. The couple had four children. A.W. developed a psychiatric illness eight years after the marriage, which required both in-patient and out-patient hospital treatment. The couple's relationship deteriorated from that time onwards. When the fourth child, a daughter, A, was born in 1974, the child went to live with P.W.'s sister, M., and her husband because A.W. was not able to cope. The idea originally was that this transfer should be temporary, until A.W.'s health improved but a few months later A.W. 'gave' the child to M. because, on account of her illness and its effects on her mental and physical health, she felt unable to cope with the requirements of caring for and bringing up the child. She felt that this could best be done by M. In 1976 P.W. and A.W. separated. The High Court in that year granted custody of A to M. After further inconclusive proceedings, during which A.W. was given access to the child, the case came for hearing in November 1979.

   A was then 5½ years old, and (the court held) regarded M. and her husband as her parents. In a long judgment (of 74 pages) Ellis, J. held that custody of the young girl should remain with M. The following passage from his judgment is worthy of particular attention:

   > In my opinion, I am not necessarily concerned with nor do I have to determine an issue of conflicting constitutional rights either as between A and her mother A.W., or between A in the custody of M and the constitutional recognition of the Family under Article 41.1.1° and 41.1.2° and 42.1. I am concerned to protect and uphold the infant's constitutional rights. In finding that this can best be achieved in the custody of M I do not think I am trespassing on the constitutional rights of A.W. or on the W. family. As already mentioned in the judgment of Walsh J. *in G.* v. *An Bord Uchtála*, there is nothing in the Constitution to indicate that in cases of apparent or alleged conflict the rights of a parent are always to be given primacy, but in any event as also stated in effect in Walsh J's judgment in that case . . . the natural (and constitutional) rights of A.W. in respect of A are preserved by her retention of her natural and statutory rights as A's guardian, even if custody be given to M. The statement in the *State (Nicolaou)* v. *An Bord Uchtála* [1966] I.R. 567, at 644 that the mother's right to the custody and care of her child was given constitutional protection by Article 40.3 of the Constitution, I do not regard as binding on me as it was not part of the *ratio decidendi* of the case and was not an issue, and in any event the guarantee given in the said Article 40.3, is a qualified one.
   >
   > If, however, there is a conflict between the constitutional rights of a legitimate child and the *prima facie* constitutional right of its mother to its custody, I am of opinion that the infant's rights which are to be determined by regard to what is required for its welfare, should prevail, even if its welfare is to be found in the custody of a 'stranger' if for good and justifiable reason, to be ascertained on the facts and in the circumstances of any particular case, valid objection can be taken to the mother's inability to provide for her child's welfare, either emanating from the mother herself or for reasons connected with the child's welfare, and not necessarily confined to failure by the parents (here A.W.) of their duty towards their children for physical or moral reasons, whereby the parents or as here the mother's custody would or could not vindicate, protect or be compatible with the child's constitutional rights including its welfare. Having regard to these conclusions I do not think it necessary for me to make a finding under Article 42.5 of the Constitution. If, however, such a finding may be regarded as necessary or material to the issues involved I hold that this is an exceptional case. I also hold that insofar as it was or is the duty of the parents, (and in the circumstances of this case, the duty of A.W.) to provide for the requirements of A specified in Article 42.1 or generally, that A.W. has failed in such for physical reasons. In my view the word 'physical' as used in Article 40.5 need not include intentional or purposeful reasons, and would include reasons of health, and hence would and does include the illness and all its detrimental effects and consequences already fully described, which have combined to prevent and render her unfit or unable to carry out her required duty or duties towards A and hence to have failed in such respect.
   >
   > I am helped in my view that an Order under Section 3 of the Act giving A into the custody of a stranger, M in furtherance of her welfare is not unconstitutional by having regard to the similarity in the wording of Article 42, 1. of the Constitution with the definition of 'welfare' in Section 2 of the Act. Such similarity accords with the view that the welfare of the child under the Act was intended to be of similar paramount consideration under the Constitution.
   >
   > Finally, it was held in *Re Frost Infants* [1947] I.R. 3 that the rights of parents are not absolute rights and that a child also had natural and imprescriptible rights of its own, and further that to afford protection to the rights of the child the Court regarded itself as having jurisdiction to control the exercise of parental rights. In my opinion, the inalienable and imprescriptible rights of the family under Article 41 of the Constitution attach to

each member of a family including the children. Therefore in my view the only way the 'inalienable and imprescriptible' and 'natural and imprescriptible' rights of the child can be protected is by the Courts treating the welfare of the child as the paramount consideration in all disputes as to its custody, including disputes between a parent and a stranger. I take the view also that the child has the personal right to have its welfare regarded as the paramount consideration in any such dispute as to its custody under Article 40.3 and that this right of the infant can additionally arise from 'the Christian and democratic nature of the State'. See *Ryan*-v-*The Attorney General* [1965] I.R. 294 (Supreme Court) and the judgment of Kenny J. in the High Court in this case. See also *O'Brien*-v-*Keogh* [1972] I.R. 144 (Supreme Court) and the judgment of Ó Dálaigh, C.J. at page 155 thereof. . . .

3. Do you think that the Constitutional issue was squarely faced and resolved in *P.W.* v. *A.W.?*
4. Would it be fair to say that the *Guardianship of Infants Act, 1964* can be consistent with Articles 41 and 42 of the Constitution only if these Articles constitute nothing to disturb the straightforward application of the welfare criterion with absolutely *no* qualifications?
5. Another case dealing with a dispute between a parent and a relation (on this occasion a grandmother) is *O'N.* v. *O'B.* unreported, High Ct., Finlay, P., January 1980 (1979 No. 503 SP.) See also *M.* v. *M.*, unreported, High Ct., Murphy, J., 2 December 1982 (1982–457 S.S.), involving a dispute between the mother of a child born outside marriage and the mother's parents who had custody of the child. Murphy, J. held that the child's welfare required that the mother be given custody, in spite of the exemplary conduct of her parents. Murphy, J. observed (at p. 25):

   . . . I bear in mind the presumption of law that the constitutional rights of the infant to welfare are ordinarily best served by entrusting the custody of [a non-marital] child to its natural mother.

6. In *P.G.* v. *C.G. & C.G.* v. *P.G.*, unreported, High Ct., Finlay, P., 12 March 1982, a marriage of two teenagers, brought about by the girl's pregnancy, was followed by separation about 18 months later. From birth, their infant son had spent most of his time with his paternal grandparents. Finlay, P. directed that the child, now 19 months old, should:

   be given into the custody of [his] mother: that the child and mother should continue to reside with [the mother's] parents and that the child should not be brought to live in any other place in Dublin and should not be brought outside the jurisdiction of this Court.

   Is it appropriate that custody of a child should be made conditional on a parent residing with particular people? If the welfare of the child is the test, what right has the parent to complain about restrictions on liberties of movement and association – even if these liberties are constitutionally protected? Cf. Freed & Foster, *Family Law in the Fifty States: An Overview*, 17 Family L.Q. 365, at 371 (1984). In the same article, at 430–438, Freed & Foster discuss recent trends in legislation in several States towards conferring access ('visitation') rights on grandparents in relation to their grandchildren. See also Zaharooff, *Access to Children: Towards a Model Statute for Third Parties*, 15 Family L.Q. 165 (1981).
7. For consideration of the position where a parent seeking custody of a child may be suffering from some form of mental illness, see Marmquist, *The Role of Parental Mental Illness in Custody Proceedings*, 2 Family L.Q. 360 (1968).

Interjurisdictional Aspects

O'D. INFANTS: O'D. v. O'D.

Unreported, High Court, Hamilton, J., 13/14/22 June 1979, as summarised in 73 Incorporated Law Society Gazette, No. 6 (July–August 1979)

This case arose from the removal in March 1979 of three infant children from the custody of their mother (the Plaintiff) in Alberta, Canada, by their father (the Defendant) who brought them to Ireland.

The Plaintiff and Defendant were married in Calgary, Alberta, in April 1965, the Plaintiff being a native of Alberta and the Defendant being a native of Derry. There were three children of the marriage, born in May 1966, May 1968 and April 1970 respectively. The Defendant was a university lecturer and the Plaintiff was employed in data processing. During the course of the marriage the Plaintiff and the Defendant lived at first in Calgary, and later in New Mexico, USA, then in Durham, England, and then again in New Mexico.

Matrimonial difficulties arose and by the year 1974 the marriage appeared to have broken down. The Plaintiff left the matrimonial home in New Mexico, taking the three children with her, and returned to Alberta. She resided continuously in Calgary with the three children from that time up to the present. The Defendant continued to live in New Mexico and visited the children from time to time but they did not leave the jurisdiction of Alberta and the Defendant at no time sought custody of them. he did, however, maintain contact with them by letter, took an interest in their education, and knew what schools they attended. The Plaintiff did not oppose this continuing relationship.

In March 1974, virtually immediately after leaving the matrimonial home, the Plaintiff applied to the Supreme Court of Alberta for a decree of judicial separation and an order granting her custody of the three children. On the 12 March 1974 she was granted an interim custody order. On the 2 December 1974 she was granted a decree of judicial separation and an order granting her custody of the three children. The Plaintiff stated that all these orders had been served on the Defendant, but the Defendant maintained throughout the proceedings that he had never been served with them.

In 1977 the Defendant applied to the New Mexican courts for a divorce. The Plaintiff, on the advice of her Canadian lawyers, did not contest the divorce, and the New Mexican court granted the Final Decree of Dissolution on the 30 March 1977. In this decree the New Mexican court granted joint custody of the three children to both parents, but ordered that the principal place of residence of the children should be with the mother. [It might well be questioned whether under the normal Private International Law rules the New Mexican court had at that date jurisdiction to deal with the custody of the children, but this question did not arise in the Irish proceedings.]

On the 1 December 1978 in a civil ceremony in New Mexico, the Defendant married his second wife who was also of Irish origin, and they continued to reside in New Mexico.

On the 16th March the Defendant intercepted the three children as they went to their different schools in Calgary and drove them across the border into the United States. He brought them to New Mexico where they remained with the Defendant and his second wife for approximately two weeks.

On the 29 March 1979 the Defendant and his second wife brought the three children to Ireland, where they took up residence with the Defendant's mother in Dublin. The Plaintiff attempted to contact the children by telephone from Canada but the Defendant refused her both custody of the children and access to them. On the 19 April 1979 the Plaintiff applied to the Supreme Court of Alberta for a further order granting her custody of the children and this order was granted.

On the 5 June 1979 the Plaintiff came to Ireland to seek custody of the children. She applied for an order of Habeas Corpus ad Subjiciendum and subsequently instituted proceedings under Section 11 of the Guardianship of Infants Act, 1964. A conditional order of Habeas Corpus was granted by the High Court (Hamilton J.) on the 9 June 1979, returnable on the 13 June 1979. At the hearing Defendant argued that the Plaintiff was an unsuitable person to have custody of the children on account of the condition of her home, her alleged alcoholism, and other factors. The Plaintiff argued that the children should be returned in her custody to Alberta, which was the proper jurisdiction to deal with the custody of the children being the jurisdiction with which they had close and continued connection. Reference was made to the following authorities: *Re H (Infants)* [1965] 3 All ER 906 and [1966] 1 All ER 886; *Re E (an infant)* [1967] 2 All ER 881; *Re T (Infants)* [1968] 3 All ER 411; *S. v. S.* (1978 unreported judgment of Finlay P.); *A. v. H.* (1978 unreported judgment of D'Arcy J.).

The Court reviewed the orders concerning the custody of the children which had been made by the courts of Alberta and New Mexico, and dealt with the desirability of the discouragement by all courts of the forcible removal of minors from one jurisdiction to another in situations which amounted to kidnapping.

Held (per Hamilton J.) that the proper forum to decide questions concerning the custody of the children was the Supreme Court of Alberta and that, providing the Irish Court was assured that no direct harm would come to the children thereby, they should be returned to the custody of the Plaintiff. In order to ascertain whether any direct harm would come to the children through their being returned to Alberta in the custody of the Plaintiff, the Court directed a psychiatric examination of the children and of the Plaintiff and the Defendant.

Postscript: In the event, subsequent to the psychiatric examination, the parties reached a settlement whereby the children were to remain in the Plaintiff's custody in Canada during all school terms, but were to visit the Defendant in Ireland, where he planned to remain, during vacations. The Defendant was to make periodical payments to the Plaintiff for the maintenance of the children, and it was agreed that all future applications concerning custody and access by made to the Courts of Alberta. The terms of this settlement were noted by the High Court in its order.

Note

For consideration of more recent English decisions, taking a somewhat different approach, see Cole, *Judicial Discretion in Child-Snatching Cases*, 129 New L.J.64 (1979).

NORTHAMPTON COUNTY COUNCIL v. A.B.F. and M.B.F.

[1982] I.L.R.M. 164 (High Ct., Hamilton, J., 1981)

Hamilton, J.:

I do not propose in the course of this judgment to deal with the facts in such a way or in such detail as to identify the infant child who is the subject matter of this application. They are adequately set forth in the affidavit filed on behalf of the applicant and the exhibits therein referred to and the affidavit of the notice party, the father of the infant child, who was born on 24 September 1977.

Briefly stated, the plaintiffs claim is for the return of the infant child to their duly appointed agent, the child having been wrongfully and illegally removed from the jurisdiction of the English courts and brought within the jurisdiction of this Court by her lawful father, who is a notice party to these proceedings, and placed in the temporary care of the defendants.

It is quite clear that if the infant child is returned to the applicants or their agent, it is proposed that she be legally adopted in spite of the wishes of her father and his lack of consent, indeed his opposition, to this proposed course. The infant child's mother appears to be willing to have the child adopted.

Under English law the position appears to be that, in certain circumstances, a child though born of lawfully married parents may, without the consent of the parents, be placed for and legally adopted.

Having regard to the orders made by the Kettering Juvenile Court, placing the infant child in the care of the applicants and the degree of comity which exists between the courts of these relevant jurisdictions, I would in the ordinary course have granted the application made on behalf of the applicants herein, both parents being English citizens who married in England, were domiciled in England and whose only child, the infant herein, was born in England and having regard to the fact that the infant had been unlawfully removed from the jurisdiction of the English courts, without considering the merits of the case.

I have however already refused the application made on behalf of applicants because the effect of granting the order sought by the applicants would have been that the infant child would have been adopted without the consent and in spite of the opposition of his lawful father, a development which is not permissible under the Irish law of adoption. . . . [Hamilton, J. quoted Article 41,1. of the Constitution. He continued:]

Counsel on behalf of the applicants has submitted and argued that only citizens of the State are entitled to the protection afforded by this Article and that it is not open to the father of the infant in this case to rely on its provisions, particularly as he had illegally taken the infant out of the jurisdiction of the English courts and into this jurisdiction.

With this submission I cannot agree. Walsh, J. stated in the course of his judgment in *McGee v Attorney General* [1974] I.R. 284, at 310:

> Articles 40, 41, 42 and 44 of the Constitution all fall within that section of the Constitution which is called 'Fundamental Rights'. Articles 41, 42 and 43 emphatically reject the theory that there are no rights without laws, no rights contrary to law and no rights anterior to law. They indicate that justice is placed above the law and acknowledge that natural rights, or human rights, are not created by law but that the Constitution confirms their existence and gives them protection. The individual has natural and human rights over which the State has no authority: and the Family as the natural primary and fundamental group of society has rights as such which the State cannot control.

At page 317 he continued: 'The natural or human rights to which I have referred earlier in this judgment are part of what is generally called the natural law'.

In the course of his judgment in *G v An Bord Uchtála* [1980] I.R. 32 he stated that he still held these views, with which I am in complete agreement.

The Supreme Court in *The State (Nicolau) v An Bord Uchtála* [1966] I.R. 567 expressly reserved for another and more appropriate case consideration of the effect of non-citizenship upon the interpretation of the Articles in question.

It seems to me however that non-citizenship can have no effect on the interpretation of Article 41 or the entitlement to the protection afforded by it.

What Article 41 does is to recognise the Family as the natural primary and fundamental unit group of society and as a moral institution possessing inalienable and imprescriptible rights antecedent and superior to all positive law, which rights the State cannot control. In the words of Walsh, J. already quoted, 'these rights are part of what is generally called the natural law' and as such are antecedent and superior to all positive law.

The natural law is of universal application and applies to all human persons, be they citizens of this State or not, and in my opinion it would be inconceivable that the father of the infant child would not be entitled to rely on the recognition of the Family contained in Article 41 for the purpose of enforcing his rights as the lawful father of the infant the subject matter of the proceeding herein or that he should lose such entitlement merely because he removed the child to this jurisdiction for the purpose of enforcing his said rights.

These rights are recognised by Bunreacht na h-Éireann and the courts created under it as antecedent and superior to all positive law: they are not so recognised by the law or the courts of the jurisdiction to which it is sought to have the infant returned.

Consequently it is for these reasons that I have at this stage refused to grant the orders sought by the applicant herein viz. that the child be returned to them or their agent.

The child however also has natural rights. As stated by the Chief Justice in *G v An Bord Uchtála* [1980] I.R., at 561, 'Having been born, the child has the right to be fed and to live, to be reared and educated, to have the opportunity of working and of realising his or her full personality and dignity as a human being. These rights of the child (and others which I have not enumerated) must equally be protected and vindicated by the State.'

It will be necessary therefore to have a full plenary hearing of this application for the purpose of ascertaining whether the child's rights are being protected before any final order can be made in this case.

Notes and Questions

1. If the Constitution affords protection to foreign families, may the members of these families, by coming to Ireland and raising the matter in judicial proceedings, seek protection under our Constitution from foreign legislation (or the practical administration or execution of the provisions of that legislation) which may not be in

harmony with our Constitution? Is this not what Hamilton J. has held in *Northampton County Council* v. *A.B.F. & M.B.F.?*

2. Is it proper that our Constitution should be capable of being invoked by foreigners who have no connection with Ireland?
3. Assuming that the Constitution may be invoked by foreigners in at least some circumstances, what limitations should there be?
4. On the question whether the Constitution protects non-citizens, see J. Kelly, *The Irish Constitution*, 374–375 (1980); Binchy, *The Need for a Constitutional Amendment*, ch. 11 of A. Flannery ed., *Abortion and the Law*, at 118–119 (1983). Professor Robert Heuston has noted that:–

> The phrase 'of the citizen' has given rise to difficulties [in Article 40.3] and elsewhere throughout the fundamental rights Articles. . . . The Supreme Court seems to be uncertain whether the constitutional guarantees protect aliens. [*State (Nicolaou) v. Attorney General* [1966] I.R. 567, at 599, 645] although in one case on the matter (*Re Singer*) [97 I.L.T.R. 130 (1963)] in which the issue might have arisen, counsel for the State expressly disclaimed any reliance on it. Clearly it would be very embarrassing for the Court, especially since the State has joined the European Economic Community, to be obliged to hold that an alien was not entitled to the same degree of protection as a citizen. On the other hand, simply as a matter of interpretation of words, it is very difficult to see how the word 'citizen' can be held to mean 'any person whether a citizen or an alien'. *Personal Rights Under the Irish Constitution*, 11 U. Br. Columbia L. Rev. 294, at 304 (1977).

5. In a stimulating commentary on the *Northampton* decision, Mr. Paul O'Connor refers to Article 29(3) of the Constitution, whereby Ireland accepts the generally recognised principles of international law as its rule of conduct in its relations with other States. Mr. O'Connor observes that:–

> It is arguable that one of these principles is that the *forum conveniens* should be permitted to settle disputes between parties. *'Kidnapping' and the Irish Courts*, 2 Ir. L.T. (n.s.) 4, at 4 (1984).

Cf. J. Kelly, *The Irish Constitution*, 181–184 (2nd ed., 1984).

6. Mr. O'Connor (*op. cit.*, at 4) also makes a jurisprudential point:

> Is it possible for the citizens of this jurisdiction to alter the natural law of constitutional amendment? If natural law is antecedent and superior to all positive law it suggests that an amendment purporting to alter the Constitution, in violation of the natural law, would not be valid.

KENT COUNTY COUNCIL v. C.S.

Unreported, High Ct., Finlay, P., 9 June 1983 (1983–290 S.S.)

Finlay, P.:

This application was brought before me by the Kent County Council ex-parte and stated originally to be an application under the *Habeas Corpus Act, 1872* seeking an order for the return by C.S. (hereinafter referred to as the Respondent) of the Infant S.S. (hereinafter referred to as the Infant) to the custody of the Applicants, the Kent County Council, and for such further order as the Court might direct.

I treated the application as seemed to me more appropriate as an application for an enquiry as to the legality of the detention of the Infant by the Respondent under Article 40 of the Constitution and the Applicants agreed to that course. I thereupon made an order directing the Respondent to appear before me on the 18th of May 1983 and to justify his detention of the Infant.

The Respondent appeared before me on that day, stated that he had applied for legal aid in order to contest the application of the Applicants, the Kent County Council, and upon his giving to me certain undertakings, that is to say, (1) not to take the Infant out of the City of Dublin and (2) not to apply for a passport or visa or to apply to have the Infant entered on his own passport, I adjourned the matter to Tuesday, 7th June, before me to permit the Respondent to prepare and present his case.

The matter came before me on the 7th June 1983 and I considered the Affidavit and Exhibits filed on behalf of the Applicant and the Respondent who was then represented by Solicitor and Counsel gave oral evidence and was cross-examined.

The material facts relating to the issues before me are not in dispute as between the evidence tendered on behalf of the Applicants and that tendered on behalf of the Respondent and I find them to be as follows.

The Respondent who is now 47 years of age has resided in England since 1956 and is an Irish citizen. Immediately prior to going to England in 1956 the Respondent married in Dublin and thereafter lived and worked in England. There were 5 children of this marriage, all of whom are now grown up. His then wife sought a divorce from him in the English courts in 1971 and was granted a decree of divorce. The Applicant then lived for some years with a married lady, Mrs. W. as she then was, and on his own evidence had 3 children by her. He apparently ceased to reside with her in or about the year 1975 and she has since remarried and is now known as Mrs. S.

In September 1979 the Respondent entered into another marriage, he then being 43 years of age and his then wife being just over 16 years of age. Of that marriage the Infant in this case was born on the 2nd September 1980. The Respondent alleges that his wife was erratic and unstable in her behaviour even prior to the birth of the Infant and became more so afterwards and he suggests that she neglected the Infant and he was much involved in its bringing up and welfare.

The Infant's mother left the Respondent eventually in the middle of June 1981 and though the Respondent's evidence on this aspect of the case, in the light of cross-examination concerning an apparent later attempt at reconciliation, was not particularly satisfactory for practical purposes they have not resided together as man and wife since that time. Approximately two weeks prior to the date on which the Infant's mother left home, the Respondent states that by reason of her failure to attend in the home that he had placed the Infant in the household and under the care of Mrs. S. with whom he had formerly lived. The Respondent states that he was still on good terms with Mrs. S. and with her present husband Mr. S. and he daily visited the Infant and saw him during all that time. An application was made by the Respondent to the Magistrates Court in England concerning the custody and access to the Infant and it came on for a preliminary hearing before the end of 1981, when a date was fixed in mid-February 1982 for a full hearing. In the intervening period, access arrangements were operated to some extent under the supervision of the Magistrates Court for the mother of the Infant and for its maternal grandmother who is still residing in England. At the commencement of February 1982 the mother of the Infant took it during one of these periods of access and brought it out of the jurisdiction of the English courts to Switzerland.

The Infant was returned to England by the mother in May of 1982 and was immediately again placed, apparently by the Respondent, in the daily custody and care of Mrs. S.

The Respondent having petitioned the courts in England for a divorce against the mother of the Infant an order was made on the 17th of August 1982 providing that the mother of the Infant was to be allowed to have certain access to the Infant who was at that time still in the custody and daily control of Mrs. S. and providing that the Social Services Department of the Kent County Council should be at liberty to apply on 48 hours notice with regard to the access arrangements provided by that order. On the 10th of November 1982 the Kent County Council applied in the divorce proceedings to intervene for the purpose of applying for an order committing the Infant to the care of Kent County Council pursuant to Section 43.1 of the *Matrimonial Causes Act, 1973* the English statute applicable. The Infant from August 1982 up to the 18th January 1983 remained in the daily custody and care of Mrs. S. with, I am satisfied, relatively constant access to the Respondent and with arranged access to his mother which was the subject matter of dispute between the parties. The divorce proceedings proper came before the High Court in England and was heard on the 13th, 14th, 17th and 18th of January 1983. At the conclusion of the hearing, His Honour Judge Callman made an order granting to the Respondent herein, who was the Petitioner in those proceedings, a decree of divorce *nisi* and made an order that the Infant should 'remain in the care of the Kent County Council with leave to place the child with the Respondent for staying access and in view to rehabilitation with the Respondent in the event of the Kent County Council deciding that care and control can be entrusted to the Respondent'. The Respondent referred to in this Order is, of course, the infant's mother. It was further ordered that access to the child be at the discretion of the local authority and that the access be supervised. It was further ordered that the child be not removed from England and Wales without leave of the court until he attained the age of 18 years and that the Respondent herein, the Petitioner in those proceedings, should not contact the Respondent in those proceedings, the mother of the Infant in any way save through the Kent County Council or through his solicitors until further order of the court. From the Schedule to the Order made in the English court which is exhibited before me, it is clear that affidavits were filed on behalf of the parties by other witnesses, such as Mrs. S. [and] by members of the staff of the Social Services and Social Welfare Section of the Kent County Council and that the court had before it a series of Court Welfare Officers reports together with a Medical Report.

From the Respondent's evidence, it would appear that immediately after the making of that order, officials of the Social Welfare Section of the Kent County Council called to Mrs. S. for the purpose of taking custody of the child and presumably for the purpose of placing it in appropriate care. The Respondent was present and informed the officials concerned that he had instructed his solicitors to apply for a stay of the order made by His Honour Judge Callman pending an appeal by him. It was then agreed apparently by the solicitors and parties acting in the case that without the necessity for returning to court a stay would in fact be put into operation and the child was left in the care and custody of Mrs. S. This is referred to in an affidavit filed on behalf of the Kent County Council as placing the child in the care of Mrs. S. The Respondent did not appeal against the order made by Mr. Justice Callman.

In March of 1983 the Respondent took the infant from the custody of Mrs. S., asserting or pretending to her that he intended to bring it to visit a brother of his who resided in England, and brought it home to this country to the house of his parents in the north side of the City of Dublin where it is presently residing.

He stated in evidence to me that he did so because he believed that under the orders of the English courts he would not be able to retain control of and custody and a proper link with the infant and that it could be placed away in someone else's care or even given in adoption.

The Respondent lost his employment in September of 1981, he states as a result of the disturbance in his life created by the break-up of his marriage and his consequent absences from work and has not since been employed. The Respondent admitted that in 1972 he was convicted of an offence associated with disputes arising from the break-up of his first marriage in which he wrote letters stating that the court was seeking to destroy him and that he would destroy his then ex-wife. It was put to him that the conviction was in respect of a threat to murder his ex-wife but he stated that the Judge in imposing upon him a sentence of one year's imprisonment in respect of that conviction stated that he had done so by reason of his attitude to the court. He also admitted having been convicted on a later occasion in 1975 of disorderly conduct and obstructing a police constable in the execution of his duty. The Respondent is at present residing with the Infant in the house of his parents . . . [H]is mother [is 76] . . . and . . . his father [is 78]. There are no other members of the Respondent's immediate family residing in Ireland, though he has got 3 brothers residing in England.

On these facts, Counsel on behalf of the Respondent has urged that the Respondent is entitled to a Constitutional right pursuant to Articles 41 and 42 of the Constitution to be regarded as the family in relation to the Infant and as such to take the responsibility for the up-bringing and education of the Infant and that he should not be deprived of that right in favour of what is in this submission described as a stranger except for the gravest of reasons consisting of a dereliction of duty by him and an immediate danger or hazard to the Infant. He has relied upon the decision of the Supreme Court [*sic*] in *Re J.M.* [1966] I.R. 295 and on [the] judgment of Hamilton J. in *Northampton County Council* v. *A.B.F.* and *M.B.F.*, [*supra*, p. 470]. Counsel on behalf of the Applicants submit that this is clearly a 'kidnapping' case and that the ordinary principle should be applied in it whereby the courts of the country in which the Infant was born, in which the parties resided during their marriage so long as it lasted and in which it is clear on the evidence it was intended that the Infant should be brought up are the appropriate courts for the determination of the welfare of the Infant.

He relies in particular on the fact that the Respondent, upon the break-up of the marriage, sought and invited the exercise by the English courts of their jurisdiction and did so as a person domiciled in England which would be a necessary pre-requisite to his obtaining a decree of divorce in that country; that only after he had exhausted those remedies in a full hearing when all the matters which were being canvassed, on one side to some extent only before me, were canvassed before the English court did he then on his own admission take the child out of the jurisdiction of those courts in plain contempt of and breach of an order of the court for the specific purpose of obtaining a different decision with regard to the custody and care of the child in these courts. He also relies on the fact that after the removal by the Respondent of the Infant out of the jurisdiction of the English courts, the Infant was made a Ward of those courts and a specific order made on the wardship side directing his return and the determination of his custody and welfare in those courts. I am satisfied that the only reasonable interpretation of the orders made within the jurisdiction of England with regard to the custody and care of this Infant is that those courts were hoping or expecting that it might be possible to place the child in the long-term care of its mother with appropriate access to its father. The child is now under 3 years of age; his mother is just approaching 20 years of age and his father is now 47 years of age. Taken in its broadest and most usual sense the family in which the Infant is a member has broken up and it is not possible any longer for the courts of this country or indeed for the courts of England to provide a unified right to the family to educate and bring up this child as a close or united family unit.

The witnesses who are material to the long-term question of the welfare of this Infant consisting of the persons who have had direct personal knowledge of the care and control of the Infant such as Mrs. S., the mother of the Infant, possibly his maternal grandmother and officers of the Social Welfare Section of Kent County Council are not ordinarily amenable to be brought before the courts in this country, nor have I any jurisdiction to force any of these persons other than the Respondent to give evidence here who do not wish to do so. The entire legal framework as a result of which this child was born of a lawful marriage in England and as a result of which a decree *nisi* in divorce has been granted in England concerning that marriage is a legal framework which is no[t] known to the law of this country. With the exception of his paternal grandparents who are aged 76 and 78 respectively and of the Respondent himself who has come to this country for the purpose which I have outlined, all the relations of the Infant consisting of uncles or consisting of his half-brothers and sisters are resident in England.

I am satisfied that there is not in this case any immediate intention on the part of the Kent County Council nor indeed any threat made by them to place this Infant for adoption with adoptive parents against the wishes of his mother and father. That, I am satisfied, is the fundamental underlying principle for the decision made by Mr. Justice Hamilton in the case of the *Northampton County Council* v. *A.B.F. and M.B.F.* [*supra*, p. 470] to which I was referred. In that case, it was the plain and immediate intention of the

County Council into whose care the child had been placed by the English courts to place it for adoption and that was against the consent of the father. The child was the child of a lawful marriage and in this country could not have been adopted either with or without the consent of the father. It was in those circumstances and I am satisfied that Mr. Justice Hamilton ordered a full plenary hearing of the merits from the point of view of the welfare of the child of the application of the County Council.

Having regard to my view of the facts of this case and the fundamental importance of the appropriate forum for the determination of the future welfare of this child being the courts in the country in which it was born and intended to be brought up, I am satisfied that there is no question of a deprivation of any of the Constitutional rights relied upon by the Respondent which should prevent me from applying the principle which I understand to be appropriate in relation to the comity between courts and in making an order for the return of the child to the care of the Kent County Council who must only deal with it in accordance with the determination of the English courts to which the Respondent who has originally invoked their jurisdiction has full access. I therefore make the order for the return of the child.

Notes

1. Does this case hold (a) that the respondent's Constitutional rights as father and as a member of a Family *had not* been infringed? (b) that there rights *would not* be infringed by an order returning the child to England? (c) that, whether or not the respondent's Constitutional rights were affected by an order returning the child to England, this order should be made on the basis of principles of private international law? Or does the case hold something entirely different on the question of the respondent's Constitutional rights?
2. See also *The State (K.M. & R.D.)* v. *Minister for Foreign Affairs, supra*, p. 152, *Re Medley, A Minor*, I.R. 6 Eq. 339 (Chy., 1871).
3. Several efforts have been made at international level to deal with the problem of international and inter-jurisdictional child abduction. In October 1980, the Hague Converence on Private International Law adopted a *Convention on the Civil Aspects of International Child Abduction*. For commentary on the Convention see Anton, *The Hague Convention on International Child Abduction*, 30 Int. & Comp. L.Q. 537 (1981); Bodenheimer, *The Hague Draft Convention on International Child Abduction*, 14 Family L.Q. 98 (1980); Farquhar, *The Hague Convention on International Child Abduction Comes to Canada*, 4 Can. J. of Family L. 5 (1983).

   The purpose of the Convention is to ensure that where children have been abducted from one country to another, they should, as a general rule, be returned to the country where they were habitually resident before the adoption. The central provisions are to be found in Articles 3, 12, 13 and 20. Article 13 provides that the removal or retention of a child is to be considered wrongful where:

   (a) it is in breach of rights of custody attributed to a person, an institution or any other body, either jointly or alone, under the law of the State in which the child was habitually resident immediately before the removal or retention; and
   (b) at the time of removal or retention those rights were actually exercised, either jointly or alone, or would have been so exercised but for the removal or retention.

   Article 12 provides that:

   > Where a child has been wrongfully removed or retained in terms of Article 3 and, at the date of the commencement of the proceedings before the judicial or administrative authority of the Contracting State where the child is, a period of less than one year has elapsed from the date of the wrongful removal or retention, the authority concerned shall order the return of the child forthwith.
   >
   > The judicial or administrative authority, even where the proceedings have been commenced after the expiration of the period of one year referred to in the preceeding paragraph, shall also order the return of the child, unless it is demonstrated that the child is now settled in its new environment.
   >
   > Where the judicial or administrative authority in the requested State has reason to believe that the child has been taken to another State, it may stay the proceedings or dismiss the application for the return of the child.

   Article 13 permits a number of exceptions to the rules prescribed in Article 12; it provides that:

   > Notwithstanding the provision of the preceeding Article, the judicial or administrative authority of the requested State is not bound to order the return of the child if the person, institution or other body which opposes its return establishes that:–

(a) the person, institution or other body having the care of the person of the child was not actually exercising the custody rights at the time of removal or retention, or had consented to or subsequently acquiesced in the removal or retention; or

(b) there is a grave risk that his or her return would expose the child to physical or psychological harm or otherwise place the child in an intolerable situation.

The judicial or administrative authority may also refuse to order the return of the child if it finds that the child objects to being returned and has attained an age and degree of maturity at which it is appropriate to take account of its views.

In considering the circumstances referred to in this Article, the judicial and administrative authorities shall take into account the information relating to the social background of the child provided by the Central Authority or other competent authority of the child's habitual residence.

Finally it is worth noting Article 20, which provides that the return of the child under the provisions of Article 12

may be refused if this would not be permitted by the fundamental principles of the requested State relating to the protection of human rights and fundamental freedom.

Should the Convention become part of Irish law? Article 20 raises some interesting issues relating to the Constitution. Do Articles 40 and 41 contain 'fundamental principles' relating to 'the protection of human rights and fundamental freedoms'? If so, of what relevance are *Northampton County Council* v. *A.B.F. & M.B.F.* and *Kent County Council* v. *C.S.* to the practical application of the central provisions of the Convention in the Irish Context?

4. Court tort law provides a useful supplement to proceedings under the *Guardianship of Infants Act, 1964* where one parent (or someone acting on his or her behalf) 'kidnaps' the child from the other parent? In its *First Report on Family Law*, p. 15 (LRC 1–1981), the Law Reform Commission recommended that a tort action for enticement should lie in such circumstances. In the United States, some courts have favoured imposition of liability in tort, whether for false imprisonment, imposition of emotional suffering or otherwise: see *Fenslage* v. *Dawkins*, 629 F. 2d 1107 (5th Cir. 1980), *Kajtazi* v. *Kajtazi*, 488 F. Supp. 15 (E.D.N.Y. 1978); but see *Friedman* v. *Friedman*, 79 Misc. 2d 646, 361 N.Y.S. 2d 108 (1974). Cf. Campbell, Comment: *The Tort of Custodial Interference – Toward a More Complete Remedy to Parental Kidnapping*, [1983] U. Illinois L. Rev. 229. Katz, *Legal Remedies for Child Snatching*, 15 Family L.Q. 103, at 114–117 (1981). A tort action for enticement may also, of course, be invoked by parents in some cases where their child is induced to leave the family to join a religious or quasi-religious cult. But may a tort action by invoked *against* parents who forcibly remove their children from religious cults and seek to convince them of the falsity of the tenets of the cults? Cf. *Peterson* v. *Sorelien*, 299 N.W. 2d 123 (Minn. 1980), cert. denied, 450 U.S. 1031 (1981) (action for false imprisonment failed). See also Bates, *Child Law and Religious Extremists: Some Recent Developments*, 10 Ottawa L. Rev. 299, at 299–303 (1978). For a comprehensive analysis of the legal and policy aspects, see Aronin, Cults, *Deprogramming, and Guardianship: A Model Legislative Proposal*, 17 Colum. J. of Law & Social Problems 163 (1982). Wardship proceedings should not be discounted: see *infra*, ch. 16.

5. See also *Cosgrove* v. *Ireland, the Minister for Foreign Affairs & the Attorney General,* [1982] I.L.R.M. p. 103 (High Ct., McWilliam, J. 1981), where damages were awarded for interference with the plaintiff's guardianship rights: passports had been wrongfully issued to his young children at his wife's request, without consulting him and contrary to his wishes; as a result, the plaintiff's wife left the country and the plaintiff's relationship with his children was effectively ended.

Chapter 16

WARDS OF COURT

It has recently been said by the authors of a comprehensive study on the subject that '[t]he law knows no greater form of protection than wardship': N. Lowe & R. White *Wards of Court*, 1 (1979). Historically, however, wardship had a somewhat less noble function. It was originally a feudal incident of tenure arising when a tenant died leaving an infant heir. The lord became guardian of the heir's land and property. Although the lord was obliged to maintain and educate the ward, and look after his land, he was entitled to keep the profits of the land until the heir came of age. Moreover, he had important influence over his heir's choice of marriage partner: *id.* See also Cross, *Wards of Court*, 83 L. Q. Rev. 200, at 200–202 (1967).

Over the centuries the Court of Wards, and later the Court of Chancery, developed an active role in protecting the personal and property interests of wards. Today jurisdiction over wards of Court is vested in the President of the High Court and in the Circuit Court. Wardship proceedings may be commenced by a third party even though the parents or guardians of a child are alive: *Shatter*, 243. For consideration of the practical aspects of wardship, see King, *Practice of Wards of Courts Office*, Lecture No. 7 of the Society of Young Solicitors, 24 February 1966, pp. 5–6 of Discussion following Lecture.

IN RE GILLS, MINORS

27 L.R.Ir. 129 (Lord Ashbourne, C., 1891)

Lord Ashbourne, C.:

This case raises an important question in reference to the practice of this Court. It appears that one of the wards of the Court, Miss Catherine Josephine Gill, having recently entered the noviciate of the Ursuline Convent at Waterford, an application was made to me by her uncle and guardian Alderman Gill to pay the entrance fee, £32, and other expenses of this minor and her brothers. This application was the first intimation made to the Court of this grave step, on the part of one of its wards, and it was only made incidentally. I at once directed the whole matter to be explained by affidavit, and the practice of the Court here and in England looked into. The guardian, Mr. Gill, made an affidavit stating that he was wholly ignorant of the practice of the Court, and that he had no intention whatever of being guilty of any disrespect to the Court; that he had done nothing whatever to encourage the ward to this step; and that he and Mrs. Gill had done all they would to show her the world and its life; and generally that he had acted entirely *bona fide*, without any knowledge whatever of anything to lead him to think he should have given the Lord Chancellor notice. I also made close inquiries into the practice of the Court, and I am informed that there is no trace of any sanction ever having been given to such a serious step by any infant ward under the care of the Court. I also communicated with England to ascertain the practice there, and I am informed by Mr. Justice Chitty, after communicating with the other Judges of the Chancery Division, and his senior chief clerk, who had been twenty-seven years in office, that there is no record of any sanction being given, or even applied for, to a female ward of Court under age, entering on a noviciate, or (to use Mr. Justice Chitty's words) 'taking any positive step leading to an irrevocable vow.' The importance, the seriousness, of the step is obvious. If a ward enters into an engagement or contract of marriage, it is the clear duty of the guardian to apprise the Court. Nay, more, if there is reason to think, or believe, or apprehend, that an engagement or understanding of marriage is likely to result from an intimacy, it may also be the duty of the guardian to communicate with the court. Entering on a noviciate, although there are no vows, and there is opportunity afforded for change of intention before the irrevocable step is taken, is plainly as grave a step for a young girl as any engagement or understanding that can be conceived. An engagement of marriage may be broken off, and an understanding of marriage may pass off. A noviciate may not be analogous, but it is no less serious. The ward is also then free to change her mind, and has as yet taken no irrevocable action, but she has taken an important initial step, satisfied a vital condition precedent to taking an irrevocable step. A binding vow to lead a religious life, and never to marry, is manifestly a decision of the most momentous character to any girl – only to be entered into after mature reflection, at an age when the judgment and discretion are fairly developed, and when notice has been given to parents and those who stand in *loco parentis.* It is not too much to ask that steps leading to an act of such a supreme character should, in the case of those who have lost their natural guardians, their parents, be deferred until the age of twenty-one years, when the Court restores them to their property and freedom from control; and, most surely, notice of any such wish or intention on the part of the ward should be brought under the notice of the Lord Chancellor, that he may have an opportunity of considering the matter, and of taking any steps that might, in his opinion, be prudent. If the parents were alive they could themselves advise delay, or give opportunities for seeing a little of the world before it was irrevocably abandoned. Nothing can replace the love, the sympathy, and the care of parents, but at least the Court, until the early age of twenty-one is reached, must stand in *loco parentis*, and not allow anything leading to a final decision to be taken without full notice. This young lady loses nearly two-thirds of her fortune if she become a nun, though I quite appreciate that she little regards this when giving up the world. At first her two brothers will benefit by this; and then if they die within a given age (and one is in very bad health), her uncle and guardian is to have all. Obviously his pecuniary interest may be advanced by this ward becoming a nun; and Serjeant Jellett is quite right in saying that that is a circumstance which made caution all the more necessary. I quite accept, however, the affidavit of Alderman Gill, and I believe that he acted, however, incautiously and mistakenly, *bona fide* and with no indirect motive. If he had been alive to and regarded the practice of the Court, which rests upon the foundations of common sense, and not upon recondite considerations, he would have given due notice of what he knew was about to take place; then he would have obviated the possibility of even a suggestion that he had given any thought whatever to his own possible advantage in the future, of which, however, I entirely acquit him.

Mrs. Margaret White, the lady superioress of the Ursuline Convent at Waterford, has also sworn a most proper affidavit, stating that she was not aware that this young lady was a ward of Court, and that whatever omission may have arisen was purely from ignorance on the part of the community, and not from any desire to deceive the Court or treat its jurisdiction with disrespect. I accept these statements in the fullest and most unreserved manner. Many of the wards of Court are being educated in convents with my full sanction, and I am glad to fall in with the views of their families in this regard, and to be able to think that female wards under age, who have lost their mothers, can thus be educated amidst pure and moral surroundings.

Notwithstanding all this, the practice of the Court has not been followed, and a serious mistake has been made. How am I now to act? Affidavits have been sworn as the health of the minor, and I have clear medical evidence that any effort to change the residence of the ward and interrupt her life would be attended with most dangerous consequences. She comes from a delicate and consumptive family; and I have such strong evidence that any shock to her wishes may develop swift and deadly disease, that I feel bound to give it every possible weight. I shall therefore, without at all sanctioning what has taken place, not disturb her residence, and I make no order on the subject. She is now in her twentieth year, and will be soon free to act exactly as she thinks right.

Mr. Gill, the guardian, has two applications before me. The first is that to continue the maintenance, and that I will accede to, as it is necessary that the wards of the Court should be duly maintained. The other is for an allowance of a sum of £150 to meet certain payments for the wards: that I shall permit, save as to the sum of £32 for the entrance of this young lady to the convent, and that having been spent without the sanction of, or notice to, the Court, and contrary to its practice, I shall disallow. . . .

Notes

1. In *Iredell* v. *Iredell*, 1 Times L. R. 260 (1885) an injunction was granted against a group of persons who had attempted to induce a ward to become a Catholic, against her father's wishes. The injunction restrained these persons from having any further communication with the ward. Commenting on *Iredell*, Lowe and White note that it 'shows that the court's powers are not limited to restraining the ward's personal relationships and theoretically wardship can be invoked to control any activity of the ward. The limiting factor in all these cases is that the court will be concerned to promote the child's welfare': *Wards of Court*, 107–108 (1979). In Ireland, would such a broad criterion offend against the Constitutional guarantees of privacy and of freedom of association, expression and religion?
2. Tort law has been invoked to control the activity of religious groups in relation to minors: cf. *Lough* v. *Ward*, [1945] 2 All E.R. 338 (King's Bench Div., Cassels, J.), McMahon & Binchy, *Irish Law of Torts*, 422–423 (1981), See also the Law Reform Commission's Working Paper No. 6–1979, *The Law Relating to Seduction and the Enticement and Harbouring of a Child*, chs. 2 and 9 and its *First Report on Family Law*, pp. 14–15 (1981). See further DeSocio, *Protecting the Rights of Religious Cults*, 8 Human Rights 38 (1979); Delgado, *Religious Totalism: Gentle and Ungentle Persuasion Under the First Amendment*, 51 S. Calif. L. Rev. (1977); *Anon., Note: Cults, Deprogrammers, and the Necessity Defence*, 80 Mich. L. Rev. 271 (1981).

IN RE J.L.

Unreported, Supreme Court, 21 December 1965 (156–1965)

Ó Dalaigh, C.J.:

This is an appeal by a minor, J.L. . . . from an order of the President of the High Court refusing the Minor's application for permission to marry.

The President has set out all the relevant facts in his judgment and it is unnecessary to recount them except in outline.

The applicant, who was born in May, 1946, is now 19½ years of age. He finds himself in wardship by reason of his having, [when a young child], drawn a prize of £6,250 in the Irish Hospital Sweepstake; this ticket had been purchased in his name by his father. The trustees of the sweepstake paid the prize money into court under the *Trustee Act, 1893*, and the applicant's father, W.L. thereupon applied to have the boy made a ward of court. This was done, the father being appointed by the Court guardian of the person and fortune.

The applicant's father is a farmer with a holding of 50 acres. The applicant left school at the age of 17, and shortly afterwards he began keeping company with a neighbouring farmer's daughter, X.Y. who is two years his senior. In August, 1964 they agreed to marry, and since that date they have regarded themselves as unofficially engaged.

Last March Miss Y. became pregnant by him and thereupon they agreed to get married at the earliest opportunity. In April the applicant sought his father's consent, but this was refused. The applicant consulted with Very Rev. B. in whose parish X.Y. resides, with a view to obtaining his consent to officiate at the marriage. Fr. B., having consulted with the Bishop of the Diocese, . . ., intimated that His Lordship was reluctant to authorise him

(Fr. B.) to perform the ceremony unless and until the Court's consent had been obtained. If the consent of the Court is forthcoming Fr. B. is prepared to perform the ceremony without delay. The parties are both Catholics.

Rev. E., C.C., who is curate in the Parish of X, has made an affidavit in which he says that he is well acquainted with the girl's family. Her father is a farmer owning 120 acres. His wife died in 1947. X is his third daughter, and Fr. E. has known her since she left the National school. Since then she has worked in and about her father's house, and has performed the duties of a housekeeper to her father in a diligent and conscientious manner. Apart from this present lapse, which he attributes to the absence of a mother's advice and guidance, Fr. E. considers X to be a girl of good character and a suitable wife for the applicant. The girl's father and family are, he says, highly respectable and industrious and are so regarded by their neighbours. The Court has heard no suggestion that the girl would not make a suitable wife for the applicant.

The applicant in his affidavit says that his father advanced two reasons for refusing to consent to the marriage, viz. (i) that he is too young and (ii) the difficulty he would have in obtaining accommodation after the marriage.

In addition to what the minor says in his affidavit as to the grounds of his father's refusal we have a letter of 10th November, 1965, written on behalf of the father by his solicitors stating that the father was not prepared to give his consent to the marriage. The letter continues: 'If it had been intimated to our client that the girl's father would have made provision for the couple his decision might have been otherwise, but in all the circumstances of the case he has decided to refuse his consent.'

The applicant's father has not made an affidavit.

The President, however, interviewed him. He told the President that he considered the applicant too young to get married. The President says that the father appears to resent the fact that the girl's father, Mr. Y., had made no approach to him to discuss the proposed marriage and was apparently unwilling to make any settlement on his daughter. As a result of a meeting which the President suggested might take place between the applicant's father and Mr. Y. it was notified to the President that Mr. Y. was not favourably disposed towards the marriage, and that, if the marriage took place, he was prepared to make a gift of £100 to his daughter but do nothing more in the way of a settlement.

The President also interviewed the applicant alone. The applicant told the President that he loves the girl and would want to marry her apart from the fact that she has become pregnant by him. He said he was not acting under compulsion by anyone. The President did not believe that any person was trying to force the applicant to marry the girl, but he did believe that he felt the compelling nature of the circumstances in which he now finds himself. The President moreover was not quite convinced that the applicant, if he were a perfectly free agent, would want to marry the girl at present.

The applicant became an employee . . . a year ago as a labourer, and he is now working with [his employers] as a lorry driver, earning a weekly wage of £10.5.0d. He has, in addition, 10 head of cattle which his father looks after for him. A sum of £240 per annum is paid out of court annually to the father for the applicant's upkeep. The applicant still resides in his father's home, but he can obtain a suitable flat in the Main Street of [a nearby town] if he is permitted to marry. In addition, to his petition for leave to marry he asks for the payment out of the funds in court the sum of £150 to meet the expenses of the proposed marriage and of the confinement of X.Y.

The President in his judgment refusing the applicant permission to marry said that he took the view that he should not override the father's wishes unless he was satisfied not merely that he was wrong but also that the father's view was unreasonable or dictated by improper motives, and he could not be so satisfied in this case. He said that he did not say the father was wrong; but, if he were prepared to hold he was, he conceived that he should not substitute his view for the father's view merely because it was his view. The father was in a better position than anyone else to know what was in his son's best interest. The applicant was too young to be contemplating marriage and he was still younger when he formed this attachment. The discrepancy in age between the applicant and the girl was of no great significance; but it was unlikely that the applicant would be contemplating marriage at his age but for the circumstance in which he found himself. The marriage, if it were to take place, would not have the approval of his father or of the girl's father. And as to the question of a proper settlement upon the marriage of a ward of court this was a matter which the Court was entitled to, and ought to consider. The President considered that the father's attitude in regard to this aspect of the matter was not unreasonable. Finally, the President adverted to the fact that, if the marriage does not take place, the child would be born out of wedlock. This was a matter intensely to be regretted; so also was an unfortunate marriage. The child's illegitimacy would not, however, be wholly unremediable; and if the applicant is genuine in what he told the President he would be prepared to make the child legitimate by marrying the girl when he comes of age and is free to do so. The President concluded by adding that he did not feel justified in giving his consent to this marriage at least so long as the father withheld his.

Mr. Finlay, for the applicant, has submitted that the paramount consideration should be the minor's best interest and that, in the circumstances of the case, it was in the applicant's interest that he should be permitted to marry. He acknowledged that the Court's consent was required for the marriage of a ward of court and that marriage without it would be a contempt. He called attention to the provision of section 19 of the *Marriages (Ireland) Act, 1844*, requiring the father's consent in the case of the marriage of an infant, but pointed out that section 3 declared that the provisions of the Act has nothing to say to the law governing the requirements of a marriage to be performed by a Catholic priest. While submitting that at common law these requirements did not include the father's consent where the parties were of an age to contract, Mr. Finlay said he was doing no more than asking the Court to give its consent without expressing any view as to whether or not the father's consent was also necessary either at common law or under the Constitution.

Mr. Lynch, for the minor's father, stated that the father had two objections to the marriage: (i) that the minor was too young and (ii) that the girl's father had not agreed to make an adequate settlement on his daughter.

At this point [the minor's father] left court in apparent dispproval of counsel's statement, or part of it. As to the first of these objections, it was given by applicant in his affidavit as the person stated to him by his father and it was repeated as an objection by the applicant's father in the interview which the President had with him. As to the second objection, it is the same objection as that stated in [the minor's solicitors'] letter of 10th November, 1965, already referred to. Counsel fairly said that the applicant's father had given different reasons at different times. [The father]'s main submission was that the court should not grant consent to the marriage unless it were shown that the father had acted unreasonably or for improper motives.

He referred to the terms of section 20 of the Act of 1844 where the tests he put forward are there enumerated as those upon which the court, in the case of marriages falling within that Act, is authorised to substitute its consent for the father's consent. The father in this instance had done nothing to forfeit his rights.

This, as the President has said, is a different and delicate matter in which one must proceed with the greatest caution.

Of the two objections advanced orally to the applicant by his father for refusing his consent to the marriage (i) his youth and (ii) the difficulty in obtaining accommodation after the proposed marriage, the applicant has reasonably met the second and the first it is not within his power to meet. Again, as to the objection stated in the letter of 10th November, 1965, viz. the failure of the girl's father to make provision for the couple, the applicant is likewise powerless to meet it. It is of some significance that the letter indicates that if this provision had been forthcoming the young man's father might well have given his consent; in other words he would no longer have advanced as an objection to the marriage the applicant's youthfulness. It is true that the father recurred to this latter objection in the interview which the President had with him; and the absence of a settlement by the girl's father had, so far as the President could discern, receded to a resentment and was coupled in the father's mind with the failure of the girl's father to approach him to discuss the proposed marriage.

In a situation of the kind which has arisen here one readily understands and sympathises with the feelings of the father of the applicant. What has occurred has been a severe trial to him, and also a grave affront to his position before his neighbours and friends. The girl's father is in like case; even more unhappily so. It is therefore wholly understandable that the courtesies and arrangements customarily preliminary to marriage in Ireland have in the circumstances been lacking. If more time were available I cannot help feeling that both parents would succeed in looking more objectively upon the situation of their children and, forgetting the resentment begotten by their children's lapse, would meet and act as persons, who sharing a common disappointment and sorrow, sought to help their children courageously remake a new life. Their children, from their side, are willing to undertake this, aided, as their religious beliefs assure them, by grace flowing from the sacrament of marriage. For the applicant this is a willing, unforced choice. If a marriage is now to be postponed many things may occur in the intervening eighteen months which will raise obstacles to harmony, happiness and even marriage itself. It is not necessary to dwell upon the position of the young woman. And while a later marriage would legitimate a child born out of wedlock it would not remove the stigma which society attaches to such, both for child and parents alike.

I return to the father's objection. The absence of a settlement in the circumstances of this case is not a matter of weight and, indeed, one may fairly say it was not put forward as such by the father in his interview with the President.

These young People could shortly look forward to a degree of security uncommon among their equals; apart from the payment out of the money in Court of a modest sum to meet the costs of the girl's confinement the applicant's fortune will remain intact and under the care of the Court until he reaches full age. Moreover, the applicant has been in steady and reasonably-paid employment and should be able to maintain himself and a wife and child. Therefore, there is not, on material grounds, any objection of substance to consent to his marriage.

I come finally to the objection of the applicant's youthfulness. This is something that is not now remediable. Ordinarily the applicant's father could have expected his son to await full age until proposing marriage. This has not happened and the father insists on withholding his consent. After the closest examination of the evidence I have reached the conclusion that it is wrong for the father to withhold his consent. His judgment of the right and just course is clouded by this most unhappy incident and most of all by his resentment of the attitude of the girl's father in the matter.

In my opinion not only is the Court not bound to follow a father's wishes which it finds to be clouded and wrong; but, on the contrary, where the consequences for the minor are likely to be grave it is the Court's duty to give its consent in disregard of the father's wishes.

After the fullest consideration I can give the matter I am satisfied that the Court should give its consent to this marriage; but, as the matter was not argued, expressing no view as to whether or not the father's views are entitled to prevail in any other forum or tribunal. All I say and all I decide is, that the circumstances of this case are such that it is, in my judgment, proper for the Court to withdraw such barrier as the wardship constitutes to this marriage.

I would also order the payment out of court of the sum asked for by the applicant.

Walsh, J. concurred.

Lavery, J. delivered a dissenting judgment, the judgment is not contained in the Court files, which include a note (probably made shortly after the decision was handed down) that it was 'not available at the moment for circulation.'

Notes

1. On this aspect of wardship, see N. Lowe & R. White, *Wards of Court*, 138–140 (1979). Marriage of a ward without the consent of the Court constitutes contempt. How do you think those guilty of contempt should be punished? Cf. *Black* v. *Creighton*, 2 L. Recorder 10 (1828). May the Court in such circumstances refuse to discharge the ward from wardship unless a settlement of his or her property is executed? Cf. *In re McLorinan, A Minor* [1935] I.R. 373 (Sup. Ct., 1934).

   In *In the Matter of Stewart, A Minor*, 2 L. Recorder 112 (1828), where a male had married a female minor without the consent of her guardian, the Court imprisoned him and ordered that he would be released only when he had gone through a proper ceremony of marriage ('the Sheriffs of the city to attend with him at the parish church') and a specified settlement had been made of the minor's property. Another case involving an order by the Court that the parties remarry to remove doubts is *In re Murray, A Minor*, 5 Ir. Eq. 266 (1842) (where the minor was a male).
2. Is the requirement of judicial consent for a ward to marry constitutional? Why should a child, because he has won a lottery, have restrictions placed on his right to marry?
3. On international aspects of wardship, see *Kent County Council* v. *C.S., supra*, p. 472: *The State (K.M. & R.D.)* v. *Minister for Foreign Affairs, supra*, p. 152; *Re Medley, A Minor*, I.R. 6 Eq. 339 (Chy., 1871); N. Lowe & R. White, *op. cit.* 102.
4. Are there any limits to the wardship jurisdiction or may the Court always act when the welfare of a child is invoked? Cf. *Re X (Wardship)*, [1975] 1 All E.R. 697 (C.A., reversing Latey, J., 1974), analysed by Everton, *High Tide in Wardship*, 125 New L. J. 930 (1975) by Rowe, *Wardship in the Law of England*, ch. 18 of 1. Baxter & M. Eberts eds., *The Child and the Courts*, at 330–331 (1978), and by Corrin, *The Extent of Wardship*, 5 Trent, L.J. 67 (1981).

INDEX